BMW Twins Owners Workshop Manual

by Jeremy Churchill

Models covered
R45. 473cc. UK only 1978 to 1985
R50. 498cc. UK 1970 to 1973, US 1969 to 1973
R60. 599cc. UK 1970 to 1978, US 1969 to 1978
R65. 649cc. UK 1978 to 1988, US 1979 to 1987
R65LS. 649cc. UK 1981 to 1985, US 1982 to 1984
R75. 745cc. UK 1970 to 1977, US 1969 to 1977
R80, R80/7, R80G/S (including Paris-Dakar version), R80GS, R80ST, R80RT, 797cc. UK 1977 on, US 1977 to 1987
R90/6, R90S. 898cc. UK and US 1973 to 1976
R100, R100/7, R100CS, R100GS, R100RS, R100RT, R100S, R100SP, R100SRS, R100ST, R100T, R100TR. 979cc. UK and US 1976 to 1984, 1987 on

(249-302)

Haynes Publishing Group
Sparkford Nr Yeovil
Somerset BA22 7JJ England

Haynes Publications, Inc
861 Lawrence Drive
Newbury Park
California 91320 USA

Acknowledgements

Our thanks are due to Gus Kuhn Motors Ltd of London for providing servicing information, Mr. C. Leighton-Thomas of Bath, Emblem Sports Cars of Pimperne, Dorset, and CW Motorcycles of Dorchester who loaned the machines on which this manual was based.

Our thanks are also due to Contact Developments of Reading who allowed us to reproduce Dell'orto carburettor illustrations.

The Avon Rubber Company supplied information on tyre care and fitting, and NGK Spark Plugs (UK) Ltd provided information on plug maintenance and electrode conditions.

© **Haynes Publishing Group 1986, 1989**

A book in the **Haynes Owners Workshop Manual Series**

Printed by J.H. Haynes & Co. Ltd, Sparkford, Nr Yeovil, Somerset BA22 7JJ, England

All rights reserved. No part of this book may be reproduced or transmitted in any form or by any means, electronic or mechanical, including photocopying, recording or by any information storage or retrieval system, without permission in writing from the copyright holder.

ISBN 1 85010 492 1

Library of Congress Catalog Card Number 89-80124

British Library Cataloguing in Publication Data
Churchill, Jeremy, *1954–*
  BMW twins owners workshop manual
  1. Motorcycles. Maintenance & repair.
  Amateurs manuals
  I. Title II. Series
  629.28'775
  ISBN 1-85010-492-1

Whilst every care is taken to ensure that the information in this manual is correct, no liability can be accepted by the authors or publishers for loss, damage or injury caused by any errors in, or omissions from, the information given.

Contents

Introductory pages

About this manual	5
Introduction to the BMW Twins	5
Model dimensions and weights	8
Ordering spare parts	9
Safety first!	10
Tools and working facilities	11
Choosing and fitting accessories	14
Fault diagnosis	17
Routine maintenance	28

Chapter 1
Engine — 59

Chapter 2
Clutch — 90

Chapter 3
Gearbox — 99

Chapter 4
Fuel system and lubrication — 118

Chapter 5
Ignition system — 147

Chapter 6
Frame and forks — 152

Chapter 7
Final drive and rear suspension — 171

Chapter 8
Wheels, brakes and tyres — 182

Chapter 9
Electrical system — 208

Chapter 10
The 1986 to 1988 models — 223

Wiring diagrams — 247

English/American terminology — 266

Conversion factors — 267

Index — 268

The R60/6 model

The R65 model

About this manual

The purpose of this manual is to present the owner with a concise and graphic guide which will enable him to tackle any operation from basic routine maintenance to a major overhaul. It has been assumed that any work would be undertaken without the luxury of a well-equipped workshop and a range of manufacturer's service tools.

To this end, the machine featured in the manual was stripped and rebuilt in our own workshop, by a team comprising a mechanic, a photographer and the author. The resulting photographic sequence depicts events as they took place, the hands shown being those of the author and the mechanic.

The use of specialised, and expensive, service tools was avoided unless their use was considered to be essential due to risk of breakage or injury. There is usually some way of improvising a method of removing a stubborn component, providing that a suitable degree of care is exercised.

The author learnt his motorcycle mechanics over a number of years, faced with the same difficulties and using similar facilities to those encountered by most owners. It is hoped that this practical experience can be passed on through the pages of this manual.

Where possible, a well-used example of the machine is chosen for the workshop project, as this highlights any areas which might be particularly prone to giving rise to problems. In this way, any such difficulties are encountered and resolved before the text is written, and the techniques used to deal with them can be incorporated in the relevant section. Armed with a working knowledge of the machine, the author undertakes a considerable amount of research in order that the maximum amount of data can be included in the manual.

A comprehensive section, preceding the main part of the manual, describes procedures for carrying out the routine maintenance of the machine at intervals of time and mileage. This section is included particularly for those owners who wish to ensure the efficient day-to-day running of their motorcycle, but who choose not to undertake overhaul or renovation work.

Each Chapter is divided into numbered sections. Within these sections are numbered paragraphs. Cross reference throughout the manual is quite straightforward and logical. When reference is made 'See Section 6.10' it means Section 6, paragraph 10 in the same Chapter. If another Chapter were intended, the reference would read, for example, 'See Chapter 2, Section 6.10'. All the photographs are captioned with a section/paragraph number to which they refer and are relevant to the Chapter text adjacent.

Figures (usually line illustrations) appear in a logical but numerical order, within a given Chapter. Fig. 1.1 therefore refers to the first figure in Chapter 1.

Left-hand and right-hand descriptions of the machines and their components refer to the left and right of a given machine when the rider is seated normally.

Motorcycle manufacturers continually make changes to specifications and recommendations, and these, when notified, are incorporated into our manuals at the earliest opportunity.

Introduction to the BMW twins

Although BMW's use of a shaft-drive motorcycle with a horizontally opposed twin-cylinder engine dates back to 1923, when the R32 model appeared, the machines described in this Manual were first introduced in 1969 to replace the high-quality R50/60/69S Earles Fork models which had been on sale since 1955, but were thought to be too unconventional in appearance to remain successful.

The major changes to the engine of the new machines were the substitution of a plain-bearing crankshaft for the previous ball-and-roller bearing component, the fitting of an electric starter and the use of a crankshaft-mounted alternator instead of the previous gear-driven dynamo. The camshaft, previously gear-driven above the crankshaft, was now mounted under the crank, driven by chain and used to drive the oil pump at its rear end; the repositioning of the camshaft had the effect of raising the cylinders for increased cornering clearance.

The most obvious changes were to the cycle parts, where a new frame gave a conventional appearance to the rear suspension, and where BMW reverted to the use of the telescopic fork; they had first used this type of front suspension in 1935 but had abandoned it in favour of Earles forks in 1955. The new suspension components were softly-sprung and gave a smooth, comfortable ride, which has become one of the marque's most popular features.

Although the machines described in this Manual have remained basically unchanged, especially by comparison with the products of the Japanese, most of their components have been modified in various degrees throughout their production life. The need to keep pace with the competition has resulted in larger-capacity engines with greatly increased power outputs and in the appearance of features such as five-speed gearboxes, disc brakes, cast alloy wheels and a much greater diversity of model types. Most of these changes can be seen by reference to the Specifications Section and/or introduction to each Chapter.

Note however that as BMW have made it a policy to offer a wide range of equipment as optional extras, with the components fitted as standard to the more expensive models being available for the basic versions, and to keep all components interchangeable where possible, many machines may be found to differ considerably from the specifications given; these refer at all times to the machines in their standard, original, form with likely variations noted where possible. For example, it is quite possible for a basic model of one year to have twin front discs and alloy wheels when it is listed as being equipped with a single disc and wire-spoked wheels, or for it to be fitted with modified components which are listed for later models.

A complete list of the models covered is given below. For reference, to assist the owner in identifying his or her machine the approximate dates of import are also given; note that these may not necessarily coincide with the actual date of sale.

Model/capacity	UK	US
R45 473cc	Aug '78 to Oct '85	–
R50/5 498cc	May '70 to Sept '73	Sept '69 to Aug '73
R60/5 599cc	April '70 to Feb '74	Sept '69 to Aug '73
R60/6 599cc	Feb '74 to June '76	Sept '73 to Aug '76
R60/7 599cc	Sept '76 to Sept '78	Sept '76 to Dec '78
R65 649cc	Aug '78 to Oct '85	Jan '79 to Dec '84
R65LS 649cc	Dec '81 to Oct '85	Jan '82 to Dec '84
R75/5 745cc	April '70 to Feb '74	Sept '69 to Aug '73
R75/6 745cc	Feb '74 to June '76	Sept '73 to Aug '76
R75/7 745cc	Sept '76 to Sept '77	Sept '76 to Aug '77
R80/7 797cc	Oct '77 to Sept '80	Sept '77 to '80
R80G/S 797cc	Introduced Oct '80	Introduced Jan '81
R80ST 797cc	Sept '82 to '84	Jan '83 to Dec '84
R80RT 797cc	Introduced August '82	Introduced Jan '83
R80 797cc	Introduced Dec '84	Introduced Jan '85
R90/6 898cc	Dec '73 to June '76	Sept '73 to Aug '76
R90S 898cc	Dec '73 to June '76	Sept '73 to Aug '76
R100/7 979cc	Sept '76 to Feb '79	Sept '76 to Dec '78
R100T 979cc	Feb '79 to Sept '80	Jan '79 to Dec '80 includes '80 ST version
R100 979cc	Oct '80 to June '84	Jan '81 to '84 – includes TR (Touring) and SP (Sport) '82, '83 versions
R100S 979cc	Sept '76 to Sept '80	Sept '76 to Dec '80
R100CS 979cc	Oct '80 to June '84	Jan '81 to Dec '81, Jan '84 to late '84
R100RS 979cc	Sept '76 to June '84 – includes SRS version of '78	Sept '76 to '84
R100RT 979cc	Feb '79 to June '84	Jan '79 to '84

Details of the 1986 on models are given in Chapter 10.

The R75/5 model

The R80ST model

The R100S model

The R100RS model

Model dimensions and weights

Overall width – of engine, except where otherwise specified:
R45, R65, R65LS .... 688 mm (27.1 in)
/5, /6 .... 740 mm (29.1 in)
/7 .... 746 mm (29.4 in)
R80ST – engine bars .... 790 mm (31.1 in)
R80 – handlebar .... 800 mm (31.5 in)
R80G/S – handlebar .... 820 mm (32.3 in)
R80RT 1983-84 – fairing .... 930 mm (36.6 in)
R80RT 1985 on – fairing .... 960 mm (37.8 in)

Overall height:
/5 .... 1040 mm (40.9 in)
R45, R60/6, R60/7, R65, R75/6, R75/7, R80/7, R100/7,
R100T, R100 .... 1080 mm (42.5 in)
R65LS .... 1090 mm (42.9 in)
R80 .... 1115 mm (43.9 in)
R80G/S, R80ST .... 1150 mm (45.3 in)
R90S, R100S, R100CS .... 1210 mm (47.6 in)
R100RS .... 1300 mm (51.2 in)
R80RT 1985 on .... 1478 mm (58.2 in)
R100RT, R80RT 1983 – 84 .... 1465 mm (57.7 in)

Seat height – unladen:
R45 and R65 up to 1980 .... 770 mm (30.3 in)
R80, R80RT 1985 on .... 807 mm (31.8 in)
R45 1981 on, R60/6, R60/7, R65 1981 on, R65LS, R75/6,
R75/7, R80/7, R100/7, R100T .... 810 mm (31.9 in)
R90S, all other 1000cc models, R80RT 1983 – 84 .... 820 mm (32.3 in)
R80ST .... 845 mm (33.3 in)
/5 .... 850 mm (33.5 in)
R80G/S .... 860 mm (33.9 in)

Overall length:
/5 .... 2100 mm (82.7 in)
R45 and R65 1981 on, R65LS .... 2110 mm (83.1 in)
R80, R80RT 1985 on .... 2175 mm (85.6 in)
/6, /7 up to 1978, R45 and R65 up to 1980, R80ST ... 2180 mm (85.8 in)
/7 1979 on .... 2210 mm (87.0 in)
R80RT 1983 – 84 .... 2220 mm (87.4 in)
R80G/S .... 2230 mm (87.8 in)

Wheelbase – with rider weighing 165 lb (75 kg) seated:
/5 up to mid-1973 (see Chapter 7) .... 1385 mm (54.5 in)
R45 and R65 up to 1980 .... 1390 mm (54.7 in)
R45 and R65 1981 on, R65LS .... 1400 mm (55.1 in)
R80ST, R80, R80RT 1985 on .... 1440 mm (56.7 in)
/5 mid-1973 on, /6, /7, R80G/S, R80RT 1983 – 84 ..... 1465 mm (57.7 in)

Ground clearance – with rider weighing 165 lb (75 kg) seated:
R45, R65, R65LS .... 105 mm (4.1 in)
/7 1981 on .... 115 mm (4.5 in)
R80, R80RT 1985 on .... 125 mm (4.9 in)
R80ST, R80RT 1983 – 84 .... 130 mm (5.1 in)
/5, /6, /7 up to 1980 .... 165 mm (6.5 in)
R80G/S .... 175 mm (6.9 in)

Kerb weight – machine with full fuel tank, tools etc:
R80G/S – 1981 model without electric starter .... 410 lb (186 kg)
R80G/S with electric starter .... 423 lb (192 kg)
R80ST .... 436 lb (198 kg)
R45, R50/5, R65 .... 452 lb (205 kg)
R65LS .... 456 lb (207 kg)
R60/5, R60/6, R75/5, R75/6, R80, R90/6 .... 463 lb (210 kg)
R60/7, R75/7, R80/7, R90S, R100/7, R100T .... 474 lb (215 kg)
R100 .... 481 lb (218 kg)
R100S, R100CS .... 485 lb (220 kg)
R80RT 1985 on .... 500 lb (227 kg)
R100RS .... 507 lb (230 kg)
R100RT 1979 – 80, R80RT 1983 – 84 .... 516 lb (234 kg)
R100RT 1981 on .... 525 lb (238 kg)

Maximum permissible weight – total of machine, passenger(s) and luggage:
/5, /6, /7 up to 1980, R45, R65, R65LS, R80G/S, R80ST ... 877 lb (398 kg)
/7 1981 on, R80, R80RT .... 970 lb (440 kg)

Ordering spare parts

When ordering replacement parts, it is essential to identify exactly the machine for which the parts are required. While in some cases it is sufficient to identify the machine by its title eg 'R75/7', the many modifications to most components mean that it is usually essential to identify the machine by its BMW **production** or model year eg '1977 R75/7'. The BMW production year starts in September of the previous calendar year, after the annual holiday, and continues until the following August. Therefore a 1977 R75/7 was **produced** at some time between September 1976 and August 1977; it may have been **sold** (to its first owner) at any time from September 1976 onwards. To avoid any further confusion, models are referred to **at all times** in this Manual by their BMW **production** or model year; to identify your own machine, record its full engine and frame numbers and take them to any BMW dealer who should have the necessary information to identify it exactly. Finally, in some cases modifications can be identified only by reference to the machine's engine or frame number; these should be noted and taken with you whenever replacement parts are required.

On all models up to 1983 the engine number is stamped on the crankcase left-hand side, immediately above the oil filler/dipstick boss. 1984 and later models have a rectangular, machined-flat surface on the crankcase left-hand side at the front, below the frame tube; the engine number is the upper of the two numbers stamped into this, the lower being a factory production code. This factory code should not be confused with the (usually 8-digit) engine number; it is to be found stamped into the crankcase, at the cylinder base on models up to 1979, underneath the oil filter cover on models from 1979 to 1983.

The frame number is stamped into the right-hand side of the steering head on all models up to 1982. On all 1983 and later models it is stamped into the right-hand lower frame tube, above the centre stand mounting. On all models the frame number is duplicated in the manufacturer's data plate, which is riveted to the steering head. A factory code which might puzzle some owners is as follows: all 500, 600, 750, 800, 900 and 1000 cc models, whether /5, /6 or /7, have the factory internal reference number '247', while R45, R65 and R65LS models have the number '248'.

To be absolutely certain of receiving the correct part, not only is it essential to have the machine's identifying title and engine and frame numbers, but it is also useful to take the old part for comparison (where possible). Note that where a modified component has superseded the original, a careful check must be made that there are no related parts which have also been modified and must be used to enable the replacement to be correctly refitted; where such a situation is found, purchase all the necessary parts and fit them, even if this means replacing apparently unworn items.

Always purchase replacement parts from an authorised BMW dealer who will either have the parts in stock or can order them quickly from the importer, and always use genuine parts to ensure the machine's performance and reliability. Pattern parts are not widely available for BMWs, being generally restricted to items such as disc brake pads, oil and air filters and exhaust system components. Unless these are of recognised quality brands which will perform as well as or better than the original, they should be avoided.

Expendable items such as lubricants, spark plugs, some electrical components, bearings, bulbs and tyres can usually be obtained at lower prices from accessory shops, motor factors or from specialists advertising in the national motorcycle press.

Location of engine number – all models up to 1983

Location of engine number – all models 1984 on

Location of frame number – all models up to 1982

Location of frame number – all models 1983 on

Manufacturer's data plate also carries frame number – early version ...

... and later version

Safety first!

Professional motor mechanics are trained in safe working procedures. However enthusiastic you may be about getting on with the job in hand, do take the time to ensure that your safety is not put at risk. A moment's lack of attention can result in an accident, as can failure to observe certain elementary precautions.

There will always be new ways of having accidents, and the following points do not pretend to be a comprehensive list of all dangers; they are intended rather to make you aware of the risks and to encourage a safety-conscious approach to all work you carry out on your vehicle.

Essential DOs and DON'Ts

DON'T start the engine without first ascertaining that the transmission is in neutral.

DON'T suddenly remove the filler cap from a hot cooling system – cover it with a cloth and release the pressure gradually first, or you may get scalded by escaping coolant.

DON'T attempt to drain oil until you are sure it has cooled sufficiently to avoid scalding you.

DON'T grasp any part of the engine, exhaust or silencer without first ascertaining that it is sufficiently cool to avoid burning you.

DON'T allow brake fluid or antifreeze to contact the machine's paintwork or plastic components.

DON'T syphon toxic liquids such as fuel, brake fluid or antifreeze by mouth, or allow them to remain on your skin.

DON'T inhale dust – it may be injurious to health (see *Asbestos* heading).

DON'T allow any spilt oil or grease to remain on the floor – wipe it up straight away, before someone slips on it.

DON'T use ill-fitting spanners or other tools which may slip and cause injury.

DON'T attempt to lift a heavy component which may be beyond your capability – get assistance.

DON'T rush to finish a job, or take unverified short cuts.

DON'T allow children or animals in or around an unattended vehicle.

DON'T inflate a tyre to a pressure above the recommended maximum. Apart from overstressing the carcase and wheel rim, in extreme cases the tyre may blow off forcibly.

DO ensure that the machine is supported securely at all times. This is especially important when the machine is blocked up to aid wheel or fork removal.

DO take care when attempting to slacken a stubborn nut or bolt. It is generally better to pull on a spanner, rather than push, so that if slippage occurs you fall away from the machine rather than on to it.

DO wear eye protection when using power tools such as drill, sander, bench grinder etc.

DO use a barrier cream on your hands prior to undertaking dirty jobs – it will protect your skin from infection as well as making the dirt easier to remove afterwards; but make sure your hands aren't left slippery. Note that long-term contact with used engine oil can be a health hazard.

DO keep loose clothing (cuffs, tie etc) and long hair well out of the way of moving mechanical parts.

DO remove rings, wristwatch etc, before working on the vehicle – especially the electrical system.

DO keep your work area tidy – it is only too easy to fall over articles left lying around.

DO exercise caution when compressing springs for removal or installation. Ensure that the tension is applied and released in a controlled manner, using suitable tools which preclude the possibility of the spring escaping violently.

DO ensure that any lifting tackle used has a safe working load rating adequate for the job.

DO get someone to check periodically that all is well, when working alone on the vehicle.

DO carry out work in a logical sequence and check that everything is correctly assembled and tightened afterwards.

DO remember that your vehicle's safety affects that of yourself and others. If in doubt on any point, get specialist advice.

IF, in spite of following these precautions, you are unfortunate enough to injure yourself, seek medical attention as soon as possible.

Asbestos

Certain friction, insulating, sealing, and other products – such as brake linings, clutch linings, gaskets, etc – contain asbestos. *Extreme care must be taken to avoid inhalation of dust from such products since it is hazardous to health.* If in doubt, assume that they *do* contain asbestos.

Fire

Remember at all times that petrol (gasoline) is highly flammable. Never smoke, or have any kind of naked flame around, when working on the vehicle. But the risk does not end there – a spark caused by an electrical short-circuit, by two metal surfaces contacting each other, by careless use of tools, or even by static electricity built up in your body under certain conditions, can ignite petrol vapour, which in a confined space is highly explosive.

Always disconnect the battery earth (ground) terminal before working on any part of the fuel or electrical system, and never risk spilling fuel on to a hot engine or exhaust.

It is recommended that a fire extinguisher of a type suitable for fuel and electrical fires is kept handy in the garage or workplace at all times. Never try to extinguish a fuel or electrical fire with water.

Note: *Any reference to a 'torch' appearing in this manual should always be taken to mean a hand-held battery-operated electric lamp or flashlight. It does **not** mean a welding/gas torch or blowlamp.*

Fumes

Certain fumes are highly toxic and can quickly cause unconsciousness and even death if inhaled to any extent. Petrol (gasoline) vapour comes into this category, as do the vapours from certain solvents such as trichloroethylene. Any draining or pouring of such volatile fluids should be done in a well ventilated area.

When using cleaning fluids and solvents, read the instructions carefully. Never use materials from unmarked containers – they may give off poisonous vapours.

Never run the engine of a motor vehicle in an enclosed space such as a garage. Exhaust fumes contain carbon monoxide which is extremely poisonous; if you need to run the engine, always do so in the open air or at least have the rear of the vehicle outside the workplace.

The battery

Never cause a spark, or allow a naked light, near the vehicle's battery. It will normally be giving off a certain amount of hydrogen gas, which is highly explosive.

Always disconnect the battery earth (ground) terminal before working on the fuel or electrical systems.

If possible, loosen the filler plugs or cover when charging the battery from an external source. Do not charge at an excessive rate or the battery may burst.

Take care when topping up and when carrying the battery. The acid electrolyte, even when diluted, is very corrosive and should not be allowed to contact the eyes or skin.

If you ever need to prepare electrolyte yourself, always add the acid slowly to the water, and never the other way round. Protect against splashes by wearing rubber gloves and goggles.

Mains electricity

When using an electric power tool, inspection light etc which works from the mains, always ensure that the appliance is correctly connected to its plug and that, where necessary, it is properly earthed (grounded). Do not use such appliances in damp conditions and, again, beware of creating a spark or applying excessive heat in the vicinity of fuel or fuel vapour.

Ignition HT voltage

A severe electric shock can result from touching certain parts of the ignition system, such as the HT leads, when the engine is running or being cranked, particularly if components are damp or the insulation is defective. Where an electronic ignition system is fitted, the HT voltage is much higher and could prove fatal.

Tools and working facilities

The first priority when undertaking maintenance or repair work of any sort on a motorcycle is to have a clean, dry, well-lit working area. Work carried out in peace and quiet in the well-ordered atmosphere of a good workshop will give more satisfaction and much better results than can usually be achieved in poor working conditions. A good workshop must have a clean flat workbench or a solidly constructed table of convenient working height. The workbench or table should be equipped with a vice which has a jaw opening of at least 4 in (100 mm). A set of jaw covers should be made from soft metal such as aluminium alloy or copper, or from wood. These covers will minimise the marking or damaging of soft or delicate components which may be clamped in the vice. Some clean, dry, storage space will be required for tools, lubricants and dismantled components. It will be necessary during a major overhaul to lay out engine/gearbox components for examination and to keep them where they will remain undisturbed for as long as is necessary. To this end it is recommended that a supply of metal or plastic containers of suitable size is collected. A supply of clean, lint-free, rags for cleaning purposes and some newspapers, other rags, or paper towels for mopping up spillages should also be kept. If working on a hard concrete floor note that both the floor and one's knees can be protected from oil spillages and wear by cutting open a large cardboard box and spreading it flat on the floor under the machine or workbench. This also helps to provide some warmth in winter and to prevent the loss of nuts, washers, and other tiny components which have a tendency to disappear when dropped on anything other than a perfectly clean, flat, surface.

Unfortunately, such working conditions are not always available to the home mechanic. When working in poor conditions it is essential to take extra time and care to ensure that the components being worked on are kept scrupulously clean and to ensure that no components or tools are lost or damaged.

A selection of good tools is a fundamental requirement for anyone contemplating the maintenance and repair of a motor vehicle. For the owner who does not possess any, their purchase will prove a considerable expense, offsetting some of the savings made by doing-it-yourself. However, provided that the tools purchased are of good quality, they will last for many years and prove an extremely worthwhile investment.

To help the average owner to decide which tools are needed to carry out the various tasks detailed in this manual, we have compiled three lists of tools under the following headings: *Maintenance and minor repair*, *Repair and overhaul*, and *Specialized*. The newcomer to practical mechanics should start off with the simpler jobs around the vehicle. Then, as his confidence and experience grow, he can undertake more difficult tasks, buying extra tools as and when they are needed. In this way, a *Maintenance and minor repair* tool kit can be built-up into a *Repair and overhaul* tool kit over a considerable period of time without any major cash outlays. The experienced home mechanic will have a tool kit good enough for most repair and overhaul procedures and will add tools from the specialized category when he feels the expense is justified by the amount of use these tools will be put to.

It is obviously not possible to cover the subject of tools fully here. For those who wish to learn more about tools and their use there is a book entitled *Motorcycle Workshop Practice Manual* available from the publishers of this manual. It also provides an introduction to basic workshop practice which will be of interest to a home mechanic working on any type of motor vehicle.

As a general rule, it is better to buy the more expensive, good quality tools. Given reasonable use, such tools will last for a very long time, whereas the cheaper, poor quality, item will wear out faster and need to be renewed more often, thus nullifying the original saving. There is also the risk of a poor quality tool breaking while in use, causing personal injury or expensive damage to the component being worked on. It should be noted, however, that many car accessory shops and the large department stores sell tools of reasonable quality at competitive prices. The best example of this is found with socket sets, where a medium-priced socket set will be quite adequate for the home owner and yet prove less expensive than a selection of individual sockets and accessories. This is because individual pieces are usually only available from expensive, top quality, ranges and whilst they are undeniably good, it should be remembered that they are intended for professional use.

The basis of any toolkit is a set of spanners. While open-ended spanners with their slim jaws, are useful for working on awkwardly-positioned nuts, ring spanners have advantages in that they grip the nut far more positively. There is less risk of the spanner slipping off the nut and damaging it, for this reason alone ring spanners are to be preferred. Ideally, the home mechanic should acquire a set of each, but if expense rules this out a set of combination spanners (open-ended at one end and with a ring of the same size at the other) will provide a good compromise. Another item which is so useful it should be considered an essential requirement for any home mechanic is a set of socket spanners. These are available in a variety of drive sizes. It is recommended that the ½-inch drive type is purchased to begin with as although bulkier and more expensive than the ⅜-inch type, the larger size is far more common and will accept a greater variety of torque wrenches, extension pieces and socket sizes. The socket set should comprise sockets of sizes between 8 and 24 mm, a reversible ratchet drive, an extension bar of about 10 inches in length, a spark plug socket with a rubber insert, and a universal joint. Other attachments can be added to the set at a later date.

Maintenance and minor repair tool kit

 Set of spanners 8 – 24 mm
 Set of sockets and attachments
 Spark plug spanner with rubber insert – 10, 12, or 14 mm as appropriate
 Adjustable spanner
 C-spanner/pin spanner
 Torque wrench (same size drive as sockets)
 Set of screwdrivers (flat blade)
 Set of screwdrivers (cross-head)
 Set of Allen keys 4 – 10 mm
 Impact screwdriver and bits
 Ball pein hammer – 2 lb
 Hacksaw (junior)
 Self-locking pliers – Mole grips or vice grips
 Pliers – combination
 Pliers – needle nose
 Wire brush (small)
 Soft-bristled brush
 Tyre pump
 Tyre pressure gauge
 Tyre tread depth gauge
 Oil can
 Fine emery cloth
 Funnel (medium size)
 Drip tray
 Grease gun
 Set of feeler gauges
 Brake bleeding kit
 Strobe timing light
 Continuity tester (dry battery and bulb)
 Soldering iron and solder
 Wire stripper or craft knife
 PVC insulating tape
 Assortment of split pins, nuts, bolts, and washers

Repair and overhaul toolkit

 The tools in this list are virtually essential for anyone undertaking major repairs to a motorcycle and are additional to the tools listed above. Concerning Torx driver bits, Torx screws are encountered on some of the more modern machines where their use is restricted to fastening certain components inside the engine/gearbox unit. It is therefore recommended that if Torx bits cannot be borrowed from a local dealer, they are purchased individually as the need arises. They are not in regular use in the motor trade and will therefore only be available in specialist tool shops.

 Plastic or rubber soft-faced mallet
 Torx driver bits
 Pliers – electrician's side cutters
 Circlip pliers – internal (straight or right-angled tips are available)
 Circlip pliers – external
 Cold chisel
 Centre punch
 Pin punch
 Scriber
 Scraper (made from soft metal such as aluminium or copper)
 Soft metal drift
 Steel rule/straight edge
 Assortment of files

 Electric drill and bits
 Wire brush (large)
 Soft wire brush (similar to those used for cleaning suede shoes)
 Sheet of plate glass
 Hacksaw (large)
 Valve grinding tool
 Valve grinding compound (coarse and fine)
 Stud extractor set (E-Z out)

Specialized tools

 This is not a list of the tools made by the machine's manufacturer to carry out a specific task on a limited range of models. Occasional references are made to such tools in the text of this manual and, in general, an alternative method of carrying out the task without the manufacturer's tool is given where possible. The tools mentioned in this list are those which are not used regularly and are expensive to buy in view of their infrequent use. Where this is the case it may be possible to hire or borrow the tools against a deposit from a local dealer or tool hire shop. An alternative is for a group of friends or a motorcycle club to join in the purchase.

 Valve spring compressor
 Piston ring compressor
 Universal bearing puller
 Cylinder bore honing attachment (for electric drill)
 Micrometer set
 Vernier calipers
 Dial gauge set
 Cylinder compression gauge
 Vacuum gauge set
 Multimeter
 Dwell meter/tachometer

Care and maintenance of tools

 Whatever the quality of the tools purchased, they will last much longer if cared for. This means in practice ensuring that a tool is used for its intended purpose; for example screwdrivers should not be used as a substitute for a centre punch, or as chisels. Always remove dirt or grease and any metal particles but remember that a light film of oil will prevent rusting if the tools are infrequently used. The common tools can be kept together in a large box or tray but the more delicate, and more expensive, items should be stored separately where they cannot be damaged. When a tool is damaged or worn out, be sure to renew it immediately. It is false economy to continue to use a worn spanner or screwdriver which may slip and cause expensive damage to the component being worked on.

Fastening systems

 Fasteners, basically, are nuts, bolts and screws used to hold two or more parts together. There are a few things to keep in mind when working with fasteners. Almost all of them use a locking device of some type; either a lock washer, lock nut, locking tab or thread adhesive. All threaded fasteners should be clean, straight, have undamaged threads and undamaged corners on the hexagon head where the spanner fits. Develop the habit of replacing all damaged nuts and bolts with new ones.

 Rusted nuts and bolts should be treated with a rust penetrating fluid to ease removal and prevent breakage. After applying the rust penetrant, let it 'work' for a few minutes before trying to loosen the nut or bolt. Badly rusted fasteners may have to be chiseled off or removed with a special nut breaker, available at tool shops.

 Flat washers and lock washers, when removed from an assembly should always be replaced exactly as removed. Replace any damaged washers with new ones. Always use a flat washer between a lock washer and any soft metal surface (such as aluminium), thin sheet metal or plastic. Special lock nuts can only be used once or twice before they lose their locking ability and must be renewed.

 If a bolt or stud breaks off in an assembly, it can be drilled out and removed with a special tool called an E-Z out. Most dealer service departments and motorcycle repair shops can perform this task, as well as others (such as the repair of threaded holes that have been stripped out).

Spanner size comparison

Jaw gap (in)	Spanner size	Jaw gap (in)	Spanner size
0.250	1/4 in AF	0.945	24 mm
0.276	7 mm	1.000	1 in AF
0.313	5/16 in AF	1.010	9/16 in Whitworth; 5/8 in BSF
0.315	8 mm	1.024	26 mm
0.344	11/32 in AF; 1/8 in Whitworth	1.063	1 1/16 in AF; 27 mm
0.354	9 mm	1.100	5/8 in Whitworth; 11/16 in BSF
0.375	3/8 in AF	1.125	1 1/8 in AF
0.394	10 mm	1.181	30 mm
0.433	11 mm	1.200	11/16 in Whitworth; 3/4 in BSF
0.438	7/16 in AF	1.250	1 1/4 in AF
0.445	3/16 in Whitworth; 1/4 in BSF	1.260	32 mm
0.472	12 mm	1.300	3/4 in Whitworth; 7/8 in BSF
0.500	1/2 in AF	1.313	1 5/16 in AF
0.512	13 mm	1.390	13/16 in Whitworth; 15/16 in BSF
0.525	1/4 in Whitworth; 5/16 in BSF	1.417	36 mm
0.551	14 mm	1.438	1 7/16 in AF
0.563	9/16 in AF	1.480	7/8 in Whitworth; 1 in BSF
0.591	15 mm	1.500	1 1/2 in AF
0.600	5/16 in Whitworth; 3/8 in BSF	1.575	40 mm; 15/16 in Whitworth
0.625	5/8 in AF	1.614	41 mm
0.630	16 mm	1.625	1 5/8 in AF
0.669	17 mm	1.670	1 in Whitworth; 1 1/8 in BSF
0.686	11/16 in AF	1.688	1 11/16 in AF
0.709	18 mm	1.811	46 mm
0.710	3/8 in Whitworth; 7/16 in BSF	1.813	1 13/16 in AF
0.748	19 mm	1.860	1 1/8 in Whitworth; 1 1/4 in BSF
0.750	3/4 in AF	1.875	1 7/8 in AF
0.813	13/16 in AF	1.969	50 mm
0.820	7/16 in Whitworth; 1/2 in BSF	2.000	2 in AF
0.866	22 mm	2.050	1 1/4 in Whitworth; 1 3/8 in BSF
0.875	7/8 in AF	2.165	55 mm
0.920	1/2 in Whitworth; 9/16 in BSF	2.362	60 mm
0.938	15/16 in AF		

Standard torque settings

Specific torque settings will be found at the end of the specifications section of each chapter. Where no figure is given, bolts should be secured according to the table below.

Fastener type (thread diameter)	kgf m	lbf ft
5mm bolt or nut	0.45 – 0.6	3.5 – 4.5
6 mm bolt or nut	0.8 – 1.2	6 – 9
8 mm bolt or nut	1.8 – 2.5	13 – 18
10 mm bolt or nut	3.0 – 4.0	22 – 29
12 mm bolt or nut	5.0 – 6.0	36 – 43
5 mm screw	0.35 – 0.5	2.5 – 3.6
6 mm screw	0.7 – 1.1	5 – 8
6 mm flange bolt	1.0 – 1.4	7 – 10
8 mm flange bolt	2.4 – 3.0	17 – 22
10 mm flange bolt	3.0 – 4.0	22 – 29

Choosing and fitting accessories

The range of accessories available to the modern motorcyclist is almost as varied and bewildering as the range of motorcycles. This Section is intended to help the owner in choosing the correct equipment for his needs and to avoid some of the mistakes made by many riders when adding accessories to their machines. It will be evident that the Section can only cover the subject in the most general terms and so it is recommended that the owner, having decided that he wants to fit, for example, a luggage rack or carrier, seeks the advice of several local dealers and the owners of similar machines. This will give a good idea of what makes of carrier are easily available, and at what price. Talking to other owners will give some insight into the drawbacks or good points of any one make. A walk round the motorcycles in car parks or outside a dealer will often reveal the same sort of information.

The first priority when choosing accessories is to assess exactly what one needs. It is, for example, pointless to buy a large heavy-duty carrier which is designed to take the weight of fully laden panniers and topbox when all you need is a place to strap on a set of waterproofs and a lunchbox when going to work. Many accessory manufacturers have ranges of equipment to cater for the individual needs of different riders and this point should be borne in mind when looking through a dealer's catalogues. Having decided exactly what is required and the use to which the accessories are going to be put, the owner will need a few hints on what to look for when making the final choice. To this end the Section is now sub-divided to cover the more popular accessories fitted. Note that it is in no way a customizing guide, but merely seeks to outline the practical considerations to be taken into account when adding aftermarket equipment to a motorcycle.

Fairings and windscreens

A fairing is possibly the single, most expensive, aftermarket item to be fitted to any motorcycle and, therefore, requires the most thought before purchase. Fairings can be divided into two main groups: front fork mounted handlebar fairings and windscreens, and frame mounted fairings.

The first group, the front fork mounted fairings, are becoming far more popular than was once the case, as they offer several advantages over the second group. Front fork mounted fairings generally are much easier and quicker to fit, involve less modification to the motorcycle, do not as a rule restrict the steering lock, permit a wider selection of handlebar styles to be used, and offer adequate protection for much less money than the frame mounted type. They are also lighter, can be swapped easily between different motorcycles, and are available in a much greater variety of styles. Their main disadvantages are that they do not offer as much weather protection as the frame mounted types, rarely offer any storage space, and, if poorly fitted or naturally incompatible, can have an adverse effect on the stability of the motorcycle.

The second group, the frame mounted fairings, are secured so rigidly to the main frame of the motorcycle that they can offer a substantial amount of protection to motorcycle and rider in the event of a crash. They offer almost complete protection from the weather and, if double-skinned in construction, can provide a great deal of useful storage space. The feeling of peace, quiet and complete relaxation encountered when riding behind a good full fairing has to be experienced to be believed. For this reason full fairings are considered essential by most touring motorcyclists and by many people who ride all year round. The main disadvantages of this type are that fitting can take a long time, often involving removal or modification of standard motorcycle components, they restrict the steering lock and they can add up to about 40 lb to the weight of the machine. They do not usually affect the stability of the machine to any great extent once the front tyre pressure and suspension have been adjusted to compensate for the extra weight, but can be affected by sidewinds.

The first thing to look for when purchasing a fairing is the quality of the fittings. A good fairing will have strong, substantial brackets constructed from heavy-gauge tubing; the brackets must be shaped to fit the frame or forks evenly so that the minimum of stress is imposed on the assembly when it is bolted down. The brackets should be properly painted or finished – a nylon coating being the favourite of the better manufacturers – the nuts and bolts provided should be of the same thread and size standard as is used on the motorcycle and be properly plated. Look also for shakeproof locking nuts or locking washers to ensure that everything remains securely tightened down. The fairing shell is generally made from one of two materials: fibreglass or ABS plastic. Both have their advantages and disadvantages, but the main consideration for the owner is that fibreglass is much easier to repair in the event of damage occurring to the fairing. Whichever material is used, check that it is properly finished inside as well as out, that the edges are protected by beading and that the fairing shell is insulated from vibration by the use of rubber grommets at all mounting points. Also be careful to check that the windscreen is retained by plastic bolts which will snap on impact so that the windscreen will break away and not cause personal injury in the event of an accident.

Having purchased your fairing or windscreen, read the manufacturer's fitting instructions very carefully and check that you have all the necessary brackets and fittings. Ensure that the mounting brackets are located correctly and bolted down securely. Note that some manufacturers use hose clamps to retain the mounting brackets; these should be discarded as they are convenient to use but not strong enough for the task. Stronger clamps should be substituted; car exhaust pipe clamps of suitable size would be a good alternative. Ensure that the front forks can turn through the full steering lock available without fouling the fairing. With many types of frame-mounted fairing the handlebars will have to be altered or a different type fitted and the steering lock will be restricted by stops provided with the fittings. Also check that the fairing does not foul the front wheel or mudguard, in any

Choosing and fitting accessories

steering position, under full fork compression. Re-route any cables, brake pipes or electrical wiring which may snag on the fairing and take great care to protect all electrical connections, using insulating tape. If the manufacturer's instructions are followed carefully at every stage no serious problems should be encountered. Remember that hydraulic pipes that have been disconnected must be carefully re-tightened and the hydraulic system purged of air bubbles by bleeding.

Two things will become immediately apparent when taking a motorcycle on the road for the first time with a fairing – the first is the tendency to underestimate the road speed because of the lack of wind pressure on the body. This must be very carefully watched until one has grown accustomed to riding behind the fairing. The second thing is the alarming increase in engine noise which is an unfortunate but inevitable by-product of fitting any type of fairing or windscreen, and is caused by normal engine noise being reflected, and in some cases amplified, by the flat surface of the fairing.

Luggage racks or carriers

Carriers are possibly the commonest item to be fitted to modern motorcycles. They vary enormously in size, carrying capacity, and durability. When selecting a carrier, always look for one which is made specifically for your machine and which is bolted on with as few separate brackets as possible. The universal-type carrier, with its mass of brackets and adaptor pieces, will generally prove too weak to be of any real use. A good carrier should bolt to the main frame, generally using the two suspension unit top mountings and a mudguard mounting bolt as attachment points, and have its luggage platform as low and as far forward as possible to minimise the effect of any load on the machine's stability. Look for good quality, heavy gauge tubing, good welding and good finish. Also ensure that the carrier does not prevent opening of the seat, sidepanels or tail compartment, as appropriate. When using a carrier, be very careful not to overload it. Excessive weight placed so high and so far to the rear of any motorcycle will have an adverse effect on the machine's steering and stability.

Luggage

Motorcycle luggage can be grouped under two headings: soft and hard. Both types are available in many sizes and styles and have advantages and disadvantages in use.

Soft luggage is now becoming very popular because of its lower cost and its versatility. Whether in the form of tankbags, panniers, or strap-on bags, soft luggage requires in general no brackets and no modification to the motorcycle. Equipment can be swapped easily from one motorcycle to another and can be fitted and removed in seconds. Awkwardly shaped loads can easily be carried. The disadvantages of soft luggage are that the contents cannot be secure against the casual thief, very little protection is afforded in the event of a crash, and waterproofing is generally poor. Also, in the case of panniers, carrying capacity is restricted to approximately 10 lb, although this amount will vary considerably depending on the manufacturer's recommendation. When purchasing soft luggage, look for good quality material, generally vinyl or nylon, with strong, well-stitched attachment points. It is always useful to have separate pockets, especially on tank bags, for items which will be needed on the journey. When purchasing a tank bag, look for one which has a separate, well-padded, base. This will protect the tank's paintwork and permit easy access to the filler cap at petrol stations.

Hard luggage is confined to two types: panniers, and top boxes or tail trunks. Most hard luggage manufacturers produce matching sets of these items, the basis of which is generally that manufacturer's own heavy-duty luggage rack. Variations on this theme occur in the form of separate frames for the better quality panniers, fixed or quickly-detachable luggage, and in size and carrying capacity. Hard luggage offers a reasonable degree of security against theft and good protection against weather and accident damage. Carrying capacity is greater than that of soft luggage, around 15 – 20 lb in the case of panniers, although top boxes should never be loaded as much as their apparent capacity might imply. A top box should only be used for lightweight items, because one that is heavily laden can have a serious effect on the stability of the machine. When purchasing hard luggage look for the same good points as mentioned under fairings and windscreens, ie good quality mounting brackets and fittings, and well-finished fibreglass or ABS plastic cases. Again as with fairings, always purchase luggage made specifically for your motorcycle, using as few separate brackets as possible, to ensure that everything remains securely bolted in place. When fitting hard luggage, be careful to check that the rear suspension and brake operation will not be impaired in any way and remember that many pannier kits require re-siting of the indicators. Remember also that a non-standard exhaust system may make fitting extremely difficult.

Handlebars

The occupation of fitting alternative types of handlebar is extremely popular with modern motorcyclists, whose motives may vary from the purely practical, wishing to improve the comfort of their machines, to the purely aesthetic, where form is more important than function. Whatever the reason, there are several considerations to be borne in mind when changing the handlebars of your machine. If fitting lower bars, check carefully that the switches and cables do not foul the petrol tank on full lock and that the surplus length of cable, brake pipe, and electrical wiring are smoothly and tidily disposed of. Avoid tight kinks in cable or brake pipes which will produce stiff controls or the premature and disastrous failure of an overstressed component. If necessary, remove the petrol tank and re-route the cable from the engine/gearbox unit upwards, ensuring smooth gentle curves are produced. In extreme cases, it will be necessary to purchase a shorter brake pipe to overcome this problem. In the case of higher handlebars than standard it will almost certainly be necessary to purchase extended cables and brake pipes. Fortunately, many standard motorcycles have a custom version which will be equipped with higher handlebars and, therefore, factory-built extended components will be available from your local dealer. It is not usually necessary to extend electrical wiring, as switch clusters may be used on several different motorcycles, some being custom versions. This point should be borne in mind however when fitting extremely high or wide handlebars.

When fitting different types of handlebar, ensure that the mounting clamps are correctly tightened to the manufacturer's specifications and that cables and wiring, as previously mentioned, have smooth easy runs and do not snag on any part of the motorcycle throughout the full steering lock. Ensure that the fluid level in the front brake master cylinder remains level to avoid any chance of air entering the hydraulic system. Also check that the cables are adjusted correctly and that all handlebar controls operate correctly and can be easily reached when riding.

Crashbars

Crashbars, also known as engine protector bars, engine guards, or case savers, are extremely useful items of equipment which can contribute protection to the machine's structure if a crash occurs. They do not, as has been inferred in the US, prevent the rider from crashing, or necessarily prevent rider injury should a crash occur.

It is recommended that only the smaller, neater, engine protector type of crashbar is considered. This type will offer protection while restricting, as little as is possible, access to the engine and the machine's ground clearance. The crashbars should be designed for use specifically on your machine, and should be constructed of heavy-gauge tubing with strong, integral mounting brackets. Where possible, they should bolt to a strong lug on the frame, usually at the engine mounting bolts.

The alternative type of crashbar is the larger cage type. This type is not recommended in spite of their appearance which promises some protection to the rider as well as to the machine. The larger amount of leverage imposed by the size of this type of crashbar increases the risk of severe frame damage in the event of an accident. This type also decreases the machine's ground clearance and restricts access to the engine. The amount of protection afforded the rider is open to some doubt as the design is based on the premise that the rider will stay in the normally seated position during an accident, and the crash bar structure will not itself fail. Neither result can in any way be guaranteed.

As a general rule, always purchase the best, ie usually the most expensive, set of crashbars you an afford. The investment will be repaid by minimising the amount of damage incurred, should the machine be involved in an accident. Finally, avoid the universal type of crashbar. This should be regarded only as a last resort to be used if no alternative exists. With its usual multitude of separate brackets and spacers, the universal crashbar is far too weak in design and construction to be of any practical value.

Exhaust systems

The fitting of aftermarket exhaust systems is another extremely popular pastime amongst motorcyclists. The usual motive is to gain more performance from the engine but other considerations are to gain more ground clearance, to lose weight from the motorcycle, to obtain a more distinctive exhaust note or to find a cheaper alternative to the manufacturer's original equipment exhaust system. Original equipment exhaust systems often cost more and may well have a relatively short life. It should be noted that it is rare for an aftermarket exhaust system alone to give a noticeable increase in the engine's power output. Modern motorcycles are designed to give the highest power output possible allowing for factors such as quietness, fuel economy, spread of power, and long-term reliability. If there were a magic formula which allowed the exhaust system to produce more power without affecting these other considerations you can be sure that the manufacturers, with their large research and development facilities, would have found it and made use of it. Performance increases of a worthwhile and noticeable nature only come from well-tried and properly matched modifications to the entire engine, from the air filter, through the carburettors, port timing or camshaft and valve design, combustion chamber shape, compression ratio, and the exhaust system. Such modifications are well outside the scope of this manual but interested owners might refer to the 'Piper Tuning Manual' produced by the publisher of this manual; this book goes into the whole subject in great detail.

Whatever your motive for wishing to fit an alternative exhaust system, be sure to seek expert advice before doing so. Changes to the carburettor jetting will almost certainly be required for which you must consult the exhaust system manufacturer. If he cannot supply adequately specific information it is reasonable to assume that insufficient development work has been carried out, and that particular make should be avoided. Other factors to be borne in mind are whether the exhaust system allows the use of both centre and side stands, whether it allows sufficient access to permit oil and filter changing and whether modifications are necessary to the standard exhaust system. Many two-stroke expansion chamber systems require the use of the standard exhaust pipe; this is all very well if the standard exhaust pipe and silencer are separate units but can cause problems if the two, as with so many modern two-strokes, are a one-piece unit. While the exhaust pipe can be removed easily by means of a hacksaw it is not so easy to refit the original silencer should you at any time wish to return the machine to standard trim. The same applies to several four-stroke systems.

On the subject of the finish of aftermarket exhausts, avoid black-painted systems unless you enjoy painting. As any trail-bike owner will tell you, rust has a great affinity for black exhausts and re-painting or rust removal becomes a task which must be carried out with monotonous regularity. A bright chrome finish is, as a general rule, a far better proposition as it is much easier to keep clean and to prevent rusting. Although the general finish of aftermarket exhaust systems is not always up to the standard of the original equipment the lower cost of such systems does at least reflect this fact.

When fitting an alternative system always purchase a full set of new exhaust gaskets, to prevent leaks. Fit the exhaust first to the cylinder head or barrel, as appropriate, tightening the retaining nuts or bolts by hand only and then line up the exhaust rear mountings. If the new system is a one-piece unit and the rear mountings do not line up exactly, spacers must be fabricated to take up the difference. Do not force the system into place as the stress thus imposed will rapidly cause cracks and splits to appear. Once all the mountings are loosely fixed, tighten the retaining nuts or bolts securely, being careful not to overtighten them. Where the motorcycle manufacturer's torque settings are available, these should be used. Do not forget to carry out any carburation changes recommended by the exhaust system's manufacturer.

Electrical equipment

The vast range of electrical equipment available to motorcyclists is so large and so diverse that only the most general outline can be given here. Electrical accessories vary from electric ignition kits fitted to replace contact breaker points, to additional lighting at the front and rear, more powerful horns, various instruments and gauges, clocks, anti-theft systems, heated clothing, CB radios, radio-cassette players, and intercom systems, to name but a few of the more popular items of equipment.

As will be evident, it would require a separate manual to cover this subject alone and this section is therefore restricted to outlining a few basic rules which must be borne in mind when fitting electrical equipment. The first consideration is whether your machine's electrical system has enough reserve capacity to cope with the added demand of the accessories you wish to fit. The motorcycle's manufacturer or importer should be able to furnish this sort of information and may also be able to offer advice on uprating the electrical system. Failing this, a good dealer or the accessory manufacturer may be able to help. In some cases, more powerful generator components may be available, perhaps from another motorcycle in the manufacturer's range. The second consideration is the legal requirements in force in your area. The local police may be prepared to help with this point. In the UK for example, there are strict regulations governing the position and use of auxiliary riding lamps and fog lamps.

When fitting electrical equipment always disconnect the battery first to prevent the risk of a short-circuit, and be careful to ensure that all connections are properly made and that they are waterproof. Remember that many electrical accessories are designed primarily for use in cars and that they cannot easily withstand the exposure to vibration and to the weather. Delicate components must be rubber-mounted to insulate them from vibration, and sealed carefully to prevent the entry of rainwater and dirt. Be careful to follow exactly the accessory manufacturer's instructions in conjunction with the wiring diagram at the back of this manual.

Accessories – general

Accessories fitted to your motorcycle will rapidly deteriorate if not cared for. Regular washing and polishing will maintain the finish and will provide an opportunity to check that all mounting bolts and nuts are securely fastened. Any signs of chafing or wear should be watched for, and the cause cured as soon as possible before serious damage occurs.

As a general rule, do not expect the re-sale value of your motorcycle to increase by an amount proportional to the amount of money and effort put into fitting accessories. It is usually the case that an absolutely standard motorcycle will sell more easily at a better price than one that has been modified. If you are in the habit of exchanging your machine for another at frequent intervals, this factor should be borne in mind to avoid loss of money.

Fault diagnosis

Contents

Introduction	1
Starter motor problems	
Starter motor not rotating	2
Starter motor rotates but engine does not turn over	3
Starter motor and clutch function but engine will not turn over	4
Engine does not start when turned over	
No fuel flow to carburettor	5
Fuel not reaching cylinder	6
Engine flooding	7
No spark at plug	8
Weak spark at plug	9
Compression low	10
Engine stalls after starting	
General causes	11
Poor running at idle and low speed	
Weak spark at plug or erratic firing	12
Fuel/air mixture incorrect	13
Compression low	14
Acceleration poor	
General causes	15
Poor running or lack of power at high speeds	
Weak spark at plug or erratic firing	16
Fuel/air mixture incorrect	17
Compression low	18
Knocking or pinking	
General causes	19
Overheating	
Firing incorrect	20
Fuel/air mixture incorrect	21
Lubrication inadequate	22
Miscellaneous causes	23
Clutch operating problems	
Clutch slip	24
Clutch drag	25
Gear selection problems	
Gear lever does not return	26
Gear selection difficult or impossible	27
Jumping out of gear	28
Overselection	29
Abnormal engine noise	
Knocking or pinking	30
Piston slap or rattling from cylinder	31
Valve noise or tapping from cylinder head	32
Other noises	33
Abnormal transmission noise	
Clutch noise	34
Transmission noise	35
Exhaust smokes excessively	
White/blue smoke (caused by oil burning)	36
Black smoke (caused by over-rich mixture)	37
Oil pressure indicator lamp goes on	
Engine lubrication system failure	38
Electrical system failure	39
Poor handling or roadholding	
Directional instability	40
Steering bias to left or right	41
Handlebar vibrates or oscillates	42
Poor front fork performance	43
Front fork judder when braking	44
Poor rear suspension performance	45
Abnormal frame and suspension noise	
Front end noise	46
Rear suspension noise	47
Brake problems	
Brakes are spongy or ineffective – disc brakes	48
Brakes drag – disc brakes	49
Brake lever or pedal pulsates in operation – disc brakes	50
Disc brake noise	51
Brakes are spongy or ineffective – drum brakes	52
Brake drag – drum brakes	53
Brake lever or pedal pulsates in operation – drum brakes	54
Drum brake noise	55
Brake induced fork judder	56
Electrical problems	
Battery dead or weak	57
Battery overcharged	58
Total electrical failure	59
Circuit failure	60
Bulbs blowing repeatedly	61

Fault diagnosis

1 Introduction

This Section provides an easy reference-guide to the more common ailments that are likely to afflict your machine. Obviously, the opportunities are almost limitless for faults to occur as a result of obscure failures, and to try and cover all eventualities would require a book. Indeed, a number have been written on the subject.

Successful fault diagnosis is not a mysterious 'black art' but the application of a bit of knowledge combined with a systematic and logical approach to the problem. Approach any fault diagnosis by first accurately identifying the symptom and then checking through the list of possible causes, starting with the simplest or most obvious and progressing in stages to the most complex. Take nothing for granted, but above all apply liberal quantities of common sense.

The main symptom of a fault is given in the text as a major heading below which are listed, as Section headings, the various systems or areas which may contain the fault. Details of each possible cause for a fault and the remedial action to be taken are given, in brief, in the paragraphs below each Section heading. Further information should be sought in the relevant Chapter.

Starter motor problems

2 Starter motor not rotating

Engine stop switch off.
Fuse blown. Check the main fuse located behind the battery side cover.
Battery voltage low. Switching on the headlamp and operating the horn will give a good indication of the charge level. If necessary recharge the battery from an external source.
Neutral gear not selected. Where a neutral indicator switch is fitted.
Faulty neutral indicator switch or clutch interlock switch (where fitted). Check the switch wiring and switches for correct operation.
Ignition switch defective. Check switch for continuity and connections for security.
Engine stop switch defective. Check switch for continuity in 'Run' position. Fault will be caused by broken, wet or corroded switch contacts. Clean or renew as necessary.
Starter button switch faulty. Check continuity of switch. Faults as for engine stop switch.
Starter relay (solenoid) faulty. If the switch is functioning correctly a pronounced click should be heard when the starter button is depressed. This presupposes that current is flowing to the solenoid when the button is depressed.
Wiring open or shorted. Check first that the battery terminal connections are tight and corrosion free. Follow this by checking that all wiring connections are dry, tight and corrosion free. Check also for frayed or broken wiring. Occasionally a wire may become trapped between two moving components, particularly in the vicinity of the steering head, leading to breakage of the internal core but leaving the softer but more resilient outer cover intact. This can cause mysterious intermittent or total power loss.
Starter motor defective. A badly worn starter motor may cause high current drain from a battery without the motor rotating. If current is found to be reaching the motor, after checking the starter button and starter relay, suspect a damaged motor. The motor should be removed for inspection.

3 Starter motor rotates but engine does not turn over

Damaged starter motor drive train. Inspect and renew component where necessary. Failure in this area is unlikely.

4 Starter motor and clutch function but engine will not turn over

Engine seized. Seizure of the engine is always a result of damage to internal components due to lubrication failure, or component breakage resulting from abuse, neglect or old age. A seizing or partially seized component may go un-noticed until the engine has cooled down and an attempt is made to restart the engine. Suspect first seizure of the valves, valve gear and the pistons. Instantaneous seizure whilst the engine is running indicates component breakage. In either case major dismantling and inspection will be required.

Engine does not start when turned over

5 No fuel flow to carburettor

No fuel or insufficient fuel in tank.
Fuel tap lever position incorrectly selected.
Tank filler cap air vent obstructed. Usually caused by dirt or water. Clean the vent orifice.
Fuel tap or filter blocked. Blockage may be due to accumulation of rust or paint flakes from the tank's inner surface or of foreign matter from contaminated fuel. Remove the tap and clean it and the filter. Look also for water droplets in the fuel.
Fuel line blocked. Blockage of the fuel line is more likely to result from a kink in the line rather than the accumulation of debris.

6 Fuel not reaching cylinder

Float chamber not filling. Caused by float needle or floats sticking in up position. This may occur after the machine has been left standing for an extended length of time allowing the fuel to evaporate. When this occurs a gummy residue is often left which hardens to a varnish-like substance. This condition may be worsened by corrosion and crystaline deposits produced prior to the total evaporation of contaminated fuel. Sticking of the float needle may also be caused by wear. In any case removal of the float chamber will be necessary for inspection and cleaning.
Blockage in starting circuit, slow running circuit or jets. Blockage of these items may be attributable to debris from the fuel tank by-passing the filter system or to gumming up as described in paragraph 1. Water droplets in the fuel will also block jets and passages. The carburettor should be dismantled for cleaning.
Fuel level too low. The fuel level in the float chamber is controlled by float height. The fuel level may increase with wear or damage but will never reduce, thus a low fuel level is an inherent rather than developing condition. Check the fuel level and make any necessary adjustment.

7 Engine flooding

Float valve needle worn or stuck open. A piece of rust or other debris can prevent correct seating of the needle against the valve seat thereby permitting an uncontrolled flow of fuel. Similarly, a worn needle or needle seat will prevent valve closure. Dismantle the carburettor float bowl for cleaning and, if necessary, renewal of the worn components.
Fuel level too high. The fuel level is controlled by the float height which may increase due to wear of the float needle, pivot pin or operating tang. Check the float height, and make any necessary adjustment. A leaking float will cause an increase in fuel level, and thus should be renewed.
Accelerator pump. On those models so equipped, repeated operation of the throttle prior to starting will cause flooding due to too much raw fuel being injected into the venturi.
Cold starting mechanism. Check the choke (starter mechanism) for correct operation. If the mechanism jams in the 'On' position subsequent starting of a hot engine will be difficult.
Blocked air filter. A badly restricted air filter will cause flooding. Check the filter and clean or renew as required.

8 No spark at plug

Ignition switch not on.
Engine stop switch off.
Fuse blown. Check fuse for ignition circuit. See wiring diagram.
Battery voltage low. The current draw required by a starter motor is

sufficiently high that an under-charged battery may not have enough spare capacity to provide power for the ignition circuit during starting. Use of the kickstart (where fitted) is recommended until the battery has been recharged either by the machine's generator or from an external charger.

Starter motor inefficient. A starter motor with worn brushes and a worn or dirty commutator will draw excessive amounts of current causing power starvation in the ignition system. See the preceding paragraph. Starter motor overhaul will be required.

Spark plug failure. Clean the spark plug thoroughly and reset the electrode gap. Refer to the spark plug section and the colour condition guide in Routine Maintenance. If the spark plug shorts internally or has sustained visible damage to the electrodes, core or ceramic insulator it should be renewed. On rare occasions a plug that appears to spark vigorously will fail to do so when refitted to the engine and subjected to the compression pressure in the cylinder.

Spark plug cap or high tension (HT) lead faulty. Check condition and security. Replace if deterioration is evident.

Spark plug cap loose. Check that the spark plug cap fits securely over the plug and, where fitted, the screwed terminal on the plug end is secure.

Shorting due to moisture. Certain parts of the ignition system are susceptible to shorting when the machine is ridden or parked in wet weather. Check particularly the area from the spark plug cap back to the ignition coil. A water dispersant spray may be used to dry out waterlogged components. Recurrence of the problem can be prevented by using an ignition sealant spray after drying out and cleaning.

Ignition or stop switch shorted. May be caused by water, corrosion or wear. Water dispersant and contact cleaning sprays may be used. If this fails to overcome the problem dismantling and visual inspection of the switches will be required.

Shorting or open circuit in wiring. Failure in any wire connecting any of the ignition components will cause ignition malfunction. Check also that all connections are clean, dry and tight.

Ignition coil failure. Check the coil, referring to Chapter 5.

Capacitor (condenser) failure. The capacitor may be checked most easily by direct substitution with a replacement item. Blackened contact breaker points indicate capacitor malfunction but this may not always occur.

Contact breaker points pitted, burned or closed up. Check the contact breaker points, referring to Routine Maintenance. Check also that the low tension leads at the contact breaker are secure and not shorting out.

Electronic ignition system fault. Refer to Chapter 5.

9 Weak spark at plug

Feeble sparking at the plug may be caused by any of the faults mentioned in the preceding Section other than those items in paragraphs 1 and 2. Check first the contact breaker assembly and the spark plug, these being the most likely culprits.

10 Compression low

Spark plug loose. This will be self-evident on inspection, and may be accompanied by a hissing noise when the engine is turned over. Remove the plug and check that the threads in the cylinder head are not damaged. Check also that the plug sealing washer is in good condition.

Cylinder head gasket leaking. This condition is often accompanied by a high pitched squeak from around the cylinder head and oil loss, and may be caused by insufficiently tightened cylinder head fasteners, a warped cylinder head or mechanical failure of the gasket material. Re-torqueing the fasteners to the correct specification may seal the leak in some instances but if damage has occurred this course of action will provide, at best, only a temporary cure.

Valve not seating correctly. The failure of a valve to seat may be caused by insufficient valve clearance, pitting of the valve seat or face, carbon deposits on the valve seat or seizure of the valve stem or valve gear components. Valve spring breakage will also prevent correct valve closure. The valve clearances should be checked first and then, if these are found to be in order, further dismantling will be required to inspect the relevant components for failure.

Cylinder, piston and ring wear. Compression pressure will be lost if any of these components are badly worn. Wear in one component is invariably accompanied by wear in another. A top end overhaul will be required.

Piston rings sticking or broken. Sticking of the piston rings may be caused by seizure due to lack of lubrication or heating as a result of poor carburation or incorrect fuel type. Gumming of the rings may result from lack of use, or carbon deposits in the ring grooves. Broken rings result from over-revving, overheating or general wear. In either case a top-end overhaul will be required.

Engine stalls after starting

11 General causes

Improper cold start mechanism operation. Check that the operating controls function smoothly and, where applicable, are correctly adjusted. A cold engine may not require application of an enriched mixture to start initially but may baulk without choke once firing. Likewise a hot engine may start with an enriched mixture but will stop almost immediately if the choke is inadvertently in operation.

Ignition malfunction. See Section 9, 'Weak spark at plug'.

Carburettor incorrectly adjusted. Maladjustment of the mixture strength or idle speed may cause the engine to stop immediately after starting. See Chapter 4.

Fuel contamination. Check for filter blockage by debris or water which reduces, but does not completely stop, fuel flow or blockage of the slow speed circuit in the carburettor by the same agents. If water is present it can often be seen as droplets in the bottom of the float bowl. Clean the filter and, where water is in evidence, drain and flush the fuel tank and float bowl.

Intake air leak. Check for security of the carburettor mounting and hose connections, and for cracks or splits in the hoses. Check also that the carburettor top is secure and that the vacuum gauge adaptor plug (where fitted) is tight.

Air filter blocked or omitted. A blocked filter will cause an over-rich mixture; the omission of a filter will cause an excessively weak mixture. Both conditions will have a detrimental affect on carburation. Clean or renew the filter as necessary.

Fuel filler cap air vent blocked. Usually caused by dirt or water. Clean the vent orifice.

Poor running at idle and low speed

12 Weak spark at plug or erratic firing

Battery voltage low. In certain conditions low battery charge, especially when coupled with a badly sulphated battery, may result in misfiring. If the battery is in good general condition it should be recharged; an old battery suffering from sulphated plates should be renewed.

Spark plug fouled, faulty or incorrectly adjusted. See Section 8 or refer to Routine Maintenance.

Spark plug cap or high tension lead shorting. Check the condition of both these items ensuring that they are in good condition and dry and that the cap is fitted correctly.

Spark plug type incorrect. Fit plug of correct type and heat range as given in Specifications. In certain conditions a plug of hotter or colder type may be required for normal running.

Contact breaker points pitted, burned or closed-up. Check the contact breaker assembly, referring to Routine Maintenance.

Igniting timing incorrect. Check the ignition timing statically and dynamically, ensuring that the advance is functioning correctly.

Faulty ignition coil. Partial failure of the coil internal insulation will diminish the performance of the coil. No repair is possible, a new component must be fitted.

Faulty capacitor (condenser). A failure of capacitor will cause blackening of the contact breaker point faces and will allow excessive sparking at the points. A faulty capacitor may best be checked by substitution of a serviceable replacement item.

13 Fuel/air mixture incorrect

Intake air leak. See Section 11.
Mixture strength incorrect. Adjust slow running mixture strength using pilot adjustment screw.
Carburettor synchronisation.
Pilot jet or slow running circuit blocked. The carburettor should be removed and dismantled for thorough cleaning. Blow through all jets and air passages with compressed air to clear obstructions.
Air cleaner clogged or omitted. Clean or fit air cleaner element as necessary. Check also that the element and air filter cover are correctly seated.
Cold start mechanism in operation. Check that the choke has not been left on inadvertently and the operation is correct. Where applicable check the operating cable free play.
Fuel level too high or too low. Check the float height and adjust as necessary. See Section 7.
Fuel tank air vent obstructed. Obstruction usually caused by dirt or water. Clean vent orifice.
Valve clearance incorrect. Check, and if necessary, adjust, the clearances.

14 Compression low

See Section 10.

Acceleration poor

15 General causes

All items as for previous Section.
Accelerator pump defective. Where so equipped, check that the accelerator pump injects raw fuel into the carburettor venturi, when the throttle is open fully. If this does not occur check the condition of the pump components and that the feed passage to the pump is not obstructed.
Timing not advancing. This is caused by a sticking or damaged automatic timing unit (ATU). Cleaning and lubrication of the ATU will usually overcome sticking, failing this, and in any event if damage is evident, renewal of the ATU will be required.
Sticking throttle vacuum piston. CD carburettors only.
Brakes binding. Usually caused by maladjustment or partial seizure of the operating mechanism due to poor maintenance. Check brake adjustment (where applicable). A bent wheel spindle or warped brake disc can produce similar symptoms.

Poor running or lack of power at high speeds

16 Weak spark at plug or erratic firing

All items as for Section 12.
HT lead insulation failure. Insulation failure of the HT lead and spark plug cap due to old age or damage can cause shorting when the engine is driven hard. This condition may be less noticeable, or not noticeable at all at lower engine speeds.

17 Fuel/air mixture incorrect

All items as for Section 13, with the exception of items 2 and 4.
Main jet blocked. Debris from contaminated fuel, or from the fuel tank, and water in the fuel can block the main jet. Clean the fuel filter, the float bowl area, and if water is present, flush and refil the fuel tank.
Main jet is the wrong size. The standard carburettor jetting is for sea level atmospheric pressure. For high altitudes, usually above 5000 ft, a smaller main jet will be required.
Jet needle and needle jet worn. These can be renewed individually but should be renewed as a pair. Renewal of both items requires partial dismantling of the carburettor.
Air bleed holes blocked. Dismantle carburettor and use compressed air to blow out all air passages.
Reduced fuel flow. A reduction in the maximum fuel flow from the fuel tank to the carburettor will cause fuel starvation, proportionate to the engine speed. Check for blockages through debris or a kinked fuel line.
Vacuum diaphragm split. Renew.

18 Compression low

See Section 10.

Knocking or pinking

19 General causes

Carbon build-up in combustion chamber. After high mileages have been covered large accumulation of carbon may occur. This may glow red hot and cause premature ignition of the fuel/air mixture, in advance of normal firing by the spark plug. Cylinder head removal will be required to allow inspection and cleaning.
Fuel incorrect. A low grade fuel, or one of poor quality may result in compression induced detonation of the fuel resulting in knocking and pinking noises. Use only the specified grade of fuel. Refer to Chapter 4. Old fuel can cause similar problems. A too highly leaded fuel will reduce detonation but will accelerate deposit formation in the combustion chamber and may lead to early pre-ignition as described in item 1.
Spark plug heat range incorrect. Uncontrolled pre-ignition can result from the use of a spark plug the heat range of which is too hot.
Weak mixture. Overheating of the engine due to a weak mixture can result in pre-ignition occurring where it would not occur when engine temperature was within normal limits. Maladjustment, blocked jets or passages and air leaks can cause this condition.
Some models are prone to pinking (see Chapter 5 for a typical example). In severe cases, compression plates may be fitted to provide a cure.

Overheating

20 Firing incorrect

Spark plug fouled, defective or maladjusted. See Section 6.
Spark plug type incorrect. Refer to the Specifications and ensure that the correct plug type is fitted.
Incorrect ignition timing. Timing that is far too much advanced or far too much retarded will cause overheating. Check the ignition timing is correct and that the advance mechanism is functioning.

21 Fuel/air mixture incorrect

Slow speed mixture strength incorrect. Adjust pilot air screw.
Main jet wrong size. The carburettor is jetted for sea level atmospheric conditions. For high altitudes, usually above 5000 ft, a smaller main jet will be required.
Air filter badly fitted or omitted. Check that the filter element is in place and that it and the air filter box cover are sealing correctly. Any leaks will cause a weak mixture.
Induction air leaks. Check the security of the carburettor mountings and hose connections, and for cracks and splits in the hoses. Check also that the carburettor top is secure and that the vacuum gauge adaptor plug (where fitted) is tight.
Fuel level too low. See Section 6.
Fuel tank filler cap air vent obstructed. Clear blockage.

22 Lubrication inadequate

Engine oil too low. Not only does the oil serve as a lubricant by preventing friction between moving components, but it also acts as a coolant. Check the oil level and replenish.

Engine oil overworked. The lubricating properties of oil are lost slowly during use as a result of changes resulting from heat and also contamination. Always change the oil at the recommended interval.

Engine oil of incorrect viscosity or poor quality. Always use the recommended viscosity and type of oil.

Oil filter and filter by-pass valve blocked. Renew filter and clean the by-pass valve.

23 Miscellaneous causes

Engine fins clogged. A build-up of mud in the cylinder head and cylinder barrel cooling fins will decrease the cooling capabilities of the fins. Clean the fins as required.

Clutch operating problems

24 Clutch slip

No clutch lever play. Adjust clutch lever end play according to the procedure in Routine Maintenance.

Clutch plate worn or warped. Overhaul clutch assembly, replacing plate if necessary (Chapter 2).

Pressure or cover plates worn or warped. Overhaul clutch assembly, replacing plates out of specification (Chapter 2).

Clutch spring broken or worn. An old or heat-damaged (from slipping clutch) spring should be renewed (Chapter 2).

Clutch release not adjusted properly. See Routine Maintenance.

Clutch inner cable snagging. Caused by a frayed cable or kinked outer cable. Replace the cable with a new one. Repair of a frayed cable is not advised.

Clutch release mechanism defective. Worn or damaged parts in the clutch release mechanism could include the pushrod, thrust bearing or thrust piston. Replace parts as necessary (Chapter 2).

Oil leaking on to clutch plate. Dismantle clutch (Chapter 2) renew clutch plate, wash off all traces of oil and trace source of leak. If the leak is from the engine refer to Chapter 1, if from the gearbox, refer to Chapter 3.

25 Clutch drag

Clutch lever play excessive. Adjust lever at bars or at cable end if necessary (refer to Routine Maintenance).

Clutch plates warped or damaged. This will cause a drag on the clutch, causing the machine to creep. Overhaul clutch assembly (Chapter 2).

Clutch release mechanism defective. Worn or damaged release mechanism parts can stick and fail to provide leverage. Overhaul clutch release mechanism (Chapter 2).

Gear selection problems

26 Gear lever does not return

Weak or broken return spring. Renew the spring.

27 Gear selection difficult or impossible

Clutch not disengaging fully. See Section 25.

Wear at external linkage (where fitted) causing excessive free play. Renew worn items.

Gearchange arms, pawls or pins worn or damaged. Wear or breakage of any of these items may cause difficulty in selecting one or more gears. Overhaul the selector mechanism.

Gearchange arm spring broken. Renew spring.

Gearchange drum stopper cam damage. Failure, rather than wear, of these items may jam the cam plates thereby preventing gearchanging. The damaged items must be renewed.

Selector forks bent or seized. This can be as a result of lack of lubrication. Though rare, bending of a shaft can result from a missed gearchange or false selection at high speed.

Selector fork end and pin wear. Pronounced wear of these items and the grooves in the cam plates can lead to imprecise selection and, eventually, no selection. Renewal of the worn components will be required.

Structural failure. Failure of any one component of the selector rod and change mechanism will result in improper or fouled gear selection.

28 Jumping out of gear

Indexing lever assembly worn or damaged. Wear of the lever and the cam with which it locates and breakage of the detent spring can cause imprecise gear selection resulting in jumping out of gear. Renew the damaged components.

Gear pinion dogs worn or damaged. Rounding off the dog edges and the mating recesses in adjacent pinion can lead to jumping out of gear when under load. The gears should be inspected and renewed. Attempting to reprofile the dogs is not recommended.

Selector forks, cam plates and pinion grooves worn. Extreme wear of these interconnected items can occur after high mileages especially when lubrication has been neglected. The worn components must be renewed.

Gear pinions, bushes and shafts worn. Renew the worn components.

Gear pinion tooth broken. Chipped teeth are unlikely to cause jumping out of gear once the gear has been selected fully; a tooth which is completely broken off, however, may cause problems in this respect and in any event will cause transmission noise.

29 Overselection

Pawl spring weak or broken. Renew the spring.

Indexing lever worn or broken. Renew the damaged items.

Stopper arm spring worn or broken. Renew the spring.

Gearchange arm stop pads worn. Repairs can be made by welding and reprofiling with a file.

Selector limiter claw components (where fitted) worn or damaged. Renew the damaged items.

Abnormal engine noise.

30 Knocking or pinking

See Section 19.

31 Piston slap or rattling from cylinder

Cylinder bore/piston clearance excessive. Resulting from wear, partial seizure or improper boring during overhaul. This condition can often be heard as a high, rapid tapping noise when the engine is under little or no load, particularly when power is just beginning to be applied. Reboring to the next correct oversize should be carried out (where possible) and a new oversize piston fitted or the cylinders and pistons should be renewed (all models 1981 on).

Connecting rod bent. This can be caused by over-revving, trying to start a very badly flooded engine (resulting in a hydraulic lock in the cylinder) or by earlier mechanical failure such as a dropped valve. Attempts at straightening a bent connecting rod from a high performance engine are not recommended. Careful inspection of the crankshaft should be made before renewing the damaged connecting rod.

Gudgeon pin, piston boss bore or small-end bearing wear or seizure. Excess clearance or partial seizure between normal moving parts of these items can cause continuous or intermittent tapping noises. Rapid wear or seizure is caused by lubrication starvation resulting from an insufficient engine oil level or oilway blockage.

Piston rings worn, broken or sticking. Renew the rings after careful inspection of the piston and bore.

32 Valve noise or tapping from the cylinder head

Valve clearance incorrect. Adjust the clearances with the engine cold.

Valve spring broken or weak. Renew the spring set.

Excessive rocker arm endfloat. Refer to Chapter 1.

Rocker arm or spindle wear. Rapid wear of a rocker arm, and the resulting need for frequent valve clearance adjustment, indicates breakthrough or failure of the surface hardening on the rocker arm tips. Similar wear in the cam lobes can be expected. Renew the worn components after checking for lubrication failure.

33 Other noises

Big-end bearing wear. A pronounced knock from within the crankcase which worstens rapidly is indicative of big-end bearing failure as a result of extreme normal wear or lubrication failure. Remedial action in the form of a bottom end overhaul should be taken; continuing to run the engine will lead to further damage including the possibility of connecting rod breakage.

Main bearing failure. Extreme normal wear or failure of the main bearings is characteristically accompanied by a rumble from the crankcase and vibration felt through the frame and footrests. Refer to Chapter 1; crankshaft repair is a task for a BMW dealer only.

Crankshaft excessively out of true. A bent crank may result from over-revving or damage from an upper cylinder component or gearbox failure. Renew the crankshaft.

Engine mounting loose. Tighten all the engine mounting nuts and bolts.

Cylinder head gasket leaking. The noise most often associated with a leaking head gasket is a high pitched squeaking, although any other noise consistent with gas being forced out under pressure from a small orifice can also be emitted. Gasket leakage is often accompanied by oil seepage from around the mating joint or from the cylinder head holding down bolts and nuts. Leakage results from insufficient or uneven tightening of the cylinder head fasteners, or from random mechanical failure. Retightening to the correct torque figure will, at best, only provide a temporary cure. The gasket should be renewed at the earliest opportunity.

Exhaust system leakage. Popping or crackling in the exhaust system, particularly when it occurs with the engine on the overrun, indicates a poor joint either at the cylinder port or at the exhaust pipe/silencer connection. Failure of the gasket or looseness of the clamp should be looked for.

Abnormal transmission noise

34 Clutch noise

Clutch plate centre splines worn. Renew the clutch plate and examine closely the gearbox input shaft.

35 Transmission noise

Bearing or bushes worn or damaged. Renew the affected components.

Gear pinions worn or chipped. Renew the gear pinions.

Metal chips jams in gear teeth. This can occur when pieces of metal from any failed component are picked up by a meshing pinion. The condition will lead to rapid bearing wear or early gear failure.

Oil level too low. Top up immediately to prevent damage to gearbox.

Gearchange mechanism worn or damaged. Wear or failure of certain items in the selection and change components can induce mis-selection of gears (see Section 27) where incipient engagement of more than one gear set is promoted. Remedial action, by the overhaul of the gearbox, should be taken without delay.

36 White/blue smoke (caused by oil burning)

Piston rings worn or broken. Breakage or wear of any ring, but particularly the oil control ring, will allow engine oil past the piston into the combustion chamber. Overhaul the cylinder barrel and piston.

Cylinder cracked, worn or scored. These conditions may be caused by overheating, lack of lubrication, component failure or advanced normal wear. The cylinder barrel should be renewed (with the piston) or rebored and the next oversize piston fitted.

Valve guides damaged or worn. This can occur as a result of valve guide failure or old age. The emission of smoke is likely to occur when the throttle is closed rapidly after acceleration, for instance, when changing gear. Renew the valve guides.

Engine oil level too high. This increases the crankcase pressure and allows oil to be forced pass the piston rings. Often accompanied by seepage of oil at joints and oil seals.

Abnormal crankcase pressure. This may be caused by blocked breather passages or hoses causing back-pressure at high engine revolutions.

37 Black smoke (caused by over-rich mixture)

Air filter element clogged. Clean or renew the element.

Main jet loose or too large. Remove the float chamber to check for tightness of the jet. If the machine is used at high altitudes rejetting will be required to compensate for the lower atmospheric pressure.

Cold start mechanism jammed on. Check that the mechanism works smoothly and correctly and that, where fitted, the operating cable is lubricated and not snagged.

Fuel level too high. The fuel level is controlled by the float height which can increase as a result of wear or damage. Remove the float bowl and check the float height. Check also that floats have not punctured; a punctured float will loose buoyancy and allow an increased fuel level.

Float valve needle stuck open. Caused by dirt or a worn valve. Clean the float chamber or renew the needle and, if necessary, the valve seat.

Oil pressure indicator lamp goes on

38 Engine lubrication system failure

Engine oil defective. Oil pump shaft or locating pin sheared off from ingesting debris or seizing from lack of lubrication (low oil level) (Chapter 1).

Engine oil screen clogged. Change oil and filter and service pickup screen (Routine Maintenance and Chapter 4).

Engine oil level too low. Inspect for leak or other problem causing low oil level and add recommended lubricant. Refer to Routine Maintenance.

Engine oil viscosity too low. Very old, thin oil, or an improper weight of oil used in engine. Change to correct lubricant. Refer to Routine Maintenance.

Camshaft or journals worn. High wear causing drop in oil pressure. Replace cam and/or bearings. Abnormal wear could be caused by oil starvation at high rpm from low oil level or improper oil weight or type (Chapter 1).

Crankshaft and/or bearings worn. Same problems as paragraph 5. Overhaul lower end. Refer to Chapter 1, crankshaft repair is a task for a BMW dealer only.

Relief valve stuck open. This causes the oil to be dumped back into the sump. Repair or replace (Chapter 4).

39 Electrical system failure

Oil pressure switch defective. Check switch according to the procedures in Chapter 9. Replace if defective.

Oil pressure indicator lamp wiring system defective. Check for pinched, shorted, disconnected or damaged wiring (Chapter 9).

Poor handling or roadholding

40 Directional instability

Steering head bearing adjustment too tight. This will cause rolling or weaving at low speeds. Re-adjust the bearings.

Steering head bearing worn or damaged. Correct adjustment of the bearing will prove impossible to achieve if wear or damage has occurred. Inconsistent handling will occur including rolling or weaving at low speed and poor directional control at indeterminate higher speeds. The steering head bearing should be dismantled for inspection and renewed if required. Lubrication should also be carried out.

Bearing races pitted or dented. Impact damage caused, perhaps, by an accident or riding over a pot-hole can cause indentation of the bearing, usually in one position. This should be noted as notchiness when the handlebars are turned. Renew and lubricate the bearings.

Steering stem bent. This will occur only if the machine is subjected to a high impact such as hitting a curb or a pot-hole. The lower yoke/stem should be renewed; do not attempt to straighten the stem.

Front or rear tyre pressures too low.

Front or rear tyre worn. General instability, high speed wobbles and skipping over white lines indicates that tyre renewal may be required. Tyre induced problems, in some machine/tyre combinations, can occur even when the tyre in question is by no means fully worn.

Swinging arm bearings worn. Difficulties in holding line, particularly when cornering or when changing power settings indicates wear in the swinging arm bearings. The swinging arm should be removed from the machine and the bearings renewed.

Swinging arm flexing. The symptoms given in the preceding paragraph will also occur if the swinging arm fork flexes badly. This can be caused by structural weakness as a result of corrosion, fatigue or impact damage, or because the rear wheel spindle is slack.

Wheel bearings worn. Renew the worn bearings.

Loose wheel spokes. The spokes should be tightened evenly to maintain tension and trueness of the rim.

Tyres unsuitable for machine. Not all available tyres will suit the characteristics of the frame and suspension, indeed, some tyres or tyre combinations may cause a transformation in the handling characteristics. Check with importer or BMW dealer for currently-approved makes of tyre. If handling problems occur immediately after changing to a new tyre type or make, revert to the original tyres to see whether an improvement can be noted. In some instances a change to what are, in fact, suitable tyres may give rise to handling deficiences. In this case a thorough check should be made of all frame and suspension items which affect stability.

41 Steering bias to left or right

Wheels out of alignment. This can be caused by impact damage to the frame, swinging arm, wheel spindles or front forks. Although occasionally a result of material failure or corrosion it is usually as a result of a crash.

Front forks twisted in the steering yokes. A light impact, for instance with a pot-hole or low curb, can twist the fork legs in the steering yokes without causing structural damage to the fork legs or the yokes themselves. Re-alignment can be made by loosening the yoke pinch bolts, wheel spindle and mudguard bolts. Re-align the wheel with the handlebars and tighten the bolts working upwards from the wheel spindle. This action should be carried out only when there is no chance that structural damage has occurred.

42 Handlebar vibrates or oscillates

Tyres worn or out of balance. Either condition, particularly in the front tyre, will promote shaking of the fork assembly and thus the handlebars. A sudden onset of shaking can result if a balance weight is displaced during use.

Tyres badly positioned on the wheel rims. A moulded line on each wall of a tyre is provided to allow visual verification that the tyre is correctly positioned on the rim. A check can be made by rotating the tyre; any misalignment will be immediately obvious.

Wheels rims warped or damaged. Inspect the wheels for runout as described in Routine Maintenance.

Swinging arm bearings worn. Renew the bearings.

Wheel bearings worn. Renew the bearings.

Steering head bearings incorrectly adjusted. Vibration is more likely to result from bearings which are too loose rather than too tight. Re-adjust the bearings.

Loosen fork component fasteners. Loose nuts and bolts holding the fork legs, wheel spindle, mudguards or steering stem can promote shaking at the handlebars. Fasteners on running gear such as the forks and suspension should be check tightened occasionally to prevent dangerous looseness of components occurring.

Engine mounting bolts loose. Tighten all fasteners.

43 Poor front fork performance

Damping fluid level incorrect. If the fluid level is too low poor suspension control will occur resulting in a general impairment of roadholding and early loss of tyre adhesion when cornering and braking. Too much oil is unlikely to change the fork characteristics unless severe overfilling occurs when the fork action will become stiffer and oil seal failure may occur.

Damping oil viscosity incorrect. The damping action of the fork is directly related to the viscosity of the damping oil. The lighter the oil used, the less will be the damping action imparted. For general use, use only one of the recommended types of oil, changing to a slightly higher or heavier oil only when a change in damping characteristic is required. Overworked oil, or oil contaminated with water which has found its way past the seals, should be renewed to restore the correct damping performance and to prevent bottoming of the forks.

Damping components worn or corroded. Advanced normal wear of the fork internals is unlikely to ocur until a very high mileage has been covered. Continual use of the machine with damaged oil seals which allows the ingress of water, or neglect, will lead to rapid corrosion and wear. Dismantle the forks for inspection and overhaul. See Chapter 6.

Weak fork springs. Progressive fatigue of the fork springs, resulting in a reduced spring free length, will occur after extensive use. This condition will promote excessive fork dive under braking, and in its advanced form will reduce the at-rest extended length of the forks and thus the fork geometry. Renewal of the springs as a pair is the only satisfactory course of action. Heavier duty springs or preload spacers are available for some models.

Bent stanchions or corroded stanchions. Both conditions will prevent correct telescoping of the fork legs, and in an advanced state can cause sticking of the fork in one position. In a mild form corrosion will cause stiction of the fork thereby increasing the time the suspension takes to react to an uneven road surface. Bent fork stanchions should be attended to immediately because they indicate that impact damage has occurred, and there is a danger that the forks will fail with disastrous consequences.

44 Front fork judder when braking (see also Section 56)

Wear between the fork stanchions and the fork legs. Renewal of the affected components is required.

Slack steering head bearings. Re-adjust the bearings.

Warped brake disc or drum. If irregular braking action occurs fork judder can be induced in what are normally serviceable forks. Renew the damaged brake components.

45 Poor rear suspension performances

Rear suspension unit damper worn out or leaking. The damping performance of most rear suspension units falls off with age. This is a gradual process, and thus may not be immediately obvious. Indications of poor damping include hopping of the rear end when cornering or braking, and a general loss of positive stability. See Chapter 7.

Weak rear springs. If the suspension unit springs fatigue they will promote excessive pitching of the machine and reduce the ground clearance when cornering. Although replacement springs are available separately from the rear suspension damper unit it is probable that if spring fatigue has occurred the damper units will also require renewal.

Swinging arm flexing or bearings worn. See Sections 40 and 41.

Bent suspension unit damper rod. This is likely to occur only if the machine is dropped or if seizure of the piston occurs. If either happens the suspension units should be renewed, as a pair (where applicable).

Abnormal frame and suspension noise

46 Front end noise

Oil level low or too thin. This can cause a 'spurting' sound and is usually accompanied by irregular fork action (Chapter 6).

Spring weak or broken. Makes a clicking or scraping sound. Fork oil will have a lot of metal particles in it (Chapter 6).

Steering head bearings loose or damaged. Clicks when braking. Check, adjust or replace (Chapter 6).

Fork clamps loose. Make sure all fork clamp pinch bolts are tight (Chapter 6).

Fork stanchion bent. Good possibility if machine has been dropped. Repair or replace tube (Chapter 6).

Excessive play in damper assembly. See Chapter 6.

47 Rear suspension noise

Fluid level too low. Leakage of a suspension unit, usually evident by oil on the outer surfaces, can cause a spurting noise. The suspension units should be renewed, as a pair (where applicable).

Defective rear suspension unit with internal damage. Renew the suspension units, as a pair (where applicable).

Brake problems

48 Brakes are spongy or ineffective – disc brakes

Air in brake circuit. This is only likely to happen in service due to neglect in checking the fluid level or because a leak has developed. The problem should be identified and the brake system bled of air.

Pad worn. Check the pad wear against the wear lines provided or measure the friction material thickness and renew the pads if necessary.

Contaminated pads. Cleaning pads which have been contaminated with oil, grease or brake fluid is unlikely to prove successful; the pads should be renewed.

Pads glazed. This is usually caused by overheating. The surface of the pads may be roughened using glass-paper or a fine file.

Brake fluid deterioration. A brake which on initial operation is firm but rapidly becomes spongy in use may be failing due to water contamination of the fluid. The fluid should be drained and then the system refilled and bled.

Master cylinder seal failure. Wear or damage of master cylinder internal parts will prevent pressurisation of the brake fluid. Overhaul the master cylinder unit.

Caliper seal failure. This will almost certainly be obvious by loss of fluid, a lowering of fluid in the master cylinder reservoir and contamination of the brake pads and caliper. Overhaul the caliper assembly.

Brake lever or pedal improperly adjusted. Adjust the clearance between the lever end and master cylinder plunger to take up lost motion, as recommended in Routine maintenance (/6, /7 up to 1980 only).

Caliper pivot seized (/6, /7 up to 1980 only).

49 Brakes drag – disc brakes

Disc warped. The disc must be renewed.

Caliper pivot, piston or pads corroded. The brake caliper assembly is vulnerable to corrosion due to water and dirt, and unless cleaned at regular intervals and lubricated in the recommended manner, will become sticky in operation.

Piston seal deteriorated. The seal is designed to return the piston in the caliper to the retracted position when the brake is released. Wear or old age can affect this function. The caliper should be overhauled if this occurs.

Brake pad damaged. Pad material separating from the backing plate due to wear or faulty manufacture. Renew the pads. Faulty installation of a pad also will cause dragging.

Wheel spindle bent. The spindle may be straightened if no structural damage has occurred.

Brake lever or pedal not returning. Check that the lever or pedal works smoothly throughout its operating range and does not snag on any adjacent cycle parts. Lubricate the pivot if necessary.

50 Brake lever or pedal pulsates in operation – disc brakes

Disc warped or irregularly worn. The disc must be renewed.

Wheel spindle bent. The spindle may be straightened provided no structural damage has occurred.

51 Disc brake noise

Brake squeal. Squealing can be caused by dust on the pads, usually in combination with glazed pads, or other contamination from oil, grease, brake fluid or corrosion. Persistent squealing which cannot be traced to any of the normal causes can often be cured by applying a thin layer of high temperature silicone grease to the rear of the pads. Make absolutely certain that no grease is allowed to contaminate the braking surface of the pads.

Glazed pads. This is usually caused by high temperatures or contamination. The pad surfaces may be roughened using glass-paper or a fine file. If this approach does not effect a cure the pads should be renewed.

Disc warped. This can cause a chattering, clicking or intermittent squeal and is usually accompanied by a pulsating brake lever or pedal or uneven braking. The disc must be renewed.

Brake pads fitted incorrectly or undersize. Longitudinal play in the pads due to omission of the locating springs (where fitted) or because pads of the wrong size have been fitted will cause a single tapping noise every time the brake is operated. Inspect the pads for correct installation and security.

52 Brakes are spongy or ineffective – drum brakes

Brake cable deterioration. Damage to the outer cable by stretching or being trapped will give a spongy feel to the brake lever. The cable should be renewed. A cable which has become corroded due to old age or neglect of lubrication will partially seize making operation very heavy. Lubrication at this stage may overcome the problem but the fitting of a new cable is recommended.

Worn brake linings. Determine lining wear using the external brake wear indicator on the brake backplate, or by removing the wheel and withdrawing the brake backplate. Renew the shoe/lining units as a pair if the linings are worn below the recommended limit.

Worn brake camshaft. Wear between the camshaft and the bearing surface will reduce brake feel and reduce operating efficiency. Renewal of one or both items will be required to rectify the fault.

Worn brake cam and shoe ends. Renew the worn components.

Linings contaminated with dust or grease. Any accumulations of

Fault diagnosis

dust should be cleaned from the brake assembly and drum using a petrol dampened cloth. Do not blow or brush off the dust because it is asbestos based and thus harmful if inhaled. Light contamination from grease can be removed from the surface of the brake linings using a solvent; attempts at removing heavier contamination are less likely to be successful because some of the lubricant will have been absorbed by the lining material which will severely reduce the braking performance.

53 Brake drag – drum brakes

Incorrect adjustment. Re-adjust the brake operating mechanism.

Drum warped or oval. This can result from overheating, impact or uneven tension of the wheel spokes. The condition is difficult to correct, although if slight ovality only occurs, skimming the surface of the brake drum can provide a cure. This is work for a specialist engineer. Renewal of the complete wheel hub is normally the only satisfactory solution.

Weak brake shoe return springs. This will prevent the brake lining/shoe units from pulling away from the drum surface once the brake is released. The springs should be renewed.

Brake camshaft, lever pivot or cable poorly lubricated. Failure to attend to regular lubrication of these areas will increase operating resistance which, when compounded, may cause tardy operation and poor release movement.

54 Brake lever or pedal pulsates in operation – drum brakes

Drums warped or oval. This can result from overheating, impact or uneven spoke tension. This condition is difficult to correct, although if slight ovality only occurs skimming the surface of the drum can provide a cure. This is work for a specialist engineer. Renewal of the hub is normally the only satisfactory solution.

55 Drum brake noise

Drum warped or oval. This can cause intermittent rubbing of the brake linings against the drum. See the preceding Section.

Brake linings glazed. This condition, usually accompanied by heavy lining dust contamination, often induces brake squeal. The surface of the linings may be roughened using glass-paper or a fine file.

56 Brake induced fork judder

Worn front fork stanchions and legs, or worn or badly adjusted steering head bearings. These conditions, combined with uneven or pulsating braking as described in Sections 50 and 54 will induce more or less judder when the brakes are applied, dependent on the degree of wear and poor brake operation. Attention should be given to both areas of malfunction. See the relevant Sections.

Electrical problems

57 Battery dead or weak

Battery faulty. Battery life should not be expected to exceed 3 to 4 years, particularly where a starter motor is used regularly. Gradual sulphation of the plates and sediment deposits will reduce the battery performance. Plate and insulator damage can often occur as a result of vibration. Complete power failure, or intermittent failure, may be due to a broken battery terminal. Lack of electrolyte will prevent the battery maintaining charge.

Battery leads making poor contact. Remove the battery leads and clean them and the terminals, removing all traces of corrosion and tarnish. Reconnect the leads and apply a coating of petroleum jelly to the terminals.

Load excessive. If additional items such as spot lamps, are fitted, which increase the total electrical load above the maximum alternator output, the battery will fail to maintain full charge. Reduce the electrical load to suit the electrical capacity.

Regulator/diode board failure.

Alternator generating coils open-circuit or shorted.

Charging circuit shorting or open circuit. This may be caused by frayed or broken wiring, dirty connectors or a faulty ignition switch. The system should be tested in a logical manner. See Section 60.

58 Battery overcharged

Diode board/regulator faulty. Overcharging is indicated if the battery becomes hot or it is noticed that the electrolyte level falls repeatedly between checks. In extreme cases the battery will boil causing corrosive gases and electrolyte to be emitted through the vent pipes.

Battery wrongly matched to the electrical circuit. Ensure that the specified battery is fitted to the machine.

59 Total electrical failure

Fuse blown. Check the main fuse. If a fault has occurred, it must be rectified before a new fuse is fitted.

Battery faulty. See Section 57.

Earth failure. Check that the main earth strap from the battery is securely affixed to the gearbox and is making a good contact.

Ignition switch or power circuit failure. Check for current flow through the battery positive lead (red) to the ignition switch. Check the ignition switch for continuity.

60 Circuit failure

Cable failure. Refer to the machine's wiring diagram and check the circuit for continuity. Open circuits are a result of loose or corroded connections, either at terminals or in-line connectors, or because of broken wires. Occasionally, the core of a wire will break without there being any apparent damage to the outer plastic cover.

Switch failure. All switches may be checked for continuity in each switch position, after referring to the switch position boxes incorporated in the wiring diagram for the machine. Switch failure may be a result of mechanical breakage, corrosion or water.

Fuse blown. Refer to the wiring diagram to check whether or not a circuit fuse is fitted. Replace the fuse, if blown, only after the fault has been identified and rectified.

61 Bulbs blowing repeatedly

Vibration failure. This is often an inherent fault related to the natural vibration characteristics of the engine and frame and is, thus, difficult to resolve. Modifications of the lamp mounting, to change the damping characteristics may help.

Intermittent earth. Repeated failure of one bulb, particularly where the bulb is fed directly from the generator, indicates that a poor earth exists somewhere in the circuit. Check that a good contact is available at each earthing point in the circuit.

Reduced voltage. Where a quartz-halogen bulb is fitted the voltage to the bulb should be maintained or early failure of the bulb will occur. Do not overload the system with additional electrical equipment in excess of the system's power capacity and ensure that all circuit connections are maintained clean and tight.

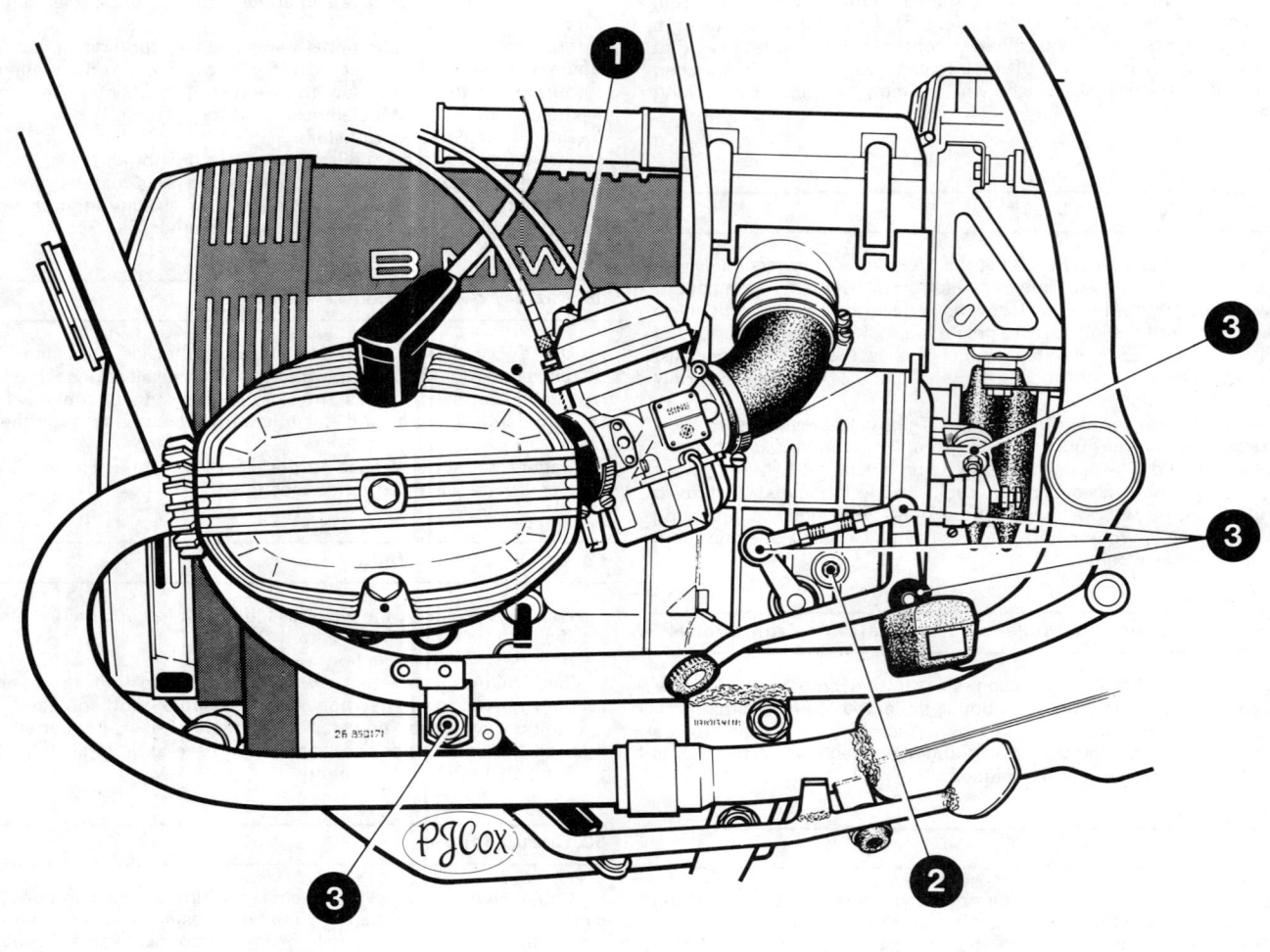

❶

Engine
Capacity:
/5, /6, /7 up to 1980 without oil cooler, R80G/S, R45,
R65 up to 1980 .... 2.25 litres (3.96 Imp pt/2.38 US qt)
/5, /6, /7 up to 1980 with oil cooler, /7 1981 on
without oil cooler, R80, R80ST, R45, R65 1981 on .... 2.50 litres (4.40 Imp pt/2.64 US qt)
/7 1981 on with oil cooler .... 2.75 litres (4.84 Imp pt/2.91 US qt)
Recommended lubricant .... Good quality HD oil suitable for 4-stroke spark ignition engines, API class SE/CC or SF/CC (see illustration in Routine maintenance for viscosities)

❷

Gearbox
Capacity .... 800cc (1.41 Imp pt/0.85 US qt)
Recommended lubricant .... Good quality hypoid gear oil API class GL-5 or to specification MIL-L-2105 B or C, viscosity SAE 90 above 5°C (41°F) SAE 80 below 5°C (41°F), alternatively SAE 80W90

❸

All greasing points .... High melting-point lithium fibre-based grease, eg Shell Retinax A

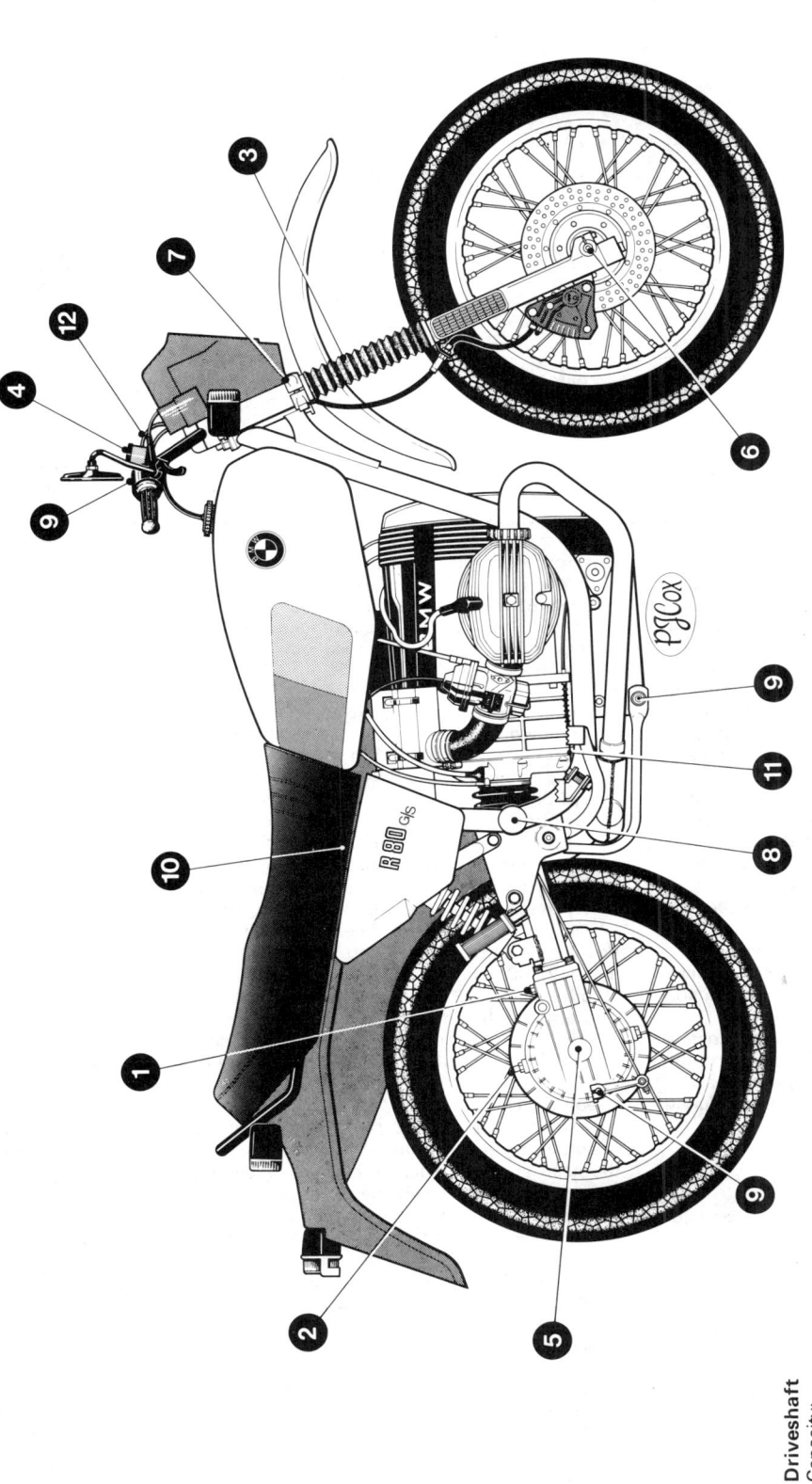

1. **Driveshaft**
   Capacity:
   /5 up to mid 1973 .... 100cc (0.18 Imp pt/0.11 US qt)
   All other models .... 150cc (0.26 Imp pt/0.16 US qt)
   Recommended lubricant .... Good quality hypoid gear oil API class GL-5 or to specification MIL-L-2105 B or C, viscosity SAE 90 above 5°C (41°F) SAE 80 below 5°C (41°F), alternatively SAE 80W90

2. **Rear bevel drive**
   Capacity:
   All models up to 1980 .... 250cc (0.44 Imp pt/0.26 US qt)
   All models 1981 on .... 350cc (0.61 Imp pt/0.37 US qt)
   Recommended lubricant .... As driveshaft type

3. **Front forks** .... Recommended brands and types only – see Chapter 6

4. **Brake fluid** .... DOT 4 (ATE SL)

5. **Rear wheel/final drive splines** .. Molykote BR2 or liquid Moly LM47L

6. **Wheel bearings** .... High melting-point lithium fibre-based grease, eg Shell Retinax A

7. **Steering head bearings** .... As wheel bearing type

8. **Swinging arm bearings** .... As wheel bearing type

9. **All greasing points** .... As wheel bearing type

10. **Battery terminals** .... Petroleum jelly or acid-free grease

11. **Control cable nipples and all other pivots** .... Engine oil or light machine oil

12. **Cables – non nylon lined** .... As above
    ATU pivots – up to 1978 models only .... Bosch grease Ft 1v4
    ATU shaft – up to 1978 models only .... Bosch grease Ft 1v22 or Ft 1v26
    Front brake master cylinder pushrod and caliper pivot pin – /6, /7 up to 1980 .... Molykote BR2 or liquid Moly LM47L

Routine maintenance
Refer to Chapter 10 for information relating to the 1986 on models

Periodic routine maintenance is a continuous process which should commence immediately the machine is used. The object is to maintain all adjustments and to diagnose and rectify minor defects before they develop into more extensive, and often more expensive, problems.

It follows that if the machine is maintained properly, it will both run and perform with maximum efficiency, and be less prone to unexpected breakdowns. Regular inspection of the machine will show up any parts which are wearing, and with a little experience, it is possible to obtain the maximum life from any one component, renewing it when it becomes so worn that it is liable to fail.

Regular cleaning can be considered as important as mechanical maintenance. This will ensure that all the cycle parts are inspected regularly and are kept free from accumulations of road dirt and grime.

All intervals are intended as a guide only; as a machine gets older it develops individual faults which require more frequent attention and if used under particularly arduous conditions it is advisable to reduce the period between each check.

For ease of reference, most service operations are described in detail under the relevant heading. However, if further general information is required, this can be found under the pertinent Section heading and Chapter in the main text.

Although no special tools are required for routine maintenance, a good selection of general workshop tools is essential. Included in the tools must be a range of metric ring or combination spanners and a selection of good quality Allen keys; all necessary tools being included in the machine's toolkit.

Service intervals – mileage:
BMW maintenance is grouped into two parts, a minor and a major service which must be carried out at the following intervals:

/5 models:
Minor service every 8000 miles (12 000 km) starting with the first 4000 miles (6000 km)
Major service every 8000 miles (12 000 km) starting with the first 8000 miles (12 000 km)
All other models:
Minor service every 10 000 miles (15 000 km) starting with the first 5000 miles (7500 km)
Major service every 10 000 miles (15 000 km) starting with the first 10 000 miles (15 000 km)

Therefore minor and major services should be carried out alternately at every 4000 miles (6000 km) for /5 models, every 5000 miles (7500 km) for all other models.

Service intervals – time:
If the machine is not used regularly, or does not cover a high mileage, BMW recommend two major services be carried out each year to preserve the machine's performance and reliability. Therefore, the minor service should be carried out every three months, the major service every six months.

Additional recommendations:
Engine oil – in normal use the engine oil should be changed every six months at the latest. If the machine is used in temperatures below 0°C (32°F), or for short, local journeys only, the oil should be changed every 2000 miles (3000 km) or three months at the latest.
Gearbox oil – must be changed at least once annually.
Driveshaft oil – must be changed at least once annually.
Rear bevel drive oil – must be changed at least once annually.
Front fork oil – must be changed at least once annually.
Hydraulic brake fluid – must be changed annually.
Wheel and steering head bearings – if conditions are very severe the bearings must be cleaned and packed with new grease every 16 000 miles (24 000 km) for /5 models, every 20 000 miles (30 000 km) for all other models. Refer to the relevant Sections of Chapters 8 and 6.
Battery – should be checked at least every month.
Air filter – should be cleaned and renewed at more frequent intervals if the machine is used in very dusty or severe conditions.

Cleaning the machine
Keeping the motorcycle clean should be considered as an important part of the routine maintenance, to be carried out whenever the need arises. A machine cleaned regularly will not only succumb less speedily to the inevitable corrosion of external surfaces, and hence maintain its market value, but will be far more approachable when the time comes for maintenance or service work. Furthermore, loose or failing components are more readily spotted when not partially obscured by a mantle of road grime and oil.

Surface dirt should be removed using a sponge and warm, soapy water; the latter being applied copiously to remove the particles of grit which might otherwise cause damage to the paintwork and polished surfaces.

Oil and grease are removed most easily by the application of a cleaning solvent such as 'Gunk' or 'Jizer'. The solvent should be applied when the parts are still dry and worked in with a stiff brush. Large quantities of water should be used when rinsing off, taking care that water does not enter the carburettors, air cleaners or electrics.

Application of a wax polish to the cycle parts and a good chrome cleaner to the chrome parts will give a good finish. Always wipe the machine down if used in the wet.

Routine maintenance

Daily (pre-ride check)

It is recommended that the following items are checked whenever the machine is about to be used. This is important to prevent the risk of unexpected failure of any component while riding the machine and with experience, can be reduced to a simple checklist which will only take a few moments to complete. For those owners who are not inclined to check all items with such frequency, it is suggested that the best course is to carry out the checks in the form of a service which can be undertaken each week or before any long journey. It is essential that all items are checked and serviced with reasonable frequency.

1 Check the tyres

Check the tyre pressures with a gauge that is known to be accurate. It is worthwhile purchasing a pocket gauge for this purpose because the gauges on garage forecourt airlines are notoriously inaccurate. The pressures, which should be checked with the tyres cold, are given in the Specifications Section of Chapter 8. Note that they are recommended by BMW **only** for the tyres fitted as standard to their machines and should be checked by reference to the tyre pressure warning label on the machine in case different types of tyre were fitted at the factory. If the machine is fitted subsequently with another make and/or type of tyre, the owner must check with the tyre manufacturer to find out if different pressures are necessary. In most cases the BMW importer will be able to help with advice on recommended tyres and pressures. Finally, ensure at all times that the pressures are suited to the load the machine is carrying and the speed at which it will be travelling.

At the same time as the tyre pressures are checked, examine the tyres themselves. Check them for damage, especially splitting of the sidewalls. Remove any small stones or other road debris caught between the treads. When checking the tyres for damage, they should be examined for tread depth in view of both the legal and safety aspects. It is vital to keep the tread depth within the UK legal limits of 1 mm of depth over three-quarters of the tread breadth around the entire circumference with no bald patches. Many riders, however, consider nearer 2 mm to be the limit for secure roadholding, traction, and braking, especially in adverse weather conditions, and it should be noted that BMW recommend minimum tread depths of 2.0 mm (0.08 in) for speeds below 80 mph (130 km/h), or 3 mm (0.12 in) for speeds above 80 mph (130 km/h), measured at the centre of the tread.

If new tyres are to be fitted, they must be of the correct size and speed or load rating, as listed in the Specifications Section of Chapter 8. However, since BMW motorcycles have proved especially sensitive to particular makes and types of tyre as well as to tyre pressures, great care must be taken when choosing new tyres. First check with the importer or a good local BMW dealer what types of currently-available tyre are approved for use on your particular model; do not forget to check the recommended tyre pressures, if different. **Do not** use any other tyre than those that are approved; if a particular make and/or type is not approved the factory, which conducts exhaustive tests, will have a very good reason for this. Once you have made your choice from the available selection, always fit front and rear tyres from the same manufacturer; never mix different tyre brands. Also, fit new inner tubes and rim tapes (where fitted) with every new tyre and use only tubes and rim tapes of the same make as the new tyre. Finally note the new pressures (if different) at all loads and speeds and keep this with the machine.

2 Check the engine oil level

The engine must have been stopped for some time so that the level settles before it can be checked accurately. Unscrew the filler plug/dipstick from its boss in the crankcase left-hand side, wipe it clean and refit it so that the plug rests on the crankcase; **do not** screw it in. Withdraw the dipstick and note the level of oil on it, which should be between the 'Max' and 'Min' lines with the machine supported upright on its centre stand.

Never allow the engine to run with the level below the 'Min' line, and do not overfill it so that the level is above the 'Max' line.

Use only a good quality, heavy duty oil suitable for 4-stroke spark ignition engines. Refer to the accompanying thermometer chart to decide what viscosity of oil is necessary at the prevailing outside temperatures. BMW recommend that a medium range multigrade, eg 10W30 is preferable to a wide range multigrade, such as 10W50, and that multigrades are preferable to monogrades.

Filler plug/dipstick must rest on crankcase as shown for accurate level to be recorded – do not screw it in

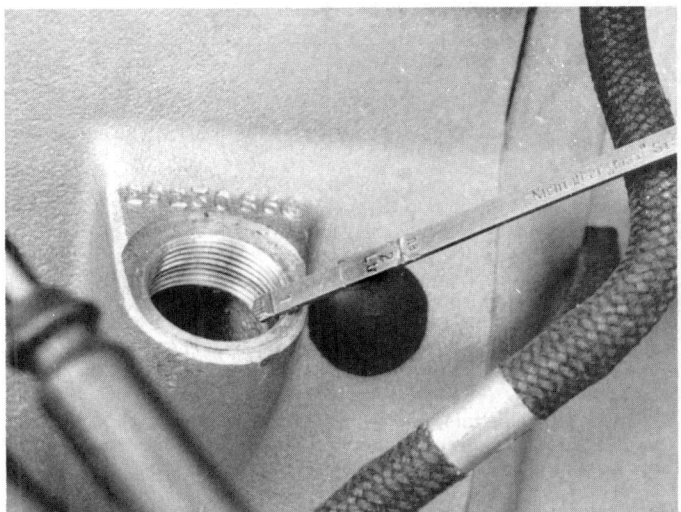
Oil level must be between 'Max' and 'Min' level lines

Use only good quality oil of specified type when topping up

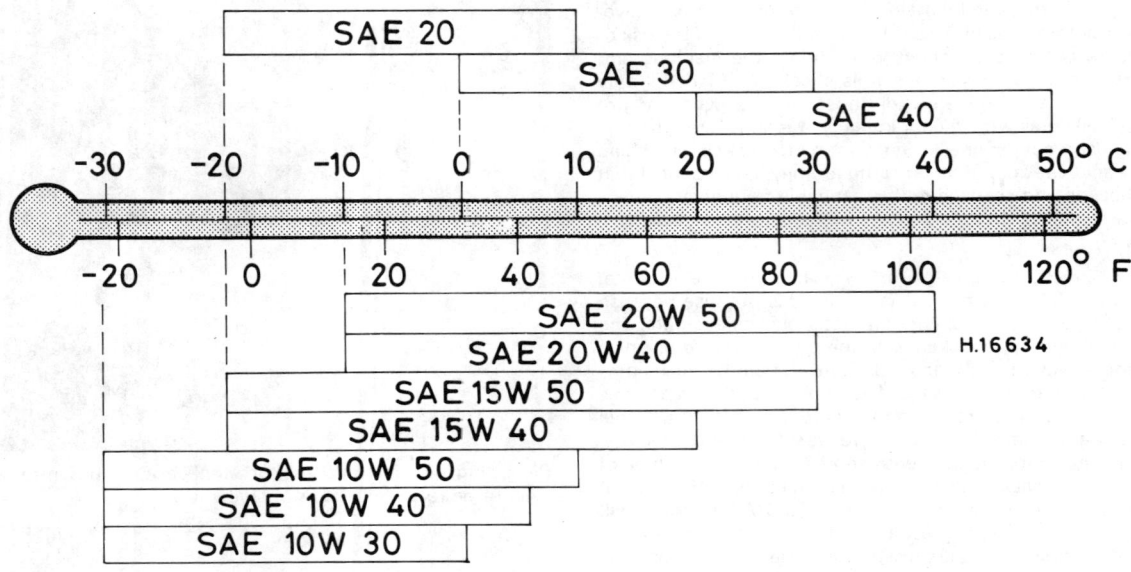

Oil viscosity selection chart

A small funnel is useful when topping up, especially if it can be carried on the machine. To fill the engine from 'Min' to 'Max' marks on the dipstick requires approximately 1.0 litre (1.76 Imp pint/1.06 US qt) on all models up to 1980, 0.85 litre (1.5 Imp pint/0.9 US qt) on all models from 1981 on. Renew the sealing washer if it is damaged or flattened and refit the dipstick, tightening it securely.

3 Check the fuel level

Checking the petrol level may seem obvious, but it is all too easy to forget. Ensure that you have enough petrol to complete your journey, or at least to get you to the nearest petrol station.

4 Legal check

Check that all lights, turn signals, horn and speedometer are working correctly to make sure that the machine complies with all legal requirements in this respect. Check also that the headlamp is correctly aimed. The vertical aim must be aligned so that with the machine standing on its wheels on level ground with the rider (and pillion passenger, if one is regularly carried) seated normally, the main beam centre (as shown on a wall 25 feet away) must be at the same height from the ground as the centre of the headlamp itself. This is adjusted by slackening the headlamp mounting bolts and tilting the headlamp to the correct angle. On machines with RS or RT fairings, ensure that the fairing headlamp glass is completely clean and dry so that there can be no reduction of the headlamp's light output. Detach the glass and clean it regularly with a suitable detergent to avoid this.

5 Check the brakes

Check that the front and rear brakes work effectively and without binding. Ensure that the rod linkages and the cables, are lubricated and properly adjusted. Check the fluid level in the master cylinder reservoir, where appropriate, and ensure that there are no fluid leaks. Should topping-up be required, use only the recommended hydraulic fluid.

6 Check the controls

Check the throttle and clutch cables and levers and the gear lever to ensure that they are adjusted correctly, functioning correctly, and that they are securely fastened. If a bolt is going to work loose, or a cable snap, it is better that it is discovered at this stage with the machine at a standstill, rather than when it is being ridden.

7 Rear suspension settings

Except for machines with Nivomat rear suspension units, ensure that the spring preload adjusters are at the correct setting for the machine's intended load. On models with two rear suspension units, ensure at all times that both are at the same setting.

8 Check the tightness of all nuts and bolts

Using the specified torque settings (where given), check that all fasteners are tightened securely, particularly the wheel spindle nuts and clamp bolts, the rear wheel fasteners (Monolever models) and the stand, footrest, suspension unit and rear subframe mounting bolts or nuts.

Minor service

1 Change the engine oil and filter

Oil changes will be much quicker if the machine is first ridden far enough to warm up the engine to normal operating temperature: this will thin the oil and ensure that any particles of dirt or debris will be retained in suspension in the oil and flushed out with it.

Place the machine on its centre stand on level ground, place a container of at least 3 litres (approx 5 Imp pints, 3 US qts) beneath the crankcase. Unscrew the dipstick.

On standard models fitted with BMW crashbars, remove the right-hand crashbar rear mounting, slacken the two front mountings and manoeuvre the bar forwards clear of the filter. Be careful not to burn your hands on the hot exhaust pipe. If an oil cooler is fitted, it is extremely awkward to remove and refit the filter with the exhaust in place; it is advisable to remove the exhaust pipes (taking great care to avoid injury) before draining the oil. Refer to Chapter 4.

On machines fitted with RS or RT fairings only, there should be sufficient room to remove and refit the oil filter with the fairing in place, especially if the hinged type of element is to be used. If BMW crashbars are also fitted, the fairing right-hand lower section should be removed (see Chapter 6) and the crashbar should be moved forwards out of the way, as described above. If an oil cooler is also fitted the exhaust pipes should be removed first, as described in Chapter 4, to make work easier. Take great care to avoid injury when handling the hot exhaust pipes.

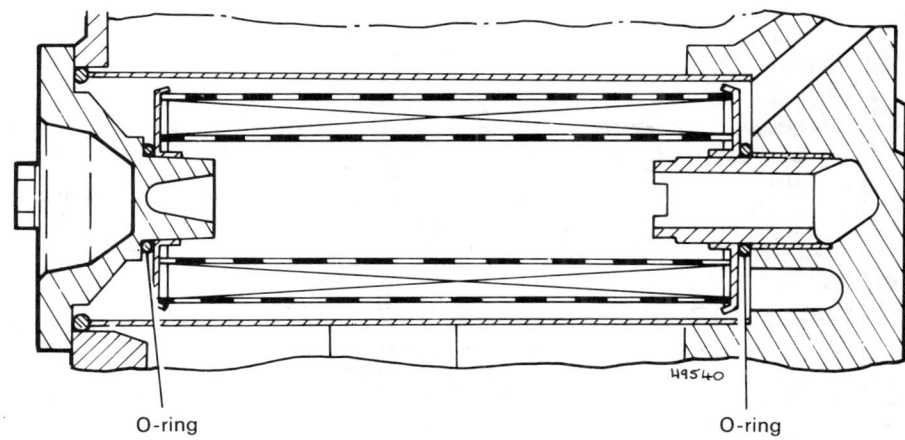

Short rigid element with two separate O-rings. Fitted to all /5, /6, /7 (except those below), R45 and R65 models. Note /7 model and later filter cover shown

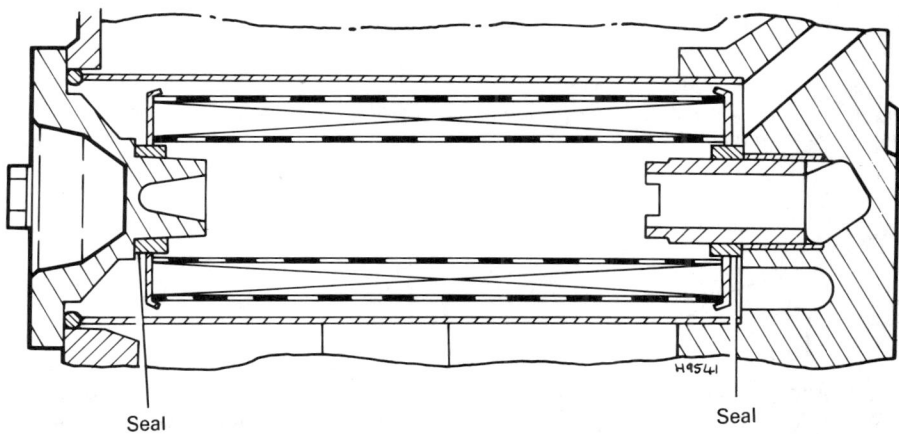

Short rigid element with two square-section seals glued in place, separate O-rings must not be used. Fitted to R80G/S and R80ST but can also be fitted to all /5, /6, /7 (except those below), R45 and R65 models

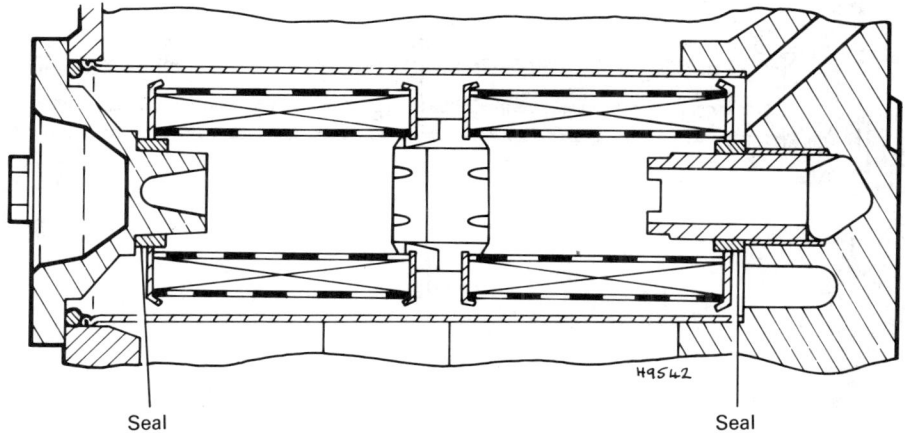

Short hinged element with two square-section seals glued in place, separate O-rings must not be used. Fitted to R100RS and R100RT machines without an oil cooler, R80 and R80RT, but can also be fitted to any standard machine fitted with an RS or RT fairing and no oil cooler

Oil filter types (continued overleaf)

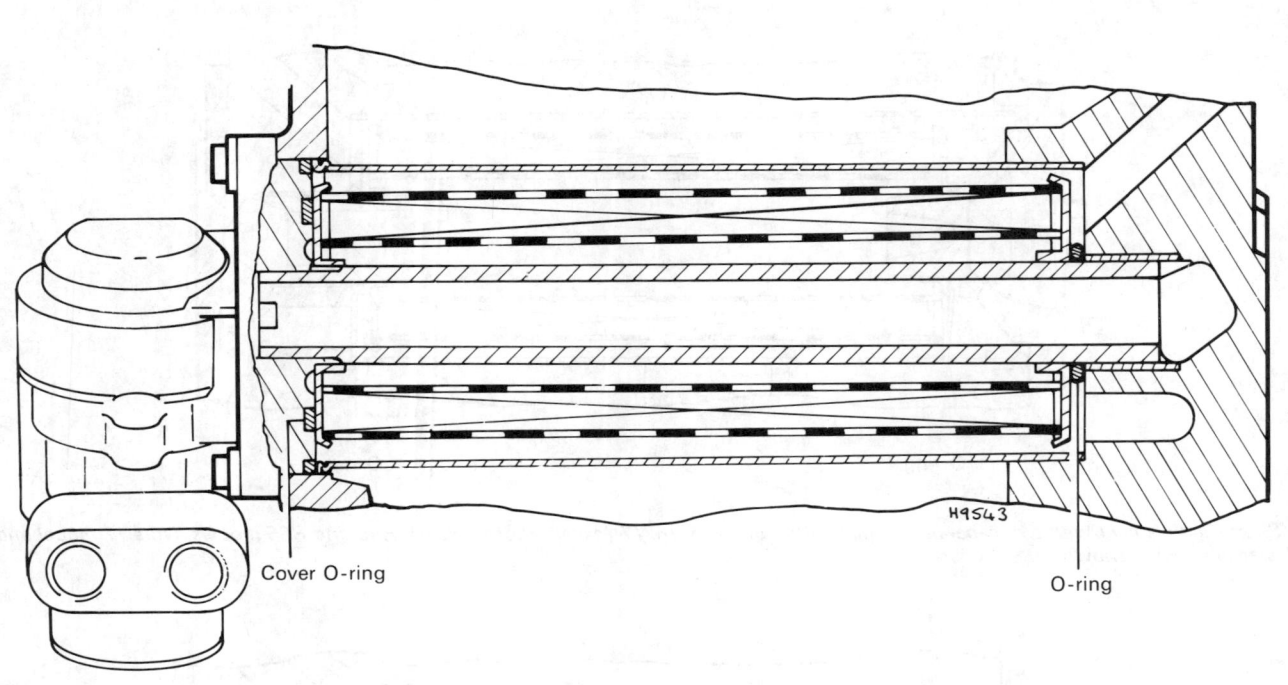

Long rigid element with one separate O-ring (note arrangement of filter cover O-rings). Fitted to R100RS and R100RT models with an oil cooler or any standard machine with an oil cooler

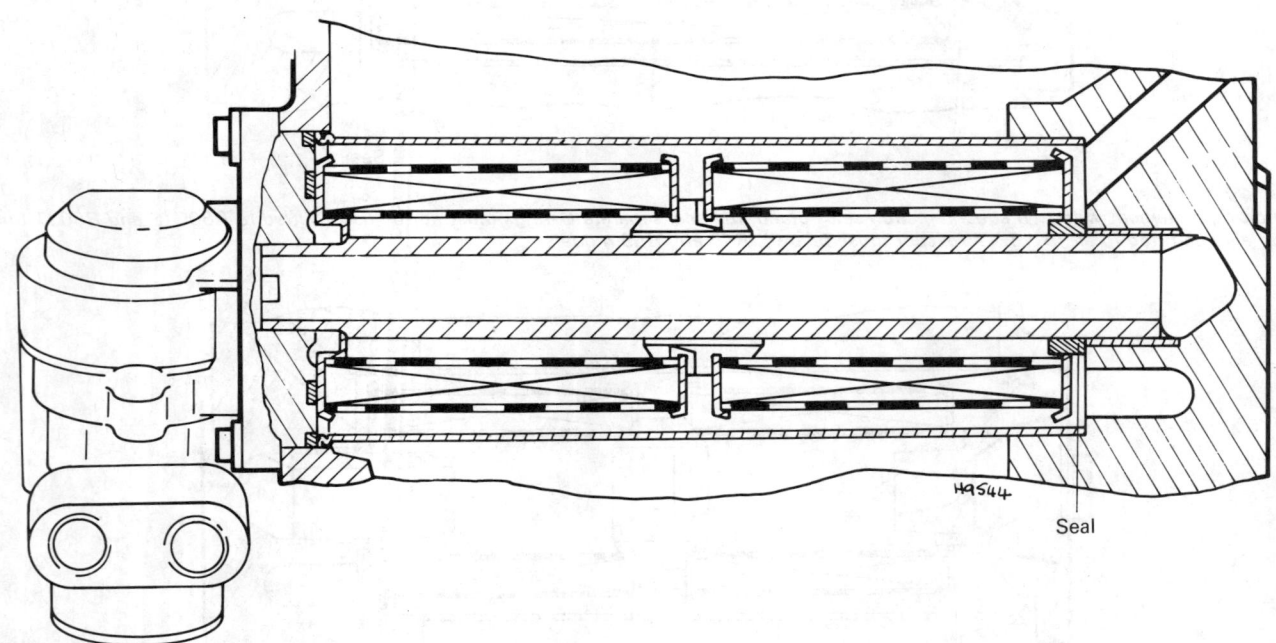

Long hinged element with one square-section seal glued in place, separate small O-ring must not be used. This element can be used instead of rigid type on machines with an RS or RT fairing and an oil cooler

Oil filter types (continued)

Routine maintenance

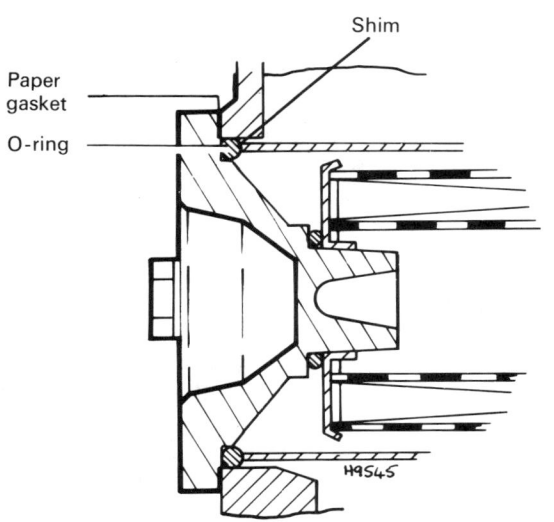

Oil filter cover seals – all models up to 1982 (except /5, /6)

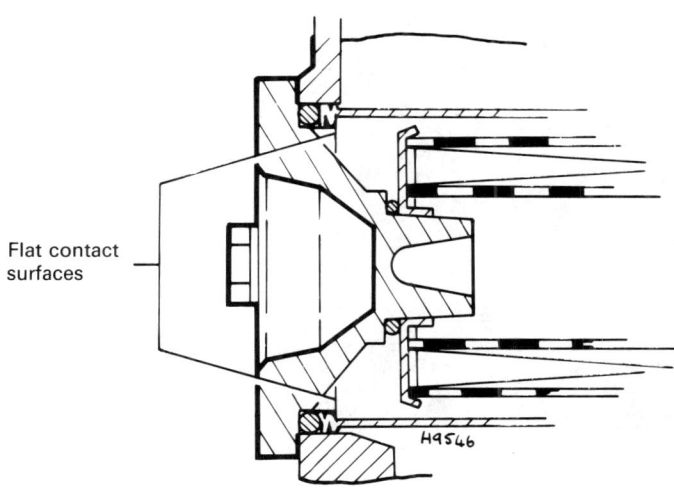

Oil filter cover seals – all models 1982 on

On machines without an oil cooler, unscrew the sump drain plug and allow the oil to drain into the container. Being careful to avoid burning your hands on the hot exhaust pipe or cylinder barrel, remove the oil filter from its chamber in the bottom right-hand front corner of the crankcase. Unscrew the three bolts or screws which retain the triangular filter cover and withdraw it. **Note:** make a careful note of the exact location, type and number of gaskets, O-rings and metal washers found as the filter components are removed. On /5 and /6 models only, remove the outer cover and gasket, unscrew the single retaining bolt that is now exposed and withdraw the inner cover. Use a bent piece of wire to hook out the filter element, noting the small O-ring at each end. On all other models the filter element is exposed as soon as the triangular cover has been removed; the accompanying illustrations will show the varying seal arrangements.

Allow the oil to drain fully from the sump and filter chamber, then wipe out the chamber with a clean, lint-free rag, and clean the sealing surfaces. Insert the new filter element. If the element with separate O-rings is to be used, ensure that the O-rings are positioned correctly on the chamber centre tube and on the filter cover boss; if an element with square-section seals is to be used, ensure that no O-rings (from previous filter types) are left in the chamber, and that the seals engage correctly on the chamber centre tube and filter cover boss. Renew all seals and gaskets (where applicable) as the filter cover is refitted; these will be supplied with a genuine BMW oil filter. Tighten securely the filter cover bolts, renew the sump drain plug sealing washer if it is flattened or damaged and refit the sump drain plug. Thoroughly clean its threads and the sump orifice and tighten the plug securely. Use the specified torque setting if possible (later models only). Fill the crankcase with the correct amount of oil, start the engine and allow it to warm up to normal operating temperature. Stop the engine and check the oil level (see pre-ride check). Top up if necessary.

The task of changing the engine oil and filter is slightly different

Unscrew the sump drain plug

Ensure that only seals appropriate to type of filter used are refitted

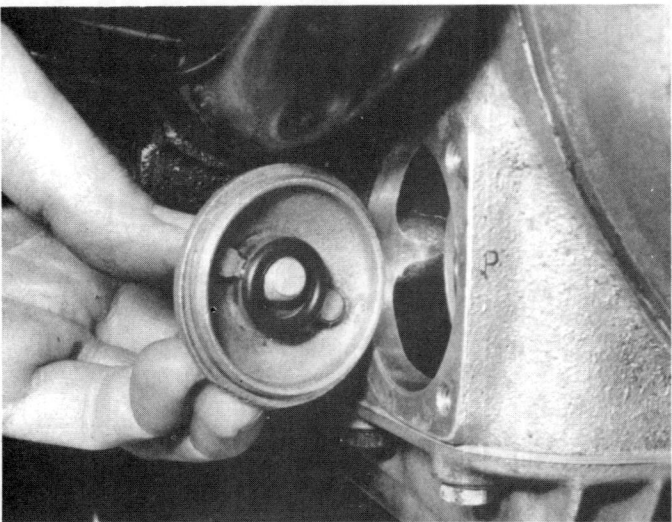

Note inner filter cover fitted to /5 and /6 models only

Ensure that all gaskets and O-rings (where fitted) are renewed before refitting filter cover

when an oil cooler is fitted. One item that is essential is the oil cooler bleed bolt, which is inserted into the base of the oil cooler adaptor in place of the standard bolt and opens the thermostatic valve by physically lifting the valve operating plunger, thus allowing the old oil to drain from the cooler and new oil to enter it on refilling. An oil cooler bleed bolt should be supplied in the toolkit of any machine fitted with an oil cooler as standard equipment and is included in the kit if the oil cooler was fitted as an optional extra. It has a longer hexagon head than a normal bolt, and a smoothly rounded tip to prevent damaging the thermostatic valve. Check very carefully that the threaded portion is exactly 23 mm (0.906 in) long; this is necessary as while too short a bolt would raise the valve plunger insuffficiently to allow free drainage of the oil, too long a bolt would damage the valve itself. It appears that some undesirably long bolts have been issued. If a bolt is found that is too long, the surplus can be removed with a hacksaw or on a grinding wheel, but it is essential that the tip is left with a smooth rounded finish. The alternative is to purchase a new bleed bolt.

Remove the single bolt that protrudes from the base of the oil cooler adaptor. Remove its sealing washer and place this over the bleed bolt. Check the length of the bleed bolt, as described above, and screw it fully into the adaptor. The oil cooler is now ready to be drained with the rest of the lubrication system; accordingly remove the dipstick and sump drain plug, then allow the oil to drain into the container. While the oil is draining, remove both spark plugs, and on 1981 and later models only, refit each into its spark plug cap and lay each on its respective cylinder head so that the metal body is touching the cylinder head finning.

When draining is complete, check the condition of the drain plug sealing washer, renewing it if necessary, then refit and tighten securely the drain plug to the specified torque setting (where given). Remove the three bolts securing the cooler adaptor to the crankcase and withdraw the adaptor taking care to catch any remaining oil from the cooler and/or filter chamber. **Note:** make a careful note of the exact location, type and number O-rings, gaskets and metal washers found as the filter is removed. Use a piece of bent wire to hook out the filter element and the separate O-ring behind it (where fitted). Wipe out the filter chamber with a clean lint-free rag and clean the sealing surfaces. Insert the new filter element. If the earlier type with a separate O-ring is to be fitted, ensure that the new O-ring is located correctly on the chamber centre tube; if the later type with a square section seal is used, ensure that the seal engages correctly on the centre tube.

Renew the adaptor sealing O-rings (and gasket, if fitted) and tighten securely the adaptor mounting bolts, then pour the specified amount of oil into the crankcase. Switch on the ignition and turn the engine over on the starter motor until the oil pressure warning lamp goes out, being careful on 1981 and later models, that the spark plugs remain in contact with the cylinder head at all times to avoid damage to the ignition system. When the oil pressure warning lamp goes out, release the starter button and switch off the ignition, because the lamp shows that fresh oil has been pumped through the cooler and filled it. Unscrew the bleed bolt and refit the original M6 x 10 mm long bolt, renewing its sealing washer if necessary, then refit both spark plugs and connect the spark plug caps to each. Check the oil level, adding oil if necessary as described above.

On all models, the oil pump pick-up filter gauze in the sump will have been cleaned at the first 600 mile (1000 km) service and does not require regular cleaning (as a part of routine maintenance) after this. It should be cleaned, however, and the sump thoroughly washed whenever the sump is removed. Refer to Chapter 4.

2 Clean the cylinder and sump cooling fins

In addition to the normal cleaning, check carefully that the cooling fins of the cylinder heads and barrels and of the sump are clean. Remove the fairing lower sections (machines with RS or RT fairings) or the sump bashplate (R80G/S) to ensure that all dirt and oil are removed which might reduce the fins' cooling ability. On machines with an oil cooler, check that the matrix is clean and unblocked; use a garden hose to flush the matrix through from behind to remove any dirt or debris.

3 Lubricate the controls and stand pivots

To grease the handlebar lever pivots, the control cables must be slackened and the pivot pins removed. Unhook the clutch cable from the actuating arm underneath the gearbox. Slacken the front brake cable (where fitted) at the drum or the master cylinder.

Remove the locknut on the lever pivot and unscrew the pin. Note the spring shim washer between the lever and the pivot housing. Disconnect the cables by pushing the inner cable into the lever until the slotted trunnion can be pulled out of the lever.

The straight-pull twistgrip should be dismantled for greasing or replacing cables. Push back the cable rubber cover. Unscrew the slotted screw in the twistgrip gear cover and remove the cover. Pull the twistgrip drum from the handlebar and unhook the cables from the block.

Grease the handlebar end, twistgrip drum gear, pinion shaft and chain. Replace the lower cable nipple in the block. With the slot in the twistgrip drum aligned with the slot in the housing, the marks on the drum gear and the pinion must be in line. This ensures that there will be

Routine maintenance

Remove handlebar lever pivot screw ...

... and withdraw lever, noting shim (where fitted)

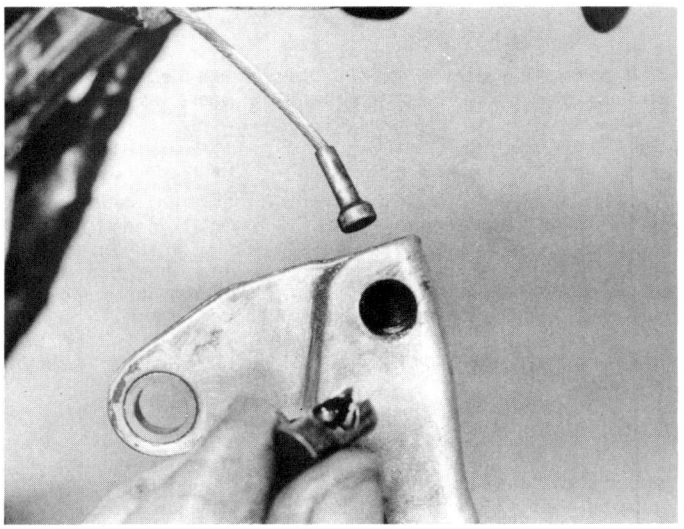
Disengage cable inner from slotted trunnion

Align twistgrip gear marks when refitting throttle cables

full throttle movement. Replace the upper cable nipple, pull back the outer cables and replace the gear cover.

Control cables on early models will require regular oiling, which is best achieved by disconnecting them and removing them from the machine. Check the outer cables for signs of damage, then examine the exposed portions of the inner cables. Any signs of kinking or fraying will indicate that renewal is required. To obtain maximum life and reliability from the cables they should be thoroughly lubricated using light machine oil. To do the job properly and quickly use one of the hydraulic cable oilers available from most motorcycle shops. Assemble the cable oiler as described by the manufacturer's instructions. Operate the oiler until oil emerges from the lower end, indicating that the cable is lubricated throughout its length. This process will expel any dirt or moisture and will prevent its subsequent ingress.

If a cable oiler is not available hang the cable upright and make up a small funnel arrangement using plasticine or by taping a plastic bag around the upper end. Fill the funnel with oil and leave it overnight to drain through.

Note that the control cables on later models (approximately from 1978 on) are lined with nylon or a similar material which **must not** be lubricated. If the cables become stiff through old age, wear, or damage, they must be renewed, although in some cases the application of one of the modern 'dry' lubricants may help.

Finish off control lubrication by applying a few drops of engine oil or light machine oil to all nipples and control pivots, and all adjuster threads.

Using a water dispersant lubricant such as WD40 or CRC5-56, spray a small amount of lubricant into all locks and electrical components.

The instrument drive cable inner wire cannot be removed from the outer casing so lubrication is not possible; the cables should be renewed if damaged, sticking or worn. To cure a squeaking cable, however, engine oil could be poured through it using the funnel arrangement described above. Ensure that all surplus oil has drained off before refitting the cable or it may work up into the instrument as the cable rotates and ruin it.

The side stand pivot is usually fitted with a grease nipple and should be lubricated with a grease gun until fresh grease can be seen. The centre stand (and side stands with no grease nipple) should be removed so that the pivots can be cleaned and greased. Check the return springs are in good condition and that their anchorages are secure. Grease all pivot components on reassembly and tighten all fasteners securely (to the specified torque settings, where given).

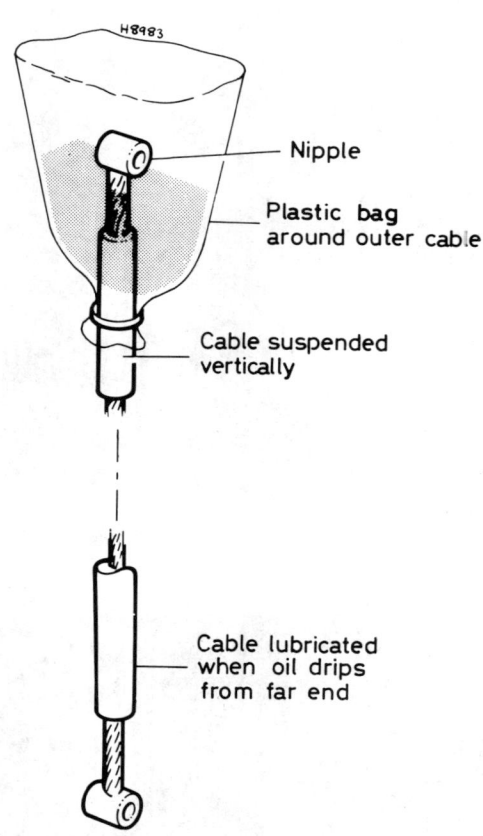

Oiling a control cable – early models only

Instrument drive cables are retained by knurled rings at their upper ends

4 Check the battery

The battery is sited underneath the seat, to the rear of the engine/gearbox unit. Raise or remove the seat and remove the tool tray to reach it. Check that the mountings are secure.

To check the battery in place, the machine must be positioned so that the battery is absolutely level. Where a black-cased battery is fitted, remove the cell filler plugs and check that the electrolyte level is 5 mm (0.2 in) above the plates. Where a battery with a translucent casing is fitted, through which the electrolyte level can be seen, the level must be between the level marks on all cells. Use only distilled water to top up to the correct height or upper level mark and refit the filler plugs.

On all models, whenever the battery is disconnected, remember to disconnect the negative (–) terminal first, to prevent the possibility of short circuits. Check that the terminals are clean and apply a thin smear of petroleum jelly (or acid-free grease) to each to prevent corrosion. On refitting, check that the vent hose is not blocked and that it is correctly routed with no kinks, also that it hangs well below any other component, particularly the exhaust system. Remember always to connect the negative (–) terminal last when refitting the battery.

Always check that the terminals are tight and that the covers are correctly refitted, also that the fuse connections are clean and tight, that the fuses are of the correct rating and in good condition, and that a spare is available on the machine should the need arise.

At regular intervals remove the battery and check that there is no pale grey sediment deposited at the bottom of the casing. This is caused by sulphation of the plates as a result of re-charging at too high a rate or as a result of the battery being left discharged for long periods. A good battery should have little or no sediment visible and its plates should be straight and pale grey or brown in colour. If sediment deposits are deep enough to reach the bottom of the plates, or if the plates are buckled and have whitish deposits on them, the battery is faulty and must be renewed. Remember that a poor battery will give rise to a large number of minor electrical faults.

If the machine is not in regular use, disconnect the battery and give it a refresher charge every month to six weeks, as described in Chapter 9.

5 Check the gearbox oil level

With the machine supported upright on its centre stand on level ground, remove the gearbox oil filler plug. On /5 models the level should be at the lowest thread of the filler plug orifice; on all other models it should be at the bottom edge of the orifice. Remove any surplus oil (/5) or allow it to trickle out (all others). If topping up is necessary use only good quality oil of the specified type. Renew the sealing washer if it is damaged or worn and refit the filler plug, tightening it to a torque setting of 28 – 31 Nm (21 – 23 lbf ft). Wash off any spilt oil.

6 Check the driveshaft oil level

With the machine supported upright on its centre stand on level ground and with the rear wheel touching the ground, remove the filler plug from the top of the **front end** of the rear bevel drive housing (see accompanying photograph). Insert a suitable rod **vertically** into the filler orifice until it touches the top of the drive shaft rear coupling. The level of oil on the rod should be 2 mm (0.08 in). If topping up is necessary, add only good quality oil of the specified type. Renew the sealing washer if it is damaged or worn and refit the filler plug. Tighten it to a torque setting of 14 Nm (10 lbf ft) on all models up to 1980, securely finger tight on all later models.

Note: *all models from 1979 on (ie those with a shock absorber in the driveshaft) – it may prove easier to check the oil level accurately by draining the swinging arm and refilling it with the exact amount of oil, carefully measured. This is described under the Major Service heading.*

7 Check the rear bevel drive oil level

The oil level must be checked with the machine supported upright on its centre stand on level ground and with the rear wheel touching the ground.

All models up to 1980 Unscrew the filler/level plug from the rear of the housing. The oil level should be at the lowest thread of the filler plug orifice. Remove any surplus oil using a syringe or similar, to prevent oil being blown on to the rear tyre via the breather. If topping up is necessary, use only good quality oil of the specified type. Renew the sealing washer if it is damaged or worn and refit the filler plug, tightening it to a torque setting of 28 – 31 Nm (21 – 23 lbf ft). Wash off any spilt oil from the housing and swinging arm.

All models 1981 on Remove the level plug from the rear of the housing. If the level is correct, oil should trickle slowly out. If the level is too high allow the surplus to drain off, until the flow is reduced to a

Routine maintenance

Remove gearbox filler plug to check oil level – /5 models ...

... gearbox filler plug – all other models

Use only good quality oil of specified type when topping up

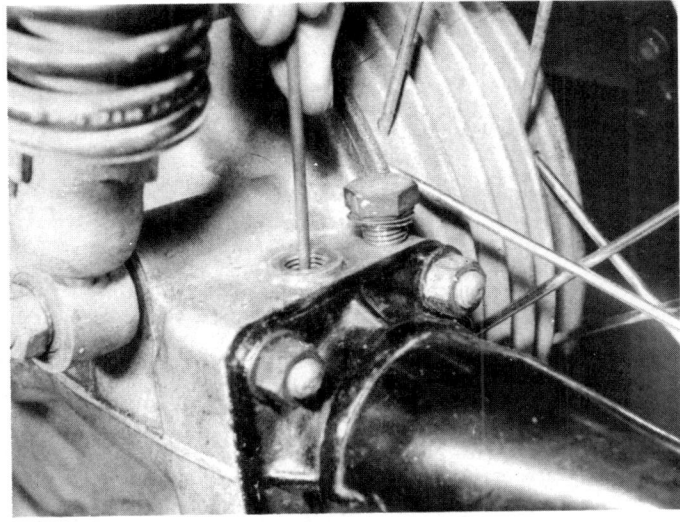

Checking the driveshaft oil level

Remove bevel drive filler/level plug to check oil level – all models up to 1980

slow trickle, to prevent oil being blown onto the rear tyre via the breather. If topping up is necessary, remove the breather/filler plug from the top of the housing and add only good quality oil of the specified type. When the level is correct renew their sealing washers if damaged or flattened and refit the plugs. Tighten the level plug to a torque setting of 10 Nm (7.5 lbf ft); the breather/filler plug should be tightened securely, using the torque setting, where specified. Wash off any spilt oil from the housing and swinging arm.

8 Clean the air filter

The air filter element should be removed for cleaning at regular intervals or performance will be reduced and fuel consumption increased.

/5, /6, /7 up to 1978

Slacken the left-hand air filter/carburettor hose clamps and the carburettor/cylinder head clamp(s) and withdraw the air hose. Unscrew the filter cover retaining screw and pull out the filter left-hand cover, holding the kickstart pedal out of the way. There is no need to disconnect the choke lever. Tap the filter lightly to remove loose particles of dirt and blow through from the inside with compressed air to clean the filter. If it is split or badly clogged it should be renewed.

Routine maintenance

Early models – removal retaining screw (arrowed) and carburettor hose ...

... then withdraw cover to release air filter element

On refitting, ensure that the element engages correctly on the three pins inside each filter cover, check that the left-hand cover is located correctly under the two metal retaining strips bolted to the gearbox top. Using two fingers inserted into the outlet aperture, guide the retaining screw into place and tighten it securely. Refit the carburettor hose and tighten the clamps securely.

/7, R45 and R65 1979-80 (UK), /7 and R65 1979 (US)

Although the filter is the same as for the models described above, due to modifications made to the crankcase breather from 1979 models onwards, the task of removal and refitting is more complicated.

Remove the fuel tank as described in Chapter 4 to expose the crankcase top surface. Remove the two Allen screws and withdraw the starter motor cover. A black rubber breather hose will be seen projecting into the left-hand half of the air filter cover; pull this clear. Proceed as described above to remove and clean the filter element.

On refitting, reverse the dismantling order but push the breather hose into place as far as possible before pushing the filter cover left-hand half into place. Refit the carburettor hose, starter motor cover and fuel tank.

All models 1981 on (UK), 1980 on (US)

Using a screwdriver, prise off from the filter top cover the four metal clips, two on each side, which retain together the two filter halves. Raise the filter upper half as much as possible and lift out the filter element to the left. The element can be cleaned using a soft brush to remove larger particles of dirt, but the most effective method is to blow the dirt away by directing a jet of compressed air from the underside of the element.

On refitting ensure that the element is inserted correctly, so that the 'Top/Oben' marking is at the rear and facing upwards and so that the rounded corners are at the front. A light application of grease around the outside edge of the element will provide a more efficient seal in exceptionally dusty or wet conditions, but ensure at all times that the filter top cover is properly seated and is securely fastened by all four metal clips.

All later models – prise off metal clips ...

... and lift off upper half to release element

Ensure filter element is refitted the correct way up

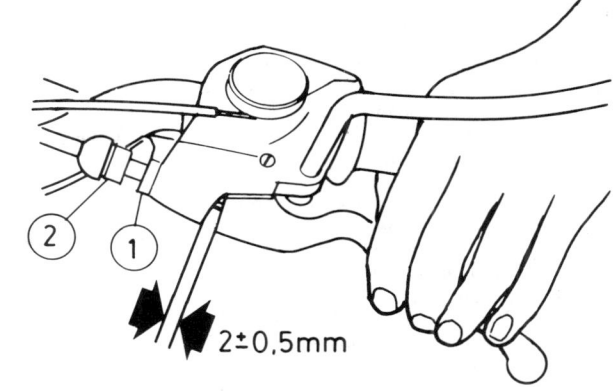

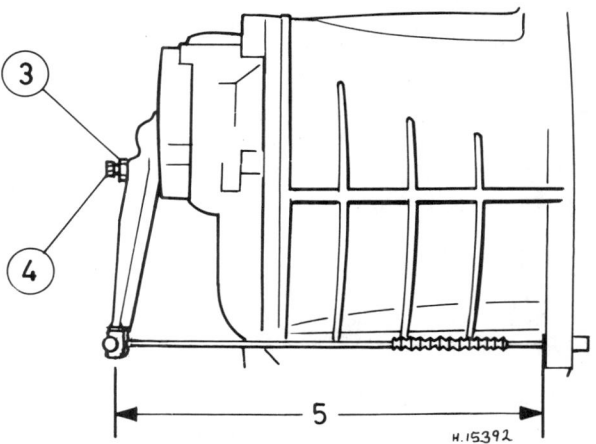

Adjusting the clutch operating mechanism – all models 1981 on

1 Locknut
2 Cable handlebar adjuster
3 Locknut
4 Adjusting screw
5 Exposed length of cable

Clutch release mechanism adjuster is on gearbox rear cover

9 Adjust the clutch

All models up to 1980

The clutch is correctly adjusted if there is 3 mm (0.12 in) free play in the cable measured between the handlebar lever butt end and the handlebar clamp (equivalent to approximately 2 mm/0.08 in of free movement at the operating lever on the gearbox) and if the operating lever is parallel to the gearbox end cover joint halfway through its travel. There must be no sign of clutch slip or drag.

To adjust the clutch first use the cable adjuster at the handlebar lever; if there is insufficient adjustment slacken the operating lever adjuster locknut and tighten the adjuster to decrease cable free play. Do not forget to ensure that the lever is parallel to the gearbox at half travel; the clutch will require greatly increased pressure to operate if the lever is acting at a severe angle on the release piston. When adjustment is correct, tighten the adjuster locknut to a torque setting of 20 – 23 Nm (15 – 17 lbf ft), then tighten the handlebar adjuster locknut. Use a grease gun to lubricate the operating lever pivot via its grease nipple until fresh grease can be seen on each side of the bearing, then apply a few drops of oil to the cable end nipples.

If the clutch still shows signs of slipping or dragging, or if it is very sudden in action, it must be dismantled for examination. On reassembly the components should be lubricated (where specified) to ensure a smooth action. Refer to Chapter 2.

All models 1981 on

The clutch is adjusted correctly if there is 2 ± 0.5 mm (0.08 ± 0.02 in) free play in the cable measured between the handlebar lever butt end and the handlebar clamp (see accompanying illustration) and the clutch operates smoothly with no sign of slip or drag.

To adjust the clutch, slacken the handlebar adjuster locknut then rotate the handlebar adjuster as necessary until the distance between the forward edge of the clutch operating lever on the gearbox and the rear edge of the cable abutment on the gearbox outer casing (ie the exposed length of clutch cable inner wire) is 201 – 203 mm (7.91 – 7.99 in). The lever should be projecting rearwards by 4° approximately. Tighten the handlebar adjuster locknut.

Slacken the locknut of the adjuster set in the clutch operating lever at the rear of the gearbox and rotate the adjusting screw until the specified clearance of 1.5 – 2.5 mm (0.06 – 0.10 in) exists as described above at the clutch handlebar lever. Tighten securely both adjuster locknuts and operate the clutch lever once or twice to settle the cable. Check that the adjustment has remained the same, resetting it if necessary. Apply a few drops of oil to all cable end nipples, adjuster threads and lever pivots.

If the clutch still shows signs of slipping or dragging, or if it is very sudden in action, it must be dismantled for examination. On reassembly the components should be lubricated, (where specified) to ensure a smooth action. Refer to Chapter 2.

10 Check the tightness of the cylinder head nuts and adjust the valve clearances

The engine must be completely cold before this task is undertaken. Remove both spark plugs and the rubber grommet from the ignition timing aperture in the crankcase. Remove both rocker covers; unscrew first the two 10 mm (spanner size) nuts at the front and rear of each rocker cover, between the second and third cylinder head fins, and remove them with their washers. Unscrew the single central cap nut on the outside of each rocker cover and tap the cover lightly with a soft-faced mallet to break the seal and release it. Be ready to catch any spilt oil and the cap nut washer.

To rotate the engine it is possible to use an Allen key in the alternator rotor retaining bolt, but it is preferable to select top gear and to rotate the engine by turning the rear wheel; this is much easier.

Turn the engine until the TDC mark (OT) appears in the crankcase aperture and check which cylinder is at TDC on the compression stroke, there should be free play at both rockers. If in doubt turn the engine over until the inlet valve on either cylinder has opened and closed again then turn the engine slowly until the TDC mark appears. If the clearances are so tight that free play cannot be detected, the cylinder head should be removed to check the valve seats.

Working in the **reverse** of the sequence shown in the accompanying illustration, **slacken** the cylinder head retaining nuts by ¼ turn each; do not slacken them further or the rocker arms may require re-aligning. Working in the sequence shown in the accompanying illustration, **tighten** the nuts to the appropriate torque setting.

When the cylinder head nuts are known to be correctly fastened use feeler gauges of appropriate thickness to measure the clearances between the inlet and exhaust valve stem tips and the ends of their respective rocker arms. If the clearance is correct a feeler gauge of the correct thickness should be a tight sliding fit. **Note:** the clearances specified in this Manual are the latest recommendation for maximum performance and reliability and least noise; the recommended

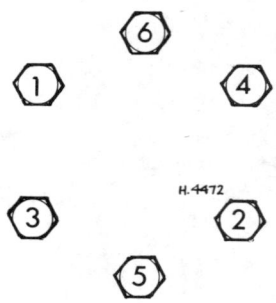

Cylinder head retaining nut tightening sequence

Removing rocker covers – unscrew two nuts at front ...

... and rear of cylinder head ...

... followed by central cap nut

Checking the valve clearances

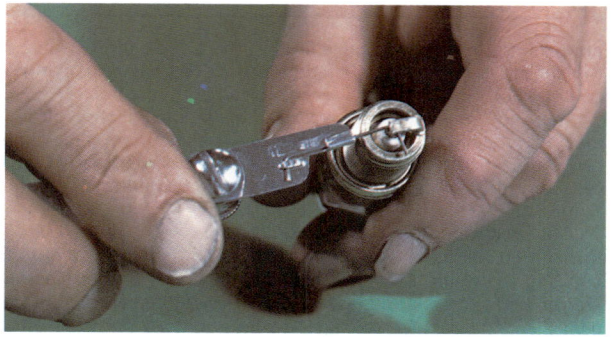
Spark plug maintenance: Checking plug gap with feeler gauges

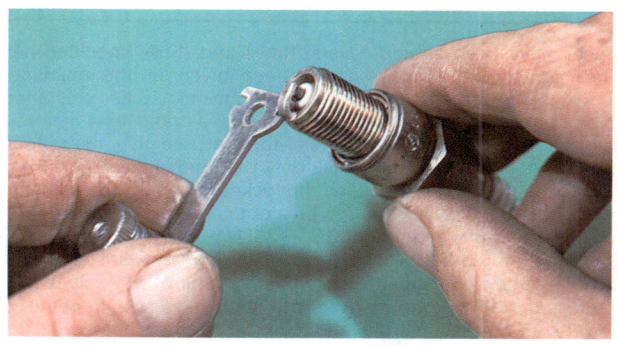
Altering the plug gap. Note use of correct tool

Spark plug conditions: A brown, tan or grey firing end is indicative of correct engine running conditions and the selection of the appropriate heat rating plug

White deposits have accumulated from excessive amounts of oil in the combustion chamber or through the use of low quality oil. Remove deposits or a hot spot may form

Black sooty deposits indicate an over-rich fuel/air mixture, or a malfunctioning ignition system. If no improvement is obtained, try one grade hotter plug

Wet, oily carbon deposits form an electrical leakage path along the insulator nose, resulting in a misfire. The cause may be a badly worn engine or a malfunctioning ignition system

A blistered white insulator or melted electrode indicates over-advanced ignition timing or a malfunctioning cooling system. If correction does not prove effective, try a colder grade plug

A worn spark plug not only wastes fuel but also overloads the whole ignition system because the increased gap requires higher voltage to initiate the spark. This condition can also affect air pollution

clearances have been altered several times and those specified here may not agree with those older settings given in the machine's handbook. Note also that BMW also recommend slacker clearances which are for use **only** during the running in of a brand-new machine. Although they are included in Chapter 1 for reference only, they should never be used at any other time; use only the normal clearances.

If adjustment is required slacken the locknut and turn the adjusting screw until the correct feeler gauge fit is obtained. Do not overtighten the locknut; a torque setting of 18 – 23 Nm (13.5 – 17 lbf ft) is specified and should be used to avoid distorting the adjuster threads and making future adjustment very difficult. When both valves have been adjusted, turn the engine over until that cylinder again comes to TDC on the compression stroke and recheck the clearances.

Note that if that cylinder has been producing excessive noise, the rockers should be checked for correct endfloat (see Chapter 1). The modified rocker assembly introduced on 1985 models is designed to reduce noise from this area and can be fitted to models from 1976 on.

If the gasket is in good condition it can be re-used. If both sealing surfaces are clean and unmarked jointing compound is not necessary, but if oil leaks have been encountered all traces of the old gasket should be removed and both mating surfaces should be carefully cleaned and checked for damage. Using a new gasket if necessary, refit the rocker cover. On all /5 and /6 models the covers are interchangeable, but on all other models they are handed and must be fitted only on the correct cylinder or there is a risk of a rocker touching the cover at high engine speeds (note also that the cover finning would then be inclined instead of horizontal). The covers can be identified either by the words 'Links' (left) or 'Rechts' (right) cast on the inside or by the letter 'L' or 'R' cast into the outside of the waisted section of each cover. Fit the washer and cap nut, then tighten the nut carefully but securely (note the specified torque setting for 1985 on models), followed by the two smaller nuts and their washers.

Turn the engine to TDC on the compression stroke for the remaining cylinder and repeat the operation.

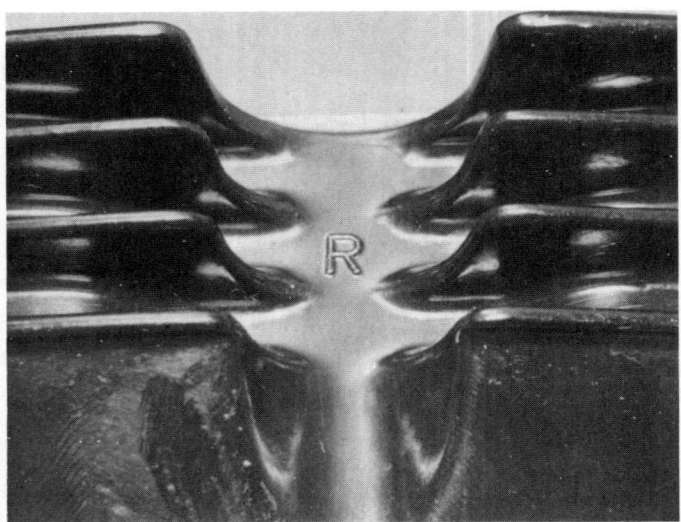

Note cast marks identifying left- and right-hand rocker covers – later models only

11 Check the spark plugs

Detach the plug leads and unscrew both spark plugs. Those specified as original equipment will prove satisfactory in most operating conditions, alternatives are available to allow for varying altitudes, climatic conditions and the use to which the machine is put. If a spark plug is suspected of being faulty it can be tested only by the substitution of a brand new (not second-hand) plug of the correct make, type and heat range.

Note that the advice of a competent BMW dealer or similar expert should be sought before the plug heat range is altered from standard. The use of too cold, or hard, a grade of plug will result in fouling and the use of too hot, or soft a grade of plug will result in engine damage due to excess heat being generated. If the correct grade of plug is fitted, however, it will be possible to use the condition of the spark plug electrodes to diagnose a fault in the engine or to decide whether the engine is operating efficiently or not. The accompanying series of colour photographs will show this clearly.

It is advisable to carry a set of new spare spark plugs on the machine, having first set the electrodes to the correct gap. Whilst spark plugs do not often fail, a new replacement is well worth having if a breakdown does occur. Ensure that the spares are of the correct heat range.

The electrode gap, which should be 0.6 – 0.7 mm (0.024 – 0.028 in), can be assessed using feeler gauges. If necessary alter the gap by bending the outer electrode, preferably using a proper electrode tool. **Never** bend the centre electrode, otherwise the ceramic insulator will crack, and may cause damage to the engine if particles break away whilst the engine is running. If the outer electrode is seriously eroded as shown in the photographs, or if the spark plug is heavily fouled, it should be renewed. Clean the electrodes using a wire brush or a sharp-pointed knife, followed by rubbing a strip of fine emery across the electrodes. If a sand-blaster is used, check carefully that there are no particles of sand trapped inside the plug body to fall into the engine at a later date. For this reason such cleaning methods are no longer recommended; if the plug is so heavily fouled it should be renewed.

Before refitting a spark plug into the cylinder head, coat the threads sparingly with a graphited grease or Copaslip to aid future removal. Use the correct size spanner when tightening the plug, otherwise the spanner may slip and damage the ceramic insulator. The plug should be tightened by hand only at first and then secured with a quarter turn on the spanner so that it seats firmly on its sealing ring. Where possible, use the specified torque setting of 20 – 30 Nm (15 – 22 lbf ft).

Never overtighten a spark plug otherwise there is risk of stripping the thread from the cylinder head, especially as it is cast in light alloy. A stripped thread can be repaired without having to scrap the cylinder head by using a 'Helicoil' thread insert. This is a low-cost service, operated by a number of dealers.

12 Check the contact breaker gap and ignition timing – all models up to 1980

/5, /6, /7 up to 1978 – contact breaker gap

Remove its three Allen screws and withdraw the engine front cover, remove both spark plugs, then insert an Allen key in the alternator rotor centre bolt and turn the engine (clockwise, looking at the alternator from the front of the machine) until the points are fully open. Check the condition of the contact breaker points. They should be an even grey colour. Slight pitting may be removed with a breaker points file. Blow out all abrasive dust. Badly pitted or worn points must be renewed. The faces of the points must be parallel when closed.

The points must be renewed as soon as pitting becomes bad. Short contact breaker points life may be due to a faulty condenser.

To replace the contact breaker points, unscrew the cheese head screw retaining the points to the backplate, and the screw retaining the cable clip. Remove the points and pull off the spade terminal from the condenser. Pull the wire out of the condenser grommet.

When replacing the contact breaker points, ensure that the pivot pin locates in the hole in the contact breaker backplate. Clean the points with solvent to remove oil or grease. Re-set the points gap, which should be 0.35 – 0.40 mm (0.014 – 0.016 in). To adjust, slacken the points fixing screw slightly. Put a screwdriver between the two pins at the top of the contact breaker backplate and turn to move the points carrier until the gap is correct. Tighten the fixing screw and recheck the gap. After adjusting the contact breaker gap, check the ignition timing.

Note: *although it provides a more accurate setting if properly applied, the use of a dwell meter is very awkward on these models as the ATU assembly is rotating immediately above the points when the engine is running. If this method is to be used, follow its manufacturer's instructions when connecting the dwell meter to the machine, start the engine (having first cleaned or renewed the points) and allow it to idle. If the meter reading is larger than that specified, the points gap must be increased and vice versa. Note that, while some meter needle flickering is normal, if the reading fluctuates wildly the ATU, camshaft and camshaft bearings should be checked carefully for wear.*

/7, R45 and R65 1979 – 80 – contact breaker gap

Remove the engine front cover which is retained by two Allen screws, then remove the single screw which retains the contact breaker

Routine maintenance

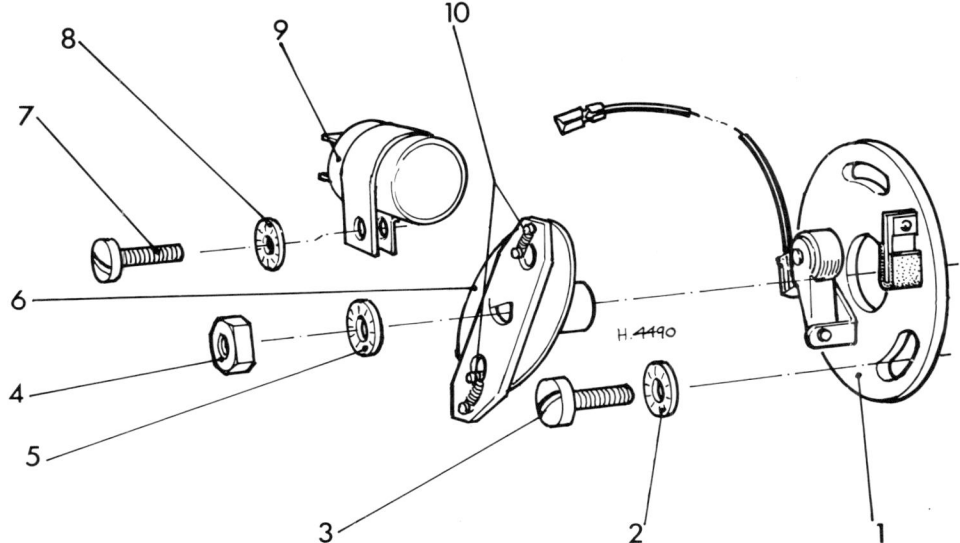

Contact breaker – all models up to 1978

1. Backplate
2. Lock washer
3. Screw
4. Nut
5. Lock washer
6. Centrifugal advance unit
7. Screw
8. Lock washer
9. Condenser
10. Springs

All models up to 1978 – contact breaker pivot pin must engage in hole in backplate

Adjust contact breaker gap when points are fully open

housing cover and withdraw the cover. Remove the spark plugs and rotate the engine clockwise, looking from the front of the machine rearwards, by using an Allen key in the alternator rotor retaining Allen bolt. Rotate the engine until the contract breaker points open to the maximum gap, then examine the condition of the contact point faces. Light burning or pitting may be reclaimed by careful dressing with a fine file or abrasive paper, but serious pitting or other damage will mean that the contact breaker assembly must be renewed.

To renew the contact breaker assembly, remove the two screws which secure the outrigger bearing plate at the forward end of the contact breaker housing, then carefully pull the bearing plate away. Remove the single screw which retains the contact breaker assembly, pull out the space terminal to disconnect the points lead, and withdraw the contact breaker assembly. Refitting is the reverse of the above procedure, but a thin smear of the grease supplied with the new assembly should be applied to the contact breaker cam and the lubricating felt, and to the camshaft where it passes through the outrigger bearing. Check that the cam lubricating felt comes into correct contact with the cam. If a white plastic cap is fitted to the contact breaker assembly or is supplied with it, the cap should be discarded as it is not intended for use on these machines and will restrict engine performance at high engine speeds.

To adjust the contact breaker gap, rotate the engine clockwise as described above until the maximum gap is obtained and measure the gap using feeler gauges which should be a light sliding fit. Note that the gap should always be checked with the outrigger bearing plate in place. The correct clearance on these models is 0.40 – 0.50 mm (0.016 – 0.020 in) and is achieved by slackening slightly the contact breaker retaining screw and inserting a screwdriver into the slot in the contact breaker backplate. The screwdriver is then turned to move the backplate until the gap is correct. Tighten securely the retaining screw and rotate the engine fully clockwise until the points are again fully open, then recheck the gap, resetting it if necessary. Once the gap is known to be correct, refit the contact breaker housing cover, and check the ignition timing.

It is preferable to use a dwell meter to set the points gap, as this provides a far more accurate setting. Connect the meter to the machine following the manufacturer's instructions, start the engine and allow it to idle. Adjust the gap as describd above until the specified reading is obtained. Note that the dwell angle (see Chapter 5 Specifications) is given in terms of degrees of crankshaft rotation or as a percentage figure; check that the correct figure is used for the meter.

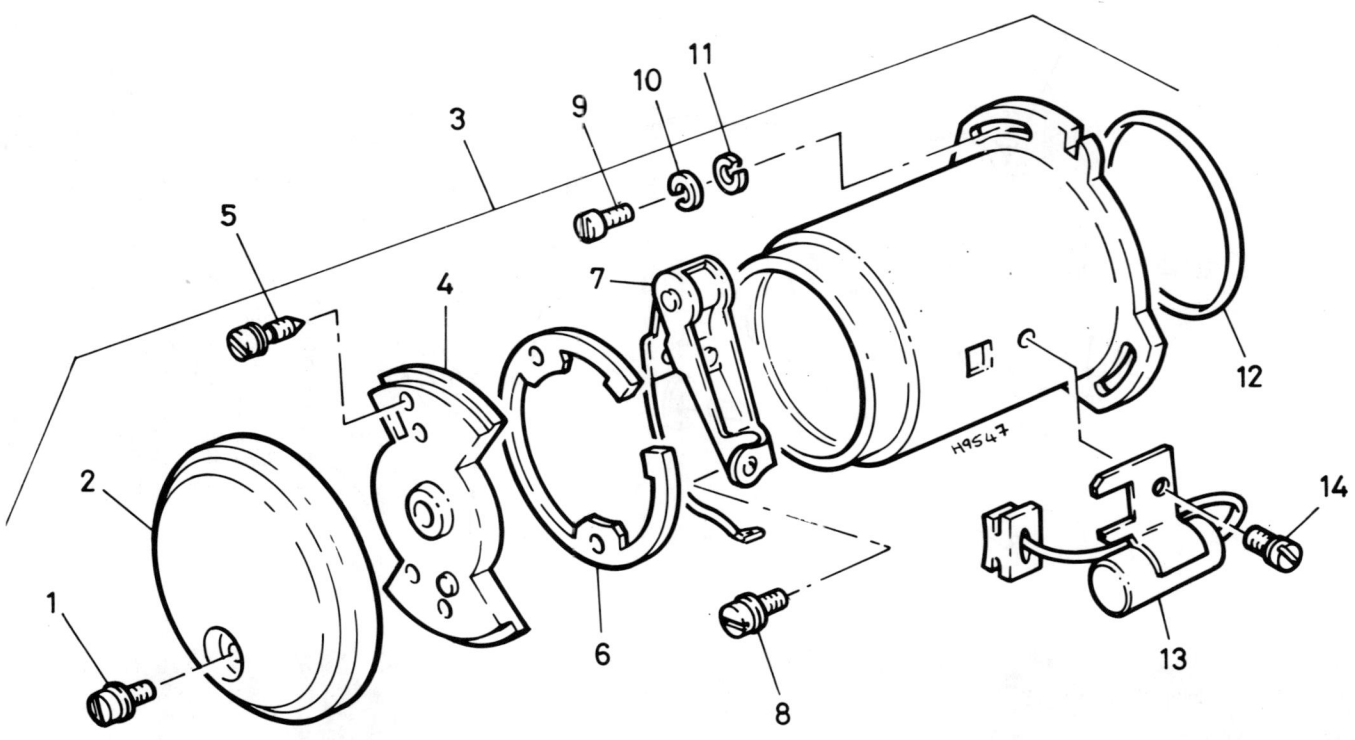

Contact breaker – all models 1979 to 1980

1 Screw
2 Housing cover
3 Contact breaker assembly
4 Outrigger bearing plate
5 Screw
6 Circlip
7 Contact breaker
8 Screw
9 Screw
10 Lock washer
11 Washer
12 O-ring
13 Condenser
14 Screw

Checking the ignition timing – all models up to 1980

The ignition timing marks stamped on the flywheel are as follows for /5 and /6 models; the static or idle speed mark is a line stamped on the flywheel (at 9° BTDC) with the letter 'S' adjacent, the full advance mark being the letter 'F'. On /7 models both marks are the same in appearance except that the static or idle speed mark is now stamped on the flywheel rim at 6° BTDC; two further lines are marked, one on each side at a distance of 6 mm (0.236 in) from the 'S' mark. As 2 mm (0.08 in) of flywheel rim movement corresponds to 1° of crankshaft rotation, these extra lines make it easier to check that the difference (if any) between cylinders does not exceed the tolerance of ± 3°.

Check the ignition timing statically with a test lamp or buzzer after the points have been checked and adjusted. Connect one lead from the lamp/buzzer to the capacitor terminal and the other lead to earth. Switch on the ignition. Remove the rubber plug from the timing mark viewing hole behind the dipstick. Also remove both spark plugs. As the engine is turned clockwise by means of an Allen key in the alternator rotor fixing screw, the lamp should light when the 'S' mark on the flywheel coincides exactly with the mark on the crankcase (see accompanying illustration). The centrifugal advance bob weights should be at rest – ie., in the retarded position. The remaining cylinder should not vary by more than 3° (equivalent to 6 mm, 0.236 in of movement at the flywheel rim) above or below the 'S' mark.

If the ignition is too advanced or retarded, adjust as follows on all models up to 1978; slacken the two cheese head screws on the contact breaker backplate. Turning the backplate clockwise retards the timing and vice versa. Tighten the two screws and recheck the timing. If timing between the cylinders is outside the 3° tolerance, check the cam drive shaft for truth, or the camshaft bearing for slackness.

To adjust the ignition timing on 1979 – 80 models, slacken the two Allen screws which fasten the contact breaker housing and rotate the housing clockwise to retard the ignition timing, or anti-clockwise to advance it. Tighten securely the housing retaining Allen screws and recheck the ignition timing.

Retarded   Correct   Advanced

Ignition timing mark positions

If one is tracing the cause of a fault such as lack of power the ignition timing should be checked on the other cylinder to discover if there is any discrepancy between the two. If such a discrepancy exists, or if the timing check reveals a fault in the ATU then the complete contact breaker housing assembly must be renewed. No parts are available with which this assembly can be reconditioned.

While the timing can be checked statically as described above, this is no longer recommended as a sufficiently accurate check, and the manufacturer advises the use of a strobe lamp instead. The best type of lamp is the more expensive xenon tube type which uses a separate power source, ie not the machine's battery. If such a lamp is not available, the machine should be taken to a BMW dealer for the work to be carried out professionally.

Connect the strobe according to the manufacturer's instructions and remove the black rubber inspection cap from the timing mark

Flywheel timing mark should align with notch in crankcase aperture as shown

Slacken retaining Allen screws and rotate distributor housing/ignition trigger unit to adjust ignition timing – all models 1979 on

viewing hole next to the dipstick. Start the engine and allow it to idle at the specified speed (see Chapter 4), then aim the strobe at the inspection aperture. The 'S' mark should align exactly with the crankcase index mark formed by a notch in the periphery of the timing mark viewing hole. Gradually increase engine speed to at least 3000 rpm and watch the timing marks. At just above idle speed (see Chapter 5) the 'S' mark should move upwards and disappear from view, and soon a white dot with the letter 'F' adjacent to it should rise into view. At full advance the 'F' mark should align exactly with the crankcase notch.

In the case of either the 'S' mark or the 'F' mark, if it appears above the crankcase notch, the ignition timing is advanced; and if below the notch, the timing is retarded. Adjust the timing as described above. Note that if the advance does not function correctly or return smoothly when the thorttle is released, the ATU mechanism is faulty. While this can be dismantled and greased on all models up to 1978 (see Major Service), it can only be cured by the renewal of the complete housing assembly on 1979 – 80 models; although there is nothing to be lost by attempting to lubricate the pivots as described for electronic ignition models (see Major Service).

13 Check the carburettors

On models with Bing carburettors release the spring clamps securing each carburettor float bowl, check that the fuel supply is switched off, tap each float bowl gently with a soft-faced mallet to break the seal and remove the float bowls. If dirt or droplets of water can be seen in the bottom of either bowl the fuel tap will require dismantling so that its filter(s) can be cleaned. If excessive amounts of dirt or water are seen the tank must be drained and cleaned out. Refer to the Major Service. Check that all jets are securely fastened and that the float bowl gasket is in good condition, then refit the float bowls and secure each with its clip. Switch on the fuel supply and check for leaks.

On R90S models switch off the fuel supply, unscrew the float bowl drain plug, detach the float bowl as described above and check the cleanliness of the fuel. Unscrew the bolt retaining each fuel banjo union, withdraw the union and clean the nylon filter gauze with a soft bristled brush. Refit the float bowl and banjo union to each carburettor, switch on the fuel supply and check for leaks.

On all models, check that there is 0.5 – 1.0 mm (0.02 – 0.04 in) free play in both throttle cables, measured at the carburettor top and use the cable adjusters to ensure that cable free play is at the correct amount and exactly the same on both carburettors. Check that the choke cable free play (where fitted) is 0.5 – 1.0 mm (0.02 – 0.04 in) and adjust, if necessary, in the same way.

Before the settings of the carburettors themselves are disturbed, the air filter must have been cleaned or renewed, the exhaust system must be in good condition, the valve clearances must have been checked and the contact breaker gap (where applicable) and ignition timing must have been checked and adjusted. Carburettors do not usually develop faults suddenly (inless a jet becomes blocked with dirt, for example) and faults which may appear to indicate a carburettor malfunction are usually due to a failure or maladjustment of another engine, ignition or induction system component. In addition to this, the engine must be warmed up to normal operating temperature.

While as a general rule carburettors should not be disturbed unnecessarily, BMW twins, especially the larger capacity models, are very sensitive to correct carburettor adjustment and particularly to correct synchronisation. If it is felt that adjustment is required, refer to the relevant Sections of Chapter 4. Owners of later model (1978 on) US models should note that local legislation may mean in practice that carburettor adjustment should be left only to a BMW dealer who has the necessary equipment to carry it out to the required standard.

Note that if rough idling and increased vibration at speed cannot be cured by carburettor adjustment, check that all jets are unblocked and

R90S only – when cleaning carburettors, do not forget filter gauze behind each fuel banjo union

the carburettor lines are undamaged. On models with Bing constant-depression carburettors check that the diaphragms are undamaged, that the O-rings sealing the pilot jets are in good condition and that the auxiliary starter carburettor levers return fully when the choke lever is closed. On earlier models it would be advisable to fit the lever return springs from later models to ensure that the levers are positively returned at all times. If this does not cure the problem carry out the compression test to check the condition of the engine (see Chapter 1).

14 Check the brakes
/5 and R60/6 – front

The front brake is adjusted corrrectly if there is 4 – 6 mm (0.16 – 0.24 in) of free play measured between the handlebar lever butt end and the handlebar clamp. If adjustment is required slacken its locknut and rotate the knurled adjuster at the handlebar lever, to give 8 – 15 mm (0.32 to 0.59 in) freeplay in the cable.

Loosen the locknut on the brake plate adjuster. Turn the centre screw fully anti-clockwise with an allen key, then turn it back until there is 4 mm (0.16 in) movement at the end of the lower brake cam lever. Tighten the locknut. Adjust the nut on the end of the inner cable, to give the correct free play at the handlebar lever.

There is no need to synchronise the action of the two brake shoes; this is achieved automatically by the action of the cable.

To check brake shoe wear on /5 and early R60/6 models the wheel must be removed from the machine. On later R60/6 models the friction material thickness can be checked through slots in the hub left-hand side. If the friction material is worn down at any point to 1.5 mm (0.06 in) or less, both shoes must be renewed. Refer to Chapter 8.

All other /6 and /7 models up to 1980 – front

The front brake is adjusted correctly if there is approximately 4 – 6 mm (0.16 – 0.24 in) of free play measured between the handlebar lever butt end and the handlebar clamp. If adjustment is required remove the fuel tank (see Chapter 4) and peel off the rubber cover from the rear of the master cylinder. Slacken the cable adjuster locknut and insert the forked feeler gauge from the machine's toolkit into the groove in the master cylinder piston. If this is not available a replacement can be cut (similar to that shown in the accompanying photograph) from a sheet of metal 1.2 mm (0.0472 in) thick. Adjustment is correct when the feeler gauge is just free to move against the master cylinder body. Tighten securely the adjuster locknut and apply a few drops of oil to

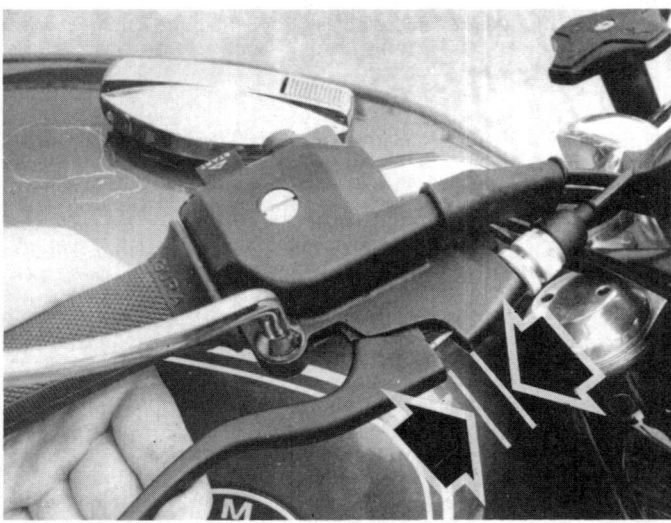

All models up to 1980 – front brake free play is measured as shown

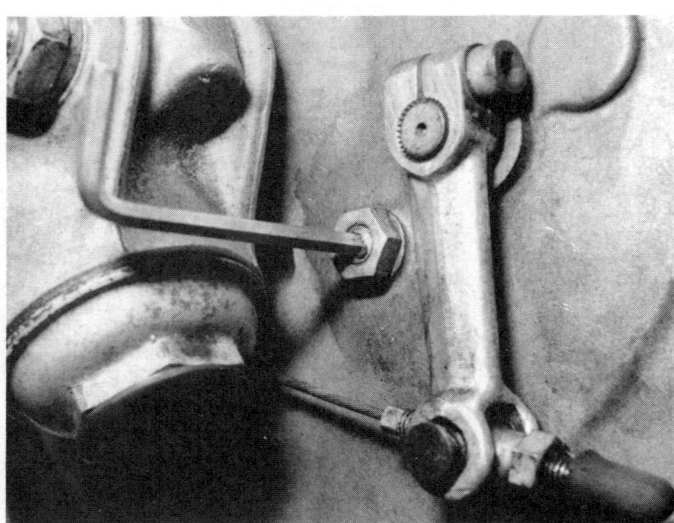

Use adjuster on brake plate to set correct shoe/drum clearance ...

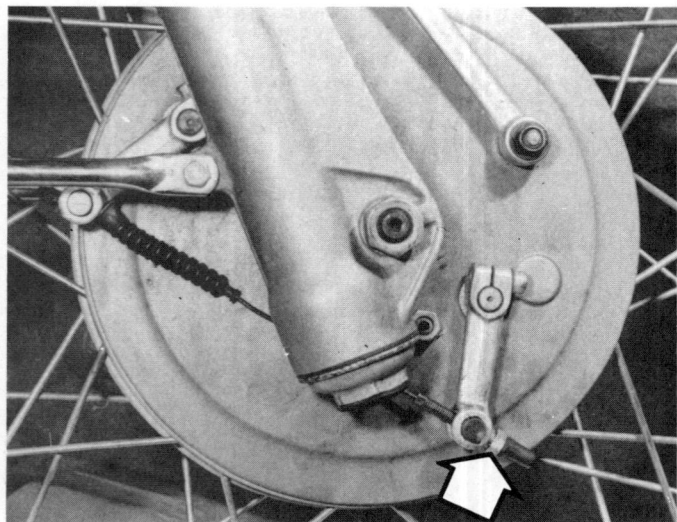

... then set correct cable free play using adjuster nut (arrowed) – cable automatically synchronises the two shoes

Later R60/6 models – brake shoe wear can be checked through slots in hub

Routine maintenance

Early disc brake models – feeler gauge is necessary to adjust mechanism free play

Do not fill master cylinder above 'Max' level line – if excessive topping-up is necessary, check system for leaks or damage

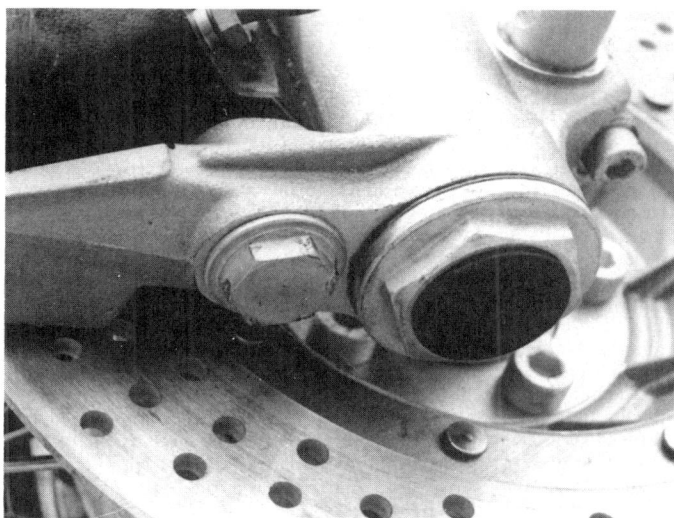

To remove swinging calipers, unscrew pivot retaining plug ...

... and use a wheel spindle clamp Allen bolt ...

the cable end nipple and to the lever pivot. At regular intervals the cable should be disconnected and the master cylinder pushrod withdrawn so that both ends can be greased with a dab of Molykote BR2 or Liquid Moly LM47L. When adjustment and lubrication are complete refit the rubber cover and the fuel tank.

The brake fluid level is monitored by the warning light on the dash panel but the level should be checked whenever the fuel tank is removed. If topping up is necessary use only the specified brake fluid from a freshly-opened sealed container. Do not fill above the 'Max' level line or fluid will be spilled when the cap and float are refitted. Brake fluid is an extremely effective paint stripper and will attack any plastic or painted components; wash off any spilt fluid with copious quantities of fresh water. Note that it is quite normal for the fluid level to drop gradually as the pads wear, but any sudden drops in level must be investigated immediately. Check all hydraulic components for signs of fluid leakage and renew any seal or component that is found to be faulty.

The amount of friction material remaining on the brake pads can be checked by looking at the caliper. Original equipment pads have painted wear limit marks; if either pad is worn so that these marks are in contact with the disc at any point, both pads must be renewed. If a twin disc system is fitted, the pads of both calipers should be renewed at the same time, even if only one is worn. Where painted wear limit marks are not provided, the pads must be renewed if any one is worn at any point to a friction material thickness of 1.5 mm (0.06 in) or less. If the pads are so fouled with dirt that they cannot be seen clearly, they must be removed and cleaned.

To renew the pads either the front wheel can be removed or the caliper(s) can be detached (in turn) from the fork leg(s). If the first course is chosen, refer to Chapter 8; if the second course is chosen, which is preferable as it permits the cleaning of the caliper pivot, proceed as follows. Unscrew the plug at the bottom of each caliper pivot and withdraw it complete with the coil spring. Unscrew one of the wheel spindle clamp Allen bolts and screw this into the thread of the caliper pivot. Extract the pivot and pull the caliper away from the disc taking care not to distort the metal brake pipe; if necessary remove the mudguard rear mounting bolt to release the brake pipe bracket. Unclip the fixed pad retaining wire clip and tap out the pad, then pull the moving pad out of the caliper piston.

If the pads are worn out or fouled with oil or grease they should be renewed immediately; there is no satisfactory way of degreasing friction material. If they are still serviceable, clean them carefully using a fine wire brush until all traces of dirt, corrosion and old friction material are removed from the friction material and the pad metal backing. Pick out any embedded particles of dirt and use fine emery cloth or similar to ease down any glazed areas.

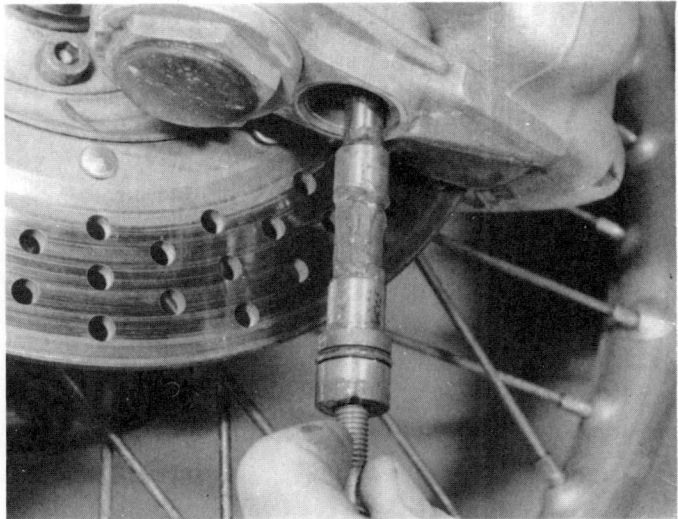
... to extract caliper pivot. Note pivot O-ring and ensure pivot is clean and well greased before refitting

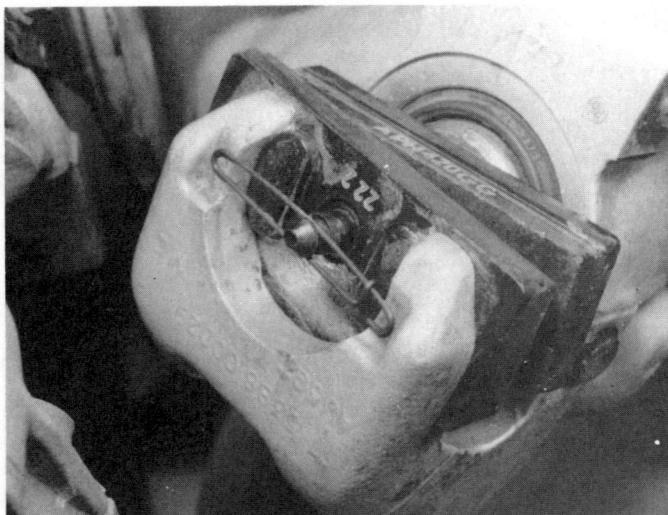
Release retaining clip to withdraw fixed brake pad

Thoroughly clean the caliper, caliper pivot and fork leg mountings, removing all traces of dirt, old grease and corrosion. Pack the caliper and fork leg pivot bores with Molykote BR2, Liquid Moly LM47L or any good quality brake caliper grease (silicone or PBC/Poly Butyl Cuprysil-based), and smear grease over the pivot itself. Note the O-ring around the pivot; this should be renewed if damaged or worn.

If new pads are to be fitted press back the caliper piston using a G-clamp or similar to make room for the new, thicker components. Renewing the O-ring on its locating pin and lubricating both pin and O-ring with a smear of the specified grease, press the moving pad into the piston bore. Fit the fixed pad to the opposite side of the caliper, ensuring that its locating shoulder engages correctly, then refit the retaining wire clip. Anchor it correctly, with the open end downwards (see accompanying photographs), and check that it is locked securely into the groove of the pad pin. Refit the caliper to the fork leg, check that the pivot is well-greased and insert it into the pivot bores rotating it to ensure that it is pressed fully into place; the pivot upper shoulder should butt firmly against the underside of the fork leg top mounting.

If the pads have been renewed, if the caliper setting has been disturbed or if the front wheel has been removed and refitted

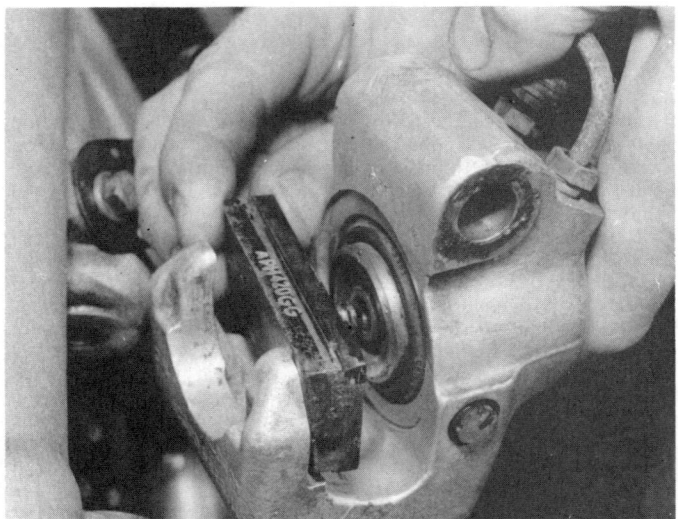
Renew O-ring if necessary and grease locating pin on refitting moving brake pad

Ensure shoulder on fixed pad engages correctly with caliper body ...

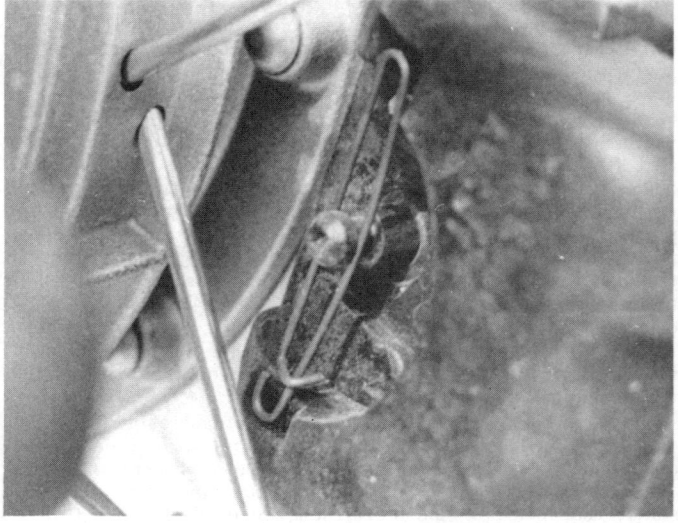
... and be careful to refit retaining wire clip correctly, as shown

(possibly) the wrong way round, the caliper must be adjusted to align the fixed pad with the disc. If this has not already been done, remove the pivot threaded plug and coil spring.

Using a broad flat-bladed screwdriver, turn the eccentric pivot until the caliper is at its outermost position, ie furthest away from the wheel spindle, then turn the pivot slowly until the fixed pad is parallel to the disc. Using a piece of chalk or a thick-nibbed felt marker, apply one or two heavy radial lines to the inside of the brake disc, then pull the caliper outwards so that the fixed pad is in firm contact with this face and rotate the wheel until the marks have been rubbed across the pad. On close examination, if the marks have been fully wiped away or rubbed along their full length, the fixed pad is parallel to the disc and the setting is correct. If the marks have been only partially abraded, this shows that the pad is angled away from or towards the disc; carefully rotate the eccentric pivot (noting that only very small movements are required) and repeat the check until the setting is correct.

When the caliper pivot is correctly set, grease the spring to prevent corrosion and refit it and the threaded plug. Tighten the plug to the specified torque setting. Check that the caliper moves smoothly and easily on its pivot; this is essential for full braking performance. If there is any doubt about this the pivot should be removed and cleaned as described above. Lubricate the pivot and pivot bearings on refitting. Repeat the operation on the remaining caliper (twin-disc system).

Apply the handlebar lever several times to bring both pads into firm contact with the disc, then check the fluid level (removing the fuel tank, if necessary). If the level is above the 'Max' mark (as it may be if new pads have been fitted) carefully remove the filler cap and soak up the surplus fluid with a clean rag to restore the level. Refit the cap and wash off any spilt fluid.

All other models – front

The hydraulic front brake fitted to later models requires no regular adjustments; pad wear is compensated for by the automatic entry of more fluid into the system from the handlebar reservoir. All that is necessary is to maintain a regular check on the fluid level and the degree of pad wear.

To check the fluid level, turn the handlebars until the reservoir is horizontal and check that the fluid level, as seen through the reservoir body, is not below the lower level mark. Remember that while the fluid level will fall steadily as the pad friction material is used up, if the level

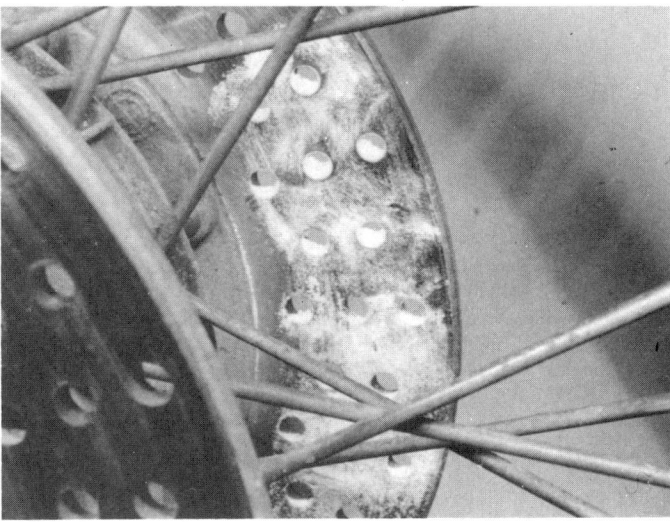

To check caliper alignment, apply marks as described to disc inner face (shown greatly exaggerated for clarity)

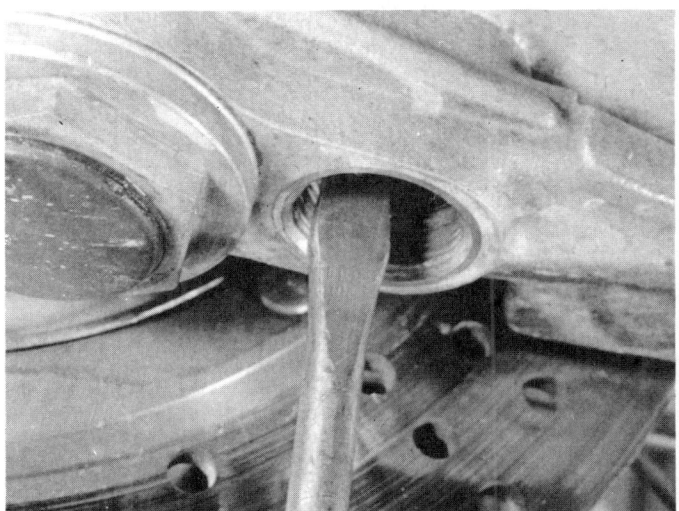

If adjustment is necessary rotate caliper pivot in very small amounts ...

... until fixed pad is parallel to disc, shown by complete removal of marks

Grease coil spring and tighten threaded plug to specified torque setting on refitting

falls below the lower level mark there is a risk of air entering the system; it is therefore sufficient to maintain the fluid level above the lower level mark, by topping-up if necessary. Do not top up to the higher level mark unless this is necessary after new pads have been fitted. If topping up is necessary, wipe any dirt off the reservoir, remove the retaining screws and lift away the reservoir cover and diaphragm. Use only good quality brake fluid of the recommended type and ensure that it comes from a freshly opened sealed container; brake fluid is hygroscopic, which means that it absorbs moisture from the air, therefore old fluid may have become contaminated to such an extent that its boiling point has been lowered to an unsafe level. Remember also that brake fluid is an excellent paint stripper and will attack plastic components; wash away any spilled fluid immediately with copious quantities of water. When the level is correct, clean and dry the diaphragm, fold it into its compressed state and fit it to the reservoir. Refit the reservoir cover (and gasket, where fitted) and tighten securely, but do not overtighten, the retaining screws.

To check the degree of pad wear, look closely at the pads from above or below the caliper. Wear limit marks are provided in the form of painted lines around the outside of the material. If either pad is worn at any point so that the mark is in contact with the disc, or if the wear limit marks have been removed completely, both pads must be renewed as a set. If the pads are so fouled with dirt that the marks cannot be seen, or if oil or grease is seen on them, they must be removed for cleaning and examination.

Unclip the plastic cover from the caliper and use a suitable drift to tap out the two pad retaining pins from the inside outwards; take care not to allow the retaining spring to fly off. Remove the central pin and withdraw both pads.

If the pads are worn to the limit marks or to a thickness of 1.5 mm (0.06 in) or less at any point, fouled with oil or grease, or heavily scored or damaged by dirt and debris, they must be renewed as a set; there is no satisfactory way of degreasing friction material. If the pads can be used again, clean them carefully using a fine wire brush that is completely free of oil or grease. Remove all traces of road dirt and corrosion, then use a pointed instrument to clean out the groove(s) in the friction material and to dig out any embedded particles of foreign matter. Any areas of glazing may be removed using emery cloth.

On reassembly, if new pads are to be fitted, the caliper pistons must now be pushed back as far as possible into the caliper bores to provide the clearance necessary to accommodate the unworn pads. It should be possible to do this with hand pressure only. If any undue stiffness is encountered the caliper assembly should be dismantled for examination as described in Chapter 8. While pushing the pistons back, maintain a careful watch on the fluid level in the handlebar reservoir. If the reservoir has been overfilled, the surplus fluid will prevent the pistons returning fully and must be removed by soaking it up with a clean cloth. Take care to prevent fluid spillage. Apply a thin smear of caliper grease to the pad retaining pins. Take care to apply caliper grease to the metal backing of the pad only and not to allow grease to contaminate the friction material. Carefully fit the pads to the caliper and hold them in place while the first retaining pin (with the spring looped over it) is refitted. Place the central pin in the pad cutouts and press the spring over it and underneath the second retaining pin which should now be pressed into place. Refit the plastic cover.

Apply the brake lever gently and repeatedly to bring the pads firmly into contact with the disc until full brake pressure is restored. Be careful to watch the fluid level in the reservoir; if the pads have been re-used it will suffice to keep the level above the lower level mark, by topping-up if necessary, but if new pads have been fitted the level must be restored to the upper level line described above by topping-up or removing surplus fluid as necessary. Refit the reservoir cover, gasket (where fitted) and diaphragm as described above.

Before taking the machine out on the road, be careful to check for fluid leaks from the system, and that the front brake is working correctly. Remember also that new pads, and to a lesser extent, cleaned pads will require a bedding-in period before they will function at peak efficiency. Where new pads are fitted use the brake gently but firmly for the first 50 – 100 miles to enable the pads to bed in fully.

If friction material of either pad is worn to the wear limit or less at any point, both pads must be renewed

Brake pads must be completely clean on refitting – ensure friction material is in contact with the disc

Insert brake pads and refit retaining pin with spring ...

Routine maintenance

... then position central pin in pad cutouts ...

... and fit second retaining pin ...

... so that pads are secured as shown

R100RS 1978 on, R100S 1979 – 80, R100RT – rear

The hydraulic disc rear brake fitted to these models is maintained in exactly the same way as described above for the front brakes of all later models. The master cylinder reservoir is situated behind the right-hand side panel. Note that the brake linkage should have 1.4 – 1.5 mm (0.055 – 0.059 in) of free play between the master cylinder piston and its operating lever; this is approximately equivalent to free play of 15 – 20 mm (0.6 – 0.8 in) at the pedal tip. This is pre-set at the factory and should not require adjustment but if necessary can be altered by slackening its locknut and disconnecting the brake rod from the pedal. Screw the rod in or out on the operating link until the clearance is correct then re-connect the rod to the pedal and tighten its locknut.

If the pads are to be removed, work is much easier if the caliper is partially removed. Unscrew the spindle retaining nut, then slacken the spindle clamp bolt. Remove the single bolt which secures the caliper mounting bracket to the rear brake torque arm, then pull the spindle out to the left. Free the brake pipe from the swinging-arm clamp and lift the caliper mounting bracket upwards off the brake disc. Hang the caliper assembly over the left-hand silencer, using a piece of cloth to prevent scratching or damage to the finish of the silencer or swinging arm.

Refitting is a straightforward reversal of the removal sequence, but remember that the wheel spindle must be greased lightly to prevent the onset of corrosion and that the rear brake pedal must be applied repeatedly to bring the brake pads back into firm contact with the disc and to restore full braking pressure before the machine is used on the road.

All other models – rear

Drum rear brake adjustment is made by placing the machine on its centre stand with the rear wheel clear of the ground, then tightening the adjuster nut at the rear end of the brake operating rod until a rubbing sound is heard as the shoes begin to contact the drum. From this point slacken the nut by 3 – 4 turns until the rubbing sound has ceased. This should produce free play of 16 – 25 mm (0.6 – 1.0 in) at the brake pedal tip.

On /5 and early /6 models the rear wheel must be removed (see Chapter 8) to check brake shoe wear, but on all models from late /6 up to 1982 (approximately) the friction material thickness can be checked through apertures in the hub left-hand side; it may be necessary to remove a rubber blanking plug from the aperture. If the friction material of either shoe is worn down at any point to 1.5 mm (0.06 in) or less, both shoes must be renewed. See Chapter 8.

From approximately 1982 on, external wear indicators were fitted in the form of a pointer attached to the brake camshaft. With the brake correctly adjusted and fully applied, the pointer should align with the 'Max' line cast on the rear bevel drive housing. As the shoes wear, the pointer will gradually move downwards. If it aligns with the 'Min' line at any time or extends beyond it, the brake shoes are worn out and must be renewed. See Chapter 8.

Use adjuster at rear end of operating rod to adjust drum rear brakes

External wear indicator is fitted to check shoe wear on later models

Special grease gun fitting is required to grease swinging arm pivot bearings

15 Grease the swinging arm pivot bearings
Prise off the black plastic cap over each bearing and pump grease in until all old grease is expelled and fresh grease can be seen. This will require a grease gun with a special conical fitting which can be pressed into the pivot shaft centre.

16 Check the tightness of all nuts, bolts and fasteners
Work methodically round the machine, checking that all nuts, bolts and screws are securely fastened. Using the specified torque wrench settings, (where given) check with particular care the engine, stand, suspension unit, rear subframe and footrest mountings, the front and rear wheel spindle nuts and spindle clamp bolts, the rear wheel mountings (Monolever models) and the clamps securing the carburettor hoses, drive shaft gaiter and fork gaiters (where fitted). Any fastener that repeatedly works loose must be secured with a new lock washer (where applicable) or with thread-locking compound.

17 Test ride
Finish off each service with a careful test ride. Check all components listed under the pre-ride check before starting and pay careful attention to all freshly-adjusted or serviced components while riding. The ride must be of sufficient length to warm up all components to normal operating temperature and a careful check must be made for any fuel, oil or brake fluid leaks that may have developed. If necessary repeat any service operation.

Major service

1 Change the engine oil and filter
Refer to the minor service operation.

2 Change the gearbox oil
The machine must be taken on a journey of sufficient length to warm up the gearbox to normal operating temperature before the oil is drained.
With the machine supported on its centre stand on level ground, remove the filler and drain plugs and allow the oil to drain into a suitable container. Renew the plug sealing washers if they are damaged or flattened. When the oil has fully drained refit the drain plug and tighten it to a torque setting of 23 – 26 Nm (17 – 19 lbf ft).
Fill the gearbox with 800 cc (1.41 Imp pint/0.85 US qt) of the specified type and viscosity of oil, then check the oil level as described in the minor service.

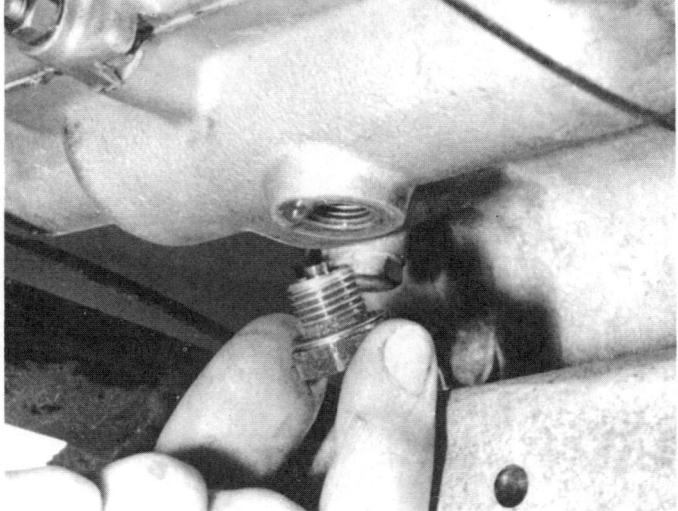
Remove gearbox drain plug to drain oil – clean magnetic pickup (where fitted)

3 Change the driveshaft oil
The machine must be taken on a journey of sufficient length to warm up the driveshaft oil to normal operating temperature before it is drained.
With the machine supported on its centre stand on level ground, remove the filler and drain plugs from the **front** end of the rear bevel drive housing and allow the oil to drain into a suitable container. Use a sheet of cardboard or similar to keep the oil off the rear wheel and tyre. Renew the plug sealing washers if they are damaged or flattened. When the oil has fully drained refit the drain plug and tighten it to the specified torque setting.
Fill the swinging arm with exactly the correct amount of the specified type and viscosity of oil, then check the oil level as described in the minor service.

4 Change the rear bevel drive oil
The machine must be taken on a journey of sufficient length to warm up the rear bevel drive to normal operating temperature before the oil is drained.

Routine maintenance

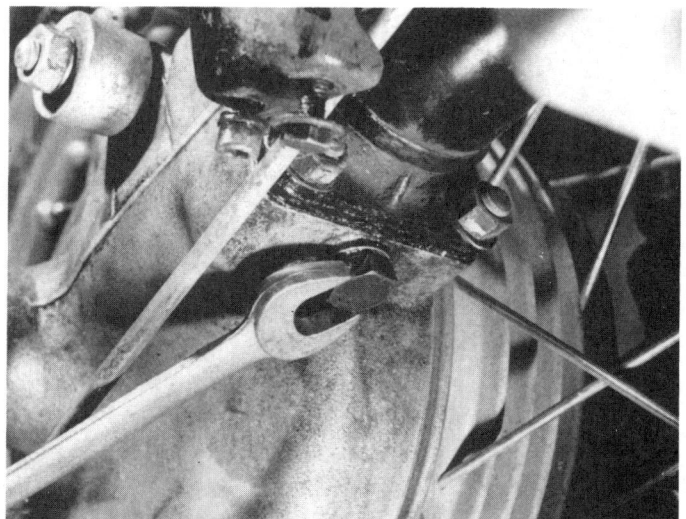
The driveshaft housing oil drain plug

The bevel drive housing oil drain plug

With the machine supported on its centre stand on level ground, remove the filler/level or filler and level plugs (as applicable) and the drain plug and allow the oil to drain into a suitable container. Use a sheet of cardboard to keep the oil off the rear wheel and tyre. Renew the plug sealing washers if they are damaged or flattened. When the oil has fully drained refit the drain plug, tightening it to the specified torque setting and pour in the correct amount of the specified type and viscosity of oil. Check the oil level as described in the minor service.

5 Clean the cylinder and sump cooling fins
Refer to the minor service operation.

6 Lubricate the controls and stand pivots
Refer to the minor service operation.

7 Check the battery
Refer to the minor service operation.

8 Renew the air filter element
Remove the old air filter element as described under the minor service operation and fit a new element.

9 Adjust the clutch
Refer to the minor service operation.

10 Clean the fuel tap filter
Turn off the fuel supply and unscrew the union nut at the base of each fuel tap. Withdraw the filter gauze and clean it with a blast of compressed air from underneath. Renew the gauze if it is split or damaged. Ensure that it is correctly located in the tap and re-connect the fuel pipe; do not overtighten the union nut. Switch on the fuel supply and check for fuel leaks. Some earlier taps have a cork seal below the filter which must be renewed if it is leaking. On R80 and R80RT 1985 on models, the filters are above the tap, inside the fuel tank. Drain the tank (see Chapter 4), remove the taps and clean the filters.

11 Check the tightness of the cylinder head nuts and adjust the valve clearances
Refer to the minor service operation.

12 Renew the spark plugs
The spark plugs should be renewed at this interval regardless of their apparent condition as they will have passed peak efficiency. Check that the new plugs are of the correct type and that they are correctly gapped before fitting them.

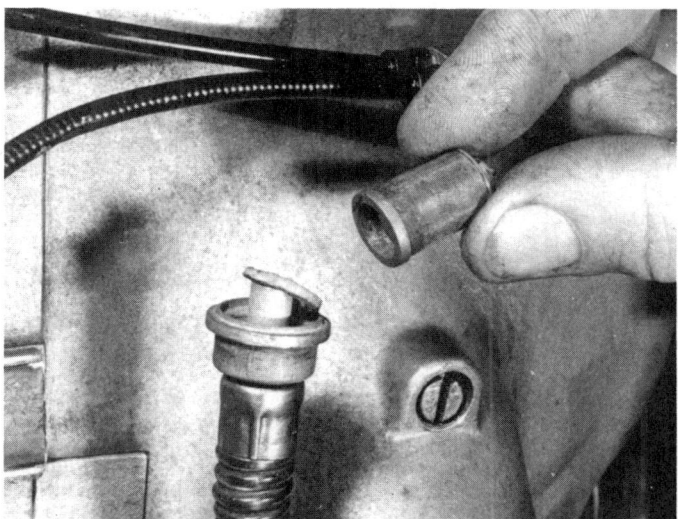
Fuel tap filter gauze must be cleaned at regular intervals

13 Grease the contact breaker cam felt and ATU pivots – all models up to 1980
While the contact breaker points are being checked, rub a small quantity of Bosch grease or similar into the cam lubricating felt. Use Ft 1v4 grease on models up to 1978, Ft 1v8 grease on all 1979-80 models.

On /5, /6 and /7 models up to 1978, grease the ATU pivots and shaft as follows. Remove its retaining nut and lock washer and withdraw the unit, noting the D-shaped hole in the centrifugal advance plate, which locates it on the camshaft extension.

Check the operation of the centrifugal advance weights. Grease the pivots with Bosch Ft 1v4 grease. Stronger springs, which delay the point at which advance commences, are available to improve low speed running for /5 and early /6 models.

The arrow stamped on the centrifugal advance plate indicates the direction of rotation.

Before refitting the ATU, grease the camshaft extension with Bosch grease Ft 1v22 or Ft 1v26. Refit the unit, tightening its retaining nut to the specified torque setting.

Remove retaining nut and washer ...

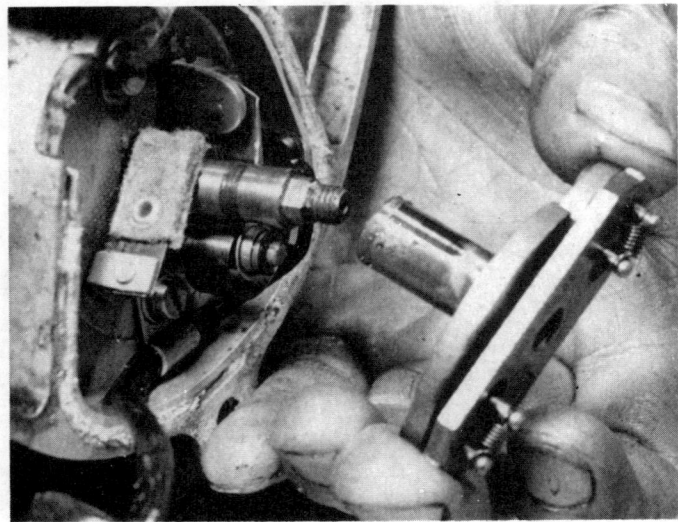
... to release ATU for examination and lubrication

14 Check the contact breaker gap (all models up to 1980) and ignition timing (all models).

For all models up to 1980, refer to the minor service operation

The electronic ignition system fitted to all models from 1981 onwards requires no routine adjustments and no maintenance other than a check at every 10 000 miles (15 000 km) to ensure that optimum performance is being maintained. Before the checking procedure is described, however, it must be stressed that this type of ignition system uses extremely high ignition voltages which may be harmful, even fatal, to anyone who touches a live component while the engine is running, or even while the ignition is switched on. Take the greatest possible care to avoid any risk of personal injury when working on the ignition system.

The actual procedures for checking and resetting the ignition timing of the electronic ignition are similar to those described under the minor service heading for the later type of contact breaker ignition, but it should be noted that attempts to check the ignition timing statically must not be made or damage will occur to the ignition components unless the owner has access to the BMW service tool that has been designed specifically for this purpose. For all practical purposes the ignition timing can only be checked dynamically using a good quality xenon tube strobe lamp which must have a power source other than the machine's battery or pulses in the machine's electrical system may produce a spurious reading.

Connect the strobe lamp according to the manufacturer's instructions and observe the timing marks as described under the minor service heading. The procedure is exactly the same with the sole exception that the full advance mark is now a white horizontal line with the letter 'Z' or 'F' adjacent to it.

If the ignition timing requires resetting, remove the crankcase front cover which is retained by two Allen screws, slacken the two Allen screws which secure the ignition trigger assembly and rotate the complete assembly in the direction necessary as described.

If the idle speed is erratic when at normal operating temperature and can be reduced from too high a speed to normal by selecting a gear, applying the brakes and just releasing the clutch to load the engine, the ignition trigger unit is probably at fault; usually through sticking weights in the ATU mechanism.

While this would normally require the renewal of the trigger unit there is nothing to be lost by attempting to lubricate the mechanism. Remove the engine front cover and trigger unit cover (two screws). Start the engine and allow it to idle. Using the extended nozzle supplied with most aerosol lubricants, inject a releasing lubricant (WD40 or similar) into the rear of the housing near the advance mechanism. Allow the surplus to drain before refitting the cover.

If this does not work the trigger unit must be renewed. See Chapter 5.

15 Check the carburettors

Refer to the minor service operation.

16 Overhaul the brakes

In addition to carrying out all the tasks listed under the minor service heading, carefully dismantle, clean and lubricate all control lever or pedal pivots, remove the wheels and dismantle drum brakes (see Chapter 8) so that the camshafts can be cleaned and greased, and check swinging caliper pivots (if not previously lubricated). Renew any worn or damaged components and reassemble. Renew the metal brake pipes if they are kinked or corroded, and the brake hoses if they are split, chafed or otherwise damaged.

Note that hydraulic brake fluid must be changed annually. It is necessary to renew the brake fluid at this interval to preserve maximum brake efficiency by ensuring that the fluid has not been contaminated and deteriorated to an unsafe degree.

Before starting work, obtain a new, full can of the specified hydraulic fluid and read carefully the Section on brake bleeding in Chapter 8. Prepare the clear plastic tube and glass jar in the same way as for bleeding the hydraulic system, open each bleed nipple by unscrewing it $1/4 - 1/2$ turn with a spanner and apply the front brake lever gently and repeatedly. This will pump out the old fluid. **Keep the master cylinder reservoir topped up at all times,** otherwise air may enter the system and greatly lengthen the operation. The old brake fluid is invariably much darker in colour than the new, making it easier to see when it is pumped out and the new fluid has completely replaced it. Where more than one bleed nipple is fitted to a system (e.g. twin front discs) repeat the operation on all bleed nipples in the system to ensure that the old fluid is completely removed. Top up the master cylinder as necessary when the operation is complete.

17 Check the swinging arm pivot bearings

With the machine supported on its centre stand on level ground, check for play by pushing and pulling alternately on the end of the swinging arm, while holding the frame firmly. Check that the swinging arm is central in the frame as described in Chapter 7. If any free play is felt, remove both bearing caps and slacken the locknuts.

Tighten both adjusters by exactly the same amount to 20 Nm (15 lbf ft), to preload the bearings. Loosen, then retighten, to 10 – 12 Nm (7.5 – 9 lbf ft). If a torque wrench is not available, tighten the adjuster with an Allen key on one side by one eighth of a turn. Tighten the adjuster locknuts to the specified torque setting. Check again that the swinging arm is exactly central in the frame; it may require some trial and error to combine the correct bearing adjustment with the correct swinging arm position. Take great care to ensure that the setting is correct.

Grease the pivot bearings as described under the minor service heading and refit the two black plastic caps.

If swinging arm pivot bearings require adjustment slacken locknuts using a slim-walled 27 mm box spanner or socket ...

... and use a torque wrench to adjust preload as described

Measure gap between swinging arm and frame on both sides to check that swinging arm is central in the frame

18 Change the front fork oil
/5, /6 and /7 up to 1980

Place the machine on its centre stand on level ground and wedge a block of wood or similar under the sump so that the front wheel is clear of the ground. Remove the black rubber plug from the bottom of each lower leg, then hold the damper rod stationary with an Allen key while the retaining nut is removed with its washer. Using the pin spanner from the toolkit unscrew the plated top cap from the top of the stanchion on early models; on later /7 models prise off the black plastic cap and unscrew the Allen screw filler plug. It should not be necessary to remove the handlebars but on machines with RS or RT fairings it will be necessary to remove the steering damper knob and handlebar safety padding.

Carefully pull downwards the fork lower legs (place a block of wood of suitable thickness under the front wheel so that the lower legs cannot drop too far) until the oil can drain out past the damper rod. Allow the oil to drain into suitable containers and use sheets of cardboard or similar to prevent oil getting on to the wheel or tyre. Wedge the front wheel securely and leave the machine as long as possible for the forks to drain fully.

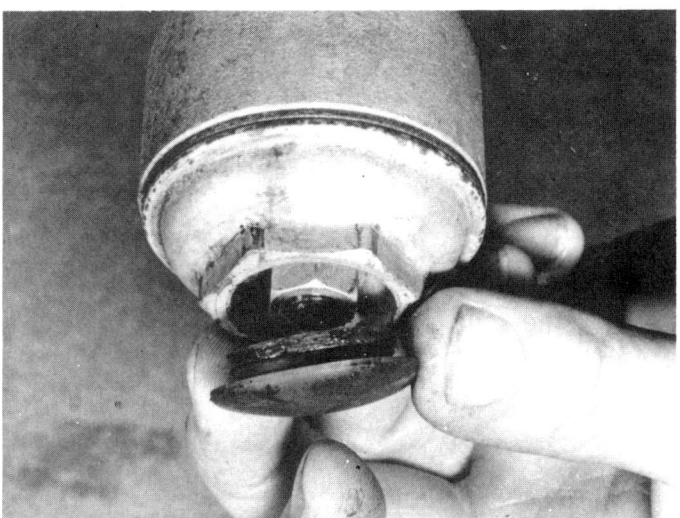
/5, /6 and /7 up to 1980 – remove rubber plugs from bottom of fork lower legs ...

... and remove damper rod retaining nuts as shown to drain fork oil

Routine maintenance

When draining is complete, lift the front wheel until the damper rod ends protrude fully through the lower leg passages, wash off any surplus oil and refit the damper rod retaining nut and washer. Use an Allen key to hold the damper rod stationary while the nut is tightened, note the specified torque setting of 23 – 26 Nm (17 – 19 lbf ft). Refit the black rubber plugs and allow the forks to extend fully (front wheel clear of the ground).

Fill each fork leg with the specified amount of one of the recommended brands of oil (see Chapter 6). **Do not** use ordinary fork oil; BMW forks are designed to work with oils of (approximately) SAE 3 viscosity. Most proprietary fork oils are up to 10 times thicker than this and will produce a very stiff ride. Note also that the specified quantity was reduced in 1977, after extensive tests, to improve damping performance. It is included for reference only; the later recommendation should be used on all models. Check the oil level by inserting a length of welding rod 1 metre (40 in) long by 5 mm (0.2 in) diameter into the fork leg until it rests on the damper piston. Withdraw the rod; the oil level on it should be 50 mm (1.97 in). Add (or remove) oil as necessary to achieve the correct level and check that the level is the same in both fork legs. Refit the plated top caps and any other disturbed components. Push the machine off its stand, apply the front brake and pump the forks up and down 5 – 10 times until the damping effect can be felt to be fully restored.

All other models

Place a sheet of cardboard against the wheel to keep oil off the brake or tyre, place a suitable container under the fork leg and remove the drain plug. On all 1000cc models, R80RT 1983-84, and R80G/S the drain plug is the smaller of the two Allen screws at the base of each fork lower leg; on all other models it is a small hexagon-headed bolt at the rear of the fork lower leg, just above the wheel spindle.

Depress the forks several times to expel as much oil as possible, then repeat the process on the remaining leg. Leave the machine for a few minutes to allow any residual oil to drain to the bottom, then pump the forks again to remove it.

Renewing their sealing washers if worn or damaged, refit and tighten the drain plugs to a torque setting of 8 Nm (6 lbf ft), then remove the fork leg top plastic plugs (where fitted) having first, on R80ST, R45 and R65 models, detached the ignition switch retaining ring and the instrument cover (or fairing top section, R65LS); on models fitted with RS or RT fairings it may prove necessary to gain sufficient working space by removing the steering damper knob (where fitted) and the handlebar safety padding.

Unscrew the Allen screw filler plugs from the centre of each fork top plug, then lift the machine on to its centre stand on level ground and wedge a block of wood or similar under the sump so that the front wheel is clear of the ground and the forks are fully extended.

Fill each leg with the specified amount of one of the recommended brands of oil (see Chapter 6). **Do not** use ordinary fork oil; BMW forks are designed to work with oils of (approximately) SAE 3 viscosity. Most proprietary fork oils are up to 10 times thicker than this and will produce a very stiff ride. Check the oil level by inserting a length of welding rod 1 metre (40 in) long by 5 mm (0.2 in) diameter into the fork leg. On all 1000cc models, R80RT 1983 – 84 and the R80G/S the rod should reach the bottom of the fork lower leg (a distance than can be checked by holding the rod against the outside of the fork leg) and should be covered with oil to a depth of 300 ± 5 mm (11.81 ± 0.59 in). On R45, R65, R65LS and R80ST models the rod should stop at the damper piston and should be covered with oil to a depth of 20 – 50 mm (0.79 – 1.97 in). Add (or remove) oil as necessary to achieve the correct level and ensure that the level is the same in both fork legs. Refit the filler plugs, tightening them to a torque setting of 9 Nm (6.5 lbf ft), followed by the plastic top plugs and/or any other disturbed components.

Push the machine off its stand, apply the front brake and pump the forks up and down 5 – 10 times until the damping effect can be felt to be fully restored.

19 Check the wheels
Wire-spoked wheels

Examine the rim for serious corrosion or impact damage. Slight deformities can often be corrected by adjusting spoke tension. Serious damage and corrosion will necessitate renewal, which is best left to an expert.

Place a wire pointer close to the rim and rotate the wheel to check it for runout. If the rim is more than 0.2 mm (0.008 in) out of true in the lateral plane or 0.5 mm (0.02 in) out of true in the axial plane, check spoke tension by tapping them with a screwdriver. A loose spoke will sound quite different from those around it. Worn bearings will also cause rim runout.

Adjust spoke tension by turning the square-headed nipples with the appropriate spoke key which can be purchased from a dealer. With the spokes evenly tensioned, remaining distortion can be pulled out by tightening the spokes on one side of the wheel and slackening those directly opposite. This will pull the rim across whilst maintaining spoke tension.

More than slight adjustment will cause the spoke ends to protrude through the nipple and chafe the inner tube, causing a puncture. Remove the tyre and tube and file off the protruding ends. The rim band protects the tube against chafing; check it is in good condition before fitting.

Check spoke tension and general wheel condition regularly. Frequent cleaning will help prevent corrosion. Replace a broken spoke immediately because the load taken by it will be transferred to adjacent spokes which may fail in turn.

Remove filler plug from top of fork leg – later models shown ...

... and add exactly the correct amount of the specified oil to each leg

Cast wheels

Note that on all 800 cc and 1000 cc models fitted with cast wheels each wheel's date of casting is stamped into it in Arabic numerals at one of the spoke crosses in the vicinity of the hub. If a **front** wheel (only) is found with a casting date before October 1982 (ie before 10/82) the machine should be taken immediately to a BMW dealer for close examination. Do not confuse this mark with a similar manufacturing mark consisting of Arabic and Roman numerals. As a result of one or two isolated cases of cracks developing in the wheel spokes (usually caused by riding over kerbstones etc) and concern amongst owners, BMW changed the method of wheel production and replaced, usually free of charge, all front wheels produced before that date. This does not apply to the R45, R65, R65LS or to R80 and R80RT 1985 on models, which all use different wheels.

Owners of R65LS models should note that due to the unique method of wheel construction, in which a softer spoke section is joined to the hard alloy rim section by a swallowtail joint, the two sections may 'work' as the machine is being ridden, causing minute cracks to appear in the paintwork at the joint between the two. If water gets into the joint it may be flung out under centrifugal force to make the cracks more obvious. If this happens a special adhesive tape is available to provide a flexible waterproof covering. A good BMW dealer should be able to fit it to your machine's wheels.

Carefully check the complete wheel for cracks and chipping, particularly at the spoke roots and the edge of the rim. As a general rule a damaged wheel must be renewed as cracks will cause stress points which may lead to sudden failure under heavy load. Small nicks may be radiused carefully with a fine file and emery paper (No 600 - No 1000) to relive the stress. If there is any doubt as to the condition of a wheel, advice should be sought from a reputable dealer or specialist repairer.

Each wheel is covered with a coating of lacquer or paint to prevent corrosion. If damage occurs to the wheel and the finish is penetrated, the bared aluminium alloy will soon start to corrode. A whitish grey oxide will form over the damaged area, which in itself is a protective coating. This deposit however, should be removed carefully as soon as possible and a new protective coating applied.

Check the lateral run out at the rim by spinning the wheel and placing a fixed pointer close to the rim edge. If the maximum run out is greater than 0.5 mm (0.02 in) the manufacturer recommends that the wheel be renewed. This is, however, a counsel of perfection; a run out somewhat greater than this can probably be accommodated without noticeable effect on steering. If warpage was caused by impact during an accident, the safest measure it to renew the wheel complete. Worn wheel bearings may cause rim run out. These should be renewed.

Note that impact damage or serious corrosion on models fitted with tubeless tyres has wider implications in that it could lead to a loss of pressure from the tubeless tyres. If in any doubt as to the wheel's condition, seek professional advice.

Wheel bearings – Monolever models rear wheel

Support the machine on its centre stand on level ground so that the rear wheel is clear of the ground. Arrange a dial gauge to bear on the outer edge of the wheel rim flange at the top of the wheel (clamping the gauge to a convenient frame tube). Grasp the wheel firmly at the top and bottom and attempt to rock it from side to side about its centre. On R80 and R80RT 1985 on models there should be no discernible play, on R80G/S and R80ST models a maximum of 0.5 mm (0.02 in) play is permissible. If these figures are exceeded, the machine should be taken to a BMW dealer for the bearings in the rear bevel drive to be checked. Note that there should be no discernible endfloat (axial play) at the wheel hub.

Wheel bearings – front, and rear (all other models)

Support the machine on its centre stand on level ground so that the wheel to be examined is clear of the ground (wedge a wooden block or similar under the sump to raise the front wheel). Grasp the wheel firmly at top and bottom and attempt to rock it from side to side about its spindle; if any play is discovered the wheel bearings require adjustment or renewal. Since adjustment requires special equipment and a range of adjuster sleeves or shims it is a task only for a competent BMW dealer. While the R65LS, R80 and R80RT 1985 on models use non-adjustable ball bearings in the front wheel, these require that the discs be removed, the hub heated and the bearings removed with an internally expanding bearing puller; the owner must decide whether or not this is a task for a dealer.

20 Check the steering head bearings

The steering head should be checked for play with the motorcycle on the centre stand and the front wheel supported clear of the ground. Grasp the fork lower legs at the bottom and alternately push and pull, feeling for any play in the bearings. The forks should fall easily to either side, if moved slightly off centre. The steering damper (where fitted) should be released.

If adjustment proves to be necessary remove the instrument cover (R45, R65, R80ST) the fairing top section (R65LS) or the handlebar safety padding (later /7 models). Depending on the tools used, it may prove advisable to remove the fuel tank to avoid the risk of damage to its paintwork and to provide more working space.

First slacken the friction-type steering damper completely, or remove the hydraulic damper.

On /5 models only, remove the headlamp fixing bolts with their chromed washers, two rubber washers and rubber sleeve. On machines with Yale-type key ignition switch, remove the large hexagonal nut and turn the headlamp to manoeuvre the switch out of the hole. Allow the headlamp to hang down, protecting paintwork with rag.

Remove the two nuts and washers from the left-hand handlebar clamp. Pull the clamp upwards until the studs disappear. Slacken the two nuts on the right-hand clamp.

Adjusting steering head bearings – /5 models – remove adjuster clamp bolt and nut ...

... and use a rod as shown to turn adjuster nut

Remove the complete damper rod on /5 models. Unscrew the centre screw in the damper knob of later models (where fitted) and remove the knob.

On /5 models only, remove the Allen screw, nut and washer from the adjuster clamp. Slacken the steering stem top nut and the bottom fork yoke stanchion clamp nuts or bolts.

On /5 models, push the 4 mm ($5/32$ in) diameter rod from the tool-kit through the slot in the adjuster clamp, to engage in a slot in the adjuster nut. On all later models, use a C-spanner on the adjuster nut. Tighten the adjuster nut until play is taken out of the bearings. Tighten the steering column top nut to the specified torque setting, whilst preventing the adjuster nut from turning. Tighten the bottom fork yoke stanchion clamp nuts or bolts to the specified torque setting and recheck the adjustment of the bearings. The steering head is correctly adjusted when the forks fall easily to one side when moved slightly off centre.

Replace and tighten the adjuster clamp bolt and nut (/5), the handlebar clamp nuts and the steering damper.

Note: *if any difficulty is experienced in achieving the correct setting, take the machine to a competent BMW dealer who has the special equipment necessary to adjust the bearings.*

21 Check the tightness of all nuts, bolts and fasteners
Refer to the minor service operation.

22 Test ride
Refer to the minor service operation.

Chapter 1 Engine
Refer to Chapter 10 for information relating to the 1986 on models

Contents

General description	1
Operations with the engine unit in the frame	2
Carrying out a compression test	3
Dismantling the engine unit: general	4
Dismantling the engine unit: removing the front engine and starter covers	5
Dismantling the engine unit: removing the cylinder heads and barrels	6
Dismantling the engine unit: removing the pistons	7
Dismantling the engine unit: removing the connecting rods	8
Dismantling the engine unit: removing the timing chain cover	9
Dismantling the engine unit: removing the timing chain and camshaft	10
Removing the engine from the frame	11
Dismantling the engine: preliminaries	12
Dismantling the engine unit: removing the oil pump	13
Dismantling the engine unit: removing the crankshaft	14
Examination and renovation: general	15
Examination and renovation: valves, spring and guides	16
Examination and renovation: cylinder heads	17
Examination and renovation: rocker assemblies	18
Examination and renovation: timing chain, sprockets and tensioner	19
Examination and renovation: pushrods, cam followers and camshaft	20
Examination and renovation: cylinder barrels	21
Examination and renovation: pistons and piston rings	22
Examination and renovation: oil seals	23
Examination and renovation: connecting rods and big-end bearings	24
Examination and renovation: crankshaft and main bearings	25
Engine reassembly: general	26
Engine reassembly: refitting the crankshaft	27
Engine reassembly: refitting the camshaft and timing chain	28
Engine reassembly: refitting the oil pump	29
Engine reassembly: refitting the timing chain cover	30
Engine reassembly: refitting the connecting rods and pistons	31
Engine reassembly: refitting the cylinder barrels	32
Engine reassembly: refitting the cylinder heads and rocker gear	33
Refitting the engine in the frame	34
Starting and running the rebuilt engine	35
Taking the rebuilt machine on the road	36

Specifications

Engine

Type .... Air-cooled horizontally-opposed transverse twin, with pushrod operated overhead valves

Dimensions:

	Bore	Stroke	Capacity (actual)
R45	70.0 mm (2.76 in)	61.5 mm (2.42 in)	473.1 cc (28.86 cu in)
R50	67.0 mm (2.64 in)	70.6 mm (2.78 in)	497.6 cc (30.35 cu in)
R60	73.5 mm (2.89 in)	70.6 mm (2.78 in)	598.8 cc (36.53 cu in)
R65, R65LS	82.0 mm (3.23 in)	61.5 mm (2.42 in)	649.2 cc (39.60 cu in)
R75	82.0 mm (3.23 in)	70.6 mm (2.78 in)	745.3 cc (45.46 cu in)
All 800cc models	84.8 mm (3.34 in)	70.6 mm (2.78 in)	797.1 cc (48.62 cu in)
R90/6, R90S	90.0 mm (3.54 in)	70.6 mm (2.78 in)	897.8 cc (54.77 cu in)
All 1000cc models	94.0 mm (3.70 in)	70.6 mm (2.78 in)	979.4 cc (59.74 cu in)

Compression ratio – standard values quoted, some machines may have been fitted with compression plates to reduce compression ratio from standard value:

R45	9.2 : 1
R50	8.6 : 1
R60	9.2 : 1
R65, R65LS*	9.2 : 1
R75	9.0 : 1
R80/7-40 kw version	9.2 : 1
R80/7-37 kw version, all other 800cc models	8.2 : 1
R90/6	9.0 : 1
R90S	9.5 : 1
R100/7	9.0 : 1
R100 (UK)	8.2 : 1
All other 1000cc models*	9.5 : 1

* *All US machines from 1980 models onwards, compression ratio was reduced to 8.2 : 1*

Chapter 1 Engine

	Idle	Maximum permissible continuous (cruising)	Maximum permissible
Recommended engine speeds – rpm:			
R45, R65, R65LS	800 – 1100	7300	7650
R50, R60/5, R60/6, R75/5, R75/6, R90/6	600 – 800	6500	7000
R60/7	800 – 1100	6500	7200
R75/7	800 – 1100	6500	7400
All 800cc models	800 – 1100	7200	7400
R90S	600 – 800	7000	7300
R100/7	800 – 1100	6800	7400
All other 1000cc models – UK – all R100T, R100S 1977, 1978 – US – all except that below	800 – 1100	7000	7400
All other 1000cc models – UK – all except those above – US – R100RS 1977	800 – 1100	7200	7400

	Maximum power (kw/hp @ rpm)	Maximum torque (Nm/lbf ft @ rpm)
Claimed engine output – DIN:		
R45	26/35 @ 7250	37.4/27.6 @ 5500
R50	24/32 @ 6400	38.3/28.3 @ 5000
R60	29/40 @ 6400	48.1/35.5 @ 5000
R65 1978 – 1980 models*	33/45 @ 7250	50.0/36.9 @ 5500
R65 1981 on models, R65LS*	37/50 @ 7250	52.3/38.6 @ 6500
R75	37/50 @ 6200	58.8/43.4 @ 5000
R80/7 – high compression version	40/55 @ 7000	62.5/46.1 @ 5500
R80/7 – low compression version	37/50 @ 7250	56.6/41.8 @ 5500
R80G/S, R80ST*	37/50 @ 6500	56.7/41.9 @ 5000
R80RT 1983, 1984 models*	37/50 @ 6500	59.0/43.5 @ 3500
R80, R80RT 1985 on models*	37/50 @ 6500	58.0/42.8 @ 4000
R90/6	44/60 @ 6500	73.0/53.9 @ 5500
R90S	49/67 @ 7000	76.0/56.1 @ 5500
R100/7	44/60 @ 6500	73.5/54.2 @ 4000
R100T – US*	44/60 @ 6500	74.6/55.1 @ 5500
R100T – UK, R100S – UK 1977, 1978, R100S – US, R100RS – US 1978, 1979, R100RT – US*	48/65 @ 6600	75.0/55.4 @ 5500
R100 – UK	49/67 @ 7000	72.0/53.1 @ 5500
R100S – UK 1979, 1980, R100RS – UK 1977 – 1980, R100RT – UK 1979, 1980 R100RS – US 1977*	51/70 @ 7250	76.0/56.1 @ 5500
R100CS, R100RS, R100RT – UK models 1981 on*	51/70 @ 7000	76.0/56.1 @ 6000

*All models 1980 on – information applies only to UK models, not available for US models

Direction of engine rotation .... Clockwise, looking at alternator from front of machine

Compression pressure – see Section 3

	All other models	R80G/S, R80ST, R80RT, R80 – 1985 model on
Good	over 10.0 bar (145 psi)	over 9.0 bar (131 psi)
Normal	8.5 – 10.0 bar (123 – 145 psi)	7.5 – 9.0 bar (109 – 131 psi)
Poor	below 8.5 bar (123 psi)	below 7.5 bar (109 psi)

Valve clearances – engine cold

	Normal		Up to first 600 mi (1000 km)	
	Inlet	Exhaust	Inlet	Exhaust
All models – latest recommendation	0.10 mm (0.004 in)	0.20 mm (0.008 in)	0.15 mm (0.006 in)	0.25 mm (0.010 in)

Valve timing – with 2.0 mm (0.08 in) valve clearance, tolerance of ± 2.5°

	R50/5, R60/5, R60/6 up to 1975	R60/6 1976, R60/7 1977	R60/7 1978
Inlet opens	40° ATDC	TDC	6° BTDC
Inlet closes	40° ABDC	40° ABDC	34° ABDC
Exhaust opens	40° BBDC	40° BBDC	46° BBDC
Exhaust closes	40° BTDC	TDC	6° BTDC

	All R75 and R90, R100/7, R100S, R100RS 1977	R80/7, R100/7, R100S, R100RS 1978	All other models
Inlet opens	10° BTDC	16° BTDC	16° BTDC
Inlet closes	50° ABDC	44° ABDC	44° ABDC
Exhaust opens	50° BBDC	56° BBDC	56° BBDC
Exhaust closes	10° BTDC	4° BTDC	4° ATDC

Chapter 1 Engine

	Inlet	Exhaust
Valves		
Head diameter:		
R45, R50	34 mm (1.34 in)	32 mm (1.26 in)
R60, R65 up to 1980	38 mm (1.50 in)	34 mm (1.34 in)
R65 1981 on, R65LS	40 mm (1.58 in)	36 mm (1.42 in)
R75, all 800cc models	42 mm (1.65 in)	38 mm (1.50 in)
R90/6, R90S, R100/7	42 mm (1.65 in)	40 mm (1.58 in)
All other 1000cc models	44 mm (1.73 in)	40 mm (1.58 in)
Head rim minimum thickness:		
/5,/6,/7	1.0 mm (0.0394 in)	1.0 mm (0.0394 in)
R80G/S, R80ST, R80, R80RT	0.8 mm (0.0315 in)	0.8 mm (0.0315 in)
R45, R65, R65LS	1.0 – 1.5 mm (0.0394 – 0.0591 in)	1.0 – 1.2 mm (0.0394 – 0.0472 in)
Head maximum runout:		
/5,/6,/7	0.025 mm (0.0010 in)	0.025 mm (0.0010 in)
R65, R80G/S, R80ST, R80, R80RT	0.020 mm (0.0008 in)	0.020 mm (0.0008 in)
Overall length:		
R50/5	102.6 – 103.0 mm (4.0394 – 4.0551 in)	102.1 – 102.5 mm (4.0197 – 4.0354 in)
R45, R65, R65LS	98.8 – 100.2 mm (3.8898 – 3.9449 in)	99.1 – 99.5 mm (3.9016 – 3.9173 in)
R60/5, R60/6	98.2 – 98.5 mm (3.8661 – 3.8780 in)	97.2 – 97.5 mm (3.8268 – 3.8386 in)
R60/7	99.2 – 99.5 mm (3.9055 – 3.9173 in)	98.2 – 98.5 mm (3.8661 – 3.8780 in)
All other models	98.4 – 98.8 mm (3.8740 – 3.8898 in)	98.4 – 98.8 mm (3.8740 – 3.8898 in)
Stem diameter:		
R45, R65, R65LS	6.945 – 6.960 mm (0.2734 – 0.2740 in)	6.945 – 6.960 mm (0.2734 – 0.2740 in)
R60/5, R60/6	7.935 – 7.950 mm (0.3124 – 0.3130 in)	7.920 – 7.935 mm (0.3118 – 0.3124 in)
All other models	7.935 – 7.950 mm (0.3124 – 0.3130 in)	7.935 – 7.950 mm (0.3124 – 0.3130 in)

Valve guides

Length overall:
- /5,/6 except R90S .... 54 mm (2.1260 in)
- R90S,/7 .... 48 mm (1.8898 in)
- R45, R65, R65LS .... 42 mm (1.6535 in)
- R80G/S, R80ST, R80, R80RT .... 44 mm (1.7323 in)

Outside diameter:
- /5,/6,/7 R80G/S, R80ST, R80RT 1983 – 84 .... 14.050 – 14.061 mm (0.5532 – 0.5536 in)
- R45, R65, R65LS .... 14 mm (0.5512 in) z6

Inside diameter:
- /5,/6,/7 .... 8 mm (0.3150 in) H7
- R45, R65, R65LS .... 7 mm (0.2756 in) H7
- R80G/S, R80ST, R80, R80RT .... 8.000 – 8.015 mm (0.3150 – 0.3156 in)

Bore in cylinder head:
- /5,/6,/7, R45, R65, R65LS .... 14 mm (0.5512 in) H7
- R80G/S, R80ST, R80, R80RT .... 14.000 – 14.018 mm (0.5512 – 0.5519 in)

Interference fit in cylinder head:
- /5,/6,/7 .... 0.032 – 0.061 mm (0.0013 – 0.0024 in)
- All other models .... N/Av

Oversizes available .... 0.1, 0.2 mm (0.004, 0.008 in)

Valve stem/guide standard clearance:	Inlet	Exhaust
R50/5	0.040 – 0.070 mm (0.0016 – 0.0028 in)	0.050 – 0.080 mm (0.0020 – 0.0032 in)
R45, R65, R65LS	0.025 – 0.055 mm (0.0010 – 0.0022 in)	0.040 – 0.070 mm (0.0016 – 0.0028 in)
R60	0.050 – 0.080 mm (0.0020 – 0.0032 in)	0.065 – 0.095 mm (0.0026 – 0.0037 in)
All other models	0.050 – 0.080 mm (0.0020 – 0.0032 in)	0.050 – 0.080 mm (0.0020 – 0.0032 in)

Inlet and exhaust valve stem/guide maximum permissible clearance – measured at top of guide:
- R45, R65, R65LS .... 0.10 mm (0.0039 in)
- All other models .... 0.15 mm (0.0059 in)

Valve seats

Outside diameter:	Inlet	Exhaust
R50/5	36.175 – 36.200 mm (1.4242 – 1.4252 in)	36.140 – 36.150 mm (1.4228 – 1.4232 in)
R45	36.2 mm (1.4252 in) h7	36.2 mm (1.4252 in) e6

		Inlet	Exhaust
R60		39.175 – 39.200 mm (1.5423 – 1.5433 in)	39.175 – 39.200 mm (1.5423 – 1.5433 in)
R65, R65LS		39.2 mm (1.5433 in) h7	39.2 mm (1.5433 in) h7
R75/5		43.175 – 43.200 mm (1.6998 – 1.7008 in)	43.140 – 43.150 mm (1.6984 – 1.6988 in)
R75/6, R90/6, R90S		43.175 – 43.200 mm (1.6998 – 1.7008 in)	43.175 – 43.200 mm (1.6998 – 1.7008 in)
R75/7, R80/7, R100/7		43.175 – 43.200 mm (1.6998 – 1.7008 in)	43.134 – 43.200 mm (1.6982 – 1.7008 in)
R80G/S, R80ST, R80, R80RT		43.175 – 43.200 mm (1.6998 – 1.7008 in)	43.134 – 43.150 mm (1.6982 – 1.6988 in)
All other 1000cc models		45.175 – 45.200 mm (1.7785 – 1.7795 in)	45.175 – 45.200 mm (1.7785 – 1.7795 in)

Bore in cylinder head – inlet and exhaust:
- R50/5 .... 36.000 – 36.025 mm (1.4173 – 1.4183 in)
- R45 .... 36 mm (1.4173 in) H7
- R60 .... 39.000 – 39.025 mm (1.5354 – 1.5364 in)
- R65, R65LS .... 39 mm (1.5354 in) H7
- All 745cc, 800cc, 900cc models, R100/7 .... 43.000 – 43.025 mm (1.6929 – 1.6939 in)
- All other 1000cc models .... 45.000 – 45.025 mm (1.7717 – 1.7727 in)

	Inlet	Exhaust
Interference fit in cylinder head:		
R50/5, R75/5	0.150 – 0.200 mm (0.0059 – 0.0079 in)	0.115 – 0.150 mm (0.0045 – 0.0059 in)
R45, R65, R65LS	N/Av	N/Av
R75/7, R80/7, R100/7, R80G/S, R80ST, R80RT 1983 – 84	0.150 – 0.200 mm (0.0059 – 0.0079 in)	0.109 – 0.150 mm (0.0043 – 0.0059 in)
All other models	0.150 – 0.200 mm (0.0059 – 0.0079 in)	0.150 – 0.200 mm (0.0059 – 0.0079 in)

Seat angle:
- Main seating face .... 45°
- At combustion chamber .... 15°
- At inlet/exhaust port .... 75°

Seat width:
- Inlet .... 1.5 mm (0.0591 in)
- Exhaust .... 2.0 mm (0.0787 in)

Seat oversizes available .... 0.2, 0.4 mm (0.0079, 0.0168 in)

Valve springs
Wire thickness .... 4.25 mm (0.1673 in)

Spring free length – approx:
- Blue or green code .... 43.5 mm (1.7126 in)
- Brown code .... 46.0 mm (1.811 in)

Spring force at test length:
- At 37.6 mm (1.4803 in) .... 27.84 – 30.16 kp (61.30 – 66.5 lb)
- At 28.5 mm (1.1221 in) .... 70.00 – 72.80 kp (154.30 – 160.5 lb)

Rocker gear
- Arm ID-/5 .... 18.032 – 18.059 mm (0.7099 – 0.7110 in)
- Bush OD-/5 .... 18.012 – 18.030 mm (0.7091 – 0.7098 in)
- Arm/bush clearance-/5 .... 0.002 – 0.047 mm (0.00008 – 0.00185 in)
- Bush ID/5 .... 14.532 – 14.559 mm (0.5721 – 0.5732 in)
- Shaft OD-/5 .... 14.512 – 14.530 mm (0.5713 – 0.5720 in)
- Bush/shaft clearance-/5 .... 0.002 – 0.047 mm (0.00008 – 0.00185 in)

Arm axial float:
- R80, R80RT 1985 .... 0.03 – 0.07 mm (0.0012 – 0.0028 in)
- All other models .... Nil, but arm must be free to move

Camshaft drive chain
Type:
- /5,/6,/7 up to 1978 .... Duplex roller chain
- All other models .... Single row roller chain

Size .... 3/8 × 7/32 in
Number of links 50

Camshaft
- Front (alternator end) bearing bore in crankcase .... 40.000 – 40.039 mm (1.5748 – 1.5763 in)
- Front flange bearing OD .... 39.984 – 40.000 mm (1.5742 – 1.5748 in)
- Front flange bearing ID .... 25.000 – 25.013 mm (0.9843 – 0.9848 in)
- Camshaft front bearing journal OD .... 24.967 – 24.980 mm (0.9830 – 0.9835 in)
- Camshaft radial clearance – at front bearing .... 0.020 – 0.046 mm (0.0008 – 0.0018 in)

Chapter 1 Engine

Rear (flywheel end) bearing bore in crankcase	24.000 – 24.021 mm (0.9449 – 0.9457 in)
Camshaft rear bearing journal OD	23.967 – 23.980 mm (0.9436 – 0.9441 in)
Camshaft radial clearance – at rear bearing	0.020 – 0.054 mm (0.0008 – 0.0021 in)
Camshaft end float	0.080 – 0.120 mm (0.0032 – 0.0047 in)
Base circle	28 mm (1.1024 in)
Cam lift:	
R50/5, R60	6.198 mm (0.2440 in)
All other models	6.756 mm (0.2660 in)
Maximum permissible runout of ATU shaft -/5,/6,/7 up to 1978	0.02 mm (0.0008 in)

Cam followers and pushrods

OD	21.955 – 21.975 mm (0.8644 – 0.8652 in)
Crankcase ID	21.985 – 22.006 mm (0.8656 – 0.8664 in)
Follower/crankcase clearance:	
Standard	0.010 – 0.051 mm (0.0004 – 0.0020 in)
Service limit	0.075 mm (0.0030 in)
Pushrod length:	
R45, R65, R65LS,/5,/6 up to 1975	N/Av
All other models	274.7 – 275.3 mm (10.8149 – 10.8386 in)

Crankshaft and main bearings

Journal dimensions	Main bearing journal dimensions are basically the same for all models, but tolerances vary depending on model and production year – see main text
Main bearing bushes	Bushes are a selective fit depending on journal dimensions and measured radial clearances – see main text – available in red, blue and green size codes for standard crankshaft, red and blue size codes for each of the three oversizes
Main bearing journal/bush clearance:	
R45 (UK), R65 (UK), R65LS (UK), all /5,/6,/7 up to 1980	0.035 – 0.065 mm (0.0014 – 0.0025 in)
/7 1981 on, R80G/S, R80ST, R65 (US), R65LS (US) – red size code bush	0.017 – 0.066 mm (0.0007 – 0.0026 in)
/7 1981 on, R80G/S, R80ST, R65 (US), R65LS (US) – blue size code bush	0.019 – 0.067 mm (0.0008 – 0.0026 in)
Crankshaft regrind stages:	
1st	0.25 mm (0.0100 in)
2nd	0.50 mm (0.0200 in)
3rd	0.75 mm (0.0300 in)
Maximum runout – at front (alternator) main bearing journal	0.02 mm (0.0008 in)
Maximum lateral runout at flywheel	0.10 mm (0.0039 in)
Crankshaft standard endfloat	0.08 – 0.15 mm (0.0032 – 0.0059 in)
Thrust washer thickness:	
Standard – red	2.483 – 2.530 mm (0.0978 – 0.0996 in)
Standard – blue	2.530 – 2.578 mm (0.0996 – 0.1015 in)
Standard – green	2.578 – 2.626 mm (0.1015 – 0.1034 in)
Standard – yellow	2.626 – 2.673 mm (0.1034 – 0.1052 in)
Wear limit – all	minus 0.20 mm (0.0079 in)

Connecting rods and bearings

Crankpin standard OD	47.975 – 47.991 mm (1.8888 – 1.8894 in)
Crankpin regrind stages:	
1st	0.25 mm (0.0100 in)
2nd	0.50 mm (0.0200 in)
3rd	0.75 mm (0.0300 in)
Connecting rod big-end ID-less bearing shells:	
/5,/6,/7 1977	52.000 – 52.010 mm (2.0472 – 2.0476 in)
All other models	52.000 – 52.015 mm (2.0472 – 2.0478 in)
Connecting rod radial clearance	0.023 – 0.069 mm (0.0009 – 0.0027 in)
Connecting rod big-end width	21.883 – 21.935 mm (0.8615 – 0.8636 in)
Crankpin width	22.065 – 22.149 mm (0.8687 – 0.8720 in)
Connecting rod axial clearance (endfloat):	
Standard	0.130 – 0.266 mm (0.0051 – 0.0105 in)
Maximum permissible	0.320 mm (0.0126 in)
Maximum weight difference between connecting rods:	
/5,/6,	6 grams (0.2116 oz)
/7, R45, R65, R65LS	± 3 grams (0.1058 oz)
R80G/S, R80ST, R80, R80RT	± 2 grams (0.0705 oz)
Note that both connecting rods must be of the same weight group, ie have the same colour-code	
Connecting rod small-end ID – less bush	24.000 – 24.021 mm (0.9449 – 0.9457 in)
Small-end bush OD	24.060 – 24.100 mm (0.9472 – 0.9488 in)
Small-end bush ID:	
Standard	22.015 – 22.020 mm (0.8667 – 0.8669 in)
Maximum permissible	22.040 mm (0.8677 in)

Chapter 1 Engine

Gudgeon pin/small-end bush clearance:
- /5,/6,/7 up to 1980 – white coded pin .... 0.015 – 0.023 mm (0.0006 – 0.0009 in)
- /5,/6,/7 up to 1980 – black coded pin .... 0.018 – 0.026 mm (0.0007 – 0.0010 in)
- /7 1981 on, R80G/S, R80ST, R80, R80RT .... 0.015 – 0.024 mm (0.0006 – 0.0009 in)
- R45, R65, R65LS .... 0.015 – 0.025 mm (0.0006 – 0.0009 in)

Gudgeon pin OD:
- /5,/6,/7 up to 1980 – white coded pin .... 21.997 – 22.000 mm (0.8660 – 0.8661 in)
- /5,/6,/7 up to 1980 – black coded pin .... 21.994 – 21.997 mm (0.8659 – 0.8660 in)
- /7 1981 on, R80G/S, R80ST, R80, R80RT – white coded pin .. 21.996 – 22.000 mm (0.8659 – 0.8661 in)
- R45, R65, R65LS .... 21.995 – 22.000 mm (0.8659 – 0.8661 in)

Gudgeon pin bore ID – in piston:
- /5,/6,/7 up to 1980 – white code
  (W stamped in piston crown) .... 22.000 – 22.003 mm (0.8661 – 0.8662 in)
- /5,/6,/7 up to 1980 – black code
  (S stamped in piston crown) .... 21.997 – 22.000 mm (0.8660 – 0.8661 in)
- /7 1981 on, R80G/S, R80ST, R80, R80RT .... 22.000 – 22.004 mm (0.8661 – 0.8663 in)
- R45 .... 22.002 – 22.007 mm (0.8662 – 0.8664 in)
- R65, R65LS .... 22.005 – 22.010 mm (0.8663 – 0.8665 in)

Gudgeon pin/piston clearance:
- /5,/6,/7 up to 1980 .... 0 – 0.006 mm (0 – 0.0002 in)
- /7 1981 on, R80G/S, R80ST, R80, R80RT .... 0 – 0.008 mm (0 – 0.0003 in)
- R45 .... 0.002 – 0.012 mm (0.0001 – 0.0005 in)
- R65, R65LS .... 0.005 – 0.015 mm (0.0002 – 0.0006 in)

Cylinders

Type:
- All models up to 1980 .... Cast iron sleeve joined to aluminium alloy finned jacket by 'Al-Fin' process
- R45, R65, R65LS 1981 on .... Aluminium alloy barrel with 'Nikasil'-plated bore
- All 1000cc and 800cc models, 1981 on .... Aluminium alloy barrel with 'Galnikal'-plated bore

Cylinder standard bore ID – at specified bore size code:

	A	B	C
R50/5	67.000 mm (2.6378 in)	67.010 mm (2.6382 in)	67.020 mm (2.6386 in)
R45	69.995 – 70.005 mm (2.7557 – 2.7561 in)	70.005 – 70.015 mm (2.7561 – 2.7565 in)	70.015 – 70.025 mm (2.7565 – 2.7569 in)
R60/5, R60/6	73.500 mm (2.8937 in)	73.510 mm (2.8941 in)	73.520 mm (2.8945 in)
R60/7	73.500 – 73.510 mm (2.8937 – 2.8941 in)	73.510 – 73.520 mm (2.8941 – 2.8945 in)	73.520 – 73.530 mm (2.8945 – 2.8949 in)
R65, R65LS	81.995 – 82.005 mm (3.2281 – 3.2285 in)	82.005 – 82.015 mm (3.2285 – 3.2289 in)	82.015 – 82.025 mm (3.2289 – 3.2293 in)
R75/5, R75/6	82.000 mm (3.2283 in)	82.010 mm (3.2287 in)	82.020 mm (3.2291 in)
R75/7	82.005 – 82.015 mm (3.2285 – 3.2289 in)	82.015 – 82.025 mm (3.2289 – 3.2293 in)	82.025 – 82.035 mm (3.2293 – 3.2297 in)
All 800cc models	84.795 – 84.805 mm (3.3384 – 3.3388 in)	84.805 – 84.815 mm (3.3388 – 3.3392 in)	84.815 – 84.825 mm (3.3392 – 3.3396 in)
R90/6, R90S	90.000 mm (3.5433 in)	90.010 mm (3.5437 in)	90.020 mm (3.5441 in)
All 1000cc models	94.005 – 94.015 mm (3.7010 – 3.7014 in)	94.015 – 94.025 mm (3.7014 – 3.7018 in)	94.025 – 94.035 mm (3.7018 – 3.7022 in)

Rebore sizes:
- /5,/6, R60/7, R75/7 – 1st .... 0.50 mm (0.020 in)
- /5,/6, R60/7, R75/7 – 2nd .... 1.00 mm (0.040 in)
- R45 and R65 up to 1980, R80/7 – 1st .... 0.25 mm (0.010 in)
- R45 and R65 up to 1980, R80/7 – 2nd .... 0.50 mm (0.020 in)
- All 1000 cc models up to 1980 .... 0.25 mm (0.010 in)
- All models 1981 on .... Rebores not possible, pistons and cylinders must be renewed if excessively worn

Maximum ovality:
- R45, R65, R65LS .... 0.005 mm (0.0002 in)
- R80G/S, R80ST, R80, R80RT – 20 mm (0.8 in) from top of bore .... 0.005 mm (0.0002 in)
- R80G/S, R80ST, R80, R80RT – 115 mm (4.5 in) from top of bore .... 0.010 mm (0.0004 in)
- All other models .... 0.010 mm (0.0004 in)

Maximum taper:
- /5,/6 .... 0.010 mm (0.0004 in)
- All other models .... 0.020 mm (0.0008 in)

Pistons

Standard OD – at specified size code:

	A	B	C
R50/5	66.960 mm (2.6362 in)	66.970 mm (2.6366 in)	66.980 mm (2.6370 in)
R45	69.955 – 69.965 mm (2.7541 – 2.7545 in)	69.965 – 69.975 mm (2.7545 – 2.7549 in)	69.975 – 69.985 mm (2.7549 – 2.7553 in)

R60/5, R60/6	73.460 mm (2.8921 in)	73.470 mm (2.8925 in)	73.480 mm (2.8929 in)
R60/7	73.470 mm (2.8925 in)	73.480 mm (2.8929 in)	73.490 mm (2.8933 in)
R65, R65LS	81.955 – 81.965 mm (3.2266 – 3.2270 in)	81.965 – 81.975 mm (3.2270 – 3.2274 in)	81.975 – 81.985 mm (3.2274 – 3.2278 in)
R75/5, R75/6	81.960 mm (3.2268 in)	81.970 mm (3.2272 in)	81.980 mm (3.2276 in)
R75/7	81.965 mm (3.2270 in)	81.975 mm (3.2274 in)	81.985 mm (3.2278 in)
All 800cc models	84.765 mm (3.3372 in)	84.775 mm (3.3376 in)	84.785 mm (3.3380 in)
R90/6, R90S	89.960 mm (3.5417 in)	89.970 mm (3.5421 in)	89.980 mm (3.5425 in)
All 1000cc models	93.960 mm (3.6992 in)	93.970 mm (3.6996 in)	93.980 mm (3.7000 in)

Standard piston/cylinder clearance:
　/5,/6 .... 0.035 – 0.045 mm (0.0014 – 0.0018 in)
　R60/7 .... 0.020 – 0.040 mm (0.0008 – 0.0016 in)
　R75/7 .... 0.019 – 0.041 mm (0.0007 – 0.0016 in)
　R80/7 .... 0.023 – 0.047 mm (0.0009 – 0.0019 in)
　R45 and R65 up to 1980 .... 0.030 – 0.050 mm (0.0012 – 0.0020 in)
　All 1000cc models up to 1980 .... 0.028 – 0.052 mm (0.0011 – 0.0021 in)
　All models 1981 on .... 0.030 – 0.040 mm (0.0012 – 0.0016 in)
Maximum permissible piston/cylinder clearance:
　/5,/6 .... 0.120 mm (0.0047 in)
　All other models .... 0.080 mm (0.0032 in)
Piston weight group .... + or – stamped in piston crown – both pistons must be of same weight group, ie carry the same marking

Piston rings
　Top:
　　Type .... Plain, rectangular section
　　Thickness:
　　　/5,/6 .... 1.790 – 1.810 mm (0.0705 – 0.0713 in)
　　　R45 .... 1.478 – 1.490 mm (0.0582 – 0.0587 in)
　　　All other models .... 1.728 – 1.740 mm (0.0680 – 0.0685 in)
　　End gap-installed:
　　　R50, R60 .... 0.25 – 0.40 mm (0.0098 – 0.0158 in)
　　　R45 .... 0.25 – 0.45 mm (0.0098 – 0.0177 in)
　　　R75/5, R75/6, R90/6, R90S .... 0.30 – 0.45 mm (0.0118 – 0.0177 in)
　　　/7 1981 on .... 0.40 – 0.65 mm (0.0158 – 0.0256 in)
　　　All other models .... 0.30 – 0.50 mm (0.0118 – 0.0197 in)
　　Side clearance:
　　　/5,/6 .... 0.060 – 0.070 mm (0.0024 – 0.0028 in)
　　　/7 .... 0.060 – 0.090 mm (0.0024 – 0.0035 in)
　　　All other models .... 0.050 – 0.082 mm (0.0020 – 0.0032 in)
　Second:
　　Type .... Plain, with stepped or tapered face
　　Thickness:
　　　/5,/6 .... 2.030 – 2.050 mm (0.0799 – 0.0807 in)
　　　/7, R45 up to 1980 .... 2.010 – 2.022 mm (0.0791 – 0.0796 in)
　　　All other models .... 1.978 – 1.990 mm (0.0779 – 0.0784 in)
　　End gap – installed:
　　　R50, R60 .... 0.25 – 0.40 mm (0.0098 – 0.0158 in)
　　　R45 .... 0.25 – 0.45 mm (0.0098 – 0.0177 in)
　　　R80G/S, R80ST, R80, R80RT .... 0.30 – 0.50 mm (0.0118 – 0.0197 in)
　　　/7 1981 on .... 0.40 – 0.65 mm (0.0158 – 0.0256 in)
　　　All other models .... 0.30 – 0.45 mm (0.0118 – 0.0177 in)
　　Side clearance:
　　　/5/6 .... 0.050 – 0.060 mm (0.0020 – 0.0024 in)
　　　All other models .... 0.040 – 0.072 mm (0.0016 – 0.0028 in)
　Oil scraper:
　　Type .... One-piece
　　Thickness:
　　　/5,/6 .... 4.010 – 4.030 mm (0.1579 – 0.1587 in)
　　　/7 .... 4.010 – 4.022 mm (0.1579 – 0.1584 in)
　　　R80G/S, R80ST, R80, R80RT, R45 1981 on .... 3.478 – 3.490 mm (0.1369 – 0.1374 in)
　　　R45 up to 1980 .... 3.510 – 3.522 mm (0.1382 – 0.1387 in)
　　　R65, R65LS .... 3.978 – 3.990 mm (0.1566 – 0.1571 in)
　　End gap – installed:
　　　R50/5, R60/5 .... 0.20 – 0.35 mm (0.0079 – 0.0138 in)
　　　R60/6, R60/7 .... 0.25 – 0.35 mm (0.0098 – 0.0138 in)
　　　R45 .... 0.25 – 0.45 mm (0.0098 – 0.0177 in)
　　　All other models .... 0.25 – 0.40 mm (0.0098 – 0.0158 in)

Chapter 1 Engine

Side clearance:
/5, /6 .... 0.030 – 0.040 mm (0.0012 – 0.0016 in)
R60/7 .... 0.020 – 0.050 mm (0.0008 – 0.0020 in)
All other models .... 0.030 – 0.062 mm (0.0012 – 0.0024 in)

Torque wrench settings

Component	Nm	lbf ft
Rocker cover cap nut – R80, R80RT 1985 on	22 – 26	16 – 18.5
Spark plugs	20 – 30	15 – 22
Valve adjuster locknuts	18 – 23	13.5 – 17
Cylinder head retaining nuts – all models up to 1980:		
1st stage	15	11
2nd stage	35	26
3rd stage	40	29.5
Standard setting	38 – 42	28 – 31
Cylinder head retaining nuts – all models 1981 on:		
1st stage	15	11
2nd stage	25	18.5
3rd stage	35	26
Standard setting	35 – 39	26 – 29
Exhaust pipe finned nuts:		
R80, R80RT 1985 on	160	118
R45 and R65 1979-80, /7 up to 1980	140 – 180	103 – 133
All other models	200 – 220	148 – 162
Connecting rod bolts	48 – 52	35.5 – 38
Flywheel mounting bolts:		
/5	58 – 62	43 – 46
R60/6 and R75/6 up to 9/74 – 10 mm bolts	60 – 65	44 – 48
R90/6 and R90S up to 9/74 – 10 mm bolts	70 – 75	52 – 55
/6 1975 on and all other models – 11 mm bolts	100 – 105	74 – 77.5
Oil pump pickup mounting bolts	9	6.5
Camshaft flange bearing – all models 1979 on	15 – 18	11 – 13.5
Sump mounting bolts	9 – 12	6.5 – 9
Alternator rotor retaining bolt	23 – 27	17 – 20
Starter motor mounting bolts	47.5	35
ATU retaining nut:		
/5, /6	6 – 7	4.5 – 5
/7 up to 1978	5 – 6	4 – 4.5
All other models	N/App	N/App
Oil filter inner cover retaining bolt – /5, /6 only	41	30
Engine oil drain plug:		
Models up to 1980	N/Av	N/Av
All models 1981 on	30 – 35	22 – 26
Oil filter cover mounting bolts	10	7.5
Engine mounting nuts:		
R80, R80RT 1985 on	54.2	40
All other models	70 – 77	52 – 57

1 General description

The engine fitted to BMW twins is horizontally opposed, with both pistons reaching the limits of their travel at the same moment. This layout cancels out all vibrations, other than the small rocking couple due to the distance between the cylinder centre lines.

The overhead valves are actuated by the camshaft, via hardened steel followers and pushrods located in tubes beneath the cylinders. The camshaft, which is below the crankshaft, is chain driven from the front of the crankshaft. It runs directly in the crankcase at the rear, and in a flanged aluminium bearing at the front. The camshaft drives the contact breaker assembly or ignition trigger and the oil pump, at the front and rear respectively.

The one-piece crankshaft is supported in large, plain main bearings, which overlap the connecting rod big-end journals. The alternator is mounted on the front of the crankshaft.

The connecting rods have split big-ends with detachable shell bearings. The gudgeon pins run in bronze bushes.

The crankcase is a one-piece tunnel housing, reinforced internally with gussets. The aluminium alloy cylinder barrels with cast iron liners, and the cylinder heads, are attached to the crankcase by four long through studs. Two additional studs hold the cylinder head to the barrel.

Pistons are cast aluminium with two compression rings and one oil control ring. The method of gudgeon pin retention was altered on 800cc and 1000cc models during the 1978 model year from the internal wire circlips fitted to all other models to external stamped circlips.

For all 1979 models on, the camshaft drive was altered significantly, a single-row chain being substituted for the old duplex type; the new chain is fitted with a connecting link to simplify dismantling work and is tensioned by a spring-assisted hydraulic tensioner.

Various modifications have been made to the various castings, both to stiffen them to accommodate the increased torque of the larger capacity engines and to reduce noise levels and oil leaks. From 1981 on the cylinder barrels were changed to the plated-bore type (see Specifications) to reduce weight and to give greater heat-dissipating properties as well as longer life.

The compression ratio is chosen for use with the specified fuels. If low grade fuels only are available, decompression plates, which replace the cylinder base gasket, may be fitted.

2 Operations with the engine unit in the frame

1 It is only necessary to remove the engine from the frame, if the crankshaft or main bearings require attention.
2 Most other work may be undertaken fairly easily with the engine still in the frame.
3 Since removing the engine, which is heavy, requires partial

dismantling of the rear drive and suspension and the removal of the gearbox, it is advantageous to do all such work with the engine in the frame.

4 Work described in the following sections refers to the left-hand side of the engine unit, unless stated otherwise in the text.

3 Carrying out a compression test

1 A good idea of the internal state of the engine can be gained by testing its compression as follows.
2 The engine must be fully warmed up to normal operating temperature and the battery fully charged for the test results to be accurate.
3 Remove both spark plugs. On models fitted with constant depression carburettors, remove the carburettors (see Chapter 4). On 1981 and later models remove the engine front cover and disconnect the three-pin plug from the ignition trigger to the main wiring loom; this is essential to prevent damage to the ignition system components.
4 Attach an accurate, good quality compression gauge (tester) to the cylinder head spark plug orifice, following its manufacturer's instructions. On machines with slide-type carburettors open the throttle fully. Spin the engine over on the starter motor and note the readings recorded.
5 After one or two revolutions the pressure should build up to a maximum figure and then stabilise; note the reading and repeat the test on the remaining cylinder. There should be no discernible difference between the two. The expected pressures are given in Specifications. If both pressures are the same and in the good or normal range then the engine is in good condition.
6 If there is a marked discrepancy between the two readings, or if either is in the poor range, the appropriate cylinder must be dismantled for checking.
7 Note that during a normal compression test one would go on to temporarily seal the piston rings by pouring a quantity of oil into the barrel and then take a second set of readings. If the pressure increased noticeably it could then be assumed that the piston rings were worn rather than the valves. Since it would be very difficult to get a full seal from such a method in a warm flat-twin engine there is little point in doing this; check the pistons and rings as well as the head gasket and valves when looking for the cause of compression loss.

4 Dismantling the engine unit: general

1 Ensure that the machine is supported firmly on the centre stand. It is less tiring if the machine can be raised off the ground on a strong, low, bench. Have blocks to hand for supporting the rear of the machine, especially if the rear wheel is to be removed.
2 For most work it is advisable to remove the fuel tank, to avoid damage – see Chapter 4.
3 Before commencing any work involving the electrical system, disconnect the battery negative (earth) lead at the speedometer clamp screw. This will be found at the rear right-hand of the gearbox, above the universal joint housing.
4 On machines fitted with RS or RT fairings it will usually be sufficient to remove the fairing lower sections (see Chapter 6), but the complete fairing can be removed to prevent any risk of damage if required.
5 Remove the exhaust system and carburettors as described in Chapter 4.

5 Dismantling the engine unit: removing the front engine and starter covers

1 First remove the fuel tank and fairing front centre section (where fitted).
2 Slacken the horn fixing screw. Unscrew the three Allen screws in the front engine cover (two only, later models) and remove the cover. Note the square rubber seal around the contact breaker lead (/5,/6 and /7 up to 1978).
3 Unscrew the two Allen screws fixing the starter cover, lift the cover, and remove from the right-hand side.

5.2 Removing the front engine cover

6 Dismantling the engine unit: removing the cylinder heads and barrels

1 Remove the exhaust pipes and the carburettors. On later US models, disconnect the 'Pure Air System' pipes at their union nuts.
2 Pull off the spark plug caps, and remove the plugs.
3 Remove the rocker covers and position the cylinder to be dismantled at TDC as described in Routine Maintenance.
4 Working in the **reverse** of the sequence shown in Fig 1.13, slacken progressively all six cylinder head retaining nuts until all pressure is released, then remove the nuts (and washers). Obtain two clearly marked containers and withdraw first all the components of the inlet rocker shaft, then the exhaust rocker shaft. Place them in their respective containers and **always** keep separate the inlet and exhaust components. Note the pillow block and spacer flat washer or conical seating and O-ring (as applicable) on each rocker bearing stud; store these with their respective rockers.
5 Withdraw the pushrods, mark inlet or exhaust, also inner and outer end, so that they can be replaced in the same position, then store with their respective rockers.
6 Pull the heads clear of the studs, taking care of the gaskets, and lay aside carefully where they will not gather dirt. Note that the gaskets have two holes at the bottom for the pushrods, which are offset to one side.
7 To protect the pistons, it is a good plan to support them before removing the barrels completely. A slotted T-shaped wooden block should be slipped over the connecting rod, between each piston skirt and the crankcase, to rest on the cylinder studs.
8 Pull the barrels and cylinder base gaskets (where fitted) off the studs noting the exact number, size and type of O-rings and gaskets fitted. The pushrod tubes and seals will remain attached to the barrels. Mark the barrels left or right, to aid replacement in the same position.
9 Do not lever the joint faces. If difficulty is experienced in removing either of the heads or barrels, proceed thus: replace the cylinder head (if removed) and the cylinder head to barrel nuts only. Make up a strap to bridge two diagonally opposed cylinder through studs, passing over the rocker cover stud, see illustration. Screw the cylinder stud nuts to the bottom of their threads. Screw the rocker cover cap nut onto its stud, fit the strap, and draw off the head and barrel by tightening the cap nut.
10 Once the head and barrel are freed from the crankcase, remove the strap and nuts, and the cylinder head nuts, and remove the head and barrel as previously described.

6.3a Do not forget two small nuts between cylinder head fins ...

6.3b ... when removing rocker covers

6.4a Remove all six cylinder head nuts before withdrawing rocker assemblies ...

6.4b ... noting spacers and O-rings (where fitted) – keep all components separate and clearly marked

6.5 Ensure pushrods are marked before removal – keep with their respective rockers

6.6 Pull cylinder head off studs and remove gasket

69

6.8 Mark cylinder barrels and note arrangement of base gaskets or seals when removing

Fig. 1.1 Engine-housing – typical

1   Oil filter inner tube
2   Oil filter outer tube
3   Stud
4   Stud
5   Spring
6   Circlip
7   Washer
8   Valve disc
9   Breather valve body
10 Plug for timing hole
11 Dowel, crankshaft thrust ring
12 Cylinder through stud
13 Spacer
14 Oil pressure switch
15 Washer
16 Bolt
17 Drain plug
18 Sealing washer
19 Sump
20 Sump gasket
21 Dowel, front crankshaft bearing
22 Collar nut
23 Lock washer
24 Nut
25 Pressure relief valve housing
26 Spring
27 Pressure relief valve plunger
28 Plug
29 Chain tensioner pivot
30 Front bearing housing
31 Crankcase
32 Dowel

Note: items 5 – 9 early type

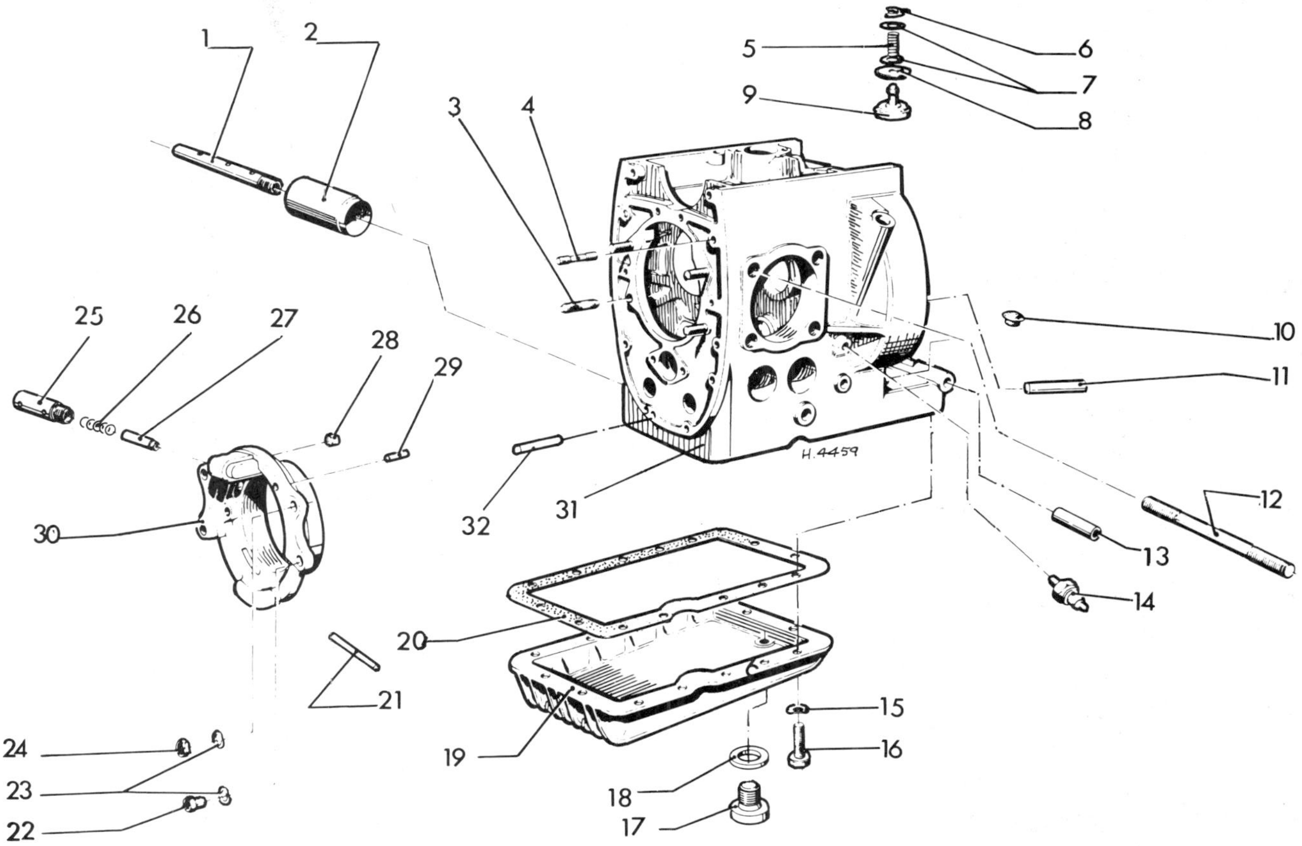

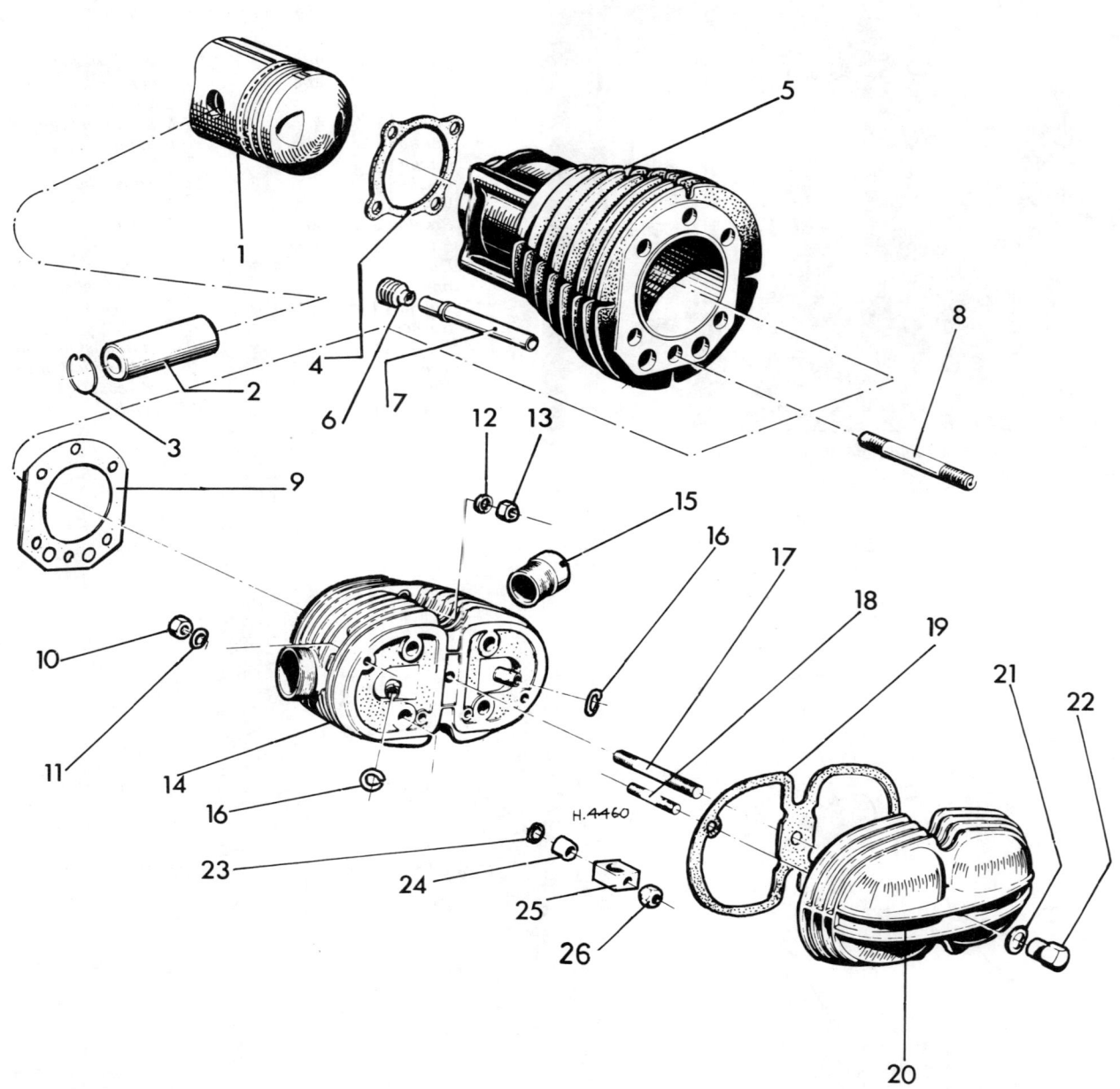

Fig. 1.2 Cylinder barrels and heads – typical

1 Piston and rings
2 Gudgeon pin
3 Circlip – early type
4 Cylinder base gasket – where fitted
5 Cylinder barrel
6 Pushrod tube seal
7 Pushrod tube
8 Cylinder head stud
9 Cylinder head gasket
10 Nut
11 Lock washer
12 Washer
13 Nut
14 Cylinder head
15 Carburettor stub
16 Circlip
17 Stud
18 Stud
19 Gasket
20 Rocker cover
21 Washer
22 Cap nut
23 O-ring – where fitted
24 Spacer
25 Rocker pillow block
26 Nut

Chapter 1 Engine

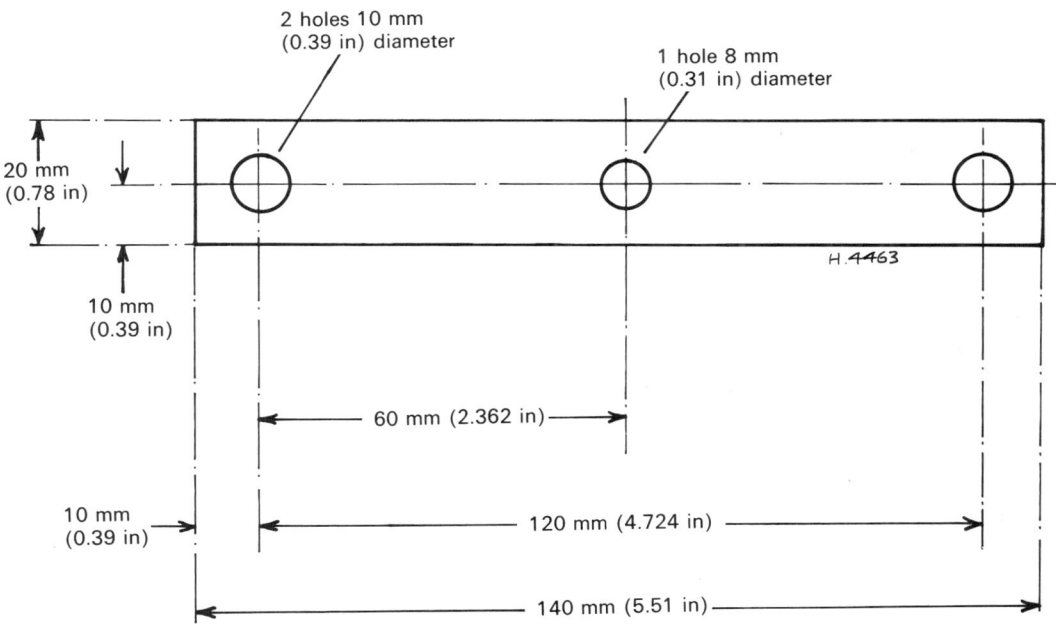

Fig. 1.3 Cylinder removing adapter 7 mm (0.27 in) thick (BMW No. 209)

7 Dismantling the engine unit: removing the pistons

1 Support the pistons with a wooden block as already described.
2 Note the arrow and the legend 'VORN' on the piston crown, indicating the front of the piston. Also the larger (inlet) valve pocket is at the rear.
3 With a small screwdriver in the slot provided, prise out a gudgeon pin wire circlip from its groove; on later 800cc and 1000cc models use circlip pliers to remove the circlips. Discard all used circlips and renew them on reassembly.
4 Heat the piston with a rag soaked in boiling water, or a hot flat iron, and push out the gudgeon pin. Do not use force, or the connecting rod may be bent, or other damage caused. Alternatively, use a special gudgeon pin removing tool.
5 Repeat for the other piston. Mark the pistons left or right to ensure that they are correctly refitted.

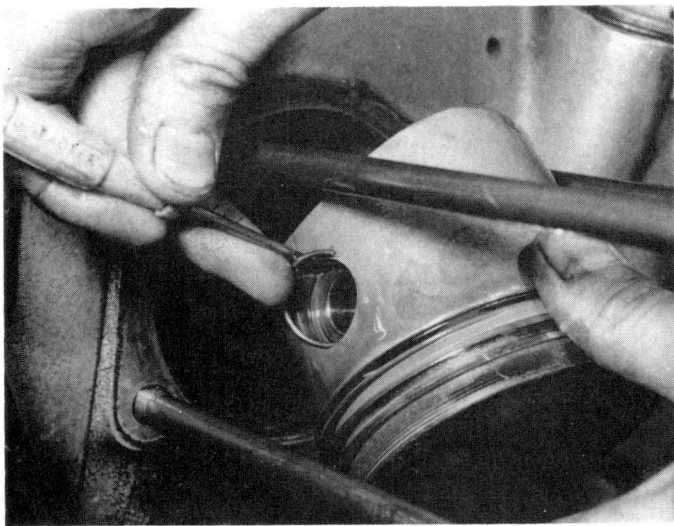

7.3 Remove retaining circlips to release gudgeon pin

7.4 Mark pistons (left or right) as soon as each is removed

8 Dismantling the engine unit: removing the connecting rods

1 Each connecting rod may be checked roughly for truth while installed in the engine. Pass a straight, close fitting bar through the small-end. Turn the engine until the bar touches the crankcase mouth, and check that it does so on both sides.
2 Do not remove the cylinder through studs unnecessarily. Unscrew them with a stud extractor, or with locknuts on their threads. Note which end screws into the crankcase.
3 To remove one connecting rod, both cylinders must be taken off. Turn the engine to top dead centre (TDC).
4 Unscrew the two connecting rod bolts with a special multi-tooth wrench through the crankcase mouth. Such a wrench may be borrowed from car specialists or bought at an auto-accessory shop. It may be possible to acquire it from a BMW dealer as tool No. 11.2.860. Take off the bearing cap, and remove the connecting rod. Note the position of the bearing cap dowel pins, towards the front (alternator) end. Mark left and right-hand rods.
5 The connecting rod bolts are not re-usable, and must be renewed.
6 Repeat for the second connecting rod.

9 Dismantling the engine unit: removing the timing chain cover

1 Remove the front engine cover, see Section 5 of this Chapter.
2 Pull off the leads to the diode plate, noting their positions, and take the wiring harness and grommet out of the cut-out in the cover.
3 Remove the alternator and ignition system components, see Chapter 9 and Chapter 5 respectively.
4 Slacken the rev-counter cable clamp screw, and withdraw the cable from the housing complete with grommet (models up to 1977 only).
5 Unscrew the nine Allen screws, and three sleeve nuts, which retain the timing chain cover. Pull off the cover.
6 If the cover is held too firmly, remove the diode plate and capacitor by unscrewing their various screws, and heat the cover to 80°C – 100°C (176° – 212°F) in the vicinity of the crankshaft bearing at the top of the cover. It should then be possible to free the cover.
7 There is an extractor available (BMW Service Tool No. 11.1.800) which bolts on to the alternator fixing bosses. These are tapped M5.

10 Dismantling the engine unit: removing the timing chain and camshaft

1 First remove the front engine cover, and timing chain cover as previously described.
2 On all models up to 1978, remove the chain tensioner circlip, push back the chain tensioner spring, and remove the tensioner blade.
3 Unscrew the lower collared nut retaining the tensioner spring, and remove the spring.
4 On all models from 1979 on, remove the single nut and the bolt which retain the fixed chain guide and remove the chain guide assembly. Using a small screwdriver, remove the circlip which retains the chain tensioner on its pivot post and gently pull the chain tensioner blade away. Disconnect the timing chain at its connecting link and remove the chain.
5 On all models, unscrew the two slotted or Allen countersunk screws retaining the front camshaft bearing. These are accessible through the holes in the camshaft sprocket, when any pair is horizontal.
6 Push out the cam followers from within the crankcase, or hook out with magnet or wire. Mark them clearly (left inlet, left exhaust etc) and store them with the valve gear.
7 On all models up to 1978, remove the timing chain assembly. Since the chain is not fitted with a joining link the two sprockets must be removed together, and as the camshaft sprocket should only be pressed off the camshaft in a suitable press, this means that the camshaft and sprocket must be removed as a single unit. This task should therefore be performed only after the gearbox, clutch and flywheel have been removed so that the oil pump can be dismantled and its inner rotor Woodruff key removed from the camshaft rear end. Refer to Section 11 and to Chapters 3 and 2 for details of the necessary preliminary dismantling operations.
8 Using BMW tool No. 11.2.600 with the appropriate adaptor or a legged puller (as shown in the accompanying photograph) extract the crankshaft sprocket. Note that this may damage the timing chain which should be renewed as a matter of course. Withdraw the crankshaft sprocket, timing chain and camshaft.
9 On all models from 1979 on the two sprockets can be withdrawn individually once the timing chain has been removed. Extract the crankshaft sprocket and bearing using BMW tool No. 11.2.600 with the appropriate grooved adaptor or a legged puller.
10 The camshaft sprocket may be removed by levering it off the camshaft using two large screwdrivers or tyre levers. Take great care to lift the sprocket evenly and not to mark the crankcase casting. The chain tensioner plunger and spring may then be removed from their housing for examination and renovation.
11 The camshaft on all models from 1979 on also cannot be removed until the preliminary dismantling operations listed in paragraph 7 above have been carried out.

8.4 Special multi-toothed wrench will be required to unscrew connecting rod bolts

9.4 Remove the clamp screw to release the rev-counter cable (where fitted)

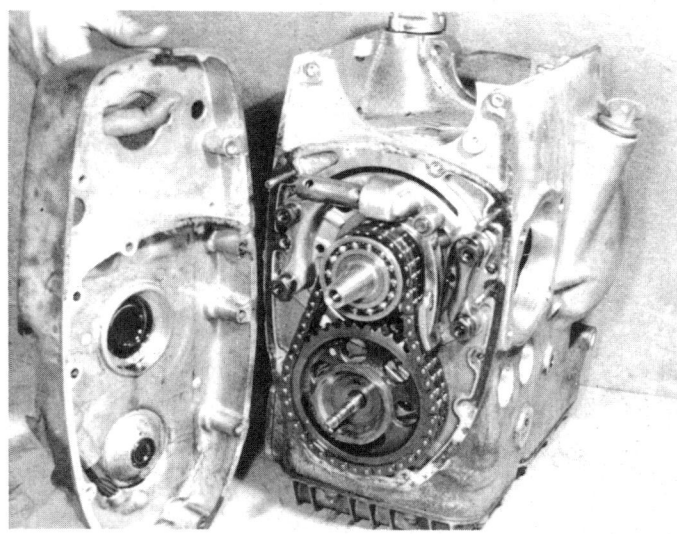

9.6 It may be necessary to heat the timing chain cover to remove it

10.2a All models up to 1978 – remove the chain tensioner circlip ...

10.2b ... and remove the tensioner components

10.5 Remove the camshaft front bearing screws (early models shown)

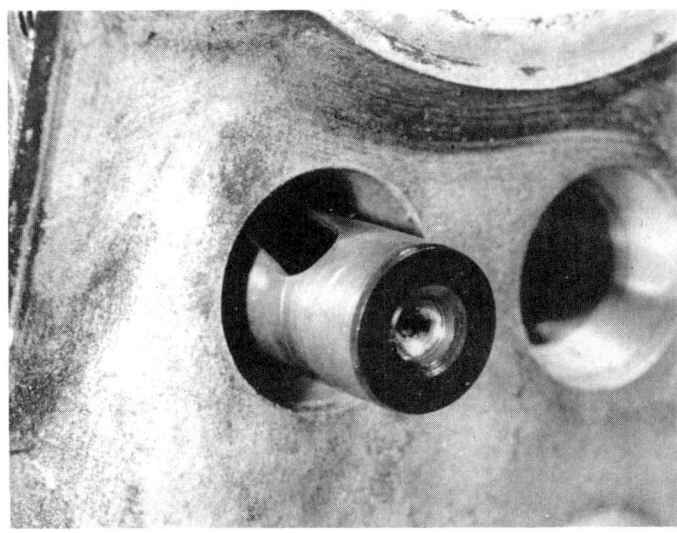

10.6 Mark the cam followers as soon as each is withdrawn (see text)

10.8 Use a suitable extractor to remove the crankshaft sprocket

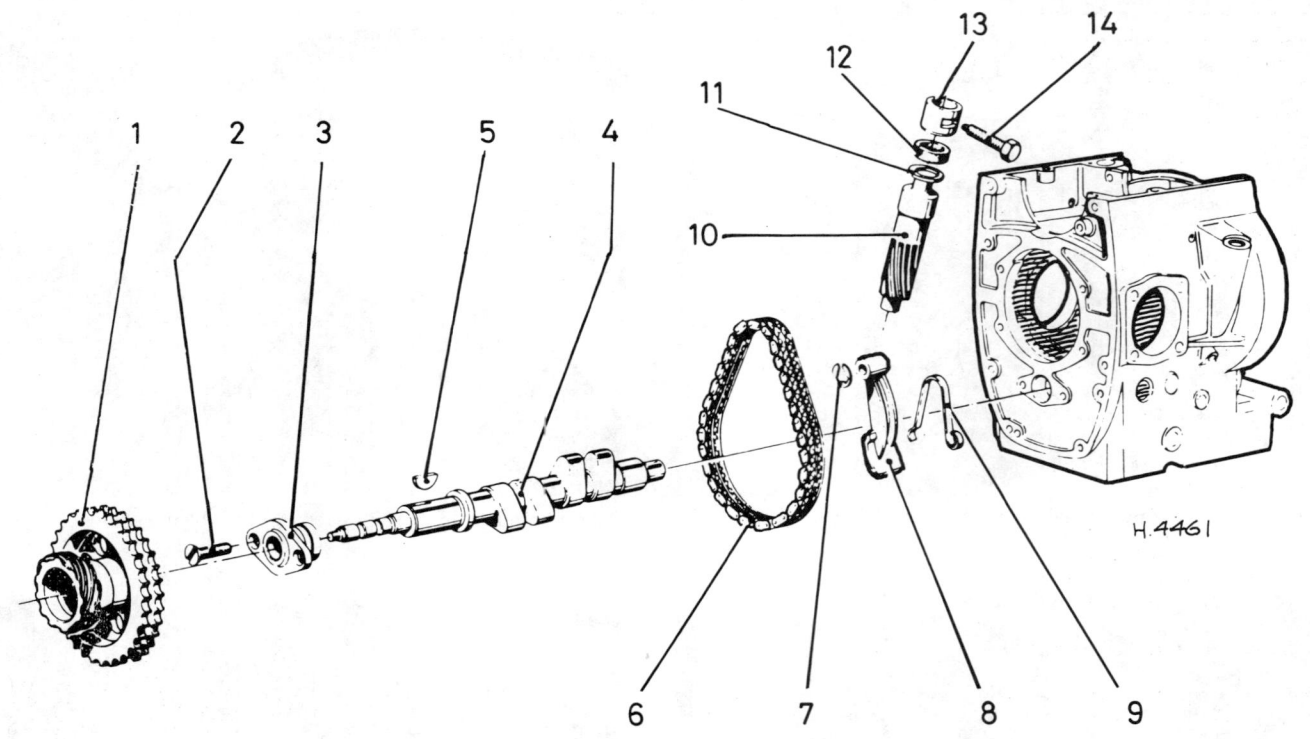

Fig. 1.4 Timing chain assembly – all models up to 1978

1 Camshaft sprocket
2 Screw
3 Camshaft bearing
4 Camshaft
5 Woodruff key
6 Timing chain
7 Circlip
8 Chain tensioner
9 Tensioner spring
10 Rev counter drive
11 Washer
12 Oil seal
13 Bush
14 Bolt

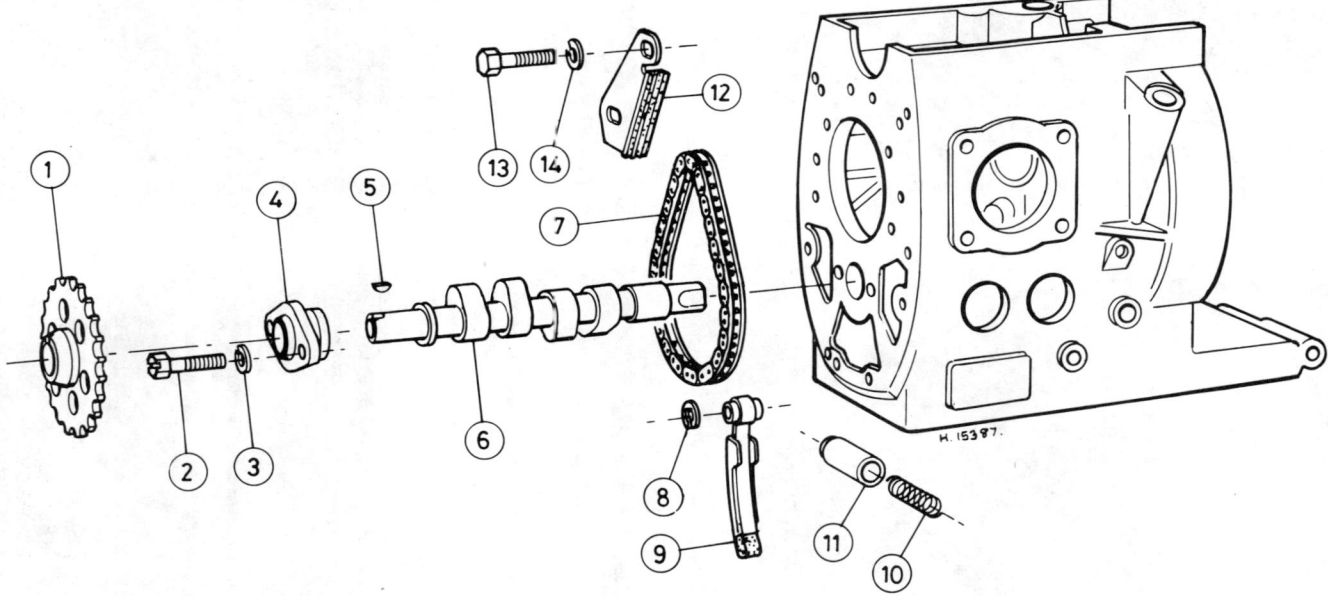

Fig. 1.5 Timing chain assembly – all models 1979 on

1 Camshaft sprocket
2 Bolt
3 Lock washer
4 Camshaft bearing
5 Woodruff key
6 Camshaft
7 Timing chain
8 Circlip
9 Chain tensioner
10 Spring
11 Plunger
12 Fixed chain guide
13 Bolt
14 Lock washer

11 Removing the engine from the frame

1 Raise or remove the seat, remove the side panels and the fuel tank (see Chapter 4).
2 Where appropriate, remove the lower fairing sections on machines fitted with RS or RT fairings; it may be advisable to remove the complete fairing to minimise the risk of damage. See Chapter 6.
3 Remove all exhaust system components. See Chapter 4.
4 Remove the engine front and starter motors covers. See Section 5.
5 Either remove all electrical and ignition components as described in Chapters 9 and 5, or disconnect all related wiring which joins the engine to the frame. Note which wires lead to which component (noting individual terminals, where necessary).
6 Referring to Routine Maintenance, drain the engine oil and remove the oil filter. Remove the oil cooler to prevent the risk of damage.
7 Disconnect the rev-counter drive cable (where fitted) and unlock the return springs of both side and centre stands. Ensure that the machine is supported securely with blocks of wood so that it cannot fall off the stand.
8 Since the engine unit, even without both cylinder heads and barrels, is heavy and unwieldy, it is advisable to remove as many more items as possible before taking the unit out of the frame, bearing in mind what work is to be undertaken on it.
9 Remove the gearbox. See Chapter 3. The clutch may be removed at this stage or after the engine has been withdrawn. See Chapter 2.
10 Make a final check that all components, electrical leads and cables have been removed which might hinder engine removal, then lift the engine unit clear of the lower frame tubes, tilting to the left to miss the upper tube, and take it out of the frame. This will require additional assistance.

12 Dismantling the engine: preliminaries

1 Before any dismantling work is undertaken, the external surfaces of the unit should be thoroughly cleaned and degreased. This will prevent the contamination of the engine internals, and will also make working a lot easier and cleaner. A high flash-point solvent, such as paraffin (kerosene) can be used, or better still, a proprietary engine degreaser such as Gunk. Use old paintbrushes and toothbrushes to work the solvent into the various recesses of the engine castings. Take care to exclude solvent or water from the electrical components and inlet and exhaust ports. The use of petrol (gasoline) as a cleaning medium should be avoided, because the vapour is explosive and can be toxic if used in a confined space.
2 When clean and dry, arrange the unit on the workbench, leaving a suitable clear area for working. Gather a selection of small containers and plastic bags so that parts can be grouped together in an easily identifiable manner. Some paper and a pen should be on hand to permit notes to be made and labels attached where necessary. A supply of clean rag is also required.
3 Before commencing work, read through the appropriate section so that some idea of the necessary procedure can be gained. When removing the various engine components it should be noted that great force is seldom required, unless specified. In many cases, a component's reluctance to be removed is indicative of an incorrect approach or removal method. If in any doubt, re-check with the text.

13 Dismantling the engine unit: removing the oil pump

1 Since it is mounted on the camshaft rear end, the oil pump cannot be withdrawn until the gearbox, clutch and flywheel have first been removed. See Chapters 3 and 2.
2 Unscrew the four countersunk screws retaining the cover plate, and remove the plate and O ring seal. If these screws are so tight that even an impact screwdriver will not loosen them, they will have to be drilled out.
3 Withdraw the inner and outer rotors with a bent wire or magnet.
4 Protect the oil pump bore with rag before extracting the Woodruff key (where fitted) from the camshaft.
5 Examination of the oil pump is described in Chapter 4.

14 Dismantling the engine unit: removing the crankshaft

1 Remove the engine from the frame, as described previously.
2 Preparatory work involves removal of the cylinder heads and barrels (Section 6 of this Chapter); pistons (Section 7); connecting rods (Section 8); clutch and flywheel (Chapter 2); oil pump (Section 13); timing chain cover (Section 9); and timing chain and camshaft (Section 10).
3 Remove the remaining three nuts from the front crankshaft bearing housing. Extract the housing (note the pressure relief valve at the top). There are two tapped holes for this purpose if a suitable extractor can be made or obtained. Otherwise, lever it off very carefully.
4 Turn the crankshaft front bobweight to the top, and pull the first big-end journal clear of the crankcase mouth. Now turn the crankshaft through 180°, so that the rear bobweight is at the top, and withdraw the crankshaft completely.
5 Prise out the rear oil seal carefully, measuring its installed depth before doing so. The open side (garter spring) of the seal faces the crankshaft.
6 Knock out, if necessary, the inner and outer thrust washers from the rear wall of the crankcase. Note the locating pegs, and the radial grooves which face outwards. The thrust washers must be replaced in the same positions; they have coloured markings.
7 The crankshaft can be removed with the engine in the frame, but the task is much easier with it out.

13.1 Oil pump cannot be removed until gearbox, clutch and flywheel have been withdrawn

14.3 Extract the crankshaft front main bearing housing

14.4a The crankshaft must be removed in two stages ...

14.4b ... with the bobweights positioned as shown to clear the crankcase

14.5 Measure the installed depth of the crankshaft rear oil seal before removing it

15 Examination and renovation: general

1 Before examining the parts of the dismantled engine unit for wear it is essential that they should be cleaned thoroughly. Use a petrol/paraffin mix or a high flash-point solvent to remove all traces of old oil and sludge which may have accumulated within the engine. Where petrol is included in the cleaning agent normal fire precautions should be taken and cleaning should be carried out in a well-ventilated place.
2 Examine the crankcase castings for cracks or other signs of damage. If a crack is discovered it will require a specialist repair.
3 Examine carefully each part to determine the extent of wear, checking with the tolerance figures listed in the Specifications section of this Chapter or in the main text. If there is any doubt about the condition of a particular component, play safe and renew.
4 Use a clean lint free rag for cleaning and drying the various components. This will obviate the risk of small particles obstructing the internal oilways, and causing the lubrication system to fail.
5 Various instruments for measuring wear are required, including a vernier gauge or external micrometer and a set of standard feeler gauges. An internal and external micrometer will be required to check wear limits. Additionally, although not absolutely necessary, a dial gauge with mounting bracket is invaluable for accurate measurement of endfloat, and play between components of very low diameter bores – where a micrometer cannot reach. After some experience has been gained the state of wear of many components can be determined visually or by feel, and thus a decision on their suitability for continued service can be made without resorting to direct measurement.

16 Examination and renovation: valves, springs and guides

1 Use a valve spring compressor to release each of the valves in turn. Keep the valves, valve springs and collets etc together in sets so that they are eventually replaced in their original location.
2 After cleaning all four valves to remove carbon and burnt oil, examine the heads for signs of pitting or burning. Examine the valve seats in the cylinder head. The exhaust valves and their seats will require the most attention because they are the hotter running. If the pitting is slight, the marks can be removed by grinding the seats and valve heads together, using fine valve grinding compound.
3 Smear a trace of fine valve grinding compound (carborundum paste) on the seat face and apply a suction grinding tool to the head of the valve. Oil the stem of the valve and insert it in the guide until it seats in the grinding compound. Using a semi-rotary motion, grind-in the valve head to its seat. Lift the valve occasionally to distribute the grinding compound more evenly. Repeat this application until an unbroken ring of light grey matt finish is obtained on both valve and seat. This denotes the grinding operation is now complete. Before passing to the next valve, make sure that all traces of the valve grinding compound have been removed from both the valve and its seat and that none has entered the valve guide. If this precaution is not observed, rapid wear will take place due to the highly abrasive nature of the carborundum base.
4 When deep pits are encountered, it will be necessary to use a valve refacing machine and valve seat cutter, set to an angle of 45°. Never resort to excessive grinding because this will only pocket the valve in the head and lead to reduce engine efficiency. If there is any doubt about the condition of a valve, fit a new one.
5 Examine the condition of the valve collets and the grooves in the valve stem in which they seat. If there is any sign of damage, new parts should be fitted. Check that the valve spring collar is not cracked. If the collets work loose or the collar splits whilst the engine is running, a valve could drop in and cause extensive damage.

6 Measure the valve stems for wear, comparing them with the unworn portion that does not extend into the valve guide. Check also the valve guides for excessive play. Check that the end of the stem is not indented from contact with the rocker arm, making tappet adjustment difficult.
7 Check the free length of each valve spring and replace all springs if any one has taken a permanent set. Worn or 'tired' valve springs have a marked effect on engine performance and should preferably be renewed during each decoke as a matter of course, especially in view of their low overall cost.
8 The valve guides are an interference fit in the cylinder head. The rocker end of the guide should be milled away down to the circlip, and the circlip removed. Heat the cylinder head to 240° – 260°C (464° – 500°F), and drive out the guide towards the combustion chamber, with a suitable drift.
9 Oversize guides are available. Drive new guides, complete with circlip into the heated cylinder head. After each has cooled, it must be reamed to the correct finished diameter.
10 After fitting new valve guides, the valve seats must be re-cut.
11 Check the sealing of the valves by pouring petrol into the inlet or exhaust ports, and checking that none leaks into the combustion chamber.

17 Examination and renovation: cylinder heads

1 Remove all traces of carbon from the combustion chambers and the inlet and exhaust ports, using a soft scraper which will not damage the surface of the valve seats. Finish by polishing the combustion chamber and ports with metal polish so that carbon does not adhere so readily. Never use emery cloth since the particles of abrasive will become embedded in the soft metal.
2 Check to make sure the valve guides are free from oil or other foreign matter that might cause the valves to stick.
3 If the valve seats are pocketed, as the result of excessive valve grinding in the past, the valve seats should be re-inserted. This is a specialist task which requires expert attention and is quite beyond the means of the average owner. Pocketed valves cause a marked fall-off in performance and reduced engine efficiency as a direct result of the disturbed gas flow.
4 Make sure the cylinder head fins are not clogged with oil or road dirt, otherwise the engine may overheat. If necessary, use a wire brush but take care not to damage the light alloy fins.
5 Check that there are no cracks, and that the valve guides are secure. Ensure that the carburettor mounting stubs are secure. If necessary refit with Loctite No. 59.

18 Examination and renovation: rocker assemblies

1 Examine carefully the outer surfaces of each rocker arm, to ensure there are no surface cracks or other signs of premature failure. The rocker arms should have a smooth surface to resist any tendency towards fatigue failure.
2 The rocker arms should be a good sliding fit on the rocker spindles without excessive play. Noisy valve gear will result from worn rocker arms and spindles and performance may drop off as a result of reduced valve lift. If play is evident, the rocker arms should be renewed and new spindles fitted.
3 Check the rocker arm adjuster and the end of the rocker which engages with the pushrod. Both these points of contact have hardened ends and it is important that the surface is not scuffed, chipped or broken, otherwise rapid wear will occur.
4 The spacer on the rocker spindle should revolve freely without end-float on /5 models. On all later models up to 1985 the rockers should be able to move freely, but without endfloat, when installed. The modified assembly introduced on 1985 models requires that shims be added as necessary to give endfloat (axial play) of 0.03 – 0.07 mm (0.0012 – 0.0028 in).

16.1 Use a valve spring compressor to release valves

16.8 To remove the valve guides, machine them down to the circlip, remove the circlip and drift out the remainder of the guide

18.4 Latest rocker assembly uses pressed-in plastic washer and must be shimmed to specified endfloat – can be fitted to earlier models, if required

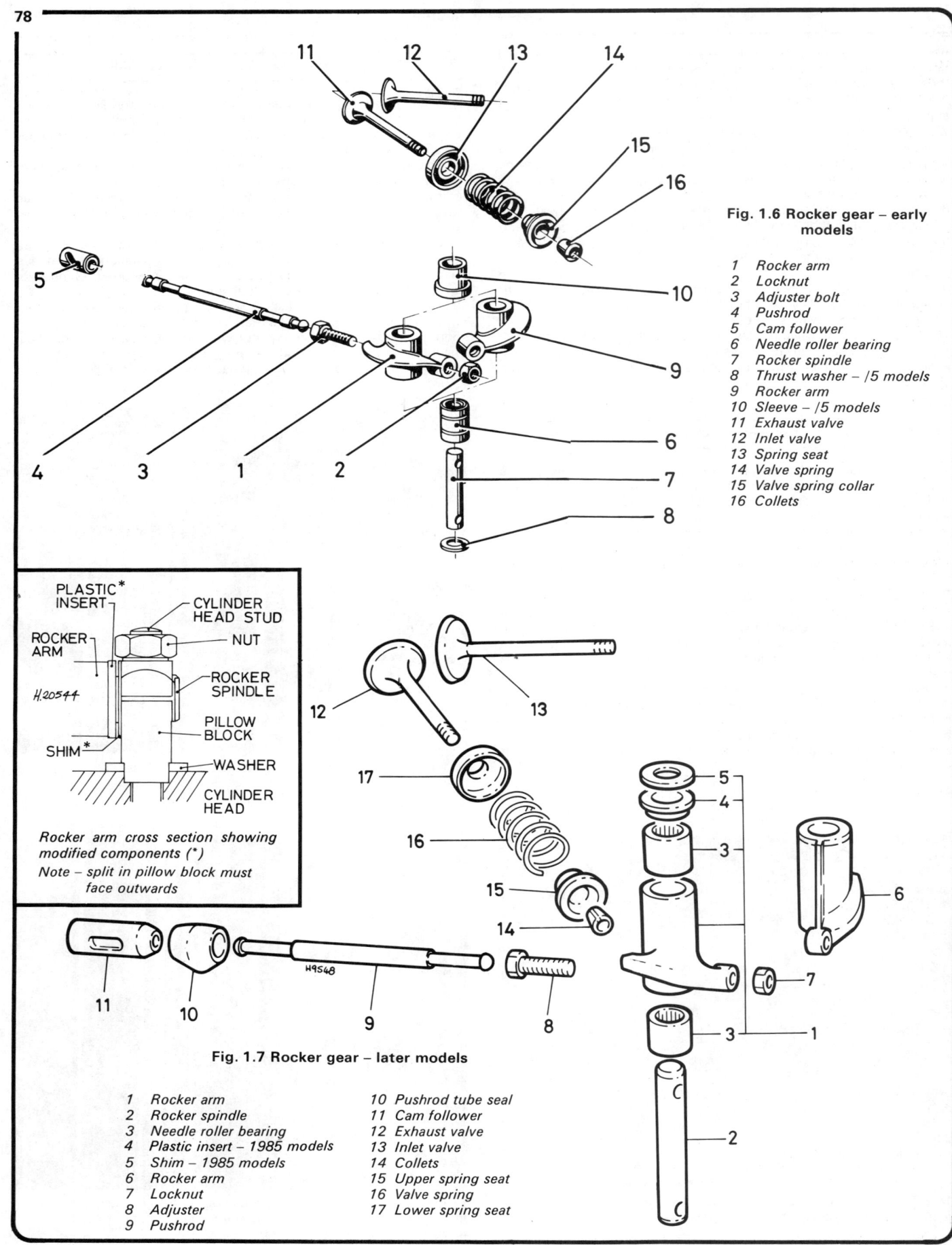

19 Examination and renovation: timing chain, sprockets and tensioner

1 It is unlikely that the timing chain and sprockets will require renewal, unless a chain breakage has damaged the teeth.
2 Check for uneven wear of the chain when still mounted on the crankcase, by removing the tensioner and turning the crankshaft a quarter turn at a time. Measure the play in the chain at each turn. If in doubt about chain condition, it should be renewed as a matter of course.
3 On early models, the timing chain is endless, and should be examined carefully when removed for broken rollers or cracked side plates or rivets damaged when extracting the sprocket.
4 Inspect the teeth of the sprockets for chipping or hooking.
5 Check that the rubber slipper surface of the chain tensioner is not damaged. It may be grooved but as long as the rollers do not make contact it is still serviceable. Check that the tensioner spring has not weakened on early models; on later models check that the tensioner plunger and spring are unworn.
6 Clean and inspect the crankshaft outrigger ball bearing without removing it from the sprocket. There must be no discernible radial play, nor any damage to the rollers or tracks. It may be extracted for replacement; chill the sprocket to aid reassembly.

20 Examination and renovation: pushrods, cam followers and camshaft

1 The camshaft is unlikely to show signs of wear unless a high mileage has been covered or there has been a breakdown in the lubrication system. Wear will be most obvious on the flanks of the cams and at the peak, where flattening-off may occur. Scuffing, or, in an extreme case, discoloration, is usually indicative of lubrication breakdown.
2 If there is any doubt about the condition of the camshaft, it is advisable to renew it whilst the engine is completely dismantled. Comparison with a new camshaft is often the best means of checking visually the extent of wear.
3 Check the cam followers for wear or damage. Again it is extremely unlikely that any has occurred. If possible compare their measured dimensions with those specified.
4 Check the pushrods for straightness by rolling them on a flat surface. Replace any that are bent, since it is impracticable to straighten them with accuracy. Check that the hardened end pieces are not loose, or the internal bearing surfaces worn, chipped or broken.
5 Check the endfloat of the front camshaft bush with a feeler gauge. If it varies from the specified dimension, refit the chain sprocket. The bush is removed after extracting the sprocket (early models only). This requires a special adaptor on the camshaft end, since the centrifugal advance spindle is rather slender.
6 Inspect the camshaft rear end bearing. This is not bushed, so cannot be replaced.
7 If, on models up to 1978, the ignition timing has been found to vary significantly from cylinder to cylinder, measure the runout of the ATU shaft. If this exceeds 0.02 mm (0.0008 in) the camshaft must be renewed; do not attempt to straighten it. If the shaft is found to be within limits measure as accurately as possible the dimensions of the camshaft front and rear bearing surfaces and calculate the radial clearance of the camshaft at each bearing. If either clearance is beyond that specified, the appropriate components must be renewed to restore accurate ignition timing.
8 While this point is not as important on later models, where the Oldham coupling between the camshaft and the distributor (contact breaker housing) or ignition trigger unit minimises the effect of camshaft bearing wear on the ignition timing, it should be remembered if trouble has been experienced in setting the timing correctly.

21 Examination and renovation: cylinder barrels

1 The usual indications of badly worn cylinder bores and pistons are excessive oil consumption and piston slap, a metallic rattle which occurs when there is little or no load on the engine. If the cylinder head end of the barrel is examined carefully, it will be observed that there is a ridge on the thrust side of each cylinder bore which marks the limit of travel of the uppermost piston ring. The depth of this ridge will vary according to the amount of wear that has taken place and can therefore be used as a guide to bore wear.
2 Bore wear is measured using a bore gauge or an internal micrometer; if these are not available take the barrels and pistons to a competent BMW dealer so that they can be checked by an expert.
3 Ovality is measured by taking four measurements, near the cylinder head end (just below the wear ridge) both along the gudgeon pin axis and at right angles to it, and at the bottom of the bore (the least worn point), again along the gudgeon pin axis and at right angles to it. If any measurement differs from its counterpart at the same height by more than the maximum limit specified, the barrel is excessively worn.
4 Taper is measured at the top (just below the wear ridge), middle and bottom of the bore, at right angles to the gudgeon pin axis. If any measurement differs from the others by more than the maximum limit specified, the barrel is excessively worn.
5 If measuring equipment is not available, a rough idea of the amount of bore wear can be obtained as follows, but should always be confirmed by an expert using accurate measuring equipment before any firm conclusions are drawn. Insert a compression ring so that it is about $1/2$ inch from the top of the bore and seated squarely in the bore by pressing it down with the skirt of the piston. Measure the ring gap with a feeler gauge, then reposition the ring below the area traversed by the piston and measure the gap again. Subtract the second reading from the first and divide the difference by three to give the piston/cylinder clearance. If this exceeds the maximum limit the bore is excessively worn.
6 On models up to 1980, if the bore is found to be excessively worn it can be rebored and an oversize piston and piston rings fitted. Check first with a BMW dealer what oversizes are available for the model in question.
7 On all models from 1981 on, if the barrels are found to be excessively worn they must be renewed with the pistons and rings. Have all components measured by an expert to confirm the amount of wear before taking such an expensive course of action.
8 Check the surfaces of each cylinder bore to ensure there are no score marks or other signs of damage that may have resulted from an earlier engine seizure or displacement of one of the circlips. Even if the bore wear is not sufficient to necessitate a rebore or renewal (as appropriate), any such damage will override this decision in view of the compression leak that will occur.
9 Check the cylinder fins for clogging with road dirt. Inspect the pushrod rubber grommets. Renew frequently, since differential expansion and their exposed position lead to oil leaks.

20.5 Measuring camshaft endfloat (early model shown)

22 Examination and renovation: pistons and piston rings

1 If rebore or barrel renewal is necessary, the pistons and rings can be discarded because they must be replaced by their oversize or new counterparts.
2 Remove all traces of carbon from the piston crown, using a soft scraper to ensure the surface is not marked. Finish off by polishing the crown with metal polish, so that the carbon will not adhere so readily. NEVER use emery cloth.
3 Piston wear usually occurs at the base of the skirt and takes the form of vertical streaks or score marks on the thrust side. If a previous engine seizure has occurred, the score marks will be very obvious. Pistons which have been subjected to heavy wear or seizure should be rejected and new ones obtained. Measure piston diameter at right angles to the gudgeon pin axis, just above the base of the piston skirt. R45 pistons should be measured at 14 mm (0.55 in) above the skirt base, R65 pistons at 18 mm (0.71 in), and R80G/S, R80ST, R80 and R80RT pistons at 27 mm (1.06 in); such precise measuring points are not given for other models but should be similar. Compare the measurement obtained with that specified (the piston size code letter will be found stamped in the piston crown).
4 If the piston has worn significantly, subtract its measured diameter from the minimum and maximum bore size measurements (see previous Section), to determine the piston/cylinder clearance. If this is more than the maximum permissible limit specified, the piston is excessively worn (assuming that the bore is within wear limits) and must be renewed.
5 Note: When either or both pistons are renewed, it is essential that the new components are of the same size code as their respective barrels (the barrel size code letter is stamped into the base flange), that both are of the same weight group (see Specifications) and, on 800cc and 1000cc models only, that both use the same type of gudgeon pin retaining circlip.
6 Remove the piston rings carefully, by expanding them sufficiently to pass over the piston. If necessary use three thin strips of metal to ease them from their grooves (see illustration). The rings are very brittle, and must not be handled roughly. Note which groove each ring came out of, and which way up on each piston.
7 Clean the ring grooves of any burnt deposits. A piece of old broken ring is useful for this, if used carefully.
8 The piston ring grooves may become enlarged in use, permitting the rings to have greater side float. It is unusual for this type of wear to occur on its own, but if the side float appears excessive, new pistons of the correct size should be fitted.
9 Piston ring wear is measured as detailed in Section 21.5. If the end gap in the two positions is nearly identical, but is greater than the recommended limit, the piston rings are worn and must be renewed.
10 The gudgeon pins must be a good sliding fit in the small-end of the connecting rods without evidence of play. Worn small-ends produce a rattle, not unlike piston slap, which will rapidly increase in intensity.

23 Examination and renovation: oil seals

1 The presence of oil in the clutch housing, or contact breaker housing, may indicate the failure of the crankshaft oil seals, or the camshaft oil seal.
2 Prise out the crankshaft rear seal carefully having first measured its installed depth. Remove the timing chain cover seals by tapping them out from the rear of the cover. Do not attempt to lever them out; the seals, especially later types, are a very tight fit in their housings and cannot be removed or refitted correctly with the cover in place without risk of damage.
3 Renew all seals as a matter of course whenever they are disturbed.
4 On installation, note that the later type of crankshaft rear seal must be soaked in engine oil for 3 hours before installation and that it must be pressed into place (spring or open side towards the crankshaft) using the special BMW tool No. 11.1.890 with adaptor No. 11.1.880. It has to be installed to a precise depth (approximately 14.4 – 14.6 mm/0.5669 – 0.5748 in) to avoid contact with the flywheel (models up to 1980) or flywheel mounting ring (all models 1981 on).
5 The crankshaft front seal should be driven into its housing when the timing chain cover is flat on a work surface, but the camshaft seal should not be fitted until the timing cover has been refitted to the engine. Both these seals should be fitted with their open or spring sides towards the crankshaft (or camshaft) and should be driven in until flush with the surrounding housing surface using as a drift a socket spanner or similar which bears only on the seal's hard outer diameter.

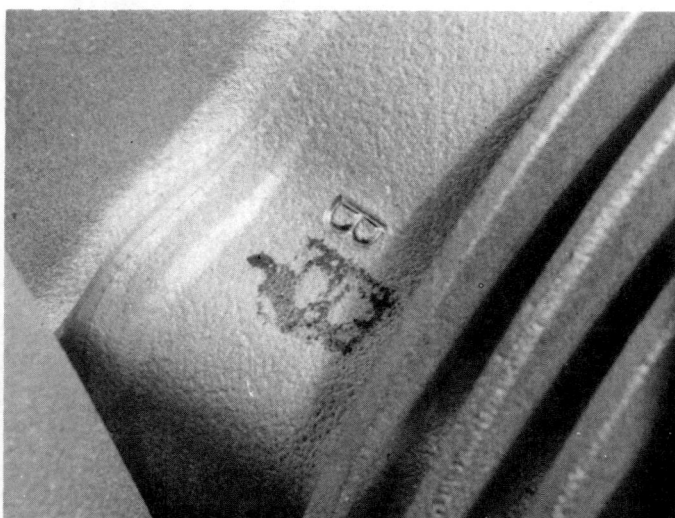

22.5 Letter stamped in barrel indicates bore size code – barrel and piston should always be the same code

Fig. 1.8 Method of removing gummed piston rings

Chapter 1 Engine

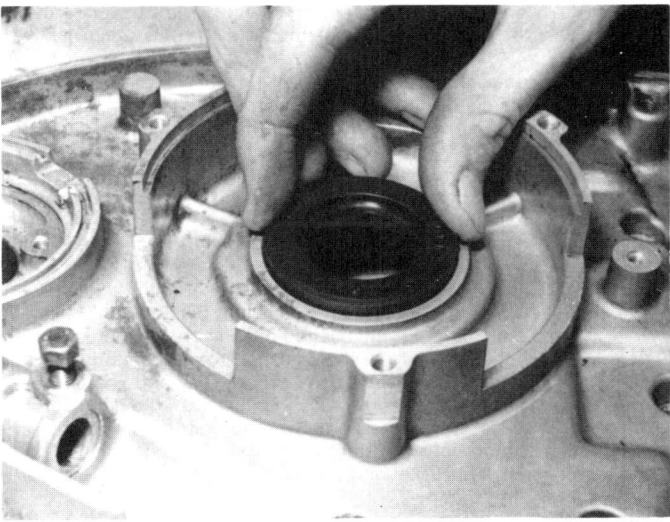

23.2 Renew all seals as a matter of course – later types are difficult to remove and refit (see text)

24 Examination and renovation: connecting rods and big-end bearings

1 Check the big-ends for wear, whilst assembled on the crankshaft, by pushing and pulling on the connecting rods. There should be no discernible play. Note that the task of assessing bearing wear by measurement requires extremely accurate measuring equipment and the skill to use it. For those owners who have this skill and equipment the various dimensions and tolerance are quoted in the Specifications Section of this Chapter, but owners are advised to entrust all crankshaft repair work to a competent BMW dealer (see Section 25).
2 When dismantled, check the big-end bearings and journal surfaces visually for scoring, wear or other damage. Treat the main bearings and journals in a similar manner. Big-end journals may be reground to three undersizes if restoration is required, but note that BMW have found that such work is often not carried out to the required standards of accuracy and recommend that the best long-term course of action is to renew the crankshaft and bearing shells.
3 If crankshaft or bearing damage is found, take great care to clean out all oilways in the crankcase and crankshaft before reassembling the engine.
4 Check that the small-end bushes are secure, and have no more than the allowable wear. If they need to be replaced, they must be pressed out. The new ones have to be turned to size in a lathe, after fitting. Each gudgeon pin should be a light sliding fit.

25 Examination and renovation: crankshaft and main bearings

1 It is recommended that if the crankshaft and main bearings show any signs of wear or damage at all the crankcase, crankshaft and bearings should be dismantled as much as possible to minimise labour charges and should be taken to a competent BMW dealer for reconditioning.
2 There is little that the average owner can do other than this as the bearing bushes must be removed and refitted using a number of special tools to prevent damage. Also the task of measuring the various

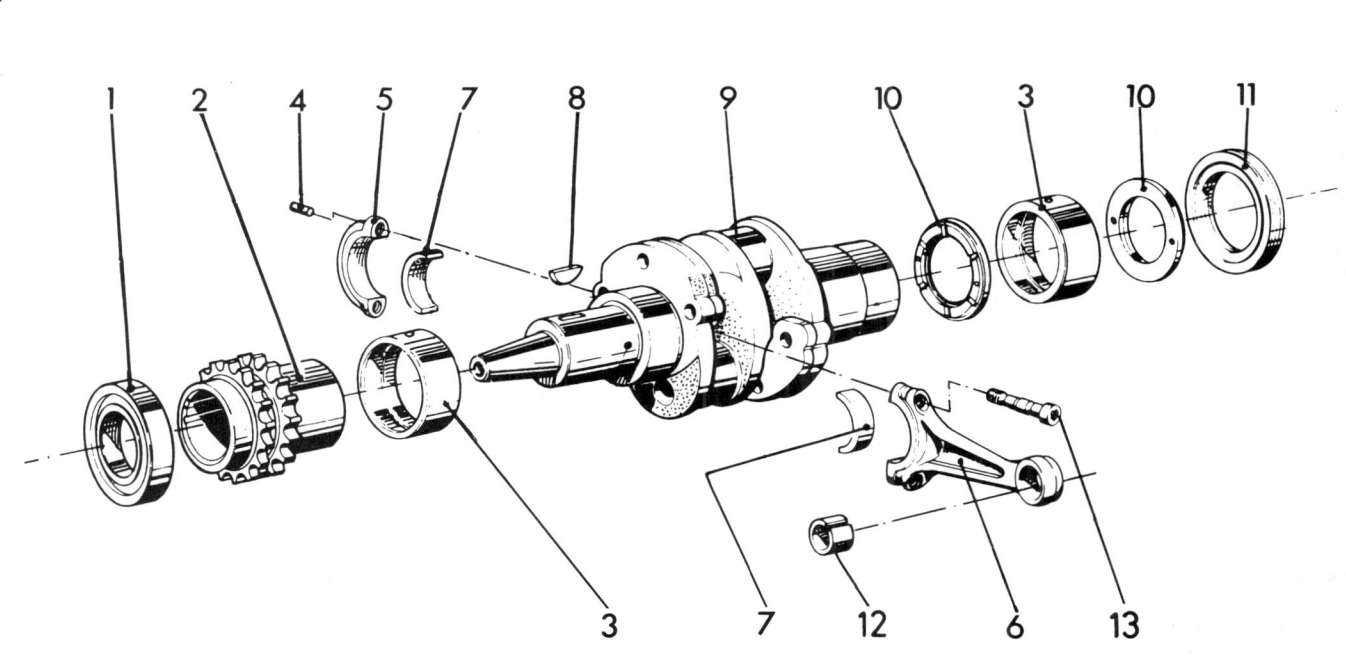

Fig. 1.9 Crankshaft – typical

1 Outrigger bearing
2 Crankshaft sprocket
3 Main bearing
4 Dowel pin
5 Big-end bearing cap
6 Connecting rod
7 Big-end bearing
8 Woodruff key
9 Crankshaft
10 Thrust washer
11 Oil seal
12 Small-end bearing
13 Bolt

components to assess wear requires specialised and extremely accurate measuring equipment as well as the skill to use it.

3 BMW manufacture these components to very close tolerances to ensure the machine's mechanical silence and longevity, but the tolerances have been changed from year to year as well as the method of bearing selection and the range of bearings available. Finally, note that while the crankshaft main bearing journals may be reground to three undersizes to compensate for wear, BMW have found that such work is often not carried out to the required standards of accuracy and recommend that the best long-term solution is to renew the crankshaft and bearing bushes.

4 If crankshaft or bearing damage is found, take great care to clean out all oilways in the crankcase and crankshaft before reassembling the engine. The cause of the damage (if other than wear due to the mileage covered) must be found and rectified before reassembly can proceed.

26 Engine reassembly: general

1 Before reassembly of the engine unit is commenced, the various component parts should be cleaned thoroughly and placed on a sheet of clean paper, close to the working area.

2 Make sure all traces of old gaskets have been removed and that the mating surfaces are clean and undamaged. Great care should be taken when removing old gasket compound not to damage the mating surface. Most gasket compounds can be softened using a suitable solvent such as methylated spirits, acetone or cellulose thinner. The type of solvent required will depend on the type of compound used. Gasket compound of the non-hardening type can be removed using a soft brass-wire brush of the type used for cleaning suede shoes. A considerable amount of scrubbing can take place without fear of harming the mating surfaces. Some difficulty may be encountered when attempting to remove gaskets of the self-vulcanising type, the use of which is becoming widespread, particularly as cylinder head and base gaskets. The gasket should be pared from the mating surface using a scalpel or a small chisel with a finely honed edge. Do not, however, resort to scraping with a sharp instrument unless necessary.

3 Gather together all the necessary tools and have available an oil can filled with clean engine oil. Make sure that all new gaskets and oil seals are to hand, also all replacement parts required. Nothing is more frustrating than having to stop in the middle of a reassembly sequence because a vital gasket or replacement has been overlooked. As a general rule each moving engine component should be lubricated thoroughly as it is fitted into position.

4 Make sure that the reassembly area is clean and that there is adequate working space. Refer to the torque and clearance setting wherever they are given. Many of the smaller bolts are easily sheared if overtightened.

27 Engine reassembly: refitting the crankshaft

1 It is assumed that the advice given in Sections 24 and 25 has been followed and that a BMW dealer has fitted new main bearing bushes, thrust washers (to restrict crankshaft endfloat to the required amount) and the crankshaft rear oil seal.

2 If this has not been done by the dealer, coat all bearing surfaces liberally with Molykote Paste G or with clean engine oil and insert the crankshaft into the crankcase, reversing the removal sequence. Refit the front main bearing housing and tighten securely its retaining nuts. Check that the crankshaft rotates smoothly.

3 Note that the flywheel mounting stub and the threaded holes for the flywheel retaining bolts must be clean and free from oil.

28 Engine reassembly: refitting the camshaft and timing chain

1 Rotate the crankshaft to the TDC position and refit the sprocket locating Woodruff key. Liberally smear with Molykote Paste G or with clean engine oil the camshaft rear bearing surfaces.

2 On all models up to 1978, assemble as a single unit the camshaft, chain and crankshaft sprocket. Align the engraved marks on the sprockets and note the position of the keyway in the crankshaft sprocket. Turn the crankshaft so that the key is in the same relative position.

3 Insert the camshaft into the crankcase (the oil pump must be removed) until the crankshaft sprocket engages the taper.

4 Ensure that the crankshaft keyway, and the engraved marks on the sprockets still align, then tap the sprocket firmly into position. Check that the crankshaft and camshaft rotate smoothly.

5 If the ball journal bearing has been removed, heat until it can be dropped onto the crankshaft sprocket.

6 Make sure that the camshaft is fully engaged in the rear bearing and refit the front bearing screws.

7 Fit the chain tensioner and spring. Recheck the timing marks.

8 On all models from 1979 on, oil the camshaft bearing surfaces and insert it into the crankcase. Fit the flanged bearing and tighten the two retaining screws, then check that the camshaft rotates smoothly.

9 Press the Woodruff key into its camshaft keyway and position the camshaft sprocket so that its keyway aligns with the key before pushing it into place. Applying counter-pressure at the camshaft rear end (via the oil pump housing) tap the sprocket fully into place.

10 Fit the crankshaft sprocket and outrigger ball bearing as described in paragraphs 4 and 5 above.

11 Insert the tensioner plunger and spring into their housing and check that they are free to move in and out. Oil them lightly.

12 Rotate the sprockets so that the timing marks are exactly aligned, then refit the chain and connect it by refitting the connecting link. Ensure that the closed end of the spring clip faces the direction of chain travel. Insert the chain tensioner blade and secure it with a circlip. Refit the chain guide assembly, ensuring that it is exactly parallel to the chain before tightening the mounting bolt and nut. The guide is slotted to permit it to be moved into the correct position. Recheck the timing marks.

13 On all models, using the notes made on removal, fit each cam follower into its original crankcase bore and ensure that all are well lubricated. Oil the crankshaft outrigger bearing and timing chain, and refit the oil pump inner rotor Woodruff key to the camshaft rear end.

29 Engine reassembly: refitting the oil pump

1 Insert both rotors into the pump housing, aligning the camshaft key and the two dots on the rotors.

2 Oil the rotors liberally with clean engine oil.

3 Ensure that the O-ring seal is correctly positioned before replacing the cover. The cover can only be fitted one way up, with the lower two screws further apart.

27.1 Check that thrust washers are securely mounted at front and rear of crankshaft rear main bearing before refitting crankshaft – locate each washer on the two locating pins

27.3 Crankshaft rear oil seal must be carefully fitted (See Section 23.4) – check that flywheel mounting stub and threaded holes are clean and free from oil

28.2a Refitting the camshaft – all models up to 1978 – fit camshaft, sprockets and chain as a single unit ...

28.2b ... ensuring that sprocket timing marks align exactly with chain slack on tensioner side

28.4 Check that crankshaft sprocket keyway aligns with key and timing marks are still aligned before tapping sprocket into place

28.5 Heat the outrigger bearing to refit – do not forget to lubricate it once it has cooled

28.6 Tighten securely the camshaft front bearing screws

28.7 Refit the chain tensioner assembly and re-check the timing marks

29.1 Align the dot on each rotor to ensure correct pump reassembly

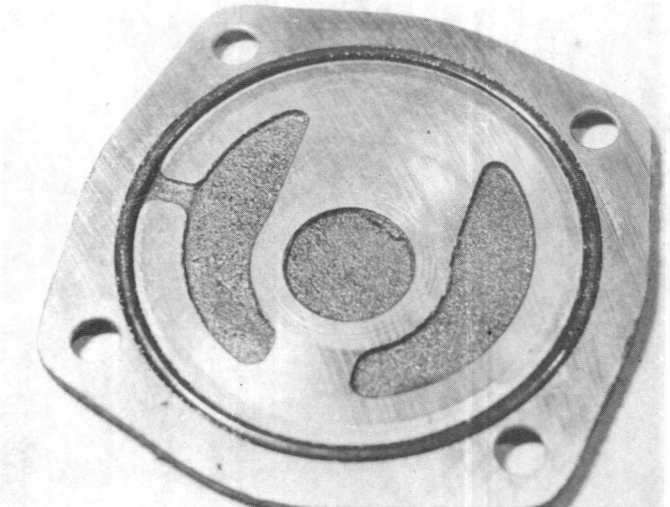

29.3 Ensure that the pump cover O-ring is correctly positioned

30 Engine reassembly: refitting the timing chain cover

1 Place the gaskets in positon on the crankcase; do not forget the two gasket strips at the top of the housing (where fitted).
2 Before refitting the cover, the diode plate, ignition components and camshaft oil seal should be removed. Heat the cover to 80° – 100°C (176° – 212°F), and tap into position on the crankcase. Centre the centrifugal advance spindle in the oil seal housing.
3 Tighten the Allen screws and nuts, starting from the centre. The two shorter screws go at the top centre.
4 Refit the camshaft oil seal.
5 Refit the diode plate, alternator, and ignition components, see Chapters 5 and 9.

31 Engine reassembly: refitting the connecting rods and pistons

1 Ensure that the surfaces in the connecting rod big-end and bearing caps are clean before fitting new bearing shells. Press the new shells into position ensuring that their locating tabs are correctly positioned.
2 Coat the big-end journals with Molykote Paste G, or oil well.
3 Always use new big-end bolts, as the original ones may have stretched.
4 Turn the crankshaft to T.D.C. and refit the connecting rods to the same journals. Both rods in an engine must have the same weight or coloured marking. The locating dowels for the bearing cap must be towards the front of the engine.
5 Check that the bearings turn freely, after tightening the bolts to the recommended torque setting.
6 Fit the piston rings to the pistons. Make sure that they are the correct way up; different markings (usually the inscription Top/Oben) to identify the top surface, have been used. Thin strips of metal are useful to assist in replacing rings, place them between the expanded ring and the piston.
7 Replace one circlip. Warm the piston and press the gudgeon pin home. The arrow cast on the piston crown and the word 'vorn' (front) must point forwards. Refit the second circlip. Make sure that both circlips seat firmly in their grooves. One end of the circlip must overlap the screwdriver slot completely (wire type only). Repeat for the second piston.

30.2 It may be necessary to heat the timing chain cover to refit it – refit oil seals as described in text

30.5 Do not fit the electrical components until the cover has cooled down (if heated)

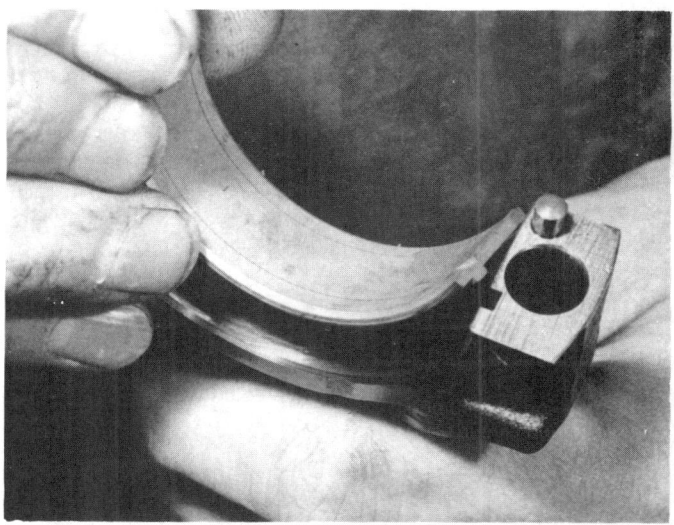

31.1 Ensure locating tabs engage correctly when refitting bearing shells

31.2 Lubricate thoroughly all journals and bearing shells

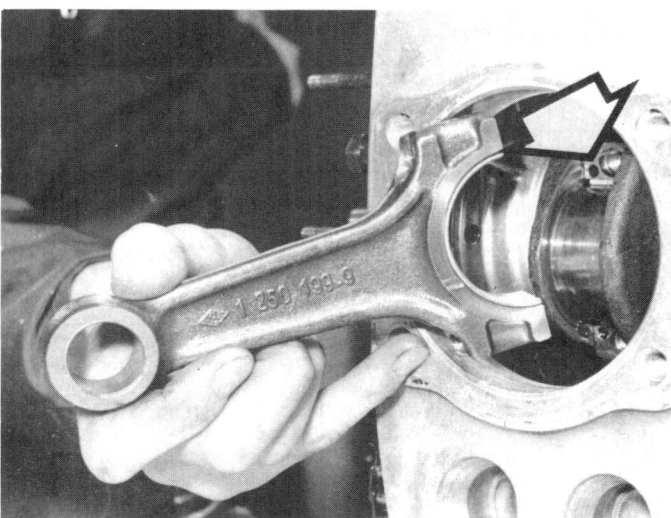

31.4 Locating dowels (arrowed) on connecting-rod and cap must be towards front (alternator) end of engine

31.5 Tighten connecting rod bolts to specified torque setting – always renew bolts

31.7a Stamped marks (see text) on piston crown show which way piston must be installed

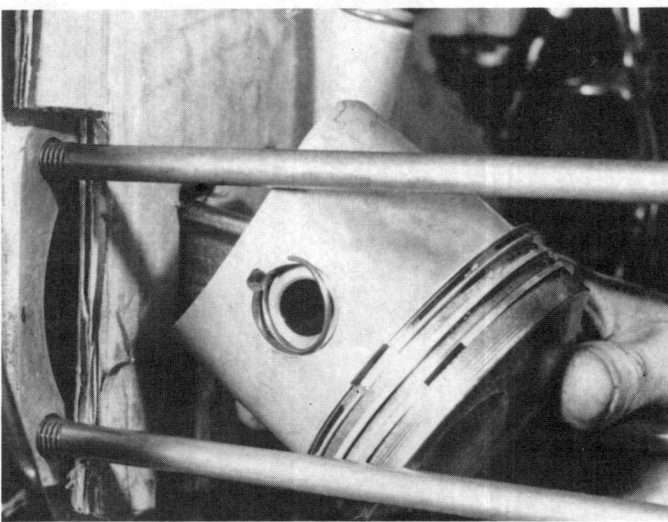

31.7b Ensure circlips are correctly seated to retain gudgeon pin – always renew circlips

32 Engine reassembly: refitting the cylinder barrels

1 Before refitting the barrels check carefully that the correct base gaskets /compression plates or O-ring seals are available. **Standard /5 and /6 models use only a base gasket**; all other models in **standard** form use a large O-ring which is inserted into a groove in the cylinder base, around the bore spigot and two smaller O-rings which are set in grooves in the cylinder base around the two upper stud holes. The O-rings should be renewed whenever they are disturbed.

2 Extra compression plates may have been fitted to any model; these, where found, should be carefully cleaned and refitted with a thin coat of Hylomar SQ32/M or similar non-setting jointing compound in additon to any other seals or gaskets appropriate to that model. Standard base gaskets should be renewed whenever the barrels are removed and should be coated similarly with jointing compound on refitting.

3 Where the base joint is sealed by O-rings, the large O-ring is 2mm (0.08 in) in diameter in standard form and should be sufficient to prevent oil leaks if the sealing faces are clean and unmarked by dents or scratches, although a thin coat of jointing compound will help to ensure this. However, if persistent oil leaks have been encountered a thicker O-ring (2.2 mm/0.009 in) is available.

4 Place the gasket, compression plate and/or O-rings in position on the barrel flange, using the jointing compound to stick them in place. Check that the push rod tube seals are in place.

5 Support the piston with a wooden block and use a piston ring clamp to compress the rings. The piston ring gaps should be positioned at 120° relative to one another. If a ring clamp is not available one may be improvised using worm-drive clips and a thin metal strip.

6 Oil the pistons and the cylinder bores with clean engine oil. Make sure the correct barrel is replaced using for identification the notes made on removal. Push the barrel onto the piston carefully, engaging the piston rings. When all three rings are entered into the bore, remove the clamp and push the barrel fully home. Repeat for the second cylinder barrel.

7 Seat the pushrod tubes firmly using the tool illustrated except for all models from 1981 on, where the seal support rings are brazed in place and cannot be moved.

32.5 Piston ring clamp can be used if required when refitting barrels – oil piston and bore

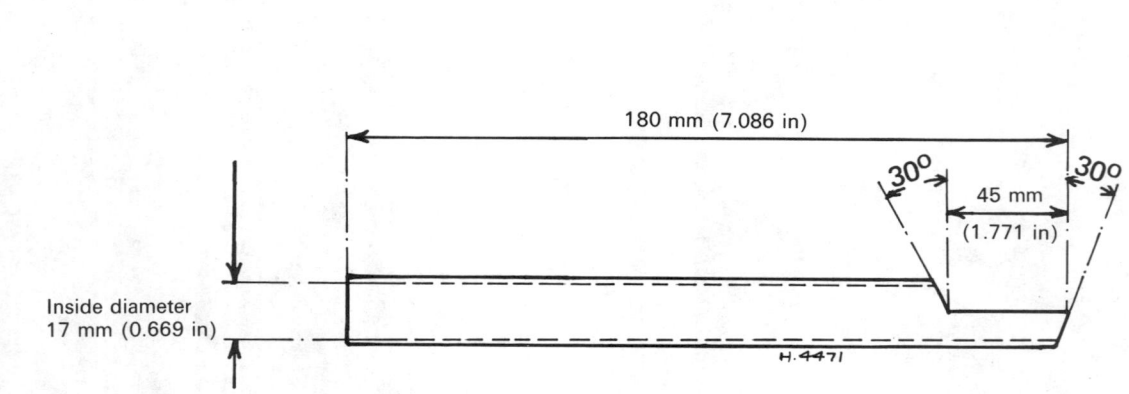

Fig. 1.10 Pushrod grommet seating tool (BMW No 11.1.600) – all models up to 1980

33 Engine reassembly: refitting the cylinder heads and rocker gear

1 Ensure that the valve spring bottom seats are fitted firmly. The marks on the valve springs must be adjacent to the cylinder head.
2 Place the upper spring collar on the valve and compress the valve spring. Replace the valve cotters, making sure that they fit firmly in the semi-circular grooves. Valve collets are in pairs, and must be kept together.
3 Release the spring compressor and seat the valve collets firmly with a few blows with a soft hammer square on the valve stem. Repeat for the other valves.
4 Valve seat sealing may be checked by pouring petrol or paraffin into the exhaust and induction ports and checking that none enters the combustion chamber.
5 Fit new cylinder head gaskets; the pushrod holes are offset to one side, so they must be aligned correctly. On 900cc models modifications to the method of locating the cylinder head meant that the two locating dowels in the barrel and their corresponding recesses in the head were removed (frame number 4.050 544 on – R90/6, 4.081, 080 on R90S). The gasket which fits the earlier type of head is no longer available, so either the dowels on earlier models must be removed (heat the barrel and draw them out with pliers) or the corresponding holes in the new gasket (see accompanying illustration) must be punched out to 14.5 mm (0.57 in).
6 Assemble the first cylinder head onto its barrel. Fit the cylinder head to barrel nuts and thick washers. Do not tighten.
7 Oil and replace the pushrods in their correct location.
8 Fit new O-ring seals (where fitted) on the cylinder through studs followed by the spacer sleeves.
9 With the tappet adjusters unscrewed, replace the rocker assemblies. Fit the four nuts. On all models from January 1980 on, ensure that the punch mark in one end of each rocker spindle is at the **top** and facing **outwards**, away from the head, so that the rocker feed oilways are correctly aligned (photo 33.9).
10 Using a jig (BMW No 200) as illustrated (on /5 models only) to hold the rocker pillow blocks, tighten the cylinder head nuts in the sequence shown. The nuts should be tightened in three stages to the specified torque setting. The function of the jig is to ensure that the rocker assembly is square. If it is not set up correctly, the result will be noisy valve gear and possibly bent pushrods and valves (very expensive). Note that the jig is not necessary on later models, which have self-aligning pillow blocks.
11 When the head is securely fastened, check that the rockers have the correct amount of endfloat and are free to move, also that the pushrods are in the centre of the tunnels. Oil the rockers liberally. Repeat the assembly instructions for the second cylinder head.
12 Reset the valve clearances as described in Routine Maintenance and replace the rocker cover.
13 1000 km (600 miles) after rebuilding the engine, the torque of the cylinder head nuts and the valve clearances should be checked. If slight oil leaks appear at the pushrod grommets, reseat with the tool illustrated (early models only).

33.1a Do not omit valve spring bottom seats

33.1b Install valve springs with paint-marked coils against cylinder head

33.2 Compress valve spring to refit cotters

33.5 Always renew head gaskets when refitting cylinder heads

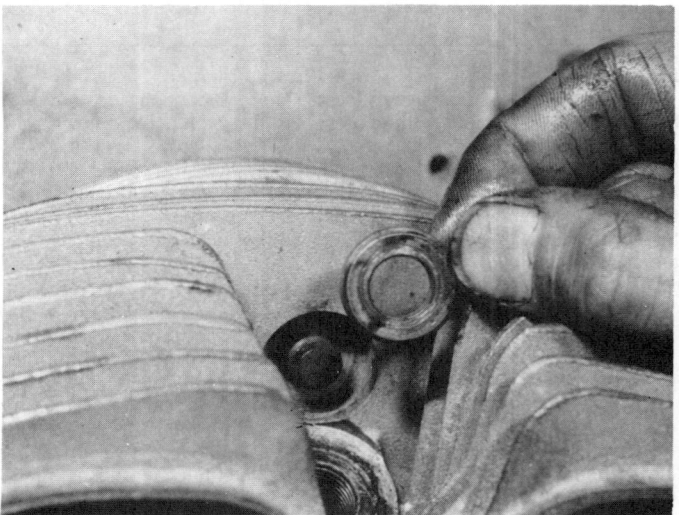
33.6 Do not forget washers before refitting retaining nuts

33.7 Ensure pushrods are refitted in their original locations

33.8 Do not forget spacers or O-rings (where fitted) before refitting rocker assemblies

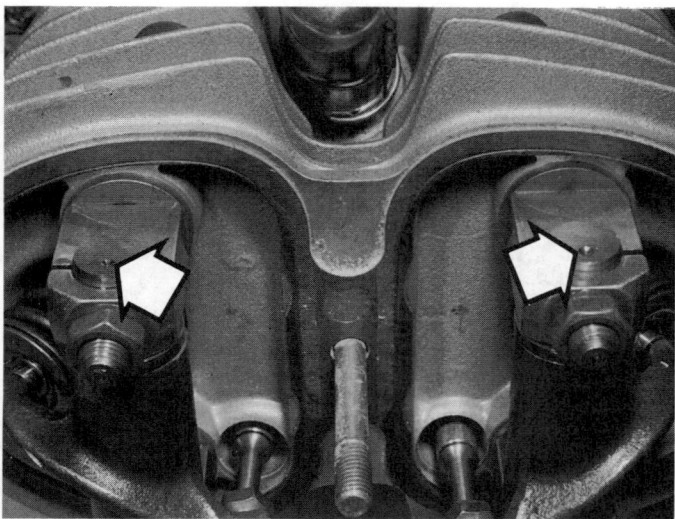
33.9 Rocker spindle punch marks (arrowed) must be at the top and face outwards – all models from early 1980 on

33.11 Check rocker endfloat carefully when tightening cylinder head nuts

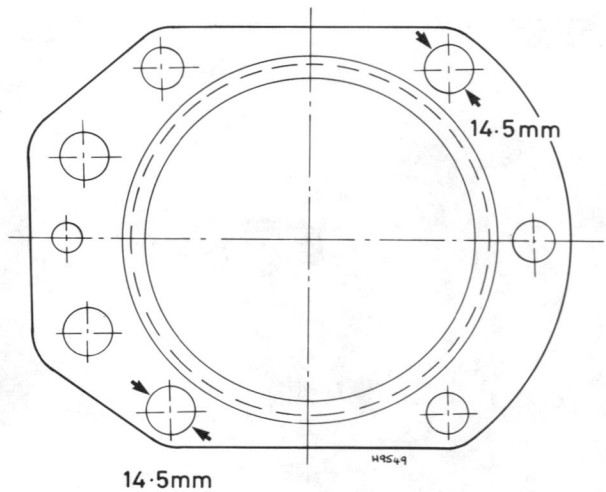
Fig. 1.11 Head gasket modifications – 900cc models

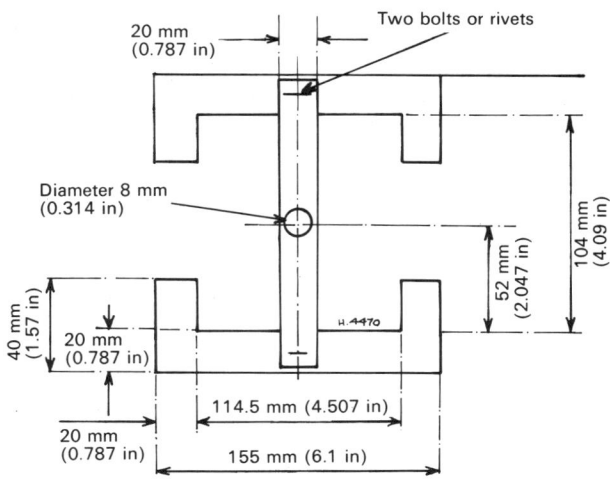

Fig. 1.12 Rocker assembly tool – thickness 20 mm (0.787 in) BMW No. 200

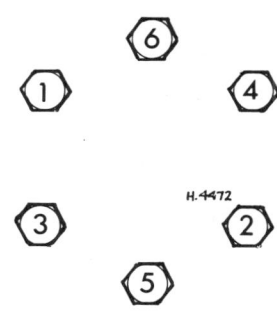

Fig. 1.13 Cylinder head nut tightening sequence

34 Refitting the engine in the frame

1 If this has not been done, refit the flywheel and clutch as described in Chapter 2.
2 Protect the frame tubes with suitable padding and enlist the aid of an assistant to lift the engine into the frame. Move it as far forwards as possible.
3 Refit the gearbox, as described in Chapter 3.
4 Hook up the stand return springs and connect the tachometer drive cable (where fitted).
5 Referring to Routine Maintenance, fit a new oil filter element and refill the engine with oil.
6 Connect to the main loom again, or refit (as appropriate) all electrical and ignition components. Check the contact breaker points gap as described in Routine Maintenance (all models up to 1980) then refit the spark plugs after checking that they are correctly gapped (see Routine Maintenance). Connect the plug leads to the spark plugs. Refit the starter motor cover.
7 Refit the exhaust system. See Chapter 4.
8 Refit the fairing components removed (where applicable).
9 Refit the fuel tank, side panels and seat.

35 Starting and running the rebuilt engine

1 Attempt to start the engine using the usual procedure adopted for a cold engine. If a kickstart is fitted this should be used in preference to the electric starter, to preserve battery charge if the engine proves reluctant to start or is difficult to turn over because of tightness caused by the fitting of new components. Do not be disillusioned if there is no sign of life initially. A certain amount of perseverance may prove necessary to coax the engine into activity even if new parts have not been fitted. Should the engine persist in not starting, check that the spark plugs have not become fouled by the oil used during re-assembly. Failing this, go through the fault-finding charts and methodically work out the problem.
2 When the engine does start, keep it running as slowly as possible to allow the oil to circulate. The oil warning light should go out almost immediately the engine has started, although in certain instances a very short delay can occur whilst the oilways fill and the pressure builds up. If the light does not go out the engine should be stopped before damage can occur, and the cause determined. Open the choke as soon as the engine will run without it. During the initial running, a certain amount of smoke may be in evidence due to the oil used in the reassembly sequence being burnt away. The resulting smoke should gradually subside.
3 Check the engine for blowing gaskets and oil leaks. Before using the machine on the road, check that all the gears select properly, and that the controls function correctly. On early models the pushrod tube seals may require seating with the tool illustrated in Fig 1.10.
4 As soon as the engine will idle smoothly, check the ignition timing as described in Routine Maintenance, then refit the engine front cover.

36 Taking the rebuilt machine on the road

1 Any rebuilt machine will need time to settle down, even if parts have been replaced in their original order. For this reason it is highly advisable to treat the machine gently for the first few miles to ensure oil has circulated throughout the lubrication system and that any new parts fitted have begun to bed down.
2 Even greater care is necessary if the engine has been rebored or if a new crankshaft has been fitted. In the case of a rebore, the engine will have to be run-in again, as if the machine were new. This means greater use of the gearbox and a restraining hand on the throttle until at least 500 miles have been covered. There is no point in keeping to any set speed limit: the main requirement is to keep a light loading on the engine and to gradually work up performance until the 500 mile mark is reached. These recommendations can be lessened to an extent when only a new crankshaft is fitted. Experience is the best guide since it is easy to tell when an engine is running freely.
3 If at any time a lubrication failure is suspected, stop the engine immediately, and investigate the cause. If an engine is run without oil, even for a short period, irreparable engine damage is inevitable.
4 When the engine has cooled down completely after the initial run, recheck the various settings, especially the valve clearances. During the run most of the engine components will have settled into their normal working locations. Check the various oil levels, particularly that of the engine as it may have dropped slightly now that the various passages and recesses have filled.

Chapter 2 Clutch

Refer to Chapter 10 for information relating to the 1986 on models

Contents

General description 1	Clutch: reassembly 5
Clutch removal 2	Clutch operating mechanism: removal, examination and
Dismantling the clutch 3	reassembly 6
Clutch: examination and renovation 4	

Specifications

Type .... Single plate dry clutch with diaphragm spring

Spring
Thickness:
  R50/5, R60/5* .... 2.4 mm (0.0945 in)
  R45 up to 1980, R60/6, R60/7, R65 up to 1980,
  R75, R80/7 .... 2.6 mm (0.1024 in)
  All 900 cc models, all 1000 cc models up to
  1980 .... 2.8 mm (0.1102 in)
  All other models .... N/Av
Pressure (fitted):
  R50/5, R60/5* .... 155 – 165 kp (342 – 364 lbf)
  R60/6, R75/5, R75/6 .... 175 – 200 kp (386 – 441 lbf)
  R60/7, R75/7, R80/7, R45 and R65 up to 1980 .... 180 – 220 kp (397 – 485 lbf)
  All 900 cc models .... 217 – 236 kp (478 – 520 lbf)
  All 1000 cc models up to 1980 .... 202 – 220 kp (445 – 485 lbf)
  All other models .... N/Av
Height (relaxed):
  R50/5, R60/5* .... 17.0 – 18.0 mm (0.6693 – 0.7087 in)
  R45 and R65 up to 1980 .... 14.7 – 15.7 mm (0.5787 – 0.6181 in)
  R75/5, all /6 models, R60/7, R75/7, R80/7 .... 18.5 – 19.5 mm (0.7283 – 0.7677 in)
  All 1000 cc models up to 1980 .... 17.1 – 17.7 mm (0.6732 – 0.6969 in)
  All other models .... N/Av

*May be fitted with stronger spring from larger capacity/later models

Clutch plate
Diameter:
  All /5, /6 and /7 models up to 1980 .... 180 mm (7.09 in)
  R45 and R65 up to 1980 .... 160 mm (6.30 in)
  All models 1981 on .... 164 – 166 mm (6.46 – 6.54 in)
Thickness:
  Standard – all models up to 1980 .... 5.75 – 6.25 mm (0.2264 – 0.2461 in)
  Standard – all models 1981 on .... 5.25 – 5.75 mm (0.2067 – 0.2264 in)
  Service limit .... 4.50 mm (0.1772 in)
Maximum runout .... 0.15 mm (0.0059 in)
Maximum vertical play .... 0.30 mm (0.0118 in)

Pressure plate
Maximum distortion .... 0.10 mm (0.0039 in)

Torque wrench settings

Component	Nm	lbf ft
Clutch lever adjuster screw locknut	20 – 23	15 – 17
Clutch cover plate/flywheel screws or bolts:		
All models up to 1980	23	17
All models 1981 on	20 – 22	15 – 16
Flywheel mounting bolts:		
/5	58 – 62	43 – 46
R60/6 and R75/6 up to 9/74 – 10 mm bolts	60 – 65	44 – 48
R90/6 and R90S up to 9/74 – 10 mm bolts	70 – 75	52 – 55
/6 1975 on and all other models – 11 mm bolts	100 – 105	74 – 77.5

1 General description

The single disc, car type, dry clutch fitted to all models is bolted directly to the flywheel, on the rear end of the crankshaft. It uses a diaphragm spring to give light operation. The spring forces a pressure plate and a clutch plate against a cover plate bolted to the flywheel. The clutch plate has bonded friction linings, and is splined to the gearbox input shaft. The clutch is cable operated via a pushrod within the gearbox input shaft.

Although the design remained principally the same, all models from 1981 on are fitted with a modified clutch which required 30% less effort to operate and is 40% lighter than the earlier unit. Early versions of this clutch suffered occasional failures of the clutch plate centre; a modified, heavy-duty plate is now used in its place, and the flywheel has been strengthened.

Clutch adjustment is described in Routine Maintenance.

Note that BMW recommend that the clutch be dismantled once a year so that the gearbox input shaft and clutch plate centre splines can be degreased, checked for wear and lubricated on reassembly. This is to preserve the clutch's smooth action and reliability.

2 Clutch removal

1 Although the clutch operating mechanism is located on the gearbox end cover and can be almost completely dismantled with the gearbox in place, if the clutch itself requires attention the gearbox must be removed to gain access to it. Refer to Chapter 3.

2 The clutch can be serviced with the engine in the frame, or it can be removed with the engine and dismantled on the bench. Refer to Chapter 1 for details of engine removal.

3 Check the gearbox input shaft and clutch plate centre splines whenever the gearbox is removed, lubricating them on reassembly, and also take the opportunity to overhaul the clutch operating mechanism.

3 Dismantling the clutch

1 Remove the gearbox. See Chapter 3, Section 2.

2 Before starting dismantling work check the clutch components for balancing marks; 1981 on models should have a white-painted mark on the cover plate, pressure plate and flywheel, which should be spaced at 120° to each other. If no marks can be seen, make your own. Using paint or a thick-nibbed felt marker, draw a line across the flywheel, pressure plate and cover plate so that these three components can be refitted in their original position by aligning their marks. Remember that they represent by far the greatest proportion of the engine's rotating mass and, if unbalanced, will produce severe vibration.

3 Note also which way round the clutch plate is fitted; the longer extended part of the centre boss usually faces towards the gearbox. It is advisable to mark the outer (rearmost) face of the clutch plate with paint or a felt marker to ensure that this is not fitted the wrong way round on reassembly.

4 On all models up to 1980, slacken the six screws round the periphery of the clutch cover plate with an impact screwdriver. These are hexagon socket cap or slotted countersunk, depending upon model.

5 Remove every other screw and replace with an M8X 50 mm (2 inch) long set screw to which a nut is fitted (or use BMW tool No. 21.2.600). Finger tighten the nut down onto the clutch ring. Now remove the remaining three clutch ring screws; on early /5 models this may release the spacers.

6 Unscrew the nuts on the temporary screws uniformly, until spring pressure is released. Remove the temporary screws and catch the spacer under each (/5 only).

7 **Warning,** the clutch diaphragm spring is held under great pressure and if this procedure is not followed, damage will be caused to both machine and person. In addition, it will be impossible to refit the clutch.

8 On all models from 1981 on slacken the six bolts or screws around the periphery of the cover, then, working on a diagonal sequence, slacken each bolt or screw by one turn at a time to release spring pressure smoothly and evenly. The pressure plate's long mounting ears should allow sufficient movement for the spring pressure to be released safely. When spring pressure is released, remove the six bolts and their lock washers. There may be a spacer behind each, fitted between the clutch cover plate and flywheel.

9 On all models, remove the cover plate, clutch plate, pressure plate (checking the balancing marks) and diaphragm spring, noting which way round the latter is fitted.

10 To ensure that the flywheel is refitted correctly on the crankshaft stub, turn the engine over until the 'OT' mark (TDC) is aligned exactly with the notch in the ignition timing aperture. **Do not** move the crankshaft once the flywheel has been withdrawn.

11 Lock the flywheel to prevent rotation while the retaining bolts are slackened. To do this, use either of the two locking tools shown in the accompanying photographs and illustration, but note that the locking tool dimensions shown in the illustration will require modification; the two drilled holes must be moved towards each other to suit the later pattern of flywheel. Once the flywheel is locked, remove the five retaining bolts and, on 1981 on models only, the washer.

12 On 1981 on models the flywheel can now be pulled off the crankshaft. If the thrust ring on the crankshaft end is to be removed tap it round until its threaded holes are halfway out of line with those of the crankshaft. Insert two suitably bent metal rods (old screwdrivers would serve) and pull off the thrust ring. Withdraw the O-ring.

13 On models up to 1980, thread two of the long set screws (or BMW tools) used to compress the spring into opposite holes in the flywheel and pull it off the crankshaft. If necessary, make up the extractor shown in the accompanying illustration and use the two set screws to pull the flywheel off. Withdraw the O-ring (where fitted).

3.5 All models up to 1980 – clutch spring pressure must be released carefully using BMW tools (alternatives shown) ...

3.9 ... to permit safe removal of clutch components

3.11a For removal and refitting flywheel can be locked using simple tool shown (on tightening) ...

3.11b ... or using fabricated copy of BMW service tool (see text)

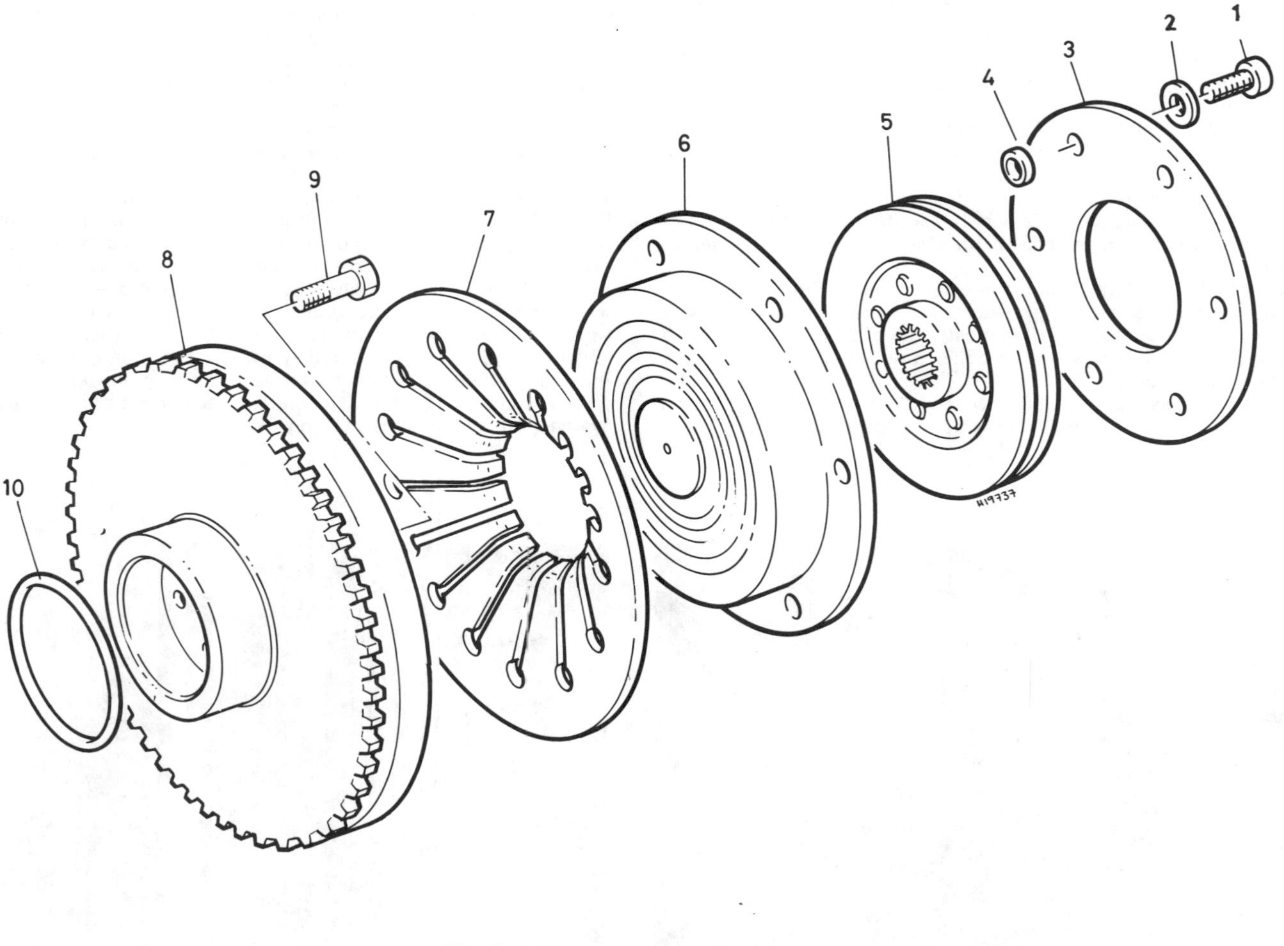

Fig. 2.1 Clutch – up to 1980 models

1 Bolt or screw	4 Spacer – /5 models only	7 Diaphragm spring	10 O-ring (later /6 and)
2 Washer – R45/65	5 Clutch plate	8 Flywheel	1979 on /7 models)
3 Cover plate	6 Pressure plate	9 Bolt – 5 off	

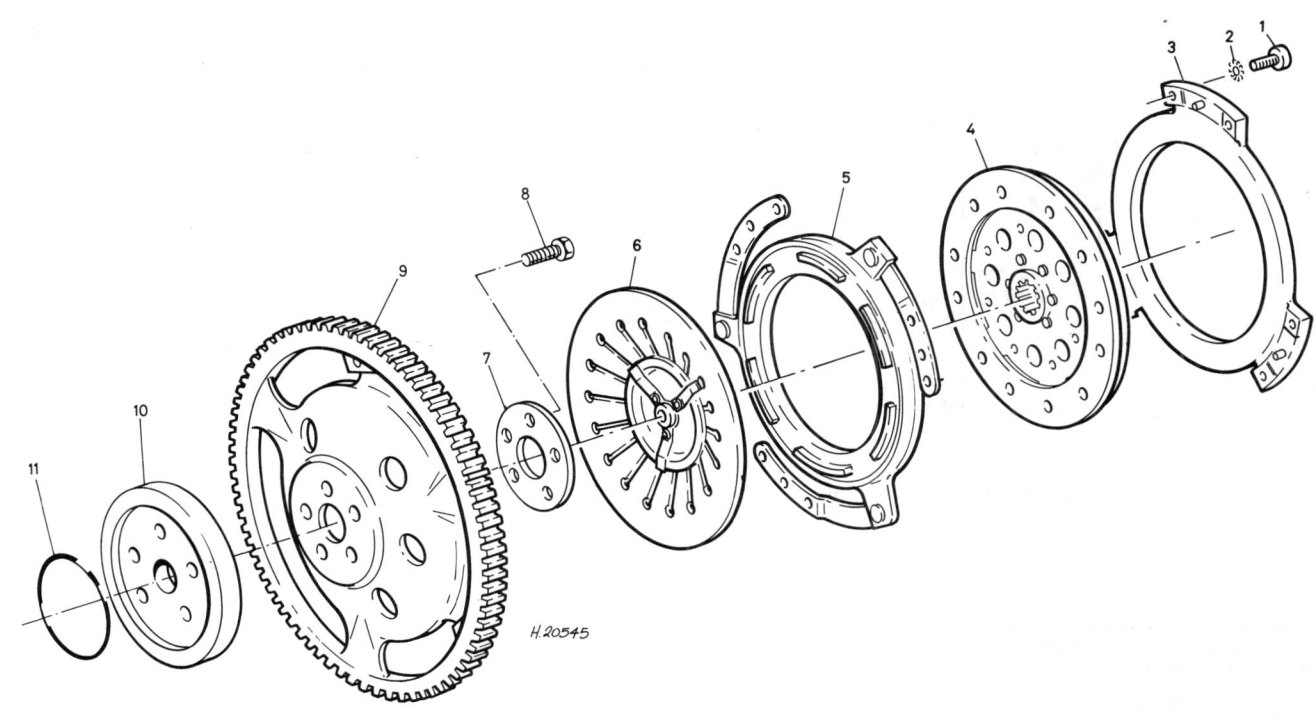

Fig. 2.2 Clutch – 1981 on models

1 Screw – 6 off	4 Clutch plate	7 Steel washer	10 Thrust ring
2 Lock washer – 6 off	5 Pressure plate	8 Bolt – 5 off	11 O-ring
3 Cover plate	6 Diaphragm spring	9 Flywheel	

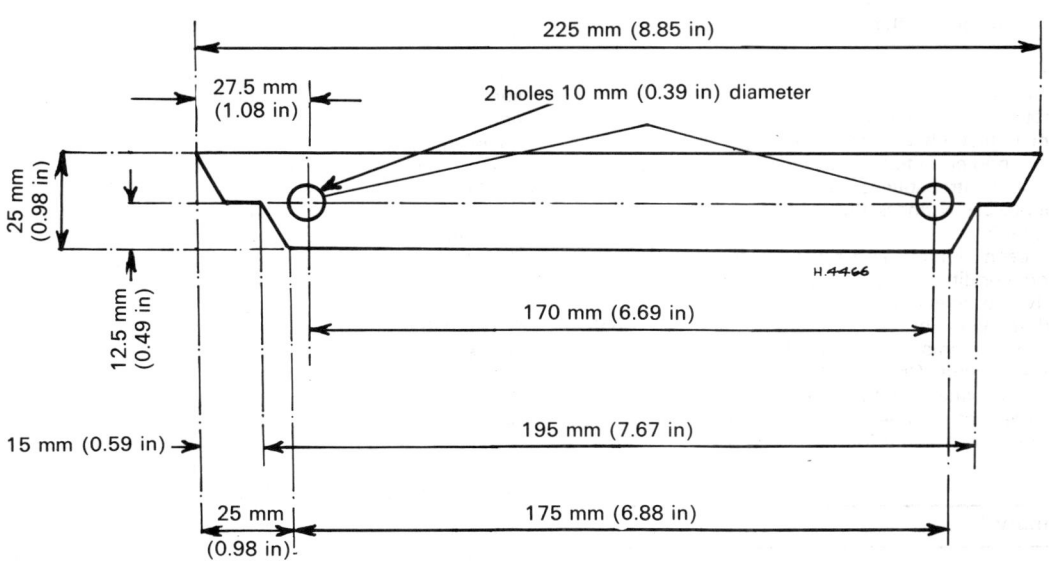

Fig. 2.3 Flywheel locking tool 6 mm (0.23 in) thick – BMW No. 208

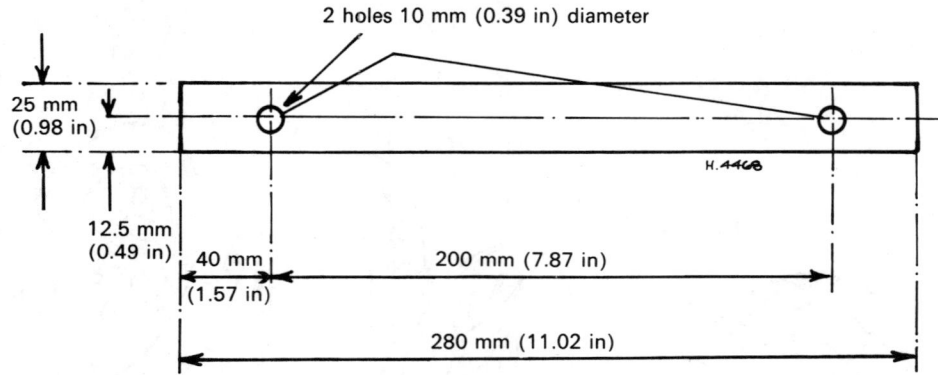

Fig. 2.4 Flywheel extracting tool – all models up to 1980 – 10 mm (0.4 in) thick – BMW No. 226

4 Clutch: examination and renovation

1 If the clutch plate is damaged in any way, or if the friction material is worn to the rivets, fouled with grease or oil, or glazed, it must be renewed as a matter of course. If it appears to be in good condition measure the thickness of the friction material at several points; if the plate is worn to 4.5 mm (0.1772 in) or less at any point, the plate must be renewed.
2 Check carefully the condition of the clutch plate centre splines and check for signs of cracking or splitting around the centre; if any damage is found the plate must be renewed.
3 Check the clutch and pressure plates for distortion and the spring pressure of the diaphragm spring. Measure the relaxed height of the spring. Also, on models up to 1980 only, lay the spring on a surface plate (or thick plate glass). With the spring laid dished side down, the difference between the height of the bent-up tabs should not exceed 0.3 mm (0.012 inches). With the spring the other way up, the maximum difference in height of the rim should be 0.8 mm (0.031 inches).
4 Inspect the teeth on the flywheel for wear or chipping. If they are badly rounded, the starter will slip.
5 If the clutch action has become sudden, with grabbing or snatching in evidence, first check the operating mechanism (see Section 6). If this is in good condition check closely the gearbox input shaft and clutch plate centre splines; renew either component if excessive wear is found. Lastly check the endfloat (axial play) of the input shaft. See Chapter 3.
6 If the clutch has been slipping and the plate friction material is found to be in good condition, the clutch cover plate should be checked very carefully and renewed.
7 If oil has found its way into the clutch housing, thoroughly degrease all clutch components and wash all traces of oil off the crankcase and gearbox castings. Check the seals at the crankshaft rear end, the oil pump cover plate and the gearbox input shaft. Check carefully that the flywheel has not been rubbing on the crankshaft seal, renewing the seal if traces of this are found.

5 Clutch: reassembly

1 The mating surfaces of the crankshaft, flywheel and thrust ring (later models only) and their threaded holes must be completely dry, clean and free from oil before reassembly. The flywheel mounting bolts **must** be renewed whenever they are disturbed; they are of the stretch type and are permanently deformed after being tightened. Where applicable, fit a new O-ring.
2 On models from 1981 on, fit the thrust ring on to the crankshaft rear end aligning the threaded holes and taking care not to damage the crankshaft seal.
3 On all models refit the flywheel. Check that the pistons are at TDC and fit the flywheel so that the OT mark (TDC) is aligned exactly with the notch in the ignition timing aperture; the mounting bolt holes in flywheel and crankshaft should align. Refit the mounting bolts; do not omit the washer (1981 on models only).
4 Lock the crankshaft by the method used on dismantling. The **new** flywheel bolts should be fitted **dry** (no oil present) and should be tightened to the specified torque setting.
5 For the next part of the operation have an assistant hold each component in place while the next is fitted. Some lubricant will be required; BMW recommend Optimol Paste PL, Staburags NBU30PTM compound, or Molykote 'U'. If these cannot be obtained locally, seek the advice of a BMW dealer. Degrease all components carefully before applying new lubricant and apply only thin smears; do not allow any lubricant on to the friction material.
6 Fit the diaphragm spring to the flywheel applying a smear of lubricant to all points of contact between the two and to the three support arms securing the spring centre. Ensure that the spring is the correct way round, then refit the pressure plate. Ensure that the balancing marks are correctly aligned; if BMW's own marks (1981 on models) are used, the pressure plate mark must be 120° away from that on the flywheel. If your own marks were made as recommended, align the pressure plate mark with that of the flywheel. Apply a smear of lubricant to all points of contact between the spring and pressure plate.
7 Fit the clutch plate to the pressure plate, ensuring that it is fitted the correct way round; the centre boss extended end should face the gearbox.
8 Refit the cover plate, aligning the balancing mark as described above. On models up to 1980 refit the three long screws with nuts or the BMW clamping tools; do not forget to fit the spacer (/5 models only) between the cover and pressure plates as each is refitted. Use a pair of needle-nose pliers or similar to hold each spacer until its screw is fitted. Tighten the nuts evenly to compress the spring sufficiently to enable the three remaining permanent screws to be fitted and tightened (do not forget the spacers, where fitted).
9 Before the screws are fully tightened, the clutch plate must be centred. The easiest way of doing this (if the gearbox is removed) is to push the gearbox input shaft into the clutch assembly and to line it up with the engine mounting stud protruding from the rear of the crankcase. If this is not possible it will be necessary to acquire the BMW centring tool No. 21.2.650 or to make up a substitute for it, as shown in the accompanying illustration. Insert the tool into the clutch plate centre splines, align the point on the end with the countersink in

the pressure plate, and leave it there while the three permanent screws are tightened. Remove the temporary clamping screws and substitute the remaining permanent screws. Working progressively and in a diagonal sequence, tighten the screws to a torque setting of 23 Nm (17 lbf ft). Remove the centring tool.

10 On all models from 1981 on, there are usually no spacers between the clutch components. However, in a few cases spacers 0.2 – 0.4 mm (0.008 – 0.016 in) thick were required to space out correctly the (older-pattern) cover plate when it was used in conjunction with the strengthened flywheel on assembly at the factory; as soon as the later-pattern cover plate became available spacers were no longer required. Therefore if spacers are found on any machine and the cover plate has not been renewed, the spacers must be refitted in their original positions on reassembly. If however the cover plate has been renewed it will automatically be of the later pattern and the spacers can be discarded.

11 Fit the cover plate, aligning its balancing mark as described in paragraph 6 above. Refit the six bolts and their lock washers (not forgetting the spacers, if fitted) and tighten them in a diagonal sequence by one turn at a time.

12 Before the bolts are fully tightened, the clutch plate must be centred, as described in paragraph 9 above. If the gearbox input shaft cannot be used, the tool for these models is BMW No. 21.2.660. This is similar to that described above but the dimensions given may be different for the later models and should be checked by measuring the diameter of the gearbox input shaft etc before a substitute is fabricated. When the clutch plate has been centred, tighten the bolts to a final torque setting of 20 – 22 Nm (15 – 16 lbf ft) and withdraw the tool (if used).

13 On all models, apply a smear of lubricant to the splines of the gearbox input shaft and the clutch plate centre before refitting the gearbox.

5.1 Flywheel and crankshaft mating surfaces and threaded holes must be completely clean and dry on reassembly

5.3a Rotate the crankshaft to exactly TDC and fit the flywheel so that ...

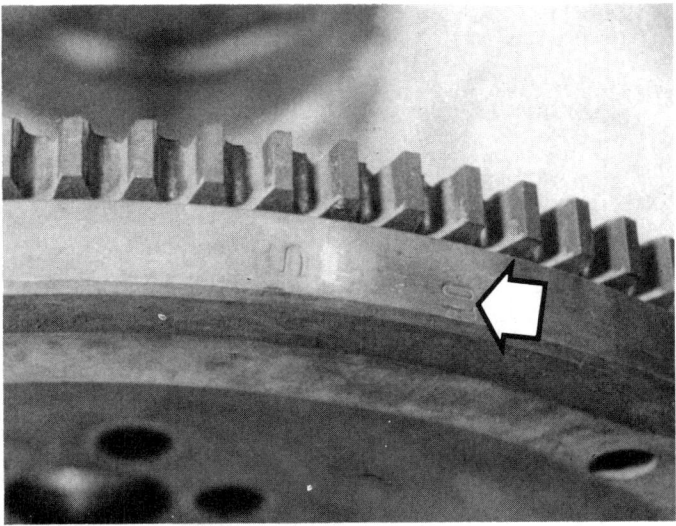

5.3b ... the OT mark (arrowed) aligns exactly with the crankcase notch – flywheel mounting bolt holes should then align exactly

5.6a Lubricate all points of contact before refitting diaphragm spring ...

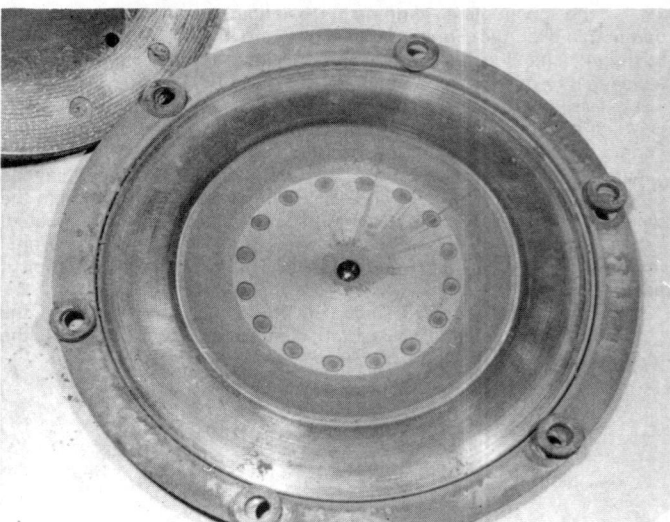

5.6b ... and pressure plate. Check balancing marks

5.8 Ensure clutch plate is fitted the correct way round. Spacers may be found on some /5 and some post-1981 models only (see text)

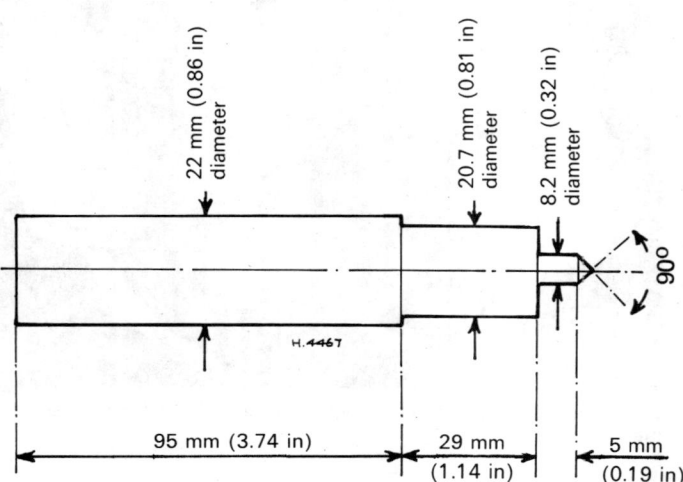

Fig. 2.5 Clutch plate centring tool – all models up to 1980

be straight, and the felt seal (where fitted) in good condition. Soak the felt in hot grease, and wrap it firmly round the pushrod. The rubber seal on the thrust piston must be undamaged.

5 If the thrust bearing or related components are worn or damaged they must be renewed. Thoroughly clean all components and pack with grease on reassembly. Check that the operating lever pivot bearing is in good condition; if wear or damage is found the lever (early models) or needle roller bearing and/or bush (later models) must be renewed.

6 Reassembly is the reverse of the dismantling sequence. If difficulty was experienced in removing the thrust components with the gearbox in the frame, they should be refitted while the gearbox is on the bench, but note that the operating lever must not be refitted until the gearbox is in place. Take care not to distort the lips of the thrust piston rubber seal (early models only) as it is refitted. Do not forget to grease all components as they are refitted. Adjust the clutch as described in Routine Maintenance.

6 Clutch operating mechanism: removal, examination and reassembly

1 Slacken the handlebar adjuster locknut, screw in the adjuster to gain the maximum cable free play and disconnect the cable from the operating lever on the gearbox.
2 The lever pivot pin is retained by a split-pin on /5 models or by a circlip on all other models up to 1980, straighten the split-pin and pull it out or remove the circlip (as applicable), then tap out the pivot pin and withdraw the lever and coil spring. On all models from 1981 on unscrew the retaining nut, pull out the pivot bolt and remove the lever noting the pivot bush.
3 Slackening its clamp (1981 on models only) withdraw the rubber sleeve and remove the thrust components. The pushrod cannot be removed from the gearbox input shaft until the gearbox has been removed from the frame. See Chapter 3.
4 Check all parts of the clutch operating linkage. The pushrod must

6.2 Remove pivot pin or bolt and withdraw clutch operating lever from gearbox rear cover

6.5 Check components for wear, renew if necessary and pack with grease on refitting

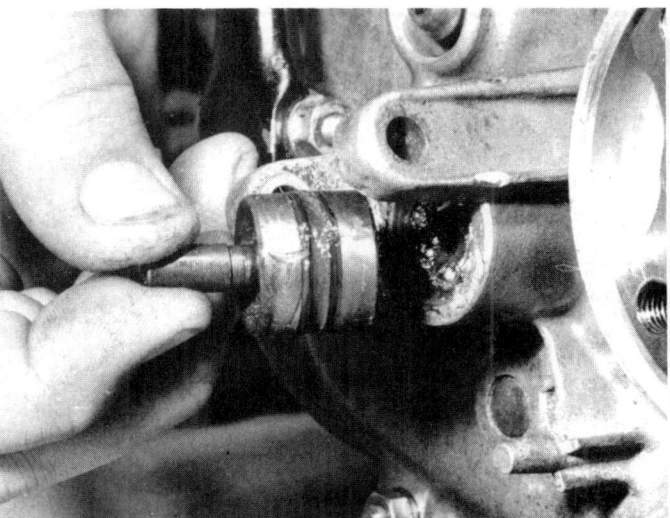

6.6 Early models only – do not distort lips of thrust piston seal on refitting

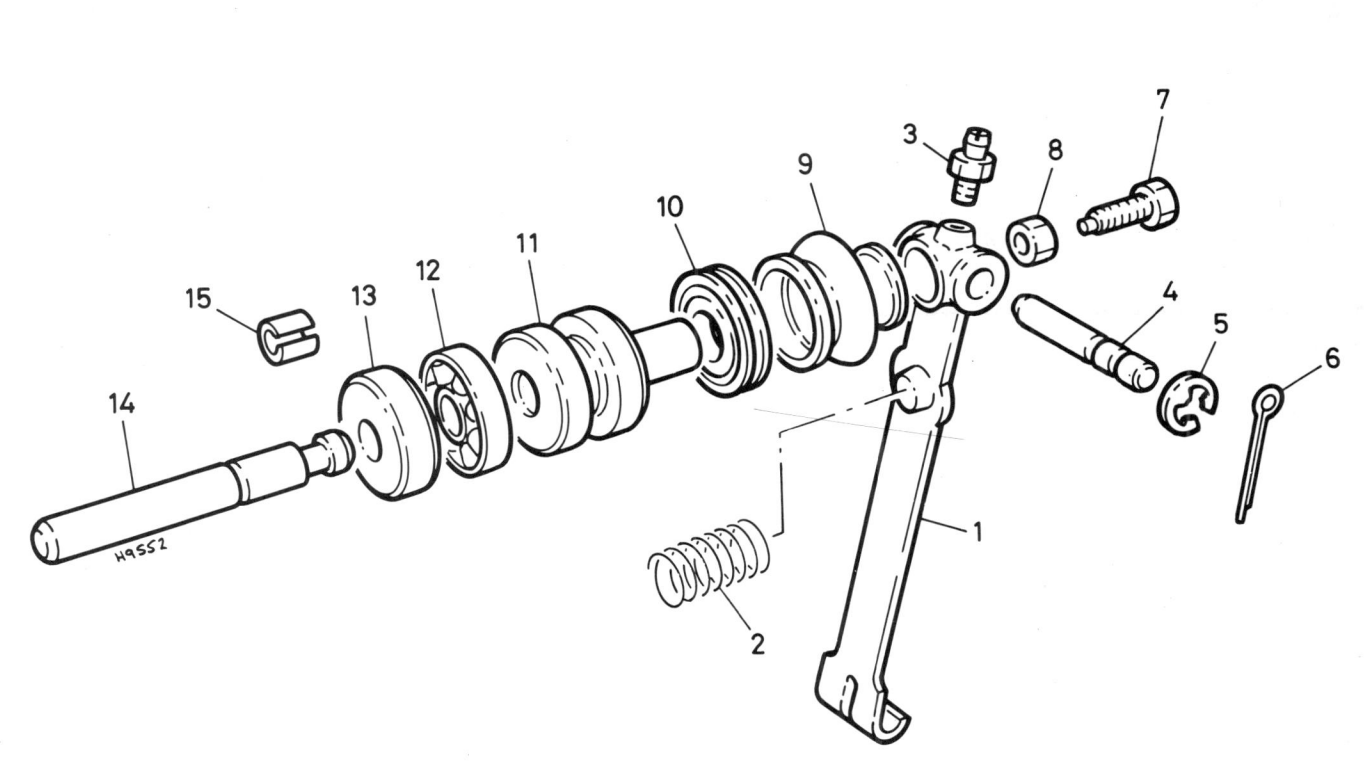

Fig. 2.6 Clutch operating mechanism – up to 1980 models

1 Clutch lever
2 Spring
3 Grease nipple
4 Pivot pin
5 Circlip – /6, /7, R45/65 models
6 Split pin – /5 models only
7 Adjuster bolt
8 Locknut
9 Sleeve
10 Sealing ring
11 Piston
12 Thrust bearing
13 Thrust washer
14 Pushrod
15 Felt ring

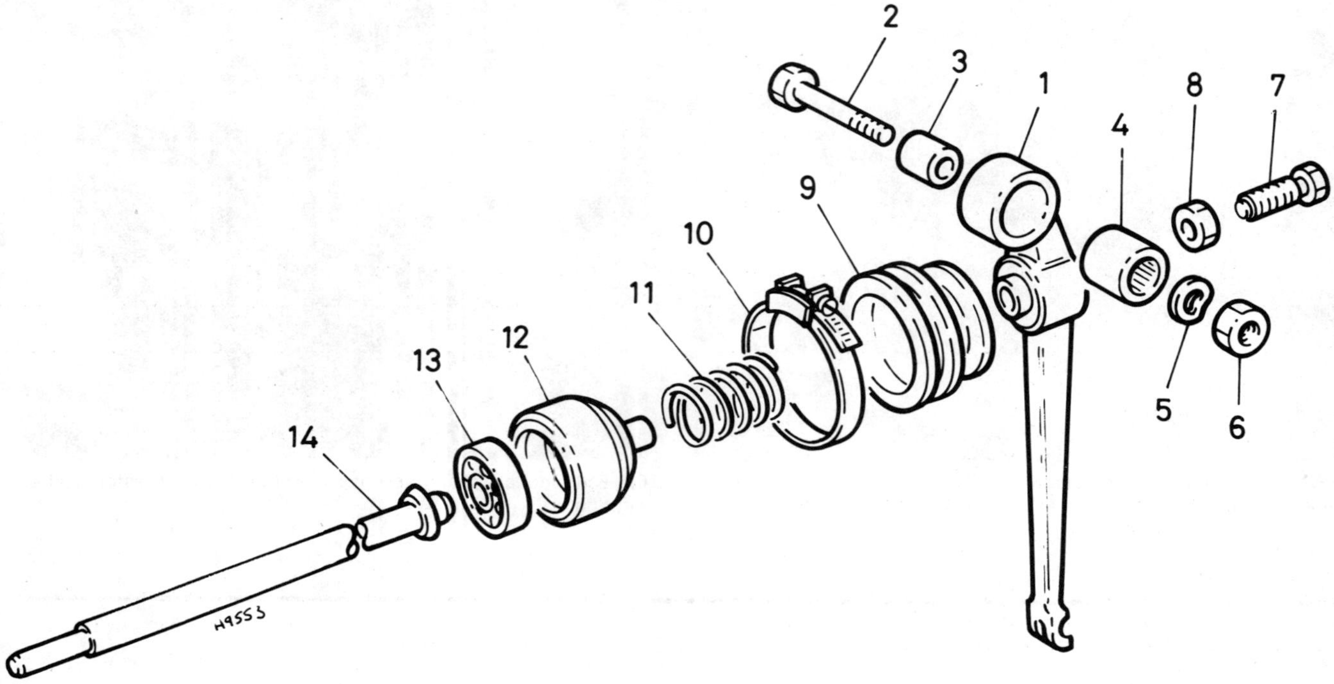

Fig. 2.7 Clutch operating mechanism – 1981 on models

1 Clutch lever
2 Pivot bolt
3 Bush
4 Needle bearing
5 Spring washer
6 Nut
7 Adjuster bolt
8 Locknut
9 Sleeve
10 Clip
11 Spring
12 Piston
13 Thrust bearing
14 Pushrod

Chapter 3 Gearbox

Refer to Chapter 10 for subsequent modifications and information relating to the 1986 on models

Contents

General description 1	Four speed gearbox gearchange mechanism: removal, examination and reassembly 10
Removing the gearbox from the frame 2	Five speed gearbox selector mechanism: dismantling, examination and reassembly 11
Dismantling the gearbox: removing the end cover 3	Four speed gearbox kickstart: removal, examination and reassembly 12
Dismantling the gearbox: removing the gear shafts and selector forks – four speed gearbox 4	Five speed gearbox kickstart: removal, examination and reassembly 13
Dismantling the gearbox: removing the gear shafts and selector forks – five speed gearbox 5	Neutral warning lamp switches: removal 14
Dismantling the gearbox: removing and replacing the end cover bearings and seals 6	Four speed gearbox: adjusting the selector forks and reassembly 15
Dismantling the gearbox: dismantling and reassembling the gear assemblies – four speed gearbox 7	Five speed gearbox: reassembly 16
Dismantling the gearbox: dismantling and reassembling the gear assemblies – five speed gearbox 8	Refitting the gearbox in the frame 17
Bearings, seals, gears and selector forks: examination and renovation 9	

Specifications

Gearbox

Type	All indirect, three shaft with gears in constant mesh	
Reduction ratios:	**/5**	**All other models**
1st	3.896:1	4.400:1
2nd	2.578:1	2.860:1
3rd	1.875:1	2.070:1
4th	1.500:1	1.670:1
5th	N/App	1.500:1
Axial float – all gear shafts	0 – 0.1 mm (0 – 0.0039 in)	
Axial float – gearchange lever shaft	0.1 mm (0.0039 in)	
Output shaft/bush clearance:		
1st gear – all models	0.005 – 0.035 mm (0.0002 – 0.0014 in)	
2nd gear – except /5	0.005 – 0.035 mm (0.0002 – 0.0014 in)	
4th gear – /5	0.005 – 0.047 mm (0.0002 – 0.0019 in)	
Axial play of free-running gear pinions – except /5	0.15 – 0.30 mm (0.0059 – 0.0118 in)	
Running clearance of gear pinions on output shaft bushes – /5 only:		
1st and 4th gear	0.040 – 0.082 mm (0.0016 – 0.0032 in)	
2nd and 3rd gear	0.025 – 0.075 mm (0.0010 – 0.0030 in)	
Output flange radial play	± 0.05 mm (0.0020 in)	
Output flange face runout	± 0.05 mm (0.0020 in)	
Clearance between ratchet/pawl and selector points on cam selector plate – all gears	0.5 mm (0.020 in) approx	

Gearbox bearings

	/5	**All other models**
Input shaft front	6304 C3 20 mm x 52 mm x 15 mm	N/Av
Input shaft rear	6304 C3 20 mm x 52 mm x 15 mm	N/Av
Layshaft front	3203 C3 17 mm x 40 mm x 17.5 mm	N/Av
Layshaft rear	6203 C3 17 mm x 40 mm x 12 mm	N/Av
Output shaft front	6403 C3 17 mm x 62 mm x 17 mm	As /5 model
Output shaft rear	6204 C3 20 mm x 47 mm x 14 mm	N/Av

Lubrication

Capacity	800cc (1.41 Imp pint, 0.85 US qt)
Recommended oil	Good quality hypoid gear oil API class GL-5 or to specification MIL-L-2105 B or C
Viscosity:	
Above 5°C (41°F)	SAE 90
Below 5°C (41°F)	SAE 80
All temperatures	SAE 80W90

Chapter 3 Gearbox

Torque wrench settings

Component	Nm	lbf ft
Gearbox/engine retaining nuts or bolts:		
All models up to 1980	20 – 24	15 – 18
All models 1981 on	33	24
Tie-rod arm stop bolts	17 – 19	12.5 – 14
Selector fork/cam bracket mounting bolts:		
All models up to 1980	23 – 25	17 – 18.5
All models 1981 on	19	14
Output flange retaining nut:		
/5, /6	220 – 240	162 – 177
/7 up to 1980, R45 and R65 up to 1980	200 – 220	148 – 162
All models 1981 on	221.5	163.5
Gearbox cover/case retaining nuts or bolts	7 – 9	5 – 6.5
Kickstart pedal cotter pin retaining nut	20 – 23	15 – 17
Gearbox oil filler plug	28 – 31	21 – 23
Gearbox oil drain plug	23 – 26	17 – 19

1 General description

The BMW four or five speed gearbox, with positive stop footchange, is bolted directly to the rear of the engine casing – making a completely integrated unit.

It differs from general motorcycle practice in being all-indirect, having three shafts. All the shafts are supported at both ends in ball or roller journal bearings.

The input shaft, which is splined to take the drive from the clutch, carries the helical drive gear with cam-type shock absorber (and the kickstart gear on /5 models). The layshaft and output shafts each have four (/5) or five (all other models) gears in constant mesh. The flange

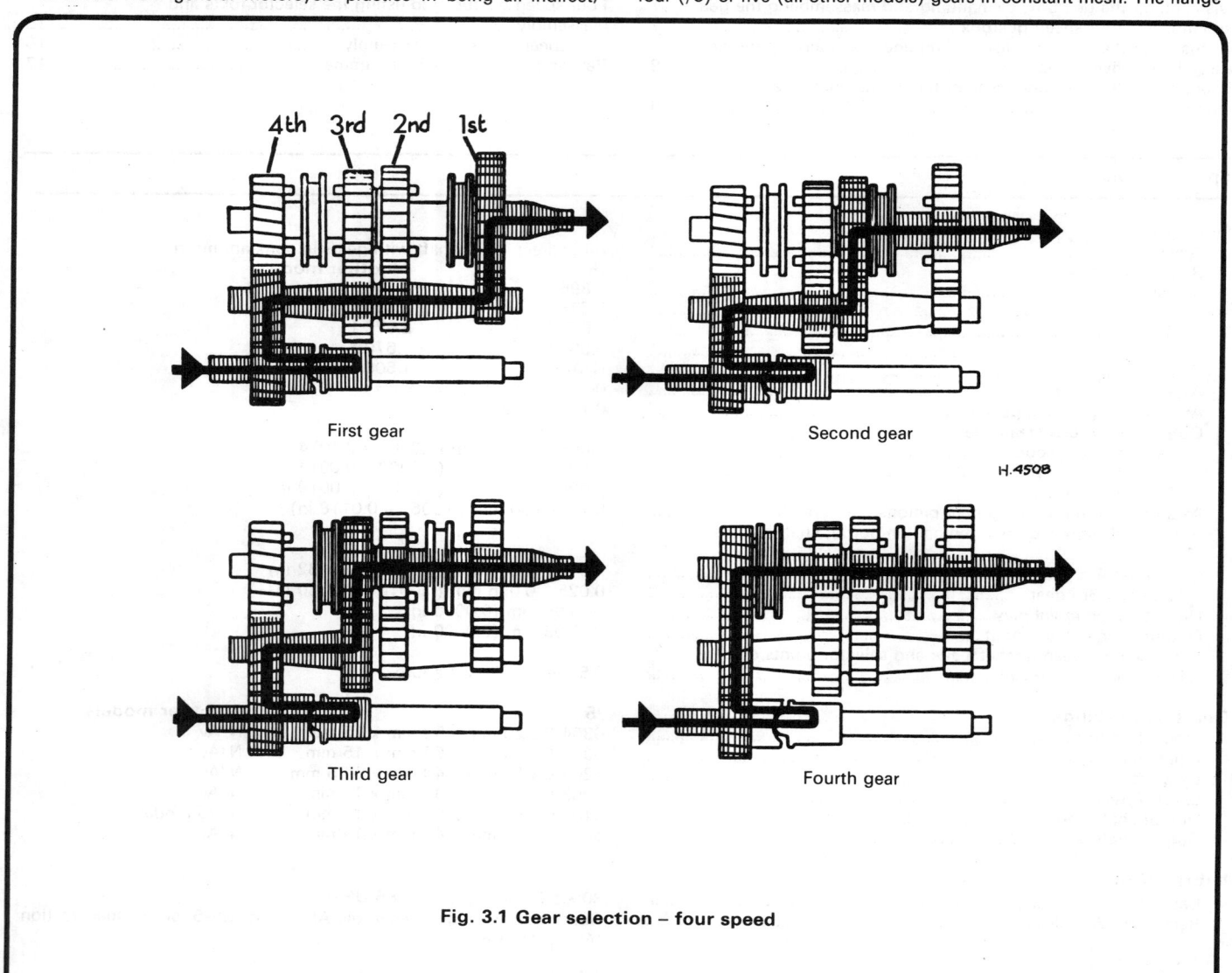

Fig. 3.1 Gear selection – four speed

Chapter 3 Gearbox

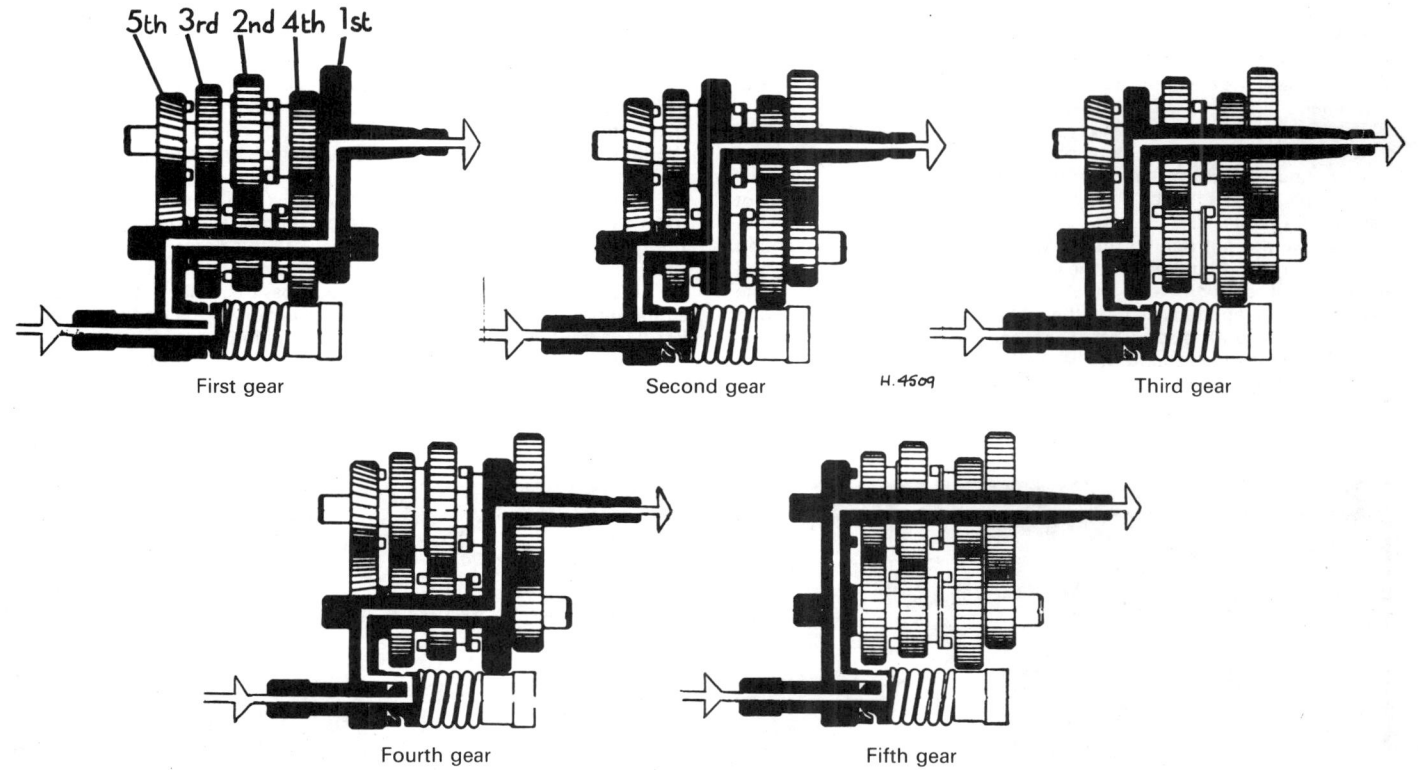

Fig. 3.2 Gear selection – five speed

for the rear drive hook joint is bolted to the end of the output shaft. The speedometer drive is also taken from the output shaft.

Gearchanging on /5 models is accomplished by two selector forks, which move two sliding dogs along the output shaft. The sliding dogs are splined on the shaft, and engage with corresponding dogs on the adjacent free-running pinions, thus coupling them to the shaft. The selector forks engage in turn with slots in the selector cam plate. This is rotated by the gear lever, via a ratchet gear. A spring loaded pawl locks the camplate in position when in gear. In neutral, a pin mounted on the camplate operates the neutral warning lamp.

The major difference between the four and five speed gearboxes, apart from the additional gear on the output and layshafts, is in the arrangement of the gearchange mechanism; and the kickstart which is optional on five speed boxes. The gear lever of the five speed gearboxes rotates two meshed camplates, via a hooked lever. The selector forks, which engage in slots in the camplates, slide gear pinions along the output and layshafts. These pinions are splined to their shafts, and have dogs which engage with corresponding dogs on the adjacent free pinions, thus coupling the free pinion to the shaft. The camplates are held positively when in gear, by a spring-loaded roller lever. The neutral warning light is operated from the camplate by a plunger switch.

Any work on the gearbox requires it to be removed from the machine. Do not dismantle more of the gearbox than is necessary to carry out the required work.

Early five speed gearboxes suffered problems with a bush in the gear selection mechanism, but this was corrected on later boxes, and the problems rectified on affected machines.

While the gearbox has remained the same in layout, many components have been altered to improve gear selection and great care is required when ordering replacement parts; most modifications can be fitted to earlier models.

The most significant change appeared in 1978, when all /7 models were fitted with an external pedal linkage pivoted from the footrest; this was successful enough to become standard equipment on nearly all other models as they were introduced, and is available, in kit form, for /5, /6, and earlier /7 models.

2 Removing the gearbox from the frame

1 Raise or remove the seat, remove the side panels and the fuel tank (see Chapter 4).
2 Where appropriate, remove the lower fairing sections on machines fitted with RS or RT fairings; it may be advisable to remove the complete fairing to minimise the risk of damage. See Chapter 6.
3 Remove all exhaust system components and the carburettors. See Chapter 4.
4 Remove the air filter element as described in Routine Maintenance. On early models (UK up to 1980, US up to 1979) disconnect the choke cables and remove the left-hand filter cover, slacken the retaining strip mounting nuts and withdraw the right-hand filter cover.

On later models disconnect the breather pipes and Pure Air System pipes (US models only), then remove the single nut and two bolts securing the filter bottom half to the gearbox.

5 If the gearbox is to be dismantled, drain the oil from it, as described in Routine Maintenance.

6 Unscrew the speedometer cable clamp screw, above the universal joint on the right of the gearbox housing and remove the battery earth lead. Withdraw the speedometer cable from the housing, together with its washer.

7 Remove the clutch operating mechanism. See Chapter 2.

8 Referring to Chapter 9, remove the battery and its carrier.

9 Disconnect the drive shaft from the gearbox, then remove the black plastic caps, slacken the locknuts and unscrew the swinging arm pivot shafts. See Chapter 7.

10 Unscrew the nut behind the brake pedal pivot, whilst preventing the pivot from rotating. Remove the wing nut on the rear brake rod, and take away the rod with pedal attached. Take out the trunnion from the brake cam lever, and replace it on the brake rod together with the wing nut. On models with disc rear brakes disconnect the brake rod at the pedal. Pull the wheel as far to the rear as possible and wedge it with a suitable block of wood placed between the tyre and the frame.

11 Where appropriate, pull back the rubber gaiter and disconnect the gearchange external linkage by removing the retaining circlip or clip at the front or rear joint. Remove the left-hand footrest and gearchange pedal.

12 Remove the engine front cover (see Chapter 1) then unscrew the engine mounting stud retaining nuts and tap out the studs. Wrap the frame tubes with suitable padding and use a jack or wooden block to take the engine's weight before the last stud is removed. If the studs are seized with corrosion, apply penetrating fluid and leave it to work before trying again. Note carefully the exact number and position of the fairing and/or exhaust pipe clamps, the stand spring anchorages and the spacers (where fitted).

13 Unscrew all gearbox/engine fasteners (two Allen screws on the left, another secured by a nut on the lower right, and a nut on the upper right) and pull the gearbox backwards until the clutch pushrod can be pushed back into the input shaft with a pair of pliers.

14 Lift the engine as far forwards as possible, check it is securely supported on the jack, then lift the gearbox on to the padding on the left-hand frame tube. Disconnect the neutral indicator switch lead and pull the gearbox carefully out to the left. Remove the clutch pushrod and any remaining thrust components (see Chapter 2).

2.4a Early models – slacken mounting nuts and bolts (arrowed) to release filter right-hand cover

2.4b Later models – disconnect breather pipes and remove filter bottom half

2.11 Disconnect gearchange external linkage (where fitted)

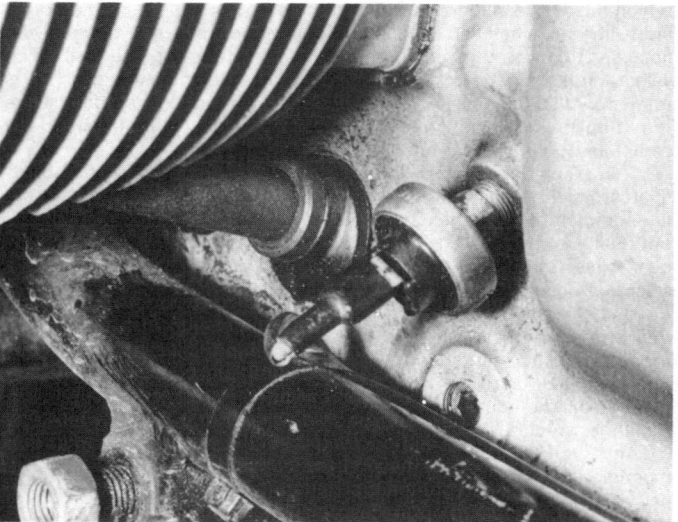

2.12a Remove engine mounting nuts and tap out mounting studs noting ...

2.12b ... the positions of the left-hand ...

2.12c ... and right-hand spring anchorages and any spacers fitted

2.13 Note positions of brackets and spacers under gearbox mounting bolts (where fitted)

2.14a Pull the gearbox to the rear and push clutch pushrod into input shaft ...

2.14b ... then disconnect the neutral warning lamp lead ...

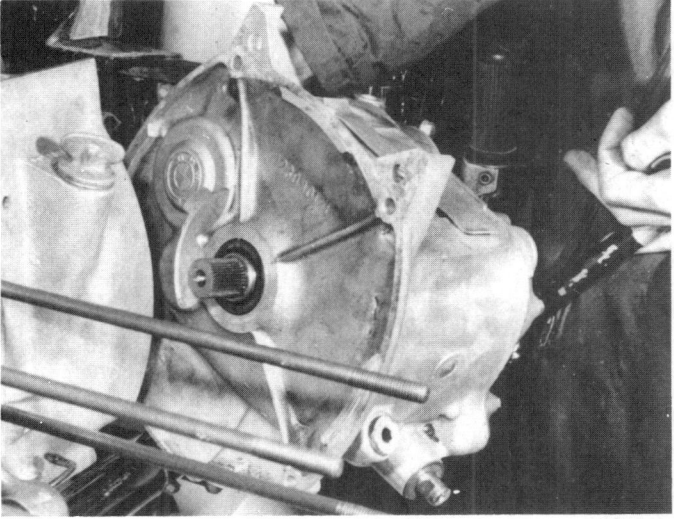

2.14c ... and remove the gearbox to the left

3 Dismantling the gearbox: removing the end cover

1 If this has not already been done, remove the clutch operating mechanism components from the end cover and withdraw the pushrod from the input shaft.
2 Remove the speedometer cable clamp screw completely. Lever out the speedometer gear bush with screwdrivers under the collar and withdraw the helical gear.
3 Hold the output flange with a suitable lever. Unscrew the centre nut and remove together with the spring washer. This nut is very tight, and requires considerable leverage to loosen.
4 Bolt a suitable plate to the output flange and draw the flange from its taper with an extractor. If necessary, release the taper with gentle knocks on the extractor screw.
5 Remove the nuts or bolts and washers which retain the gearbox end cover. There are seven nuts on four speed gearboxes and nine bolts on the five speed.
6 Heat the end cover to 80° – 100°C, (176° – 212°F); depress the kickstart (if fitted) slightly, and pull off the cover. The output and layshaft bearings of four speed boxes and all three bearings of five speed boxes, will remain on their shafts. It may be necessary to tap the output shaft gently with a soft hammer. Discard the gasket; it should not be refitted.
7 Remove the shims from inside the output and layshaft bearing housings and put aside in a safe place.

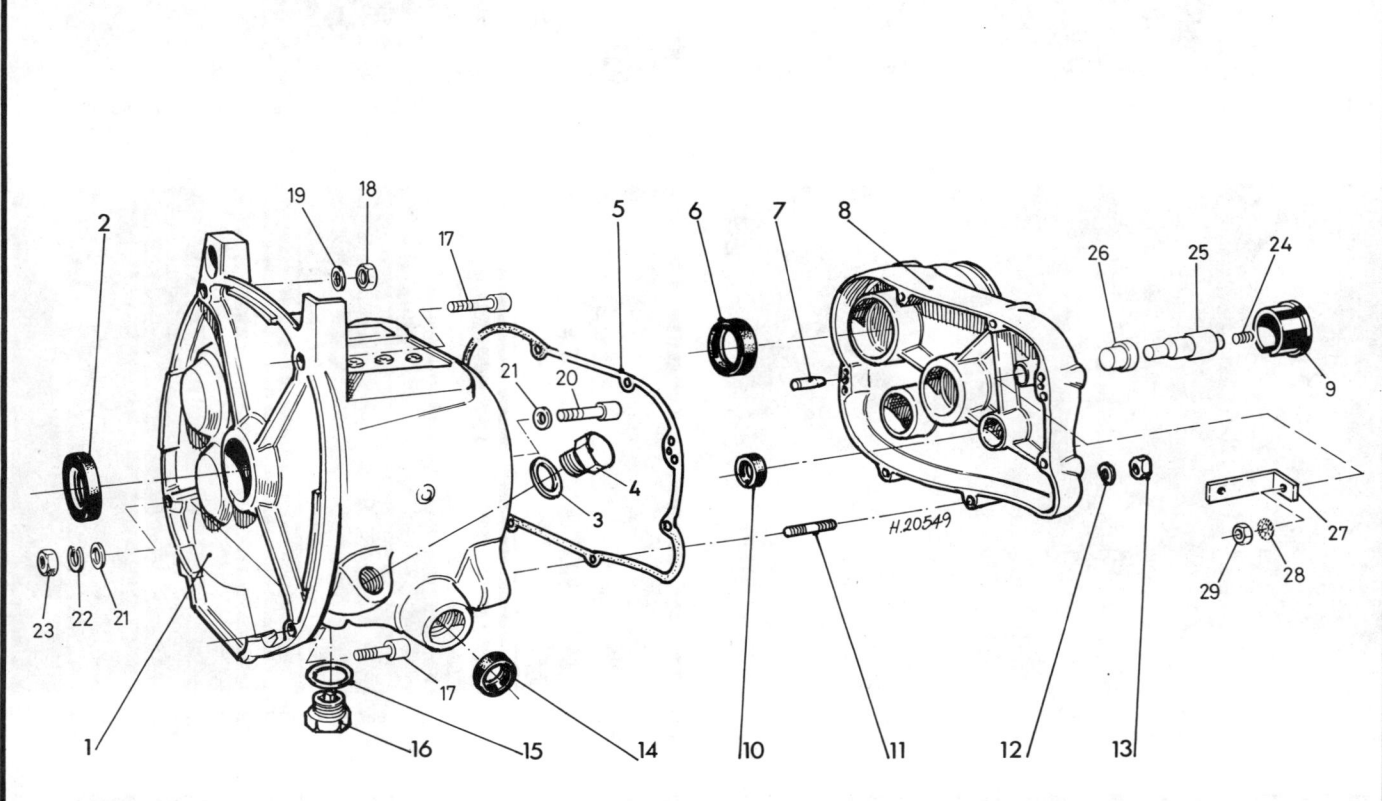

Fig. 3.3 Gearbox housing – four speed

1 Gearbox housing
2 Input shaft oil seal
3 Gasket
4 Filler plug
5 End cover gasket
6 Output shaft oil seal
7 Dowel – 2 off
8 End cover
9 Neutral indicator switch cover
10 Kickstart shaft oil seal
11 Stud – 7 off
12 Lock washer – 7 off
13 Nut – 7 off
14 Gearchange shaft oil seal
15 Gasket
16 Drain plug
17 Bolt – 2 off
18 Nut
19 Washer
20 Bolt
21 Washer – 2 off
22 Lock washer – 4 off
23 Nut
24 Grub screw
25 Neutral switch
26 Bush
27 Switch contact
28 Lock washer
29 Nut

3.2a Lever out the speedometer gear bush ...

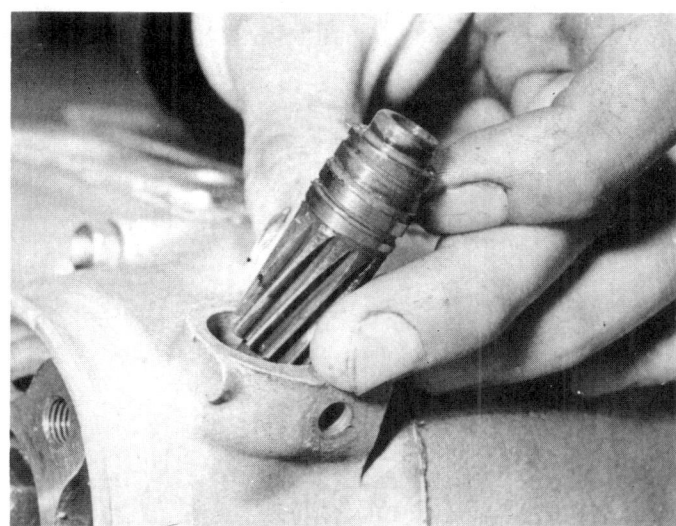

3.2b ... and remove the helical gear

3.3 Bolt a lever to the output flange to hold it while removing retaining nut

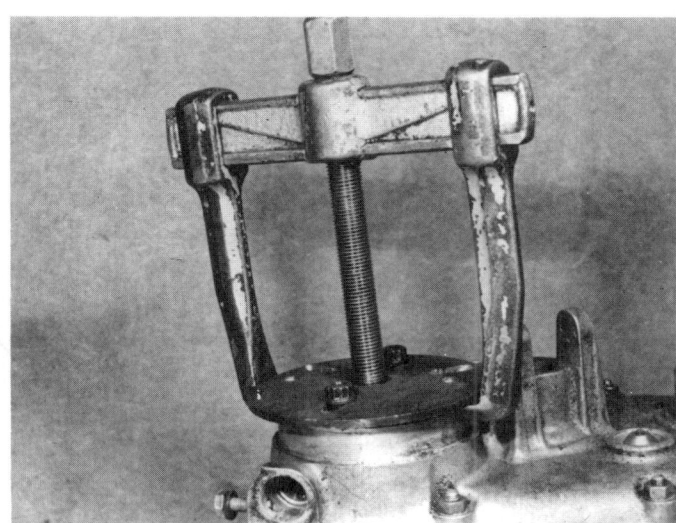

3.4 A suitable plate bolted to the output flange will provide purchase for an extractor

3.6 Depress kickstart (where fitted) slightly to remove gearbox end cover

3.7 Carefully note position and number of shims before removing – store with shafts

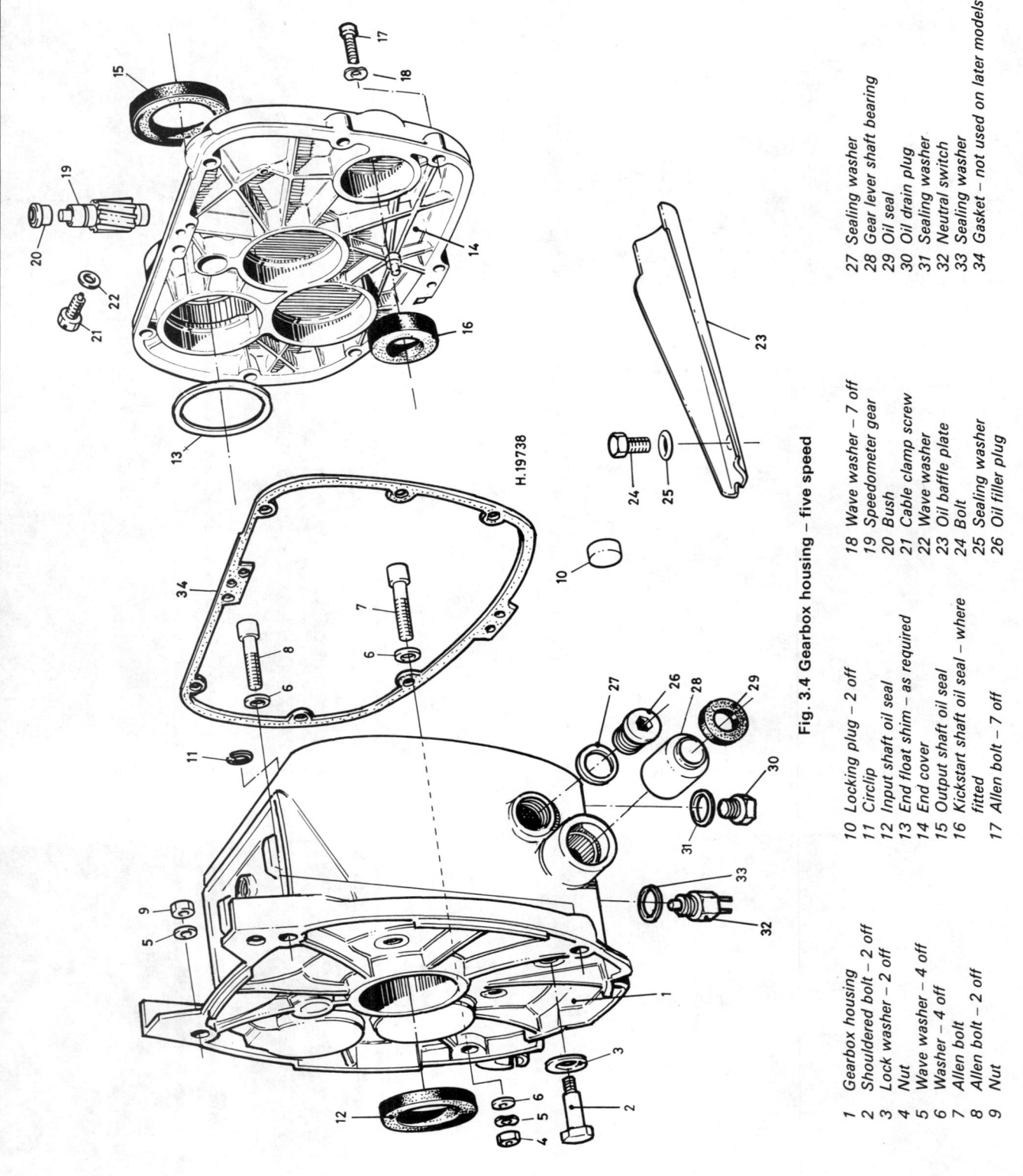

Fig. 3.4 Gearbox housing – five speed

1 Gearbox housing
2 Shouldered bolt – 2 off
3 Lock washer – 2 off
4 Nut
5 Wave washer – 4 off
6 Washer – 4 off
7 Allen bolt
8 Allen bolt – 2 off
9 Nut
10 Locking plug – 2 off
11 Circlip
12 Input shaft oil seal
13 End float shim – as required
14 End cover
15 Output shaft oil seal
16 Kickstart shaft oil seal – where fitted
17 Allen bolt – 7 off
18 Wave washer – 7 off
19 Speedometer gear
20 Bush
21 Cable clamp screw
22 Wave washer
23 Oil baffle plate
24 Bolt
25 Sealing washer
26 Oil filler plug
27 Sealing washer
28 Gear lever shaft bearing
29 Oil seal
30 Oil drain plug
31 Sealing washer
32 Neutral switch
33 Sealing washer
34 Gasket – not used on later models

4 Dismantling the gearbox: removing the gear shafts and selector forks – four speed gearbox

1 Mark each selector fork and eccentric adjuster to enable them to be replaced in the same position. Keep each fork and adjuster together.
2 Unscrew the two hexagon socket cap screws in the top of the gearbox, retaining the eccentric adjusters and remove with washers. Withdraw the plate between the selector forks and the gearbox housing.
3 Heat the clutch end of the gearbox housing to 80° – 100°C (176° – 212°F). Extract the output shaft, together with the layshaft and the selector forks from the housing.
4 While the housing is still warm, tap the input shaft out from the clutch end. Use a soft hammer and don't damage the splines. All bearings should remain on their respective shafts.
5 Invert the gearbox and allow the oil baffle to drop out of the output shaft bearing housing.

5 Dismantling the gearbox: removing the gear shafts and selector forks – five speed gearbox

1 Unscrew the hexagon socket cap screw in the centre of the gear lever, and remove the lever.
2 Unscrew the two shouldered bolts inside the clutch end of the gearbox. Tilt the selector cam bracket to disengage the forks from the cams and remove the bracket.
3 Heat the clutch end of the gearbox housing to 80° – 100°C (176° – 212°F), and gently tap out the input shaft from the clutch end, without damaging the splines. The bearing remains in the housing.
4 While the housing is still hot, withdraw the selector fork shaft that has two forks on it. Take out the two selector forks. This should be possible without removing the input shaft.
5 Unscrew the crosshead screw retaining the oil baffle plate and remove the plate.
6 Reheat the clutch end of the gearbox housing and extract the output and layshafts with the remaining selector fork. Both bearings remain on their shafts.

6 Dismantling the gearbox: removing and replacing the end cover bearings and seals

1 Note that output shaft oil seal faces outwards – ie, the open side (garter spring) is towards the output flange. Push the seal out carefully, if it is to be replaced later.
2 Lever the kickstart shaft oil seal carefully out of the cover, after removing the shaft.
3 On four speed gearboxes, tap out the input shaft flanged bush and dished shim from the input bearing, after removing the kickstart intermediate gear.
4 Heat the cover to 80° – 100°C (176° – 212°F), and tap out the bearing.
5 Avoid disturbing the neutral indicator contact on the end cover, since this requires re-setting with a jig (four speed gearbox).
6 On five speed gearboxes, all bearings remain on their shafts.
7 To refit the input shaft bearing, again heat the end cover. In addition the bearing may be chilled.
8 Replace the flanged bush and shim. The raised perimeter of the shim should face the bearing.
9 Refit the kickstart intermediate gear and circlip (the shoulder on the gear faces the cover).
10 Tap a new output shaft seal into place, correct way up. Note that on 1981 – 82 models the black seal should only be replaced by the later bluish-green item. Also press a new kickstart shaft seal into the cover.

4.1 Mark each selector fork and eccentric adjuster before removing – four speed gearbox

4.2 Remove the plate between the selector forks and housing

6.3 Four speed gearbox – tap out input shaft flanged bush and shim before removing bearing

6.10a Ensure that output shaft seal is of correct type and is fitted the right way round

6.10b Take care not to damage seal on installation

7 Dismantling the gearbox: dismantling and reassembling the gear assemblies – four speed gearbox

1 Lever the thrust washer off the input shaft and remove the coil spring and kickstart gear.
2 Compress the shock absorber spring in a vice and prise out the wire circlip underneath the kickstart ratchet.
3 Remove the kickstart ratchet, shock absorber spring, shock absorber cam and input gear pinion.
4 Check the clutch end bearing in position. If it is necessary to remove the bearing, push it off the shaft towards the kickstart gear end. Remove the oil retaining plate and spacer.
5 When reassembling the input shaft, compress the shock absorber spring to replace the wire circlip. If the circlip is distorted or loose, it should be renewed. Push on the thrust washer after the coil spring. The thrust washer must be tight enough on the shaft to retain the compressed spring. If it does not do so, it must be renewed.

6 Extract the first gear with bearing from the output shaft (this is the gear at the tapered output flange end). There is a thrust washer between the bearing and the gear.
7 Take off the first gear floating bush and the second thrust washer and sliding dog.
8 Remove the external circlip, followed by the splined washer and the second and third gears.
9 Remove the external circlip from the other end of the shaft. Extract the helical fourth gear and bearing. There is a thrust washer between the gear and the bearing and between the gear and the sliding dog. Remove the floating bush, sliding dog and thrust washers.
10 If the central bush on the shaft is worn or damaged, the complete shaft must be renewed.
11 Assemble in reverse order. The third gear is the smaller of the two gears with dogs. Replace all washers and bushes in the same places.
12 The layshaft is a complete forged item and cannot be split. If, after cleaning, the bearings are found to require removal for replacement, draw them from the shaft with an extractor.

7.1 Lever the thrust washer off the input shaft rear end to release coil spring and kickstart gear

7.2 Shock absorber spring must be compressed safely to allow retaining circlip to be removed

7.6a Apply extractor to output shaft 1st gear pinion to remove shaft rear bearing ...

7.6b ... noting presence of thrust washer between bearing and gear

7.7a Remove 1st gear pinion, followed by floating bush and second thrust washer ...

7.7b ... then remove sliding dog

7.8a Remove circlip and splined washer, then ...

7.8b ... withdraw the 2nd gear pinion ...

7.8c ... followed by the 3rd gear pinion

7.9a Remove circlip from output shaft front end, then ...

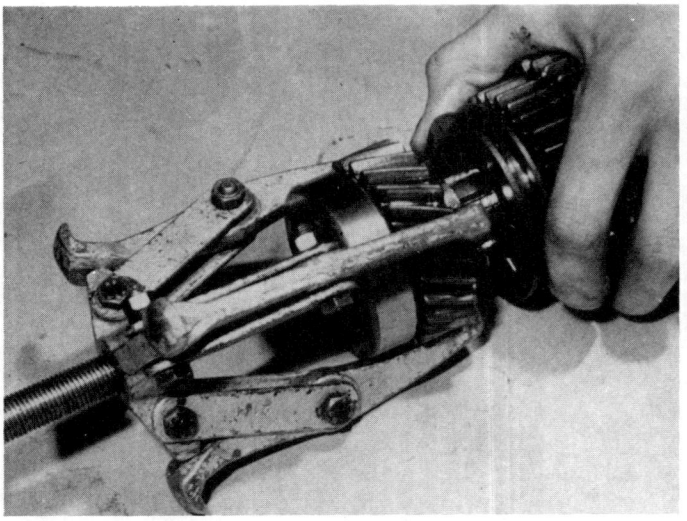

7.9b ... apply extractor to 4th gear pinion to remove front bearing ...

7.9c ... noting the thrust washer between bearing and gear

7.9d Remove 4th gear pinion, followed by floating bush, second thrust washer ...

7.9e ... and the sliding dog

Chapter 3 Gearbox

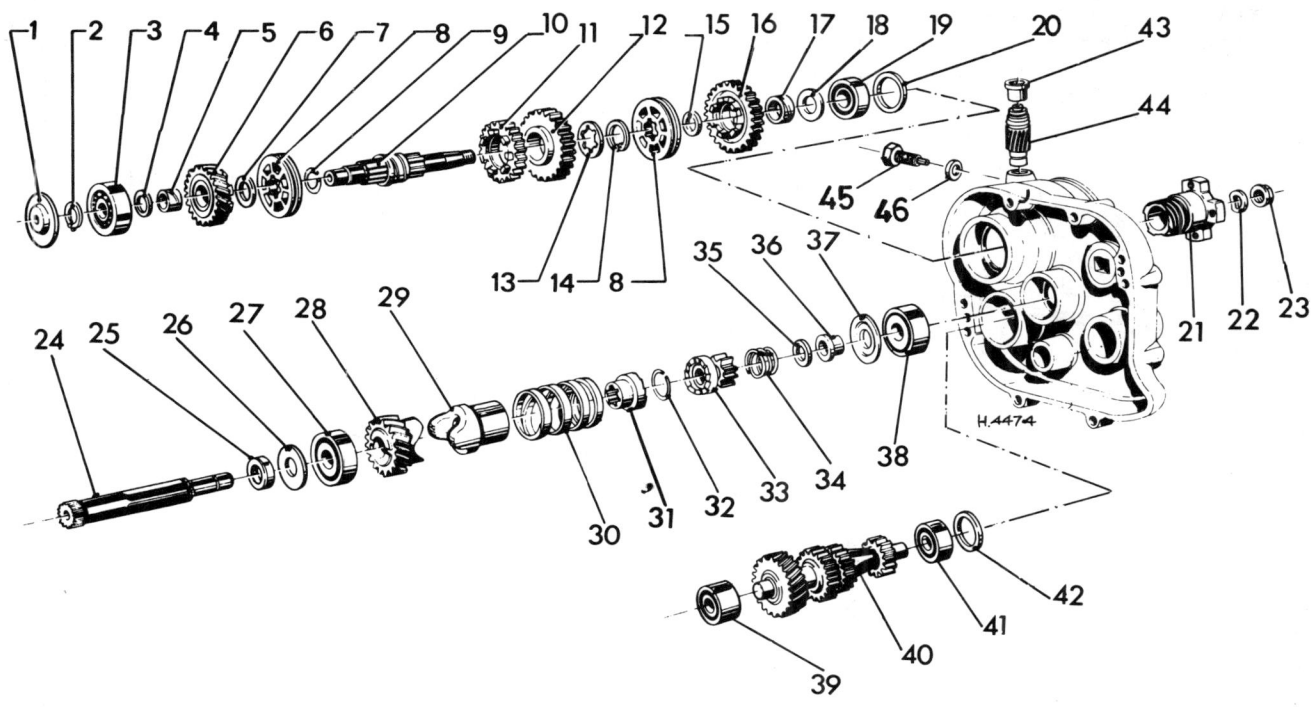

Fig. 3.5 Gear assemblies – four speed

1 Oil baffle
2 Circlip
3 Ball journal bearing
4 Thrust washer
5 Fourth gear floating bush
6 Fourth gear
7 Thrust washer
8 Sliding dog
9 Wire circlip
10 Output shaft
11 Third gear
12 Second gear
13 Splined washer
14 Circlip
15 Thrust washer
16 First gear
17 First gear floating bush
18 Thrust washer
19 Ball journal bearing
20 End float shim – as required
21 Output flange
22 Lock washer
23 Shouldered nut
24 Input shaft
25 Spacer
26 Oil retaining plate
27 Ball journal bearing
28 Input gear pinion
29 Shock absorber cam
30 Shock absorber spring
31 Kickstart ratchet
32 Wire circlip
33 Kickstart gear
34 Kickstart ratchet spring
35 Thrust washer
36 Flanged bush
37 Dished shim
38 Ball journal bearing
39 Double row ball journal bearing
40 Layshaft
41 Ball journal bearing
42 End float shim – as required
43 Speedo gear bush
44 Speedo gear
45 Speedo cable clamp screw
46 Lock washer

8 Dismantling the gearbox: dismantling and reassembling the gear assemblies – five speed gearbox

1 Pull off the input shaft rear bearing with an extractor and remove the dished shim.
2 Compress the shock absorber spring in a vice and remove the circlip retaining the kickstart gear or spring seat. Remove the gear, shock absorber spring, shock absorber cam and helical pinion.
3 Pull the first gear wheel and bearing off the output shaft, together (at taper end of shaft). There is a thrust washer between the gear and the bearing. Remove the first gear bush, a further thrust washer and the fourth gear. Remove the circlip and the splined thrust washer, followed by the second gear.
4 Take off the circlips from the other end and pull off the helical fifth gear together with the bearing. Remove the thrust washer and the third gear. Take off the remaining circlip and splined thrust washer.
5 The central bush on the shaft cannot be removed; the complete shaft must be replaced if it is faulty.
6 If it is necessary to remove the layshaft bearings for replacement, they should be pulled off with a suitable extractor. The layshaft cannot be dismantled further.

9 Bearings, seals, gears and selector forks: examination and renovation

1 Wash the bearings thoroughly in a high flash point solvent. Do not pull bearings off their shafts if they can be cleaned and checked in place. Do not 'spin' a dry bearing. If any radial play is evident, or if the bearing feels rough when turned, it should be renewed. Examine the inner and outer raceways and the balls for damage.
2 Check garter seals, including gearchange and kickstart shaft seals, for scratches, damage, or relaxed springs. Note the moulded oil thrower ridges on the closed side of the seal. When replacing with new seals, ensure that the moulded arrow points in the direction of rotation of the shaft.
3 Examine each of the gear pinions to ensure there are no chipped, rounded or broken teeth and that the dogs on the ends of the pinions are not rounded. Worn dogs are a frequent cause of jumping out of gear; renewal of the pinions concerned is the only effective remedy. Check that the inner splines are in good condition and the pinions are not slack on the shafts. Bushed pinions require special attention in this respect, since wear will cause them to rock.
4 Check both the input and the output shafts for worn splines,

damaged threads and other points at which wear may occur, such as the extremities which pass through the bearings. If signs of binding or local overheating are evident, check both shafts for straightness.

5 Examine the selector forks to ensure they are not twisted or badly worn. Wear at the fork end will immediately be obvious; check the arm in conjunction with the groove with which it normally engages. Do not overlook the pin which engages with the camplate track; this is subject to wear.

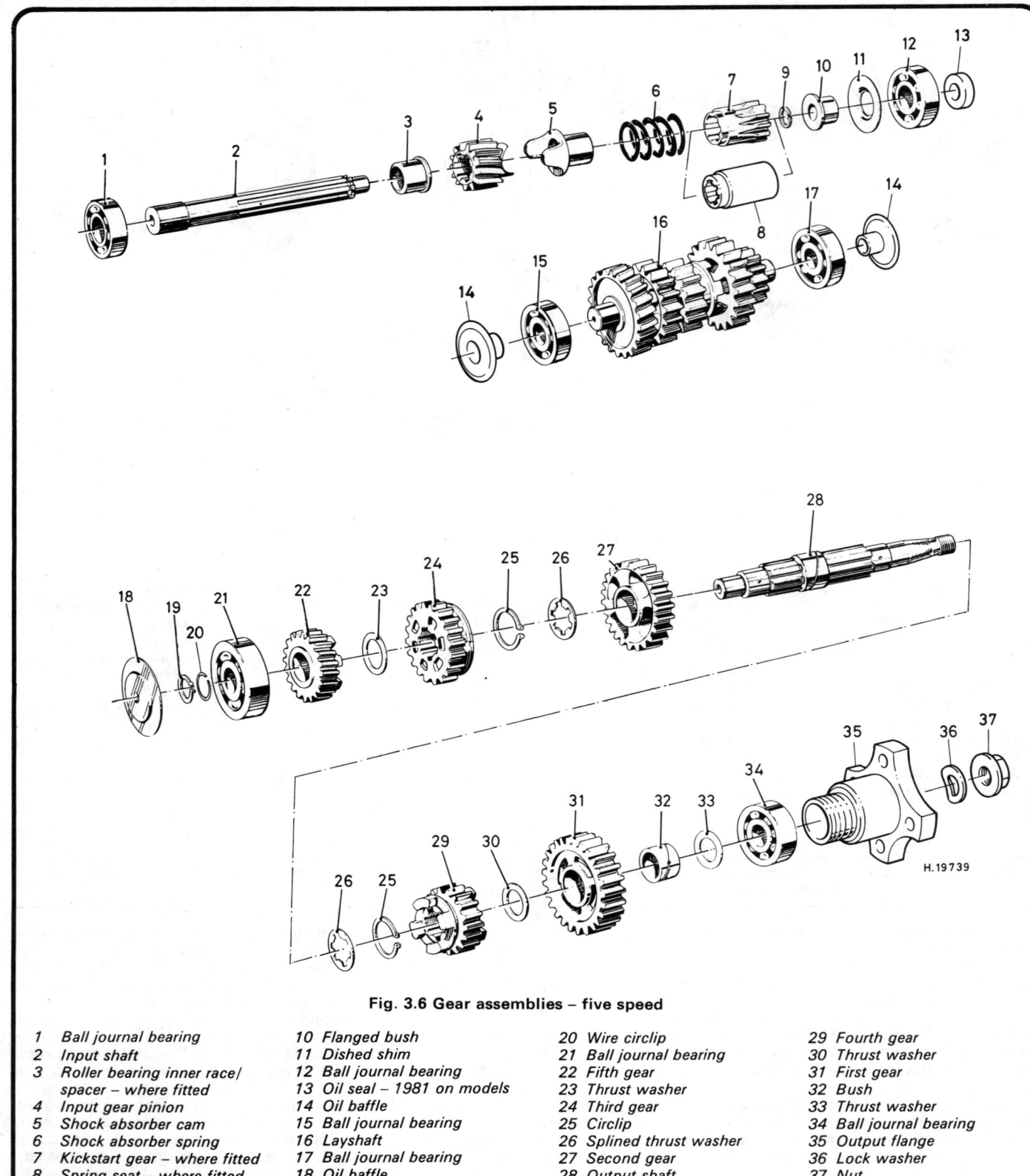

Fig. 3.6 Gear assemblies – five speed

1 Ball journal bearing
2 Input shaft
3 Roller bearing inner race/spacer – where fitted
4 Input gear pinion
5 Shock absorber cam
6 Shock absorber spring
7 Kickstart gear – where fitted
8 Spring seat – where fitted
9 Circlip
10 Flanged bush
11 Dished shim
12 Ball journal bearing
13 Oil seal – 1981 on models
14 Oil baffle
15 Ball journal bearing
16 Layshaft
17 Ball journal bearing
18 Oil baffle
19 Circlip
20 Wire circlip
21 Ball journal bearing
22 Fifth gear
23 Thrust washer
24 Third gear
25 Circlip
26 Splined thrust washer
27 Second gear
28 Output shaft
29 Fourth gear
30 Thrust washer
31 First gear
32 Bush
33 Thrust washer
34 Ball journal bearing
35 Output flange
36 Lock washer
37 Nut

Chapter 3 Gearbox

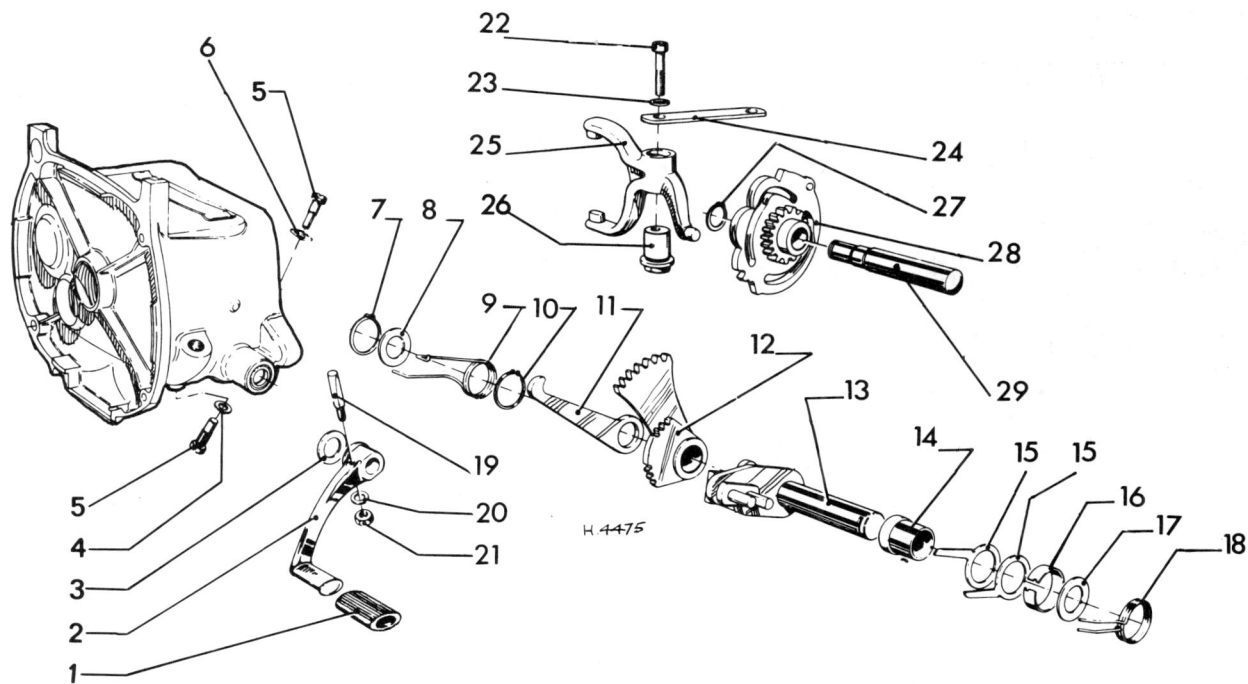

Fig. 3.7 Gear selection mechanism – four speed

1 Gearchange rubber
2 Gearchange lever
3 End float shim
4 Shim – as required
5 Limiting bolt
6 Tab washer
7 Circlip
8 Washer
9 Pawl spring
10 Circlip
11 Pawl
12 Gear selector quadrant
13 Gear lever shaft
14 Spacer sleeve
15 Detent fingers
16 Leaf spring
17 Shim
18 Return spring
19 Cotter
20 Washer
21 Nut
22 Allen screw – 2 off
23 Shim
24 Backing plate
25 Selector fork – 2 off
26 Eccentric adjuster – 2 off
27 Circlip
28 Selector camplate
29 Camplate spindle

10 Four speed gearbox gearchange mechanism: removal, examination and reassembly

1 The gear shafts and selector forks must first be removed, see Section 4.
2 Remove the external circlip on the camplate shaft, followed by the camplate.
3 Remove the external circlip of the pawl shaft, then the washer and pawl spring. Remove the second external circlip, the pawl and the selector quadrant.
4 After unscrewing the cotter nut, knock out the cotter pin with a soft hammer and pull the gearchange lever and shim off the shaft.
5 Withdraw the gearchange shaft from within the gearbox housing, complete with the selector assembly.
6 Check all parts of the gearchange mechanism for wear. The slots in the camplate may wear, especially where they change direction. The pawl and the notches in the camplate, the selector quadrant rack and pinion and the selector ratchet teeth and pawl, are all subject to wear. Remove any burrs. The springs, if unbroken, may be weakened. If the machine has covered a high mileage, it is advisable to renew them, to avoid a breakdown due to fracture. Worn gear selector parts will cause poor gear selection and possibly allow the gears to jump out of engagement.
7 The correct sequence for reassembling the selector mechanism is as follows: the shouldered sleeve slides over the shaft, with its shoulder abutting the selector lever (this has the two pegs on it). The two fingers, assembled inside the leaf spring slide onto the shouldered sleeve. The fingers are bent at one end and should bend away from the selector lever. Position the fingers one each side of the shorter peg. The spacer washer goes on next, followed by the return coil spring, with the ends bending towards the selector lever and one each side of the longer peg.
8 Insert the assembly into the gearbox housing, with the legs of the return spring on either side of the peg in the housing. Fit the gearchange lever with shim.
9 Check the endfloat of the gearchange shaft and adjust if necessary by using a shim of different thickness.
10 Fit the selector quadrant; the ratchet faces the selector lever. The teeth of the pawls on the selector lever must be equidistant from the first teeth on the selector ratchet. It may be necessary to bend the return spring legs to achieve this.
11 Fit the pawl and circlip and the pawl spring, washer and circlip.
12 When replacing the camplate, the second tooth from the top of the selector quadrant rack must engage with the marked tooth on the camplate pinion.
13 The clearance between the selector cam and the pawl, when the selector lever is against its limit stop in second to fourth gears, should be approximately 2 mm (0.080 inches) in both directions (dimension x, see Fig. 3.8). If necessary, adjust the respective limit stop by fitting different shims. The upper stop has a tab washer, which should be replaced if it is removed.
14 Note that in neutral position, the warning light contact is at two o'clock with the end cover joint horizontal.

10.2 Remove circlips to release camplate and selector components – camplate shown in neutral position

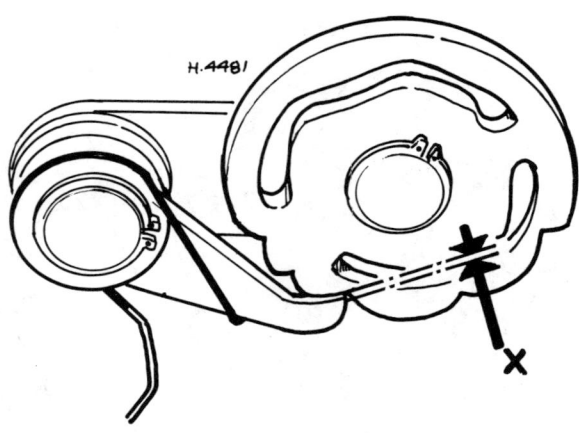

Fig. 3.8 Clearance between selector cam and pawl (Sec 10)

11 Five speed gearbox selector mechanism: dismantling, examination and reassembly

1 The selector bracket has to be removed first, as described in Section 5.2 of this Chapter.
2 Remove the two circlips from the camplate spindles. Pull off both camplates.
3 Remove the circlip on the selector lever shaft and pull out the shaft with selector pawl and spring.
4 The camplate indexing lever with the roller follower is also retained with a circlip.
5 Check all parts of the gearchange mechanism for wear, particularly the camplate slots where they change direction. Check the selector pawl and engaging pins and the gear teeth on the camplates.
6 Make sure that the selector lever spring, selector pawl spring and indexing lever spring are sound. It is advisable to renew these if the machine has covered a high mileage, while the gearbox is stripped.
7 Make sure the nylon roller on the indexing lever is in good condition.
8 When replacing the selector lever return spring, the two legs of the spring must be on either side of the peg in the selector bracket.
9 The selector camplates must be positioned with the first teeth of the gears in mesh.

12 Four speed gearbox kickstart: removal, examination and reassembly

1 Remove the kickstart intermediate gear retaining circlip and pull the gear off its shaft. Note the shoulder on the gear faces the cover.
2 Unscrew the kickstart lever cotter nut and knock out the cotter with a soft hammer. Do not damage the threads, or the cotter will have to be replaced. Pull the kickstart lever off the shaft.
3 Ensure that the kickstart shaft is not burred by the cotter pin and dress with a fine flat file if necessary. Push the shaft, with ratchet and spring, out of the housing.
4 Hold the kickstart shaft in a vice with soft jaws and remove the return spring end from the hole in the shaft, using pliers.
5 If the gearbox is stripped and has done a high mileage, it is advisable to renew the spring, to avoid breakdown.
6 When replacing a spring, wind it up clockwise until the end can be inserted in the hole in the shaft.

7 Check the kickstart ratchet teeth on the input shaft for wear. If the teeth are badly worn, the kickstart could slip, with painful results! The ratchet spring should also be renewed after a high mileage. It is unlikely that either the kickstart ratchet or intermediate pinion will require renewal.
8 When replacing the quadrant and shaft in the end cover, insert the end of the spring in the cover, using pliers.

13 Five speed gearbox kickstart: removal, examination and reassembly

1 The kickstart on five speed gearboxes is fitted as an optional extra only except on R80G/S models.
2 Remove the circlip retaining the intermediate gear assembly to the kickstart shaft, and take off the assembly with the washer.
3 Unscrew the kickstart lever cotter nut and knock out the cotter. Try not to damage the threads. Pull off the kickstart lever.
4 Make sure that the cotter has not damaged the kickstart shaft. Remove any burrs with a fine flat file. Pull out the kickstart shaft from the end cover with the dished washer and return spring.
5 Inspect the gear teeth, including the one on the input shaft. Renew the return spring if necessary.

14 Neutral warning lamp switches: removal

1 The neutral warning lamp switch on four speed gearboxes is in the end cover. It consists of a contact on the camplate, making contact with a blade on the end cover.
2 Do not remove the end cover contact unnecessarily, as it requires a jig to re-set it. If it is removed, the insulating bush and centre bolt in the end cover should be replaced using sealing compound.
3 If the remainder of the electrical circuit is in good order, but the lamp does not light when the gearbox is in neutral, the blade contact may be bent to complete continuity. This requires removal of the end cover.
4 The neutral warning light switch on five speed gearboxes is a sealed unit screwed into the bottom of the gearbox. To renew the switch, drain the gearbox oil, remove the engine rear mounting stud and nuts, tap out the crankcase central spacer, then disconnect its wires and unscrew the switch; fit a new sealing washer on reassembly.

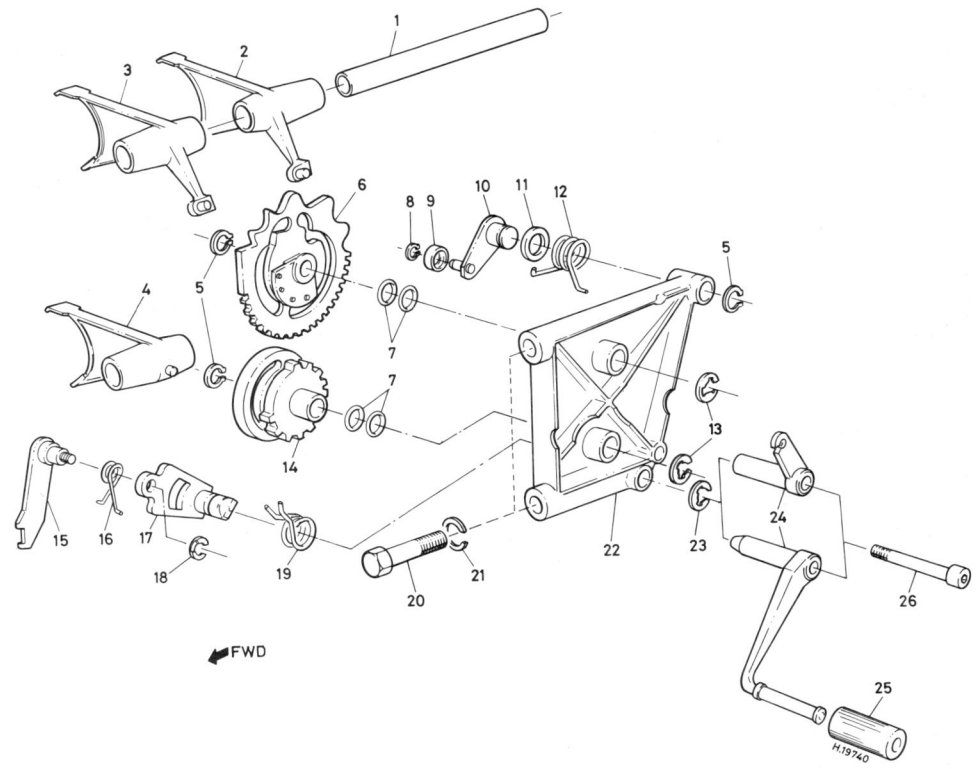

Fig. 3.9 Gear selection mechanism – five speed

1 Selector fork shaft
2 Selector fork – first and second gears
3 Selector fork – fifth gear
4 Selector fork – third and fourth gears
5 Circlip
6 Selector camplate – output shaft
7 O-rings – early/6 models only
8 Circlip
9 Roller
10 Camplate indexing lever
11 Shim
12 Spring
13 Circlip
14 Selector camplate – layshaft
15 Selector pawl
16 Spring
17 Selector lever
18 Circlip
19 Spring
20 Shouldered bolt – 2 off
21 Lock washer – 2 off
22 Selector cam bracket
23 Circlip
24 Gear lever/linkage front arm – as fitted
25 Rubber
26 Allen screw

12.1 Remove circlip to release kickstart intermediate gear

12.8 Kickstart return spring outer end should engage in cover as shown

15 Four speed gearbox: adjusting the selector forks and reassembly

1 If the selector forks require adjustment due to new parts being fitted, or to check the setting, this must be done before the input shaft is replaced.
2 Heat the gearbox housing to 80° – 100°C (176° – 212°F), and fit the output shaft and layshaft, with the selector forks engaged in the sliding dogs. The forks must be replaced in the same position. Engage the selector fork pins in the camplate.
3 Replace the plate between the forks and the housing and the eccentric adjusters in their respective forks. Align the marks previously made, and tighten the hexagon socket cap screws. When tightening the lower fork screw, engage second gear.
4 Now put the gears into neutral. Check that the sliding dogs are midway between the gears with the aid of a mirror. Adjust if necessary by turning the eccentric adjuster.
5 Also check that when a gear is engaged, the sliding dogs engage the full length of the dogs on the gears, but do not touch the gears. Arrive at an optimum setting for both of the above.
6 Mark the selector forks and eccentric adjusters clearly and remove the gear assemblies. The gearbox may now be reassembled.
7 Reheat the gearbox housing. With a suitable tube that will pass over the shaft to locate on the input gear, tap the input shaft into the housing. Do not tap the end of the shaft, as the bearing may not seat properly.
8 Drop the output shaft oil baffle into the housing, raised centre section downwards. Fit the output and layshafts, together with the selector forks, into the housing. Take care to avoid damaging the selector forks. Engage the pegs with the camplate.
9 To measure the axial play in the shafts, special jigs are required. The axial play is adjusted by shims in the end cover.
10 Refit the eccentric adjusters, the plate between the selector forks and the housing and the screws. Align the marks on the forks and adjusters and tighten the screws.
11 Retain the shaft endfloat shims with grease and apply a thin coat of Loctite 573 (or equivalent) sealant; do not fit a new gasket. If the end cover retaining nuts are tightened to a torque setting of 7 – 9 Nm (5 – 6.5 lbf ft) there is no risk of oil leakage and the shaft endfloat is much easier to set precisely, without the give of a gasket.
12 Heat the end cover, depress the kickstart slightly and put the cover in position. Engage the kickstart gears and tap the cover home fully. Tighten the retaining nuts as specified.
13 Check that in neutral, the warning lamp switch closes, using a flashlamp and battery. If it does not do so, the end cover must again be removed and the switch contact bent towards the camplate.
14 To refit the output flange, use a suitable solvent to degrease completely the tapers of the shaft and flange, tap the flange on to the shaft and lock it by the method used on dismantling. Coat the nut with a viscous oil and refit it, tightening it to a torque setting of 220 – 240 Nm (162 – 177 lbf ft).

16 Five speed gearbox: reassembly

1 Before reassembling the gear shafts, heat the housing to 80° – 100°C (176° – 212°F).
2 Drop the output shaft oil baffle into the housing, raised central part downwards. Fit the output and layshafts, together with the third and fourth gear selector forks, into the housing. The short ends of the fork guides should be adjacent to one another. Tap the selector fork shaft into the housing.
3 Replace the third selector fork on the layshaft. The longer guide end faces downwards.
4 Turn the selector mechanism to neutral and refit the bracket, engaging the selector fork pegs.
5 While the housing is still hot, replace the input shaft.
6 The measurement of axial play in the shafts should be carried out at this stage. Using a depth gauge, measure the distance between the top of the shaft bearing and the housing joint surface. Next measure the depth of the shaft bearing housing in the end cover. Subtract the two dimensions and place shims in the housing to reduce the difference to 0.1 mm (0.040 in). Use grease to retain the shims.
7 Apply a thin coat of Loctite 573 (or equivalent) sealant; do not fit a new gasket. If the end cover retaining nuts or bolts are tightened to a torque setting of 7 – 9 Nm (5 – 6.5 lbf ft) there is no risk of oil leakage and the shaft axial play is much easier to set precisely without the give of a gasket.
8 Heat the end cover to 80° – 100°C (176° – 212°F) before refitting. Depress the kickstart slightly (where fitted) to engage the kickstart gears. Tighten the retaining nuts or bolts as specified.
9 To refit the output flange, use a suitable solvent to degrease completely the tapers of the shaft and flange, tap the flange on to the shaft and lock it by the method used on dismantling. Coat the nut with a viscous oil and refit it, tightening it to the specified torque setting.

17 Refitting the gearbox in the frame

1 Having checked that the clutch operating mechanism components are greased and refitted and that the input shaft splines are greased (see Chapter 2), manoeuvre the gearbox into the frame and re-connect the neutral indicator switch lead. Offer up the gearbox to the rear of the engine and refit the engine/gearbox fasteners; tighten them to the specified torque setting.
2 Check that the engine mounting studs are clean, straight and well-greased to prevent corrosion. Manoeuvre the engine/gearbox unit into position and refit the studs (longer stud to the rear). **Do not** forget to refit the spacers (one each side at the rear stud, between the engine and frame), stand spring anchorages (double anchorage on the left-hand side) and fairing or exhaust pipe clamps in their original positions. When all components are in place and the engine is seated securely but without strain on its mountings tighten them to the specified torque setting. Remove the padding from the frame tubes and refit the engine front cover.
3 Refit the gearchange linkage, pedal and left-hand footrest.
4 Referring to Chapter 7 and Routine Maintenance, refit the swinging arm and connect the driveshaft again, then refill the swinging arm with oil.
5 Grease the pivot bearings, reassemble the rear brake mechanism and adjust it as described in Routine Maintenance.
6 Refit the battery and carrier.
7 Reassemble the clutch operating mechanism (see Chapter 2) and adjust it as described in Routine Maintenance.
8 Reconnect the speedometer cable and battery earth lead to the gearbox, then (if it was drained) fill the gearbox with oil as described in Routine Maintenance.
9 Refit the air filter assembly, carburettors and exhaust system. Check that the carburettors are correctly adjusted. See Chapter 4.
10 Refit the fairing components, the fuel tank, the side panels and the seat.

15.4 Using a mirror to check selector fork setting – four speed gearbox

15.8 Raised centre of oil baffle faces forwards, as shown

15.14 Thoroughly degrease tapers when refitting output flange – do not damage seal

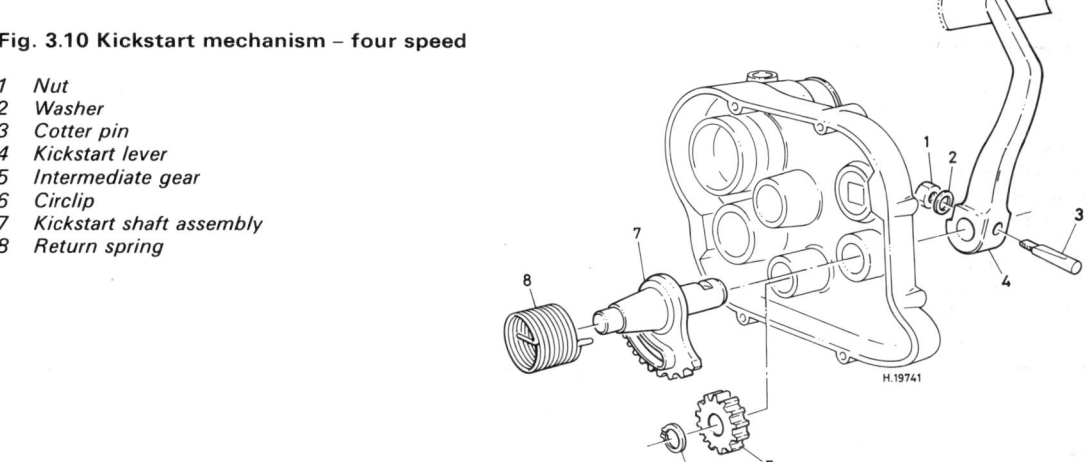

Fig. 3.10 Kickstart mechanism – four speed

1 Nut
2 Washer
3 Cotter pin
4 Kickstart lever
5 Intermediate gear
6 Circlip
7 Kickstart shaft assembly
8 Return spring

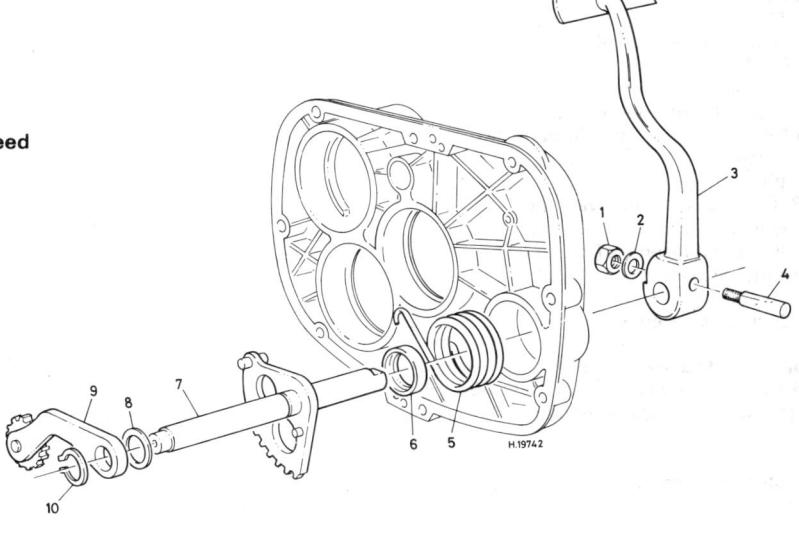

Fig. 3.11 Kickstart mechanism – five speed

1 Nut
2 Washer
3 Kickstart lever
4 Cotter pin
5 Return spring
6 Dished washer
7 Kickstart shaft assembly
8 Washer
9 Intermediate gear assembly
10 Circlip

Chapter 4 Fuel system and lubrication

Refer to Chapter 10 for subsequent modifications and information relating to the 1986 on models

Contents

General description 1	Carburettors: adjustment 10
Fuel tank: removal and refitting 2	Pure air system: general 11
Fuel taps: removal, examination and refitting 3	Exhaust system: removal and refitting 12
Carburettors: removal and refitting 4	Oil pump: examination and renovation 13
Carburettor overhaul: Bing slide type 5	Oil pump pick-up filter gauze: cleaning 14
Carburettor overhaul: Dell'orto 6	Crankcase breather: examination 15
Carburettor overhaul: Bing constant-depression type 7	Oil pressure relief valve 16
Carburettor adjustment and exhaust emissions: general note 8	Oil pressure warning lamp 17
Carburettors: checking the settings 9	

Specifications

Fuel tank capacity

	Litre	Imp gal	US gal
/5 1972 on, /6 except R90S:			
Overall	18.0	3.96	4.76
Including reserve of	2.0	0.44	0.53
R80ST:			
Overall	19.0	4.18	5.02
Including reserve of	2.0	0.44	0.53
R80G/S:			
Overall	19.5	4.29	5.15
Including reserve of	2.0	0.44	0.53
/5 1970-71, R45, R65, R65LS, R80, R80RT 1985 on:			
Overall	22.0	4.84	5.81
Including reserve of	2.0	0.44	0.53
R80G/S Paris – Dakar version:			
Overall	32.0	7.04	8.45
Including reserve of	2.0	0.44	0.53
All other models:			
Overall	24.0	5.28	6.34
Including reserve of	3.0	0.66	0.79

Recommended fuel grade

R50/5, R100 (UK) 1981 on, all 800cc models (except R80/7 with high compression engine), all US models 1980 on .... Regular (2-star) grade to German DIN 51 600 standard or equivalent, minimum octane number 91 (RON/research method) or 82 (MON/motor method)

All other models .... Super, premium, high-test (4-star) grade to German DIN 51 600 standard or equivalent, minimum octane number 98 (RON/research method) or 88 (MON/motor method)

Note: *refer to Chapter 10, Section 6 for more information relating to fuel recommendations.*

Chapter 4 Fuel system and lubrication

Carburettor type

R50, R60	Bing concentric float slide type
R90S	Dell'orto concentric float slide type
All other models	Bing constant depression

Carburettors

	R50/5	R60/5, R60/6	R60/7
Type, LH	1/26/113	1/26/111	1/26/123
Type, RH	1/26/114	1/26/112	1/26/124
Choke size	26 mm (1.02 in)	26 mm (1.02 in)	26 mm (1.02 in)
Main jet	135	140	140
Needle jet	2.68	2.68	2.68
Jet needle	4	4	4
Needle clip position – grooves from top	3rd	2nd	2nd
Idle jet	35	40	40
Float weight	10 grams (0.3527 oz)	10 grams (0.3527 oz)	10 grams (0.3527 oz)
Throttle valve	22 – 570	20 – 570	20 – 570
Pilot air screw – turns out from fully closed	1/2 – 1 1/2	1/4 – 1 1/4	1/4 – 1 1/4

Carburettors

	R90S
Type, LH	PHM 38BS
Type, RH	PHM 38BD
Choke size	38 mm (1.50 in)
Main jet	155
Needle jet	2.60
Jet needle	K4
Needle clip position – grooves from top	3rd
Choke jet	77·46/70
Idle jet	60
Idle air jet diameter	1.2 mm (0.046 in)
Pilot mixture screw – turns out from fully closed	1 – 1 1/2
Bypass bore diameter	1.4 mm (0.055 in)
Float valve diameter	3.0 mm (0.12 in)
Float chamber vent bore diameter	2.5 mm (0.09 in)
Float weight	10 grams (0.3527 oz)
Accelerator pump jet	0.35
Quantity injected per stroke	0.4 cc (0.0244 cu in)

Carburettors

	R45 1979	R45 1980	R45 1981 on	R65 1979	R65 1980
Type, LH:					
UK	64/28/201	64/28/301	64/28/303	64/32/2030	64/32/3030
US	N/App	N/App	N/App	64/32/203	64/32/303
Type, RH:					
UK	64/28/202	64/28/302	64/28/304	64/32/2040	64/32/3040
US	N/App	N/App	N/App	64/32/204	64/32/304
Choke size	28 mm (1.10 in)	28 mm (1.10 in)	28 mm (1.10 in)	32 mm (1.26 in)	32 mm (1.26 in)
Main jet	123	123	105	140	140 US up to 1/80, 140 UK, 145 US 1/80 on
Needle jet	2.66	2.66	2.66	2.66	2.66
Jet needle	46 – 241	46 – 241	46 – 241	46 – 241	46 – 241
Needle clip position – grooves from top	2nd	2nd	2nd	3rd (UK), 2nd (US)	3rd
Idle jet	45	45	45	45	45
Pilot mixture screw – turns out from fully closed	1/2	1/2	1/2	1/2	1/2 (UK), 3/4 (US)

Carburettors

	R65 1981, 1982 R65LS 1982	R65 and R65LS 1983 on	R75/5, R75/6	R75/7	R80/7 1978
Type, LH:					
UK	64/32/307	64/32/347	64/32/9	64/32/13	64/32/201
US	64/32/325	64/32/335	64/32/9	64/32/13	64/32/201
Type, RH:					
UK	64/32/308	64/32/348	64/32/10	64/32/14	64/32/202
US	64/32/326	64/32/336	64/32/10	64/32/14	64/32/202
Choke size	32 mm (1.26 in)	32 mm (1.26 in)	32 mm (1.26 in)	32 mm (1.26 in)	32 mm (1.26 in)
Main jet	148 (UK), 145 (US)	138 (UK), 135 (US)	135	145	145
Needle jet	2.64 (UK), 2.66 (US)	2.64	2.70	2.66	2.66
Jet needle	46 – 241	46 – 242	46 – 241	46 – 241	46 – 241
Needle clip position – grooves from top	4th (UK), 3rd (US)	3rd	3rd	3rd	3rd (UK), 2nd (US)
Idle jet	45 (UK), 40 (US)	45 (UK), 40 (US)	45 44-950	50	50 (UK), 45 (US)
Pilot mixture screw – turns out from fully closed	1/2 (UK), 3/4 (US)	1/2 (UK), 3/4 (US)	1/2 – 1	1/2 – 1	1/2 – 1 (UK), 1/2 (US)

Chapter 4 Fuel system and lubrication

Carburettors	R80/7 1979	R80/7 1980	R80G/S and R80ST up to 5/83	R80RT up to 5/83	R80G/S, R80ST and R80RT 5/83 on
Type, LH:					
UK	64/32/201	64/32/201	64/32/305	64/32/305	64/32/349
US	64/32/221	64/32/321	64/32/321	64/32/321	64/32/351
Type, RH:					
UK	64/32/20	64/32/202	64/32/306	64/32/305	64/32/350
US	64/32/222	64/32/322	64/32/322	64/32/322	64/32/352
Choke size	32 mm (1.26 in)	32 mm (1.26 in)	32 mm (1.26 in)	32 mm (1.26 in)	32 mm (1.26 in)
Main jet	145	145 (UK), 150 (US)	145 (UK), 150 (US)	145	135 (UK), 132 (US)
Needle jet	2.66	2.66	2.64 (UK), 2.66 (US)	2.66	2.68 (UK), 2.66 (US)
Jet needle	46 – 241	46 – 241	46 – 241	46 – 241	46 – 242
Needle clip position – grooves from top	3rd (UK), 2nd (US)	3rd	4th (UK), 3rd (US)	4th (UK), 3rd (US)	4th (UK), 3rd (US)
Idle jet	50 (UK), 45 (US)	50 (UK), 45 (US)	45 (UK), 40 (US)	50 (UK), 40 (US)	45
Pilot mixture screw – turns out from fully closed	1/2 – 1 (UK), 1/2 (US)	1/2 – 1 (UK), 3/4 (US)	3/4	3/4	3/4

Carburettors	R80G/S (US) R80, R80RT 1985	R90/6	R100/7 1977	R100/7 1978	R100T 1979
Type, LH:					
UK	64/32/353	64/32/11	64/32/19	64/32/19	94/40/103
US	64/32/357	64/32/11	64/32/19	64/32/223	94/40/107
Type, RH:					
UK	64/32/354	64/32/12	64/32/20	64/32/20	94/40/104
US	64/32/358	64/32/12	64/32/20	64/32/224	94/40/108
Choke size	32 mm (1.26 in)	32 mm (1.26 in)	32 mm (1.26 in)	32 mm (1.26 in)	40 mm (1.58 in)
Main jet	130 (R80G/S) 135 (R80, R80RT)	150	150	150	170 (UK), 160 (US)
Needle jet	2.68 (UK), 2.66 (US)	2.68	2.68	2.68 (UK), 2.66 (US)	2.66 (UK), 2.64 (US)
Jet needle	46 – 251	46 – 241	46 – 241	46 – 241	46 – 241
Needle clip position – grooves from top	3rd	1st	3rd	3rd (UK), 2nd (US)	3rd (UK), 2nd (US)
Idle jet	45	45 44 – 950	50	45	45
Pilot air screw – turns out from fully closed	3/4	1/2 – 1	1	1 – 1 1/4 (UK), 1/2 (US)	1 – 1 1/4 (UK), 1/2 (US)

Carburettors	R100T 1980	R100 1981 on	R100S 1977	R100S 1978	R100S 1979
Type, LH:					
UK	94/40/103	94/40/111	94/40/103	94/40/103	94/40/105
US	94/40/109	94/40/113	94/40/103	94/40/107	94/40/107
Type, RH:					
UK	94/40/104	94/40/112	94/40/104	94/40/104	94/40/106
US	94/40/110	94/40/114	94/40/104	94/40/108	94/40/108
Choke size	40 mm (1.58 in)	40 mm (1.58 in)	40 mm (1.58 in)	40 mm (1.58 in)	40 mm (1.58 in)
Main jet	170 (UK), 165 (US)	160	170	170 (UK), 160 (US)	170 (UK), 160 (US)
Needle jet	2.66	2.66	2.66	2.66 (UK), 2.64 (US)	2.68 (UK), 2.64 (US)
Jet needle	46 – 241	46 – 341	46 – 341	46 – 341	46 – 341
Needle clip position – grooves from top	3rd (UK), 2nd (US)	3rd (UK), 2nd (US)	3rd	3rd (UK), 2nd (US)	2nd
Idle jet	45	45	45	45	45
Pilot mixture screw – turns out from fully closed	1 – 1 1/4 (UK), 1 (US)	1 – 1 1/4 (UK), 1 (US)	1 – 1 1/4	1 – 1 1/4 (UK), 1/2 (US)	1 – 1 1/4 (UK), 1/2 (US)

Carburettors	R100S 1980	R100CS 1981 on	R100RS 1977	R100RS 1978-79, R100RT 1979	R100RS and R100RT, 1980
Type, LH:					
UK	94/40/105	94/40/111	94/40/105	94/40/105	94/40/105
US	94/40/109	94/40/113	94/40/105	94/40/107	94/40/109
Type, RH:					
UK	94/40/106	94/40/112	94/40/106	94/40/106	94/40/106
US	94/40/110	94/40/114	94/40/106	94/40/108	94/40/110
Choke size	40 mm (1.58 in)	40 mm (1.58 in)	40 mm (1.58 in)	40 mm (1.58 in)	40 mm (1.58 in)
Main jet	170 (UK), 165 (US)	160	170	170 (UK), 160 (US)	170 (UK), 165 (US)

Chapter 4 Fuel system and lubrication

Needle jet	2.68 (UK), 2.66 (US)	2.66	2.68	2.68 (UK), 2.64 (US)	2.68 (UK), 2.66 (US)
Jet needle	46 – 341	46 – 341	46 – 341	46 – 341	46 – 341
Needle clip position – grooves from top	2nd	3rd (UK), 2nd (US)	2nd	2nd	2nd
Idle jet	45	45	45	45	45
Pilot mixture screw – turns out from fully closed	1 – 1¼ (UK), 1 (US)	1 – 1¼ (UK), 1 (US)	1 – 1¼	1 – 1¼ (UK), ½ (US)	1 – 1¼ (UK), 1 (US)

Carburettors   R100RS and R100RT, 1981 on
Type, LH:
  UK 94/40/111
  US 94/40/113
Type, RH:
  UK 94/40/112
  US 94/40/114
Choke size .... 40 mm (1.58 in)
Main jet 160
Needle jet 2.66
Jet needle .... 46 – 341
Needle clip position – grooves from top .... 3rd (UK), 2nd (US)
Idle jet 45
Pilot mixture screw – turns out from fully closed .... 1 – 1¼ (UK), 1 (US)

Carburettor passages and auxiliary starting carburettor – Bing constant depression type only
Starter jet:
  R100/7 70
  All other 1000cc models 80
  All other models 60
Starter air jet diameter .... 2.0 mm (0.08 in)
Diameter of passages in rotary valve:
  R80G/S, R80ST .... 2.0/1.2/0.7/0.6 mm (0.08/0.05/0.03/0.02 in)
  All other models .... 2.0/1.2/0.7 mm/ (0.08/0.05/0.03 in)
Rotary valve diaphragm:
  R75/5 .... 65 – 811
  R75/6, R90/6 .... 65 – 810
  All other models .... N/Av
Control plunger weight:
  R75/5, R75/6 .... 102 gram (3.5975 oz)
  R90/6 .... 106 gram (3.7386 oz)
Float weight:
  R75/5 .... 10 gram (0.3527 oz)
  R75/6, R90/6 .... 13 gram (0.4585 oz)
Idle air jet diameter .... 1.0 mm (0.039 in)
Bypass bore – R75/5, R75/6 .... 1.0 mm (0.039 in)
Bypass bore 1 – except R75/5, R75/6:
  All 1000cc models except R100/7 .... 0.80 mm (0.032 in)
  All other models .... 0.70 mm (0.028 in)
Bypass bore 2-except R75/5, R75/6 .... 0.65 mm (0.026 in)
Idle outlet passage diameter .... 1.0 mm (0.039 in)
Float valve diameter .... 2.5 mm (0.098 in)
Float chamber vent bore – except R80G/S, R80ST:
  All 1000cc models .... 2.0 mm (0.079 in)
  All other models .... 4.0 mm (0.158 in)

Carburettor tune-up data
Idle speed:
  /5, /6 .... 600 – 800 rpm
  All other models .... 800 – 1100 rpm
CO level at idle speed – all (US) models 1978 on .... 2 ± 0.5%

Engine lubrication system
Type .... Pressure-fed, wet sump
System pressure – oil temperature 80°C (176°F):
  At 800 rpm .... 1.0 – 2.0 bar (14.5 – 29.0 psi)
  At 4000 rpm .... 4.0 – 5.0 bar (58.0 – 72.5 psi)
Filter bypass valve opens at .... 1.5 bar (21.8 psi)
Pressure relief valve opens at .... 5.0 bar (72.5 psi)
Relaxed length of relief valve spring .... 68.0 mm (2.6772 in)
Oil pressure warning lamp lights below .... 0.2 – 0.5 bar (2.9 – 7.3 psi)

Recommended oil	Good quality HD oil suitable for 4-stroke spark ignition engines, API class SE/CC or SF/CC
Viscosity	Depends on outside temperatures – see chart in Routine Maintenance

Engine oil capacity:

	At oil change – lit/Imp pint/US qt	At oil and filter change/engine rebuild – lit/Imp pint/US qt
/5,/6,/7 up to 1980 without oil cooler, R80G/S, R45 and R65 up to 1980	2.00/3.52/2.11	2.25/3.96/2.38
/5,/6,/7 up to 1980 with oil cooler, /7 1981 on without oil cooler, R80, R80ST, R80RT, R45 and R65 1981 on	2.25/3.96/2.38	2.50/4.40/2.64
/7 1981 on with oil cooler	2.50/4.40/2.64	2.75/4.84/2.91

Oil pump

Type	Eaton (Hypo-trochoidal)
Delivery rate @ 6000 rpm	1400 lit (308 Imp gal/370 US gal) per hour
Outer rotor OD:	
R45, R65, R65LS, R80G/S, R80ST, R80, R80RT	56.950 – 57.050 mm (2.2421 – 2.2461 in)
All other models	57.075 – 57.100 mm (2.2470 – 2.2480 in)
Pump body ID	57.200 – 57.246 mm (2.2520 – 2.2538 in)
Outer rotor/pump body clearance:	
R45, R65, R65LS, R80G/S, R80ST, R80, R80RT	0.150 – 0.296 mm (0.0059 – 0.0117 in)
All other models	0.100 – 0.171 mm (0.0039 – 0.0067 in)
Rotor height:	
/5,/6	13.966 – 13.984 mm (0.5498 – 0.5505 in)
All other models	13.955 – 13.985 mm (0.5494 – 0.5506 in)
Pump body depth	14.010 – 14.025 mm (0.5516 – 0.5522 in)
Pump body/rotor clearance (rotor endfloat):	
/5,/6	0.026 – 0.059 mm (0.0010 – 0.0023 in)
All other models	0.025 – 0.070 mm (0.0009 – 0.0028 in)
Inner rotor/outer rotor clearance:	
/5,/6	0.12 – 0.30 mm (0.0047 – 0.0118 in)
All other models	0.12 – 0.20 mm (0.0047 – 0.0079 in)
Pump end cover maximum wear depth	0.05 mm (0.0020 in)

Torque wrench settings

Component	Nm	lbf ft
Carburettor threaded stubs:		
All models up to 1980	12 – 14	9 – 10
All models 1981 on	50	37
Exhaust pipe finned nuts:		
R80, R80RT 1985 on	160	118
R45 and R65 1979 – 80, /7 up to 1980	140 – 180	103 – 133
All other models	200 – 220	148 – 162
Exhaust chamber clip bolts – R80, R80RT 1985 on	21	15.5
Sump mounting bolts	9 – 12	6.5 – 9
Oil pump pickup mounting bolts	9	6.5
Oil filter inner cover retaining bolt – /5, /6 only	40	29.5
Oil filter cover mounting bolts	10	7.5
Oil cooler banjo bolts	19.5	14.5
Engine oil drain plug – 1981 on models only	30 – 35	22 – 26

1 General description

The carburettors are gravity fed with petrol from the tank astride the top frame tube. On /5, /6 and /7 models, each carburettor is provided with a tap, with a reserve position, while other models are fitted with a single tap. In addition, there is a connecting tube between each petrol supply pipe. There is also a detachable fuel filter at each petrol tap.

Both carburettors breathe through a dry paper cartridge-type air filter, above the gearbox.

Three types of carburettor are fitted, all having concentric float chambers. Bing slide type carburettors are fitted to the R50 and R60 models; with the carburettors on the R60/6 and R60/7 models having a cold starting slide instead of a tickler. All other models have Bing constant velocity carburettors with an auxiliary starting carburettor, except for the R90S model which has Dellorto slide-type carburettors with a cold starting device and accelerator pump. The carburettors are operated by twin cables from the handlebar twist grip. The cold starting device on most models is operated by the lever on the left-hand air filter cover up to (US) 1979 and (UK) 1980 models, after which it was handlebar-mounted.

On all models, fuel level is controlled by a plastic double float, which cuts off fuel supply by means of a needle valve.

On the slide-type carburettors, the slide and its attached needle vary the quantity of air passing through the carburettor venturi and the quantity of fuel passing through the needle jet, simultaneously. A needle-activated accelerator pump enriches the mixture on acceleration. At small throttle openings, fuel is sucked from the float chamber via a pilot jet by air passing through an additional passage which by-passes the main venturi.

The accelerator pump on Dell'orto carburettors is operated by the throttle slide. As the slide rises, it depresses a lever to which a diaphragm is attached. The diaphragm acts as a pump and injects petrol directly into the induction tract.

The constant velocity carburettors are controlled by a butterfly valve and a vacuum piston in front of the butterfly attached to a diaphragm.

The pressure in the throat in front of the vacuum piston drops as the butterfly is opened. Since the space above the diaphragm is connected to the throat and the space below the diaphragm is maintained at atmospheric pressure, as the butterfly is opened the vacuum piston will rise until equilibrium is reached. A needle attached to the vacuum piston controls the quantity of fuel entering the choke, simultaneously with the rise or fall of the vacuum piston.

The idling system functions independently of the main jet system in a similar manner to that of the slide-type carburettors.

The starting device is a complete auxiliary carburettor integral with the main carburettor and having a rotary slide.

The high pressure lubricating system with a full flow filter, uses an Eaton-type trochoidal gear pump driven directly by the camshaft. Oil is

Chapter 4 Fuel system and lubrication

drawn from the wet sump through a strainer and is pumped through the cartridge filter. A spring loaded ball-type bypass valve set in the end of the filter housing ensures that the oil supply is maintained even if the filter becomes blocked; if the pressure difference exceeds the set amount the bypass valve opens and allows unfiltered oil to circulate around the engine. From the filter, oil passes via an annular passage in the front camshaft bearing flange to the front crankshaft bearing, hence to the rear crankshaft bearing. From the rear crankshaft bearing passages direct the oil to the cylinder walls and to the ends of the upper cylinder studs. The oil continues up the cylinder stud holes to lubricate the valve mechanism, and drains down the push rod tubes. The big ends are lubricated via oilways leading from the main bearings. The timing chain dips into the sump oil and lubricates the crankshaft outrigger bearing by splash. During 1980 the crankcase and front main bearing cap were modified to provide an oil feed direct to the crankshaft front main bearing from the filter; passages then direct oil to the camshaft and to the rear main bearing.

An oil cooler has been fitted as standard equipment only to R100RS models from 1978 onwards and to R100RT models from 1980 onwards but may be encountered on other models as it has been offered as an optional extra for the other models in the range. The cooler receives its supply from an adaptor placed over the end of the filter chamber, oil being fed from the pump, through the oil filter and into the oil cooler before it returns to circulate around the engine components. A thermostatic valve is fitted in the adaptor to ensure that the cooler is in use only when the oil temperature exceeds 80°C (176°F), opening progressively until full flow is reached at approximately 110°C (230°F).

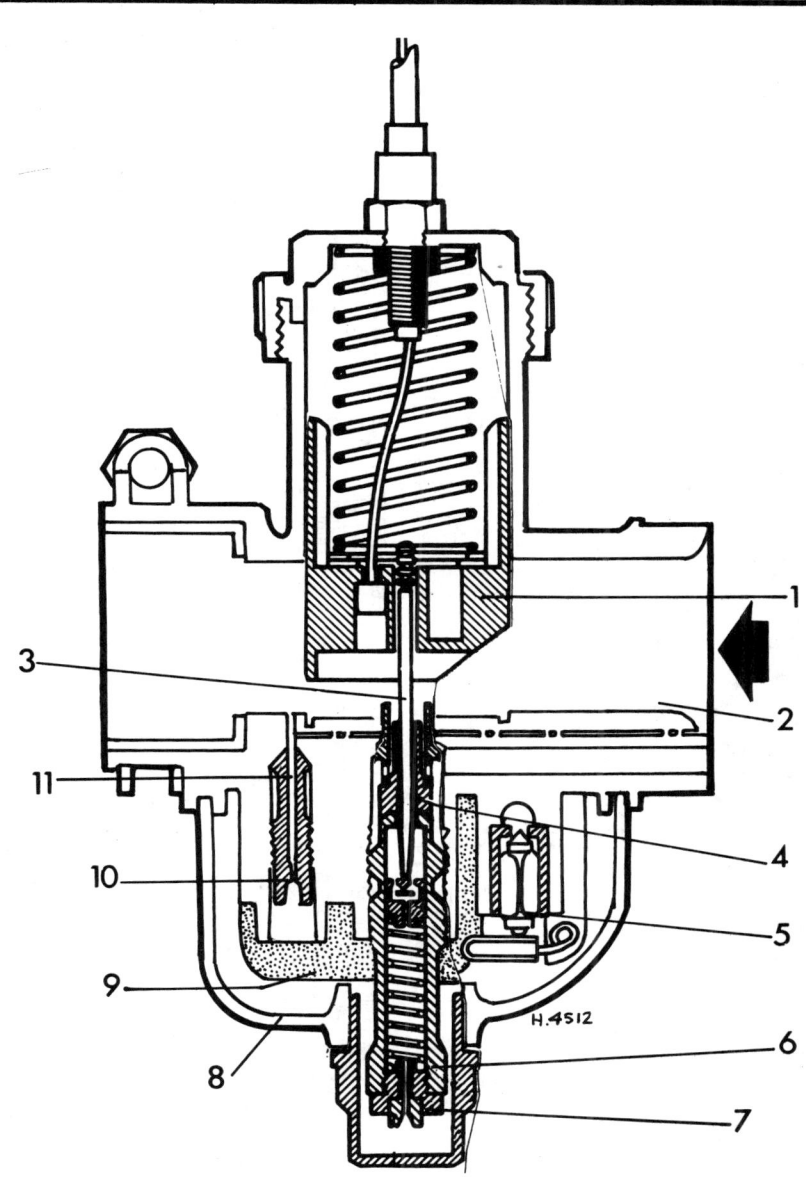

Fig. 4.1 Carburettor operation – Bing slide-type

1 Throttle slide
2 Venturi
3 Needle
4 Needle jet
5 Float needle
6 Accelerator pump
7 Main jet
8 Float chamber
9 Float
10 Pilot jet
11 Pilot air passage

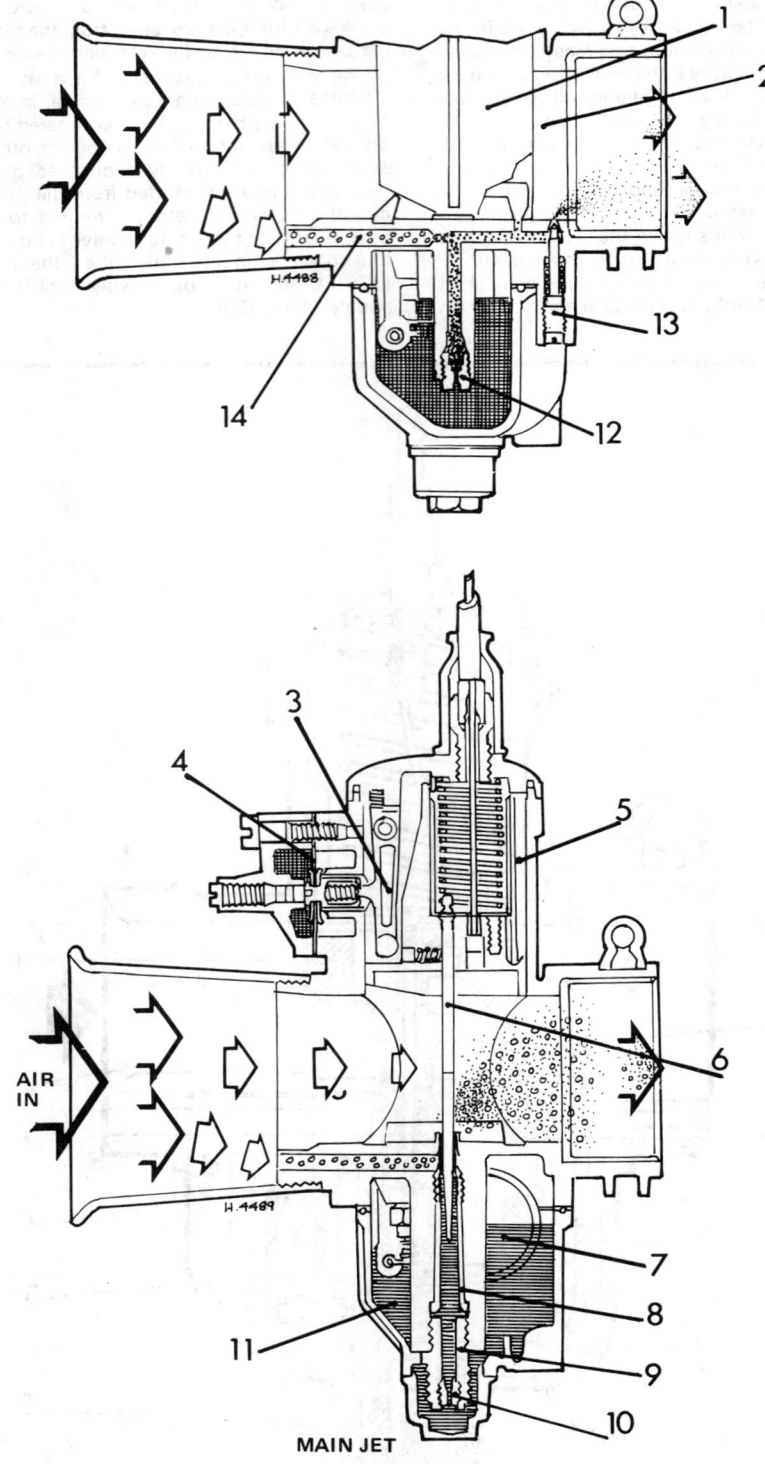

Fig. 4.2 Carburettor operation – Dell'orto

1 Throttle slide
2 Venturi
3 Accelerator pump lever
4 Diaphragm
5 Slide
6 Needle
7 Float
8 Atomiser and needle jet
9 Main jet holder
10 Main jet
11 Float chamber
12 Pilot jet
13 Mixture regulating screw
14 Pilot air passage

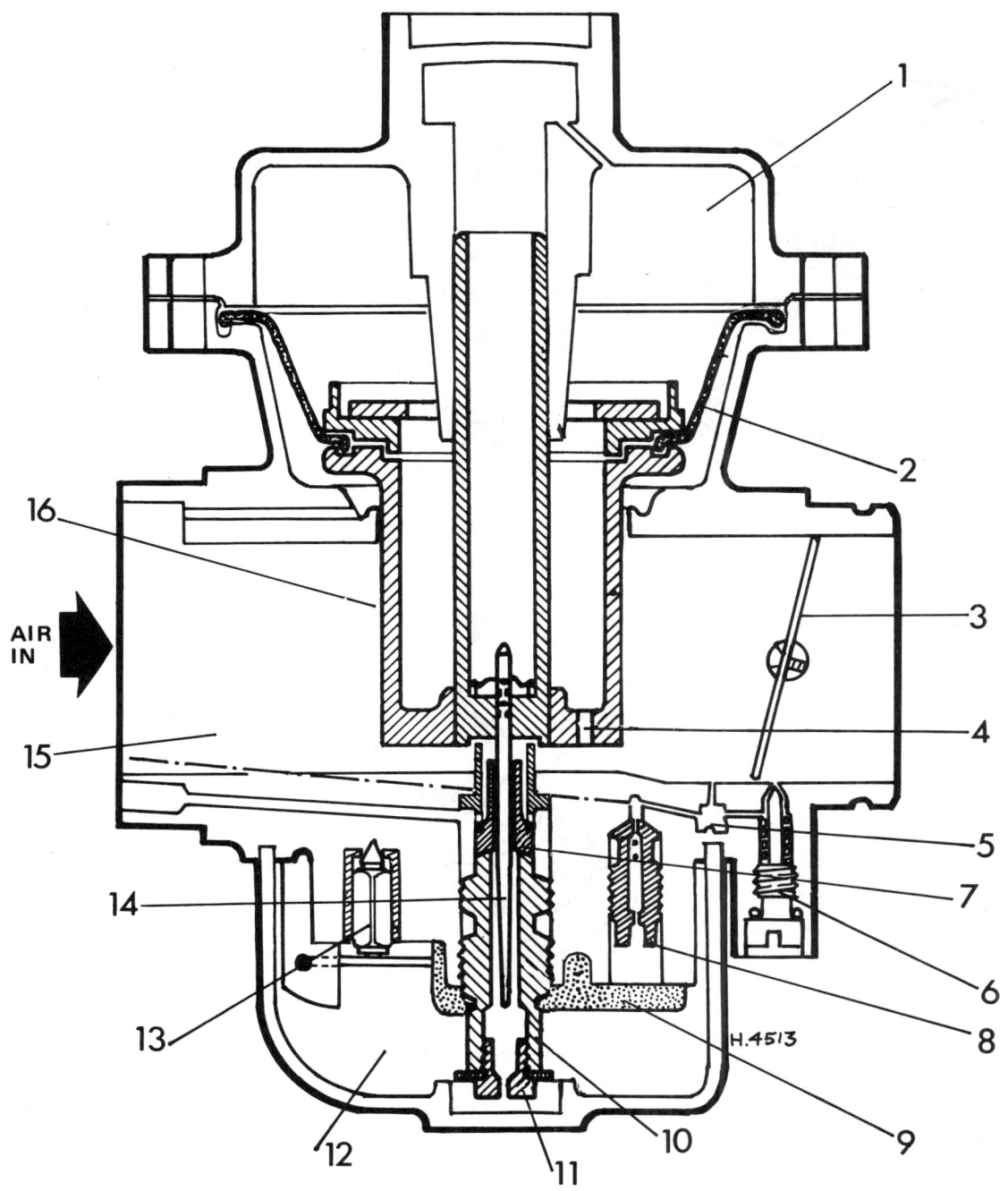

Fig. 4.3 Carburettor operation – Bing vacuum type

1 Vacuum chamber
2 Diaphragm
3 Butterfly valve
4 Vacuum chamber connecting passages
5 Pilot air passage
6 Mixture regulating screw
7 Needle jet
8 Pilot
9 Float
10 Main jet holder
11 Main jet
12 Float chamber
13 Float needle
14 Needle
15 Venturi
16 Vacuum piston

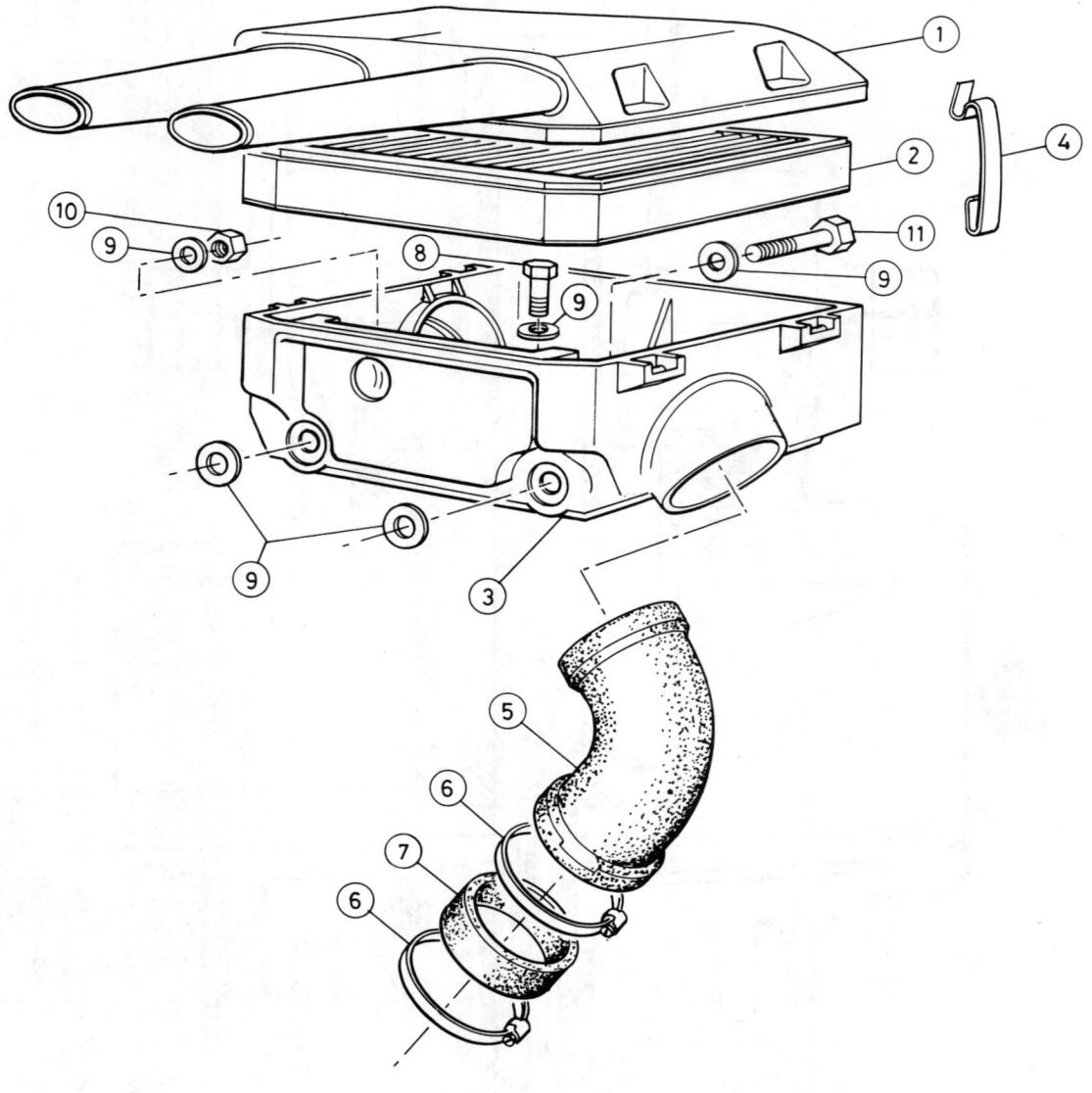

Fig. 4.4 Air filter – later models

1 Top cover	4 Spring clip	7 Sleeve	10 Nut
2 Filter element	5 Carburettor intake hose	8 Bolt	11 Bolt
3 Filter housing	6 Hose clamp	9 Washer	

2 Fuel tank: removal and refitting

R45, R65, R65 LS, R80G/S, R80ST

1 Unlock and raise or remove the dualseat, remove the tool tray and wedge it on the mudguard to prevent the seat falling shut. Pull the breather/overflow tube off its union on the tank underside. Switch off the fuel tap(s).
2 Pull the fuel feed pipe(s) off the tap(s) and unhook the rubber retaining strap from the frame top tube, while pressing down on the rear of the tank. Lift the tank at the rear and pull it backwards until it clears the front mounting then lift it at the front and withdraw it.
3 Reverse to refit the tank. Switch on the fuel supply and check for leaks.

All other models

4 Unlock and raise the dualseat, remove the tool tray and wedge it on the mudguard to prevent the seat falling shut. Pull the breather/overflow hose off its union on the tank underside. Switch off the fuel taps.
5 Where possible, pull the fuel feed pipes off the taps; where the pipes are crimped in place unscrew the tap lower union nut to release each pipe.
6 On R80 and R80RT 1985 on models, pull out the circlips retaining the tank to its rear mountings. On all other models, unscrew the two retaining nuts. Lift the tank at the rear and pull it backwards until it clears the front mounting, then lift it at the front and withdraw it.
7 Reverse the removal procedure to refit, taking care that the tank seats correctly on its mountings. Reconnect or re-route the breather hose and fuel feed pipes, switch on the fuel supply and check for leaks.

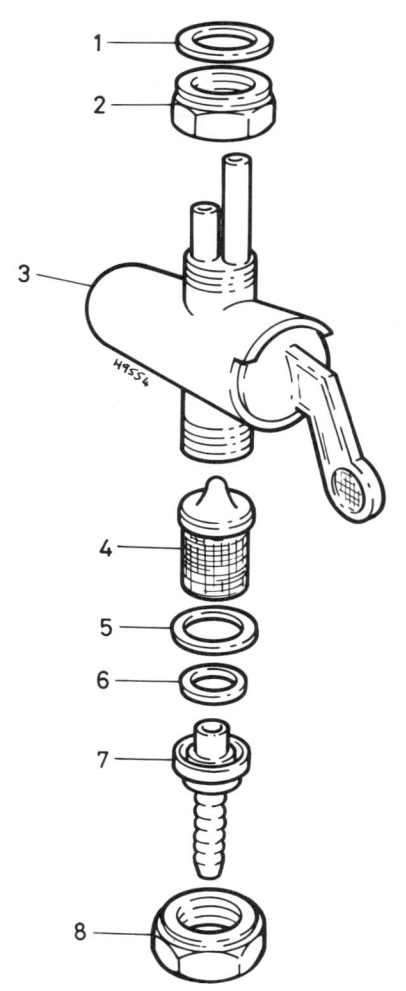

Fig. 4.5 Fuel tap – early type

1 Sealing washer
2 Tank union nut
3 Fuel tap
4 Filter gauze
5 Sealing washer
6 Sealing washer
7 Tap spigot
8 Bottom union nut

2.4 Where fitted, pull tank breather/overflow hose off its union

2.6a Latest models – tank is secured by two circlips at the rear

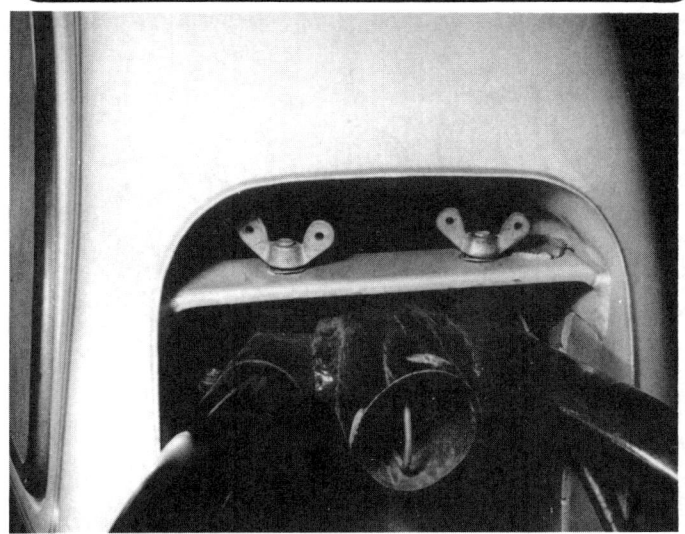

2.6b Earlier models – tank is secured by two nuts (wingnuts or black plastic) at the rear

2.6c Lift tank at rear to clear mountings and manoeuvre backwards to remove

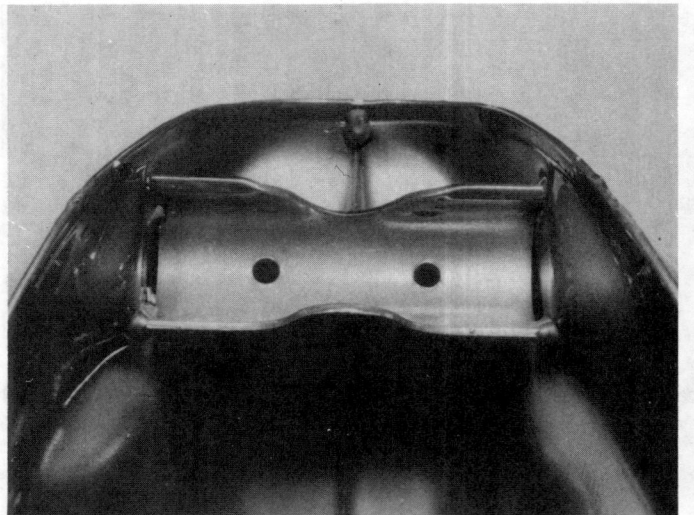

2.7a Mounting bracket on tank nose ...

2.7b ... must engage fully with frame mounting rubber

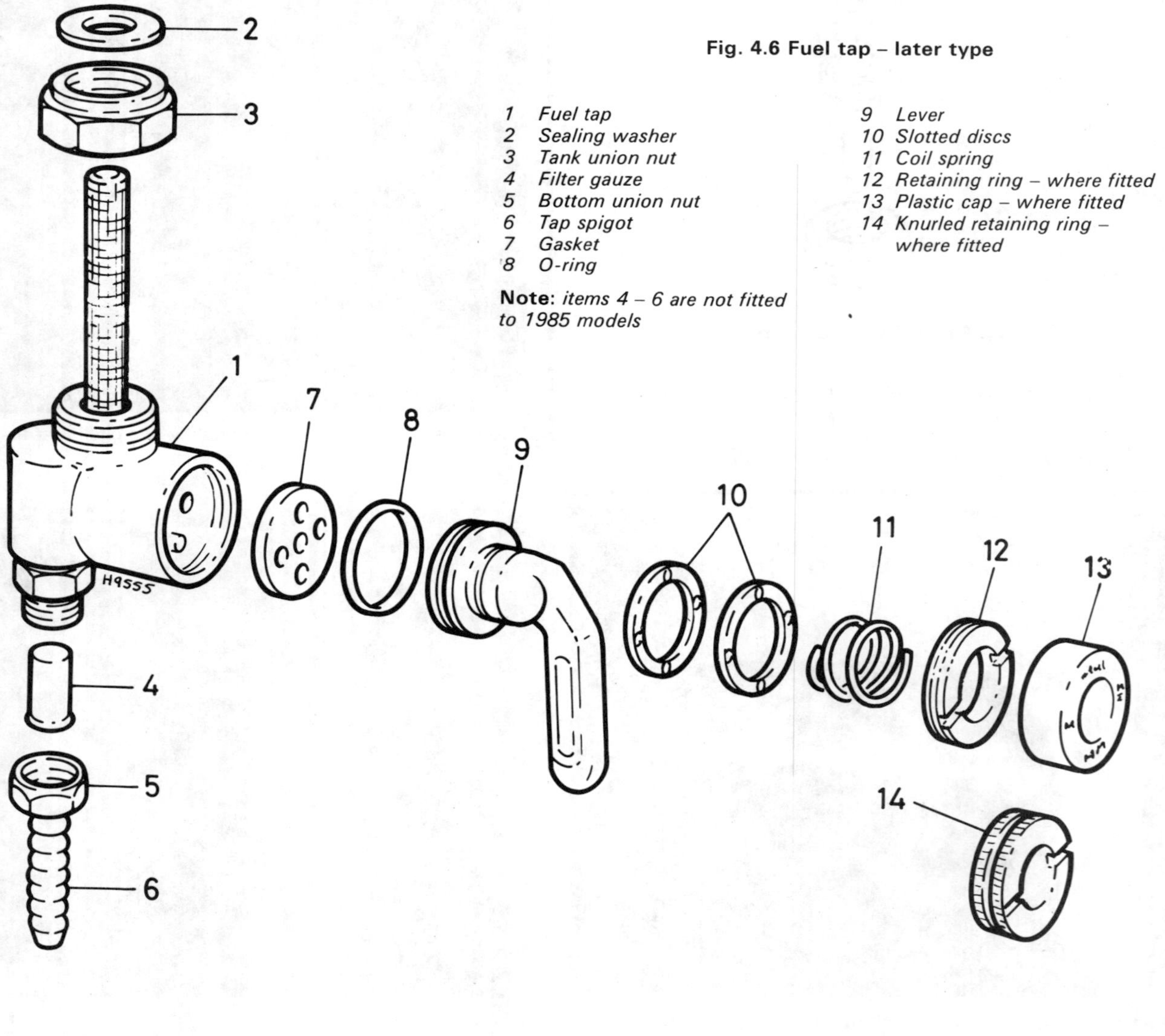

Fig. 4.6 Fuel tap – later type

1 Fuel tap
2 Sealing washer
3 Tank union nut
4 Filter gauze
5 Bottom union nut
6 Tap spigot
7 Gasket
8 O-ring
9 Lever
10 Slotted discs
11 Coil spring
12 Retaining ring – where fitted
13 Plastic cap – where fitted
14 Knurled retaining ring – where fitted

Note: *items 4 – 6 are not fitted to 1985 models*

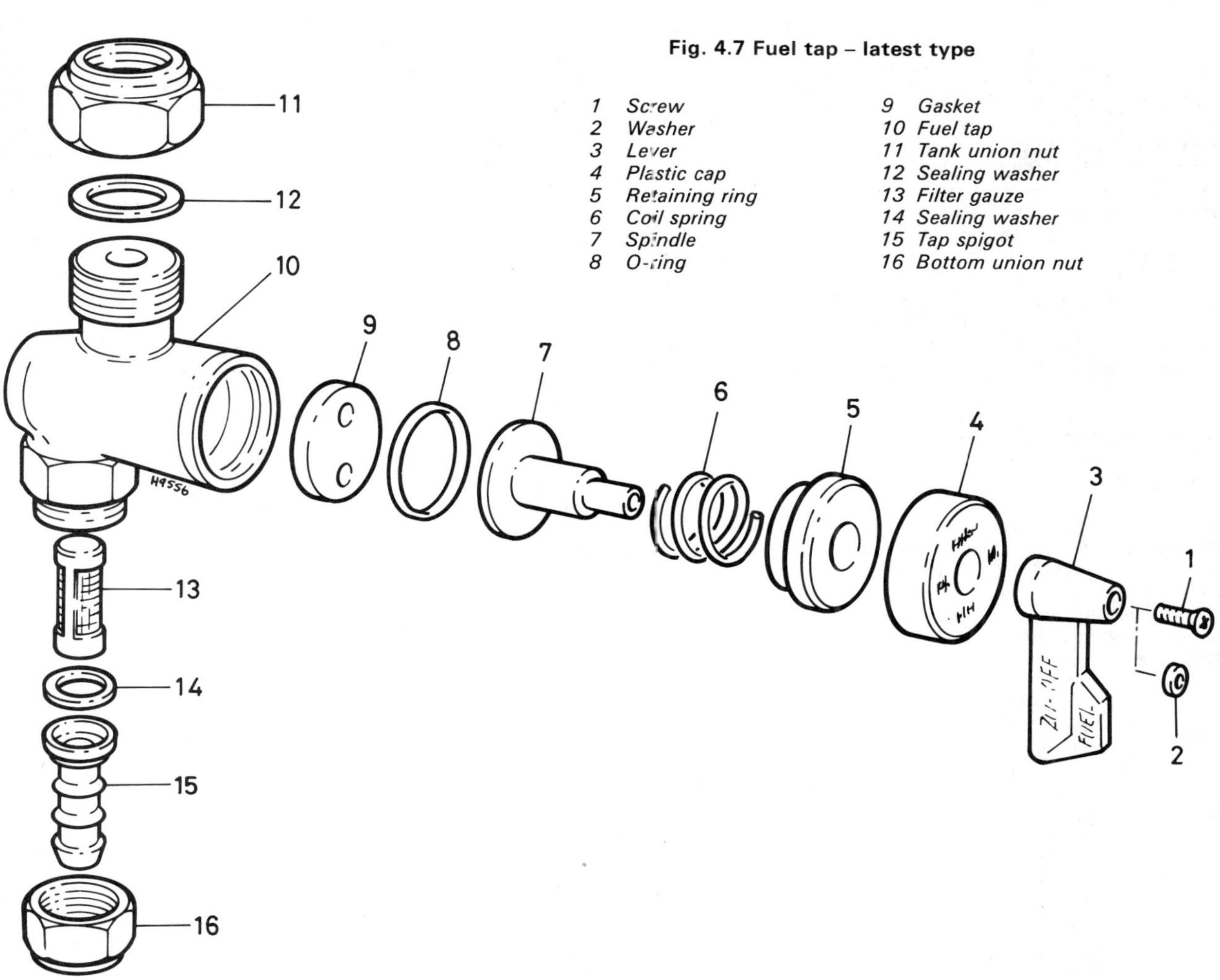

129

Fig. 4.7 Fuel tap – latest type

1 Screw
2 Washer
3 Lever
4 Plastic cap
5 Retaining ring
6 Coil spring
7 Spindle
8 O-ring
9 Gasket
10 Fuel tap
11 Tank union nut
12 Sealing washer
13 Filter gauze
14 Sealing washer
15 Tap spigot
16 Bottom union nut

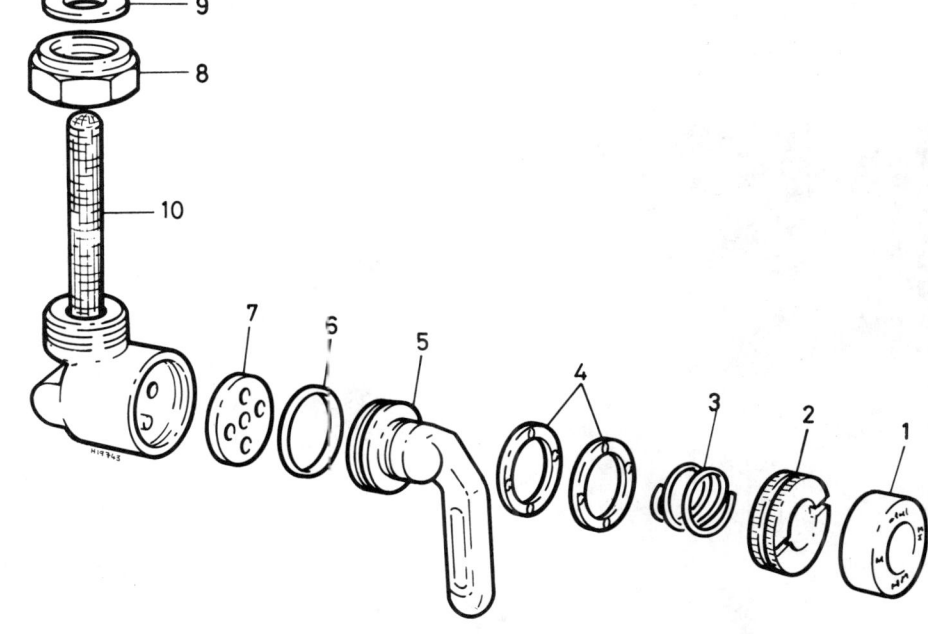

Fig. 4.8 Fuel tap – R80, R80RT 1985 on

1 Plastic cap
2 Knurled retaining ring
3 Coil spring
4 Slotted discs
5 Lever
6 O-ring
7 Gasket
8 Tank union nut
9 Sealing washer
10 Fuel tap

3 Fuel taps: removal, examination and refitting

1 Disconnect the fuel feed pipes and place a suitable container under each tap. Switch the taps to reserve and allow all the fuel to drain out. Take all necessary precautions to prevent the risk of fire.
2 When the fuel has completely drained, slacken the bottom union nut, where fitted (if not removed to disconnect the fuel pipes), and remove the nut, tap spigot and filter gauze. The tap mounting nut has a normal right-hand thread at the tank stub; holding the tap body steady with a spanner applied to the cast hexagon in the tap lower body, turn the union nut to the **left** (standing at the side of the machine, looking down at the tap) to unscrew it. Catch any surplus fuel that spills out.
3 Where a filter gauze is fitted inside the tank, detach it and check it for splits or other damage; clean it as described in Routine Maintenance. Where nylon stack pipes are fitted note carefully which pipe fits into which tap aperture before removing them.
4 On the earliest type, the tap cannot be dismantled further. Blow through it with the lever in the on and reserve positions to check that it is clear; blockages may be cleared by a blast of compressed air. If the tap is leaking or if a blockage cannot be cleared, the tap must be renewed.
5 On the later types of tap unscrew the retaining screw (where fitted) and withdraw the tap lever. Prise off the plastic cap (manoeuvring it over the lever, where applicable) and unscrew the knurled retaining ring. Withdraw the lever components. If the gaskets are of cork they should be removed and replaced by the later rubber type as corks swell or shrink unevenly if not fully wetted by the fuel and can thus cause either stiff tap action or leakage.
6 Thoroughly clean all components and check for signs of wear or damage, especially the mating surfaces of the tap body, lever and gasket. Renew the sealing O-ring and the union nut gaskets if they are damaged or worn. Note that the tap detent positions are provided by the two slotted discs; check that these are clean and unworn.
7 On reassembly place the gasket in the tap body ensuring that all fuel passages are aligned. Fit the sealing O-ring to the lever and apply a thin smear of grease to it to prevent damage on refitting. On taps with a cranked lever, assemble the two slotted discs, the coil spring (where fitted) and the knurled retaining ring onto the lever and fit it as a single unit. On all taps apply a smear of grease to all lever components to prevent corrosion and to lubricate them.
8 On taps with lever coil springs, tighten securely the knurled retaining ring; the spring will ensure that the tap is sealed but easy to operate. On earlier taps without the coil spring tighten the ring until the desired operating force is reached. Refit the remaining tap components by reversing the dismantling sequence. Where the tap positions are marked on the plastic cap, ensure that the cap is refitted so that the marks are correct.
9 Fit a new gasket to the union nut on refitting the tap to the tank. The wider plain portion of the union nut should be uppermost; engage its threads simultaneously on those of the tank and tap. Turn the nut to the right to tighten it, holding the tap steady with a spanner applied to the cast hexagon. Do not overtighten the union nut.
10 When the taps are refitted, correct the fuel pipes again, pour the drained fuel back into the tank and switch on the fuel supply. Check carefully for leaks.

4 Carburettors: removal and refitting

1 Switch off the fuel tap(s) and disconnect the fuel feed pipe(s).
2 On R50 and R60 models unscrew the knurled ring on top of each carburettor and withdraw the throttle slide. R60/6 and R60/7 carburettors also have a cold starting slide: unscrew the hexagonal nuts and extract the slides. Tape the throttle slides to the top frame tube in a safe position.
3 On Dell'orto carburettors, fitted to the R90S models, unscrew the two mixing chamber top retaining screws of each carburettor and remove the throttle slide complete with accelerator pump lever. Note the O-ring seal in the mixing chamber top. Unscrew the cold starting slide and withdraw. Tape the throttle slides to the top frame tube.
4 On all models, slacken the clips on the air hoses and on the carburettor to cylinder head joints. Pull off the fuel pipe and withdraw the carburettors and air hoses.
5 To disconnect constant-depression carburettors, raise the auxiliary carburettor lever and detach the cable nipple. Pull the inner cable through the adjuster. Unscrew the throttle cable adjuster, slip the inner cable through the slot in the abutment and detach the barrel nipple from the lever. Repeat for the second carburettor.
6 Note the difference between the left and right-hand carburettors and lay them aside carefully.
7 Replace in the reverse order to removal. Insert each throttle slide carefully, entering the needle into the jet. Do not oil the slides. Make sure the lug on the mixing chamber top engages with the notch in the carburettor body of Bing slide type carburettors.
8 Make sure that all the hose clips are tight, making air-tight joints. If this is not so, the mixture will be weakened with possible damage to the pistons. Check that all controls work smoothly and are correctly adjusted.

3.9 Wider plain portion of tap union nut must be upwards – care is required when removing and refitting taps

4.5a Removing constant-depression carburettors – disengage carburettor from air hoses ...

Chapter 4 Fuel system and lubrication

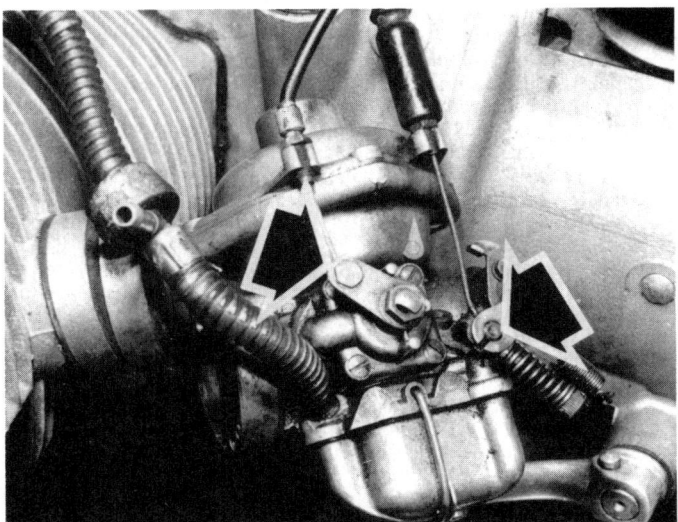

4.5b ... then disconnect fuel pipe and control cables (cable nipples arrowed)

Fig. 4.9 Carburettor assembly – Bing slide type

1	Main jet cover	21	Fuel pipe adapter
2	Gasket	22	Throttle slide
3	Float bowl clip	23	Needle
4	Float bowl	24	Needle clip
5	Float	25	Washer
6	Float pivot	26	Throttle slide spring
7	Main jet	27	Mixing chamber top
8	Accelerator pump	28	Adjuster locknut
9	O-ring seal	29	Throttle cable adjuster
10	Pilot jet	30	O-ring seal
11	Needle jet	31	Mixing chamber ring
12	Needle jet holder	32	Tickler spring
13	Float bowl gasket	33	Tickler
14	Float needle	34	Tickler cap
15	Carburettor body	35	Split cotter pin
16	Spring	36	Insulating washer
17	Slide stop screw	37	Insulating bush
18	Pilot air screw	38	Clamp bolt
19	Spring	39	Clamp
20	Gasket	40	Nut

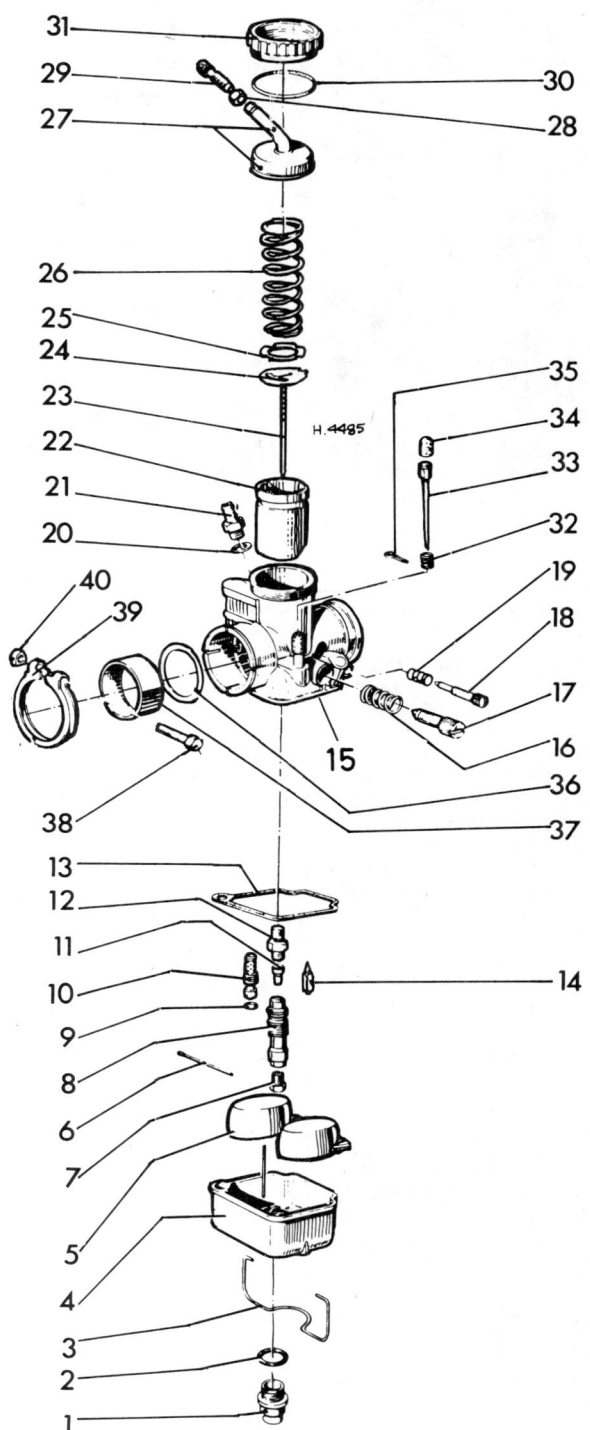

5 Carburettor overhaul: Bing slide type

1 Remove each carburettor as previously described. Dismantle them separately, so that parts are not interchanged.
2 Push back the spring clip, and remove the float bowl.
3 Unscrew the main jet holder and the mixing tube. The needle jet should drop out. Unscrew the pilot jet. Blow through the jets to clear.
4 Inspect the needle jet and the needle for wear. After a considerable mileage, the jet may become oval then it should be renewed. Check the O-ring seal on the pilot jet.
5 Inspect the throttle slide for wear, replace if necessary. The needle must be replaced with the clip in the correct groove.
6 If it is necessary to remove the throttle stop or pilot air screws, screw them in until they seat lightly, recording the exact number of turns necessary to do this, then unscrew them. On refitting reverse this procedure to return each screw to its original setting.
7 Extract the float pivot pin using pliers. It is splined at one end. Remove the twin float and allow the float needle to drop out. Check the conical tip of the needle for wear or damage. Shake the float to check that there is no petrol in it, which would indicate a leak. Replace the pivot pin carefully the same way round.
8 Clean the float bowl and check the float chamber gasket.
9 Insert the throttle slide into the mixing chamber carefully, ensuring that the needle enters the needle valve. Do not oil the slide. The slide cutaway is on the intake side.
10 The mixing chamber top ring should be screwed up hand tight. Ensure that the locating lug on the mixing chamber top engages with the notch in the carburettor body.
11 Jet sizes and needle position, are selected by the manufacturers after exhaustive testing with the recommended fuel. They should only be altered in exceptional circumstances.

Chapter 4 Fuel system and lubrication

5.1 Bing slide carburettor – R50 and R60

6 Carburettor overhaul: Dell'orto

1 Remove the carburettors as described in Section 4. Dismantle them separately to avoid mixing their components.
2 Unscrew the fuel filter cover screw and remove the screw, seal, filter cover and filter screen. Wash the screen in petrol.
3 Unscrew the float bowl nut and remove with sealing ring. Remove the float bowl and O-ring seal.
4 Unscrew the main jet, main jet holder and needle jet. Blow through the jets to ensure that they are clear.
5 Unscrew the starting jet and check the O-ring seal. Unscrew the pilot jet, and the accelerator pump valve. Blow through to clear.
6 Pull out the float pivot pin and remove the twin float. Drop out the float needle and unscrew the needle valve. Check the O-ring seal underneath the needle valve and inspect the float needle tip for wear. Check the plastic float for leaks by shaking to see if any petrol is inside.
7 Clean the float bowl and nut. Inspect the float chamber O-ring seal and fit firmly in its groove before replacing the float bowl. Ensure that all O-ring seals are replaced without damage.

8 Unscrew the accelerator pump jet cover with O-ring seal – this is opposite the fuel filter – and remove the accelerator pump jet with its O-ring seal. Blow through the jet. It should not be necessary to dismantle the accelerator pump. **Do not** move the pump adjuster screw – this is set by the factory.
9 Check the condition of the O-ring seal in the mixing chamber top. Inspect the throttle needle and needle jet for wear. The jet may be worn oval after considerable mileage when it should be renewed.
10 Jet sizes and needle position are selected by the manufacturers after testing with the recommended fuel. Changes are only necessary in exceptional circumstances.
11 If it is necessary to remove the throttle stop or pilot mixture screws, screw them in until they seat lightly, recording the exact number of turns necessary to do this, then unscrew them. On refitting reverse this procedure to return each screw to its original setting.
12 Throttle slide or mixing chamber tops should not be interchanged as the accelerator pumps will then need readjusting.
13 Insert the throttle slide into the mixing chamber carefully, making sure that the needle goes into the needle jet. The accelerator pump lever is on the intake side.

6.1 Dell'orto carburettor – R90S

Fig. 4.10 Carburettor assembly – Dell'orto type PHM BD or BS

1 Mixing chamber top screw
2 Mixing chamber top
3 Pivot, accelerator pump lever
4 Spring
5 Accelerator pump lever
6 Adjuster cover
7 Cable adjuster
8 Adjuster locknut
9 Adjuster body
10 Choke spring
11 Choke slide
12 Choke body
13 Screw
14 Choke body gasket
15 Accelerator pump diaphragm
16 Spring
17 Jet cover, accelerator pump
18 O-ring seal
19 Accelerator pump jet
20 O-ring seal
21 Accelerator pump valve
22 O-ring seal
23 Accelerator pump body
24 Locknut
25 Regulating screw, accelerator pump
26 O-ring seal
27 Screw
28 Spring washer
29 Adjuster cover
30 Adjuster
31 Adjuster locknut
32 Cable guide
33 Nut
34 Throttle spring
35 Needle clip
36 Throttle slide
37 Needle
38 O-ring seal, mixing chamber top
39 Nut, clamp screw
40 Insulating bush
41 Clamp screw
42 Clamp
43 O-ring seal
44 Flat washer
45 Spring
46 Pilot mixture screw
47 O-ring seal
48 Flat washer
49 Spring
50 Pilot air adjusting screw
51 Filter screen
52 Filter cover
53 O-ring seal
54 Bolt, filter cover
55 Accelerator pump valve
56 Pilot jet
57 O-ring seal
58 Float needle assembly
59 Starting jet
60 O-ring seal
61 Atomiser
62 Main jet holder
63 Main jet
64 Float
65 Float pivot
66 Float bowl O-ring seal
67 Float bowl
68 Gasket
69 Main jet cover

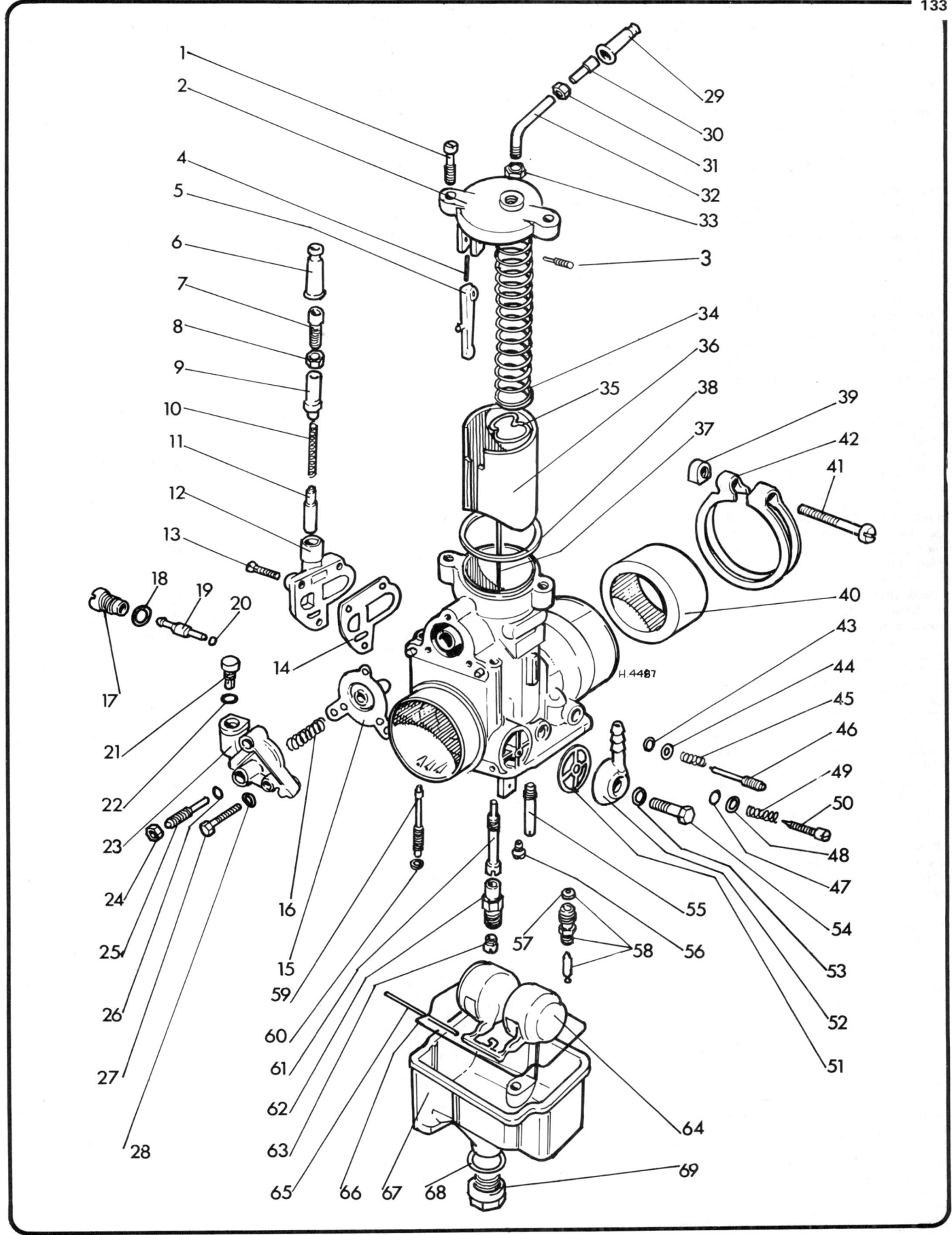

7 Carburettor overhaul: Bing constant-depression type

1 Remove each carburettor as described in Section 4. Dismantle them separately so that parts are not interchanged.
2 Push back the retaining clip and remove the float chamber.
3 Unscrew the main jet and main jet holder; the needle jet should drop out. Unscrew the pilot jet. Blow through the jets to clear them.
4 Unscrew the countersunk screws and remove the vacuum chamber cover. The screws may be very tight and great care is needed to avoid damage to the casting. Remove the diaphragm with slide and needle carefully and check the diaphragm for splits or tears.
5 Inspect the needle and needle jet for wear. The needle jet may be worn oval after a considerable mileage. The needle and plunger must be renewed as a complete assembly. Check the O-ring seal on the pilot jet.
6 When reassembling the throttle slide, ensure that the tab on the diaphragm locates in the recess in the carburettor body. This positions the pressure equalising passages in the throttle slide on the butterfly side of the choke. Do not oil the damper rod.
7 The cable abutments on the vacuum chamber cover must be above the butterfly and choke levers. Tighten the screws diagonally.
8 If correctly installed, the vacuum piston should move in both directions under its own weight.
9 Check the float and float needle as described in Section 5.7.
10 Clean the float bowl and check the condition of the gasket.
11 Do not forget to replace the washer under the main jet.
12 If it is necessary to remove the throttle stop or pilot mixture screw, screw each in until it seats lightly, recording the exact number of turns necessary to do so, then unscrew it. On refitting, reverse this procedure to return each screw to its original setting.
13 Unscrew the four countersunk screws and remove the auxiliary starting carburettor. Note the gasket and check its condition. Wash the rotary slides in petrol. Do not interchange the two starting carburettors – they are handed.
14 Jet sizes are selected by the manufacturers after testing with the recommended fuels, and should need changing only in exceptional circumstances.

8 Carburettor adjustment and exhaust emissions: general note

1 In some countries legal provision is made for describing and controlling the types and levels of toxic emissions from motor vehicles.
2 In the USA exhaust emission legislation is administered by the Environmental Protection Agency (EPA) which has introduced stringent regulations relating to motor vehicles. The Federal law entitled the Clean Air Act, specifically prohibits the removal (other than temporary) or modification of any component incorporated by the vehicle manufacturer to comply with the requirements of the law. The law extends the prohibition to any tampering which includes the addition of components, use of unsuitable replacement parts or maladjustment of components which allows the exhaust emissions to exceed the prescribed levels. Violations of the provisions of this law may result in penalties of up to $10 000 for each violation. It is strongly recommended that appropriate requirements are determined and understood prior to making any change to or adjustments of components in the fuel, ignition, crankcase breather or exhaust systems.
3 To help ensure compliance with the emission standards some manufacturers have fitted to the relevant systems fixed or pre-set adjustment screws as anti-tamper devices. In most cases this is restricted to plastic or metal limiter caps fitted to the carburettor pilot adjustment screws, which allow normal adjustment only within narrow limits. Occasionally the pilot screw may be recessed and sealed behind a small metal blanking plug, or locked in position with a thread-locking compound, which prevents normal adjustment.
4 It should be understood that none of the various methods of discouraging tampering actually prevents adjustment, nor, in itself, is re-adjustment an infringement of the current regulations. Maladjustment, however, which results in the emission levels exceeding those laid down, is a violation. It follows that no adjustments should be made unless the owner feels confident that he can make those adjustments in such a way that the resulting emissions comply with the limits. For all practical purposes a gas analyser will be required to monitor the exhaust gases during adjustment, together with EPA data of the permissible Hydrocarbon and CO levels. Obviously, the home mechanic is unlikely to have access to this type of equipment or the expertise required for its use, and, therefore, it will be necessary to place the machine in the hands of a competent motorcycle dealer who has the equipment and skill to check the exhaust gas content.

9 Carburettors: checking the settings

1 The various jet sizes, throttle valve cutaway (on slide type carburettors) and needle position are predetermined by the manufacturer and should not require modification. Check with the Specifications list at the beginning of this Chapter if there is any doubt about the sizes fitted. If a change appears necessary it can often be attributed to a developing engine fault unconnected with the carburettor(s). Although carburettors do wear in service, this process occurs slowly over an extended length of time and hence wear of the carburettor is unlikely to cause sudden or extreme malfunction. If a fault does occur check first other main systems, in which a fault may give similar symptoms, before proceeding with carburettor examination or modification.
2 Where non-standard items, such as exhaust systems, air filters or camshafts have been fitted to a machine, some alterations in carburation may be required. Arriving at the correct settings often requires trial and error, a method which demands skill born of previous experience. In many cases the manufacturer of the non-standard equipment will be able to advise on correct carburation changes.
3 As a rough guide, up to $1/8$ throttle is controlled by the pilot jet, $1/8$ to $1/4$ by the throttle valve cutaway, $1/4$ to $3/4$ throttle by the needle position and from $3/4$ to full by the size of the main jet. These are only approximate divisions, which are by no means clear cut. There is a certain amount of overlap between the various stages. The above remarks apply only in part to constant velocity carburettors which utilise a butterfly valve in place of the throttle valve. The first and fourth stages are controlled in a similar manner. The second stage is controlled by the by-pass valve which is uncovered as soon as the throttle valve (piston) is opened. During the third stage the fuel passing through the main jet is metered by the needle jet working in conjunction with the piston needle (jet needle).
4 If alterations to the carburation must be made, always err on the side of a slightly rich mixture. A weak mixture will cause the engine to overheat which may cause engine seizure. Reference to the colour chart in Routine Maintenance will show how, after some experience has been gained, the condition of the spark plug electrodes can be interpreted as a reliable guide to mixture strength.

7.1 Bing constant depression carburettor – all other models

7.2a Prise back the clip and withdraw the float chamber ...

7.2b ... then drive out the float pivot pin, remove the float ...

7.2c ... and withdraw the float needle

7.3a Unscrew the main jet, with its washer ...

7.3b ... and unscrew the main jet holder ...

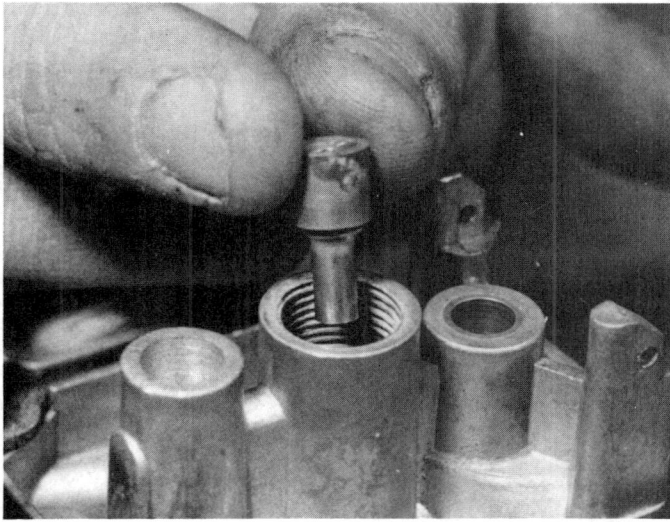
7.3c ... to release the needle jet

7.3d Unscrew the pilot jet – renew its O-ring if damaged or worn

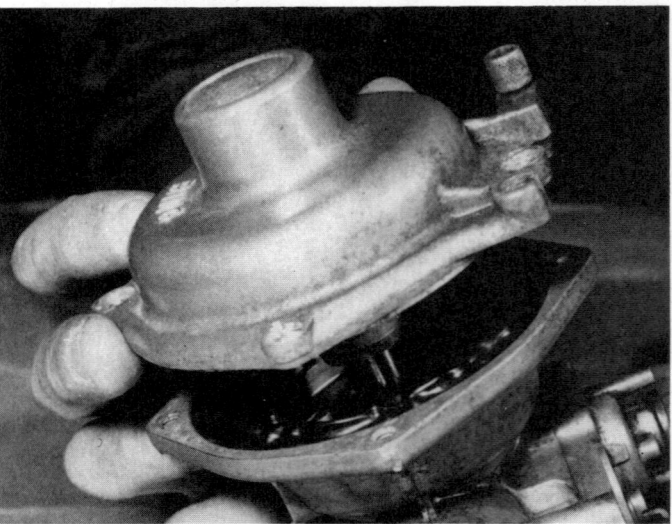

7.4 Vacuum chamber is retained by four screws – take care not to tear the diaphragm

7.6 Diaphragm locating tab must engage in carburettor body recess

7.13 Take care not to interchange components when dismantling auxiliary starting carburettors – rotary valves are handed

Fig. 4.11 Carburettor assembly – Bing constant-depression type

1. Float bowl clip
2. Float bowl
3. Float pivot
4. Float
5. Main jet
6. Main jet washer
7. Main jet holder
8. Needle jet
9. Needle jet holder
10. Float needle
11. Float bowl gasket
12. O-ring seal
13. Pilot jet
14. Pilot mixture screw
15. O-ring seal
16. Spring
17. Butterfly stop screw
18. Spring
19. Bush
20. Carburettor body
21. Auxiliary carburettor slide
22. Gasket
23. Spring
24. Gasket
25. Auxiliary carburettor cover
26. Screw
27. Spring circlip
28. Auxiliary carburettor lever
29. Nipple
30. Washer
31. Nut
32. Screw
33. Butterfly and shaft
34. O-ring seal
35. Return spring
36. Lock washer
37. Nut
38. Butterfly lever
39. Butterfly lever
40. Screw
41. Lock washer
42. Spring anchorage
43. Vacuum piston
44. Diaphragm
45. Diaphragm support
46. Lock washer
47. Screw
48. Vacuum chamber top
49. Screw
50. Adjuster locknut
51. Cable adjuster

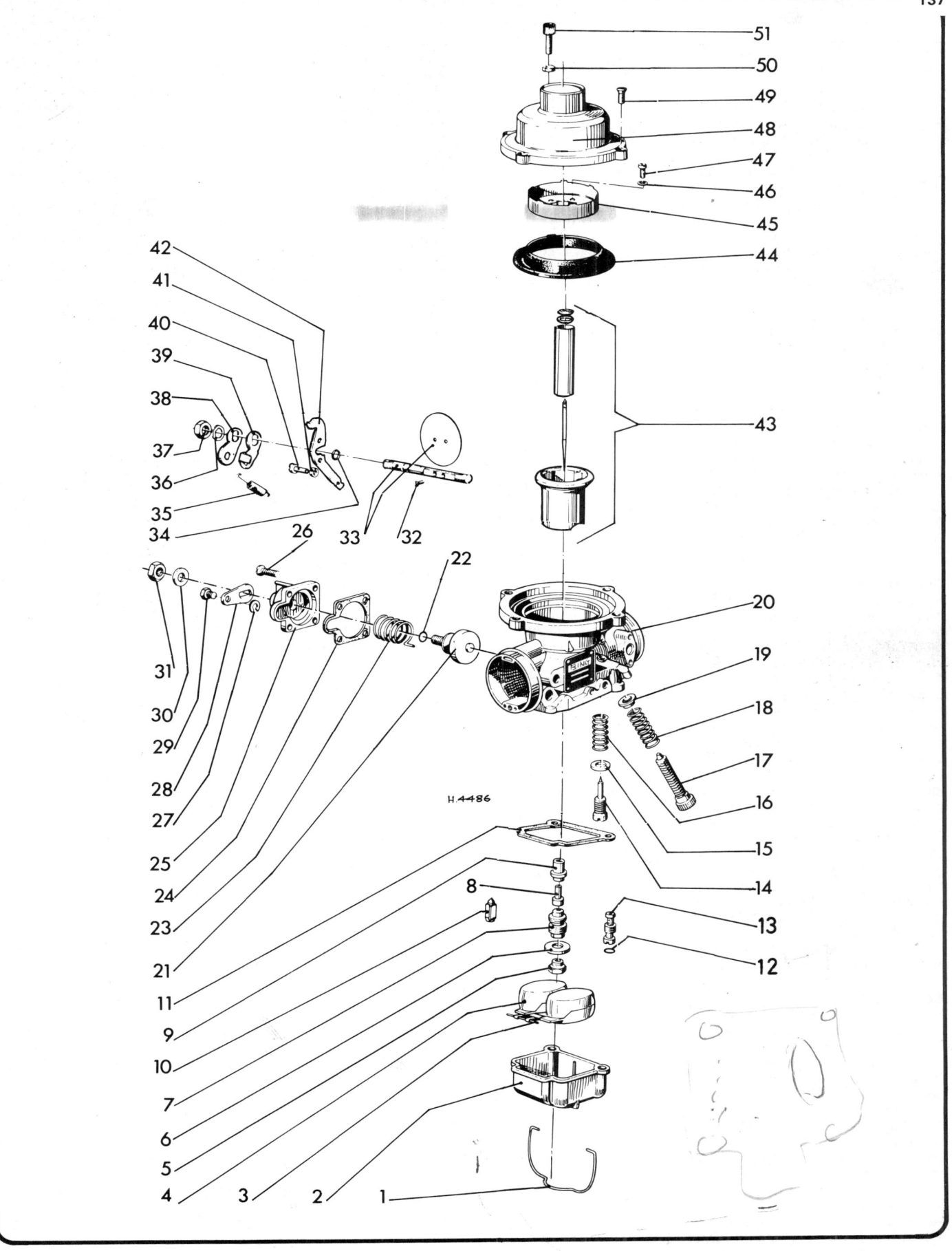

10 Carburettors: adjustment

All models

1 Before the carburettors are adjusted they must be removed and cleaned as described in the previous Sections of this Chapter. Check that all jet sizes and other settings are correct; then check the fuel level as follows.

2 Remove the float bowl and check that when the float lever is just touching the float needle the float is parallel with the float chamber flange. The float lever may be bent carefully to adjust. Note that this can also be checked with the carburettor in place on the machine. Switch on the fuel supply with the float hanging down, then slowly raise the float and note the point at which the fuel supply is cut off; the base of the float should be parallel with the float chamber.

3 With the carburettors known to be clean and in good condition, refit them to the machine. Check that the air filter element is clean or renewed, that the air hoses are free from splits or other leaks, that the valve clearances are correctly set, that the spark plugs are correctly gapped and the contact breaker gap (where applicable) and ignition timing are correct.

4 Adjust both throttle and choke cables to have exactly the same amount of free play on both carburettors; free play should be 0.5 – 1.0 mm (0.02 – 0.04 in); ensure that the control cables are in good condition and working smoothly. If the carburettors are to be set up from scratch, increase throttle cable free play to about 4.0 mm (0.16 in) so that there is no chance of the slide or butterfly hanging on a tight cable and interfering with adjustment.

5 Start the engine and allow it to warm up to normal operating temperature. When it is fully warmed up fully close the twistgrip, check that the choke lever is completely returned and allow the engine to idle. Note: do not allow it to idle for more than ten minutes at a time or it may overheat.

Slide carburettors

6 Detach each plug lead in turn, and check the idling speed of each cylinder alternately. Regulate the firing of the cylinder deviating most from the specified idling speed to that of the other cylinder. While a plug lead is detached, insert an adaptor (Beru EPI or similar) into the plug cap to prevent damage to the cap by the spark.

7 Turn the throttle stop screw clockwise to increase or anti-clockwise to decrease engine speed.

8 When both cylinders are idling at the same speed, turn the pilot air screw (Bing carburettors) or the pilot mixture screw (Dell'orto carburettors) carefully in both directions until the best tick-over is achieved.

9 Having found the best mixture on one carburettor, recheck the idling speed and adjust the throttle stop screw if necessary. Repeat the procedure on the other carburettor.

10 Readjust the throttle cables to give the original 0.5 – 1 mm (0.02 – 0.04 inches) free play.

11 To adjust the transition from idling to partial load, open the twist grip slightly to increase engine speed. Again remove each plug lead in turn and check that each cylinder runs at the same speed. If necessary, adjust the cable of the slower cylinder to have less free play (unscrew the adjuster). Tighten adjuster locknuts.

12 If a carburettor fails to respond to adjustment the pilot jet and airways should be cleaned. The free play in the throttle cable must be maintained to avoid difficulty in setting the slow running.

Constant depression carburettors – models up to 1978

13 If the engine idles with reasonable smoothness proceed to the instruction in paragraph 14. If it refuses to idle or is very rough, set the adjusting screws of each carburettor to the basic setting, ie: turn the throttle stop screws until they just touch the butterfly levers, then turn clockwise a full turn. Tighten the pilot mixture screws fully until they seat lightly, then unscrew them by the specified number of turns. Slacken the cables.

14 Adjust the pilot mixture screws of both carburettors until the best idling is achieved.

15 Now adjust each carburettor alternately. Unscrew the throttle stop screw a fraction of a turn at a time, then re-adjust the pilot mixture pilot screw. Repeat until the cylinder being adjusted ceases to run after a few strokes when the other plug lead is disconnected.

16 Re-adjust the throttle cables to give an equal movement in both of 0.5 – 1 mm (0.02 – 0.04 inches). Open the throttle to increase idling speed slightly. Remove each plug lead in turn and check that each cylinder idles at the same speed. Adjust the throttle cable of the slowest cylinder if necessary. Tighten the adjuster locknuts.

17 If a carburettor fails to respond to adjustment, clean the pilot jet and air passageways. It is essential that the free play in the throttle cables is maintained; there will be difficulty in setting the slow running if it is not.

Constant depression carburettors – notes on adjusting later models

18 While the tasks of removing and refitting, dismantling and reassembly, and cleaning and adjustment are identical for all models, one or two points must be borne in mind, particularly on later models. The first is that the carburation should never be altered or disturbed unless absolutely necessary, and in the event of a fault developing, all other possibilities should be checked before the carburettors are touched. The second point is that all BMWs, particularly the later models, are very sensitive to carburettor settings and will run very roughly if the carburettors are not balanced correctly.

19 If the owner is in any doubt about his ability to adjust the carburettors of his machine correctly, it is recommended that the machine is taken to a BMW dealer for the work to be carried out professionally. Owners in the US should take note of the comments made in Section 8 and ascertain whether local laws permit such work to be carried out by unauthorised personnel before attempting it themselves.

20 The final note on carburettor adjustment concerns 1981 and subsequent models. The electronic ignition system fitted to these models uses an extremely high ignition voltage which can have harmful, possibly even fatal, effects on anyone who touches live ignition components while the engine is running or even while the ignition is switched on. An added point to be borne in mind is that the ignition system components may be damaged if, for example, a spark plug is detached while the engine is running.

21 For the reasons mentioned above it is no longer possible to adjust the carburettors of the 1981 and subsequent models by the time-honoured method of removing one spark plug cap so that the other cylinder can be set, and vice versa. While the carburettors can be balanced accurately by returning the throttle stop and mixture screws to their basic positions, as described in paragraph 13 above, and then by juggling settings to achieve the desired smoothness and throttle response, this method is very time-consuming and requires a great deal of skill and experience as well as a rather sensitive ear, if sufficiently accurate results are to be achieved. For this reason, the use of vacuum gauges is recommended.

22 On looking at the forward edge of the carburettors from underneath, a protrusion will be seen adjacent to that which holds the pilot mixture screw, this second protrusion being sealed by a plain blanking screw; this is the take-off point provided for the use of vacuum gauges; note that on earlier models it may be on the side. Remove the blanking screws and attach a vacuum gauge tube to each. With the engine fully warmed up to normal operating temperature, rotate each mixture regulating screw by small increments each way until the point is found at which the idling speed is fastest. Owners in the US should note that an exhaust gas analyser will be required to ensure that the levels of CO in the exhaust are within the permitted limits of 1.5 – 2.5% at idle speed; if this item of equipment is not available adjustments must be made at the throttle stop screws only, as described below, and the machine then taken to a BMW dealer for the mixture regulating screws to be set correctly.

23 For UK owners, and for US owners who have the necessary equipment, once the mixture regulating screws have been set, the throttle stop screws must be rotated to achieve a constant smooth idling speed of 800 – 1100 rpm with each carburettor set to give the same vacuum gauge reading, indicating that the two are correctly balanced. Note that it does not matter what the gauge reading is, the important point is that the reading is the same for both carburettors.

24 Note that the throttle and choke cables for each carburettor must have 0.5 – 1 mm (0.02 – 0.04 in) of free play, measured in vertical movement of the outer cable at the adjuster on the carburettor, and that the excess free play set when returning the carburettors to the basic position at the start of the adjustment sequence must be removed by adjustment when the work is complete. An adjuster is provided at the upper end of each junction box so that all but the slightest trace of free play can be eliminated from the junction box/throttle twistgrip cable and from the junction box/choke lever cable.

10.2 If level is correct float should be parallel with body flange – bend float lever (arrowed) to adjust

10.8a Bing slide carburettor – throttle stop screw 1, pilot air screw 2

10.8b Dell'orto carburettor – throttle stop screw 1, pilot mixture screw 2

10.13 Bing constant-depression carburettor – throttle stop and pilot mixture screws (arrowed)

10.22a Bing constant-depression carburettor, vacuum gauge take-off point can be here ...

10.22b ... or at the side of the carburettor, as here

11 Pure air system: general

1 Introduced on all US models from 1980 on, a system of 10.5 mm diameter tubes takes pure air from the filter chamber and passes it directly into the exhaust ports, thus reducing emissions by burning up the previously unburned hydrocarbons remaining in the exhaust gases. No pump is necessary to inject the air, the venturi action provided by the exhaust gases passing over the aperture in each exhaust port being sufficient to draw air through the one-way valves in the filter chamber and into the exhaust port itself.

2 The second part of the system was introduced on 1981 models but is available as a kit for fitting to 1980 models. It comprises two rubber tubes which lead from each carburettor inlet tract to a connector in front of the air filter casing; a rubber tube leads from this connector to the left-hand valve of the two valves situated in the filter chamber itself. Another tube links the two valves inside the filter chamber. The function of this part of the system is to use the vacuum created in the inlet tract to shut off the air supply to the exhaust ports by closing the valves when the throttle is closed during deceleration, and to prevent the severe popping and banging in the exhaust system that would result if air were still injected into the exhaust on the overrun.

3 The system is very simple in operation, having no moving parts and requiring no maintenance or adjustment. If a fault is suspected in any part of the system, check very carefully for slack connections, split or damaged pipes, sticking valves or any other damage. Any component that is found to be worn or damaged should be renewed immediately. Repairs are not advised in view of the possibly illegal nature of such an action, as discussed in Section 8.

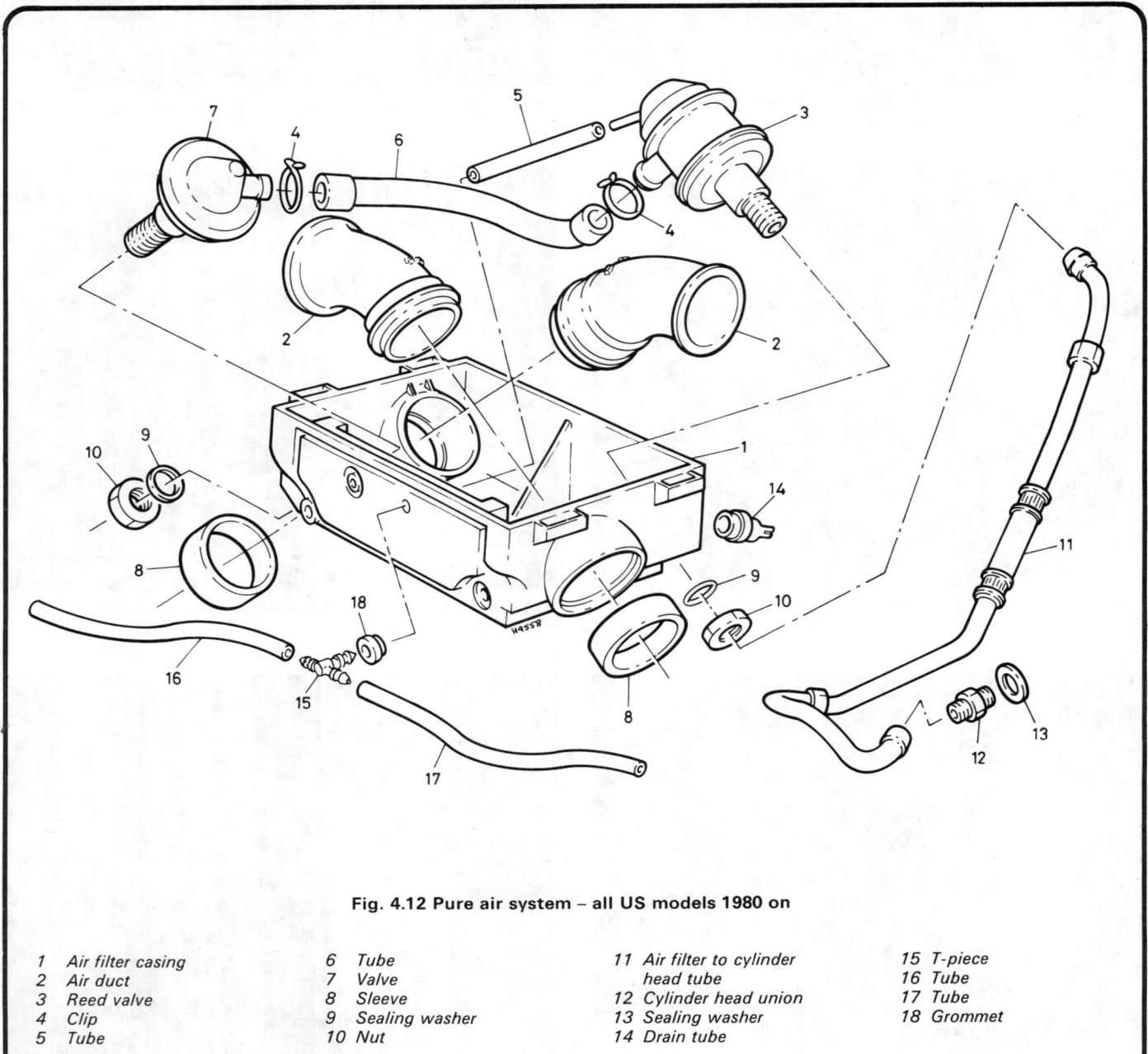

Fig. 4.12 Pure air system – all US models 1980 on

1	Air filter casing
2	Air duct
3	Reed valve
4	Clip
5	Tube
6	Tube
7	Valve
8	Sleeve
9	Sealing washer
10	Nut
11	Air filter to cylinder head tube
12	Cylinder head union
13	Sealing washer
14	Drain tube
15	T-piece
16	Tube
17	Tube
18	Grommet

Note: items 3 – 7 and 15 – 18 1981 on models only

Chapter 4 Fuel system and lubrication

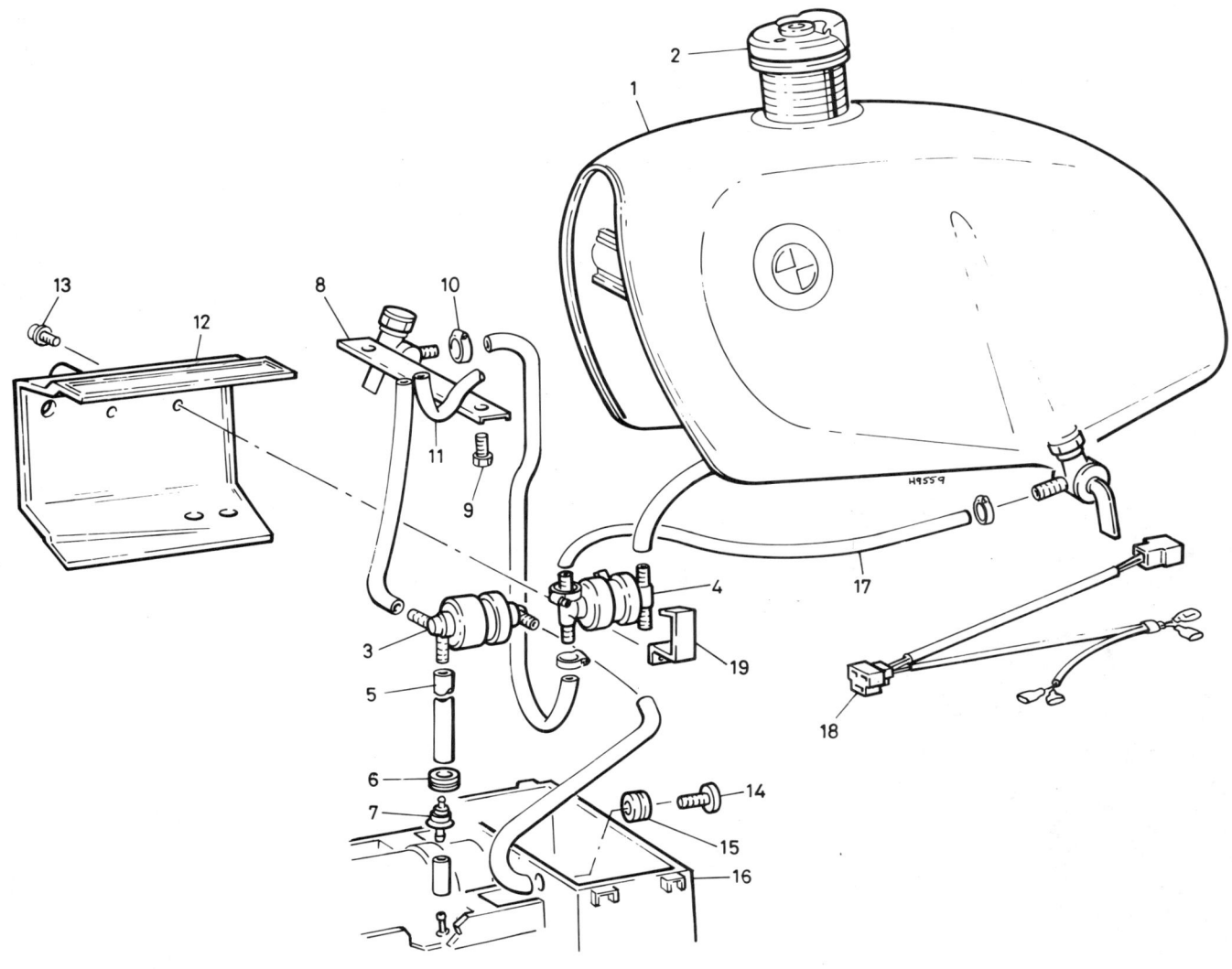

Fig. 4.13 Evaporative Emission Control System – California 1985 models only

Refer to Chapter 10 for further details of the Evaporative Emission Control System

1 Fuel tank
2 Filler cap
3 Air vent solenoid
4 Fuel shut-off solenoid
5 Vacuum hose
6 Grommet
7 Pressure relief valve
8 Bracket
9 Bolt – 2 off
10 Clamp – 2 off
11 Tank overflow drain tubing
12 Starter motor cover
13 Allen screw – 4 off
14 Pipe fitting
15 Grommet
16 Air filter casing lower half
17 Fuel feed pipe
18 Wiring loom extension
19 Clamp

12 Exhaust system: removal and refitting

All models – exhaust finned nuts

1 Note that it is not necessary to unscrew the exhaust pipe finned nuts completely when removing the pipes; they can be slackened one or two turns to release the clamp washer and tapered ring, allowing the pipes to be tapped forwards out of the head.

2 At regular intervals however the finned nuts should be removed so that the threads can be thoroughly cleaned, using a wire brush. Scrub all traces of dirt and corrosion from the cylinder head stubs and from the nuts themseves, and use a soft wire brush to clean the clamp washer and ring. Clean the plated exhaust pipe in the usual way. On reassembly, place the nut over the exhaust pipe end (facing the correct way round) followed by the triangular-section compression ring and the clamp ring; ensure that the tapered surfaces engage each other.

Apply a smear of high-temperature anti-corrosion compound such as Copaslip to the threads before refitting the nut.

3 It is a worthwhile investment to purchase either the BMW special tool 18 0 600 or one of the proprietary equivalents to slacken and tighten the nuts with the minimum risk of damage. Never use a punch to slacken or tighten them.

4 If the nuts are found to be locked in place with corrosion, apply a liberal quantity of penetrating fluid to the threads and allow time for it to work before attempting to slacken the nut; use only the special tool or the fins may be bent or broken. If this fails, the nuts can be heated in an attempt to loosen them. If the nuts are still locked in place, or if you suspect that they are cross-threaded it is better to cut the nut across with a hacksaw and to open it up using a hammer and chisel than to risk stripping the threads of the cylinder head stub; new nuts, while expensive, are cheaper than attempting to repair stripped threads.

Chapter 4 Fuel system and lubrication

R80G/S, R80ST

5 Remove the left-hand side panel and remove the two silencer mounting bolts, slacken its clamp bolt, and work it off the primary silencer stub.
6 Slacken the exhaust pipe/primary silencer clamps and the exhaust finned nuts and use a soft-faced mallet to tap out the exhaust pipes. Remove the primary silencer.
7 Reassembly is the reverse of the dismantling sequence; apply a smear of high temperature anti-corrosion compound to all pipe stubs (and the finned nuts, if removed). Tighten the mountings securely.

R80, R80RT 1985 on

8 Remove their mounting bolts, slacken their retaining clamps and withdraw the silencers.
9 Slacken the finned nuts, the front balance pipe clamp bolts, and the exhaust pipe/crossover chamber clamps and use a soft-faced mallet to tap out the exhaust pipes. Remove the crossover chamber.
10 Reassembly is the reverse of the removal sequence. Fit the exhaust pipes to the cylinder heads and crossover chamber and partially tighten the finned nuts. Check that the pipes are correctly aligned before tightening the front balance pipe clamp bolts. Apply a smear of high-temperature anti-corrosion compound to all pipe stubs (and the finned nuts, if removed). Tighten the mountings securely.

All other models

11 Slacken the exhaust pipe to silencer clips. Remove the two silencer bolts of each silencer from beneath the rear footrest bracket. The silencers can now be pulled rearwards, free of the exhaust pipes.
12 Slacken the clamp screws of the front (all models) and rear (1981 on models only) balance pipes. Remove the engine rear mounting nuts (noting the footrest original positions on early models) and release the pipe clamps.
13 Slacken the finned nuts and use a soft faced mallet to tap the pipes forward.
14 Reassembly is the reverse of the above. Apply a smear of high-temperature anti-corrosion compound to all pipe stubs (and the finned nuts, if removed). Do not fully tighten any fasteners until all components are correctly refitted and aligned without strain on their mountings; then tighten the balance pipe clamp screws, the finned nuts, the pipe clamps (aligning the footrests again, where applicable), the pipe/silencer clamps and the silencer mounting bolts.

12.1 While finned nuts need not be unscrewed to remove exhaust pipes, they should be removed at regular intervals for cleaning

12.2 Ensure tapered faces of compression and clamp rings engage each other – apply anti-corrision compound to stub threads

12.11a Slacken silencer clips – note exhaust pipe clamp on front footrest mounting

12.11b Silencers are each retained by two bolts on footrest bracket

Chapter 4 Fuel system and lubrication

12.12 Slacken fully balance pipe clamp screws

12.13 Finned nuts need only be slackened to release exhaust pipes

13 Oil pump: examination and renovation

1 The oil pump is driven from the rear end of the camshaft. Oil pump removal is described in Chapter 1.

2 Inspect the O-ring seal in the oil pump cover; if it is distorted or damaged it should be renewed. Clean the O-ring seal groove and seat the seal firmly.

3 Check the clearances between the outer rotor and pump body and between the inner and outer rotors, with a feeler gauge. Check the clearance between the rotor face, and the oil pump housing flange surface by holding a straight edge across the flange. All clearances are given in the specifications section of this Chapter. Measurements should be made with the pump dry.

4 Inspect the rotors and the pump housing for scoring or damage.

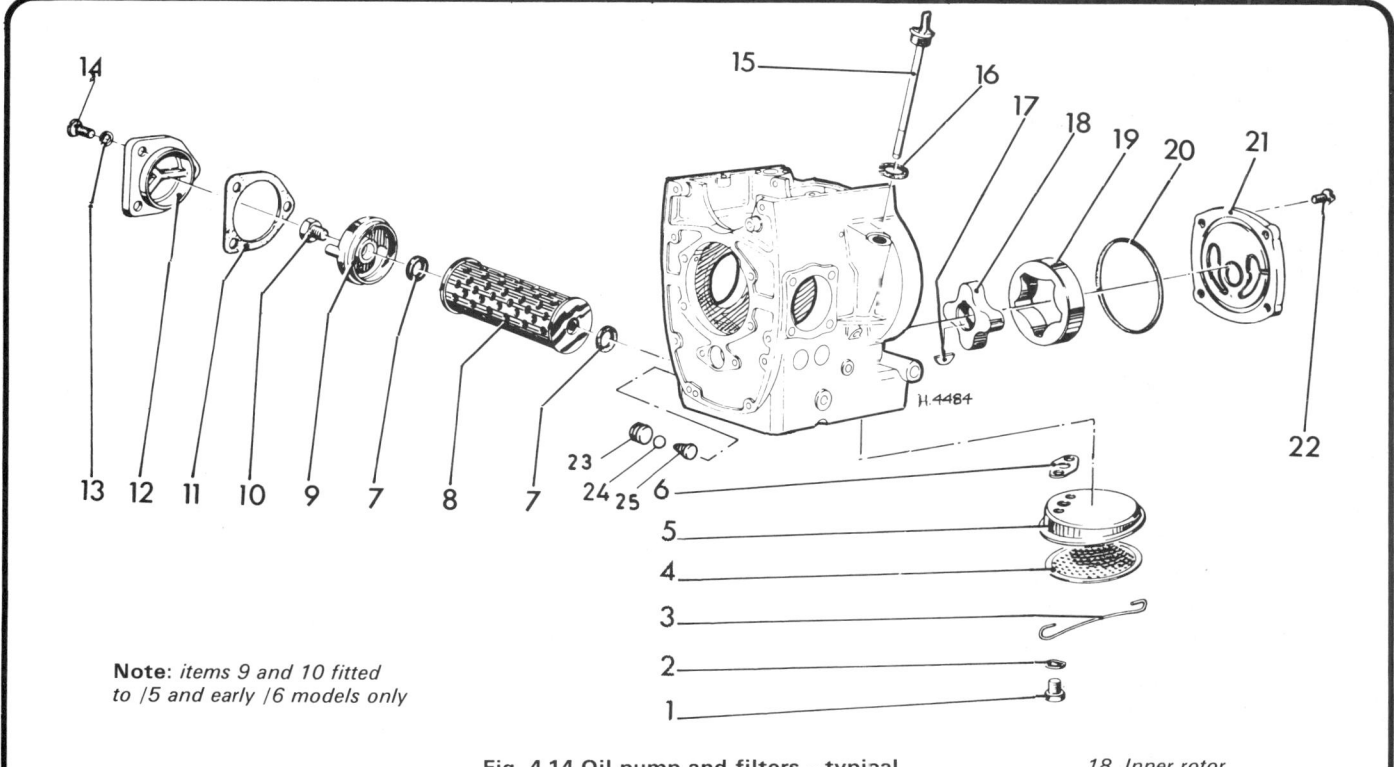

Fig. 4.14 Oil pump and filters – typical

1 Bolt
2 Lock washer
3 Wire clip
4 Strainer screen
5 Strainer body
6 Gasket
7 O-ring seal
8 Filter cartridge
9 Filter end plate
10 Bolt
11 Gasket
12 Filter cover plate
13 Lock washer
14 Screw
15 Dipstick
16 Gasket
17 Woodruff key – where fitted
18 Inner rotor
19 Outer rotor
20 O-ring seal
21 End plate
22 Screw
23 Threaded plug
24 Filter bypass valve ball
25 Filter bypass valve spring

Note: items 9 and 10 fitted to /5 and early /6 models only

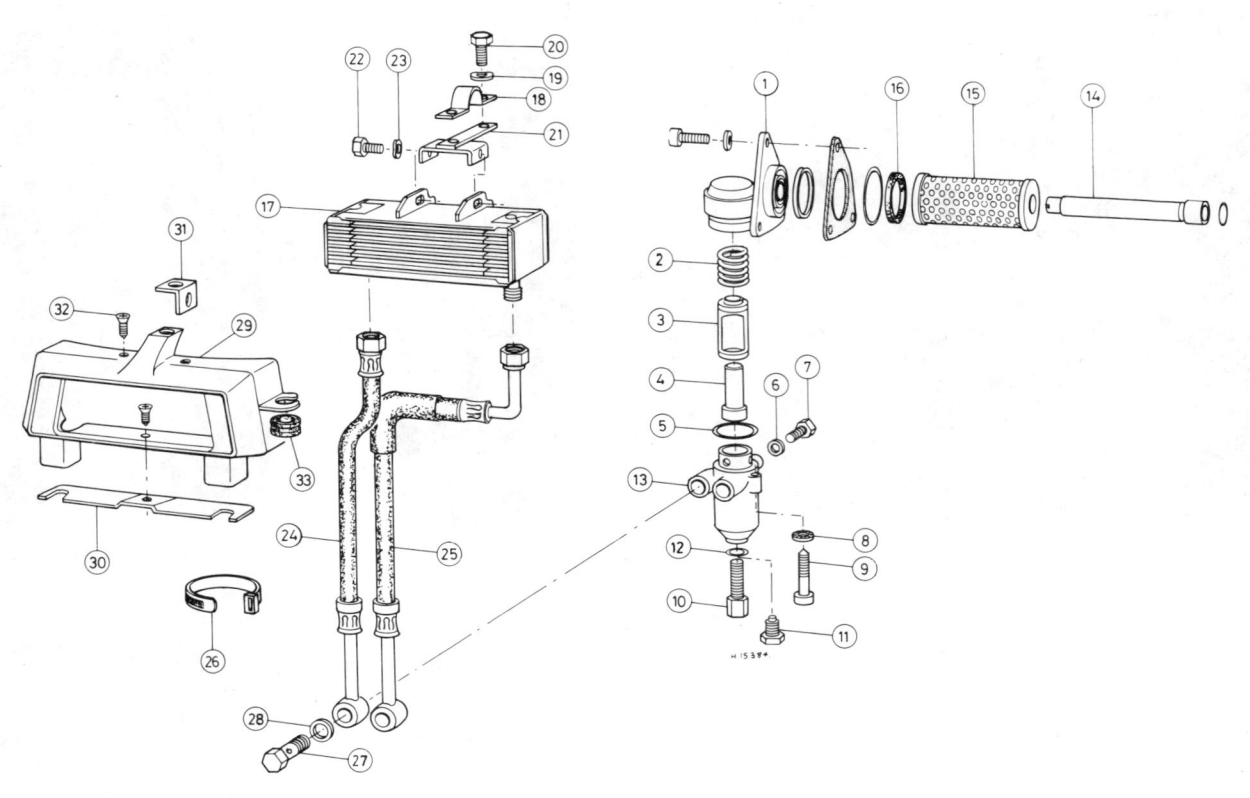

Fig. 4.15 Oil cooler and filter assembly – R100RS 1978 on and R100RT 1980 on

1 Filter chamber cover
2 Spring
3 Plunger
4 Thermostatic valve
5 O-ring
6 O-ring
7 Bolt
8 Lock washer
9 Bolt
10 Bleed bolt
11 Blanking bolt
12 O-ring
13 Valve housing
14 Filter shaft
15 Filter
16 Seal
17 Oil cooler
18 Clamp
19 Wave washer
20 Bolt
21 Top mounting bracket
22 Bolt
23 Wave washer
24 Inlet pipe
25 Outlet pipe
26 Pipe tie
27 Banjo union bolt
28 Sealing washer
29 Oil cooler cover
30 Mounting plate
31 Mounting bracket
32 Screw

13.2 Renew O-ring and check pump cover for wear or damage

13.3a Checking the oil pump for wear – measuring outer rotor/pump body clearance, ...

Chapter 4 Fuel system and lubrication

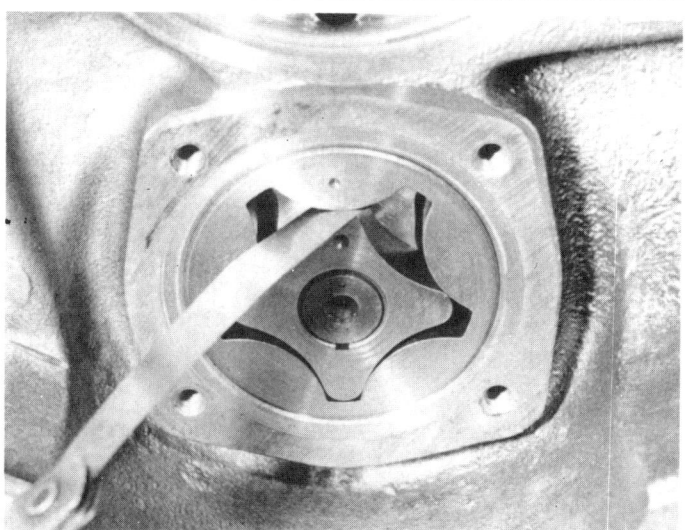

13.3b ... inner rotor/outer rotor clearance, ...

13.3c ... and pump body/rotor clearance (rotor endfloat)

14 Oil pump pick-up filter gauze: cleaning

1 The filter gauze should be cleaned at the first 600 mile/1000 km service and whenever the sump is removed after this.
2 Referring to Routine Maintenance, drain the engine oil and remove the oil filter.
3 Unscrew the retaining bolts around the periphery of the sump, tap it with a soft faced mallet to break the seal and withdraw it. Carefully remove all traces of the old gasket from both mating surfaces and thoroughly clean the sump (inside and outside). Use a clean lint-free rag to wipe down the inside of the crankcase.
4 Unclip the wire retainer holding the filter gauze and wash the gauze to remove all particles of foreign matter. Check that the pump pick-up spacer is undamaged; the earlier plastic type should be replaced by the later component to prevent any risk of cracking. If the pick-up body is removed, thoroughly degrease its threads, apply a few drops of Loctite 242 thread locking compound and tighten the mounting bolts to a torque setting of 9 Nm (6.5 lbf ft).
5 On reassembly, fit the gauze to the pick-up and secure with the wire clip. Smear both sides of the new sump gasket with Hylomar SQ32/M or a similar non-setting jointing compound. Working in a diagonal sequence, tighten the sump retaining bolts to a torque setting of 9-12 Nm (6.5 – 9 lbf ft).
6 Refit the sump drain plug and oil filter, then refill the crankcase with oil as described in Routine Maintenance.

14.4 Unclip wire retainer to release pump pick-up filter gauze

15 Crankcase breather: examination

1 The breather is located at the rear right-hand side of the engine housing beneath the starter cover. It is untimed and recycles oil-saturated air through the engine via the carburettors.
2 Remove the starter cover; see Chapter 1.
3 Unscrew the two hexagon socket cap screws (three on later models) and remove the breather cover.
4 Remove the circlip (early models only). Note in which groove it was fitted – there are two. The top one is for R50/5, R60/5, R60/6 and R75/6 models. The bottom one is for R75/5, R90/6, R90S models. Remove the washer, spring, washer and the valve disc.
5 If there is any doubt about the condition of the early type of breather it should be discarded and replaced by the later type. This is a simple reed-valve unit which has no working parts and requires no maintenance. In the unlikely event of its failure, it should be renewed.
6 Owners of early models should note that the later type is a straight replacement and will eliminate the 'plopping' sound of the original, especially when the engine is being started from cold.
7 When replacing the breather cover, pass the breather hose through the hole in the air filter cover.

14.5 Thoroughly clean all components and renew sump gasket on reassembly

Chapter 4 Fuel system and lubrication

15.5 Early type of breather (shown) should be replaced by later reed-valve type

15.6 Remove single screw to dismantle reed-valve type breather

16 Oil pressure relief valve

1 The oil pressure relief valve consists of a spring-loaded plunger. It is situated on the front crankshaft bearing housing.
2 Slacken the horn fixing screws, unscrew the three fixing screws and remove the front engine cover. Next remove the timing chain cover. See Chapter 1.
3 Unscrew the pressure relief valve housing and extract the plunger and spring.
4 Check that the plunger moves freely in the housing and measure the relaxed length of the spring – see specifications section of this Chapter.
5 The plunger should be fully to the right (looking at the engine from the front). If it sticks it should be removed and any burrs should be polished away. Alternatively replace it by the plunger with two chamfered faces fitted to the large-capacity six-cylinder BMW cars.

17 Oil pressure warning lamp

1 The oil pressure warning lamp, which comes on when the ignition is switched on, should extinguish at idling speed. It is operated by a switch on the left of the engine housing, below the dipswitch.
2 If the lamp flashes, or remains on, check the oil level in the sump or that the filter is not clogged. If these are in order, check the electrical system for faults. If the lamp comes on when slowing down from high speed, again check the oil level and the filter. If these are OK, the main bearings or big end bearings may be worn, or the oil pressure relief valve or oil pump faulty. Have the oil pressure checked with a gauge. If the pressure is low, overhaul the engine.

16.1 Oil pressure relief valve is fitted in crankshaft front main bearing housing

17.1 Oil pressure warning lamp switch is screwed into crankcase left-hand side, below barrel

Chapter 5 Ignition system

Refer to Chapter 10 for information relating to the 1986 on models

Contents

General description 1	Ignition control unit: removal and refitting 5
Contact breaker/ignition trigger: removal and refitting 2	Electronic ignition system: testing 6
Condenser: removal and refitting 3	Elimination of persistent pre-ignition – all R60 models 7
Ignition HT coil(s): removal and refitting 4	

Specifications

Ignition system type
All models up to 1980	Battery and coil contact breaker triggered
All models 1981 on	Battery and coil, triggered by transistorised electronic system using Hall-effect transmitter

Ignition timing
Static:
/5, /6	9° ± 3° BTDC
/7 up to 1978	6° ± 3° BTDC
All other models	6° BTDC

Advance beings at:
/5	800 rpm
/6, /7	1550 rpm
All other models	1500 rpm

Full advance at:
/5	2800 – 3200 rpm
All other models	3000 rpm (minimum)

Advance range:
/5, /6, /7 up to 1978	25° ± 2°
All other models	26°

Contact breaker
Gap:
/5, /6, /7 up to 1978	0.35 – 0.40 mm (0.014 – 0.016 in)
/7, R45 and R65 1979-80	0.40 – 0.50 mm (0.016 – 0.020 in)

Dwell angle:
/5	110° ± 1° (60 – 61%)
/6, /7 up to 1978	78° ± 1° (43 – 44%)
/7, R45 and R65 1979 – 80	120° ± 3° (65 – 68%)

Contact breaker spring pressure:
/5, /6, /7 up to 1978	450p
/7, R45 and R65 1979 – 80	N/Av
Maximum permissible runout of ATU shaft – /5, /6, /7 up to 1978	0.02 mm (0.0008 in)

Condenser capacity
/5, /6, /7 up to 1978	0.2 microfarad – 25%
/7, R45 and R65 1979 – 80	0.2 microfarad ± 20%

Ignition HT coil
Type:
R45 1981 on, R65 1981 on, R65LS, R80G/S, R80ST, R80, R80RT 1985	Bosch 12V twin coil
All other models	Bosch E6V single coil (x2)

Spark gap – all models up to 1980:
At 300 sparks per minute, 3V	8.0 mm (0.32 in)
At 3600 sparks per minute	13.5 mm (0.53 in)

Winding resistances – all models 1981 on:
Primary:
Single coil – terminals 15 to 1	0.67 – 0.77 ohm
Twin coil – terminals 15 to 1	1.15 – 1.32 ohm

Secondary:
Single coil – terminals 15 to 4	3.70 – 5.30 K ohm
Twin coil – terminals 4a to 4b	7.50 – 9.15 K ohm

Spark plugs
Make .... Bosch
Type: ....

	Bosch New designation	Bosch Previous designation
All 800cc models	W7D	W175T30
All R75, R90/6, R90S, R100/7 up to 1978, all US 1000cc models 1981 on	W6D	W200T30
R45, R60/7, R65, R65LS, all 1000cc models (except R100/7 1977 – 78) up to 1980, all UK 1000cc models 1981 on	W5D	W225T30
R50/5, R60/5, R60/6	W5D1	W230T30

Gap .... 0.6 – 0.7 mm (0.024 – 0.028 in)

Torque wrench settings

Component	Nm	lbf ft
Spark plugs	20 – 30	15 – 22
ATU retaining nut:		
/5, /6	6 – 7	4.5 – 5
/7 up to 1978	5 – 6	4 – 4.5

1 General description

On models up to 1978, the single contact breaker is operated by a cam attached to the centrifugal advance unit, which in turn is mounted on the front of the camshaft. The contact breaker interrupts the low tension circuit of the twin ignition coils at a pre-set moment. A high tension voltage is thus induced in the coils, which jumps the spark plug gaps and ignites the petrol/air mixture.

The ignition coils are slung below the top frame tube. The capacitor, mounted above the alternator, minimises sparking across the contact breaker points and helps intensify the high tension current.

The machines produced during the 1979 and 1980 model years were fitted with a modified type of contact breaker assembly. An Oldham coupling was fitted between the camshaft and the contact breaker to eliminate variations in ignition performance by removing high-frequency vibration, and the contact breaker assembly was fitted in a separate housing bolted to the front of the timing chain cover, this housing having an outrigger bearing to provide more rigid support for the contact breaker camshaft end.

The ignition system fitted to all BMW models from 1981 onwards is a transistor-controlled type which contains no mechanical components other than a centrifugal advance and retard unit mounted in the trigger assembly. When the ignition is switched on battery voltage is fed to the primary windings of the ignition HT coils via the control unit, a secondary circuit being fitted in the control unit to protect the coils from overheating by switching the supply off after 1.5 seconds. This circuit remains in operation until the engine is rotated usually by operating the electric start button. The control unit also provides a supply of approximately 5 volts to the trigger assembly, which is a self-contained unit mounted on the forward end of the camshaft.

As the engine rotates, a Hall-effect transistor fitted in the trigger assembly picks up the variations in magnetic flux produced by the cutouts in a specially-shaped rotor passing across a magnetic gate and sends a weak impulse back to the control unit. The control unit senses this impulse and switches off the current to the primary windings of the HT coils which induces a high tension pulse in the secondary windings of the coils, the pulse being fed to the appropriate spark plug via the HT lead and suppressor cap.

2 Contact breaker/ignition trigger: removal and refitting

All models up to 1978
1 Remove the front engine cover and the ATU described in Routine Maintenance. Disconnect the battery (earth) lead.
2 To remove the contact breaker assembly, mark the backplate and the surrounding casting, so that the contact breaker can be replaced in exactly the same position for quick re-timing. Unscrew the two cheese head screws (one retains the cable clip) and remove the spring washers and backplate.
3 Before refitting the centrifugal advance unit, grease the cam lubricating felt and the pivot with the recommended grease. Adjust the points gap and check the ignition timing. See Routine Maintenance.

All 1979 – 80 models
4 Remove the engine front cover and disconnect the battery earth lead. Remove both spark plugs and turn the engine over until the contact breaker gap is at its widest. Unscrew the two retaining Allen screws, disconnect the low-tension lead and withdraw the unit. Do not move the crankshaft.
5 On refitting turn the units' shaft until the points are at their widest gap, then refit the unit ensuring that it engages correctly with the camshaft. Tighten the bolts, connect the lead and check the points gap and ignition timing.

All models 1981 on
6 If it is necessary to remove the ignition trigger assembly, great care must be taken to ensure correct ignition timing on refitting. The assembly is contained in a separate housing which is secured to the timing chain cover by two Allen screws, and is connected to the control unit by a three-pin connector block. Its removal is therefore an extremely simple operation, but unless one has access to the BMW service tool developed to provide accurate static ignition timing, the following procedure must be adopted before the assembly is withdrawn.
7 Check that the ignition is switched off, then remove the two spark plugs and rotate the engine until the 'S' mark is aligned exactly with the crankcase index mark. Slacken and remove the two screws which retain the chrome-plated cover to the front of the trigger assembly, withdraw the cover and note carefully the exact position of the shaped rotor relative to the fixed pick-up or magnetic gate. Ensure that the rotor is in this position when the trigger assembly is refitted. Note that this is merely an approximation of the correct trigger assembly position, and that the ignition timing should be checked as soon as possible after the engine is started. See Routine Maintenance. It is preferable, however, to have the use of the BMW service tool mentioned previously when carrying out this task, and it should be noted that the same tool may be used to test the operation of the trigger assembly, a point worth bearing in mind if one is attempting to trace a fault in the ignition system. Again the trigger assembly is likely to prove an expensive component and it may well prove worth while to return the machine to a BMW dealer for accurate testing before the trigger assembly is actually disturbed.

3 Condenser: removal and refitting

All models up to 1978
1 If the engine is difficult to start, or suffers a persistent misfire, especially when hot, it is possible that the capacitor is faulty. To check, separate the contact breaker points by hand, with the ignition switched on. If a spark occurs across the points and if they have a blackened and burnt appearance, the capacitor may be regarded as unserviceable.
2 The capacitor cannot be tested; it may have an intermittent fault. Replace with the correct capacitor only.

Chapter 5 Ignition system

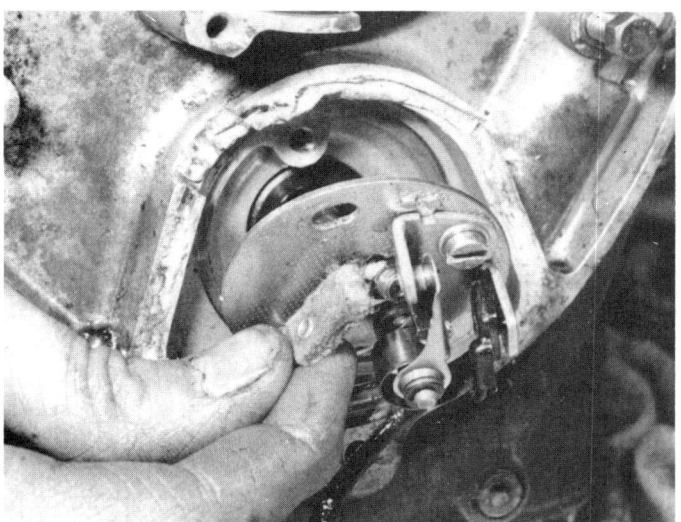

2.2 Models up to 1978 – mark contact breaker backplate and timing chain cover before removal so that backplate can be correctly refitted

3.3 Location of condenser – all models up to 1978

3 Pull off the two leads to the capacitor, unscrew the slotted cheese head screw and remove the spring washer and capacitor and clip. Ensure that the capacitor is earthed well when replacing.

All 1979-80 models

4 The capacitor (condenser) is retained by a single screw to the outside of the contact breaker housing. If it is thought to be faulty (see above) it must be renewed. Remove the single screw and disconnect the lead.

4 Ignition HT coil(s): removal and refitting

1 The ignition coils are sealed and generally give a very long service. If a weak spark suggests a faulty coil, it should be checked by a specialist. The coils are slung below the top frame tube.
2 It is unlikely that both coils will fail simultaneously. If the complete ignition system fails, it is more likely that the contact breaker, capacitor, or wiring, is at fault.
3 To remove the coils, first remove the petrol tank. See Chapter 4. Disconnect the battery earth lead.
4 Pull off the two blade terminals from the coils. Unscrew the two hexagon socket cap screws and remove the coils. Pull off the high tension lead. Note that an earth tag is fitted underneath the front screw of the left-hand ignition coil.

4.3 Remove the fuel tank to expose the ignition HT coil(s)

5 Ignition control unit: removal and refitting

1 The control unit is bolted to an alloy heat sink which is in turn bolted to the top of the front brake hose junction block, the complete assembly being mounted on the frame top tube immediately to the rear of the steering head. When removing and refitting the control unit, hold each bolt with a close-fitting ring spanner while slackening or tightening its securing nut to prevent the control unit from moving, and be very careul to tighten each bolt by just enough to retain the control unit securely.
2 It is easily cracked, and therefore rendered useless, if any of the retaining bolts are overtightened. Note also that the flat top surface of the heatsink must be clean and dry and completely free from corrosion if adequate heat transfer is to be maintained. The manufacturer recommends the application of a heat transferring, anti-corrosion compound such as Curil K2, GC Silicone Compound 25 or Dow-Corning Heat Sink Compound 340, to the heat sink mating surface to prevent the onset of such corrosion while the machine is in use. Remember that if the control unit is allowed to overheat its useful life will be drastically shortened.

5.1 Ignition control unit is mounted on frame top tubes – post-1981 models only

6 Electronic ignition system: testing

Important note *The first thing to remember is that electronic ignition systems use extremely high ignition voltages which may be harmful or even fatal. Take great care to avoid contact with live components while the engine is running or even while the ignition is switched on. Remember also never to allow the system to operate with either one of the HT leads isolated as the very high voltages may damage one or more of the components in the system.*

1 When testing the ignition system note that problems can be broken down as follows.

  a) Faulty spark plugs, suppressor caps, or HT leads
  b) Loose, broken, or corroded connections, or damaged wiring
  c) Wear or damage of the advance mechanism
  d) Faulty electronic components

The above are arranged in the order in which they are most likely to be found, and with the exception of item d) should provide no undue problem during fault diagnosis. A dry battery and bulb test circuit or a pocket multimeter can be used to trace wiring faults, and faults in the HT side can be tested most easily by the substitution of the suspect component. Tracing faults in the trigger assembly or in the control unit requires the use of basic test equipment such as a multimeter but it should be noted that if either of these units is found to be faulty it must be renewed as there are no parts available with which either can be reconditioned.

2 If symptoms should arise which indicate a fault in the ignition system, commence fault-finding by checking first the spark plugs, the spark plug caps, the HT leads and the wiring as outlined above. It is essential that all wiring connections are clean and free from all traces of dirt or corrosion, and that each connection is securely fastened. If these checks fail to isolate the fault, the problem lies either in the power supply to the ignition system or in the ignition components.

3 To check the power supply to the HT coils, use a multimeter set to the appropriate scale or a voltmeter to measure the voltage between each HT coil terminal 15 and a suitable earth point when the ignition is switched on. The figure obtained should be equal to the battery output voltage. If any discrepancy is found, the voltage drop must be measured. Switch off the ignition and disconnect the wire from any coil terminal 1, then connect the meter between the battery positive (+) terminal and that coil's terminal 15. Using a spare length of wire, connect terminal 1 of the coil to be tested to a suitable earth point. Switch on the ignition and note the reading obtained, then switch the ignition off as soon as possible and repeat the test on the remaining coil. Do not leave the coil terminal 1 connected to the earth for longer than one minute or the coil windings will be damaged by overheating. In the case of both coils the voltage drop, or difference between the battery output voltage and the reading obtained, must not be more than 1.5 volts. If a greater difference is found check carefully all earth connections, the battery connections, the ignition switch, the engine kill switch, and the wiring between these components and between the coils and control unit until the fault is traced and rectified.

4 The power supply to the control unit is checked by measuring the voltage between terminals 2 and 4 with the ignition switched on. Pull back the rubber cover from the control unit connecting plug and insert the meter probes into the relevant terminals of the plug itself so that the test is made with the control unit fully connected. A reading equal to the battery output voltage should be obtained, but if a discrepancy is found, check the feed wire between the ignition switch and the control unit and rectify any faults that may be discovered. Check particularly carefully the three-pin plug which connects the separate ignition harness to the main wiring loom.

5 The power supply to the trigger assembly is measured only when the correct voltage is known to be reaching the control unit itself, as described above. Switch off the ignition and connect the meter between terminals 5 and 3 of the control unit in the same way as described for the control unit test. Switch on the ignition and note the reading obtained, which should be at least 5 volts. If the correct reading is not obtained, the fault lies in either the control unit or in the trigger assembly and it will be necessary to obtain a milliammeter to trace the faulty component.

6 When a milliammeter is available, disconnect the control unit connecting plug, withdraw terminal 5 from the plug and connect the plug again to the control unit so that terminal 5 only is disconnected, then connect the milliammeter between the detached end of the

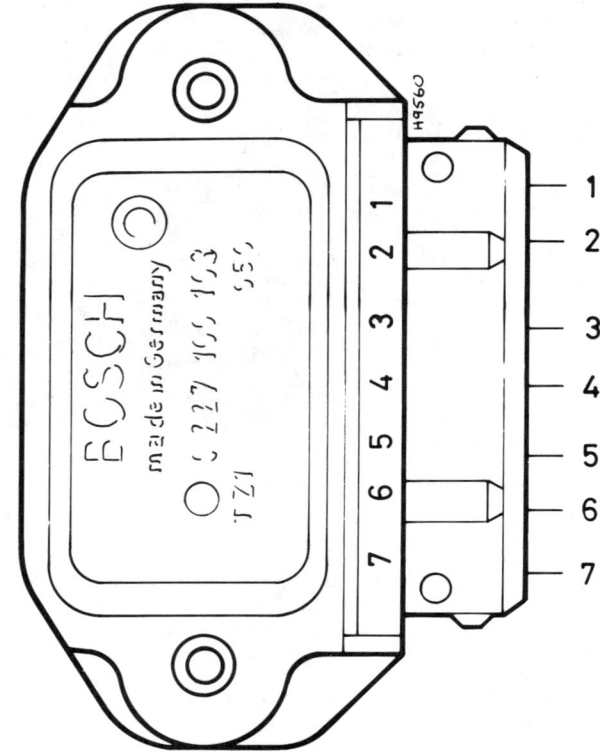

Fig. 5.1 Electronic ignition control unit terminals

Terminal 1 goes to terminal 1 on ignition HT coil
Terminal 2 goes to terminal 31 (frame earth)
Terminal 3 goes to ignition trigger −
Terminal 4 goes to terminal 15 on ignition HT coil, then to switches
Terminal 5 goes to ignition trigger +
Terminal 6 goes to ignition trigger 0
Terminal 7 – not used

terminal 5 wire and terminal 4 of the control unit. Switch on the ignition and note the reading obtained. If a reading of 3 – 20 milliamps is obtained, the control unit is faulty and must be renewed, but if the reading is more or less than 3 – 20 milliamps, it is the trigger assembly that is faulty and must be renewed.

7 If after conducting the above tests the fault has not been found, the problem lies in the components of the ignition system as all other possibilities will have been eliminated. The simplest method of checking these components is as follows. Remove the crankcase front cover which is secured by two Allen screws and disconnect the three-pin plug which connects the trigger assembly to the control unit. Connect one end of a spare length of wire to the centre terminal of that half of the plug which leads to the control unit, then remove the spark plugs, connect each to its respective plug cap and lay the plugs on the cylinder heads so that the metal portion of the spark plug body is in firm contact with the cylinder head finning. Switch on the ignition and touch the bared end of the length of the wire briefly to earth several times, thus simulating the action of the trigger assembly. Sparks should appear at the spark plug electrodes each time the wire is earthed. If this is the case, the control unit and coils are proven to be in good working order and the fault lies in the trigger assembly which must be renewed.

8 If, on conducting the above test, sparks do not appear at the spark plug electrodes, the fault must lie in the control unit itself or in the ignition HT coils. While the control unit cannot be checked by the private owner, the elimination of the HT coils will indirectly prove its effectiveness. Checking the condition of the HT coils will require the

use of a multimeter set to the relevant resistance scale, or of an ohmmeter. The procedure is essentially the same for both types of coil fitted to the BMW models described in this Manual. First disconnect the low tension leads and the HT lead from the coil to be tested, then connect the meter across the two low tension lead spade terminals 15 and 1, noting the reading obtained which should be within the limits given below.

HT coil primary windings:
Single coil 0.67 – 0.77 ohm
Twin coil 1.15 – 1.32 ohm

9 To check the coil secondary windings, two slightly different methods are required. On those machines fitted with two individual HT coils, connect the meter between terminal 15 and the HT lead terminal, but on those machines fitted with a single twin coil, connect the meter between the two HT lead terminals. The readings obtained should be as follows.

HT coil secondary windings:
Single coil 3.7 – 5.3 K ohm
Twin coil 7.5 – 9.15 K ohm

In the case of both types of coil, if the readings obtained for either the primary or the secondary windings differ appreciably from those given, the coil should be considered faulty and renewed, although it should be noted that if there is any doubt about the test results, the suspect coil should be taken to a BMW dealer or to a competent auto-electrician for accurate testing on a spark-gap tester.

10 In the event that the coils are found to be in satisfactory condition, the control unit must be considered faulty by simple virtue of the fact that all other possibilities will have been eliminated at this stage, assuming that the tests described above have been carried out with sufficient care. In view of the fact that the control unit is likely to be an expensive item, it is recommended that the complete machine is returned to a BMW dealer for accurate testing to save unnecessary expense.

7 Elimination of persistent pre-ignition – all R60 models

1 This section applies to the owners of R60/5, R60/6 and R60/7 models sold in the UK, but may well be of benefit to the owners of other BMW models. Some R60 machines have suffered from persistent pre-ignition pinking or knocking during acceleration, a problem that was not solved by any of the usual checks of the ignition timing or mixture strength, or by decarbonisation.

2 To counter this problem the factory introduces a few modifications although it must be stressed that these modifications should be made only on the machines described above, and that they should only be made when the problem persists after the ignition timing has been checked and found to be accurate, after the carburettors have been checked, and after the combustion chambers and piston crowns have been cleaned of all carbon deposits. It should be noted, furthermore, that the factory recommends the use only of premium grade fuel with an octane number of at least 98 (research method) in these machines and in all BMW models up to 1980 (US) and 1981 (UK).

3 The first modification is to fit a compression plate 0.7 mm (0.03 in) thick between each cylinder barrel and the crankcase, thus lowering the compression ratio from 9.2:1 to 8.6:1. These plates can be ordered under BMW Part number 11 11 1 335 650. To ensure an oil-tight seal when fitting them, smear both sides of each plate with a non-setting jointing compound such as Hylomar SQ32/M and fit them with two new O-rings, BMW Part number 11 11 1 262 141.

4 The above modification should cure most cases, but if the problem still persists the following have proved successful. First, set the ignition timing in exactly 6 degrees BTDC, no tolerance being permissible. Second, richen the mixture at $1/4 - 3/4$ throttle openings by raising the jet needle, ie by fitting the needle clip in the lowest notch of the needle. Third, fit spark plugs with a thermal value of 200, ie Bosch W200T30/W6D, Champion N7Y etc.

Chapter 6 Frame and forks

Refer to Chapter 10 for subsequent modifications and information relating to the 1986 on models

Contents

General description 1	Frame: examination and renovation 8
Front forks: removal 2	Steering damper: removal and examination 9
Front forks: dismantling 3	Footrests, stands and controls: general 10
Front forks: examination and renovation 4	Fairing: removal and refitting 11
Front forks: reassembly 5	Instruments: removal and refitting 12
Front forks: refitting 6	Speedometer and rev-counter cables: replacing 13
Steering head bearings: removal, examination and refitting 7	

Specifications

Frame .... Duplex cradle type of welded tubular steel, with bolted-on rear subframe

Front forks
- Type .... Hydraulically damped, coil sprung, telescopic
- Suspension travel:
  - /5, /6 .... 208 mm (8.19 in)
  - /7, R80G/S, R80RT 1983 – 84 .... 200 mm (7.87 in)
  - R45, R65, R65LS, R80ST, R80, R80RT 1985 on .... 175 mm (6.89 in)
- Stanchion OD:
  - R80, R80RT 1985 on .... 38.425 – 38.450 mm (1.5128 – 1.5138 in)
  - All other models .... 35.925 – 35.950 mm (1.4144 – 1.4154 in)
- Lower leg ID:
  - R80, R80RT, 1985 on .... 38.500 – 38.539 mm (1:5158 – 1.5173 in)
  - All other models .... 36.000 – 36.025 mm (1.4173 – 1.4183 in)
- Stanchion/lower leg clearance:
  - R80, R80RT 1985 on .... 0.050 – 0.114 mm (0.0020 – 0.0045 in)
  - All other models .... 0.05 – 0.10 mm (0.0020 – 0.0039 in)
- Stanchion maximum warpage .... 0.10 mm (0.0039 in)
- Stanchion installed height (test length) – from top of stanchion to top machined surface of bottom yoke:
  - /5, /6, /7 up to 1980 .... 160 mm (6.2992 in)
  - /7 1981 on, R80G/S, R80RT 1983 – 84 .... 161 mm (6.3386 in)
  - R45, R65, R65LS, R80ST .... 190 mm (7.4803 in)
  - R80, R80RT 1985 on .... 162 mm (6.3779 in)

Chapter 6 Frame and forks

Damper piston OD:	
/5, /6, /7 up to 1980	27.600 – 27.800 mm (1.0866 – 1.0945 in)
R80, R80RT 1985 on	29.800 – 30.000 mm (1.1732 – 1.1811 in)
All other models	27.530 – 27.700 mm (1.0839 – 1.0906 in)
Stanchion ID:	
R80, R80RT 1985 on	30.850 – 31.150 mm (1.2146 – 1.2264 in)
All other models	27.850 – 28.150 mm (1.0965 – 1.1083 in)
Damper piston/stanchion clearance:	
/5, /6, /7 up to 1980	0.05 – 0.55 mm (0.0020 – 0.0217 in)
R80, R80RT 1985 on	0.85 – 1.35 mm (0.0335 – 0.0532 in)
All other models	0.15 – 0.62 mm (0.0059 – 0.0244 in)
Fork spring free length:	
Early /5, /6*	530 – 542 mm (20.8661 – 21.3385 in)
/5, /6, /7 up to 1980 – except those below	567 – 579 mm (22.3228 – 22.7952 in)
R100RS and R100RT up to 1980 – also any standard model fitted with full fairing, twin front disc brakes or HD suspension	543 – 555 mm (21.3779 – 21.850 in)
R45, R65, R65LS, R80ST	490 – 502 mm (19.2913 – 19.7637 in)
/7 1981 on, R80G/S, R80RT 1983 – 84	539 – 551 mm (21.2204 – 21.6929 in)
R80, R80RT 1985 on	472 – 484 mm (18.5826 – 19.0551 in)

May be fitted with stronger spring listed for later models

Fork spring wire diameter:	
Early /5, /6	N/Av
/5, /6, /7 up to 1980 (except R100RS, R100RT) – standard spring	4.00 mm (0.1575 in)
R80, R80RT 1985 on	4.30 mm (0.1693 in)
All other models	4.25 mm (0.1673 in)

	At oil change – cc/ Imp fl oz/US fl oz	At rebuild – cc/ Imp fl oz/US fl oz
Fork oil capacity – per leg:		
/5, /6, /7 1977*	265/9.33/8.96	280/9.86/9.47
/5, /6, /7 up to 1980	235/8.27/7.95	250/8.80/8.45
/7 1981 on, R80G/S, R80RT 1983 – 84	220/7.74/7.44	220 – 230/7.74 – 8.10/7.44 – 7.78
R45, R65, R65LS, R80ST	190/6.69/6.42	190 – 200/6.69 – 7.04/6.42 – 6.76

	At oil change – cc/Imp fl oz/US fl oz
R80 1985 on	300 ± 10/10.56 ± 0.35/10.14 ± 0.34
R80RT 1985 on	320 ± 10/11.26 ± 0.35/10.82 ± 0.34

Original recommended quantity, reduced to improve damping performance – use later recommendation

Fork oil level – forks fully extended:	
/5, /6, /7 1977*	437 mm (17.2 in) maximum from top surface of fork top plug to top of oil
/5, /6, /7 up to 1980	50 mm (1.97 in) above damper piston
R45, R65, R65LS, R80ST	35 ± 15 mm (1.38 ± 0.59 in) above damper piston
/7 1981 on, R80G/S, R80RT 1983 – 84	300 ± 5 mm (11.81 ± 0.20 in) above base of fork lower leg/damper rod Allen screw
R80, R80RT, 1985 on	N/Av

Only applies if original fork oil quantity recommendation has been used

Recommended fork oil:	
Manufacturer	Type
Aral	1010 shock absorber oil
Aral	P3441 shock absorber oil
Bel-Ray	SAE 5 Fork Oil with 'Seal Swell'
BP	Aero Hydraulic
BP	BP-Olex HLP2849
Castrol	Fork Oil Extra Light
Castrol	DB Hydraulic fluid
Castrol	Shock Absorber Oil 1-318
Castrol	LHM – only for temperatures below 0°C (32°F)
Castrol	AWH15
Esso	Univis J13
Golden Spectro	Suspension Fluid Very Light
Mobil	Aero HFA
Mobil	DTE 11
Premium Fork Lubricant	Spectro SAE 10 – for competition use only
Shell	Aero Fluid 4
Shell	4001

Steering head bearings

Type	Taper roller
Reference number	32 028 (FAG), or 320/28X (SKF or Timkin)
Size	28 mm x 52 mm x 16 mm

Torque wrench settings

Component	Nm	lbf ft
Steering stem top nut:		
/5, /6, /7 up to 1980	120 – 130	88.5 – 96
R45, R65, R65LS	80 – 90	59 – 66
R80, R80RT 1985 on	106.8	79
All other models	120	88.5

Component	Nm	lbf ft
Steering adjuster clamp ring – /5	10 – 12	7.5 – 9
Fork leg top plug:		
/7 up to 1980	120 – 130	88.5 – 96
R80, R80RT 1985 on	93.8 – 119.8	69 – 88.5
All other models	120	88.5
Fork yoke clamp bolts:		
R45, R65, R65LS	40 – 45	29.5 – 33
/6, /7 up to 1980	35 – 40	26 – 29.5
/5 – bottom yoke nuts	33 – 35	24 – 26
R80, R80RT 1985 on	25.3 – 33.3	18.5 – 24.5
All other models	40	29.5
Fork brace mounting bolts – R80, R80RT 1985 on	13 – 17	9.5 – 12.5
Front mudguard bracket mounting bolts – 8 mm	20 – 25	15 – 18.5
Front mudguard stay mounting bolts – 6 mm – /5, /6	2.5	2
Damper piston and damper rod lower threaded plug – /5, /6, /7 up to 1980	25 – 27	18.5 – 20
Lower leg bottom cap – /5, /6, /7 up to 1980	80 – 100	59 – 74
Damper rod/lower leg fastener:		
8 mm nut /5, /6, /7 up to 1980	23 – 26	17 – 19
Allen screw – R45, R65, R65LS	30 – 40	22 – 29.5
Allen screw R80, R80RT 1985 on	13 – 17	9.5 – 12.5
Allen screw all other models	35	26
Fork oil filler plug – R45, R65, R65LS, all other models 1981 on	9	6.5
Fork oil drain plug – R45, R65, R65LS, all other models 1981 on	8	6
Rear frame section mounting bolts:		
/5, /6, /7, R80RT 1983 – 84	25	18.5
R80G/S, R80ST, R80, R80RT 1985 on	22 – 24	16 – 18
R45, R65, R65LS	15 – 17	11 – 12.5
Centre stand mountings:		
Early models – cadmium-plated bolts	30 – 35	22 – 25
Later models – plastic-coated bolts or plated nuts	43 – 48	32 – 35.5
R80, R80RT 1985 on	26 – 32	19 – 23.5
Side stand pivot pin – all models from 1/83 on	16 – 20	12 – 15

1 General description

The front forks are of the conventional coil-sprung hydraulically damped type with a characteristically (for BMW) long travel. Five types of fork are fitted to the machines described in this Manual. /5, /6 and /7 models up to 1980 all share the same type. R45 and R65 models, when introduced, were fitted with a new type developed by Fichtel and Sachs which are simpler in design but have a shorter travel; these forks are also used on the R65LS. All /7 models from 1981 on, the R80G/S and the R80RT 1983 – 84 use a modified version of the Fichtel and Sachs forks which retain the long travel of the original design but have better damping and, due to the use of some Teflon components, are quieter in operation. Although not a separate type in its own right, the R80ST uses forks which combine the stanchion and damping mechanism layout of the later /7 models with the lower leg and spring of the R45/65 forks; the effect of this is to convert the R80G/S cycle parts into a good-handling road-going version. The last fork type, developed for the K100 series, is fitted in slightly modified form to the R80 and R80RT 1985 on models.

On some models the forks can be stiffened by fitting either stronger springs (/5, /6 and /7 up to 1980) or preload spacers at the bottom of the lower legs (/7 1981 on, R80G/S, R80RT 1983 – 84). Note that these models can also be fitted with heavy-duty rear suspension units, if required. Consult a local BMW dealer for full details.

The steering head bearings are of the taper-roller type. The frame is a full cradle type of welded tubular steel with a bolted-on rear subframe.

2 Front forks: removal

1 The bulk of the fork components can be examined by withdrawing the lower legs while the stanchions remain clamped in the yokes. If the fork legs are to be removed as a complete unit, proceed as follows.
2 Remove the front wheel. See Chapter 8, Section 2. Remove its mounting bolts or nuts and withdraw the front mudguard.
3 Remove the brake calipers (or brake backplate) from the fork legs, wedge a piece of wood between the pads and secure the calipers out of harm's way.
4 Remove the fuel tank. See Chapter 4, Section 2.
5 Depending on the owner's skill and the work being performed, remove the fairing (RS and RT, where fitted). While not strictly necessary (except in the case of the S-type fairing) the removal of the fairing creates extra working space and prevents any risk of fairing damage. On models fitted with 'S'-type fairings, the fairing must be removed. See Section 11.
6 Remove the steering damper knob and handlebar safety padding (where fitted). On R45, R65, R80ST and R65LS models, remove the ignition switch retaining ring, pull out the turn signal repeater and remove the instrument top cover (removing the fairing top half, R65LS). Before removing the fork legs, read Section 3 paragraph 10.
7 On R45, R65 and R65LS models, slacken the fork yoke pinch bolts and pull the fork legs down and away from the machine.
8 On all other models remove the handlebars and, taking care not to stretch, trap or distort the control cables, brake hose (where fitted) or electrical wiring, move them as far to the rear as possible. Remove the plated top cap from each fork leg using a peg spanner (/5, /6 and /7 up to 1978) or prise off the rubber or plastic top cap (all later models), then unscrew the fork leg top plugs.
9 Remove the plugs slowly and with care as they will be under some pressure from the fork springs; lay a thick piece of rag over the plug while unscrewing the last few turns to prevent any risk of the plug flying off and causing personal injury or damage to the machine. When they are removed, collect the washer (or fairing mounting bracket – 'S'-type fairings) under each.
10 Remove the spring top seat (where fitted) and carefully withdraw the springs, noting which way up they are fitted.
11 Slacken fully the bottom yoke pinch bolts or nuts and pull each stanchion downwards out of the yokes, using penetrating fluid to release any corrosion that may have formed. It is permissible to remove each clamp bolt and to spring the bottom yoke slightly apart by inserting a screwdriver into the slot in each clamp, if the stanchion cannot be released by hand, but it must be noted that great care must be taken not to overstress or otherwise weaken the bottom yoke.

2.2a Remove the front mudguard – /5 models ...

2.2b ... mountings also secure hydraulic pipe brackets on later models

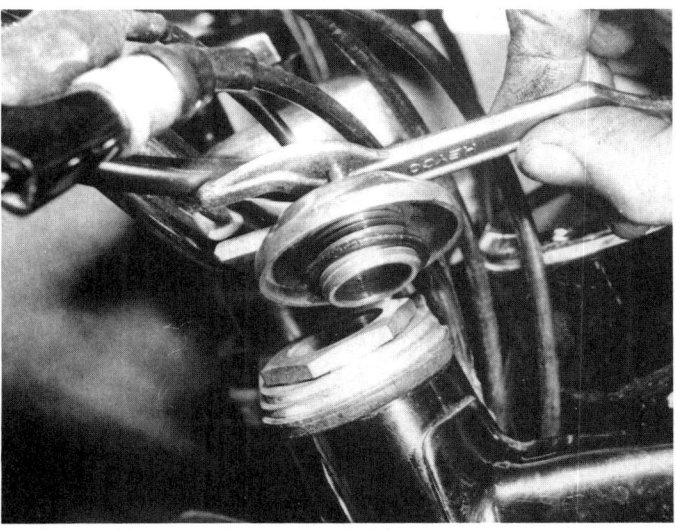

2.8a Peg spanner is required to remove filler plug on early models ...

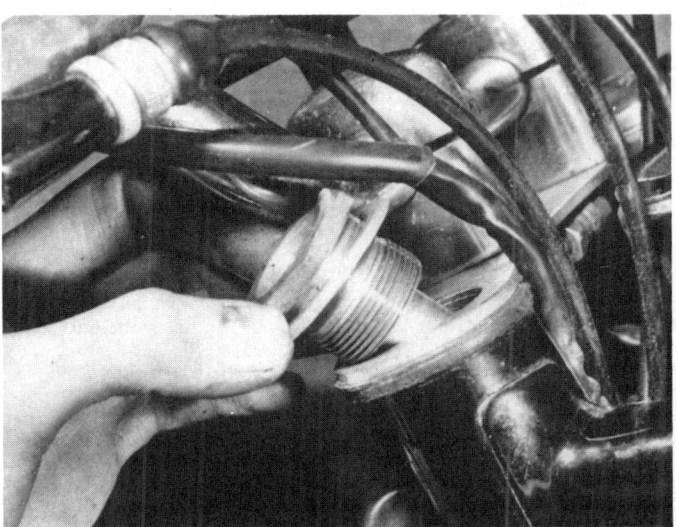

2.8b ... so that fork top plugs can be removed

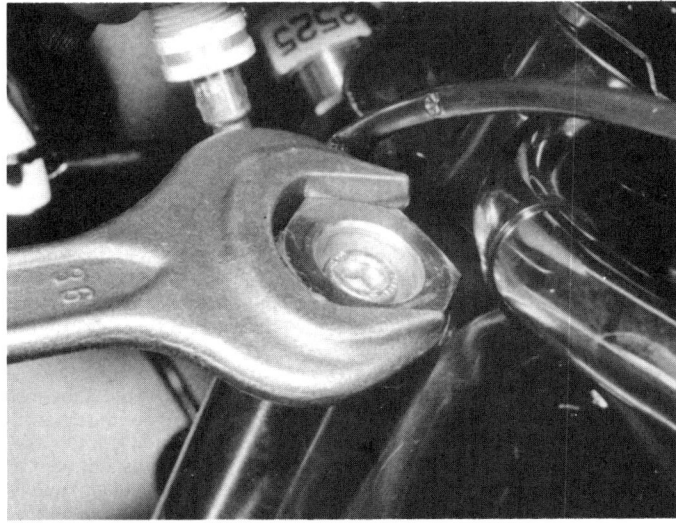

2.8c On later models top plug can be unscrewed complete with Allen headed filler plug

2.9 Top plugs may be under pressure from fork springs – take care when removing plugs and note which way up springs are fitted

2.11a Slacken bottom yoke pinch bolts or nuts ...

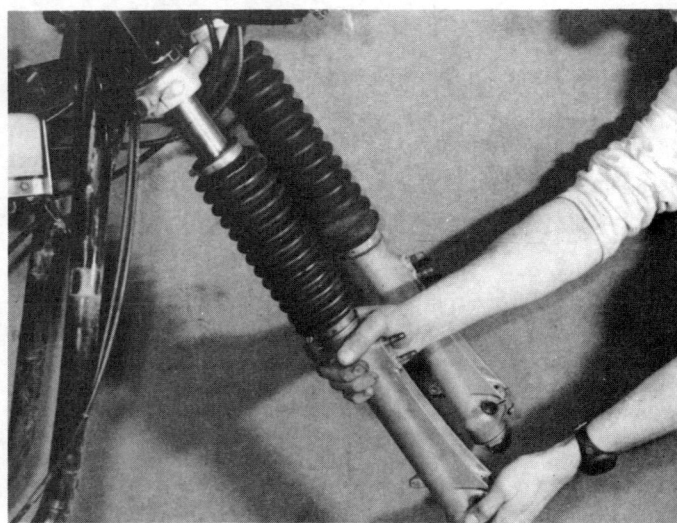

2.11b ... and pull fork leg downwards to remove

3 Front forks: dismantling

/5, /6, /7 up to 1980

1 Remove the fork legs from the machine as described in the previous Section. Invert them over a suitable container and pump them to expel as much oil as possible.
2 Slacken the gaiter top and bottom clips (where fitted) and pull the fork lower leg off the stanchion, after removing completely the damper rod lower nut and washer. Pull the gaiter off the lower leg and unscrew the bottom cap, noting the rubber buffer inside. Discard the gasket.
3 Remove the internal circlip from the bottom of the stanchion and unscrew the threaded ring using the peg spanner in the tool kit. (From frame numbers R50/5 2904276, R60/5 2941811, R75/5 2997998, there are two rings and a valve plate). Extract the thick rubber buffer and the damper rod. The damper rod **must** be removed through the bottom end of the stanchion. **Note:** do not remove the damper rod unnecessarily, as it is tricky to replace. Remove and discard the soft metal washer from the lower end of the damper rod. It is unlikely that the damper unit will need to be dismantled further, but if it is extremely dirty the piston and lower threaded plug can be unscrewed (if care is taken to hold the damper rod without damaging it) so that the components can be thoroughly cleaned. Note the spring-loaded ball valve in the lower plug. Tighten the threaded plugs to the specified torque setting on reassembly.

/7 1981 on and R80G/S, R80ST, R80RT 1983 – 84

4 Remove the fork legs from the machine as described in the previous Section. Invert them over a suitable container and pump them to expel as much oil as possible. Collect and store the spring bottom seat which should drop out (not R80ST).
5 Using an Allen key of suitable size, slacken the larger Allen screw situated at the bottom of each fork lower leg. This task is sometimes complicated by the fact that the damper rod assembly rotates with the screw so that nothing is achieved; to prevent this happening, temporarily refit the fork spring and top plug, tap smartly on the head of the Allen screw with a suitable hammer and a soft metal drift to jar the threads free, then push the fork lower leg up the stanchion as far as possible to compress the fork spring and to lock the damper assembly using spring pressure. If this fails to work, a more positive means of locking the damper assembly can be used.
6 Using a vice whose jaws have been padded with soft alloy or wooden covers, clamp the fork lower leg securely in the horizontal position, ensuring that the vice is clamped only on the wheel spindle lug to prevent distortion or damage to the lower leg casting. Push the stanchion fully into the lower leg; except for R80ST models and obtain a length of wooden dowel that will fit inside the stanchion and is long enough to rest on the head of the damper assembly while projecting beyond the stanchion upper end, then grind a coarse taper on one end of the dowel so that it fits securely into the head of the damper assembly. Using a pair of Mole grips or a similar tool to provide the necessary leverage, apply pressure to the damper assembly to prevent it from rotating and unscrew the Allen screw.
7 On R80ST models the damper rod head has a hexagonal upper end using a slim 13 mm socket spanner and the necessary extensions, hold the damper rod end and unscrew the Allen screw. On R80G/S models slacken their clamps and remove the fork gaiters. On all models, pull the lower leg off the stanchion and pull the damper rod seat off the damper rod, if it has not stuck at the bottom of the lower leg.
8 **Note:** the damper assembly is difficult to refit and should not be disturbed unless necessary. Remove the circlip from the bottom of the stanchion; on later models (it has not been possible to establish a precise date) with the spring loaded valve housing, the housing may be ejected with some force as the circlip is removed. Wrap a thick rag around the base of the stanchion to prevent the loss of any components. Withdraw the damper assembly carefully, noting the precise order of installation and the fitted positions of all components.
9 Remove the dust seal (where fitted) from the top of the lower leg, lever out the fork oil seal taking care not to scratch the housing, and invert the lower leg to tap out the damper rod seat (if not removed already) and the preload spacer (where fitted).

R45, R65, R65LS

10 Remove the fork legs from the machine as described in the previous Section and unscrew the damper rod Allen screw (see paragraph 5 above). Obtain two blocks of wood and cut V-shaped notches in them so that the stanchion can be clamped securely upright in a vice at its upper end without risk of distorting it; failing this, refit the fork leg to the machine and tighten the top and bottom yoke pinch bolts. With the stanchion held securely, have an assistant press the top plug as far as possible into the stanchion against spring pressure (use a T-handled Allen screwdriver in the fork oil filler plug) while the retaining circlip is removed. The quickest method is to tap it downwards out of its groove, turn it until it is nearly vertical and pull it out with a pair of pliers. Slowly allow the spring pressure to push the top plug upwards out of the stanchion until all pressure is released.
11 Remove the top plug and withdraw the spring, noting which way up it is fitted.

12 Unscrew the damper rod Allen screw using the method described above for the R80ST (paragraph 7), if it slackened but then rotated with the damper rod. Remove the lower leg.

13 **Note:** the damper rod assembly is difficult to refit and should not be disturbed unless necessary. Remove the circlip from the bottom of the stanchion and withdraw the damper assembly carefully, noting precisely the order of installation and the fitted positions of all components.

14 Pull the damper rod seat off the damper rod or tip it out of the lower leg. Lever out the fork oil seal, taking care not to scratch or damage its housing in the top of the lower leg.

R80, R80RT 1985 on

15 Although very different components are used, the forks of these models are dismantled in the same way as these of the /7 1981 on models. Refer to paragraphs 4 – 9 above, noting the following points:

1. There are no separate top or bottom spring seats
2. The damper rod should be held (if necessary) by the method described in paragraph 6
3. There is no separate damper rod seat
4. The valve housing is not of the spring-loaded type

3.2a Dismantling early type fork legs – remove damper rod nut and washer

3.2b Lower leg bottom cap can be unscrewed if required – discard gasket

3.3a Remove circlip from stanchion lower end ...

3.3b ... and unscrew threaded nozzle(s) ...

3.3c ... then pull out the thick buffer ring ...

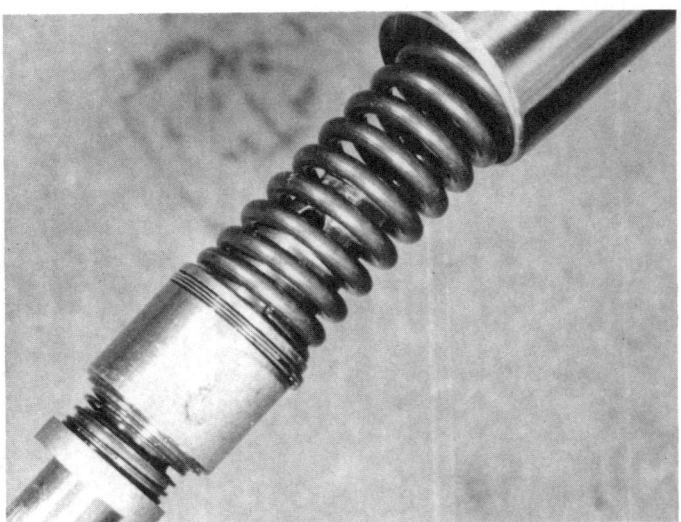

3.3d ... followed by the damper rod

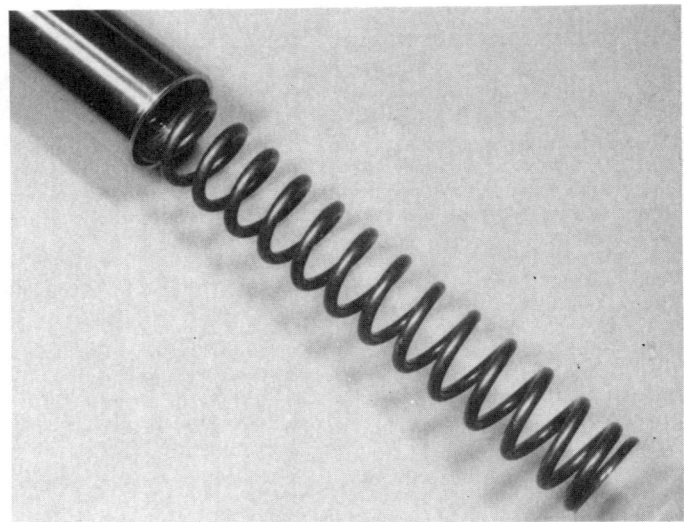

3.11 Note which way up spring is fitted as it is removed

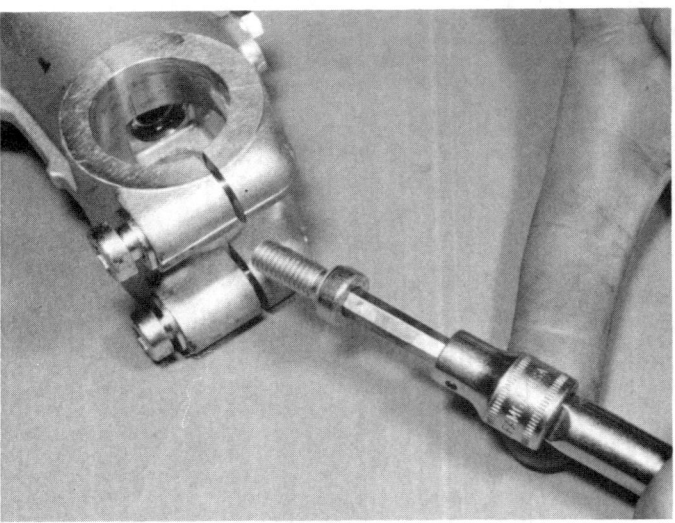

3.15a Damper rod must be locked to permit removal of retaining Allen screw ...

3.15b ... so that stanchion can be removed from fork lower leg

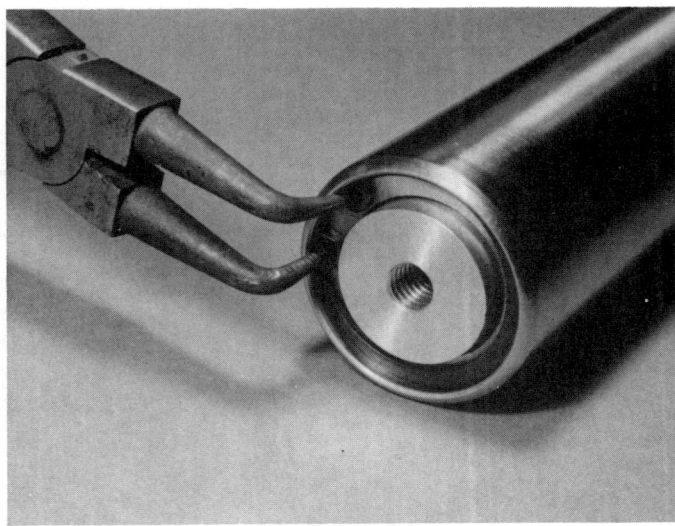

3.15c Remove circlip from stanchion lower end ...

3.15d .. and note number and thickness of shims ...

Fig. 6.1 Front forks – /5, /6, /7 up to 1980

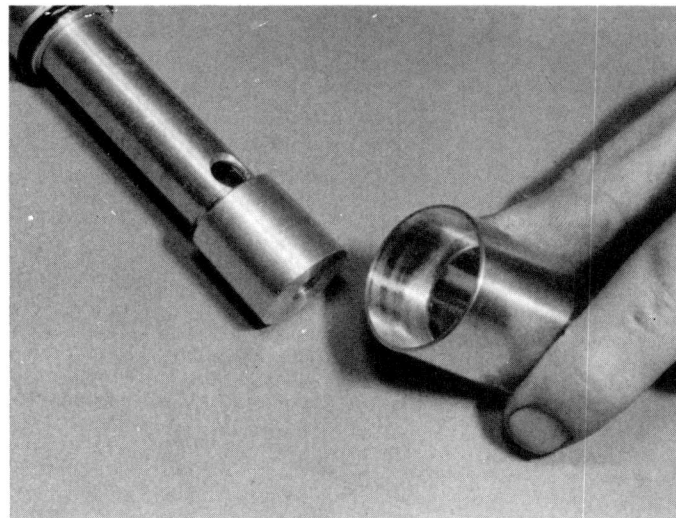

3.15e ... which prevent valve housing endfloat. Damper rod can then be withdrawn

1. Top cap
2. Sealing washer – up to 1977 only
3. Filler plug – 1978 on
4. Sealing washer – 1978 on
5. Fork top plug
6. Metal washer
7. Fork spring
8. Stanchion
9. Damper piston wiper rings – 3 off per leg
10. Damper piston
11. Rubber washer – later models only
12. Damper valve plate
13. Damper valve spring
14. Damper rod
15. Ball
16. Spring
17. Damper rod lower threaded plug
18. Soft metal washer
19. Buffer
20. Threaded ring – not fitted to early /5 models
21. Damper valve plate
22. Threaded ring
23. Circlip
24. Clip – only with gaiter
25. Gaiter – where fitted
26. Felt ring – only with dust excluder
27. Dust excluder – where fitted
28. Oil seal
29. Fork lower leg
30. Stud – 2 off per leg, /5 only
31. Washer
32. Spindle clamp bolt
33. Gasket
34. Rubber buffer
35. Bottom cap
36. Wave washer
37. Nut
38. Rubber plug

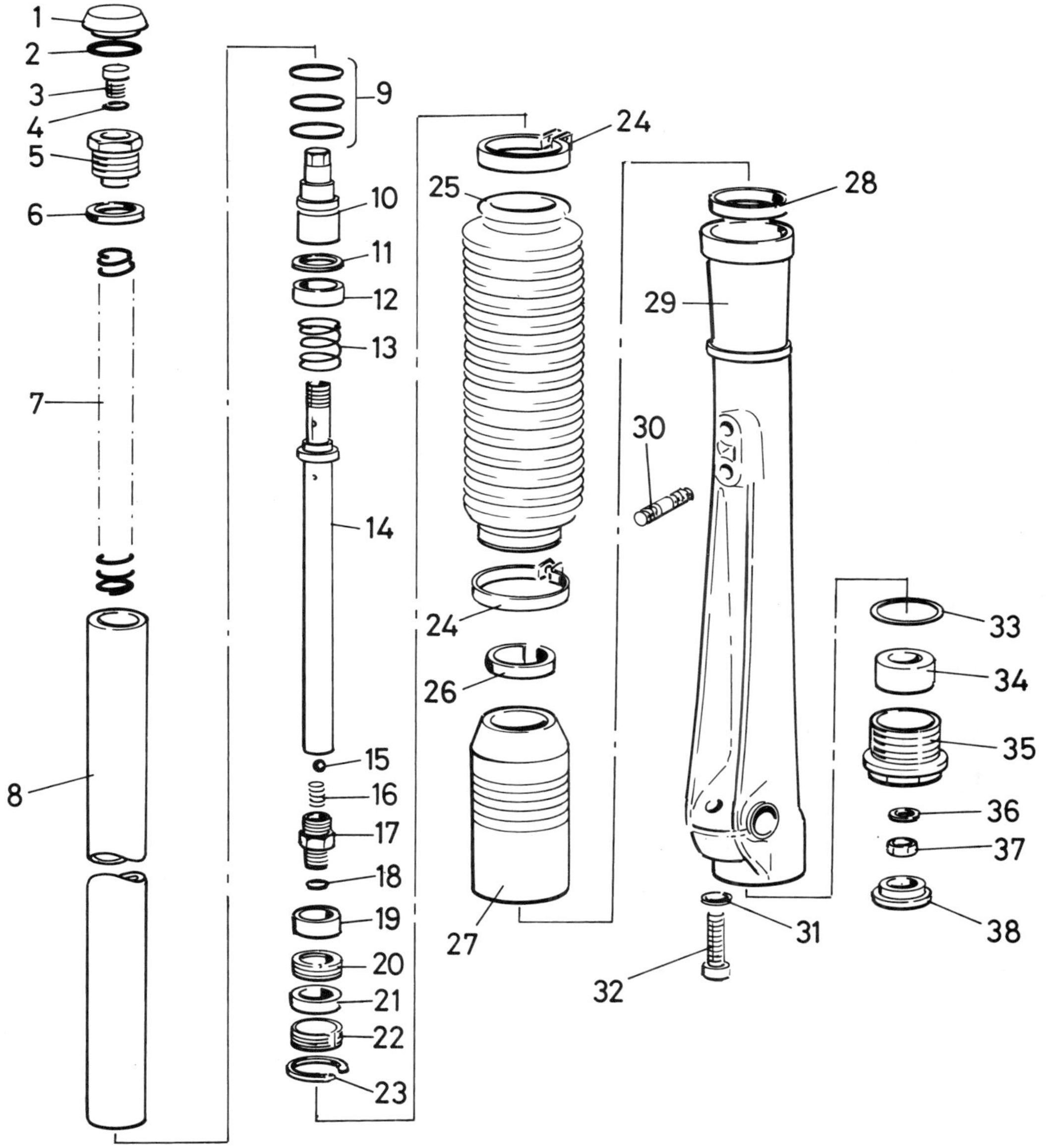

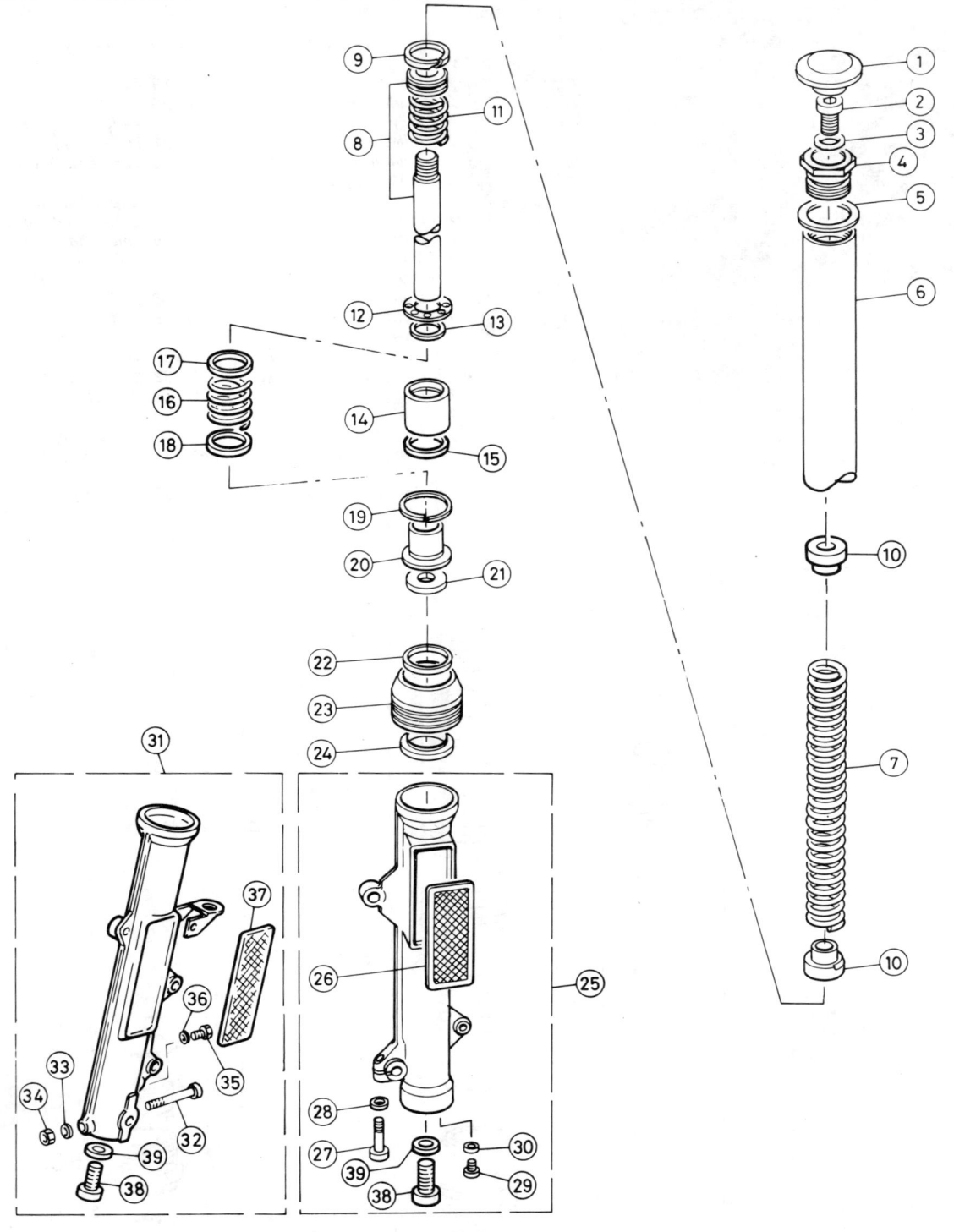

Fig. 6.2 Front forks – /7 1981 on, R80G/S, R80ST, R80RT 1983 to 1984

1　Top cap
2　Filler plug
3　Sealing washer
4　Fork top plug
5　Metal washer
6　Stanchion
7　Fork spring
8　Damper rod
9　Damper piston ring
10　White nylon spring seats
11　Rebound spring
12　Perforated washer
13　Valve washer
14　Valve housing – early version
15　Shim – as required – early version
16　Valve spring – later version
17　Upper valve housing – later version
18　Lower valve housing – later version
19　Circlip
20　Damper rod seat
21　Preload spacer – where fitted
22　Felt ring
23　Dust excluder
24　Oil seal
25　Fork lower leg – except R80ST
26　Reflector
27　Spindle clamp bolt
28　Washer
29　Drain plug
30　Sealing washer
31　Fork lower leg – R80ST
32　Spindle clamp bolt
33　Washer
34　Nut
35　Drain plug
36　Sealing washer
37　Reflector
38　Damper rod Allen screw
39　Sealing washer

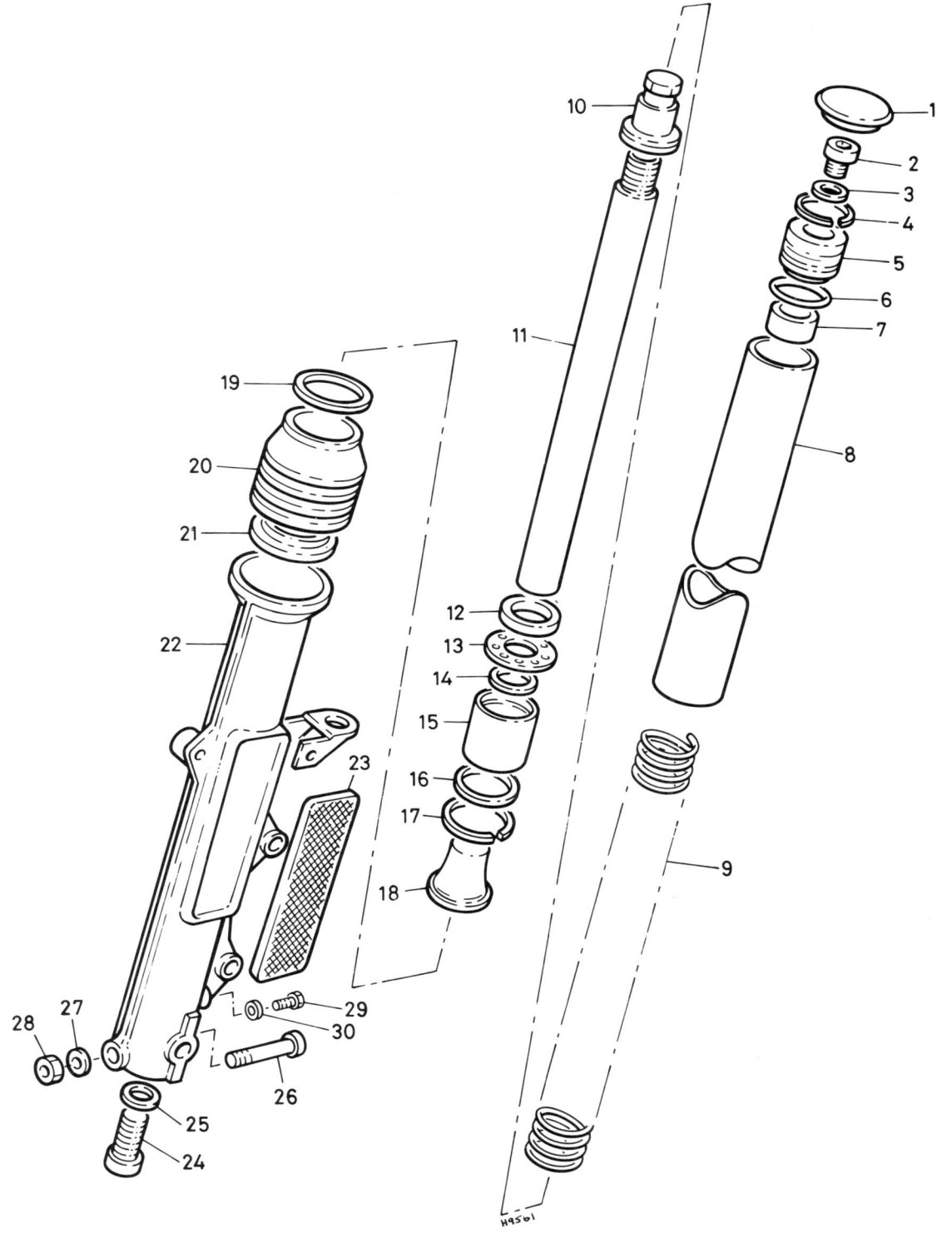

Fig. 6.3 Front forks – R45, R65, R65LS

1 Top cap
2 Filler plug
3 Sealing washer
4 Circlip
5 Top plug
6 O-ring
7 Spring top seat
8 Stanchion
9 Fork spring
10 Damper piston
11 Damper rod
12 Buffer
13 Perforated washer
14 Valve washer
15 Valve housing
16 Shim – as required
17 Circlip
18 Damper rod seat
19 Felt ring
20 Dust excluder
21 Oil seal
22 Fork lower leg
23 Reflector
24 Damper rod Allen screw
25 Sealing washer
26 Spindle clamp bolt
27 Washer
28 Nut
29 Drain plug
30 Sealing washer

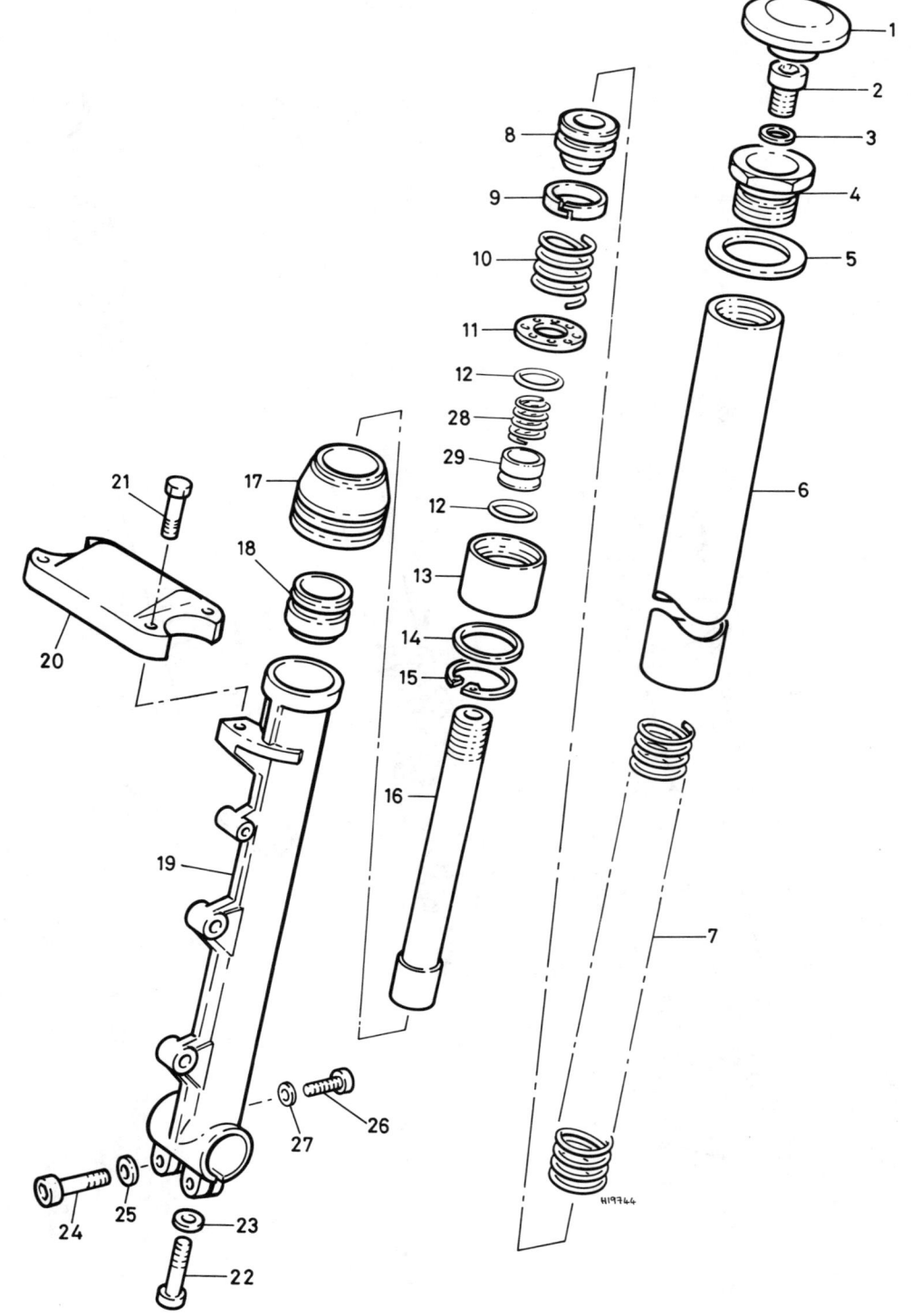

Fig. 6.4 Front forks – R80 and R80RT 1985 on
Note: modified damper components introduced April 1985

1 Top cap
2 Filler plug
3 Sealing washer
4 Fork top plug
5 Metal washer
6 Stanchion
7 Fork spring
8 Damper piston
9 Damper piston ring
10 Rebound spring
11 Perforated washer
12 O-ring 1 off early models, 2 off later models
13 Valve housing
14 Shim – as required
15 Circlip
16 Damper rod
17 Dust excluder
18 Oil seal
19 Fork lower leg
20 Fork brace
21 Bolt
22 Damper rod Allen screw
23 Sealing washer
24 Spindle clamp bolt – 2 off
25 Washer – 2 off
26 Drain plug
27 Sealing washer
28 Valve spring – later models
29 Valve – later models

4 Front forks: examination and renovation

1 If the forks have been damaged in an accident, it is essential to inspect both fork yokes, the stanchions and the sliders, for distortion and hairline cracks. Distorted components must be renewed, no attempt being made to re-align them.
2 Stanchions may be checked for straightness by rolling them along a flat surface.
3 Check the lower fork yoke by clamping the steering column horizontally in a vice with soft jaws. Fit the stanchions to the yoke, with the upper ends projecting the specified test length beyond the top machined face of the yoke.
4 Take a sight across two straight edges laid across the extreme ends of the stanchions. Check for parallelism by measuring between the stanchions at each end, at right angles. Fit the top fork yoke and screw on the steering column top nut, and the two stanchion top nuts with spacer washers. They should all go on without any apparent strain.
5 The fork sliders are not bushed; the stanchions bear directly in the alloy casting. If the sliders are worn or scored they must be renewed. Permissible clearance is given in the Specifications Section of this Chapter.
6 The oil seal should be renewed whenever it is disturbed. It may be prised out carefully with a screwdriver. Grease and refit a new seal with the open side (garter spring) facing downwards; the top edge of the seal must be flush with the top of the fork lower leg.
7 Check the condition of the ring(s) on the damper piston and the action of the damper valve. The damper rings must not be distorted. Also renew all gaskets and O-rings.
8 Check the telescopic gaiters for cracks or wear and check the condition of the felt ring inside the R90S type gaiter. Charge the felt with oil. It is important that the gaiters are in good condition, as they keep grit from the oil seals. Dirt and grit will ruin these seals and may score the fork sliders.
9 In many cases, modifications have been made to the damping mechanism components, usually to reduce noise. In most cases these modified components can be fitted to earlier model forks. Check with a BMW dealer if any modifications have been made to your machine's forks. For example, all R45/65 models from 1981 on were fitted with a plastic valve disc running in a modified valve housing; these parts can be fitted to earlier models but the shortened later-pattern damper rod seat will also be required.
10 Measure the spring free lengths; if either has settled to less than the specified length, both springs must be renewed.

5 Front forks: reassembly

1 Ensure that all components are absolutely clean on reassembly and smear clean fork oil over each component as it is refitted.
2 Reassembly is the reverse of the dismantling procedure, noting the following points.
3 If the damper rod was removed, great care must be taken to ensure that the piston wiper rings or seal are not damaged as they are refitted to the stanchion. BMW have special guides with tapered internal faces to help refitting. If these are not available, the rod must be inserted very carefully into the stanchion. It may help to use feeler gauge blades as shown in the accompanying photograph to feed in the rings. Once fitted, the damper rod should slide with ease inside the stanchion.
4 Refit the various components to the damper rod, ensuring that all are fitted in the correct order and the correct way round.
5 /7 models 1981 on, R80G/S, R80ST and R80RT 1983 – 84 – the early version of these forks uses shims to remove all clearance between the valve housing and the damper rod retaining circlip, as do all R45 and R65 models, all R65LS models and the R80 and R80RT 1985 on models; this is to prevent the valve housing rattling audibly. Check that there is no clearance when the damper assembly is refitted to the stanchion; if necessary remove the circlip and add shims to remove the clearance. Shims are available in thicknesses of 0.1, 0.2, 0.3 and 0.5 mm (0.004, 0.008, 0.012 and 0.020 in).
6 Later versions of these forks (/7 1981 on, R80G/S, R80ST, R80RT 1983 – 84 only — it is not clear when the change was made) are fitted with an upper and lower valve housing and an additional rebound spring is fitted between the two. To refit the circlip with this type of damper assembly have an assistant hold the damper rod and press the lower valve housing up into the stanchion while you refit the circlip.
7 On all models up to 1980, place the rubber buffer in the lower leg bottom cap (flat side uppermost). Apply a smear of sealant to the cap threads (do not refit the gasket) and tighten the cap to the specified torque setting of 80 – 100 Nm (59 – 74 lbf ft). Fit a new soft metal washer to the bottom of the damper rod, fit the fork spring to the stanchion to push the damper rod as far as possible out of the stanchion lower end and insert the assembly into the lower leg. As soon as the damper rod end protrudes through the bottom cap, refit the retaining nut and washer and tighten them securely while holding the damper rod stationary with an Allen key. Refit the rubber plug and pull the stanchion out to full extension.
8 Where applicable, refit the fork gaiter. Clamp the stanchion at the fully-extended position by tightening its top clamp.
9 On all other models fit the damper rod seat (where fitted) to the damper rod. On /7 1981 on models (etc) do not forget to press the preload spacers (if fitted) down to the bottom of the fork lower leg. Use the fork spring as described above to maintain pressure on the damper rod head, insert the stanchion assembly into the lower leg, then refit and tighten to the specified torque setting the damper rod Allen screw.
10 Refit the fork spring (do not forget the spring seats, where fitted).
11 On R45, R65 and R65LS models refit the fork top plug. Renew its sealing O-ring seal and apply a smear of oil to lubricate it. Reverse the removal procedure to fit the retaining circlip (if it was distorted in any way on removal it must be renewed) and check that it is seated properly before releasing the plug.

4.6 Fork oil seal should be renewed as a matter of course

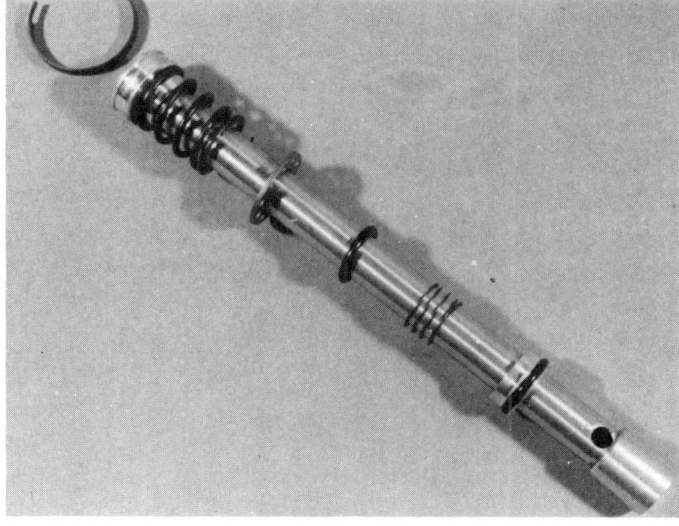

4.7a Check valve passages are clear and damper rod components for wear

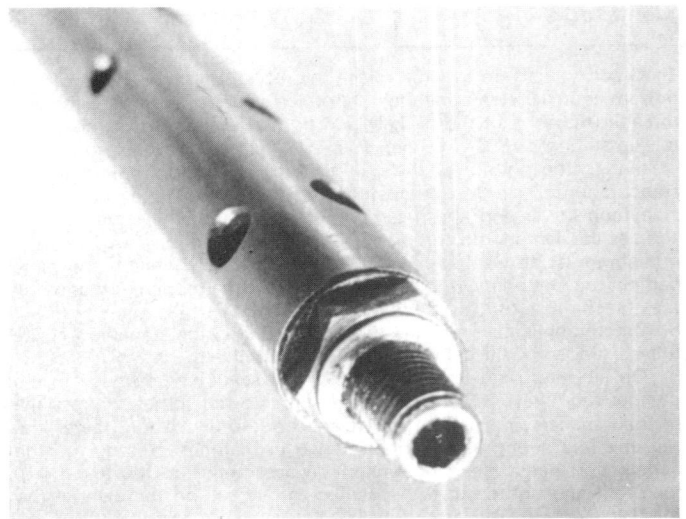

4.7b Do not forget to renew soft metal washer on damper rod bottom end – early models

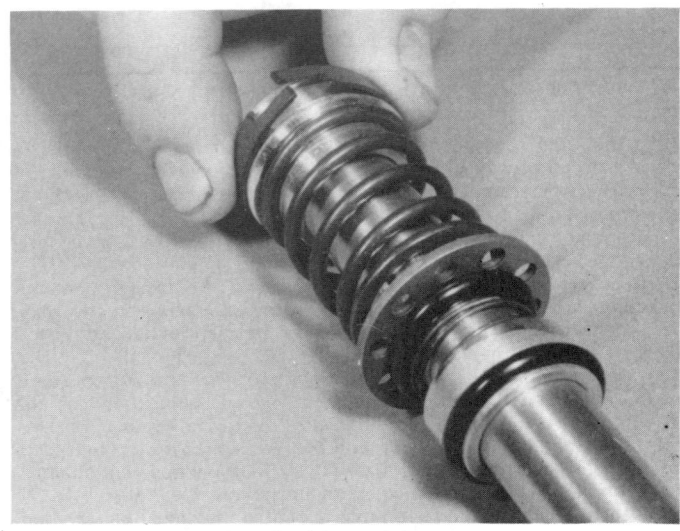

5.3a Damper piston wiper ring(s) are delicate ...

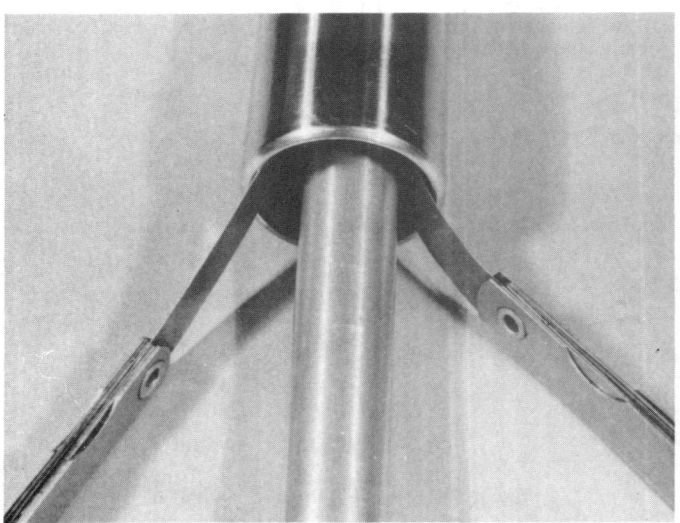

5.3b ... and must not be damaged on refitting to stanchion

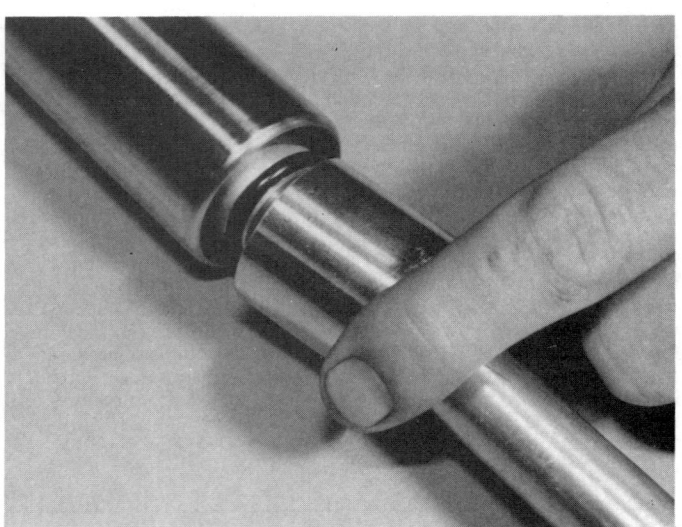

5.5a Refitting valve housing – some later models (see text) ...

5.5b ... shims must be added to eliminate housing endfloat

5.8 Where fitted, gaiters can be used to clamp fork leg at full extension for easier refitting

6 Front forks: refitting

1 On R45, R65 and R65LS models slide each stanchion into the yokes until it is flush with the top surface of the top yoke, then tighten the pinch bolts.
2 On all other models slide the stanchion up through the bottom yoke until it rests against the underside of the top yoke. Refit the fork top plug (and washer) then tighten it to the specified torque setting.
3 On all models, fill the forks with oil as described in Routine Maintenance. If they have been dismantled a larger amount of oil (see Specifications) will be required to bring the level up to the correct measurement. Refit the filler plugs and top caps as described.
4 Working methodically in the reverse of the dismantling sequence refit all disturbed components.
5 Tighten all fasteners securely to the correct torque settings, where given.
6 Where gaiters are fitted raise the upper end against the underside of the bottom yoke. Note that a hole in the gaiter top end must engage with a hollow breather dowel in the yoke. Check that the gaiters are straight and tighten the top clamp; do not tighten the bottom clamp (except R80G/S) until the front mudguard has been refitted.
7 When the front mudguard and wheel have been refitted, push the machine off its stand, apply the front brake and pump the forks up and down to align the legs and their mountings. Working from the top downwards tighten all fasteners to their specified torque settings.
8 Check that all controls are correctly adjusted, that all components are securely fastened and that the suspension works smoothly before using the machine.

7 Steering head bearings: removal, examination and refitting

1 Remove the front forks. See Chapter 2.
2 Remove the steering stem top nut and withdraw the top yoke complete with the instruments. On some models the instrument mounting bracket may have to be unbolted from the bottom yoke. Allow the headlamp assembly and turn signals to hang down clear of the bottom yoke. Where applicable disconnect the turn signal wires.
3 On /5 models, slacken the hexagon socket cap screw of the steering column adjuster nut clamp, remove the clamp and unscrew the adjuster nut. On all other models, simply unscrew the adjuster nut. Take off the top ball race cover.
4 Pull the bottom yoke downwards, out of the steering head, assisting by tapping the steering column with a soft hammer. Take care not to damage the threads. Remove the upper ball journal inner race from the steering head.
5 The lower bearing inner race must be pulled off the steering column but only if it requires renewal.
6 Clean and examine the outer bearing tracks whilst in the steering head. Since the forks rotate through only a small angle, the commonest damage to the bearings is brinelling. This is indenting of the roller tracks by the rollers, generally due to maladjustment. It can be felt, when turning the forks, by the steering seeming to 'index' in one position.
7 Outer races must be extracted using an internally-expanding bearing puller. When refitting, clean the housings and make sure that the races seat squarely. Use the old races as drifts. Do not interchange parts of bearings.
8 Grease the bearings before reassembly. Fit the lower bearing inner race onto the steering column and place the upper bearing inner race into the steering head. Insert the steering column carefully into the steering head, holding the upper bearing in place. Continue reassembly in reverse order of dismantling.
9 Check that all control cables and wiring are correctly routed as components are refitted.
10 Adjust the steering head bearings as described in Routine Maintenance when the forks have been refitted.

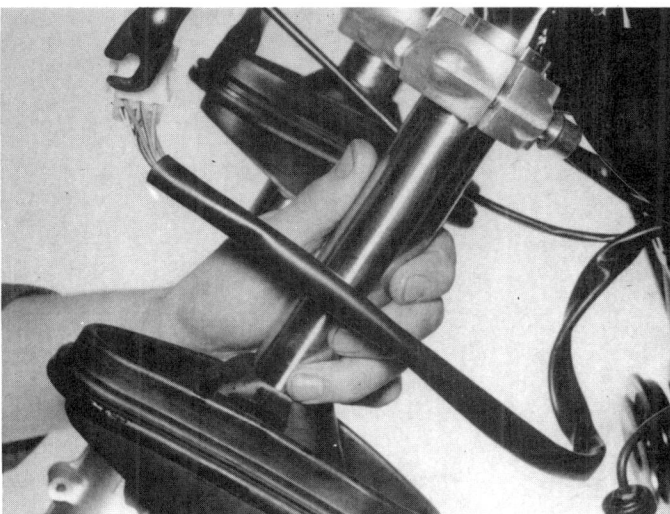

6.2 Ensure all components are in place before refitting fork legs

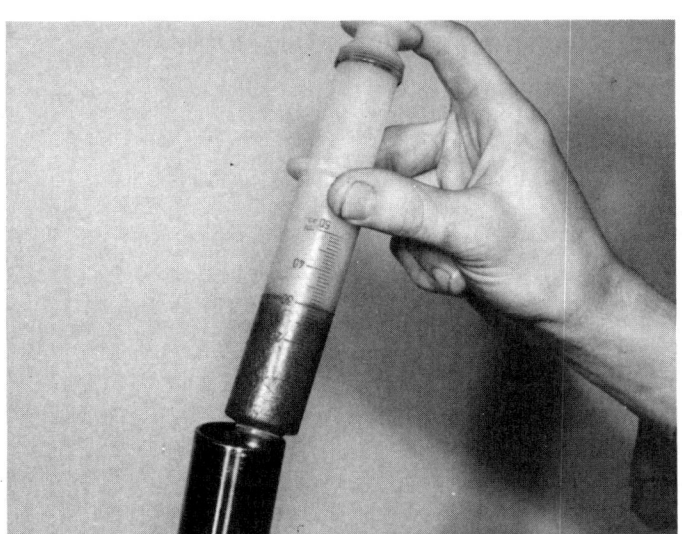

6.3 Fill each leg with correct amount of specified oil – check level

6.6a Where gaiters are fitted, breather hole in gaiter top ...

6.6b ... must engage with dowel in bottom yoke

6.7 Align fork legs carefully before tightening fork brace mounting bolts

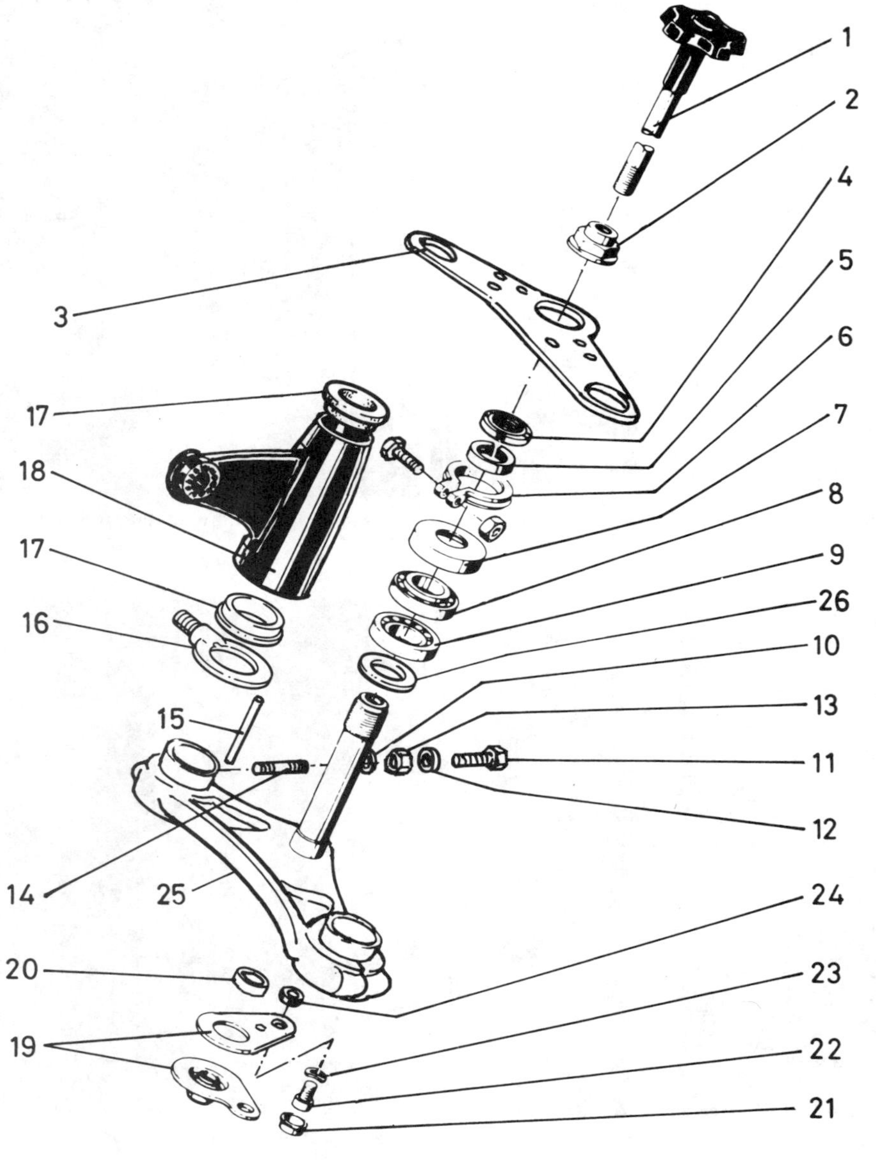

Fig. 6.5 Steering head – typical

1. Steering damper
2. Steering column nut
3. Top yoke
4. Adjuster nut
5. Split round nut – /5 only
6. Adjuster clamp ring – /5 only
7. Dust cover
8. Tapered roller bearing
9. Tapered roller bearing
10. Washer – /5 only
11. Allen screw – later models
12. Washer – later models
13. Nut – /5 only
14. Stud – /5 only
15. Roll pin – only fitted with fork gaiters
16. Indicator mounting
17. Rubber rings
18. Headlamp bracket
19. Damper plates – /5 only
20. Damper rod rubber ring – /5 only
21. Washer – /5 only
22. Allen screw – /5 only
23. Lock washer – /5 only
24. Nut – /5 only
25. Bottom yoke
26. Sealing washer

8 Frame: examination and renovation

1 The frame is unlikely to require attention unless accident damage has occurred. In some cases, renewal of the frame is the only satisfactory remedy if the frame is badly out of alignment. Only a few frame specialists have the jigs and mandrels necessary for resetting the frame to the required standard of accuracy, and even then there is no easy means of assessing to what extent the frame may have been over-stressed.
2 After the machine has covered a considerable mileage, it is advisable to examine the frame closely for signs of cracking or splitting at the welded joints. Rust corrosion can also cause weakness at these joints. Minor damage can be repaired by welding or brazing, depending on the extent and nature of the damage.
3 Remember that a frame which is out of alignment will cause handling problems and may even promote 'speed wobbles'. If misalignment is suspected, as a result of an accident, it will be necessary to strip the machine completely so that the frame can be checked, and if necessary, renewed.
4 BMW specifically advise against fitting a sidecar to any of the machines described in this Manual.

9 Steering damper: removal and examination

1 There are two types of steering damper fitted – the friction type on the /5 range, and an hydraulic damper on all others, where fitted. An hydraulic damper is available as an optional extra on /5 machines.
2 To remove the friction type damper, unscrew and remove the damper rod. Take off the circlip and washer retaining the lower damper plate to the bottom fork yoke and remove the damper plate. Unscrew the hexagon socket cap screw and nut which fixes the upper damper plate to the frame and remove the upper plate. Remove the damper rod rubber sleeve from within the steering column.
3 Hydraulic dampers are removed by unclipping the wire retainers at each end of the damper and pulling them out of their holes. It will be necessary to remove the fairing centre section to do this (R100RS and R100T only). The damper will then pull off the balljoints. If it is desired to remove the damper operating gear, unscrew the two screws retaining the gear housing to the lower fork yoke and remove the housing. Unscrew the crosshead screw in the centre of the damper knob and remove the knob. Pull the gear and damper rod out from underneath the steering head.
4 Examine hydraulic dampers for leaks and uniformity of damping action. It is highly unlikely that friction type dampers will require attention. Check the security of fixing of both types.

10 Footrests, stands and controls: general

1 At regular intervals (see Routine Maintenance) all footrests, the stands, brake pedal and gearchange lever or linkage should be checked and lubricated. Check that all mountings are securely fastened using the specified torque settings if given.
2 If necessary, dismantle the assembly so that all pivot points and bearing surfaces can be cleaned and greased. Return springs, where fitted, must be in good condition with no trace of fatigue and must be securely mounted.
3 If accident damage is to be repaired, check that the component is not cracked or broken. Such damage may be repaired by welding if the pieces are taken to an expert but since this will destroy the finish renewal is the most satisfactory course of action. If a component is bent it can be straightened after heating the affected area to a dull cherry red with a blowlamp or welding torch. Again the finish will be destroyed but painted surfaces can be repainted easily, while chromed surfaces can only be replated.

9.2 Remove circlip to release friction-type steering damper lower plate

9.3 Unclip wire retainers to release hydraulic steering damper

10.1 All control pivots should be dismantled for cleaning and greasing at regular intervals

11 Fairing: removal and refitting

R65LS
1 To remove the lower section unscrew the two self-tapping screws on the right and left then lift the fairing rear covers at an angle and remove them. Slacken the two Allen screws which clamp each turn signal lamp stalk.
2 Remove the front turn signal lamp lenses, lift out the reflectors and disconnect the wires. Withdraw the lamp assemblies. Unscrew the two lower section mounting bolts which fasten it to two brackets projecting up from the headlamp brackets; renew the rubber mountings if perished or damaged. Pull the lower section forward, disengaging its mounting grommets from the fairing top section and pull the turn signal wires inwards to release the lower section.
3 To remove the top section of the fairing unscrew the ignition switch retaining ring, press in the top section at the front, just above the headlamp, to release the clips, disengage it from the lower section mounting grommets and slide it upwards and backwards until the turn signal repeater can be pulled out and the fairing top section removed. Reverse to reassemble.

S-type fairing
4 Remove the nut, bolt, and washer fixing the tubular fairing stay to the upper fork yoke bracket on each side. Remove each flashing indicator lens and reflector and detach the wires from the rear of the reflectors. Slacken the indicator clamp bolts and pull both housings from the stalks. Detach the leads to the clock and voltmeter, and pull out the illuminating bulb holders.
5 Flex the bottom of the fairing to disengage it from the indicator stalks and remove the fairing. There is a slotted dished washer behind the grommet on the indicator stalk. The screen is attached by rivets which must be drilled out to remove it. On refitting, the rivets must be fitted using a special BMW tool No. 009510.

RS-type fairing
6 Where the fairing lower sections are split, they can be eased over the exhaust pipes. If they are not split, the exhaust system must be removed. See Chapter 4.
7 Removing the nine screws around its periphery, pull the fairing front centre section downwards slightly, press to the rear at the top and withdraw it.
8 Remove the single bolt securing the fairing lower sections to their bottom mounting brackets and the single bolt securing the upper mounting bracket. Remove the five self-tapping screws from the top edge of each lower section and remove the sections. If they are split, very carefully ease them apart by just enough to pass over the exhaust pipes.
9 Pull down the fork gaiters and carefully disengage the brake pipes from their locating slots. Remove the seven screws and remove the fairing top centre section.
10 Disconnect the six-pin electrical plug then unscrew its retaining ring and pull the ignition switch clear of the fairing instrument panel.
11 Remove the four nuts (two each side) from the mirror/fairing mountings. With an assistant working on the opposite side, remove the single retaining bolt securing each side of the fairing to the mounting bracket. Being very careful to avoid damage lift the fairing forwards off the machine. This is a two-man task if damage is to be avoided.
12 Refitting is the reverse of the removal sequence. The gaiters are a persistent problem; BMW recommend that they are glued to the fairing at six evenly-spaced points using Sicomet 8200 adhesive. Ensure they are folded correctly before glueing them. Do not overtighten any of the fasteners as their threaded bushes could easily be torn out of the plastic. Note that the windscreen is mounted as described for the S-fairing.

RT-type fairing
13 Where the fairing lower sections are split, they can be eased over the exhaust system. If they are not split, the exhaust pipes must be removed. See Chapter 4.
14 Removing the nine screws around its periphery, pull the fairing front centre section downwards slightly, press to the rear at the top and withdraw it.
15 Remove the single bolt securing each fairing lower section to its bottom mounting bracket and the single bolt securing the upper mounting bracket. To remove the latter remove the two screws securing the cover next to the luggage locker lids and remove the lids. Remove the three screws in the air plenum chambers and remove the lower sections. If they are split, ease them apart very carefully by just enough to pass over the exhaust pipes.
16 Pull down the fork gaiters and carefully disengage the brake pipes from their locating slots. Remove the seven screws and remove the fairing top centre section.
17 Press away the rubber trim surrounding the headlamp glass and unscrew the four retaining screws, then remove the headlamp glass and tunnel. Detach the two clips securing the electrical wiring to the two front lower areas of the mounting bracket and disconnect the wires at the six-pin block connector.
18 Unscrew the retaining ring and pull the ignition switch clear of the fairing instrument panel.
19 With an assistant working on the opposite side remove the bolts (two on each side) which retain the fairing to the mounting bracket upper arms (accessible through the headlamp aperture) and lower arms. Lift the fairing forwards off the machine. Be very careful; this is a two man task if damage is to be avoided.
20 Refitting is the reverse of the removal sequence. The gaiters are a persistent problem; BMW recommend that they are glued to the fairing at six evenly-spaced points using Sicomet 8200 adhesive. Ensure they are folded correctly before glueing them. Do not overtighten any of the fasteners as their threaded bushes could be easily torn out of the plastic.
21 To remove the windscreen on 1979 – 80 models, first remove the two screws holding each locking catch. Remove the parking lamp assembly and unscrew from the inside the two nuts which retain the screen holder. Detach the rubber sealing strip and withdraw the screen.
22 On refitting reverse the removal procedure. Do not forget to fit the two O-rings to the screen holder pegs, and do not overtighten the retaining nuts. The thicker end of the locating rod plastic guide on the adjusting mechanism must face inwards.
23 The procedure for 1981 on models differs only in the adjuster assembly. Unscrew the star-shaped knob and take off the underlay washer, then remove the two bolts retaining each baseplate and withdraw the baseplates. Proceed with the rest of the removal sequence.
24 Once the fairing has been removed, the plenum chamber can be detached if required (four screws). The air outlet retaining ring can then be unscrewed and the outlet removed.

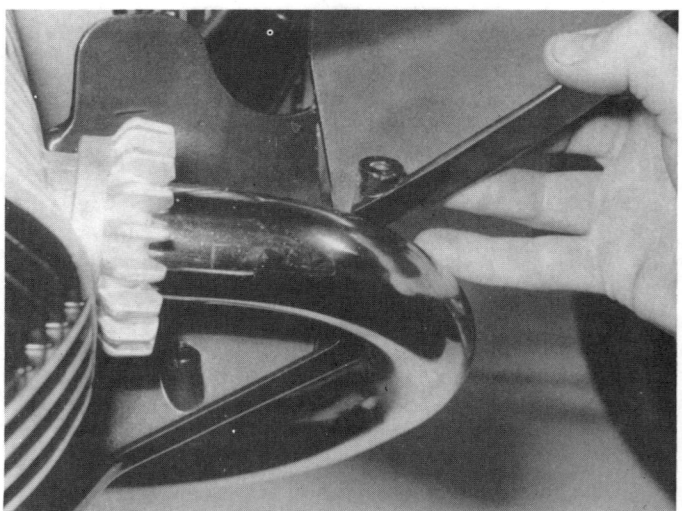

11.13 RS- and RT- fairing removal – exhaust pipes need not be removed if lower sections are split

11.14 Remove all retaining screws and carefully remove front centre section

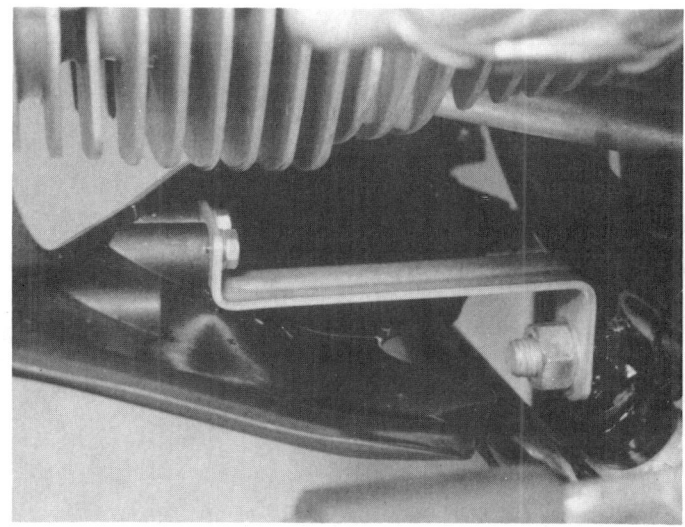

11.15a Lower section bottom mounting may have one or two bolts

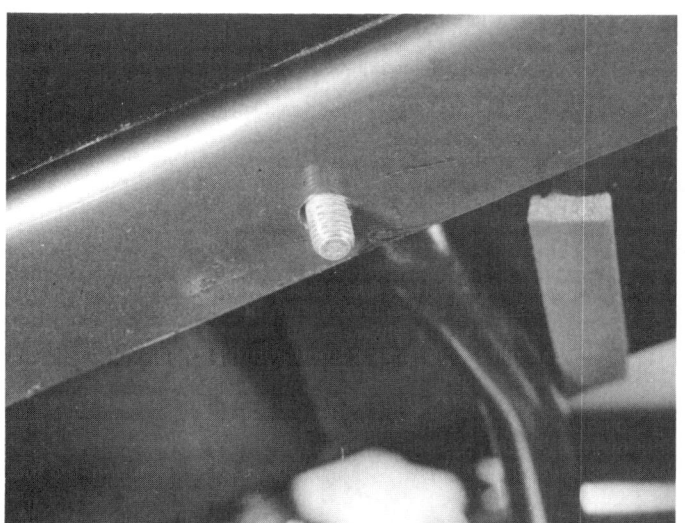

11.15b To unscrew lower section top mounting bolt ...

11.15c ... access must be gained to storage compartments – RT only

11.16a Slide brake pipes through locating slots to disengage ...

11.16b ... and slide down fork gaiters to release fairing top centre section

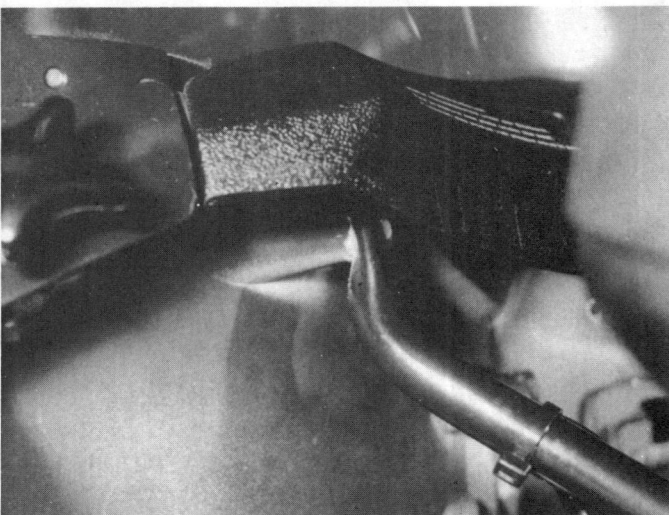

11.19a Fairing top mounting is difficult to reach ...

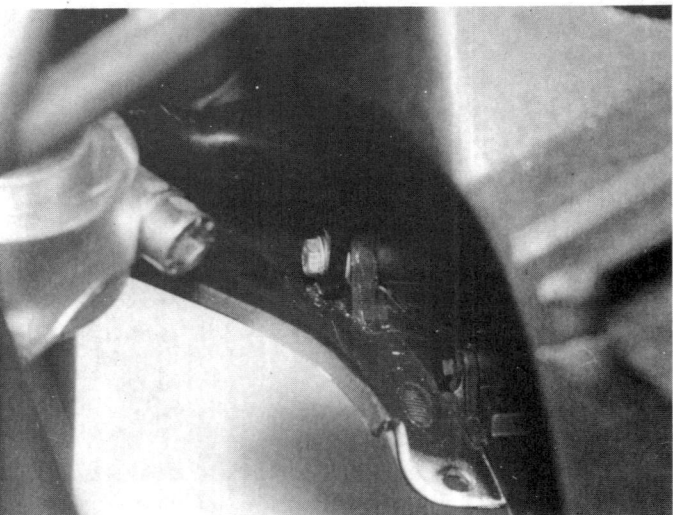

11.19b ... as is the lower mounting

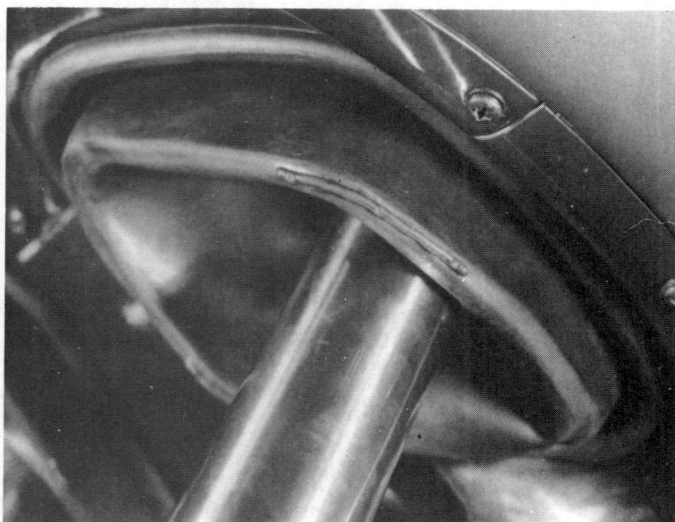

11.20 Fold gaiter correctly before glueing into place (see text). Do not overtighten mounting bolts or screws

12 Instruments: removal and refitting

1 /5 models have a combined speedometer and rev-counter mounted in the headlamp. All other models have separate instruments in a housing attached to the top fork yoke.

2 To remove the /5 instrument, first prise the headlamp rim off the bottom of the shell. Disconnect the battery earth lead and unplug the flasher relay, and the warning lamps in the instrument shell. Withdraw the drive cables. Unscrew the two securing nuts and remove the retaining strap. Lift the instrument out of the top of the housing.

3 On all other models except the R45, R65, R65LS, R80G/S and R80ST, the instrument housing must first be removed. Unscrew the knurled rings and withdraw both drive cables. Slacken the three hexagon head screws at the rear of the housing and lift the housing off the bracket. Remove the crosshead screw in the centre of the plug beneath the housing and unplug it. The housing can now be taken off completely. Remove the lower cover (three screws) and lamp holder (six screws). Unscrew the self-tapping screws on the instrument requiring replacement, and lift out the instrument head.

4 The instruments cannot be repaired. Remember that you must have a functioning speedometer accurate within ± 10% at 30 mph, in the UK. If the odometer continues to record when the speedometer fails to function, the instrument head is faulty and requires renewal or repair.

5 The voltmeter and clock fitted in the handlebar fairing of the R90S models are retained by a strap with two knurled nuts. Pull off the electrical connections and lamp and withdraw the instrument from the top of the dashboard.

6 To remove the instruments on R45, R65, R65LS and R80ST models take off the fairing top section (R65LS only) see Section 11; on all other models remove the ignition switch retaining ring and unscrew the two screws retaining the instrument surround; lift away the complete instrument cover and detach the turn signal repeater to release it. Disconnect the speedometer drive cable and pull out the instrument lighting bulb holder, then unplug the rev-counter multi-pin plug, noting the semi-circular pin. Remove the two nuts retaining either instrument and remove it.

7 On R80G/S models remove from the rear the four screws (two each side) which retain it and lift away the instrument housing front cover, pulling off the fork gaiter breather hoses (Note: refit these hoses before refitting the front cover on reassembly). Slacken the headlamp mountings and, pull the headlamp forwards off its bracket. Disconnect the speedometer drive cable, remove its retaining nut and withdraw the speedometer. The warning lamp unit is adjacent.

13 Speedometer and rev-counter cables: replacing

1 Faulty instrument drive cables are often indicated by jerky movement of the instrument needle, if not by complete immobility.

2 To remove the cables at the instrument end on /5 models, first remove the headlamp. Prise the headlamp rim off the bottom of the shell with a screwdriver. Disconnect the battery earth lead and unplug the flasher relay. The rev-counter cable is behind the speedometer cable, when looking into the headlamp shell. Unscrew the knurled retaining ring, and pull the cable out of the instrument. If the rev-counter cable is to be removed, first disconnect the speedometer cable.

3 Drive cables on all other models, having removed the fairing upper section (R65LS only) are immediately accessible underneath the instrument housing. Simply unscrew the knurled ring and withdraw the cable.

4 The other end of the speedometer cable is above the rear drive universal joint, at the rear right-hand side of the gearbox, slacken the clamping screw and withdraw the cable. Remove the petrol tank (Chapter 4). Unclip the strap around the rubber cable tidy on the top frame tube and remove the speedometer cable. Pull the cable out of the headlamp grommet (/5). Note the route of the cable for replacement.

5 To remove the other end of the rev-counter cable, take off the front engine cover: slacken the horn fixing screws, remove the three hexagon socket cap screws and take off the cover. Slacken the drive cable clamp screw and withdraw the cable. Pull off the cable grommet and draw the cable out of the headlamp shell (/5.)

6 Check to see if the outer cable is compressed or damaged. There must be no sharp bends in the cable.

Chapter 7 Final drive and rear suspension

Refer to Chapter 10 for information relating to the 1986 on models

Contents

General description 1	Swinging arm: examination and renewing bearings and seals 6
Rear bevel drive housing: removal 2	Driveshaft: removal, examination and refitting 7
Rear bevel drive: examination and renovation 3	Swinging arm and driveshaft: refitting 8
Rear bevel drive housing: refitting 4	Rear suspension units: adjustment, removal and examination 9
Swinging arm and driveshaft: removal 5	Nivomat suspension units: general 10

Specifications

Driveshaft
Type .... Enclosed shaft with needle roller bearing universal joint at gearbox end and splined coupling at rear end. Fitted with spring-loaded face cam shock absorber from 1979 models on

Oil quantity:
    /5 models up to mid 1973 .... 100 cc (0.18 Imp pint, 0.11 US qt)
    All other models .... 150 cc (0.26 Imp pint, 0.16 US qt)
Recommended oil .... Good quality hypoid gear oil API class GL-5 or to specification MIL-L-2105 B or C

Viscosity:
    Above 5°C (41°F) .... SAE 90
    Below 5°C (41°F) .... SAE 80
    All temperatures .... SAE 80W90

Rear bevel drive
Type .... Helical-cut crownwheel and pinion gears
Final drive ratio:
    R100S, R100CS, (US) R100T, (US) R100, (US) R100RS
    1978 on, (US) R100RT 1980 on 2.91:1 (32/11T)
    R90S, (UK) R100RS, (US) R100RS 1977, R100T (except US
    1980 model), (UK) R100RT, (US) R100RT 1979, (UK) R100 ..... 3.00:1 (33/11T)
    R90/6, R100/7 .... 3.09:1 (34/11T)
    R75, R80, R80/7 with high compression engine 3.20:1 (32/10T)
    R60/5, R60/6, R60/7 1977, R80/7 with low-compression
    engine, R80G/S, R80ST, R80RT 3.36:1 (37/11T)
    R65, R65LS 3.44:1 (31/9T)
    R50/5, R60/7 1978 .... 3.56:1 (32/9T)
    R45 .... 3.89:1 (35/9T)
Tooth backlash:
    All models up to 1980 .... 0.15 - 0.20 mm (0.0059 - 0.0079 in)
    All models 1981 on .... 0.08 - 0.14 mm (0.0032 - 0.0055 in)
Crownwheel lateral play – without seal:
    All models up to 1980 .... Nil
    All models 1981 on .... 0.10 mm (0.0039 in)
Oil quantity:
    All models up to 1980 .... 250 cc (0.44 Imp pint, 0.26 US qt)
    All models 1981 on .... 350 cc (0.61 Imp pint, 0.37 US qt)
Recommended oil .... Good quality, hypoid gear oil API class GL-5 or to specification MIL-L-2105 B or C

Viscosity:
    Above 5°C (41°F) .... SAE 90
    Below 5°C (41°F) .... SAE 80
    All temperatures .... SAE 80W90

Chapter 7 Final drive and rear suspension

Rear suspension

Type:
- R80G/S, R80ST, R80, R80RT 1985 on .... Single coil sprung suspension unit with gas-assisted hydraulic damping acting on a swinging arm which also encloses the drive shaft (BMW 'Monolever')
- All other models .... Twin coil sprung hydraulically-damped suspension units acting on a pivoted fork, right-hand tube enclosing the driveshaft

Suspension travel:
- /5, /6, /7 except R100RT, R80RT 1983-84 .... 125.0 mm (4.92 in)
- R100RT – with Nivomats .... 85.5 mm (3.37 in)
- R45, R65, R65LS .... 110.0 mm (4.33 in)
- R80G/S .... 170.0 mm (6.69 in)
- R80ST .... 153.0 mm (6.02 in)
- R80, R80RT 1985 on .... 121.0 mm (4.76 in)

Spring free length:
- /5, /6, /7, R80RT 1983-84 .... 251 mm (9.8819 in)
- R45, R65, R65LS .... 240 – 248 mm (9.4488 – 9.7638 in)
- R80G/S .... 272 – 276 mm (10.7086 – 10.8661 in)
- R80, R80RT 1985 on .... 212 – 214 mm (8.3464 – 8.4252 in)
- All other models .... N/Av

Spring wire diameter:
- /5, /6, /7, R80RT 1983-84 .... 7.46 – 7.54 mm (0.2937 – 0.2969 in)
- R45, R65, R65LS .... 7.50 mm (0.2953 in)
- R80G/S .... 11.00 mm (0.4331 in)
- R80, R80RT 1985 on .... 10.40 mm (0.4094 in)
- All other models .... N/Av

Swinging arm pivot bearings:
- Type – all models .... Taper roller
- Reference number and size – all models up to 1/81 .... 30203 (A) 17 mm x 40 mm x 12 mm
- Reference number and size – all models 1/81 on .... 32203 17 mm x 40 mm x 17 mm

Torque wrench settings

Component	Nm	lbf ft
Driveshaft flange/output flange 12-sided bolts:*		
/5, /6 – bolts 14.5 mm long	24 – 26	18 – 19
R80, R80RT 1985 on – bolts 13.0 mm long	31.6 – 39.6	23 – 29
All other models – bolts 13.0 mm long	38 – 42	28 – 31
Rear coupling/driveshaft retaining nut:		
/5, /6	240 – 260	177 – 192
/7 up to 1978	200 – 220	148 – 162
Rear bevel drive/swinging arm mounting nuts:		
Early models	N/Av	N/Av
/7 1981 on, R45 and R65 1981 on, R65LS, R80RT 1983-84	47	34.5
R80G/S, R80ST, R80, R80RT 1985 on*	65	48
Bevel drive pinion retaining nut:		
/5, /6	100 – 110	74 – 81
/7 up to 1980, R45 and R65 up to 1980	150 – 165	111 – 122
All models 1981 on	165	122
Drive pinion assembly/bevel drive housing retaining threaded ring:		
All models up to 1980	100 – 120	74 – 88.5
All models 1981 on	118	87
Bevel drive cover/housing retaining nuts:		
All models up to 1980	18 – 21	13.5 – 15.5
All models 1981 on	17.7	13
Oil filler plug – swinging arm:		
All models up to 1980	14	10
All models 1981 on	Screwed in securely and fastened finger-tight	
Oil drain plug – swinging arm:		
All models up to 1980	14 – 17	10 – 12.5
R80, R80RT 1985 on	14	10
All other models	15.7	11.5
Oil filler plug – rear bevel drive:		
All models up to 1980	28 – 31	21 – 23
R80, R80RT 1985 on	20	15
All other models	N/Av	N/Av
Oil level plug – rear bevel drive – 1981 on models only	10	7.5
Oil drain plug – rear bevel drive:		
All models up to 1980	23 – 26	17 – 19
R80, R80RT 1985 on	22	16
All other models	25.5	19
Swinging arm pivot shafts:		
To preload bearings	20	15
Normal setting	10 – 12	7.5 – 9
Swinging arm pivot shaft locknuts:		
/5, /6, R45 and R65 up to 1980	100 – 110	74 – 81
All other models	100 – 120	74 – 88.5

Chapter 7 Final drive and rear suspension

Component	Nm	lbf ft
Suspension unit top mounting eye/damper rod:		
/5, /6, R45 and R65 up to 1980	30 – 34	22 – 25
/7 up to 1980	34 – 39	25 – 29
R45 and R65 1981 on, R65LS, /7 1981 on R80RT 1983-84	36 – 40	26.5 – 29.5
R80, R80G/S, R80ST, R80RT 1985 on	15	11
Suspension unit mountings – all pivoted fork models:		
Both upper mountings, right lower mounting	35 – 40	26 – 29.5
Left lower mounting	30 – 35	22 – 26
Suspension unit mountings – all 'Monolever' models:		
R80G/S, R80ST – upper and lower	43 – 48	32 – 35.5
R80, R80RT 1985 on – upper and lower	29.3	21.5

* Only applicable if BMW special tool is used – see text

1 General description

The drive is taken from the gearbox output shaft via a hook-type universal joint. The rear driveshaft passes through the right-hand swinging arm tube, which also serves as an oil bath.

The helical bevel drive pinion and crownwheel are housed in an aluminium alloy oil bath case. They are splined to the driveshaft and rear wheel respectively. Both crownwheel and pinion are supported in ball and needle roller bearings.

In mid-1973 (frame numbers up to 2906304 (R50/5), 2942996 (R60/5) and 2997998 (R75/5) the wheelbase of the machine was increased by extending the length of the swinging arm and driveshaft.

The shock absorber fitted into the rear driveshaft of all models from 1979 onwards is a spring-loaded face cam type which is very similar in design and construction to that fitted to the gearbox input shaft.

It should be noted that the new driveshaft assembly is available as a kit that can be fitted to all earlier series 7 models, to all series 6 models, and to all long wheelbase series 5 models (1973 onwards). Earlier series 5 models can be equipped as well, but will require the purchase of the necessary components such as the later swinging-arm assembly.

In 1981 the R80G/S appeared with a single sided swinging arm rear suspension called 'Monolever' by BMW. Although radically different in appearance, the layout is essentially the same as that of all other models. The bevel drive housing had been stiffened to take the extra stress; the new version is lighter and stronger than the original and is now fitted to all other models in the range.

Rear suspension unit(s) are conventional coil spring hydraulically damped types except for the R100RT from 1981 on. This model is fitted with Boge 'Nivomat' self-levelling suspension; it is described in greater detail in the relevant Section. Nivomat suspension can be supplied as an optional extra for any /5, /6 or /7 model or the R80RT 1983-84 models and may also be found on these models.

2 Rear bevel drive housing: removal

1 The bevel drive housing is bolted to the driveshaft housing (swinging arm). It may be removed as a complete assembly with the swinging arm, or individually, as follows:
2 Remove the rear wheel. See Chapter 8.
3 Drain the bevel drive and driveshaft oil. See Routine Maintenance.
4 Unscrew the wing nut from the rear brake rod, remove the trunnion from the brake cam lever and replace both on the brake rod.
5 Remove the nut and washer from the (right-hand) suspension unit lower mounting stud (not necessary on R80G/S, R80ST).
4 Unscrew the four nuts that fix the bevel drive housing to the swinging arm and remove them together with washers. Tap the housing with a soft-faced mallet to break the seal.
5 Pull the bevel drive housing rearwards, clear of the holes in the swinging arm, disengage from the suspension unit lower fixing eye, and remove. Note the gasket.

3 Rear bevel drive: examination and renovation

1 Dismantling the bevel drive is beyond the scope of the majority of amateur mechanics. Wear or damage will be indicated by a high pitched whine. Backlash between the crownwheel and pinion may be assessed by holding the output shaft firmly and rotating the input shaft in both directions. Any lateral play in the crownwheel can be felt by pulling and pushing the output driveshaft.
2 A faulty output shaft oil seal will be indicated by excessive oil in the brake drum, or around the wheel spindle nut.
3 The helical drive coupling and rear wheel drive splines should be examined for wear or damage.
4 If any wear or damage is found or suspected, take the unit to a BMW dealer for reconditioning.

2.4 Remove bevel drive mounting nuts ...

2.5 ... to release bevel drive housing

4 Rear bevel drive housing: refitting

1 Clean the swinging arm/bevel drive mating surfaces carefully. Where a gasket is used coat both sides of it with a thin smear of Hylomar SQ32/M or similar non-setting jointing compound and stick it to the housing flange; if no gasket is used apply a thin coat of Loctite 638 or similar sealant.
2 Offer up the housing to the rear of the swinging arm and push it in to place, rotating the drive flange to engage the input pinion teeth with the driveshaft rear coupling. Refit the retaining nuts (and washers).
3 On models with pivoted fork rear suspension, refit the wheel spindle to align the housing then tighten the retaining nuts securely (to the specified torque setting, where given). Remove the spindle.
4 On 'Monolever' models the retaining nuts must be tightened securely. Note that the torque setting specified can be applied accurately **only** by using the special crowsfoot-type spanner BMW No. 33.1.620; do not try to approximate the torque setting by applying a measured pull to a spanner of known length. If the special tool is not available, tighten the nuts securely and take the machine to a BMW dealer for the torque to be checked.
5 Refit the rear wheel and connect the rear brake. Adjust the brake as described in Routine Maintenance. Fill the driveshaft and bevel drive housings with oil, as described in Routine Maintenance.

5 Swinging arm and driveshaft: removal

1 The swinging arm and driveshaft can only be removed as a single unit. Before starting work, read Section 8, paragraphs 5 and 6, concerning the driveshaft bolts.
2 Working as described in Routine Maintenance, drain the driveshaft oil. The bevel drive housing need not be drained, unless it is to be dismantled, but should be kept upright to prevent the loss of oil through the breather.
3 Slacken the clips retaining the universal joint gaiter. Push the gaiter back and unscrew the four 12-sided bolts with a ring spanner. Prevent the driveshaft from turning by applying the rear brake (if the bevel drive has not been removed), or by engaging top gear. Discard the bolts.
4 Remove the wing nut from the rear brake rod and the trunnion from the brake cam lever, replacing both on the brake rod. Undo the nut behind the footbrake pedal pivot, preventing the pivot from turning while doing so. Remove the footbrake with brake rod attached.
5 Remove the bevel drive if desired, see Section 2, otherwise remove the rear wheel only, see Chapter 8.
6 Unscrew the nut from the left-hand suspension unit lower mounting bolt and remove it together with washer. Withdraw the bolt. If the bevel drive has not been removed, remove the nut and washer from the right-hand suspension unit lower mounting stud. Pull the unit off the stud.
7 Remove the caps from the swinging arm bearing adjusters, slacken the adjuster locknuts and unscrew both adjusters completely with an Allen key. Support the swinging arm whilst doing so. Remove the swinging arm.

6 Swinging arm: examination and renewing bearings and seals

1 The taper roller swinging arm bearings are supported on adjustable stub spindles, which are secured into the frame.
2 Remove the swinging arm as described in Section 5 of this Chapter.
3 Do not remove the swinging arm bearing seals unless they or the bearings are to be replaced. The seals are easily damaged when being removed. Note that the flange on the spacer should be adjacent to the bearing, that is, trapped behind the lip seal.
4 Lever out the seals if necessary, with a screwdriver. Take out the bearing inner races and clean and inspect them. Clean the bearing inner races whilst they are in the swinging arm and inspect for brinelling (indenting) of the tracks. If necessary lever the outer races from their housings and remove the grease retainer from the left-hand bearing housing.
5 When assembling, clean and grease the bearings. Do not interchange bearing parts. Fit the flange on the spacer adjacent to the bearing, then tap the seal into place. The open side of the lip seal should face the bearing.
6 If the driveshaft gaiter is split or torn it should be renewed.

5.3 Unscrew 12-sided bolts to separate driveshaft flange from gearbox

5.7 Removal of plastic cap exposes each swinging arm pivot shaft and locknut

6.4 Note grease retainer behind left-hand pivot bearing

6.5a Pack bearings with grease on refitting

6.5b Spacer is refitted with flange adjacent to bearing

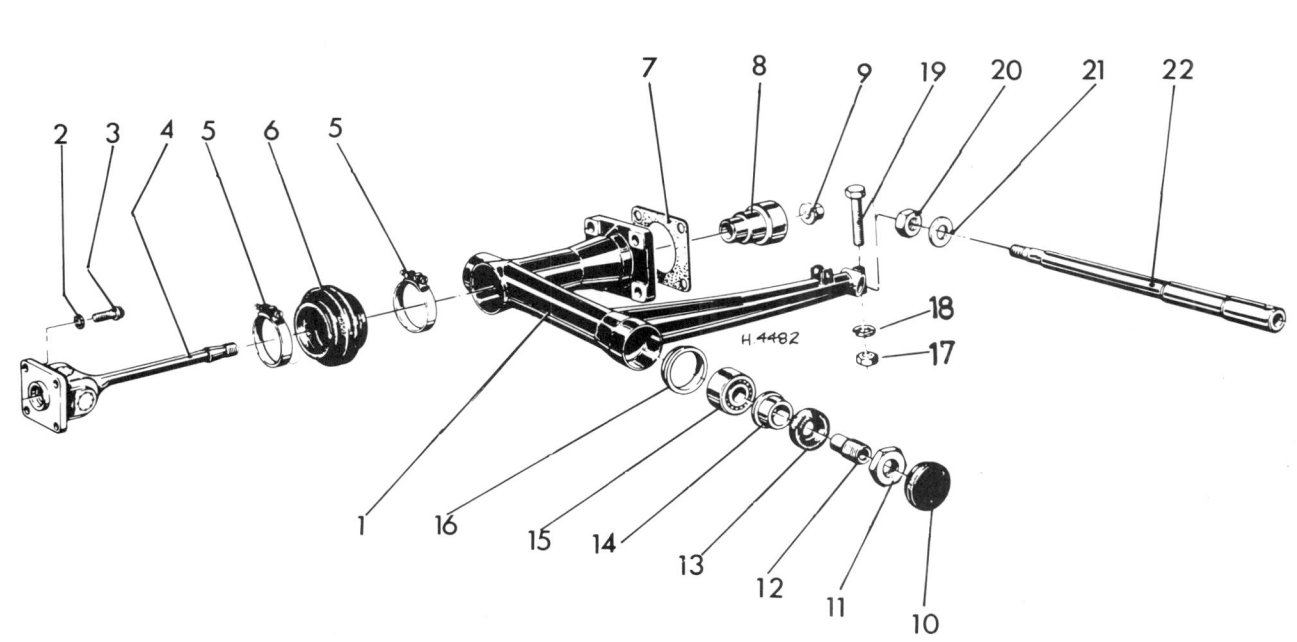

Fig. 7.1 Swinging arm and driveshaft – all models up to 1978

1 Swinging arm
2 Lock washer
3 Twelve point bolt
4 Driveshaft
5 Gaiter clip
6 Gaiter
7 Gasket
8 Rear coupling
9 Nut
10 Dust cap
11 Locknut
12 Pivot shaft
13 Oil seal – where fitted
14 Thrust sleeve – where fitted
15 Tapered roller bearing
16 Grease retainer
17 Nut
18 Lock washer
19 Bolt
20 Nut
21 Washer
22 Rear wheel spindle

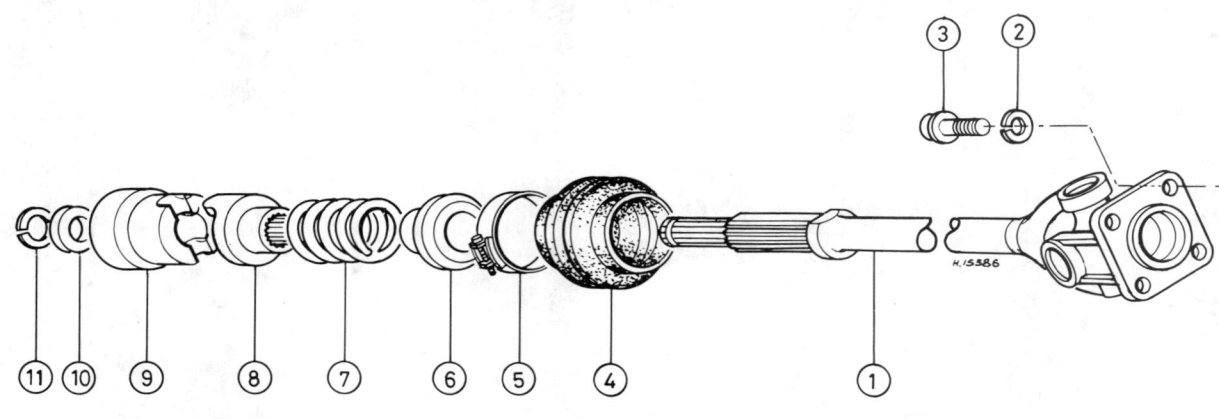

Fig. 7.2 Driveshaft – 1979 on models

1 Driveshaft
2 Lock washer (where fitted)
3 Bolt
4 Gaiter
5 Gaiter clamp
6 Spring seat
7 Shock absorber spring
8 Shock absorber front cam
9 Shock absorber rear cam
10 Spacer
11 Circlip

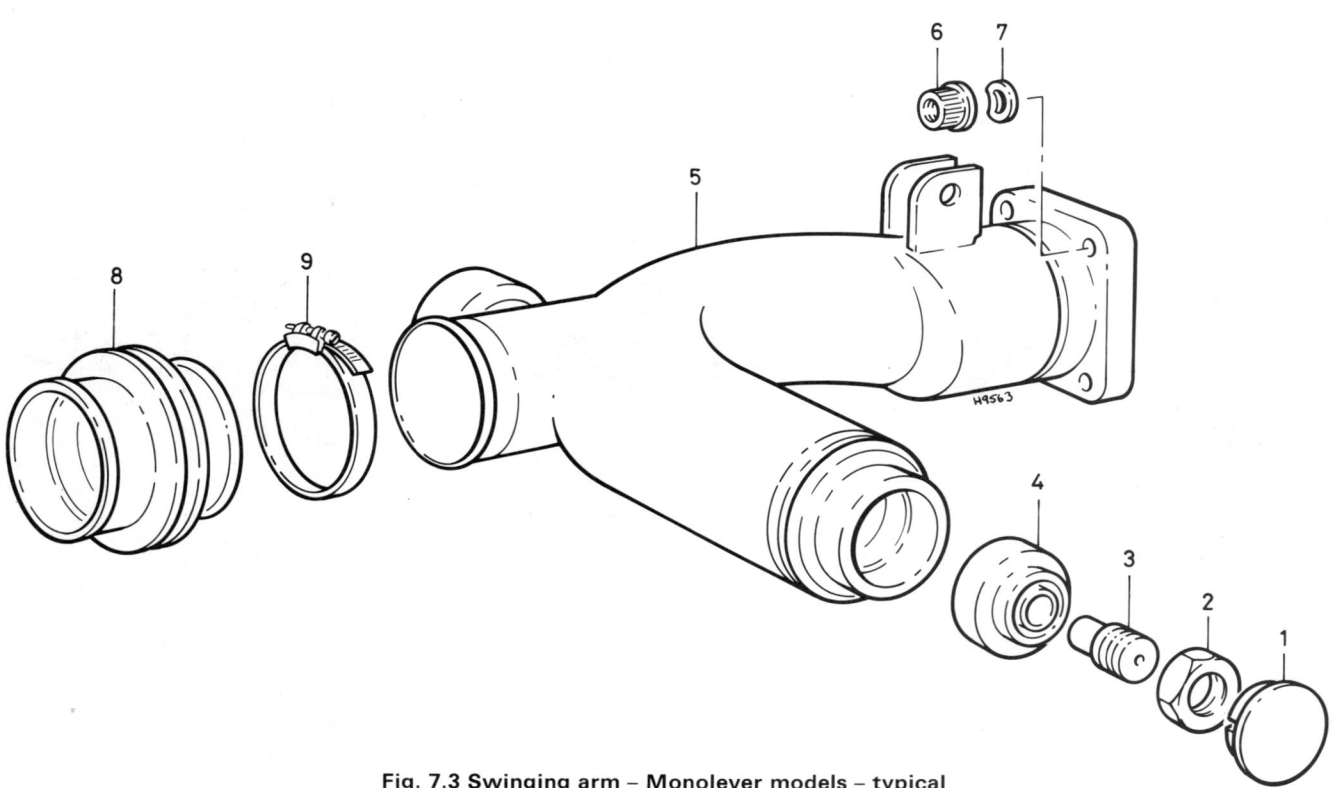

Fig. 7.3 Swinging arm – Monolever models – typical

1 Dust cap
2 Locknut
3 Pivot shaft
4 Tapered roller bearing
5 Swinging arm
6 Nut
7 Washer
8 Gaiter
9 Clamp – 2 off

7 Driveshaft: removal, examination and refitting

All models up to 1978

1 The universal joint bearings are riveted and cannot be replaced. If they are worn, the complete shaft must be replaced. There should be no appreciable play in the bearings and no roughness.
2 Worn universal joint bearings will cause considerable vibration, as also will a bent driveshaft or universal joint flange. Take great care when dismantling and reassembling not to bend either.
3 Examine the helical splines on the output drive coupling for wear or chipping.

Chapter 7 Final drive and rear suspension

4 If it is necessary to remove the driveshaft, the swinging arm should be held in a vice with soft jaws. Prevent the shaft from rotating and unscrew the nut inside the splined drive coupling. This nut is very tight. Use a suitable extractor to release the drive coupling from its taper. Give a sharp blow on the end of the extractor spindle if necessary.

5 Before refitting the coupling, it is essential to clean the internal and external tapers with degreasing agent. **(Do not use petrol)**. Tighten the nut to the specified torque setting.

All models 1979 on

6 Dismantling and reassembly are simpler than on the older type, but it must be noted that a suitable spring compressor must be first obtained or fabricated, the special BMW tool being number 26 1 700.

7 The tool required must compress the shock absorber spring by pressing inwards the rear shock absorber cam. The BMW tool achieves this by the use of a flat metal strip which fits over the flange at the driveshaft forward end. Two long threaded rods are secured to this strip and pass up the outside of the swinging arm to project beyond the rear end of the swinging arm and driveshaft. A shaped adaptor is placed over the two rods and slid down to bear on the rear face of the shock absorber rear cam, whereupon pressure is applied to the shock absorber spring by tightening evenly two nuts, one on each threaded rod.

8 It should be possible to obtain the BMW tool or to fabricate a close approximation of it. Once the shock absorber spring is safely compressed, use a sharp-pointed instrument to prise out the plain wire clip which retains the assembly. The metal spacer, the two cams, the shock absorber spring, and the spring seat can be removed from the rear of the driveshaft once the tool had been released. The driveshaft is then pulled out of the swinging arm from the front.

9 On reassembly, refit the driveshaft and its components in the reverse of the dismantling order, ensuring that each is well lubricated to prevent the onset of corrosion. It is essential that the retaining circlip is in good condition; renew it if in the slightest doubt. Compress the shock absorber spring using the tool employed on dismantling, fit the circlip carefully over the driveshaft rear-end, and slide it along the shaft and into its groove in the shaft splines. Check that the circlip is correctly seated before releasing the tool. Note that if the tool is not available, the swinging arm assembly should be removed from the machine and taken to a BMW dealer for the work to be carried out. Do not try and dismantle the driveshaft assembly without a safe means of compressing the shock absorber spring, or there is a severe risk of personal injury.

7.4 To release driveshaft (early models) unscrew rear coupling retaining nut and extract coupling

7.7a Driveshaft removal (later models) – special tool is required ...

7.7b ... to compress shock absorber spring safely ...

7.7c ... so that retaining circlip can be removed

7.8a With circlip removed and spring pressure released, withdraw spacer noting recessed face ...

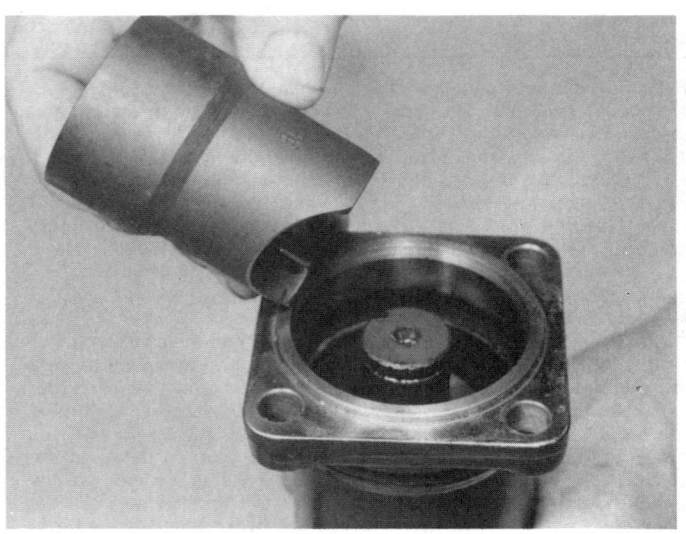

7.8b ... followed by shock absorber rear cam ...

7.8c ... shock absorber front cam ...

7.8d ... shock absorber spring ...

7.8e ... and the spring seat

7.8f Pull driveshaft forwards out of swinging arm

Chapter 7 Final drive and rear suspension

8 Swinging arm and driveshaft: refitting

1 Insert the swinging arm/driveshaft assembly into the frame and screw the adjusters in to finger tightness. Ensure that the distances between the swinging arm bearing housings and the frame mountings are the same on both sides. If necessary reposition the adjusters to achieve this.
2 Adjust the swinging arm bearings as described in Routine Maintenance.
3 Refit the suspension unit(s) and tighten the mountings to the specified torque settings.
4 Refit the bevel drive housing and/or the rear wheel, connect the brake rod again and adjust it as described in Routine Maintenance. Using a suitable solvent thoroughly degrease the gearbox output flange and driveshaft flange and their threaded holes.
5 The driveshaft twelve-sided head retaining bolts **must** be renewed whenever they are disturbed; they are of the stretch type which deform permanently on tightening. Also they must be fitted **dry** (no oil on the threads) and **must** be tightened to the specified torque setting. Note also that the type fitted to all models up to 1980 (14.5 mm/0.57 in long, with a spring washer) should be replaced by the later type (13.0 mm/0.51 in long, without a spring washer); testing has shown that if correctly fitted the bolts do not slacken in service if the spring washer is not fitted, but the shorter bolts are necessary to prevent the risk of damage to the gearbox output shaft oil seal. Models from 1981 on are all fitted with the shorter bolts and no spring washers as standard.
6 Fit the new bolts as described above and tighten them to the specified torque setting. On models up to 1980 be careful to use the torque wrench setting appropriate to the type of bolts fitted. **Note:** On all models the torque setting is specified to take into account the leverage which results from the use of the special crowsfoot-type spanner BMW tool No. 00.2.560; do **not** attempt to approximate it using any other means (such as applying a measured pull at the end of a spanner of known length). Use **only** the BMW tool to tighten the bolts; if necessary take the machine to a BMW dealer for the work to be done.
7 Refit the driveshaft gaiter and tighten its clamps securely. Fill the driveshaft housing (and bevel drive, if drained) with oil to the correct level as described in Routine Maintenance.

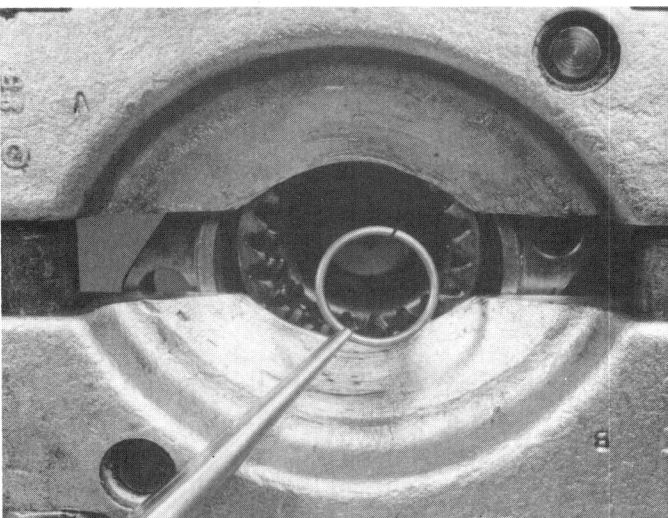

7.9a On refitting, renew circlip if necessary

7.9b Expand the circlip as shown to fit it over the shaft rear end

7.9c Check that circlip is seated securely in spacer recess, as shown

8.2 Adjust pivot bearings to correct preload – ensure swinging arm is central in the frame

9 Rear suspension units: adjustment, removal and examination

1 The two-way hydraulically damped suspension units may be adjusted to three spring load settings. Adjustment is effected by turning the lever below the spring, except on 'Monolever' models, which are adjusted with a C-spanner.

  For solo riding – lever facing forwards
  For solo riding with luggage – lever pointing outwards
  For two-up riding – lever facing rearwards

Both levers **must** be set to the same position (twin suspension units only). Faulty dampers may be suspected if handling becomes unpredictable, or if the rear end of the machine bounces up and down when depressed and released. Oil leaks will indicate a faulty oil seal.
2 Place the machine on its centre stand on level ground and wedge a block of wood or similar under one of the silencer mounting points so that the rear wheel is clear of the ground. Remove the nuts, bolts and washers fixing the suspension unit(s) to the rear sub-frame at the top. Remove the nut, bolt and washer fixing the left hand suspension unit to the swinging arm. Depress the rear of the machine in order to withdraw the bolt above the silencer. Remove the nut and washer from the right-hand suspension unit lower stud. Take off both units.
3 Select the softest position, compress the spring and unscrew the top fixing eye from the damper rod. There are two flats at the top of the rod to accept a spanner. Take off the spring cover and spring. Note the rubber buffer on the damper rod.
4 Check damper action by pulling and pushing on the damper-rod. It should require more effort to pull it out than to push it in. In both directions, the action must be uniform over the total length of the stroke. If oil is escaping, the damper rod seal is faulty. It is not possible to renovate the dampers, they can only be renewed.
5 Check the spring free length (see Specifications). Stronger springs are available for use when heavy loads are habitually carried.
6 If the Silentbloc rubber bushes in the suspension unit mounting eyes need renewing, they may be pressed out.
7 Replace the suspension units in the same position, otherwise the load adjusting levers will point into the spokes.

10 Nivomat suspension units: general

1 Nivomat suspension units, developed in conjunction with the manufacturers, Boge, require no adjustment or maintenance and are self-adjusting to provide the same ride height, ground clearance, suspension travel and performance for all loads up to the maximum permissible and at all speeds. Spring preload (or its equivalent) and damping action are adjusted automatically to be relatively soft during low-speed solo use and become progressively harder as the need arises.
2 The unit functions as follows (refer to the accompanying illustration): the pump rod is resiliently mounted to the top of the unit, the piston rod being attached to the bottom. As the suspension moves, the relative movement of these two components causes oil to be sucked from the low-pressure chamber via passages to the pump intake valve, from where it is forced through the pump check valve into the high-pressure chamber. This pressurises the gas, which is kept separate by a rubber diaphragm, increases the pressure in the unit's working parts and raises the spring preload to raise the machine to a pre-determined ride height. When this has been reached a valve opens to allow the oil to flow through the unit back to the low-pressure chamber. Damping action is provided by the pumping action itself, in addition to the spring-loaded damper valves. Note that if the load limit is exceeded, a safety valve prevents excessive pressure from building up; this means that the full ride height will not be reached.
3 It is important to remember that the ride height and suspension travel will not reach their full values until the units have pumped themselves up. Therefore if the first few miles of a journey are on a completely smooth road, the rear suspension may not be ready to take sudden bumps. Also if the load is suddenly altered, ie if the rider takes all his weight on his legs when stopped at a traffic light, if a pillion passenger mounts or dismounts, or if luggage is added or removed, the rear suspension will take a little while to adjust itself to the new requirements. This is not a fault, merely a function of the system's design and should not cause problems once the rider is familiar with it.

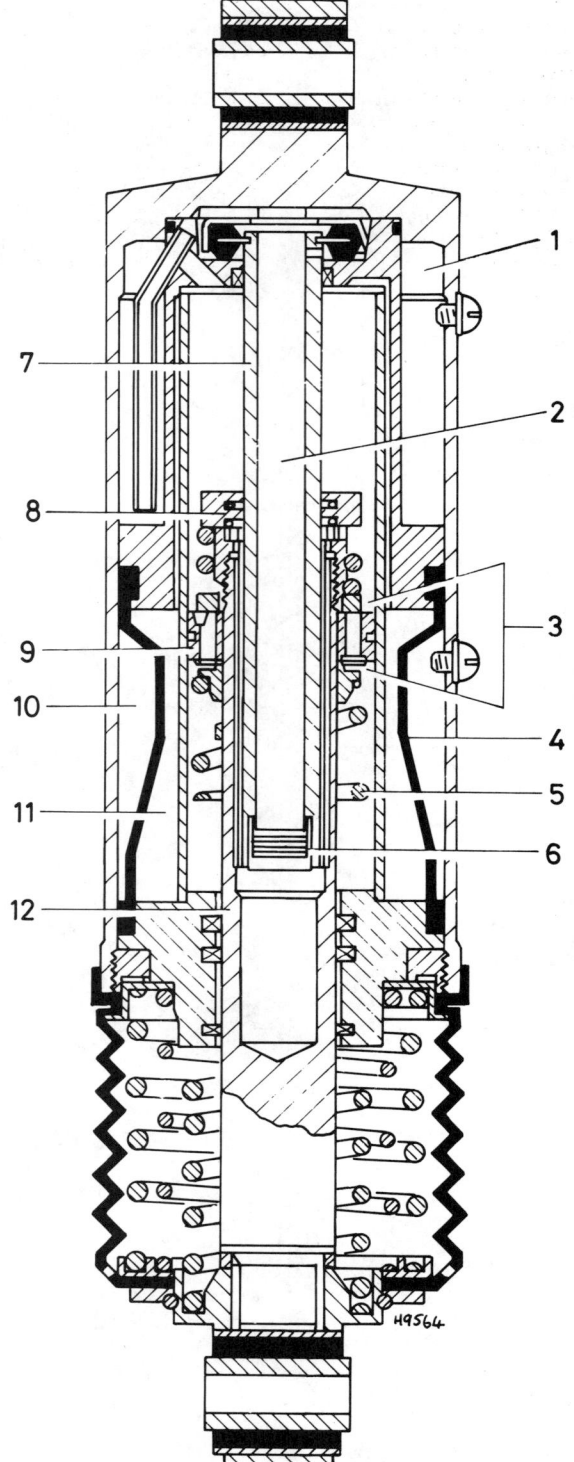

Fig. 7.4 Nivomat suspension unit

1 Low pressure chamber
2 Ride height control passage
3 Damper spring loaded valves
4 Rubber diaphragm
5 Rebound spring
6 Pump intake valve
7 Hollow pump rod
8 Pump check valve
9 Damper piston
10 Gas (high pressure)
11 High pressure chamber
12 Piston rod

4 To test the units, place a load on the rear of the machine, sufficient to noticeably compress the suspension, then with the machine stationary but on its wheels press down on its rear end (20 to 25 strokes of approximately 15 – 20 mm /$^{1}/_{2}$ – $^{3}/_{4}$ in). The units should be seen to pump themselves up to the normal ride height.

5 Units manufactured before August 1981 have a silver-painted lower mounting eye. All units manufactured after this date have a black-painted lower mounting eye and were modified to give softer damping for a more comfortable solo ride. In addition to this, units manufactured from January 1982 on (identified by the letter 'L', or subsequent in alphabetical order, being stamped in the lower mounting eye) have an additional spring underneath the rubber gaiter to increase the speed at which the units reach their set ride height.

6 This additional spring should have been fitted by dealers or parts depots to all units with black mounting eyes (and to remaining stocks of earlier units). If the units fitted to your machine are slow to reach full ride height or do not reach it at all, check that the additional spring has been fitted before suspecting a fault in the units.

7 **Warning**: do not attempt to dismantle the units or to alter their performance. **Do not** touch the two screws in the unit body. If any fault is suspected in the rear suspension performance take the machine to a BMW dealer for attention. Note that a light film of oil on the damper piston rod does not necessarily indicate a fault, although any serious oil leakage will obviously warrant instant attention by a dealer.

8 If faulty, the units must be renewed as a matched pair which have the same part number, even if only one is actually at fault.

Chapter 8 Wheels, brakes and tyres

Refer to Chapter 10 for subsequent modifications and information relating to the 1986 on models

Contents

General description 1	Rear disc brake master cylinder: removal, examination and
Front wheel: removal and refitting 2	refitting 10
Rear wheel: removal and refitting 3	Bleeding the hydraulic brake system 11
Wheel bearings: removal, examination and refitting 4	Tyres: removal, repair and refitting – tubed tyres 12
Drum front brake: examination and renovation 5	Valve cores and caps: tubed tyres 13
Drum rear brake: examination and renovation 6	Tyres: removal and refitting – tubeless tyres 14
Hydraulic brake overhaul: general 7	Puncture repair and tyre renewal – tubeless tyres 15
Caliper: removal, examination and refitting 8	Tyre valves: description and renewal – tubeless tyres 16
Front brake master cylinder: removal, examination and	Wheel balancing 17
refitting 9	

Specifications

Wheels

Type:

R65LS	BMW cast aluminium, compound type
R45, R65, R80, R80/7 1979 – 80, R80RT, R100, R100S 1979 on, (US) R100CS, (UK) R100CS 1982 on, R100RS 1978 on, R100T, R100RT	Cast aluminium alloy
All other models	Wire spoked

Size:

	Front	Rear
/5 up to early 1972*	1.85B x 19	1.85B x 18
/5 early 1972 on, R60/6, R60/7, R75/6, R75/7, R80/7 1978, R90/6, R90S, R100/7, R100S, R100RS 1977 (std)	1.85B x 19	2.15B x 18
R100RS 1977 (optional cast wheels) R80/7 1979 – 80, R100T, R80ST		
R100RS 1978 – 80, R100S and R100RT 1979 – 80	1.85B x 19	2.50B x 18
R80RT 1983 – 84, R100, R100CS	1.85B x 19	2.75C x 18
R100RS and R100RT, 1981 on	2.15B x 19	2.50B x 18
R45, R65	2.15B x 19	2.75C x 18
R65LS	1.85B x 18	2.50B x 18
R80G/S 1981	2.15B x 18	2.50B x 18
R80G/S 1982 on	1.85B x 21	2.15B x 18
R80, R80RT 1985 on	1.85B x 21	2.50B x 18
	MT H2 2.50 x 18E	MT H2 2.50 x 18E

*For frame numbers, see Section 1

Rim maximum runout:

Lateral-spoked wheels	0.2 mm (0.0079 in)
Lateral-cast wheels	0.5 mm (0.0197 in)
Radial-spoked wheels	0.5 mm (0.0197 in)
Radial-cast wheels	0.9 mm (0.0354 in)

Wheel bearings – reference number and size:

/5, /6, /7, R45, R65, R80RT 1983 – 84 – front and rear, R65LS – rear, R80G/S and R80ST – front	30203 (A) 17 mm x 40 mm x 12 mm
R65LS – front (ball journal)	6203 17 mm x 40 mm x 12 mm
R80, R80RT 1985 on – front (ball journal)	6005 25 mm x 47 mm x 12 mm
Maximum play of rear bevel drive bearings – cold – measured at rim R80G/S, R80ST	0.5 mm (0.0197 in)

Brakes

Type:

	Front	Rear
/5, R60/6	2LS drum-cable operated	SLS drum-rod operated
R45, R60/7, R65 (UK), R75/6, R75/7, R80 (UK), R80/7 1978, R80G/S, R80ST (UK), R80RT 1985 on (UK), R90/6, R100/7	Single hydraulic disc	SLS drum-rod operated
R65 (US), R65LS, R80 (US), R80/7 1979 – 80, R80RT 1983 – 84, R80RT 1985 on (US), R90S, R100S 1977 – 78, R100RS 1977, R100T, R100, R100CS	Twin hydraulic discs	SLS drum-rod operated
R100RS 1978 on, R100S 1979 – 80, R100RT	Twin hydraulic discs	Single hydraulic disc

Drum brake

Drum standard ID:

R65LS – rear	220 mm (8.6614 in)
All other models – front (where fitted) and rear	200 mm (7.8740 in)

Chapter 8 Wheels, brakes and tyres

Drum maximum ID:
    R65LS – rear .... 221.5 mm (8.7205 in)
    All other models – front (where fitted) and rear .... 201.5 mm (7.9331 in)
Drum maximum ovality .... 0.02 mm (0.0008 in)
Brake shoe friction material minimum thickness .... 1.5 mm (0.0591 in)

Disc brake

Disc diameter:
    /7 up to 1980 – front .... 264 mm (10.39 in)
    R80, R80RT 1985 on .... 285 mm (11.22 in)
    All other models – front, /7 rear .... 260 mm (10.24 in)
Disc standard thickness:
    R80, R80RT 1985 on – single disc .... 5.0 mm (0.1969 in)
    R80, R80RT 1985 on – twin disc .... 4.0 mm (0.1575 in)
    All other models .... N/Av
Disc minimum thickness:
    R80, R80RT 1985 on .... N/Av
    All other models .... 4.6 mm (0.1811 in)
Disc maximum runout:
    Lateral .... 0.2 mm (0.0079 in)
    Radial .... 0.3 mm (0.0118 in)
Brake pad friction material minimum thickness .... 1.5 mm (0.0591 in)
Front brake master cylinder piston OD:
    R45 and R65 single disc 1982 on, R80G/S 1982 on, R80ST .. 12.00 mm (0.4724 in)
    R45 and R65 single disc up to 1981, R80G/S 1981,
    (UK) R80 and R80RT 1985 on – twin disc .... 13.00 mm (0.5118 in)
    (UK) R80 and R80RT 1985 on – single disc, R80 (US) .. 14.00 mm (0.5512 in)
    R60/7, R75/6, R75/7, R80/7 1978, R90/6, R100/7 .. 14.29 mm (0.5626 in)
    R45 and R65 twin disc 1982 on, R65LS, R80RT 1983 – 84,
    (US) R80RT 1985 on, all 1000cc models 1982 on .. 15.00 mm (0.5906 in)
    R90S up to 1975, also any standard /6 with optional twin
    discs up to 1975 .... 15.86 mm (0.6244 in)
    R45 and R65 twin disc up to 1981, all 1000cc 1981 models .. 16.00 mm (0.6299 in)
    R90S 1976, also any standard /6 1976 with optional twin
    discs, R80/7 1979 – 80, all 1000cc models (except
    R100/7) up to 1980, also any standard /7 with optional
    twin discs .... 17.46 mm (0.6874 in)
Rear brake master cylinder piston OD:
    All models up to 1980 .... 15.80 mm (0.6221 in)
    All models 1981 on .... 14.29 mm (0.5626 in)
Rear brake master cylinder piston/operating lever free play ..... 1.4 – 1.5 mm (0.0551 – 0.0591 in)
Brake caliper piston OD:
    R45, R65, R65LS .... 36 mm (1.4173 in)
    R80 and R80RT 1985 on – single disc .... 48 mm (1.8898 in)
    /6 1976, /7 (front) up to 1980 .... 40 mm (1.5748 in)
    All other models – front or rear .... 38 mm (1.4961 in)

Tyres

Note: *check with BMW importer/dealer for currently approved makes and types of tyre*

Type:
    R80, R80RT 1985 on .... Tubeless
    All other models .... Tubed

Size:

	Front	Rear
R50, R60, R75, R80RT 1983 – 84	3.25S19	4.00S18
R80/7, all 900cc and 1000cc models	3.25H19	4.00H18
R45, R65 up to 1980	3.25S18	4.00S18
R65 1981 on, R65LS	3.25H18	4.00H18
R80G/S	3.00 – 21 48R	4.00 – 18 64R
R80ST	100/90H19	120/90H18 or 120/90 – 18 65H
R80, R80RT 1985 on	90/90 – 18 51H	120/90 – 18 65H

Recommended minimum tread depth – measured at centre of tread:
    Up to 80 mph (130 km/h) .... 2.0 mm (0.08 in)
    Above 80 mph (130 km/h) .... 3.0 mm (0.12 in)
Tyre maximum lateral runout – measured at sidewall .... 1.7 mm (0.0669 in)
Tyre maximum radial runout – measured at centre of tread ..... 1.5 mm (0.0591 in)

Tyre pressures – tyres cold

	Front – psi (bar)		Rear – psi (bar)	
	Solo	Pillion	Solo	Pillion
/5, /6:				
Up to 87 mph (140 km/h)	28 (1.9)	29 (2.0)	26 (1.8)	31 (2.1)
*Above 87 mph (140 km/h)	28 (1.9)	31 (2.1)	29 (2.0)	33 (2.3)
R45, R65, R65LS, R80RT 1983 – 84, /7:				
Up to 81 mph (130 km/h)	28 (1.9)	31 (2.1)	26 (1.8)	29 (2.0)
81 – 100 mph (130 – 160 km/h)	28 (1.9)	31 (2.1)	29 (2.0)	32 (2.2)
Above 100 mph (160 km/h)	31 (2.1)	31 (2.1)	32 (2.2)	33 (2.3)

	Front – psi (bar)		Rear – psi (bar)	
	Solo	Pillion	Solo	Pillion
R80ST:				
Up to 81 mph (130 km/h)	28 (1.9)	31 (2.1)	29 (2.0)	32 (2.2)
Above 81 mph (130 km/h)	31 (2.1)	31 (2.1)	32 (2.2)	35 (2.4)
R80G/S	28 (1.9)	31 (2.1)	26 (1.8)	32 (2.2)
R80, R80RT 1985 on	32 (2.2)	34 (2.4)	36 (2.5)	42 (2.9)

* Increase pressures by 3 psi (0.2 bar) if travelling at maximum speed for long periods
Note: pressures apply to original equipment tyres only – check with tyre manufacturer if non-standard tyres are fitted

Torque wrench settings

Component	Nm	lbf ft
Front wheel spindle retainer:		
R80, R80RT 1985 on – Allen screw	31 – 35	23 – 26
All other models – nut	45 – 50	33 – 37
Front wheel spindle clamp bolt:		
All models up to 1980	15 – 17	11 – 12.5
/7 1981 on, R80RT 1983 – 84	17	12.5
R45 and R65 1981 on, R65LS, R80G/S, R80ST	14 – 16	10 – 12
R80, R80RT 1985 on	13 – 17	9.5 – 12.5
Rear wheel fasteners:		
R80G/S (frame numbers 6.250.001 – 6.250.820) – 3 x 12 mm nut	100 – 110	74 – 81
R80G/S (frame number 6.250.821 on), R80ST – 3 x 12 mm nut	85	63
R80, R80RT 1985 on – 4 x 12 mm bolt	98 – 112	72 – 83
All other models – spindle nut	45 – 50	33 – 37
Rear wheel spindle clamp bolt – except Monolever models:		
All models up to 1980	14 – 18	10 – 13.5
All models 1981 on	17	12.5
Brake disc mounting nuts or bolts	22 – 24	16 – 18
Swinging caliper pivot retaining plug:		
/6	60 – 65	44 – 48
/7 up to 1980	40 – 45	29.5 – 33
Brake caliper mounting bolts:		
R80G/S, R80ST	35	26
R80, R80RT 1985 on	30 – 34	22 – 25
All other models	N/Av	N/Av
Metal brake pipe unions	8 – 11	6 – 8
Metal brake pipe/brake hose union – all models 1981 on	12 – 15	9 – 11

1 General description

The types of wheel and brake fitted to each model are given in the Specification Section of this Chapter.

Wire-spoked wheels consist of a light alloy rim joined to a full-width light alloy hub by a number of steel spokes. Note that on /5 models (frame numbers (R50/5) 2903 756, (R60/5) 2939 207, (R75/5) 2983 280, and later) the rear rim width was increased. If the rear rim of an earlier model is to be renewed at any time, it should be replaced by the wider rim to improve the machine's stability. On R80G/S and R80ST models if the rear wheel requires re-spoking or a new rim, it should be taken to a BMW dealer. The rim offset from the hub varies according to the year of production and must be checked only by an expert or there is a risk of the tyre rubbing on the frame.

Refer to Routine Maintenance for details of the regular checks required for all wheels, and for details of the cast alloy wheels fitted to various models.

The hydraulic disc brakes fall into two distinct types. /6 and /7 models up to 1980 use single-piston swinging calipers manufactured for BMW by ATE; the calipers pivot on eccentric pivots to permit accurate pad alignment and are pressurised via a master cylinder mounted on the frame top tube, under the fuel tank. A warning lamp is fitted to give notice of low fluid level, and a control cable links the handlebar lever to the master cylinder. R45 and R65 models, and all other models from 1981 on use a conventional handlebar-mounted master cylinder manufactured by Magura which pressurises one (or two) twin-piston fixed calipers made by Brembo (R45, R65 and R65LS models may also be fitted with virtually identical calipers made by ATE). Later models are fitted as standard with brake pads whose friction material is semi-metallic in composition to improve brake response in wet weather. The discs were plain on /6 models up to 1974, after which, except for R80 and R80RT 1985 on models with single discs, they were drilled to give better wet-weather braking response; these holes produce a characteristic buzzing whine when the brakes are applied.

Refer to Routine Maintenance for any information on servicing the wheels, brakes and tyres that is not included in this Chapter.

2 Front wheel: removal and refitting

All models – general

1 Place the machine on its centre stand and wedge a wooden block or similar under the sump so that the front wheel is clear of the ground. On machines fitted with twin disc brakes mark the hub as shown in the accompanying photograph so that it is refitted the original way round; this avoids having to reset the calipers (early models) and prevents premature pad wear (later models).

2 During wheel removal make a careful note of any washers and spacers fitted; these must be refitted in their original locations. Also wedge a piece of wood between the brake pads; do not apply the brake lever.

3 When the wheel has been refitted, tighten the spindle nut (or Allen screw) to its specified torque setting, then push the machine off its stand and apply the front brake (having refitted the calipers, where applicable). Pump the forks up and down several times to align the fork lower legs on the spindle, then raise the machine on to its centre stand and tighten the spindle clamps to their specified torque settings. On all models with disc brakes apply the lever repeatedly to bring the pads back into contact with the disc(s).

4 Check that the brake and front forks operate correctly, that the wheel is free to rotate easily, and that all disturbed fasteners are correctly tightened before riding the machine.

Chapter 8 Wheels, brakes and tyres 185

/5 models and R60/6

5 Unscrew the Allen screw and nut of the torque arm upper anchorage. Remove the wheel spindle nut and washer on the right-hand side.
6 Slacken the spindle clamp bolt on the left-hand fork lower leg (and the right-hand on R60/6) and withdraw the spindle using a tommy bar.
7 Pull the wheel forwards, remove the brake plate and take out the wheel completely.
8 Before refitting the spindle it should be cleaned and greased lightly. Reverse the dismantling procedure to refit the wheel. See notes above.

R80, R80RT 1985 on

9 If a twin disc system is fitted, remove either caliper. If the single disc system is fitted it is just possible to remove the wheel with the caliper in place, but work is a great deal easier if the caliper is removed. Unscrew the brake hose mounting at the fork leg and remove the two caliper mounting bolts. Withdraw the caliper.
10 Unscrew the Allen screw which secures the spindle retaining collar on the right-hand side and withdraw it with the collar. Slacken the spindle clamp bolts, insert a tommy-bar into the spindle and pull out the spindle with a twisting motion. Note the two spacers.
11 On refitting, grease the spindle to prevent corrosion and reverse the removal procedure. The wider of the two spacers fits against the hub right-hand side. Hold the spindle with the tommy-bar and tighten the Allen screw to the specified torque setting. Refit the caliper, if removed, and tighten its mounting bolts securely. See notes above for remainder of refitting procedure.

All other models

12 On models from 1981 on (or any R45 or R65) with a twin-disc system, remove one of the calipers. Unscrew the brake hose mounting at the fork leg and remove the two caliper mounting bolts. Withdraw the caliper.
13 Remove the wheel spindle nut and washer on the left-hand side.
14 Slacken the wheel spindle clamp screw on both fork lower legs and withdraw the spindle, using a tommy bar. Note the spacer(s) (where fitted).
15 On refitting, grease the spindle to prevent corrosion and reverse the removal procedure. Do not forget to refit the spacer(s) in their previously-noted positions. Tighten the spindle nut (do not omit the washer) to the specified torque setting. Refit the caliper (where removed) and tighten its mounting bolts securely. See general notes.

2.1 Mark front hubs of twin-disc models as shown before removal to ensure correct refitting

2.5 Drum brake models – release brake torque arm at its upper mounting

2.8a Wheel spindle should be cleaned and greased on reassembly

2.8b Do not tighten spindle clamp bolts until fork legs are correctly aligned

2.9a If brake caliper is to be removed ...

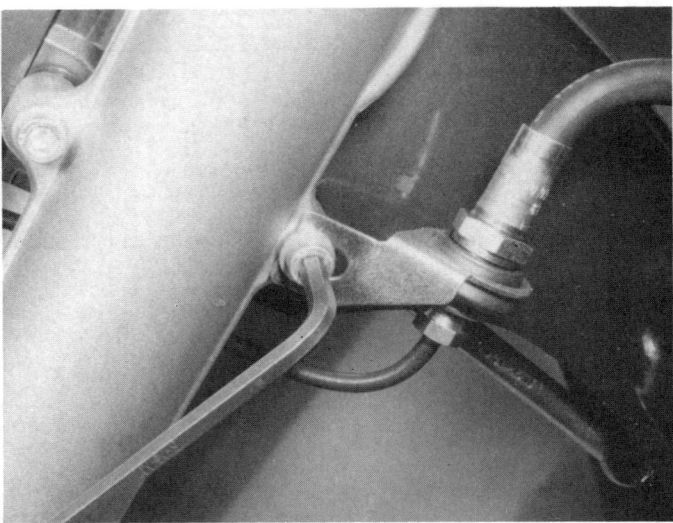

2.9b ... slacken (or remove) hose mounting to prevent damage to hose

2.10 Spindle retaining collar is secured by an Allen screw – R80, R80RT 1985 on

2.11a Note wider spacer on hub right-hand side ...

2.11b ... while narrower spacer is on hub left-hand side

2.13 Wheel spindle nut is on left-hand side on all other models – do not omit washer

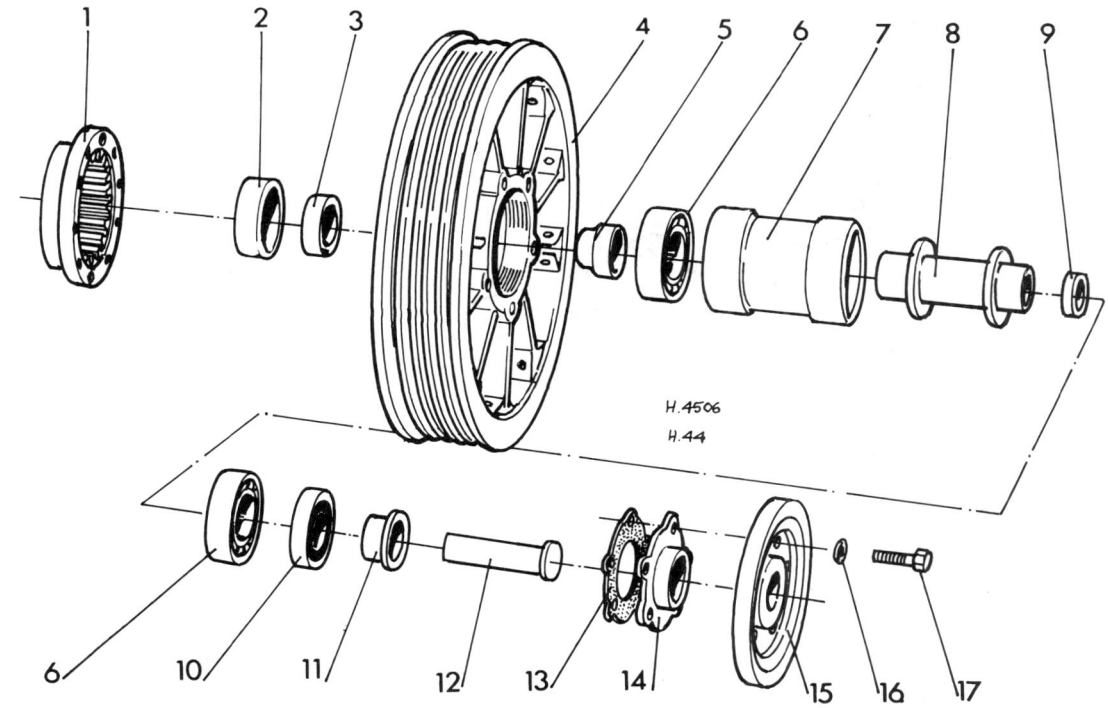

Fig. 8.1 Drum brake wheel hub – up to 1974

1 Rear drive coupling (rear wheel only)
2 Felt seal housing
3 Seal
4 Hub
5 Thrust sleeve
6 Tapered roller bearing
7 Outer spacer sleeve
8 Inner spacer sleeve
9 Adjuster sleeve
10 Seal
11 Thrust sleeve
12 Reducing sleeve, front wheel
13 Gasket
14 Bearing cap
15 Wheel disc – /5 only
16 Lock washer
17 Bolt

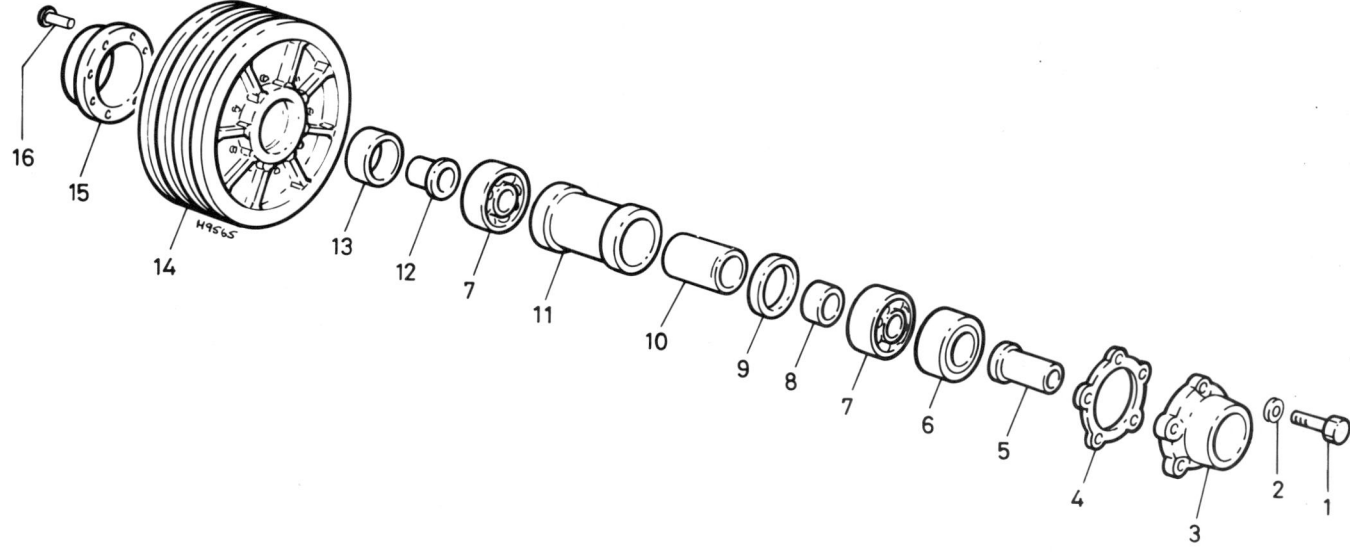

Fig. 8.2 Drum brake wheel hub – 1975 on

1 Bolt
2 Washer
3 Cap
4 Gasket
5 Thrust sleeve
6 Oil seal
7 Tapered roller bearing
8 Adjuster sleeve
9 Seal
10 Inner spacer sleeve
11 Outer spacer sleeve
12 Thrust sleeve
13 Seal
14 Hub
15 Rear drive coupling – rear wheel only
16 Rivet

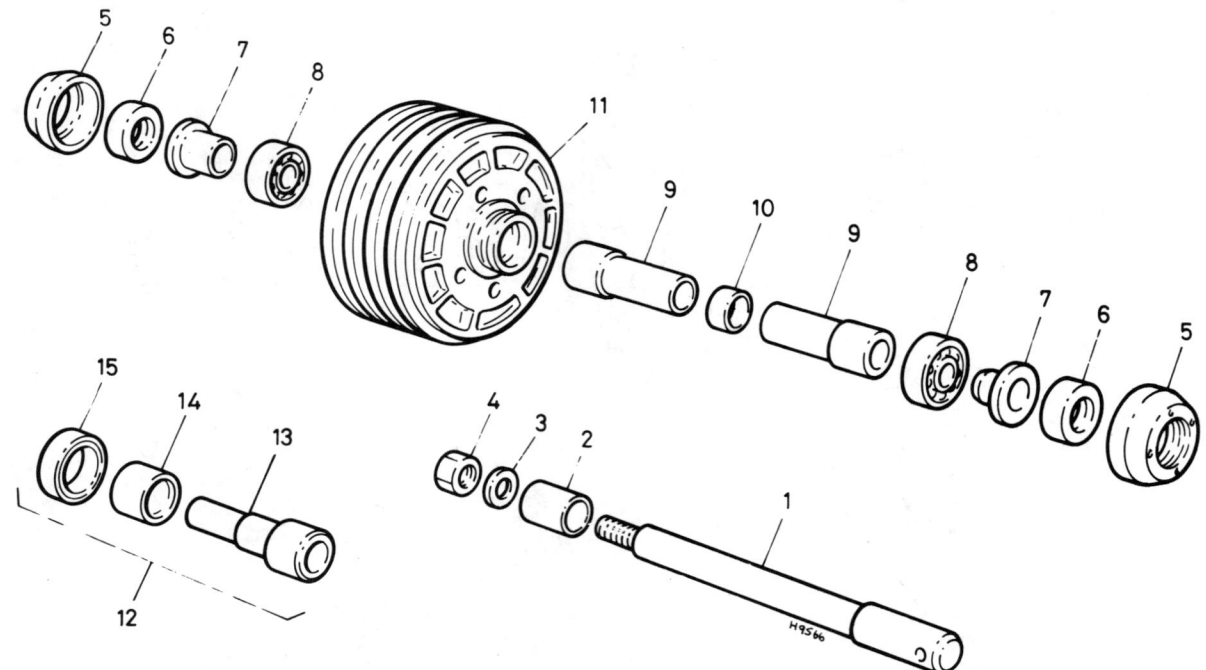

Fig. 8.3 Front spoked wheel hub – up to 1974

1 Wheel spindle	5 Cap	9 Reducing sleeves – where fitted	12 Reducing sleeve assembly – where fitted
2 Spacer	6 Seal	10 Adjuster sleeve	13 Reducing sleeve
3 Washer	7 Thrust sleeve	11 Hub	14 Thrust sleeve
4 Nut	8 Tapered roller bearing		15 Oil seal

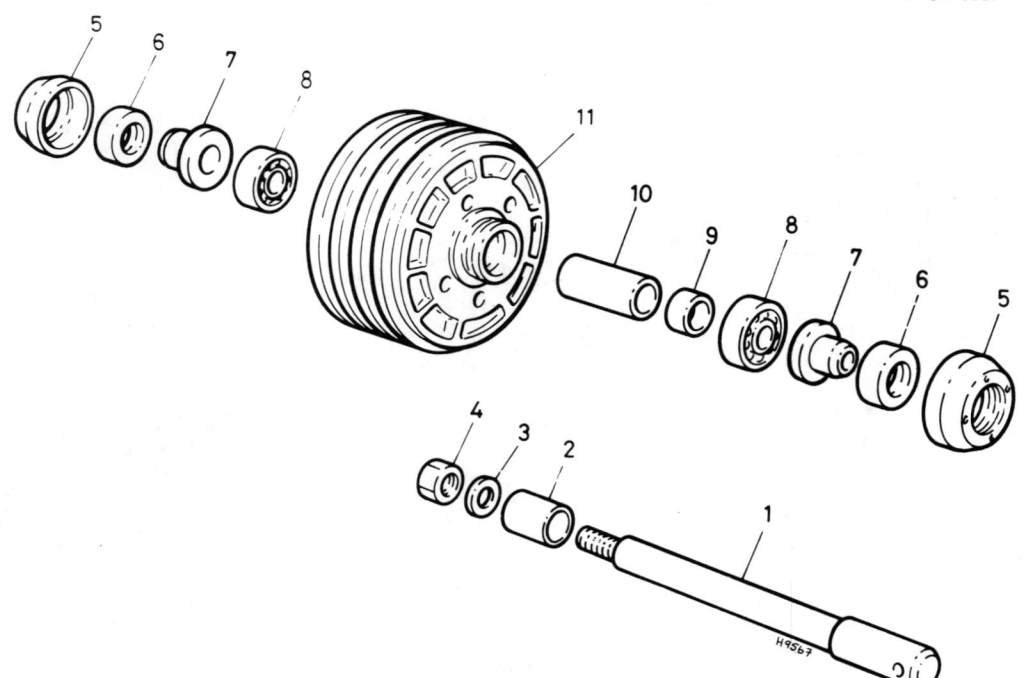

Fig. 8.4 Front spoked wheel hub – 1975 on

1 Spindle	4 Nut	7 Thrust sleeve	10 Spacer
2 Spacer	5 Cap	8 Tapered roller bearing	11 Hub
3 Washer	6 Seal	9 Adjuster sleeve	

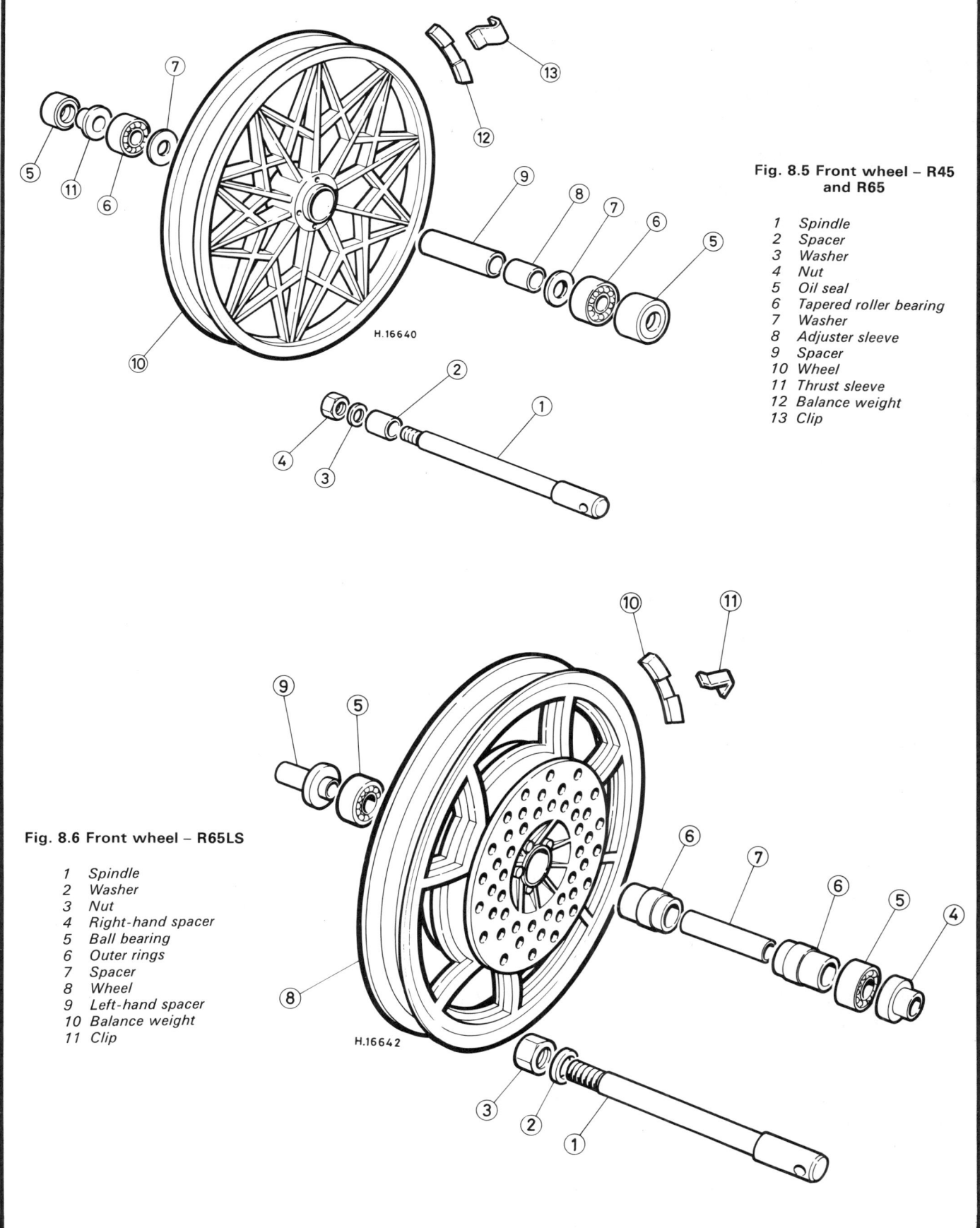

Fig. 8.5 Front wheel – R45 and R65

1 Spindle
2 Spacer
3 Washer
4 Nut
5 Oil seal
6 Tapered roller bearing
7 Washer
8 Adjuster sleeve
9 Spacer
10 Wheel
11 Thrust sleeve
12 Balance weight
13 Clip

Fig. 8.6 Front wheel – R65LS

1 Spindle
2 Washer
3 Nut
4 Right-hand spacer
5 Ball bearing
6 Outer rings
7 Spacer
8 Wheel
9 Left-hand spacer
10 Balance weight
11 Clip

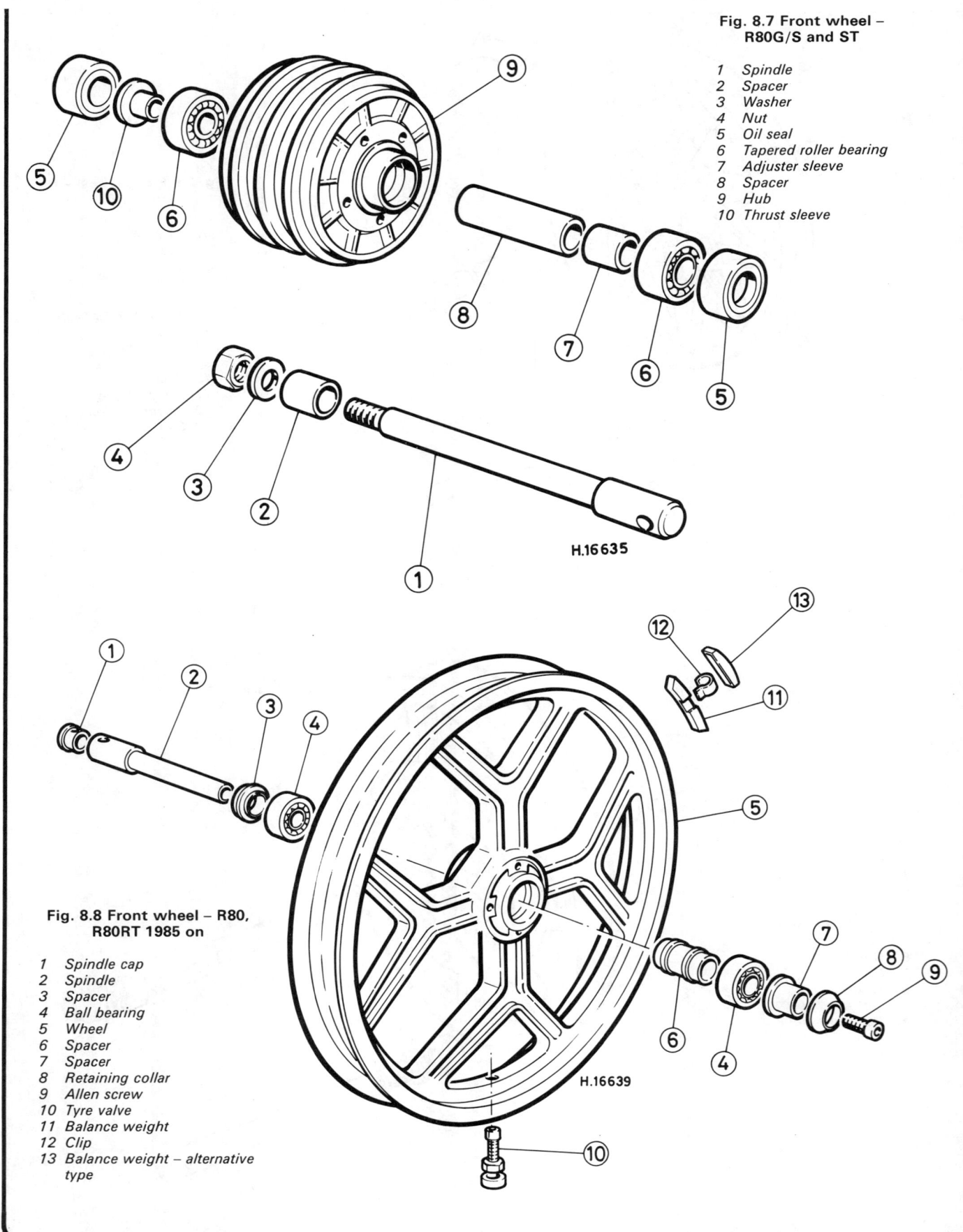

Chapter 8 Wheels, brakes and tyres

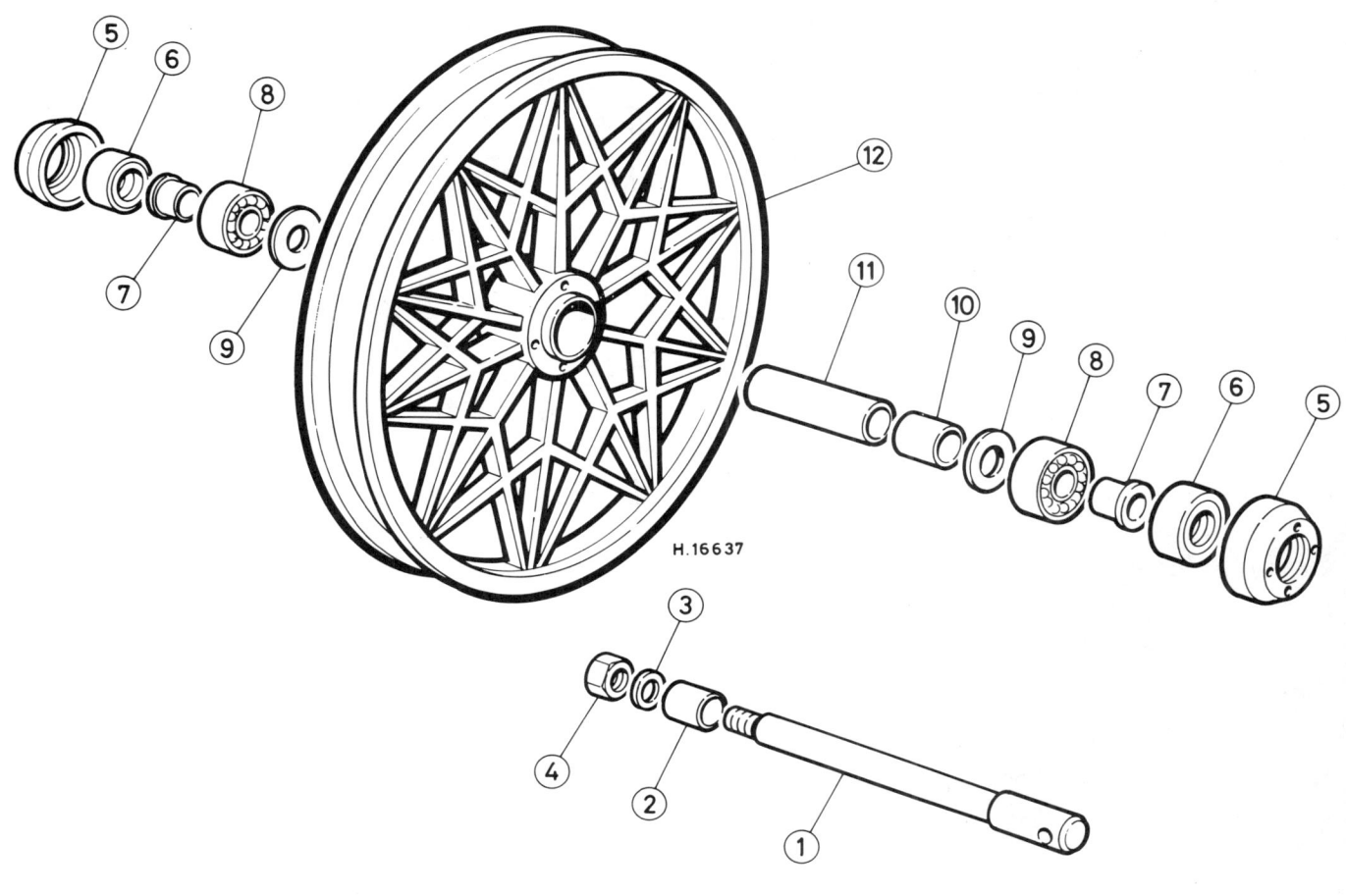

Fig. 8.9 Front cast wheel – all other models

1 Spindle
2 Spacer
3 Washer
4 Nut
5 Cap – all models up to 1978
6 Oil seal
7 Thrust sleeve
8 Tapered roller bearing
9 Metal washer
10 Adjuster sleeve
11 Spacer
12 Wheel

3 Rear wheel: removal and refitting

Monolever models
1 Place the machine on its centre stand and support it with a block of wood under a convenient point so that the rear wheel is clear of the ground.
2 R80ST – rotate the wheel until only one of the mounting nuts is at the top; working space is minimal and it may also be necessary to remove the brake adjusting nut.
3 Applying the rear brake to prevent rotation, unscrew the mounting nuts or bolts. Withdraw the wheel, rocking it lightly to release it.
4 On refitting, check that the mating surfaces of the wheel and bevel drive mounting flange are completely clean and free from grease.
5 Fit the rear wheel and mounting nuts or bolts. Ensure that the conical spacers under the nut or bolt heads engage correctly with the wheel tapered surfaces. Tighten the mountings securely using a torque wrench or the machine's own tools. With its own tubular extension the wheel nut spanner provided will need only normal hand pressure to tighten the mounting to approximately the correct torque setting. Check the tightness of the mountings with a torque wrench as soon as possible.

Models with disc rear brakes
6 Place the machine on its centre stand and rotate the rear suspension unit spring preload adjusters (where applicable) to the hardest position. Unscrew the retaining nut on the spindle right-hand end, then remove the nut and its washer and slacken the spindle clamp bolt in the swinging-arm left-hand fork end. Slacken and remove the single bolt which secures the caliper mounting bracket to the rear brake torque arm, then pull the spindle out to the left using a tommy bar in the hole provided in the spindle left-hand end. Free the brake pipe from the swinging-arm clamp and lift the caliper mounting bracket upwards off the brake disc. Hang the caliper assembly over the left-hand silencer, using a piece of cloth to prevent scratching or damage to the finish of the silencer or swinging-arm. Wedge a piece of wood between the pads to prevent fluid leakage and caliper damage should the rear brake pedal inadvertently be applied while the wheel is removed. The wheel itself is removed by pulling to the left and out to the left rear of the machine.
7 Refitting is a straightforward reversal of the removal sequence, but remember that the wheel spindle must be greased lightly to prevent the onset of corrosion and that the rear brake pedal must be applied

192 Chapter 8 Wheels, brakes and tyres

repeatedly to bring the brake pads back into firm contact with the disc and to restore full braking pressure before the machine is used on the road.

All other models
8 Put the motorcycle on the centre stand. Turn the suspension unit adjusting levers to the hardest spring setting.
9 Unscrew the spindle nut on the right-hand side, and remove the nut and washer.
10 Slacken the spindle clamp bolt on the left-hand swinging-arm and withdraw the spindle using a tommy bar.
11 Pull the wheel to the left to disengage the splines and remove. It may prove necessary to tilt the machine to the right to withdraw the wheel.
12 Before replacing the spindle, it should be greased lightly; apply a smear of Molykote BR2 or Liquid Moly LM47L to the drive flange splines. Rotate the spindle when inserting. Tighten the spindle clamp bolt last. The tommy bar hole in the spindle should be horizontal.
13 Reset the suspension units.

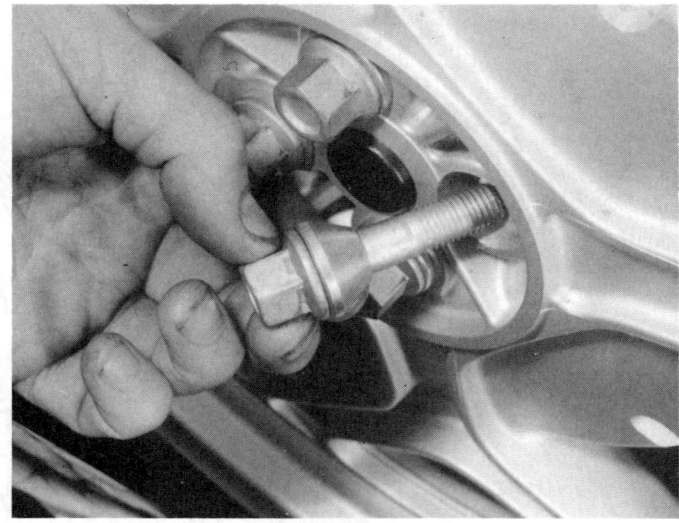

3.5a Rear wheel refitting, Monolever models – ensure conical spacers are refitted as shown

3.5b Mounting nuts or bolts should be tightened to specified torque settings

3.9 Remove rear wheel spindle nut ...

3.10 ... and slacken spindle clamp bolt to release spindle

3.11 Pull wheel off driving splines and remove from machine

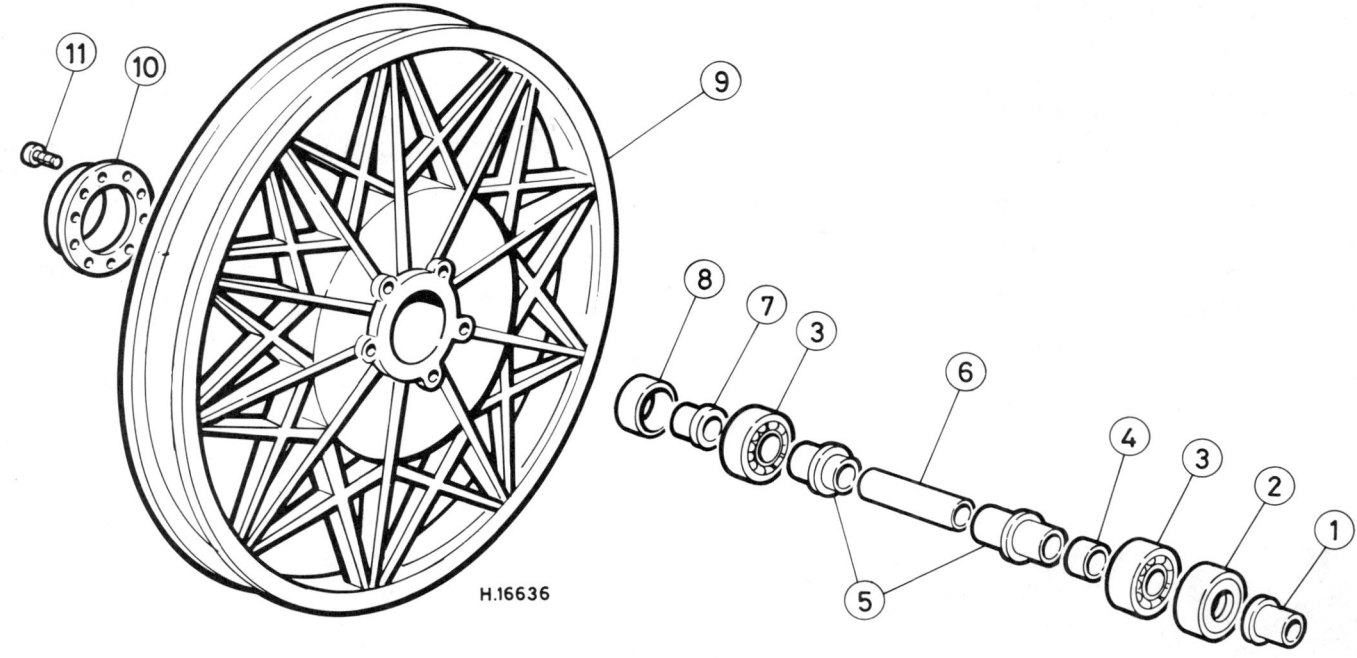

Fig. 8.10 Rear cast wheel – typical

1 Thrust sleeve
2 Oil seal
3 Tapered roller bearing
4 Adjuster sleeve
5 Outer rings
6 Spacer
7 Thrust sleeve
8 Seal
9 Wheel
10 Drive coupling
11 Rivet

4 Wheel bearings: removal, examination and refitting

1 Check the wheel bearings as described in Routine Maintenance. Except for the two cases outlined below, bearings are of the taper-roller type which are adjusted by fitting sleeves of different thicknesses. Since special equipment is required to measure the amount of bearing friction at a given preload and since it is necessary to have a range of sleeves available for fitting, it is recommended that the wheels are taken to a competent BMW dealer for reconditioning whenever bearing play is discovered.
2 Note that on Monolever models the rear wheel bearings are part of the rear bevel drive housing, the dismantling of which is beyond the scope of this Manual.
3 On R65LS, R80 and R80RT 1985 on models the front wheel bearings are of the ball journal type and are sealed for life. If play is discovered, the bearings must be renewed. Remove the brake discs (R65LS). Remove the tyre (and inner tube R65LS). Being very careful to avoid the risk of personal injury or of distorting the wheel, heat the wheel (BMW recommend the use of a hot plate) to approximately 80°C (176°F) and use an internally-expanding bearing puller to extract the bearings. While the hub is still warm tap in the new bearings, until they are flush with the hub, using as a drift a socket spanner which bears only on the bearing outer race. Do not omit the central spacer (and support rings, R65LS) if removed. When the hub has cooled, refit the brake discs, tyre and inner tube (as applicable).
4 On all other models, if the bearings are to be dismantled for cleaning and greasing, proceed as follows referring to the accompanying illustrations. Remove the wheel from the machine as described in Section 2 or 3.

Drum front wheels and wire-spoked drum rear wheels
5 Withdraw the reducing sleeve from the front wheel hub.
6 On /5 models, unscrew the five Allen screws and remove with spring washers. Remove the chrome cover and the bearing cap with oil seal and thrust sleeve. Note the gasket.
7 R60/6 front wheels and /6 and later rear wheels, have no cover. Unscrew the five Allen screws and remove with spring washers. Remove the bearing cap as above.
8 Heat the wheel hub to 80° – 100°C (176° – 212°F). The complete bearing assembly may be driven out of the hub from the brake drum side, using the wheel spindle as a drift. Use a soft hammer to avoid damaging the spindle.
9 Clean the bearings in high flash-point solvent; do not interchange races. Examine the raceways and rollers for chipping or damage. If any bearing damage or wear is found, the bearings must be renewed and the adjustment checked; this is a task for a BMW dealer. Renew the oil seals if damaged or worn.
10 Grease the bearings before reassembly. Heat the wheel hub to 80° – 100°C (176° – 212°F). Assemble from the left-hand side as a complete assembly built on the spindle or individually. Remove the spindle and left-hand thrust sleeve, if fitted as a complete assembly. Fit the bearing cap and gasket centring the lip seal on the wheel spindle before tightening the screws. Replace the thrust sleeve and the reducing sleeve on the front wheel.

Wire-spoked disc front wheels and all cast wheels
11 Unscrew the bearing cap on each side with a peg spanner (front wheels up to 1978) and remove the inner sleeve. On front wheels from 1979 on, lever out the seals from each side after pulling out the inner sleeves. On early models the bearing will come out with the inner sleeve, while on later models it can be pulled out. On early model cast rear wheels the pressure sleeve must be removed and the seal extracted with an internally-expanding bearing puller; on later models remove as described for front wheels.
12 To remove the bearing outer races, heat the hub to 80°C (176°F) and tap them out (wire-spoked wheels) or draw them out with an internally-expanding bearing puller (cast wheels).
13 Wash all components in a suitable solvent and check for signs of wear or damage. If bearing wear is found, take the wheel to a BMW dealer for new bearings to be fitted and adjusted.
14 Grease all components thoroughly on refitting. The hub must be heated so that the bearing outer races can be tapped in with a suitable drift and the seals (later models) must be driven home until they are flush with their housings. Tighten the bearing caps securely (early models).

4.5 Where fitted, withdraw reducing sleeve from front hub

4.6 /5 models only – unscrew five retaining screws to release cover plate

4.8 Complete bearing assembly can be drifted out after hub has been heated

4.10a On reassembly, insert right-hand bearing first ...

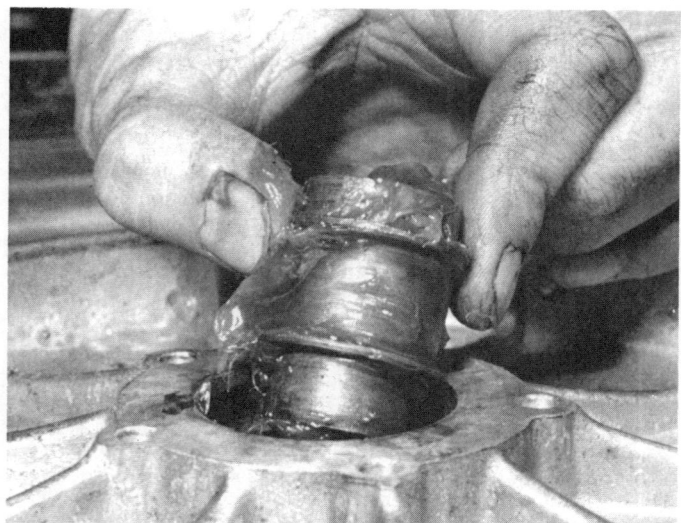

4.10b ... followed by the inner spacer ...

4.10c ... the outer spacer ...

Chapter 8 Wheels, brakes and tyres

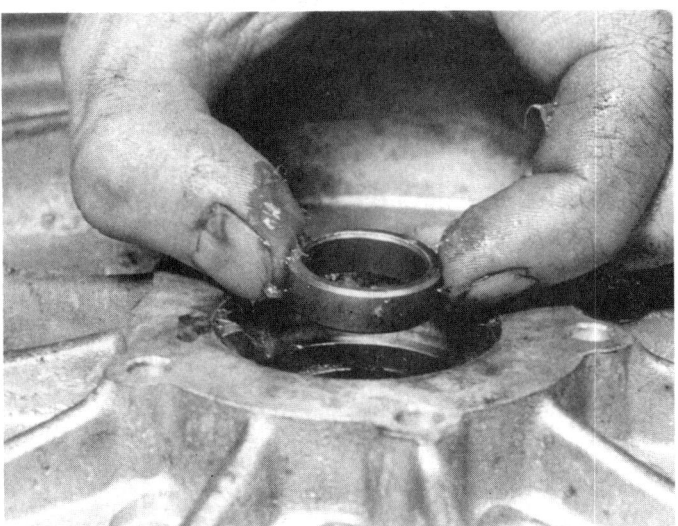

4.10d ... the adjuster sleeve ...

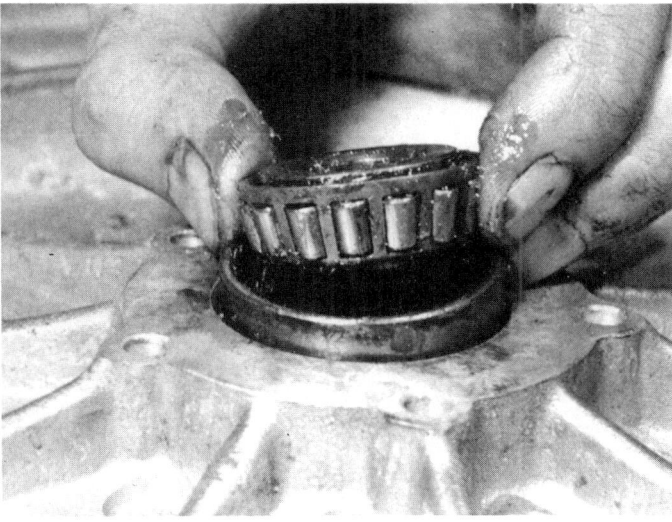

4.10e ... and the left-hand bearing

4.10f Rear wheels – fit the bearing cap and left-hand thrust sleeve

5 Drum front brake: examination and renovation

1 It is convenient to withdraw the brake plate in unit with the front wheel. This requires the front brake cable to be disconnected.
2 Slacken the adjuster at the brake end of the control cable to allow both brake cam levers to be compressed sufficiently to withdraw the slotted trunnions.
3 Remove the front wheel as described in Section 2 of this Chapter, but including the brake plate assembly.
4 Take off the brake plate, use a rag soaked in solvent to wipe the dust from the brake drum and inspect the braking surface for scoring.
5 If the linings are damaged, worn to less than the minimum thickness at any point or fouled with grease, they must be renewed. Do not chamfer the ends of the linings.
6 To remove the brake shoes, remove the external circlips from the pivots. Pull both shoes from the backplate complete with springs. The springs are of different strengths. The stronger springs go at the front of the brake plate. Refit the shoes in the same position, if they are not being renewed. Clean and grease the pivots and brake cams lightly.

5.2 Slacken brake cable adjuster and withdraw slotted trunnions

5.4 Remove wheel from machine and withdraw brake backplate

5.6a Remove retaining circlips ...

5.6b ... and note positions of shoes and return springs before removal

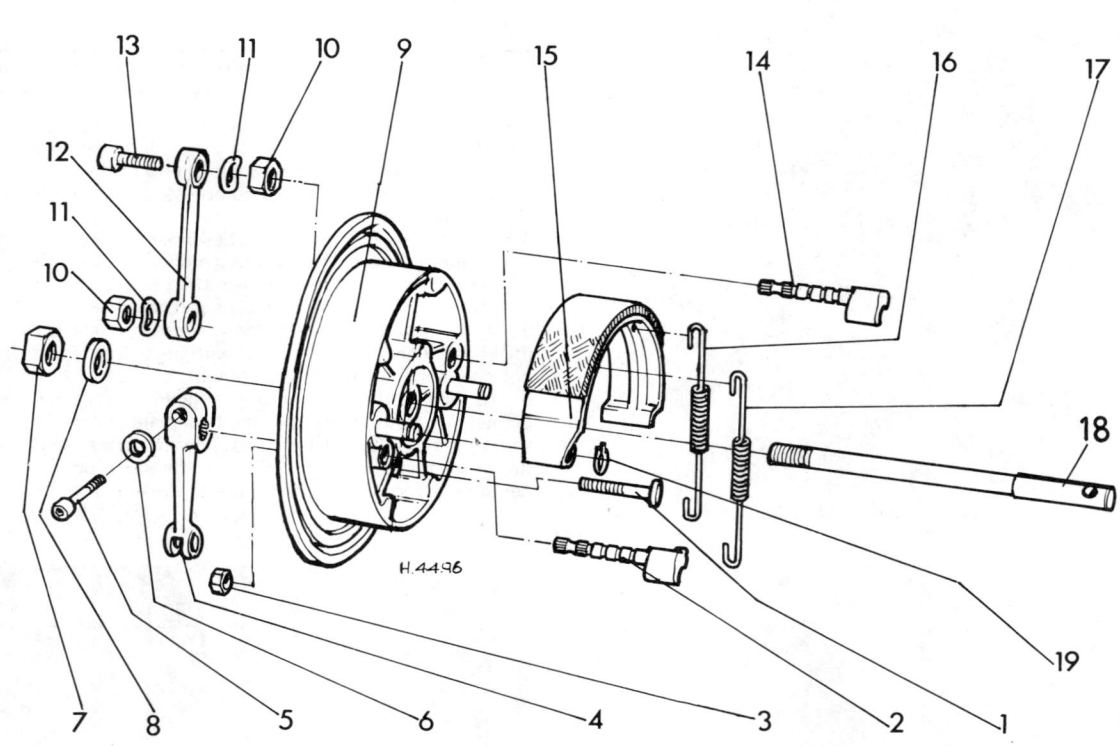

Fig. 8.11 Front drum brake – /5, R60/6

1 Eccentric adjuster
2 Lower brake cam
3 Adjuster locknut
4 Brake cam lever – 2 off
5 Lever pinch bolt – 2 off
6 Lock washer
7 Nut
8 Washer
9 Brake backplate
10 Nut
11 Lock washer
12 Brake torque arm
13 Allen screw
14 Upper brake cam
15 Brake shoe – 2 off
16 Lower return spring
17 Upper return spring
18 Front wheel spindle
19 Circlip – 2 off

Chapter 8 Wheels, brakes and tyres

6 Drum rear brake: examination and renovation

1 Remove the rear wheel. See Section 3.
2 If the brake shoe friction material is damaged, fouled with grease or oil, or worn at any point to a thickness of 1.5 mm (0.06 in) or less, the shoes must be renewed. This can be done without removing the bevel drive.
3 Disconnect the rear brake rod. On all Monolever models, use a screwdriver to displace the circlip from the shoe pivot. Note the flat on the brake cam end washer. The brake shoe adjacent to this flat should be levered away from the bevel housing with a screwdriver. Unhook the shoe return springs, and remove both shoes. Mark the shoes to replace in the same position. Linings are bonded to the shoes which must be exchanged. Do not chamfer the ends of the linings.
4 Use a rag soaked in solvent to remove all dust from the brake drum and inspect for scoring. Scored drums have to be skimmed in a lathe, which entails turning the linings also to the new diameter.
5 Clean and lightly grease the brake cam and pivot. Renew the O-rings or seals set on the camshaft, if worn.
6 If there is excessive oil on the brake linings, the bevel drive output shaft seal may be faulty and should be checked immediately, or the oil may be leaking through a faulty seal on the brake camshaft. Check the seals very carefully if this is found. On 1981 and later models a later type of camshaft has four O-ring grooves; check that these are of the correct depth and that the O-rings are correctly seated.

6.3a Note flat on brake cam end washer (arrowed)

6.3b Carefully lever shoes off and unhook return springs

6.5 Where fitted, wear indicator pointer must be correctly aligned on reassembly (if disturbed)

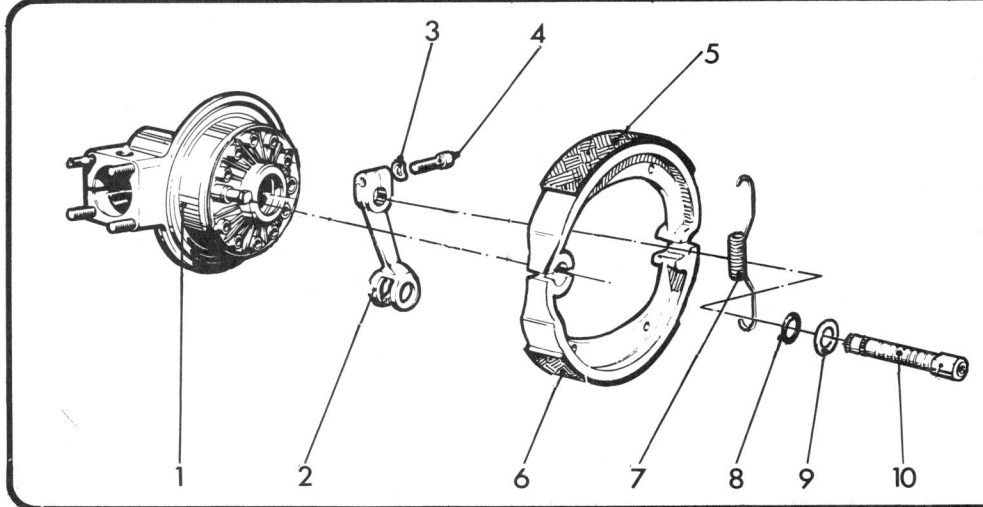

Fig. 8.12 Rear drum brake – typical

1 Rear bevel drive
2 Brake cam lever
3 Lock washer
4 Pinch bolt
5 Upper brake shoe
6 Lower brake shoe
7 Return spring – 2 off
8 Felt seal – O-ring on later models
9 Washer
10 Brake cam

7 Hydraulic brake overhaul: general

1 Before starting work on any component of a hydraulic brake system, note the following:
2 Caliper overhaul should be preceded by removing the pads, as described in Routine Maintenance.
3 Check carefully with a BMW dealer exactly what replacement parts are available to recondition the components; there is no point in attempting to dismantle an assembly if lack of pistons and seals means that it cannot be repaired.
4 Remember that brake fluid is an excellent paint stripper and will also attack plastic components. If any is spilt, wash it off as soon as possible with fresh water. Use only new fluid from a freshly-opened sealed container as it is hygroscopic, which means that it absorbs water from the air. This eventually lowers the fluid's boiling point to an unsafe degree; fluid should never be re-used.
5 The brake discs can be checked for warpage by clamping a dial gauge to the fork leg; if runout exceeds the maximum limit specified, the disc(s) should be renewed. If they are worn at any point to less than the minimum specified thickness, or if they become scored for any reason, braking efficiency will be impaired. The discs should then be renewed; they are held on by bolts with a shim between the disc and the bolts or nuts on some models. Renew the tab washers and bend up their locking tabs on refitting.
6 Examine the flexible hoses for cracks or scuffing. At the first sign of damage, they must be renewed. First drain the system. Unscrew the unions at each end of the hose and remove the hose. The grommet which holds the hose in the brake on the frame may be slipped out of the bracket.
7 Check all unions for tightness. Rigid and flexible tubes must not rub on an adjacent part.
8 If fluid leaks around the brake pads, the caliper seals are faulty. The handlebar lever will feel 'spongy'. Complete failure of the brakes, although there is pressure at the handlebar lever, may indicate a seized piston. In either case, the unit must be removed for servicing.

8 Caliper: removal, examination and refitting

Single piston swinging caliper

1 Remove the dust cap(s) from the bleed nipple(s), attach a length of tubing to each (where fitted) from a suitable container and open the bleed nipples one full turn. Apply the brake lever repeatedly until all the fluid has drained. Disconnect the metal brake pipe at the caliper gland nut and place a plastic bag over the end of each pipe to prevent any fluid dripping out.

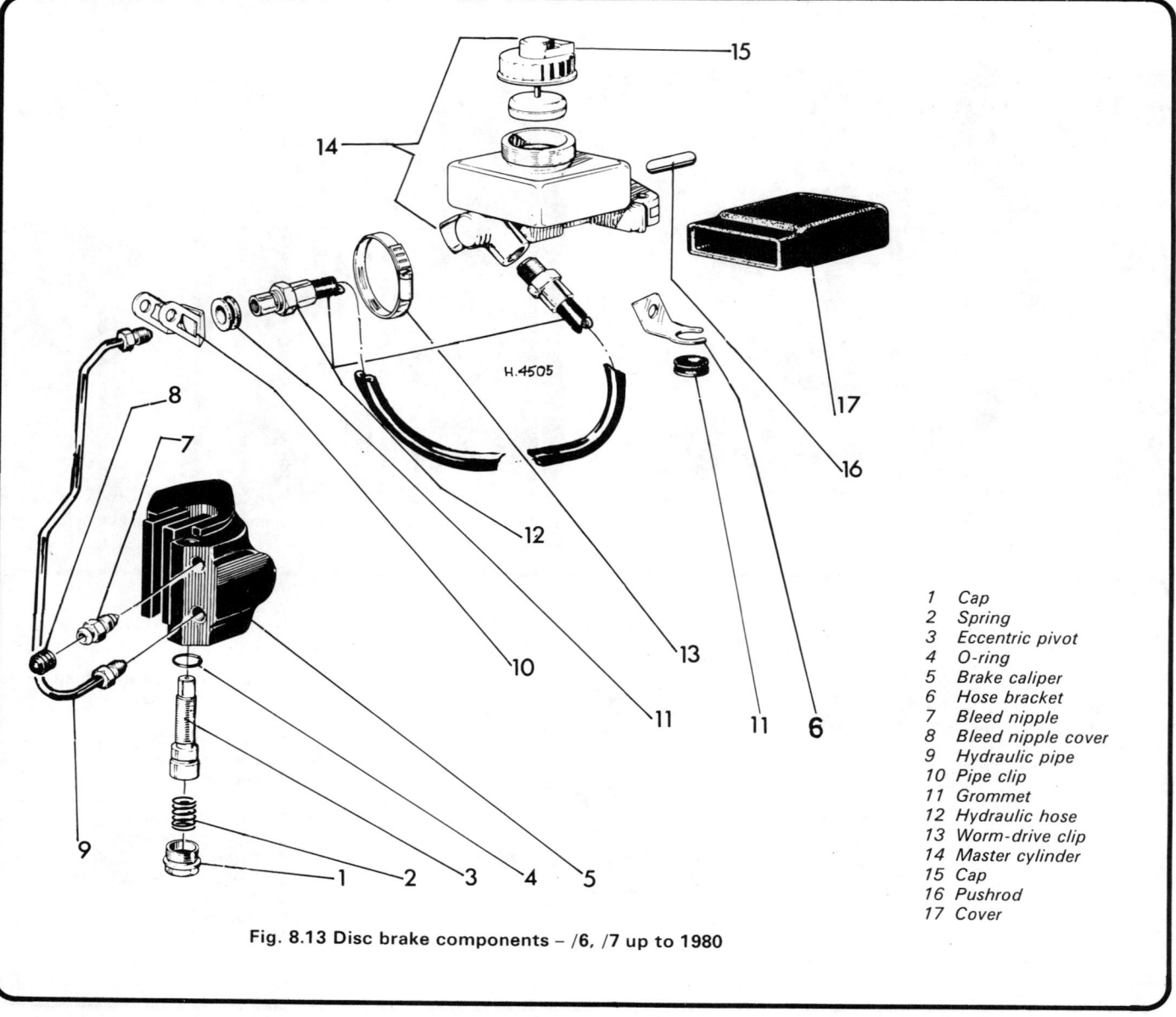

1 Cap
2 Spring
3 Eccentric pivot
4 O-ring
5 Brake caliper
6 Hose bracket
7 Bleed nipple
8 Bleed nipple cover
9 Hydraulic pipe
10 Pipe clip
11 Grommet
12 Hydraulic hose
13 Worm-drive clip
14 Master cylinder
15 Cap
16 Pushrod
17 Cover

Fig. 8.13 Disc brake components – /6, /7 up to 1980

Chapter 8 Wheels, brakes and tyres

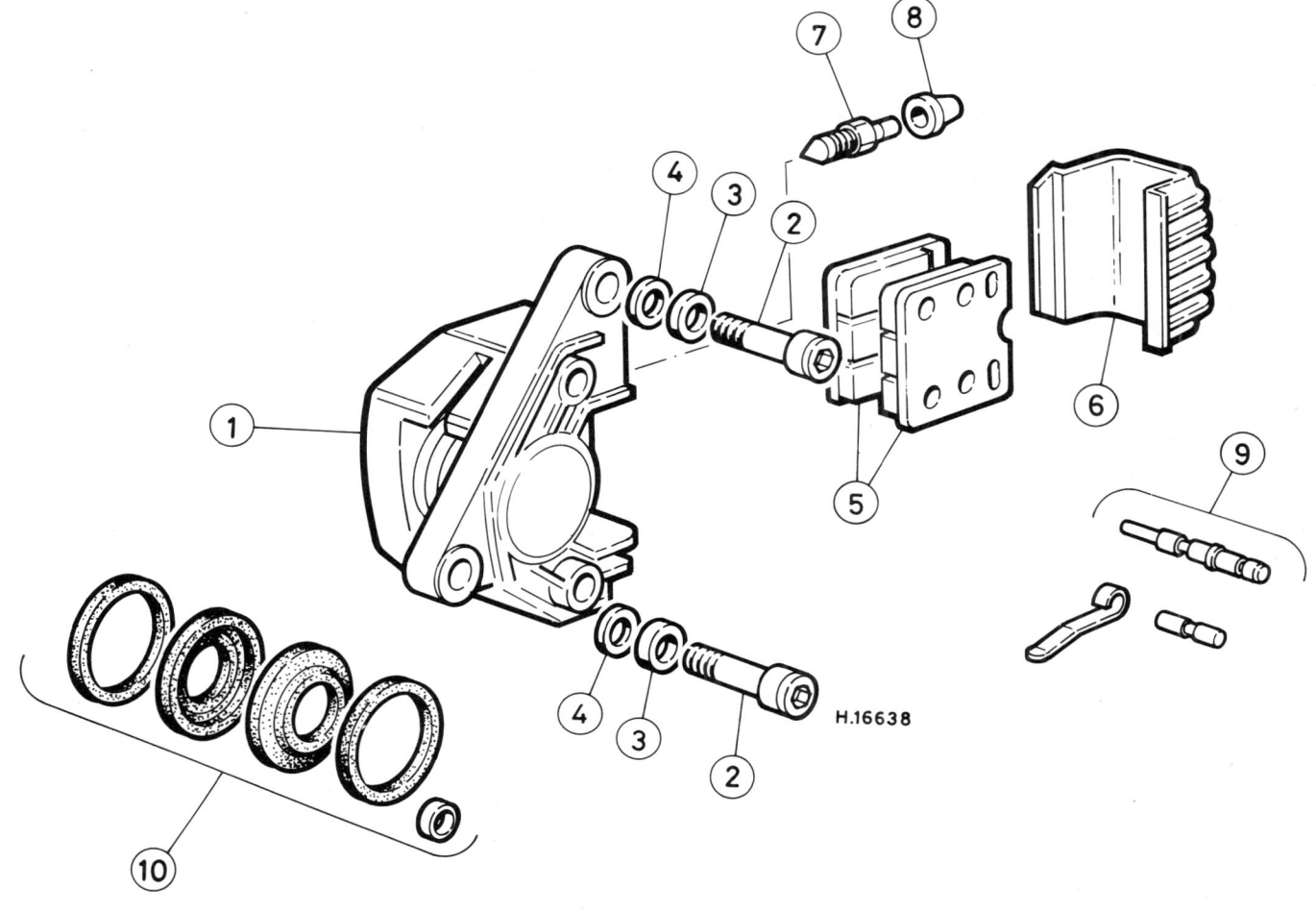

Fig. 8.14 Front brake caliper – all other models (typical)

1 Caliper assembly
2 Bolt
3 Spacer
4 Washer
5 Brake pads
6 Cover
7 Bleed nipple
8 Dust cap
9 Pad retaining pins and spring
10 Seal kit

2 Remove the caliper(s) from the forks as described in Routine Maintenance.
3 Wrap the caliper in thick rag and apply a jet of compressed air to the brake pipe orifice to eject the piston. Remove the seals, noting carefully how each is fitted.
4 Examine the caliper components. If the piston or the caliper bore is scratched, scored or corroded they must be renewed.
5 Clean all components thoroughly with new brake fluid prior to reassembly. Clean the caliper pivot components as described in Routine Maintenance and check for wear by reassembling them and feeling for free play. If any is felt, the worn components must be renewed. Soak the new seals in clean hydraulic fluid before refitting them to the caliper.
6 Smear the piston and caliper bore with clean brake fluid and refit the piston, taking care not to dislodge the seals. Press the piston fully into the caliper bore, refit the caliper to the machine and connect the brake pipe again tightening securely the union nut.
7 Refit the pads and adjust the caliper (see Routine Maintenance). Repeat the operation on the other caliper (twin-disc systems only). Fill the system with clean fluid and bleed it to remove all trapped air. See Section 11.

Twin piston fixed caliper
8 The caliper assemblies fitted to all other models are identical in design and construction whether fitted to the front or to the rear brake. In both cases, it will be necessary to remove the caliper from the machine before dismantling work can be undertaken. Before this is done, however, it should be noted that few components appear to be available to recondition the caliper assembly, and the advice of a local BMW dealer should be sought to clarify this point before work is started. In some cases it would appear that the only solution to a caliper fault is the renewal of the complete assembly.
9 The caliper units should be removed for overhaul if there has been any evidence of weeping from the seals. Note that seals can sometimes leak enough to admit air to the system without allowing the fluid to leak out. Whatever the case, immediate investigation is warranted. Start by disconnecting the brake pipe(s) at the caliper gland nut and block the open pipe end with a suitable wooden or rubber plug. This will prevent the ingress of contaminants and the loss of hydraulic fluid.
10 Take great care during the dismantling and reassembly sequences, that no hydraulic fluid is allowed to come into contact with any painted or plastic parts. It will quickly destroy both of these surfaces, and if accidentally splashed, should be washed off immediately. Remove the plastic caliper cover and the pads as described in Routine Maintenance. Remove the caliper unit(s) from the fork leg by slackening and removing the two mounting bolts or as described in Routine Maintenance for rear brakes.
11 Remove the two socket screws which retain the caliper halves, to give access to each piston assembly. Remove the dust seal and withdraw the piston and seals from each side. Examine all the components carefully. The seals should be renewed as a matter of course. The working surface of the piston should be highly polished

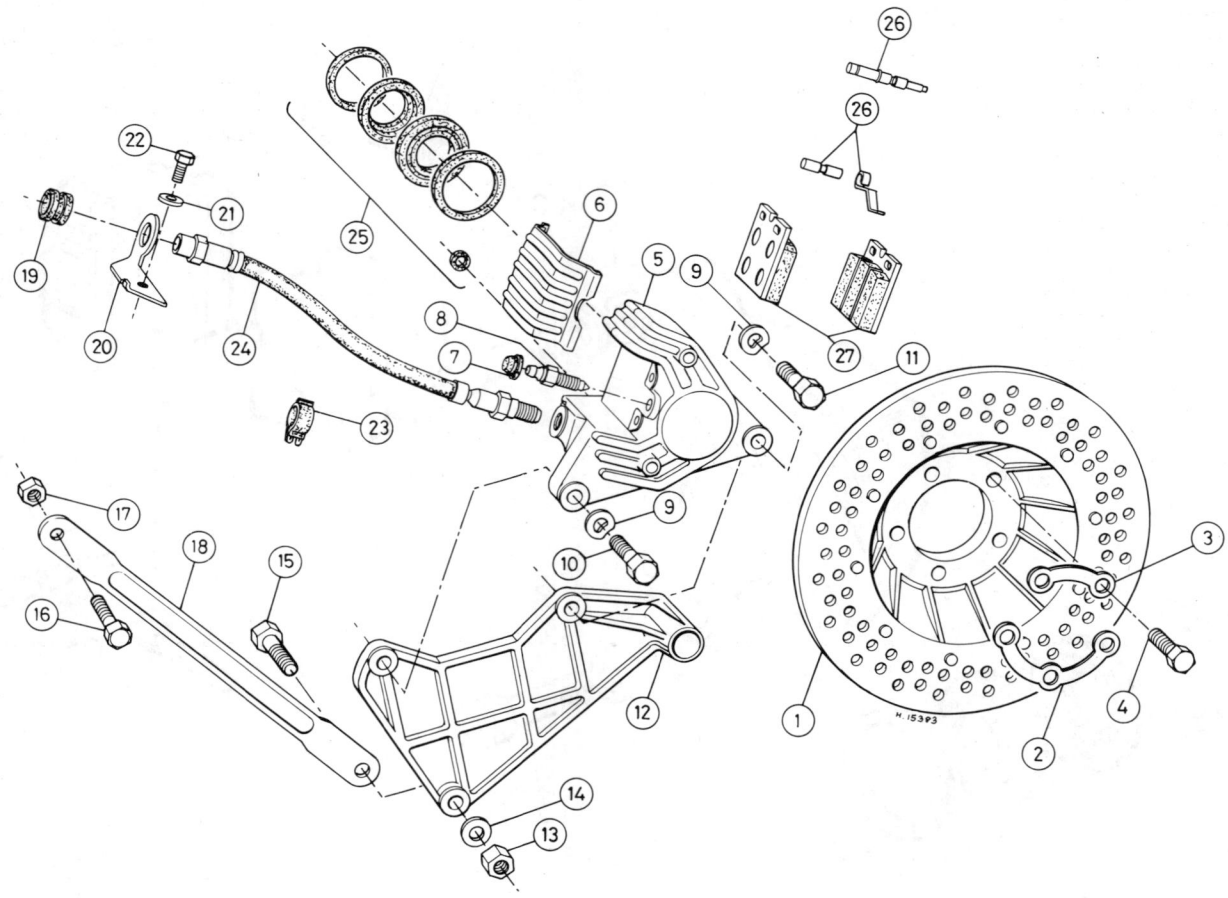

Fig. 8.15 Rear brake caliper and disc

1 Brake disc	8 Bleed nipple	15 Bolt	22 Bolt
2 Tab washer	9 Wave washer	16 Bolt	23 Hose clamp
3 Tab washer	10 Bolt	17 Nut	24 Hydraulic hose
4 Bolt – 5 off	11 Bolt	18 Torque arm	25 Hydraulic seals
5 Caliper	12 Caliper mounting bracket	19 Grommet	26 Pad retaining pins and spring
6 Caliper cover	13 Nut	20 Bracket	
7 Bleed nipple cap	14 Washer	21 Washer	27 Brake pads

with no scores or corroded areas. If these are evident, the piston must be renewed or it will rapidly destroy the new seals. The caliper bores are least likely to exhibit signs of wear or corrosion damage but if such evidence is present, it will necessitate renewal of the caliper body as a unit.

12 The component parts should be cleaned thoroughly with new brake fluid prior to reassembly. On no account use petrol (gasoline) or paraffin (kerosene) as these will ruin the seals. Reassemble, by reversing the dismantling sequence, ensuring that all parts are kept clinically clean. Lubricate the seal and piston with hydraulic fluid prior to fitting them to the caliper. Make sure that the brake pipe is fitted correctly. Before using the machine, bleed the brake system. See Section 11.

9 Front brake master cylinder: removal, examination and refitting

/6, /7 up to 1980 – cable-operated cylinder
1 Remove the fuel tank. See Chapter 4.
2 Drain the hydraulic fluid. See Section 8.
3 Remove the rubber cap over the operating lever. Disconnect the front brake inner cable from the cylinder lever and unscrew the adjuster completely. Unscrew the brake hose union or unions, and pull off the wires to the fluid level warning and stop lamp switches. Unscrew the worm drive clip which clamps the cylinder to the top frame tube and remove the cylinder.
4 Unscrew the pressure switch from the front of the cylinder.
5 If the unit is faulty, take it to a good BMW dealer for advice; it has not been possible to discover any information to help the owner in dismantling the assembly. While a repair kit is listed, the simplest solution may well be to purchase a new master cylinder. Ensure the correct size of cylinder is ordered.
6 Renew all sealing washers on refitting and tighten securely the pressure switch and brake hose union(s). Reverse the removal procedure to refit. Fill the system with clean, new fluid and remove any trapped air bubbles by bleeding. See Section 11.

All other models – handlebar-mounted cylinder
7 To dismantle the system, attach clear plastic tubing to the bleed nipple of each of the brake calipers, open the nipples by one full turn, and apply the front brake lever repeatedly to expel all the fluid. When no more fluid can be seen issuing from the nipples, tighten down each one. Slacken and remove the single screw which retains the twistgrip top cover, then remove the cover and disconnect the throttle cable.

Unscrew the single clamping screw and withdraw carefully the right-hand switch cluster from the rear of the twistgrip assembly.

8 The task of disconnecting the hydraulic hose from the master cylinder is a problem which must be left largely to the owner's skill and ingenuity to solve. For those machines which have a banjo union at this point, the brake hose leaving the master cylinder at right angles, there is no real problem although the task is awkward due to the tight confines of the available working space, especially if a fairing is fitted. Cover all surrounding components with a layer of clean cloth to prevent fluid spilling on to delicate components, then slacken and remove the banjo bolt. For those machines (generally the models with flat handlebars) in which the brake hose is screwed straight into the master cylinder body, the task of disconnecting becomes virtually impossible without major dismantling work, for example the removal of part of the fairing (where fitted) or of the handlebars. It is suggested that the simplest solution in the long run may well be to remove the fuel tank and to disconnect the brake hose at the junction block mounted on the frame to the rear of the steering head.

9 Whichever method is chosen, once the brake hose, throttle cable and electrical leads have been disconnected from the twistgrip assembly, slacken the clamping screws and remove the twistgrip assembly with the brake hose, where applicable, from the handlebar. Unscrew the pivot bolt retaining nut, then withdraw the pivot bolt and brake lever. If it is necessary to separate the fluid reservoir from the master cyinder, slacken and remove the three screws which retain the reservoir cap, and withdraw the cap, the gasket and the rubber diaphragm, then slacken and remove the single screw which passes upwards through the master cylinder into the reservoir body. The reservoir is then pulled off with a twisting motion as if unscrewing it. Note that the sealing O-ring fitted over the reservoir spigot must be renewed whenever the joint is disturbed in this way, regardless of its apparent condition.

10 If the brake hose is of the screwed-in type described above, and was disconnected at the junction block as suggested, remove it from the master cylinder body by unscrewing it. Slacken and remove the two Allen screws which fasten the master cylinder to the twistgrip body, and separate the master cylinder from the twistgrip. Using a suitable sharp-pointed instrument prise out the circlip from the master cylinder right-hand end, then pull out the piston assembly and return spring. Examine all the components closely, renewing any that are found to be worn or in any way damaged. Remember that it is essential that the master cylinder is maintained at peak efficiency if the brakes are to be in a safe and usable condition.

11 Carefully clean and lubricate all components prior to reassembly, using only clean hydraulic fluid. Reassembly is the reverse of the dismantling procedure described above, remembering that the use of new seals is recommended at all applicable joints and brake hose unions. Refill the system and remove all traces of air bubbles by bleeding as described in Section 11, then wash off any surplus brake fluid using copious quantities of fresh water and check for any fluid leaks which may subsequently appear.

12 Remember to check that the throttle cable is adjusted correctly and functioning properly, that any disturbed electrical circuits are operating correctly, that all the nuts and bolts are securely fastened, and that the brakes themselves are operating correctly and efficiently before the machine is taken out on the road.

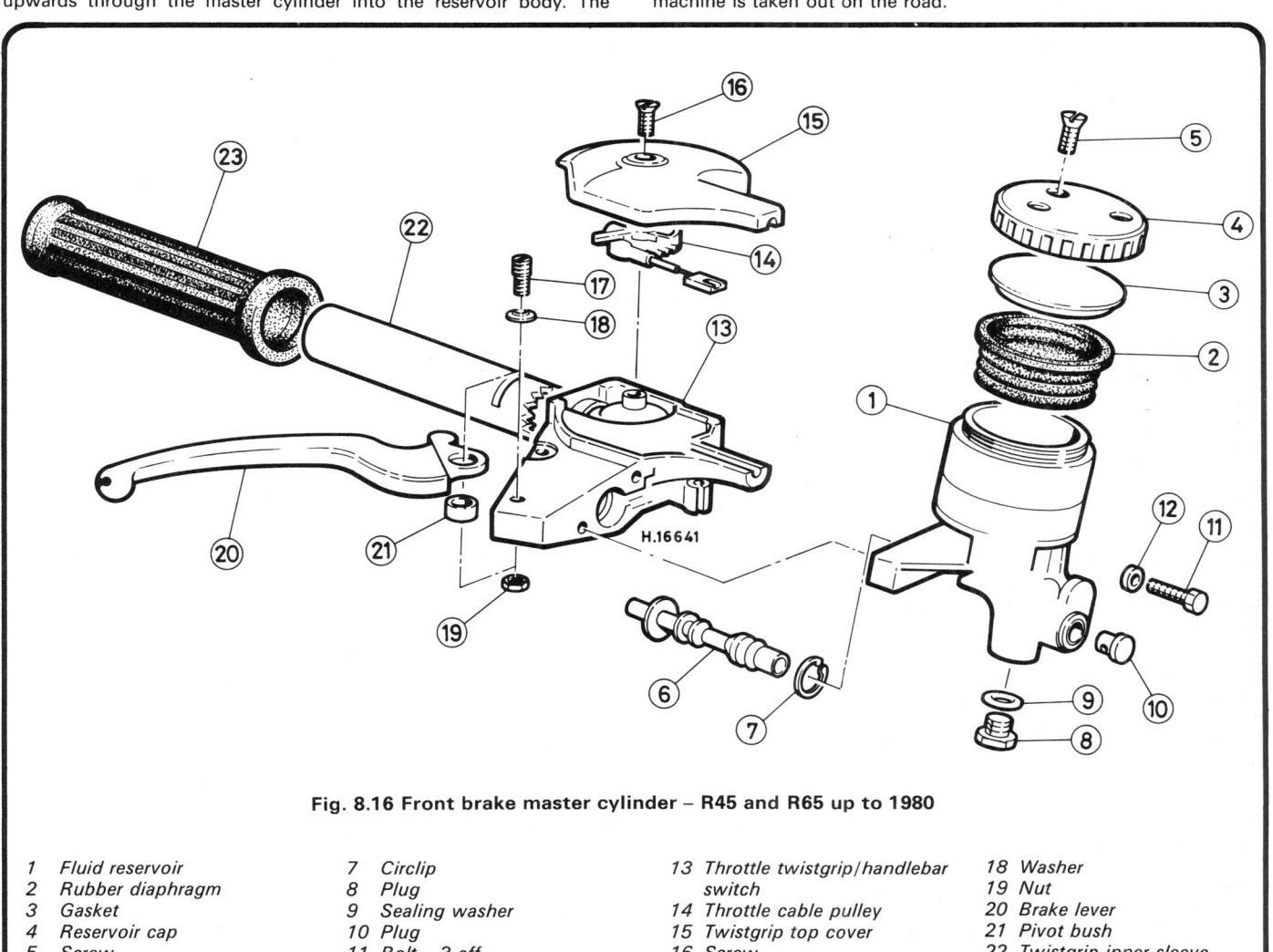

Fig. 8.16 Front brake master cylinder – R45 and R65 up to 1980

1   Fluid reservoir
2   Rubber diaphragm
3   Gasket
4   Reservoir cap
5   Screw
6   Piston assembly
7   Circlip
8   Plug
9   Sealing washer
10 Plug
11 Bolt – 3 off
12 Washer – 2 off
13 Throttle twistgrip/handlebar switch
14 Throttle cable pulley
15 Twistgrip top cover
16 Screw
17 Pivot bolt
18 Washer
19 Nut
20 Brake lever
21 Pivot bush
22 Twistgrip inner sleeve
23 Twistgrip rubber

Chapter 8 Wheels, brakes and tyres

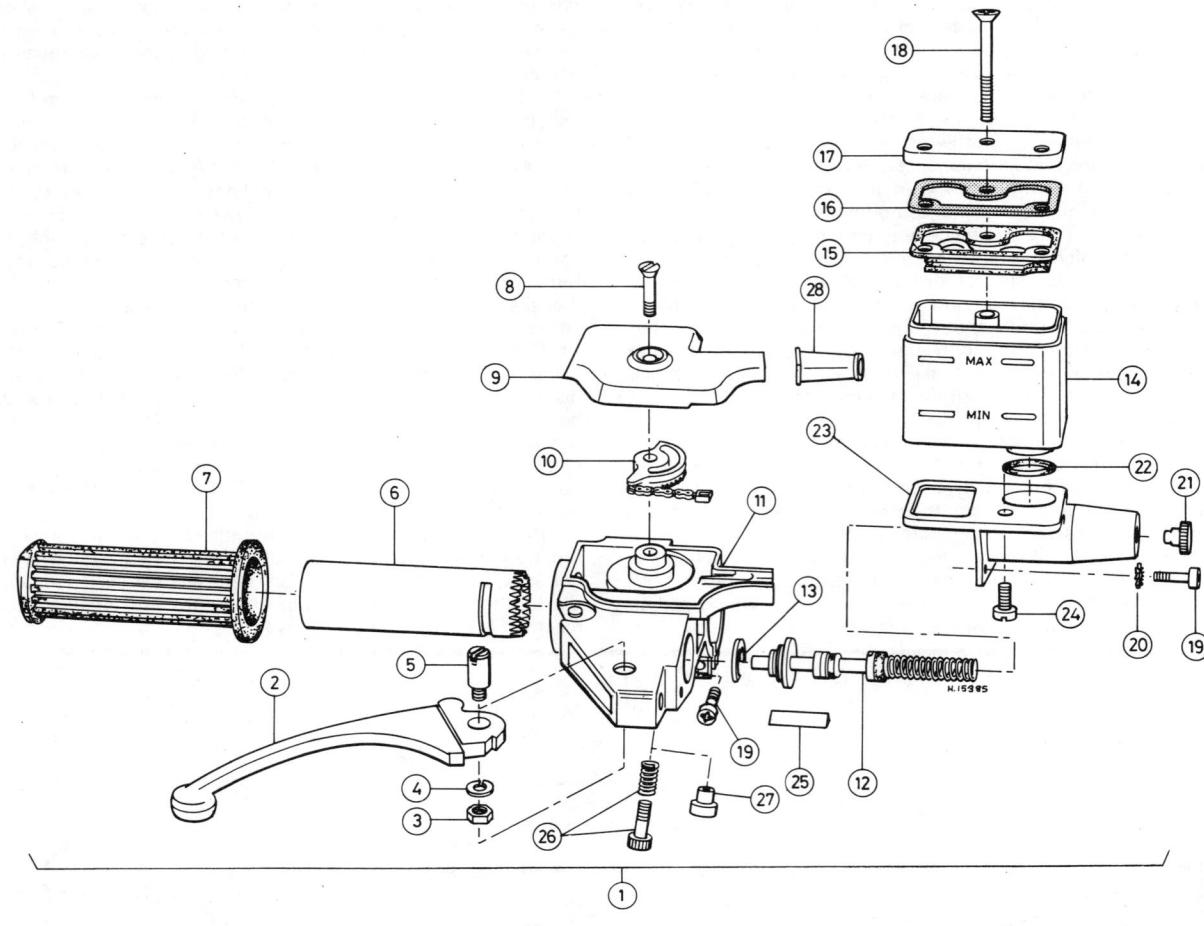

Fig. 8.17 Front brake master cylinder – all other models (typical)

1 Master cylinder and throttle twistgrip
2 Brake lever
3 Nut
4 Washer
5 Pivot bolt
6 Twistgrip inner sleeve
7 Twistgrip rubber
8 Screw
9 Twistgrip top cover
10 Throttle cable pulley
11 Throttle twistgrip/handlebar switch
12 Piston assembly
13 Circlip
14 Fluid reservoir
15 Rubber diaphragm
16 Gasket
17 Reservoir cap
18 Screw – 3 off
19 Allen screw – 2 off
20 Washer – 2 off
21 Plug
22 O-ring
23 Master cylinder
24 Screw
25 Wedge
26 Screw and spring
27 Plug
28 Boot

10 Rear disc brake master cylinder: removal, examination and refitting

1 To remove the master cylinder attach a clear plastic tube to the caliper bleed nipple, open the bleed nipple by one full turn and drain the fluid from the system by operating the brake pedal until no more fluid can be seen issuing from the nipple. Remove the rear wheel as described in Section 3 of this Chapter, then remove the right-hand sidepanel, disconnect the terminals from the fluid reservoir cap, and slacken and remove the single bolt which clamps the fluid reservoir to the frame. Disconnect the fluid reservoir/master cylinder pipe at the hose clamp on the master cylinder top and withdraw the fluid reservoir. Unscrew the gland nut which secures the metal brake pipe to the rear of the master cylinder, then disconnect and remove the brake pedal at the clevis pin which connects it to the master cylinder brake rod. Slacken and remove the single bolt which secures the master cylinder brackets to the frame, then unscrew the two Allen screws which form the exhaust right-hand silencer mounting and also pass through the master cylinder bracket.
2 Manoeuvre the master cylinder assembly clear of the frame and unscrew the two bolts to detach the mounting bracket. Remove the operating linkage from the front end of the master cylinder and push out the piston components by passing a slim rod up through the brake pipe orifice in the rear of the cylinder body.
3 Carefully examine the seals and piston, renewing all the components as a set if there is the slightest doubt about their condition, although the seals should be renewed as a matter of course whenever they are disturbed. If the slightest trace of damage is found in the master cylinder bore, the master cylinder should be renewed as a complete assembly.
4 Carefully clean each component and lubricate it with clean hydraulic fluid, then reassemble and refit the assembly following the reverse of the above instructions. Refill the system with clean brake fluid and bleed it, as described in Section 11 to remove all traces of air. Wash off all surplus hydraulic fluid and check that the brake operates correctly and efficiently before using the machine on the road.
5 When refitting the master cylinder, note that the adjustable brake rod between the pedal and the master cylinder operating arm should be adjusted so that there is 1.4 – 1.5 mm (0.055 – 0.059 in) of free play between the tip of the operating lever and the master cylinder piston when the brake pedal is in the at-rest position.

Chapter 8 Wheels, brakes and tyres

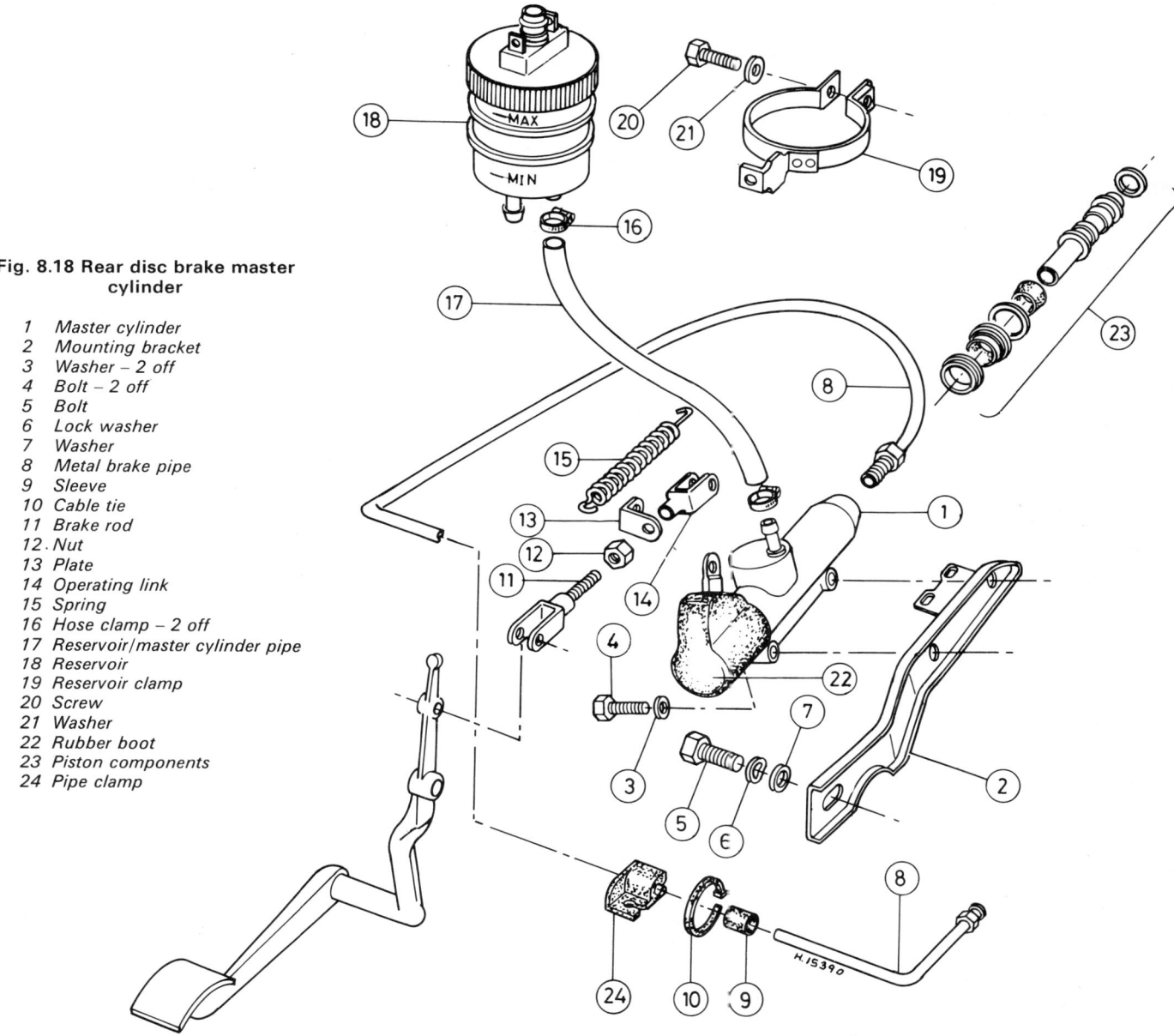

Fig. 8.18 Rear disc brake master cylinder

1 Master cylinder
2 Mounting bracket
3 Washer – 2 off
4 Bolt – 2 off
5 Bolt
6 Lock washer
7 Washer
8 Metal brake pipe
9 Sleeve
10 Cable tie
11 Brake rod
12 Nut
13 Plate
14 Operating link
15 Spring
16 Hose clamp – 2 off
17 Reservoir/master cylinder pipe
18 Reservoir
19 Reservoir clamp
20 Screw
21 Washer
22 Rubber boot
23 Piston components
24 Pipe clamp

11 Bleeding the hydraulic brake system

1 The method of bleeding a brake system of air and the procedure described below apply equally to either a front brake or rear brake of the hydraulically actuated type.
2 If the brake action becomes spongy, or if any part of the hydraulic system is dismantled (such as when a hose is replaced) it is necessary to bleed the system in order to remove all traces of air. The procedure for bleeding the hydraulic system is best carried out by two people.
3 Check the fluid level in the reservoir and top up with new fluid of the specified type if required. Keep the reservoir at least half full during the bleeding procedure; if the level is allowed to fall too far air will enter the system requiring that the procedure be started again from scratch. Refit the cap onto the reservoir to prevent the ingress of dust or the ejection of a spout of fluid.
4 Remove the dust cap from the caliper bleed nipple and clean the area with a rag. Place a clean glass jar below the caliper and connect a pipe from the bleed nipple to the jar. A clear plastic tube should be used so that air bubbles can be more easily seen. Where a twin piston caliper is fitted two bleed nipples are usually used. If this is the case a pipe should be fitted to each nipple, and the two nipples operated simultaneously. This approach can be adopted where two separate calipers are fitted. Place some clean hydraulic fluid in the glass jar so that the pipe(s) are immersed below the fluid surface throughout this operation.
5 If parts of the system have been renewed, and thus the system must be filled, open the bleed nipple about one turn and pump the brake lever until fluid starts to issue from the clear tube. Tighten the bleed nipple and then continue the normal bleeding operation as described in the following paragraphs. Keep a close check on the reservoir level whilst the system is being filled.
6 Operate the brake lever as far as it will go and hold it in this position against the fluid pressure. If spongy brake operation has occurred it may be necessary to pump the brake lever rapidly a number of times until pressure is achieved. With pressure applied, loosen the bleed nipple about half a turn. Tighten the nipple as soon as the lever has reached its full travel and then release the lever. Repeat this operation until no more air bubbles are expelled with the fluid into the glass jar. When this condition is reached, the air bleeding operation should be complete, resulting in a firm feel to the brake operation. If sponginess is still evident continue the bleeding operation; it may be that an air bubble trapped at the top of the system has yet to work down through the caliper.

7 When all traces of air have been removed from the system, top up the reservoir and refit the diaphragm and cap or cover. Check the entire system for leaks, and check also that the brake system in general is functioning efficiently before using the machine on the road.
8 Brake fluid drained from the system will almost certainly be contaminated, either by foreign matter or more commonly by the absorption of water from the air. All hydraulic fluids are hygroscopic, that is, they are capable of drawing water from the atmosphere, and thereby degrading their specifications. In view of this, and the relative cheapness of the fluid, old fluid should always be discarded.
9 Great care should be taken not to spill hydraulic fluid on any painted cycle parts; it is a very effective paint stripper. Also, the plastic glasses in the instrument heads, and most other plastic parts, will be damaged by contact with this fluid.

12 Tyres: removal, repair and refitting – tubed tyres

1 To remove the tyre from either wheel, first detach the wheel from the machine. Deflate the tyre by removing the valve core, and when the tyre is fully deflated, push the bead away from the wheel rim on both sides so that the bead enters the centre well of the rim; this will require some care and effort on cast wheels. Remove the locking ring and push the tyre valve into the tyre itself.
2 Insert a tyre lever close to the valve and lever the edge of the tyre over the outside of the rim. Very little force should be necessary; if resistance is encountered it is probably due to the fact that the tyre beads have not entered the well of the rim, all the way round. If aluminium rims are fitted, damage to the soft alloy by tyre levers can be prevented by the use of plastic rim protectors.
3 Once the tyre has been edged over the wheel rim, it is easy to work round the wheel rim, so that the tyre is completely free from one side. At this stage the inner tube can be removed.
4 Now working from the other side of the wheel, ease the other edge of the tyre over the outside of the wheel rim that is furthest away. Continue to work around the rim until the tyre is completely free from the rim.
5 If a puncture has necessitated the removal of the tyre, reinflate the inner tube and immerse it in a bowl of water to trace the source of the leak. Mark the position of the leak, and deflate the tube. Dry the tube, and clean the area around the puncture with a petrol soaked rag. When the surface has dried, apply rubber solution and allow this to dry before removing the backing from the patch, and applying the patch to the surface.
6 It is best to use a patch of self vulcanizing type, which will form a permanent repair. Note that it may be necessary to remove a protective covering from the top surface of the patch after it has sealed into position. Inner tubes made from a special synthetic rubber may require a special type of patch and adhesive, if a satisfactory bond is to be achieved.
7 Before replacing the tyre, check the inside to make sure that the article that caused the puncture is not still trapped inside the tyre. Check the outside of the tyre, particularly the tread area, to make sure nothing is trapped that may cause a further puncture.
8 BMW recommend that punctures are repaired by patching only in an emergency; normally the tube must be renewed. If the tube is patched, treat it as a temporary repair only and renew it at the earliest opportunity.
9 If a new tyre is to be fitted, BMW recommend that the tube (and rim tape, on wire-spoked wheels) must be renewed as well. The tube must be of the same make as the tyre. Check with the importer or a BMW dealer for approved tyre makes and types before buying one.
10 When fitting the tyre note first the arrows indicating the direction of rotation. If only one arrow is found this is to be fitted pointing in the direction of rotation on rear wheels, but **opposite** to the direction of rotation, to accept braking loads, on **front** wheels. Where two arrows (marked 'Front wheel' and 'Rear wheel') are provided, fit the tyre as indicated by them.
11 To ensure correct wheel balance, check the tyre sidewall for a spot of paint. On most German makes of tyre this indicates the lightest point of the tyre (check this point with the tyre manufacturer, to be safe) and must be fitted next to the valve on wire-spoked wheels. On machines with cast wheels, check the rim carefully. If a circular stamp is found this indicates the heaviest point on the rim; align the tyre paint mark with it on refitting. If no stamp is found align the tyre paint mark with the valve.

12 To replace the tyre, inflate the inner tube for it just to assume a circular shape but only to that amount, and then push the tube into the tyre so that it is enclosed completely. Lay the tyre on the wheel at an angle, and insert the valve through the rim tape and the hole in the wheel rim. Attach the locking ring on the first few threads, sufficient to hold the valve captive in its correct location. Deflate the inner tube.
13 Starting at the point furthest from the valve, push the tyre bead over the edge of the wheel rim until it is located in the central wall. Continue to work around the tyre in this fashion until the whole of one side of the tyre is on the rim. It may be necessary to use a tyre lever during the final stages.
14 Make sure there is no pull on the tyre valve and again commencing with the area furthest from the valve, ease the other bead of the tyre over the edge of the rim. Finish with the area close to the valve, pushing the valve up into the tyre until the locking ring touches the rim. This will ensure that the inner tube is not trapped when the last section of bead is edged over the rim with a tyre lever.
15 Check that the inner tube is not trapped at any point. Reinflate the inner tube, and check that the tyre is seating correctly around the wheel rim. On cast alloy wheels, up to 2.5 – 4.5 bar (36 – 63 psi) will be necessary to push the tube over the rim safety hump. There should be a thin rib moulded around the wall of the tyre on both sides, which should be an equal distance from the wheel rim at all points. If the tyre is unevenly located on the rim, try bouncing the wheel when the tyre is at the recommended pressure. It is probable that one of the beads has not pulled clear of the centre well.
16 Always run the tyres at the recommended pressures and never under or over inflate. The correct pressures for original equipment tyres are given in the Specifications Section of this Chapter; if non-standard tyres are fitted, check with the manufacturer for recommended pressures.
17 Tyre replacement is aided by dusting the side walls, particularly in the vicinity of the beads, with a liberal coating of french chalk. Washing up liquid can also be used to good effect, or a proprietary tyre-fitting lubricant.
18 Never replace the inner tube and tyre without the rim tape in position (wire-spoked wheels). If this precaution is overlooked there is a good chance of the ends of the spoke nipples chafing the inner tube and causing a crop of punctures.
19 Never fit a tyre that has a damaged tread or sidewalls. Apart from legal aspects, there is a very great risk of a blowout, which can have very serious consequences on a two wheeled vehicle.
20 Tyre valves rarely give trouble, but it is always advisable to check whether the valve itself is leaking before removing the tyre. Do not forget to fit the dust cap, which forms an effective extra seal. Lock the valve locking ring against the dust cap, not the rim, to prevent the valve from being torn out of the tube if the tyre should creep on the rim. If the valve tilts at an angle while the machine is in use, this indicates that the tyre is creeping and should be refitted.

12.10 Arrows on tyre sidewall indicate direction of rotation – see text

Chapter 8 Wheels, brakes and tyres

12.11 Paint spot on tyre sidewall is normally aligned with valve – check carefully

13 Valve core and caps: tubed tyres

1 Valve cores seldom give trouble, but do not last indefinitely. Dirt under the seating will cause a puzzling 'slow-puncture'. Check that they are not leaking by applying spittle to the end of the valve and watching for air bubbles.
2 A valve cap is a safety device, and should always be fitted. Apart from keeping dirt out of the valve, it provides a second seal in case of valve failure, and may prevent an accident resulting from sudden deflation.
3 Remember always to lock the valve locking ring against the dust cap so that if the tyre starts to creep on the rim there will be some warning of this (from the angle of the valve) and the tyre can be repositioned before the valve is torn out of the tube.

14 Tyres: removal and refitting – tubeless tyres

1 It is strongly recommended that should a repair to a tubeless tyre be necessary, the wheel is removed from the machine and taken to a tyre fitting specialist who is willing to do the job or taken to an official dealer. This is because the force required to break the seal between the wheel rim and tyre bead is considerable and considered to be beyond the capabilities of an individual working with normal tyre removing tools. Any abortive attempt to break the rim to bead seal may also cause damage to the wheel rim, resulting in an expensive wheel replacement. If, however, a suitable bead releasing tool is available, and experience has already been gained in its use, tyre removal and refitting can be accomplished as follows.
2 Remove the wheel from the machine by following the instructions for wheel removal as described in the relevant Section of this Chapter. Deflate the tyre by removing the valve insert and when it is fully deflated, push the bead of the tyre away from the wheel rim on both sides so that the bead enters the centre well of the rim. As noted, this operation will almost certainly require the use of a bead releasing tool.
3 Insert a tyre lever close to the valve and lever the edge of the tyre over the outside of the wheel rim. Very little force should be necessary: if resistance is encountered it is probably due to the fact that the tyre beads have not entered the well of the wheel rim all the way round the tyre. Should the initial problem persist, lubrication of the tyre bead and the inside edge and lip of the rim will facilitate removal. Use a recommended lubricant, a diluted solution of washing-up liquid or french chalk. Lubrication is usually recommended as an aid to tyre fitting but its use is equally desirable during removal. The risk of lever damage to wheel rims can be minimised by the use of proprietary plastic rim protectors placed over the rim flange at the point where the tyre levers are inserted. Suitable rim projectors may be fabricated very easily from short lengths (4 – 6 inches) of thick-walled nylon petrol pipe which have been split down one side using a sharp knife. The use of rim protectors should be adopted whenever levers are used and, therefore, when the risk of damage is likely.
4 Once the tyre has been edged over the wheel rim, it is easy to work around the wheel rim so that the tyre is completely freed on one side.
5 Working from the other side of the wheel, ease the other edge of the tyre over the outside of the wheel rim, which is furthest away. Continue to work around the rim until the tyre is freed completely from the rim.
6 Refer to the following Section for details relating to puncture repair and the renewal of tyres. Check with the importer or with a BMW dealer for a list of approved makes and types of tyre before purchasing; fit only those recommended. See also the remarks relating to the tyre valves in Section 16.
7 Refitting of the tyre is virtually a reversal of removal procedure. If the tyre has a balance mark (usually a spot of coloured paint) indicating its lightest point, as on the tyres fitted as original equipment, this must be positioned alongside the circular stamp mark on the rim which indicates the wheel's heaviest point. If no stamp mark is found, align the tyre mark with the valve. Similarly any arrow indicating direction of rotation must be fitted pointing the right way. If only one arrow is found this must be fitted pointing in the direction of rotation on **rear** wheels, but **opposite** to the direction of rotation, to accept braking loads, on **front** wheels. Where two arrows (marked 'Front wheel' and 'Rear wheel') are provided, fit the tyre as indicated by them.
8 Starting at the point furthest from the valve, push the tyre bead over the edge of the wheel rim until it is located in the central well. Continue to work around the tyre in this fashion until the whole of one side of the tyre is on the rim. It may be necessary to use a tyre lever during the final stages. Here again, the use of a lubricant will aid fitting. It is recommended strongly that when refitting the tyre only a recommended lubricant is used because such lubricants also have sealing properties. Do not be over generous in the application of lubricant or tyre creep may occur.
9 Fitting the upper bead is similar to fitting the lower bead. Start by pushing the bead over the rim and into the well at a point diametrically opposite the tyre valve. Continue working round the tyre, each side of the starting point, ensuring that the bead opposite the working area is always in the well. Apply lubricant as necessary. Avoid using tyre levers unless absolutely essential, to help reduce damage to the soft wheel rim. The use of the levers should be required only when the final portion of bead is to be pushed over the rim.
10 Lubricate the tyre beads again prior to inflating the tyre, and check that the wheel rim is evenly positioned in relation to the tyre beads. Inflation of the tyre may well prove impossible without the use of a high pressure air hose. The tyre will retain air completely only when the beads are firmly against the rim edges at all points and it may be found when using a foot pump that air escapes at the same rate as it is pumped in. This problem may also be encountered when using an air hose on new tyres which have been compressed in storage and by virtue of their profile hold the beads away from the rim edges. To overcome this difficulty, a tourniquet may be placed around the circumference of the tyre, over the central area of the tread. The compression of the tread in this area will cause the beads to be pushed outwards in the desired direction. The type of tourniquet most widely used consists of a length of hose closed at both ends with a suitable clamp fitted to enable both ends to be connected. An ordinary tyre valve is fitted at one end of the tube so that after the hose has been secured around the tyre it may be inflated, giving a constricting effect. Another possible method of seating beads to obtain initial inflation is to press the tyre into the angle between a wall and the floor. With the airline attached to the valve additional pressure is then applied to the tyre by the hand and shin, as shown in the accompanying illustration. The application of pressure at four points around the tyre's circumference whilst simultaneously applying the airhose will often effect an initial seal between the tyre beads and wheel rim, thus allowing inflation to occur.
11 Having successfully accomplished inflation, increase the pressure to 40 psi and check that the tyre is evenly disposed on the wheel rim. This may be judged by checking that the thin positioning line found on each tyre wall is equidistant from the rim around the total circumference on the tyre. If this is not the case, deflate the tyre, apply additional lubrication and reinflate. Minor adjustments to the tyre position may be made by bouncing the wheel on the ground.

12 Always run the tyre at the recommended pressures and never under or over-inflate. The correct pressures for original equipment tyres are given in the Specifications Section of this Chapter; check with the tyre manufacturers (if non-standard tyres are fitted) and use their recommended pressures, if different.

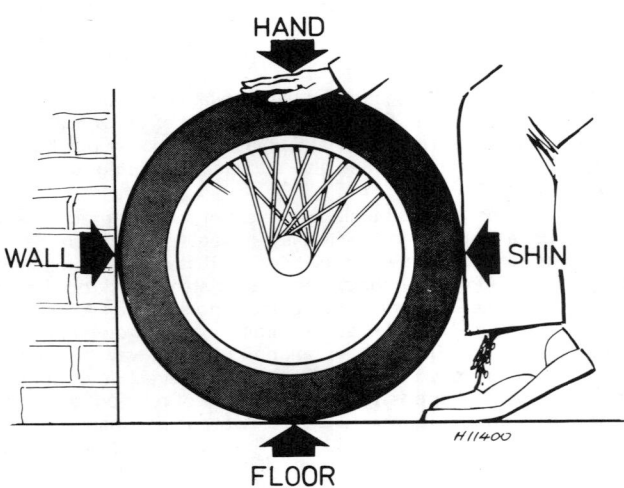

Fig. 8.19 Method of seating the beads on tubeless tyres

15 Puncture repair and tyre renewal – tubeless tyres

1 If a puncture occurs, the tyre should be removed for inspection for damage before any attempt is made at remedial action. The temporary repair of a punctured tyre by inserting a plug from the outside should not be attempted. Although this type of temporary repair is used widely on cars, the manufacturers strongly recommend that no such repair is carried out on a motorcycle tyre. Not only does the tyre have a thinner carcase, which does not give sufficient support to the plug, the consequences of a sudden deflation are often sufficiently serious that the risk of such an occurrence should be avoided at all costs.
2 The tyre should be inspected both inside and out for damage to the carcass. Unfortunately the inner lining of the tyre – which takes the place of the inner tube – may easily obscure any damage and some experience is required in making a correct assessment of the tyre condition.
3 There are two main types of tyre repair which are considered safe for adoption in repairing tubeless motorcycle tyres. The first type of repair consists of inserting a mushroom-headed plug into the hole from the inside of the tyre. The hole is prepared for insertion of the plug by reaming and the application of an adhesive. The second repair is carried out by buffing the inner lining in the damaged area and applying a cold or vulcanised patch. Because both inspection and repair, if they are to be carried out safely, require experience in this type of work, it is recommended that the tyre be placed in the hands of a repairer with the necessary skills, rather than repaired in the home workshop.
4 BMW provide an emergency repair kit for tubeless tyres as part of the machine's toolkit. This can be used, following the instructions provided, to repair holes up to 4 mm (0.16 in) in diameter but note that a repaired tyre should not be ridden above 37 mph (60 km/h) or for more than 250 miles (400 km). The kit is an emergency repair only; the tyre should be renewed as a safety precaution as soon as possible.
5 In the event of an emergency, the only recommended 'get-you-home' repair is to fit a standard inner tube of the correct size. If this course of action is adopted, care should be taken to ensure that the cause of the puncture has been removed before the inner tube is fitted. It will be found that the valve hole in the rim is considerably larger than the diameter of the inner tube valve stem. To prevent the ingress of road dirt, and to help support the valve, a spacer should be fitted over the valve.
6 In the event of the unavailability of tubeless tyres, ordinary tubed tyres may be fitted to these wheel rims. Use tyres of an equivalent type and grade to ensure their suitability. It is recommended that the advice of the tyre manufacturer or a reputable supplier is sought to ensure that a compatible replacement tyre is fitted.

16 Tyre valves: description and renewal – tubeless tyres

1 It will be appreciated from the preceding Sections that the adoption of tubeless tyres has made it necessary to modify the valve arrangement, as there is no longer an inner tube which can carry the valve core. The problem has been overcome by fitting a separate tyre valve which passes through a close-fitting hole in the rim, and which is secured by a nut and locknut. The valve is fitted from the rim well, and it follows that the valve can be removed and replaced only when the tyre has been removed from the rim. Leakage of air from around the valve body is likely to occur only if the sealing seat fails or if the nut and locknut become loose.
2 The valve core is of the same type as that used with tubed tyres, and screws into the valve body. The core can be removed with a small slotted tool which is normally incorporated in plunger type pressure gauges. Some valve dust caps incorporate a projection for removing valve cores. Although tubeless tyre valves seldom give trouble, it is possible for a leak to develop if a small particle of grit lodges on the sealing face. Occasionally, an elusive slow puncture can be traced to a leaking valve core, and this should be checked before a genuine puncture is suspected.
3 The valve dust caps are a significant part of the tyre valve assembly. Not only do they prevent the ingress of road dirt in the valve, but also act as a secondary seal which will reduce the risk of sudden deflation if a valve core should fail.

17 Wheel balancing

1 It is customary on all high performance machines to balance the wheels complete with tyres and tube. The out of balance forces which exist are eliminated and the handling of the machine is improved in consequence. A wheel which is badly out of balance produces through the steering a most unpleasant hammering effect at high speeds.
2 Some tyres have a balance mark on the sidewall, usually in the form of a coloured spot. This mark must be in line with the tyre valve or rim stamp mark. Refer to Sections 12 and 14. Even then the wheel may require the addition of balance weights, to offset the weight of the tyre valve itself.
3 If the wheel is raised clear of the ground and is spun, it will probably come to rest with the tyre valve or the heaviest part downward and will always come to rest in the same position. Balance weights must be added to a point diametrically opposite this heavy spot until the wheel will come to rest in ANY position after it is spun.
4 The wheels should be removed from the machine and mounted on a stand to eliminate brake or final drive drag. For wire spoked wheels, weights are available from BMW in 10, 15 and 20 gram sizes; these are clipped around the nipple of the appropriate spoke. For cast wheels, weights are available from BMW in 5, 10, 15, 20, 25 and 30 gram sizes; these are attached to the rim by a spring clip, using special pliers.
Note: all models – the sum of the weights fitted to any rim must not exceed 60 grams (2 oz).
5 Most tyre-fitting specialists have wheel-balancing equipment which can be used to balance the wheels in a very short time, making the labour charge reasonable.

Tyre removal: Deflate inner tube and insert lever in close proximity to tyre valve

Use two levers to work bead over the edge of rim

When first bead is clear, remove tyre as shown

Tyre fitting: Inflate inner tube and insert in tyre

Lay tyre on rim and feed valve through hole in rim

Work first bead over rim, using lever in final section

Use similar technique for second bead, finish at tyre valve position

Push valve and tube up into tyre when fitting final section, to avoid trapping

Chapter 9 Electrical system

Refer to Chapter 10 for subsequent modifications and information relating to the 1986 on models

Contents

General description 1	Diode board: removal 9
Electrical system: general information and preliminary checks 2	Voltage regulator: removal 10
	Fuses: replacing 11
Wiring: layout and examination 3	Starter motor: removal 12
Battery: removal and refitting 4	Starter motor: overhaul 13
Battery: examination and maintenance 5	Relays: location and testing 14
Charging system: testing 6	Switches: general 15
Alternator: removal 7	Horn: location and adjustment 16
Alternator: overhaul 8	Bulbs: renewal 17

Specifications

Electrical system
Voltage	12
Earth (Ground)	Negative (−)
Fuses	8A (x 2)

Battery
	Manufacturer	Capacity
/5	Varta	15Ah
/6	Varta	25Ah (30Ah optional)
/7 up to 1980	Varta	28Ah (30Ah optional)
/7 1981 on, R80RT 1983-84	BMW – Mareg	28Ah (30Ah optional)
R45 and R65 up to 1980	Varta	16Ah
R45 and R65 1981 on, R65LS, R80G/S with electric start, R80ST	BMW – Mareg	16Ah
R80G/S without electric start	BMW – Mareg	9Ah
R80, R80RT 1985 on	BMW – Mareg	20Ah (30Ah optional)

Alternator
Type:
/5	Bosch 0.120.340.001 G1 14V 13A 19
/6 except R90S	Bosch 0.120.340.002 G1 14V 20A 21/280W
R90S	Bosch 0.120.340.003 G1 14V 17A 22/238W
All 1000cc models up to 1980	Bosch 0.120.340.005 G1 14V 18A 22/240W
All other models	Bosch 0.120.340.004 G1 14V 20A 21/280W

Rated output:
/5	180W/14V 13A
R90S	238W/14V 17A
All 1000cc models up to 1980	250W/14V 18A
All other models	280W/14V 20A
Charge starts at	980 rpm

Chapter 9 Electrical system

Maximum speed	10 000 rpm
Slip ring minimum OD	26.8 mm (1.0551 in)
Slip ring maximum distortion	0.06 mm (0.0024 in)
Brush minimum length	see text
Resistance between phase outputs	0.62 ohm
Resistance between slip rings – exciter winding:	
/5, /6	6.21 – 7.59 ohm
All other models	3.40 – 3.74 ohm

Diode board (rectifier) – type

/5	Bosch 0.197.002.001 RS20/1 A1A
All other models	Bosch 0.197.002.003 D120 915 158 14V 20A

Voltage regulator

Type:	
/5, /6 (except R90S) up to 1973	Bosch 0.190.601.013 AD 1/14V
R90S, /6 1974 on, /7 up to 1980, R45 and R65 up to 1980	Bosch 0.190.601.009 AD 1/14V
All models 1981 on	Wehrle E1051 B/14V
No load regulated voltage	13.55 – 14.25 volts
Regulated voltage under load – @ 5000 rpm:	
All models up to 1980	13.9 – 14.8 volts
All models 1981 on	13.5 – 14.2 volts

Starter motor

Manufacturer	Bosch
Type:	
/5, /6 up to 1974	0.001.157.007 DF12V 0.5HP
/6 1975 on	N/Av DF12V 0.6HP
All other models	0.001.157.023 DF12V 0.7 HP
Brush minimum length – see text	11.5 mm (0.4528 in)
Current strength:	
/5, /6 up to 1974	290A
All other models	320A
Commutator minimum OD	33.0 mm (1.2992 in)
Commutator undercut	0.5 mm (0.0197 in)
Armature axial float	0.10 – 0.15 mm (0.0039 – 0.0059 in)
Starter relay:	
/5	Stribel SR9570
/6	Stribel type 1357 104.3 SR9572
All other models	Bosch 0.332.014.118

Turn signal relay

/5	Hella 91 M2E2 x 21W-12V
/6, /7 up to 1980	Hella TBB26 1 – 4 x 21W-12V
/7 1981 on	Hella TBB53 DOT2 (4) x 21W ± 0.5W-12V
R45 and R65 up to 1980, R80G/S, R80ST	Bosch 0.335.200.043. 12V2 (4) x 21W 13-7W
All other models 1981 on	Wehrle 12V2 (4) x 21W 13-7W

Horn

/5	Bosch 0.320.123.013-12V 400HZ or Hella B31-12V OH3
/6	Bosch 0.320.143.025-12V 400HZ
/7 – single horn	Fiamm 410HZ
/7 – twin horn	Fiamm 410HZ and 510HZ
All other models	Bosch 0.320.043.029-12V 335HZ

Bulbs

	/5	/6, /7, R80, R80RT	R80G/S	R45, R65, R65LS, R80ST
Headlamp	12V, 45/40W	12V, 60/55W	12V, 60/55W	12V, 60/55W
Parking lamp	12V, 4W	12V, 4W	12V, 4W	12V, 4W
Neutral indicator	12V, 2W	12V, 1.2W	12V, 3W	12V, 3W
Oil pressure warning	12V, 2W	12V, 1.2W	12V, 3W	12V, 1.2W
Charge warning	12V, 4W	12V, 3W	12V, 3W	12V, 1.2W
Main beam warning	12V, 2W	12V, 1.2W	12V, 3W	12V, 3W
Turn signal repeater(s)	12V, 2W	12V, 2W	12V, 3W	12V, 3W
Brake fluid warning – /6 and /7 up to 1980 only	N/App	12V, 1.2W	N/App	N/App
Instrument lighting	12V, 2W	12V, 3W	12V, 3W	12V, 3W
Additional instrument lighting	N/App	12V, 2W	N/App	N/App
Stop/tail lamp	12V, 21/5W	12V, 21/5W	12V, 21/5W	12V, 21/5W
Turn signal lamp	12V, 21W	12V, 21W	12V, 21W	12V, 21W

Torque wrench settings

Component	Nm	lbf ft
Alternator rotor retaining bolt	23 – 27	17 – 20
Starter motor mounting bolts	47.5	35

Chapter 9 Electrical system

1 General description

The charging system consists of a 12 volt three-phase alternator which has a rotor fixed to the front of the crankshaft, rotating within a stator screwed to the crankcase. The rotor is not permanently magnetised, energising current being supplied by the charge warning lamp circuit via two brushes bearing on slip rings.

The ac voltage generated is rectified to dc by the diodes on the plate above the alternator, and regulated by the voltage regulator mounted on the right-hand side of the top frame tube. Early models use a mechanical regulator; all models from 1981 on are fitted with an electronic regulator.

If the system is functioning correctly, the charge warning lamp will extinguish when engine speed exceeds idle. Since the charge warning lamp circuit provides the alternator rotor energising current, it is important to replace it with a bulb of the same wattage.

The starter motor is series-wound and operates on direct current, having a pinion with a slipping clutch arrangement. The starter pinion is engaged by a solenoid mounted on top of the starter. A transistor-controlled relay prevents engagement of the starter whilst the engine is running. The relay is mounted on the left side of the top frame tube. In addition, on the /6 range, the starter motor cannot be operated with the machine in gear. A clutch-operated switch allows the starter motor to operate only with the clutch disengaged.

Before commencing work on any part of the electrical system, disconnect the battery earth lead.

2 Electrical system: general information and preliminary checks

1 In the event of an electrical system fault, always check the physical condition of the wiring and connectors before attempting any of the test procedures described here and in subsequent Sections. Look for chafed, trapped or broken electrical leads and repair or renew these as necessary. Leads which have broken internally are not easily spotted, but may be checked using a multimeter or a simple battery and bulb circuit as a continuity tester. This arrangement is shown in the accompanying illustration. The various multi-pin connectors are generally trouble-free but may corrode if exposed to water. Clean them carefully, scraping off any surface deposits, and pack with silicone grease during assembly to avoid recurrent problems. The same technique can be applied to the handlebar switches.

2 A sound, fully charged battery is essential to the normal operation of the system. There is no point in attempting to locate a fault if the battery is partly discharged or worn out. Check battery condition and recharge or renew the battery before proceeding further.

3 Many of the test procedures described in this Chapter require that voltages or resistances be checked. This requires the use of some form of test equipment such as a simple and inexpensive multimeter of the type sold by electronics or motor accessory shops.

4 If you doubt your ability to check safely the electrical system entrust the work to a BMW dealer. In any event have your findings double checked before consigning expensive components to the scrap bin.

3 Wiring: layout and examination

1 The wiring harness is colour-coded and will correspond with the accompanying wiring diagram. When socket connectors are used, they are designed so that reconnection can be made in the correct position only.

2 Visual inspection will usually show whether there are any breaks or frayed outer coverings which will give rise to short circuits. Occasionally a wire may become trapped between two components, breaking the inner core but leaving the more resilient outer cover intact. This can give rise to mysterious intermittent or total circuit failure. Another source of trouble may be the connectors and sockets, where the connector has not been pushed fully home in the outer housing, or where corrosion has occurred.

3 Intermittent short circuits can often be traced to a chafed wire that passes through or is close to a metal component such as a frame member. Avoid tight bends in the lead or situations where a lead can become trapped between casings.

4 Battery: removal and refitting

/5 models

1 Lift the dual seat and remove the tool tray and side covers where fitted.

2 Unclip the two rubber retaining straps. Take off the battery cover, and disconnect the battery leads – negative lead first. Pull the vent pipe from the spigot at the top left of the battery. Unscrew the two hexagon socket cap screws fixing the top of the battery carrier to the frame, tilt the battery backwards and lift clear. On refitting, the positive terminal must be on the left.

/6, /7 and R80RT 1983-84

3 Place the machine on its centre stand, lift out the tool tray and wedge it on the rear mudguard so that the seat cannot fall closed. Unhook the rubber band and disengage both side panels from their (rear) frame clips; it may be necessary to remove its front retaining screw and to lift the grab handle out of the way.

4 On models up to 1980 it is permissible to use either of two methods to remove the battery. The first involves dismantling the air cleaner assembly so that the battery can be removed forwards; this is more complex than the second method which is described below.

5 Unscrew the two battery strap nuts and remove the strap. Remove the terminal covers and disconnect the battery leads – negative (earth) lead first. Pull the vent pipe from the spigot at the top left of the battery.

6 On models up to 1980 only, slacken the rear subframe two lower mounting bolts and remove fully the two upper mounting bolts and nuts. Allow the subframe to pivot backwards (ensuring that the tail lamp electrical lead is not stretched or damaged) until the rear wheel touches the ground. Remove the nuts retaining the battery tray to the frame rubber mounting bushes and pivot the battery and tray backwards against the rear mudguard. Lift out the battery, manoeuvring the tail lamp lead to avoid trapping it against the frame.

7 On all models from 1981 on it is merely necessary to disconnect the tail lamp lead at the six-pin block connector near the battery positive terminal. Lift out the battery.

8 On reassembly, fit the batttery with its positive terminal on the left. Reverse the dismantling sequence to refit. Ensure that the subframe mounting bolts are tightened to the correct torque setting.

R45, R65, R65LS, R80 and R80RT 1985 on

9 Detach the side panels. On R45, R65 and R65LS models unclip each panel at the front rubber mounting then pull it up and forwards off its two rear mountings. On R80 and R80RT models remove the single retaining screw at the bottom edge of each cover, pull the covers out

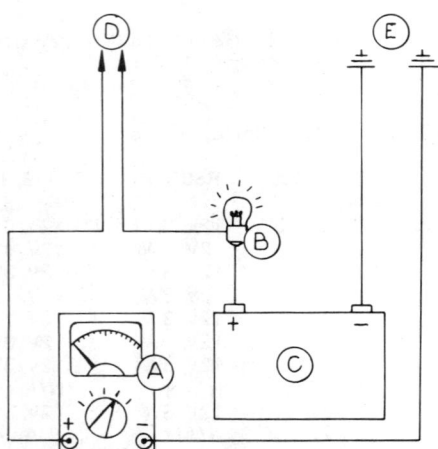

Fig. 9.1 Simple continuity test circuits

A Multimeter
B Bulb
C Battery
D Positive probe
E Negative probe

Chapter 9 Electrical system

slightly at the bottom and downwards at the front; then disengage each from its upper rear mounting. Raise the seat and remove the tool tray.

10 Unhook the rubber retaining strap(s), withdraw the terminal cover (where fitted) and disconnect the terminals – negative (earth) terminal first. Pull the vent tube off its spigot on the battery casing. On R45, R65, and R65LS models disconnect the tail-lamp at the six-pin block connector near the battery positive terminal.

11 Lift the battery up and to the rear and manoeuvre it out of the frame.

12 Refitting is the reverse of the above. The battery must be fitted with its positive terminal on the left.

R80G/S, R80ST

13 Place the machine on its centre stand, then unlock the dual seat, raise it at the rear and withdraw it. Lift out the tool tray. Detach the right-hand side panel by pulling it out at the rear and then forwards. If the extra access is needed detach the silencer cover by unscrewing the three retaining screws and pulling it outwards slightly. Pull it down and to the rear to disengage the top mountings, then pull it to the front and withdraw it.

14 Unhook the battery retaining straps, remove the terminal cover and disconnect the terminals – negative (earth) terminal first. Pull the vent tube off its spigot.

15 Remove the suspension unit top mounting bolt and lower the wheel to the ground; swing the unit to the rear. Lift the battery up and to the rear and manoeuvre it out of place.

16 Refitting is the reverse of removal. Tighten the suspension unit mounting bolt to the specified torque setting.

All models

17 Once the battery had been removed, the battery tray mounting nuts or bolts can be unscrewed to release the tray. Withdraw it from the machine, if required.

5 Battery: examination and maintenance

1 To check the battery thoroughly it is best to disconnect it and remove it from the machine; always disconnect the negative (−) terminal first to prevent the risk of short circuits damaging any component. Batteries can be dangerous if mishandled. See 'Safety First' and note the precautions described for handling them. Wear overalls or old clothing in case of accidental acid spillage. Clean the outside of the battery carefully, and remove any deposits from the terminals, which should be coated with petroleum jelly prior to installation. Connect the negative (−) terminal last.

2 When new, the battery is filled with an electrolyte of dilute sulphuric acid having a specified gravity of 1.280 at 20°C (68°F). Subsequent evaporation, which occurs in normal use, can be compensated for by topping up with distilled or demineralised water only. Never use tap water as a substitute and do not add fresh electrolyte unless spillage has occurred.

3 The state of charge of a battery can be checked using a hydrometer.

4 The normal charge rate for a battery is $1/10$ of its rated capacity, thus for a 28 ampere hour unit charging should take place at 2.8 amp. Exceeding this figure could cause the battery to overheat, buckling the plates and rendering it useless. Few owners will have access to an expensive current-controlled charger, so if a normal domestic charger is used, check that after a possible initial peak, the charge rate falls to a safe level. If the battery becomes hot during charging **stop**. Further charging will cause damage. Note that cell caps should be loosened and vents unobstructed during charging to avoid a build-up of pressure and risk of explosion also that both battery terminals should be disconnected before charging takes place.

5 After charging, top up with distilled water as required, then check the specific gravity and battery voltage. Specific gravity should be above 1.250 and a sound, fully charged battery should produce 15-16 volts. If the recharged battery discharges rapidly if left disconnected it is likely than an internal short caused by physical damage or sulphation has occurred. A new battery will be required. A sound item will tend to lose its charge at about 1% per day.

4.2a Battery removal, /5 models – unhook straps, remove carrier mounting screws ...

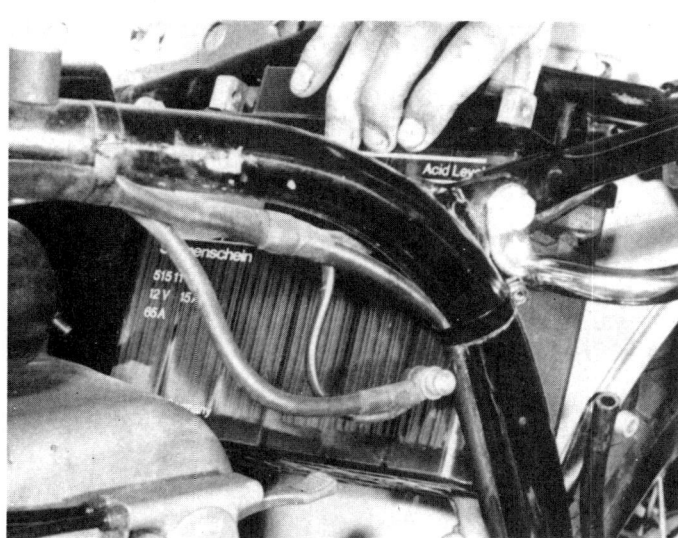

4.2b ... and tilt battery backwards to remove

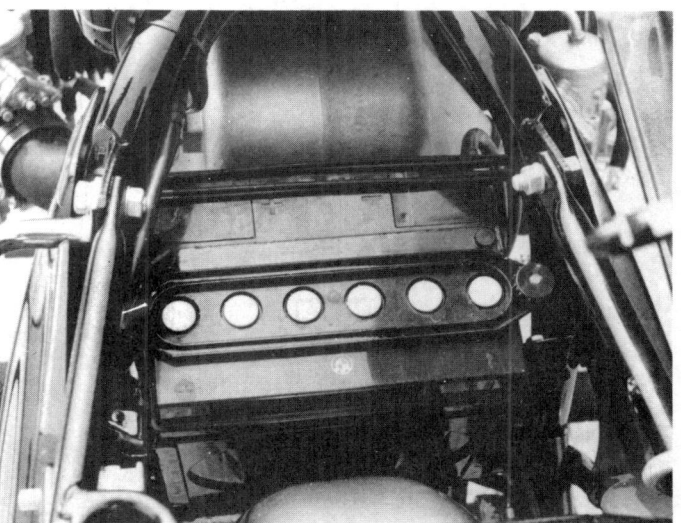

4.5 Later models – battery is retained by metal strap and two plastic nuts

5.1a Always disconnect battery at negative terminal first, before checking electrical components

5.1b Ensure vent pipe is routed correctly, well clear of other components, and is not kinked

6 Charging system: testing

Regulator check

1 Remove the fuel tank. See Chapter 4.
2 Remove the engine front cover. See Chapter 1.
3 Refer to the accompanying illustrations to identify the various terminals mentioned.
4 With the engine stopped and the ignition switched off, disconnect the B+/30 lead (heavy-gauge red or black wire) from the diode board.
5 Connect a voltmeter set to read over 15 volts between the B+/30 diode board terminal and the alternator earthed brush terminal (can be marked as D+ or D– on either the alternator or in the wiring diagrams).
6 Start the engine. At just over idle speed a reading of 13.55-14.25 volts should be obtained. Stop the engine. If a significantly lower reading is obtained check the alternator.
7 Reconnect the B+/30 lead to the diode board, then connect the voltmeter first between the diode board D+ (it may be more convenient to make the connection at the regulator D+ terminal if the back of the diode board cannot be reached) terminal and a good earth point on the frame. Start the engine and note the reading obtained, then stop the engine and repeat the test between the B+/30 terminal and earth.
8 If a difference in voltage of up to 0.5 volt is found, the regulator is faulty. If the difference is between 1.5-4.0 volts the diode board is at fault.

Alternator and regulator quick test

9 This test should only be carried out if the charge warning light remains permanently on while the engine is running.
10 Remove the fuel tank and front engine cover.
11 With the engine stopped and the ignition switched off disconnect the regulator three-pin plug. Using a spare length of wire connect the D+ (blue wire) to the DF (blue/black wire) terminals on the plug.
12 Start the engine and increase speed to 1000-2000 rpm. If the charge warning light goes out, the regulator is faulty, if it stays on, the alternator is faulty.

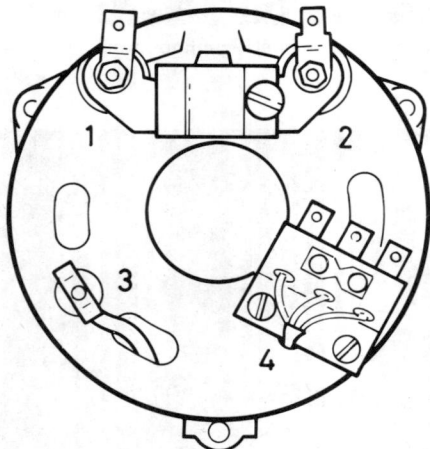

Fig. 9.2 Alternator connections

1 Earthed brush, should be marked D– or D+, brown wire
2 Insulated brush, should be marked DF, blue/black wire (black on later models)
3 Additional output to diode board – not on /5 models, should be marked Y, black wire
4 Output to diode board – disregard for charging system check, should be marked D or D–, black wire.

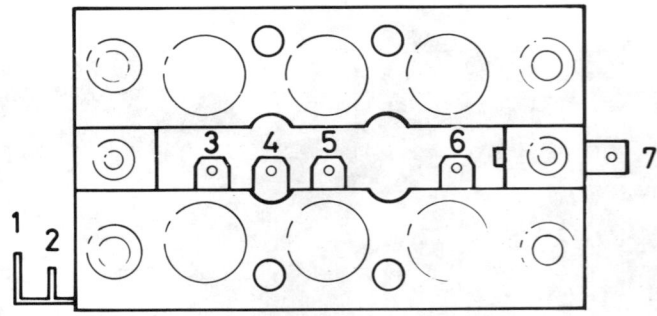

Fig. 9.3 Diode board connections – seen from rear

1 B+/30 Red or black wire
2 Not used
3 Diode No 1
4 Diode No 2   black wires in three-pin socket
5 Diode No 3
6 D+ Blue wires
7 Y Black wire – not on /5 models

Chapter 9 Electrical system 213

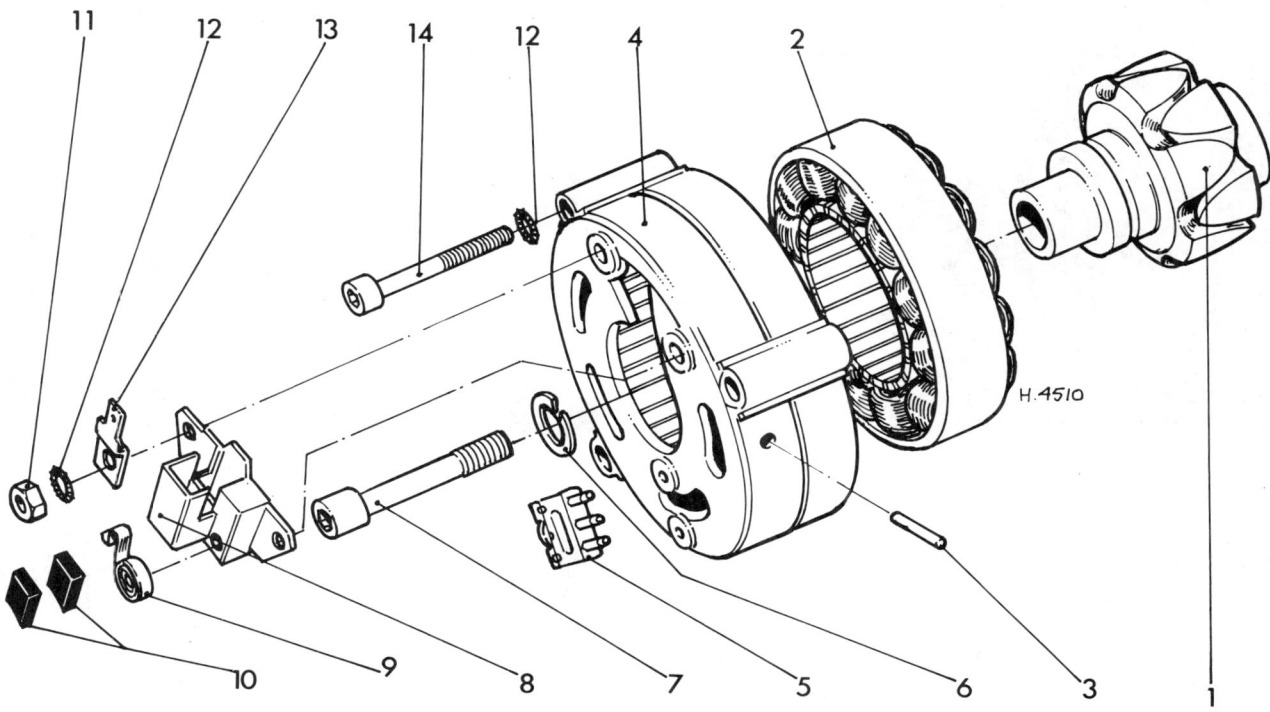

Fig. 9.4 Alternator

1 Rotor
2 Stator
3 Spring dowel pin – 2 off
4 Alternator housing
5 Three-pin connector
6 Lock washer
7 Rotor retaining bolt
8 Brush holder
9 Brush spring
10 Brush
11 Nut
12 Lock washer
13 Terminal
14 Allen screw – 3 off

7 Alternator: removal

1 Disconnect the battery negative (earth) lead.
2 Slacken the horn fixing screws.
3 Unscrew the three hexagon socket cap screws and remove the front engine cover.
4 Pull off the three-pin output socket from the alternator plug. Pull off the two leads to the brush holder terminals and the third alternator lead on all later models. The wire colours are given in the accompanying illustration.
5 Pull up the alternator brushes and wedge them clear of the slip rings with the ends of the brush springs.
6 Unscrew the three Allen screws and withdraw the stator. To remove the rotor unscrew its retaining Allen bolt. Note that the bolt will slacken and then tighten for a while before it is released. Obtain a length of metal rod approximately 6 mm (0.24 in) in diameter and 40 – 50 mm (1.6 – 2.0 in) long. Insert this into the rotor centre, refit the rotor retaining bolt and tighten it on to the end of the rod. The threads in the rotor itself, near its front end, will allow the centre bolt to push against the head of the rod as it is tightened and draw off the rotor. If the rotor proves stubborn, tap smartly on the bolt head to jar the rotor free.
7 Withdraw the rotor.

7.5 Disconnect alternator leads and wedge brushes with spring tails

7.6a Remove three Allen screws to release stator

7.6b To remove stator, unscrew retaining Allen bolt ...

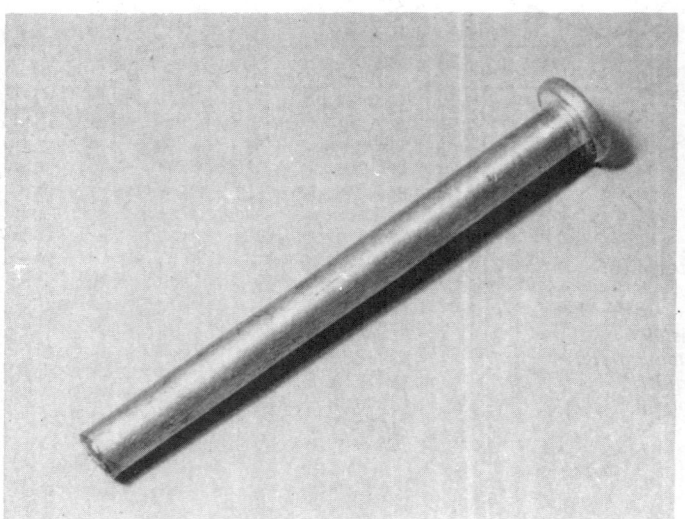

7.6c ... insert extractor pin (see text) ...

7.7 ... tighten retaining bolt on to pin to draw off rotor

8 Alternator: overhaul

1 The only alternator components which wear in use are the brushes. Check that they are free to move in their holders and that they are kept under firm pressure against the slip rings by their springs.

2 Brushes should normally be renewed when they have worn to 50% or less of their original length. Unfortunately there is some doubt about the original length. BMW make no recommendations and do not specify lengths, and Bosch specify an original length of 10 mm (0.4 in) which gives a minimum length of 5 mm (0.2 in). However, the brand new brushes on the R80RT model featured in this Manual measured 16.5 mm (0.65 in) and those purchased for the author's R100/7 measured 16 mm (0.63 in), which would give a minimum length of 8 mm (0.32 in). The second set of brushes mentioned were coloured black from the tip to exactly half-way, from where they became copper coloured; it is reasonable to assume that this is intended to be a form of wear limit indicator in which the brushes are to be renewed if no more black material can be seen.

3 Owners are advised to treat brushes as suspect if they are worn to 8 mm or less. If a friendly BMW dealer will allow you to measure the new brushes in his spares department you can calculate the minimum length and compare this with the length of those fitted. Whenever new brushes are fitted, measure their length, calculate the minimum length and note this (mark it on the inside of the engine front cover with a felt marker).

4 The two nuts on the brush holder, visible from the front of the alternator stator, retain the blade terminals only.

5 To replace the brushes, unscrew the two nuts accessible from inside the stator housing, remove the spring washers and take off the brush housing. Note the insulating washers and bush on the right-hand stud (viewed from the front of the housing).

6 When soldered new brushes in position, do not allow solder to run down the brush tails towards the brushes. Note that the brush tails locate in slots behind the brushes.

7 Clean dirty slip rings with petrol, or if necessary very fine glass paper. **Do not** use emery paper. Scored slip rings must be skimmed in

Chapter 9 Electrical system

a lathe, but this must not reduce their diameter to less than the minimum specified.

8 Applying up to 40 volts ac, check for continuity between both slip rings in turn and each of the rotor steel claw poles; no continuity (ie infinite resistance) should be found. Check the exciter winding by measuring the resistance across the slip rings; the reading obtained should be similar to that specified.

9 Measure the resistance between each pair of terminals on the stator output three-pin plug. The reading obtained should be close to that specified.

9 Diode board: removal

1 If the test described in Section 6 proves the diode board to be faulty, it must be renewed, but your findings should always be confirmed by a BMW dealer or an auto-electrical expert before this is done.
2 Remove the engine front cover and disconnect the battery negative (earth) lead.
3 Remove the four retaining nuts or Allen screws and their washers, withdraw the diode board and unplug the wires leading to it.

10 Voltage regulator: removal

1 The voltage regulator, mounted on the right-hand side of the top frame tube, is not adjustable. If it is suspected of being faulty, it should be checked by a BMW dealer or an auto-electrical specialist.
2 To remove, unplug the three-pin plug, unscrew the two screws and remove the regulator with its shield plate.

11 Fuses: replacing

1 A blown fuse can be recognised by the melted metal strip. If a fuse blows repeatedly, the electrical system should be checked to eliminate the fault. Do not put in a fuse of a higher rating – another item may be damaged – or a fire result. The same applies to replacing the fuse with wire. Spare fuses of the correct rating should always be carried.
2 Remove the headlamp.
3 On /5 models, the two fuses are located in two holders attached to the inside of the headlamp shell. On /6 and /7 models the fuses are mounted on the terminal board at the back of the headlamp shell. On all other models they are mounted in a box at the rear of the frame top tube. Raise or remove the seat, lift out the tool tray, unscrew the knurled ring and withdraw the cover.

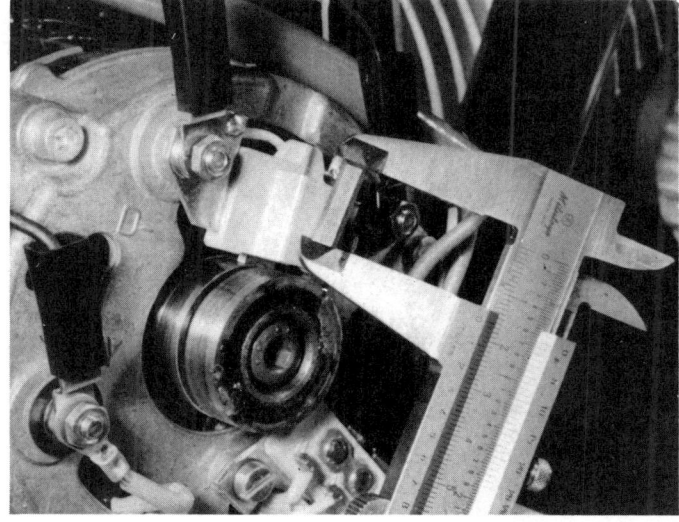

8.2 Measuring alternator brush length – see text for lengths specified

9.3 Diode board is mounted on timing chain cover

10.1a Location of voltage regulator – early mechanical type ...

10.1b ... and later electronic type

11.3 Location of fuses – later models

12 Starter motor: removal

1 Remove the air filter and both covers; see Chapter 3. Remove the petrol tank; see Chapter 4. Slacken the horn fixing screws, unscrew the three fixing screws and remove with the front engine cover. Disconnect the battery earth (negative) lead.
2 Unscrew the two screws, tilt the starter cover and take off to the right.
3 Detach the starter relay lead from the spade terminal on the solenoid. Unscrew the hexagonal nut, remove the spring washer and the heavy gauge starter cable.
4 Remove the two bolts, nuts and washers at the rear of the starter motor. Also remove the hexagonal bolt which is accessible through a hole in the timing chain cover.
5 Lift the starter motor clear of its housing.

13 Starter motor: overhaul

1 To renew the brushes, remove the two nuts, washers and the starter motor end bracket. Note that there are two additional washers under the bracket. Unscrew the two screws and remove with the washers and dustcap.
2 Remove the circlip and the shims from the armature shaft.
3 Unscrew the two long starter housing screws. These have the threaded extensions for fixing the end bracket. Take off the commutator cover. Examine the brushes and ensure that they move freely.
4 Pull up the springs of the two brushes attached to the brush holder, partly withdraw the brushes and wedge them in raised position with the springs. Pull up the springs of the remaining two brushes attached to the field coils and remove the brushes completely. Remove the brush holder backplate.
5 If the brushes have worn to half their original length, they must be renewed. However the original length is not known. Refer to Section 8, paragraphs 2 and 3; again BMW do not make any recommendations and while Bosch specify a length of 11.5 mm (0.45 in) it is not clear whether this is the original length or the wear limit. Owners should proceed according to the advice given in Section 8. When renewing the brushes do not allow solder to run up the copper brush tails, towards their heads.
6 Clean the commutator with fine glass paper, not emery. Ensure that the commutator segments are undercut, that is the insulation between each segment should be 0.5 mm (0.020 inch) below the commutator surface. Use a hacksaw blade ground to the correct thickness to undercut the insulation. If the commutator is badly scored, it must be skimmed to a fine surface finish. Do not reduce the diameter below 33 mm (1.299 inch). Note the washer and insulating washer on the armature shaft.
7 When refitting the commutator cover, position the brush holder backplate so that the long screws pass through the two slots in the edge of the plate.
8 To remove the starter pinion, first detach the field coil lead from the solenoid. Unscrew the retaining screws and remove the solenoid, disengage from the pinion engaging lever.
9 Remove the brush holder plate as previously described. Pull the armature with pinion and pinion housing out of the starter body.
10 Unscrew the engaging lever pivot screw and take out the armature with engaging lever.
11 Push the thrust ring clear of the wire circlip and remove the circlip. Take off the starter pinion assembly.
12 A new pinion housing bush may be pressed into place, after soaking it in engine oil for 30 minutes. The end of the bush should be flush with the housing.
13 Inspect the field coils for scorching or charring. Electrical checking of the armature and field coils and renewal of the field coils, has to be left to a specialist.
14 Before reassembly, coat the quick thread and the engaging ring with Bosch silicone grease Ft 2 v 3. Check the armature endfloat, which is adjusted by means of shims.

12.3 Disconnect starter motor leads

12.4 Starter motor front mounting bolt is accessible through hole in timing chain cover

13.8 Disconnect field coil lead (arrowed) from solenoid

13.14 Armature endfloat is controlled by shims

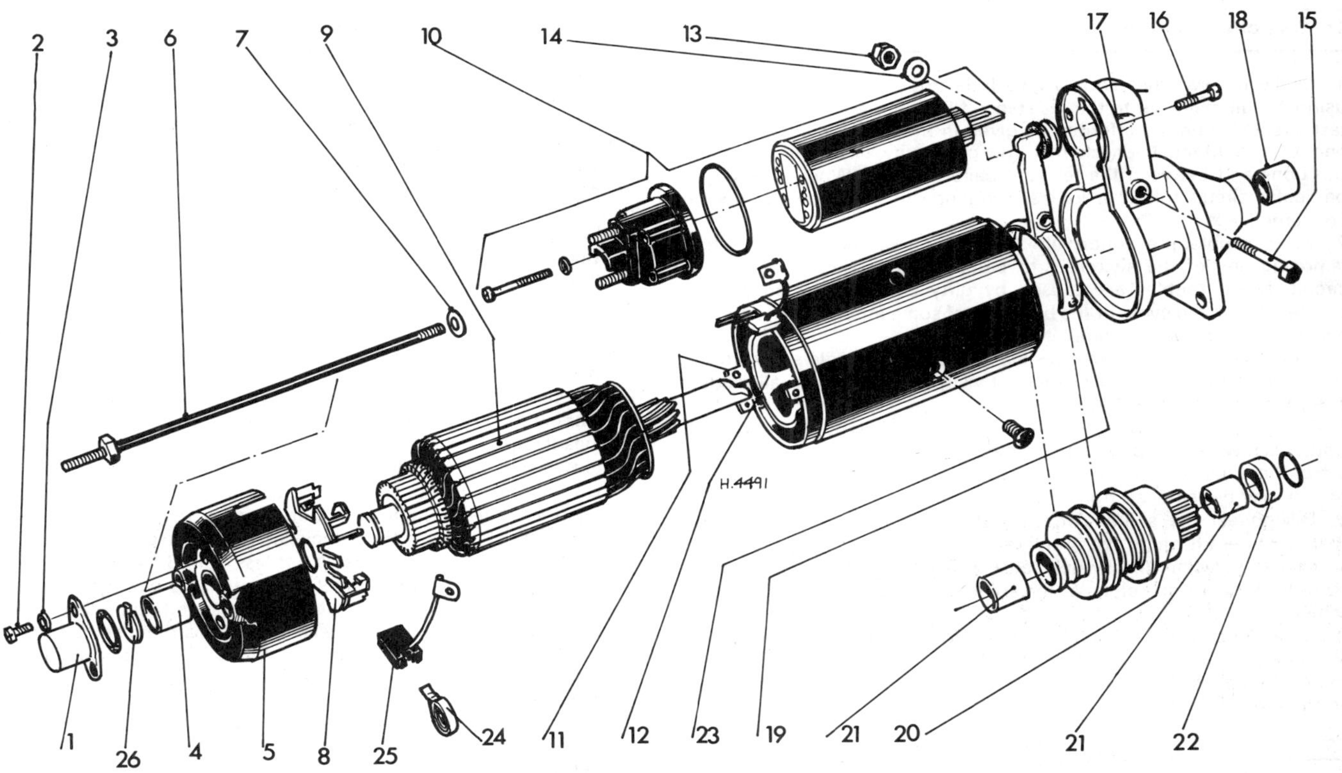

Fig. 9.5 Starter motor

1 End cap
2 Screw
3 Spring washer
4 Bush
5 Commutator cover
6 Stud
7 Spring washer
8 Brush carrier
9 Armature
10 Starter solenoid
11 Insulating strip
12 Field coil
13 Nut
14 Spring washer
15 Pivot bolt
16 Countersunk screw
17 Drive housing
18 Bronze bush
19 Lever
20 Starter pinion
21 Bush
22 Stop ring
23 Countersunk screw
24 Brush spring
25 Brush set
26 Circlip

14 Relays: location and testing

1 The various relays are mounted on the frame top tubes (with the exception of the light relay which is in the headlamp), under the fuel tank. In some cases (usually early models only) the wires have separate connectors, but usually the relays are pressed into a connecting plug.
2 If a relay which has individual wires leading to it, is removed at any time, make a written note as each wire is removed, showing which colour wire should be connected to each terminal (the numbers are stamped into the relay itself). Use the colours of the wires shown in the diagrams at the back of this Manual to indentify each relay.
3 If a relay is suspected of being faulty, it must be renewed; repairs are not possible.
4 In the case of the turn signal relay note that the battery must be checked and found to be fully charged, the bulbs must be in working order and of the correct wattage, and the lamp wiring and earth connections must be in good condition. All these should be checked before the relay is suspected.
5 The starter and horn relays on /7 models (where fitted) are almost identical in appearance and may be interchanged or incorrectly fitted if care if not taken. To check this detach the battery negative terminal lead and touch it several times to the terminal post. If a clicking sound is heard the wrong relay is fitted (starter in place of horn) and is being energised. If the correct horn relay is fitted, no clicks will be heard. If the starter relay is incorrect it will be impossible to start the machine, so the fault will be evident.

15 Switches: general

1 While the switches should give little trouble, they can be tested using a multimeter set to the resistance function or a battery and bulb test circuit. Using the information given in the wiring diagrams at the end of this Manual, check that full continuity exists in all switch positions and between the relevant pairs of wires. When checking a particular circuit follow a logical sequence to eliminate the switch concerned.
2 As a simple precaution always disconnect the battery before removing any of the switches, to prevent the possibility of a short circuit. Most troubles are caused by dirty contacts, which can be cleaned, but in the event of the breakage of some internal part, it will be necessary to renew the complete switch.
3 Note that handlebar switches are secured by a single screw to the rear of the handlebar lever clamp or twistgrip assembly on all models except /5 and /6 up to 1975.
4 The early models' switches are removed by taking out the two small slotted screws above and beneath the switch tumbler. Pull the switch out of the housing and remove the slotted screw within. The complete switch may be removed from the handlebar.
5 Disconnect the switch wires inside the headlamp and pull the switch harness through the grommet.
6 When replacing the switch, ensure that it seats correctly in its housing. If necessary, chamfer the spigots of new switches slightly to achieve this.
7 On all models, note that if a switch is found to be faulty it can only be renewed. There is little to lose, therefore, by attempting to dismantle and repair it although whether this is successful or not depends entirely on the owner's skill.

16 Horn: location and adjustment

1 A single or twin horn arrangement is fitted according to the model. Each horn is mounted on a resilient steel bracket on the frame front downtubes. If the horn fails to operate, or works feebly, it can be adjusted by slackening the locknut and turning the adjuster screw in or out by a small amount until the best sound is obtained.
2 If the horn fails to work at all, first check that power is reaching it by disconnecting the wires. Substitute a 12 volt bulb, switch on the ignition and press the horn button. If the bulb lights, the circuit is proved good and the horn is at fault; if the bulb does not light, there is a fault in the circuit which must be found and rectified. On twin-horn systems check the relay first.
3 To test the horn itself, connect a fully-charged 12 volt battery directly to the horn. If it does not sound, a gentle tap on the outside may free the internal contacts. If this fails, the horn must be renewed as repairs are not possible, but there is little to be lost by attempting to dismantle the horn and repair it; Fiamm horns for example can be dismantled and their contacts can be cleaned quite easily.

17 Bulbs: renewal

Headlamp and parking lamp

1 On machines with RS fairings unscrew the four knurled nuts and withdraw the headlamp glass and light tunnel. Unscrew the single screw at the bottom of the rim and remove the unit.
2 On machines with RT fairings peel back the rubber trim at each corner of the headlamp glass and unscrew the four cross-head screws, taking care not to crack the glass. Remove the glass and light tunnel. Unscrew the single screw at the bottom of the headlamp rim and withdraw the headlamp reflector unit.
3 On R80G/S models remove the four screws to release the headlamp trim then slacken both headlamp retaining bolts and pull forwards the reflector unit.
4 On all other models unscrew the single screw at the bottom of the headlamp rim and pull away the headlamp reflector unit.
5 To remove the headlamp bulb from the reflector unit on /5 models, push the bulb carrier down, turn anticlockwise, and remove the reflector with the bulb. Pull the bulb from the spring. When replacing, ensure that the indexing tab aligns with the notch. Push the pilot bulb out of the reflector from the inside (through the main bulb hole). Avoid touching the inside surface of the reflector. The pins on the bulb must locate in the notches in the reflector. When the headlamp bulb carrier is replaced, the pilot bulb contact must be at the top.
6 To remove the headlamp bulb from the reflector unit on all other models: pull off the main bulb socket. Hinge back the wire retaining clip and pull the bulb out, it is located by notches. Pull the pilot bulb holder out of the reflector, press the bulb inwards and turn anticlockwise to remove, except on models fitted with RS or RT fairings. Remove the two lens retaining screws from the parking lamp set in the fairing above the headlamp, remove the lens and withdraw the bulb.
7 Before replacing bulbs, ensure that the contacts are clean.
8 When replacing the headlamp, hook the rim over the top of the shell and push the bottom of the rim over the retaining clips at the bottom of the shell. Ensure that it is firmly fitted, since it doesn't bounce!
9 Headlamp beam height is adjusted by slackening the two headlamp fixing bolts fixing the lamp to the fork brackets and pivoting the headlamp. Tyre pressures should first be checked and the rider should be seated normally.
10 UK lighting regulations stipulate that the lighting system must be arranged so that the light does not dazzle a person standing in the same horizontal plane as the vehicle, at a distance greater than 25 feet from the lamp, whose eye level is not less than 3 feet 6 inches above that plane. It is easy to approximate this setting by placing the machine 25 feet away from a wall, on a level road, and setting the beam height so that it is concentrated at the same height as the distance from the centre of the headlamp to the ground. In addition, the headlamp must be capable of being dipped.

Turn signal and stop/tail lamp

11 Unscrew the two screws securing the lamp lens, remove the lens and reflector and separate. Check the condition of the gasket.
12 Check the electrical connections on the rear of the reflector, particularly the earths.
13 The bulbs are bayonet type; the rear/stop lamp bulb has double filaments, with off-set pins to ensure correct orientation. Always replace turn signal bulbs with those of the correct rating, or the flashing rate will be upset.
14 When replacing the lenses, note that they are marked 'TOP'. Do not over-tighten the screws and break the lenses.

Instrument and warning lamps

15 Dismantle the instruments as described in Chapter 6. Withdraw the bulbs and renew them. Use only bulbs of the correct rating, especially on the charge warning lamp which supplies the current to excite the alternator.

14.1a Turn signal relay and warning lamps (arrowed) are inside headlamp shell – /5 only

14.1b Location of relays – /7 (and later /6) ...

14.1c ... and later models. Use wire colours to identify each relay, if in doubt

17.5a Headlamp bulb removal, /5 models – withdraw bulb carrier with bulb ...

17.5b ... then pull bulb off carrier spring. Do not touch glass envelope of quartz-halogen bulbs

17.5c Pilot bulb pins locate on notches – /5 models

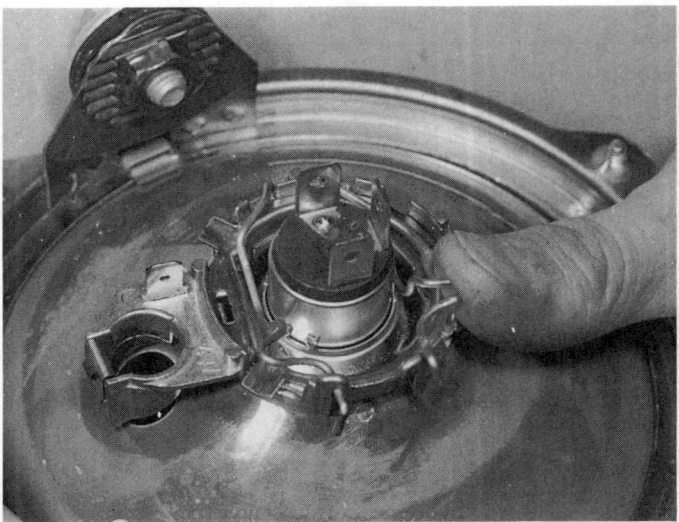

17.6a Release wire clip to withdraw headlamp bulb on later models

17.6b Parking (pilot) lamp bulb is separately mounted in RS or RT fairings

17.11 Remove retaining screws to release lamp lens – keep reflector clean

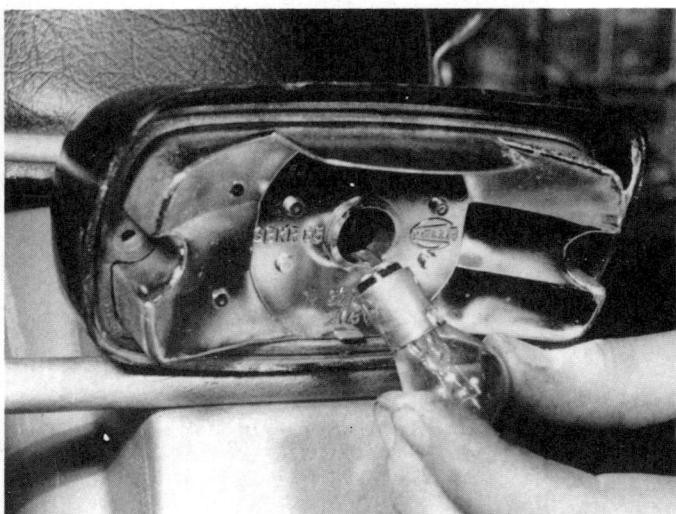

17.12 Stop/tail lamp bulb has offset retaining pins to ensure correct fitting

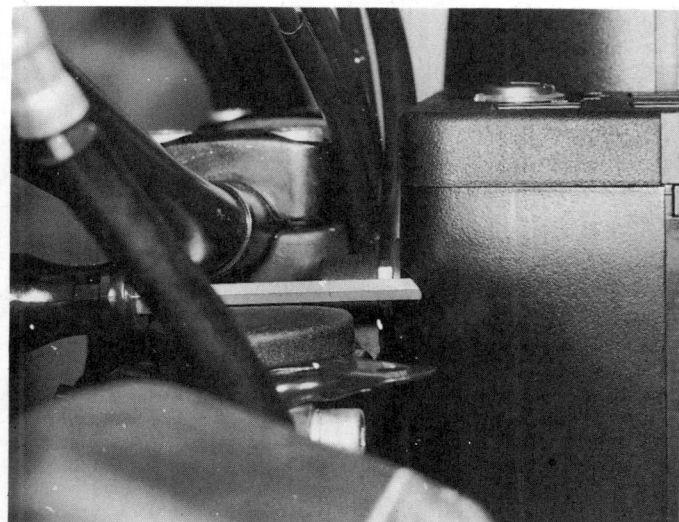

17.15a Instrument panel bulb renewal – R80G/S – remove four screws from rear of headlamp

17.15b Bulb holders are of bayonet fitting and carry capless bulbs

The R65 model

The R80RT model

The R100RS model

The R100RT model

Chapter 10 The 1986 to 1988 models

Contents

Introduction	1
Routine maintenance: modified service intervals	2
Routine maintenance: revised procedures	3
Crankshaft rear oil seal: refitting – R80GS and R100GS models	4
Gearbox: modifications – all models	5
Recommended fuel: general – all models	6
Evaporative Emission Control System: general – US R80, R80RT, R100RS and R100RT models	7
Exhaust system: general	8
Front forks: damper rod assembly overhaul – all R45/65 models and all other models from 1981 on	9
Front forks: modifications – R65, R80, R80RT, R100RS and R100RT models	10
Front forks: damping components alignment – R65, R80, R80RT, R100RS and R100RT models	11
Front forks: general – R80GS and R100GS models	12
Fairing mounting: modification – all RT models	13
Dualseat mounting: repair – R80GS and R100GS models	14
Instrument mountings: general – R100RS and R100RT models	15
Final drive and rear suspension: general – all models except the R80GS and R100GS	16
Rear bevel drive housing: removal – R80GS and R100GS models	17
Rear bevel drive housing: refitting – R80GS and R100GS models	18
Swinging arm and driveshaft: removal and refitting – R80GS and R100GS models	19
Driveshaft: general – R80GS and R100GS models	20
Wheel track offset: all models	21
Rear suspension unit: general – R80GS and R100GS models	22
Wheels, brakes and tyres: general	23
Rear wheel: removal and refitting	24
Wheel rim: repair – R80GS and R100GS models	25
Tubeless tyre valves: renewal – later models	26
Battery: removal and refitting	27
Diode board (rectifier): testing – all models	28
Fuses: general – R80GS and R100GS models	29
Valeo starter motor: servicing – R80GS and R100GS models	30
Stop lamp and clutch interlock switches: general	31

Specifications

Information is given only where different from that given for the equivalent earlier model in the Specifications Sections of Chapters 1 to 9. For R80GS, R100GS, R100RS and R100RT models, information is given only where available.

Model dimensions and weights

Overall width – of handlebars or fairing:
    R65, R100RS .... 800 mm (31.5 in)
    R100RT .... 960 mm (37.8 in)
    R80GS, R100GS .... 1000 mm (39.4 in)

Overall height:
    R65 .... 1115 mm (43.9 in)
    R80GS, R100GS .... 1165 mm (45.9 in)
    R100RS .... 1380 mm (54.3 in)
    R100RT .... 1478 mm (58.2 in)

Seat height – unladen:
    R65, R100RS, R100RT .... 807 mm (31.8 in)
    R80GS, R100GS .... 850 mm (33.5 in)

Overall length:
    R65, R100RS, R100RT .... 2175 mm (85.6 in)
    R80GS, R100GS .... 2290 mm (90.2 in)

Wheelbase – rider seated:
    R65, R100RS, R100RT .... 1440 mm (56.7 in)
    R80GS, R100GS .... 1513 mm (59.6 in)

Ground clearance – rider seated:
    R65, R100RS, R100RT .... 125 mm (4.9 in)
    R80GS, R100GS .... 170 mm (6.7 in)

Kerb weight:
    R65 .... 452 lb (205 kg)
    R80GS, R100GS .... 463 lb (210 kg)
    R100RS .... 505 lb (229 kg)
    R100RT .... 516 lb (234 kg)

Maximum permissible total weight:
    R65, R100RS, R100RT .... 970 lb (440 kg)
    R80GS, R100GS .... 926 lb (420 kg)

Routine maintenance

Engine oil capacity – at oil and filter change:
- R80GS .... 2.25 litres (3.96 Imp pint)
- R100GS .... 2.50 litres (4.40 Imp pint/2.64 US qt)
- Driveshaft oil – R80GS, R100GS .... None
- Rear bevel drive oil – R80GS, R100GS .... 260 cc (0.46 Imp pint/0.28 US qt)

Specifications relating to Chapter 1

Engine

Compression ratio:
- R65 .... 8.7:1
- R100GS 8.5:1
- R100RS, R100RT 8.45:1

Recommended engine speeds – rpm:

	Idle	Max cruising	Max permissible
R100RS 1987	800 – 1100	7200	7400
All 1988 models	800 – 1100	7000	7250

Claimed engine output – DIN:

	Maximum power (kw/hp @ rpm)	Maximum torque (Nm/lbf ft @ rpm)
R65	35/48 @ 7250	47.8/35.3 @ 3500
R80GS	37/50 @ 6500	61.0/45.0 @ 3750
R100GS – UK	44/60 @ 6500	76.0/56.1 @ 3750
R100GS – US	43/58 @ 6500	76.0/56.1 @ 3750
R100RS, R100RT	44/60 @ 6500	74.0/54.6 @ 3500

Compression pressure – R65 .... As R80 1985 on

Valve timing – R100GS, R100RS, R100RT
- Inlet opens .... 10° BTDC
- Inlet closes .... 50° ABDC
- Exhaust opens .... 50° BBDC
- Exhaust closes .... 10° ATDC

Valves and valve seats

Valve head diameter:

	Inlet	Exhaust
All later 800 cc models (approx June 1987 on), R100GS, R100RS, R100RT	42 mm (1.65 in)	40 mm (1.58 in)

Valve seat angle – main seating face:

All later 800 cc models (approx June 1987 on), R100GS, R100RS, R100RT	45°	30°

Specifications relating to Chapter 2

Clutch diaphragm spring – R100GS, R100RS, R100RT .... These models are fitted with a thicker spring identified by a blue paint dot – no further information is available

Specifications relating to Chapter 4

Fuel tank capacity

	Litre	Imp gal	US gal
R100RS, R100RT – US 1988 models:			
Overall	21.0	N/App	5.55
Reserve	5.0	N/App	1.32
R65, R80, R80RT, R100RS, R100RT – UK 1988 models:			
Overall	22.0	4.84	N/App
Reserve	5.0	1.10	N/App
R65, R80, R80RT, R100RS – UK and US 1986 – 87 models:			
Overall	22.0	4.84	5.81
Reserve	2.0	0.44	0.53
R100GS – US:			
Overall	21.7	N/App	5.73
Reserve	4.7	N/App	1.24
R80GS, R100GS – UK:			
Overall	26.0	5.72	N/App
Reserve	4.7	1.03	N/App

Recommended fuel grade – see Section 6 for full details

All models 1985 on with blue spot on cylinder head fin .... Unleaded or leaded regular petrol (gasoline)*

*Regular is defined as:
- Unleaded .... Regular grade petrol (gasoline) to German DIN 51607 standard or equivalent, minimum octane rating of 91 Research Method (RM/RON), 82.5 Motor Method (MM/MON)
- Leaded .... Regular grade petrol (gasoline) to German DIN 51600 standard or equivalent, minimum octane rating of 91 Research Method (RM/RON), 82.5 Motor Method (MM/MON)

Chapter 10 The 1986 to 1988 models

Carburettor
- R80GS — As late UK R80G/S, except that the needle clip position is now 3rd from top
- R100GS, R100RS, R100RT – US models — As US R80, R80RT 1985 on

	R65 – UK and US	R100GS – UK	R100RS, R100RT – UK
Carburettor			
Type LH:			
UK	64/32/359	94/40/123	64/32/363
US	64/32/361	N/App	N/App
Type RH:			
UK	64/32/360	94/40/124	64/32/364
US	64/32/362	N/App	N/App
Choke size	32 mm (1.26 in)	40 mm (1.58 in)	32 mm (1.26 in)
Main jet	130	150	135
Needle jet	2.66	2.66	2.66
Jet needle	46 – 251	46 – 371	46 – 251
Needle clip position – grooves from top	3rd	3rd	3rd
Idle jet	45 (UK) 40 (US)	45	45
Pilot mixture screw – turns out from fully closed	3/4	3/4 – 1	3/4 – 1

Engine lubrication system

Engine oil capacity:

	At oil change	At oil and filter change
R80GS	2.00 lit (3.52 Imp pint)	2.25 lit (3.96 Imp pint)
R100GS	2.25 lit (3.96 Imp pint/2.38 US qt)	2.50 lit (4.40 Imp pint/ 2.64 US qt)

Specifications relating to Chapter 5

Spark plugs
- Make and type – all models 1986 on .... Bosch W7DC
- Electrode gap – all models 1987 on:
  - Standard .... 0.6 – 0.7 mm (0.024 – 0.028 in)
  - Maximum .... 0.9 mm (0.036 in)

Specifications relating to Chapter 6

All specifications
- R65 .... As 1985 on R80
- R100RS, R100RT .... As 1985 on R80RT

Front forks – R80GS, R100GS
- Manufacturer .... Marzocchi
- Suspension travel .... 225 mm (8.86 in)
- Stanchion OD .... 39.936 – 39.975 mm (1.5723 – 1.5738 in)
- Lower leg ID .... 40.160 – 40.199 mm (1.5811 – 1.5826 in)
- Stanchion maximum warpage .... 0.10 mm (0.0039 in)
- Stanchion installed height (test length) .... 180 mm (7.0866 in)
- Fork spring free length .... 445 – 450 mm (17.5197 – 17.7165 in)
- Fork spring wire diameter .... 4.67 – 4.73 mm (0.1839 – 0.1862 in)
- Fork oil capacity – per leg:

	At oil change	At rebuild
Right-hand – cc/Imp fl oz/US fl oz	440 ± 10/15.49 ± 0.35/ 14.88 ± 0.34	470 ± 10/16.54 ± 0.35/ 15.89 ± 0.34
Left-hand – cc/Imp fl oz/US fl oz	410 ± 10/14.43 ± 0.35/ 13.86 ± 0.34	470 ± 10/16.54 ± 0.35/ 15.89 ± 0.34

- Recommended fork oil:
  - Aral .... Weich (soft) telescopic fork oil – for winter use
  - Aral .... Hart (firm) telescopic fork oil – only for temperatures above 15°C (59°F)
  - Shell (Italy) .... EB/B/33 – approved by Marzocchi

Torque wrench settings – R80 and R80RT (late 1985 on), R65, R100RS, R100RT

Component	Nm	lbf ft
Fork leg top nut	107	79
Oil filler plug	20	15
All other torque settings	As R80/R80RT 1985 on (see Chapter 6)	

Torque wrench settings – R80GS, R100GS

	Nm	lbf ft
Fork leg top slotted nut	40	29.5
Oil filler plug	10.5	7.5
Handlebar clamp bolts	20 – 24	15 – 18
Steering stem top nut	107	79
Fork leg top plug	18 – 22	13 – 16
Top and bottom fork yoke pinch bolts	13.2 – 16.8	9.5 – 12.5
Fork brace mounting bolts	13.2 – 16.8	9.5 – 12.5
Oil drain plug	5.3 – 6.7	4 – 5
Damper rod Allen screw	13 – 17	9.5 – 12.5
Rear frame section mounting bolts	16	12
Centre stand mountings	41.8	31

Specifications relating to Chapter 7

Driveshaft – R80GS, R100GS
  Type .... Enclosed shaft incorporating bonded rubber damper, needle roller bearing universal joint at both front and rear ends
  Oil quantity and type .... None – all bearings sealed for life
  Rear splined coupling lubricant .... Staburags NBU 30 PTM compound, Optimol Paste PL, Uni Moly C220 Slip Agent or equivalent

Rear bevel drive
  Reduction ratio:
    R65 .... 3.36:1 (37/11T)
    R80GS 3.20:1 (32/10T)
    R100GS 3.09:1 (34/11T)
    R100RS, R100RT 3.00:1 (33/11T)
  Tooth backlash – R80GS, R100GS .... 0.07 – 0.16 mm (0.0028 – 0.0063 in)
  Taper roller bearing preload – R80GS, R100GS ... 0.05 – 0.10 mm (0.0020 – 0.0039 in)
  Oil quantity – R80GS, R100GS .... 260 cc (0.46 Imp pint, 0.28 US qt)
  Recommended oil .... As earlier models

Rear suspension – R65, R100RS, R100RT .... As 1985 R80, R80RT

Rear suspension – R80GS, R100GS
  Type .... Single coil sprung suspension unit with gas-assisted hydraulic damping acting on a swinging arm, (which encloses the driveshaft) via a pivoted 'floating' rear bevel drive housing – movement controlled by a separate torque arm (BMW Paralever)
  Suspension travel .... 180 mm (7.09 in)
  Spring free length .... 307 – 311 mm (12.0866 – 12.2441 in)
  Spring wire diameter .... 11.71 – 11.89 mm (0.4610 – 0.4681 in)
  Pivot bearings:

	Swinging arm	Bevel drive housing
Type	Taper roller	Taper needle roller
Reference number (size – mm)	32203 (17 x 40 x 17)	N/Av (17 x 32 x 10)

Torque wrench settings – R80GS, R100GS

Component	kgf m	lbf ft
Driveshaft flange to output flange 12-sided bolts	35 – 45	26 – 33
Bevel drive housing pivots:		
Left-hand bearing pivot stub	98 – 112	72 – 83
Right-hand bearing pivot shaft	6.8 – 7.8	5 – 5.5
Right-hand bearing pivot shaft locknut	98 – 112	72 – 83
Swinging arm pivots:		
Pivot shafts – to preload bearings	18 – 22	13 – 16
Pivot shafts – normal setting	8 – 12	6 – 9
Pivot shaft locknuts	95 – 119	70 – 88
Bevel drive housing torque arm mountings:		
Front-to frame	38 – 46	28 – 34
Rear-to housing	31 – 35	23 – 26
Rear suspension unit mountings	26 – 32	19 – 23.5
Bevel drive pinion retaining nut	180 – 220	133 – 162
Bevel drive cover/housing retaining bolts	19 – 23	14 – 17
Oil filler plug – rear bevel drive	18 – 22	13 – 16
Oil drain plug – rear bevel drive	22 – 28	16 – 21

Specifications relating to Chapter 8

All specifications
  R65 .... As 1985 on R80
  R100RS, R100RT .... As UK 1985 on R80/R80RT with twin front discs

Wheels – R80GS, R100GS
  Type .... Wire-spoked in cross-over pattern

	Front	Rear
Size:		
R80GS up to frame number 6 245 617	1.85 x 21 MT	2.50 x 17 MT
All later R80GS, R100GS	1.85 x 21 MT H2	2.50 x 17 MT H2

  Wheel bearings .... As 1985 R80/R80RT

Brakes – R80GS, R100GS
  Brake disc standard thickness .... 6 mm (0.2362 in)/minimum 5.4 mm (0.2126 in)
  All other information .... As 1985 on UK R80/R80RT with twin front disc

Tyres – R80GS, R100GS
  Type:
    R80GS up to frame number 6 245 617 .... Tubed
    All later R80GS, R100GS .... Tubeless

Chapter 10 The 1986 to 1988 models

Size:
Front ....
Rear ....

Tyre pressures – R80GS, R100GS ....

Specifications relating to Chapter 9

Electrical system – R80GS, R100GS
Fuses ....

Battery
Manufacturer ....
Capacity:
R65 and R80G/S, 1986 on models ....
All models 1987 on ....

Starter motor – R80GS, R100GS
Manufacturer ....
Type ....
Brush standard length – measured ....

Bulbs
R80GS, R100GS ....
All other models ....

R80GS	R100GS
90/90 – 21 54 S	90/90 – 21 54 T
130/80 – 17 65 S	130/80 – 17 65 T

As 1985 on R80/R80RT

7.5A (x 2) – Brown

BMW – Mareg

20 Ah (30 Ah optional for R65)
25 Ah (30 Ah possible on R100RS, R100RT)

Valeo
06F 80091 D6RA 7 12V 0.7kw
14 mm (0.5512 in)

As R80G/S
As R80/R80RT

1 Introduction

1 The first nine Chapters of this manual cover all BMW twins sold in the US and UK from 1969 to 1985. This Chapter covers those later models sold subsequently, mentioning only those points which require an alteration in servicing procedures or specifications.
2 To use this manual when working on one of these later models therefore, first check always in this Chapter. If no information is given that is relevant to the task in hand, then it can be assumed that the procedure or specification required is unchanged from that given in Chapters 1 to 9.
3 Note that since most later models are based on the R80 and R80RT 1985 models described in the previous Chapters, the information required will usually be found under the heading of these models.
4 **Note:** As explained in the preliminary sections of this Manual, machines in Chapters 1 to 9 are identified by their BMW model or production year which starts well in advance of the calendar year (see Ordering spare parts). Except in one or two cases, where modifications have been introduced during a production run, this practice is continued in this Chapter.
5 Given below is a brief description of the models covered in this Chapter followed by their dates of import, which will assist owners in identifying their machines.

1986 model year
6 With the '248-type' models (R45, R65, R65LS) having been discontinued at the end of 1985, the new R65 (usually known as the R65/85, or 'Monolever' model') was introduced. This consisted of a slightly detuned 650 cc engine transplanted into the cycle parts of the R80/85 model, using K100-type front forks and Monolever rear suspension, as well as the quieter exhaust system.
7 Apart from minor modifications to components such as brake master cylinder sealing diaphragms, and a black-finished fork brace and lower legs, the R80, R80RT and R80G/S models continued unchanged. In the US, the evaporative emission control system, fitted to 1985 California models, was now fitted to all 800 cc 49-state models; note that the R65 was not required to comply with this legislation.

1987 model year
8 Apart from the modifications described elsewhere in this Chapter the R65, R80 and R80RT continued unchanged in both the US and the UK.
9 In the US the R80G/S was discontinued at the end of 1986, but in the UK 1987 models received detail alterations such as black rocker covers, a fork brace as standard, and revised paintwork and graphics.
10 During 1987 BMW responded to strong customer pressure by re-introducing the 1000 cc twins. At first a limited production run of models were released in RS trim; these proved so successful that a further batch were assembled, although none in fact reached the US until the 1988 production year.
11 The R100RS employed a detuned 1000 cc engine transplanted, like the R65, into the transmission and cycle parts of the R80/85 model; it is of course distinguished by the fitting of the R100RS-type fairing that remained virtually unchanged since its introduction in 1976.
12 The engine is tuned to produce as broad a spread of torque as possible consistent with a power output of 60 bhp; BMW now state that this is a comfortable maximum output for their flat-twin engine.

1988 model year
13 In the UK the R80G/S was replaced by the Paralever-type R80GS and the R65, R80 and R80RT continued unchanged. The R100RT model was introduced, featuring an RT fairing on the R80/85-type cycle parts and using an identical detuned 1000 cc engine to that of the R100RS.
14 In the US the 650 cc and 800 cc models were discontinued, being replaced by the R100RS and R100RT.
15 In both the US and UK the R100GS was introduced; it is accompanied by the R80GS in the UK. These 'trail-bike' style models feature similar engines and transmissions to their road-oriented counterparts but differ most noticeably in the styling and suspension. Marzocchi front forks are fitted that were developed in conjunction with BMW, but the single most obvious feature is the new rear suspension.
16 The R80GS and R100GS are fitted with BMW's Paralever rear suspension in which two further pivots are installed at the rear end of the swinging arm, so that the rear bevel drive housing is permitted a certain amount of movement in the same plane as the suspension. This effectively increases the radius of wheel movement and, by linking the housing to the frame with a separate torque arm and the suspension unit, forms a virtually parallelogram-shaped linkage.
17 The effect is to remove most of this pitching, which permits the use of long-travel suspension. To allow the system to work effectively, the brake rod is replaced by a cable and the driveshaft features a second universal joint, placed next to the splined coupling at its rear end.

Model	UK	US
R65 649 cc	Oct '85 to Dec '88	Nov '85 to '87
R80 797 cc	Oct '85 on	Nov '85 to '87
R80RT 797 cc	Oct '85 on	Nov '85 to '87
R80G/S 797 cc	Oct '85 to Sep '87	Nov '85 to '86
R80GS 797 cc	Sept '87 on	Not imported
R100GS 979 cc	Sept '87 on	Oct '87 on
R100RS 979 cc	June '87 on	Oct '87 on
R100RT 979 cc	Sept '87 on	Oct '87 on

2 Routine maintenance: modified service intervals

1988 on US models
1 Owners should note that the specified service intervals for the 1988 on US models (R100GS, R100RS, R100RT) have been revised. The interval is now 4000 miles (6000 km). Furthermore, BMW now recommend that only one major service is necessary each year if the machine does not cover a high mileage.

2 In practice this means that the intervals are now as follows:

Minor service every 8000 miles (12 000 km), starting with the first 4000 miles (6000 km), or every six months at least.

Major service every 8000 miles (12 000 km), starting with the first 8000 miles (12 000 km), or at least once annually.

3 All other intervals remain the same as shown in the Routine maintenance section of this manual.

UK models
4 Owners should note that for all later UK models, BMW now recommend that only one major service is necessary each year if the machine does not cover a high mileage. This means that the minor service must be carried out at least every six months and the major service at least once annually. All other intervals remain the same.

3 Routine maintenance: revised procedures

Engine oil and filter – R100GS
1 Place the machine on its centre stand, remove the dipstick and engine oil drain plug and allow the oil to drain into a suitable container, as described in the Routine maintenance section of this manual.

2 While the oil is draining, unscrew the two banjo union bolts securing the oil cooler pipes to the adaptor, secure the pipes out of the way and unscrew the three bolts securing the adaptor over the filter chamber. As the adaptor is withdrawn, note carefully the number and location of the seals. Hook out the old filter element, wipe out the chamber and fit a new element, metal end facing outwards.

3 New sealing O-rings will usually be provided with a genuine BMW oil filter; use grease to stick these in place on the adaptor and refit it to the crankcase. Tighten the adaptor mounting bolts securely, then refit the oil cooler pipes. Fit new sealing washers if necessary and tighten the banjo bolts carefully but securely, ensuring that the pipes are positioned well clear of the exhaust system. Refit the engine oil drain plug, having renewed its sealing washer if necessary, and tighten to the specified torque setting.

4 Refill the crankcase with the specified amount of oil, then start the engine and allow it to idle for a few minutes until the fresh oil is fully distributed around the engine. Switch off the engine, allow one or two minutes for the oil level to settle, then check it using the dipstick and top up if necessary.

Driveshaft oil – R80GS, R100GS
5 Note that there is no oil in the swinging arm on Paralever equipped models. Owners should check the condition of the driveshaft joints and splined coupling whenever the assembly is dismantled and should apply a thin smear of the specified grease to the splines on reassembly. All bearings are sealed for life and cannot be lubricated.

Swinging arm pivot bearings – R80GS, R100GS
6 BMW state that due to the considerable expansion and contraction as the suspension moves through its travel, the 'Paralever' swinging arm has to be vented via the swinging arm pivot bearings. This, coupled with the use of sealed bearings, means that the swinging arm pivot bearings must **not** be greased using a grease gun or similar, in spite of the instructions in some BMW Rider's Handbooks.

3.1 R100GS model – ensure oil cooler matrix is kept clear of dirt at all times

3.2a Disconnect oil cooler pipes at banjo union bolts (arrowed) before removing adaptor ...

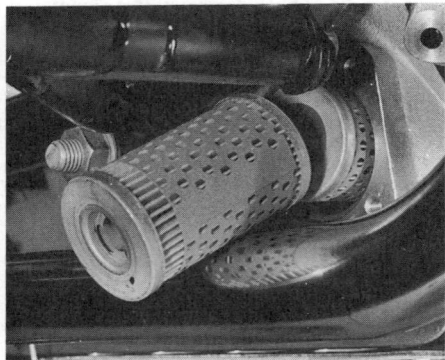

3.2b ... to release oil filter. Note which end is outermost

3.3 Ensure seals are correctly installed before refitting adaptor

3.11 Sidestand pivot is integral with crashbars on R100GS model

Spark plug renewal – all models 1987 on

7 Owners should note that the manufacturer now recommends that spark plugs are renewed automatically, regardless of age or apparent condition, if the electrode gap is ever found to have widened to the maximum limit or more. If this ever proves necessary both plugs should be renewed as a set. Note however that the spark plugs should be renewed at every major service (ie once annually, at least) and so should not reach this limit at all, under normal running conditions. If the electrodes are found to be eroding much more quickly than normal the cause must be found and rectified as soon as possible.

Rear bevel drive oil – R80GS, R100GS

8 As a separate level plug is not fitted, follow the procedure for models up to 1980 in Routine Maintenance. Note revised oil capacity.

Air filter element – all models

9 Whenever the air filter element is renewed, check carefully that its frame seats correctly into the edge of the filter lower half. It may be necessary to pare some material away carefully from the edge of the element frame, particularly at the rear bottom edge (underneath the 'Top/Oben' marking) until the element seats correctly. Modified filters have been developed which are fitted to all new machines and replace all older items in dealers stocks.

Checking the rear suspension – R80GS, R100GS

10 When checking the rear suspension on these models, do not forget to check the bevel drive housing pivot bearings as well as the swinging arm pivots, and do not confuse the two if free play is detected. Check the torque arm mountings, the gaiters, and all fasteners.

Checking the stand pivots – R100GS

11 When carrying out the regular check of the controls and stand pivots, note that the side stand is mounted on the crashbars; check, therefore, that the crashbar mountings are securely fastened whenever the stand itself is checked.

4 Crankshaft rear oil seal: refitting – R80GS and R100GS models

1 A new type of oil seal is fitted at the crankshaft rear end and gearbox output shaft, the latter being discussed in the following Section.

2 Instead of a feather-edged lip which relies for its efficiency upon a garter spring, the new type of seal incorporates a lip of a PTFE material (eg Teflon) which is not pre-shaped on delivery and relies upon its own inherent elasticity for the required contact pressure.

3 Before installation the seal must be shaped, for two hours, so that the crankshaft thrust ring will pass through it with the minimum of effort and risk of damage. This is best achieved by pressing the seal on to the BMW service tool, No. 11.1.880, which is specified as the installing drift.

4 If the specified tool is not available the seal can be shaped by pressing it carefully over the thrust ring; first polish away any burrs or sharp edges from the thrust ring using fine abrasive paper so that the seal lip is not damaged on installation. Whichever method is used, take care not to damage the spiral on the seal lip.

5 Once shaped, the seal can be tapped into place as described in Chapter 1, with its open side inwards (towards the crankshaft). Remember that the seal must be driven in to exactly the correct depth so that there is no risk of contact with the flywheel.

6 When refitting the thrust ring, note that the seal will bed in more rapidly if no oil or grease is present (ie installed dry); again take care not to damage the seal as the thrust ring is inserted.

5 Gearbox: modifications – all models

Gearbox/engine mountings

1 On all later models the upper right-hand engine to gearbox fastener is changed from a stud to a bolt. The bolt may be hexagon-headed or of the Allen type, depending on the year and model.

Meshing angle – input gears

2 From gearbox number Z or ZSA 58 225 on (during the 1982 model year) the meshing angle of the helical-cut input gear train was altered to 17.5°. Gears cut to this angle are identified by a cross or star marking on one end and cannot be interchanged with the older type. Gearboxes fitted with these gears are identified by a spot of blue paint on the air filter housing contact surface.

Uprated input shaft shock absorber

3 From gearbox number 115 167 onwards (introduced to production machines in March 1985) a new input shaft assembly was fitted which featured redesigned and strengthened shock absorber components. Individual components are not interchangeable with the earlier type but the complete shaft assembly can be fitted to any gearbox with the 17.5° input gear meshing angle (see above). Gearboxes with the uprated shock absorber can be identified by the black-painted panel amongst the ribs under the air filter housing contact surface.

Output shaft front bearing

4 From March 1985 on the two circlips (items 19 and 20, Fig. 3.6) at the front end of the output shaft were deleted; the output shaft groove is no longer machined and the front bearing is of a modified type. The modified bearing can be fitted to earlier gearboxes if required, in which case the two circlips should not be refitted.

Output shaft oil seal – R80GS, R100GS

5 Since these models do not carry oil in the swinging arm, BMW have gone to some lengths to ensure that no oil leaks into the swinging arm from the gearbox. The output shaft rear bearing is double sealed to minimise the amount of oil that actually reaches the seal and the vent passages on the speedometer drive have been opened out.

6 A new type of seal is used which does not have the usual feather-edged lip which relies for its efficiency upon a garter spring, but has a single lip of a PTFE material (eg Teflon) which is not pre-shaped on delivery.

7 On installation the seal lip must first be shaped, for two hours, to prevent damage to it by the speedometer drive worm. This is best achieved by pressing the seal on to the BMW service tool, No. 23.1.750, which is specified as the installing drift. Once the seal lip is shaped in this way it will retain its shape and will use its own inherent elasticity to maintain contact pressure.

8 If the specified tool is not available and a mandrel of the same diameter as the output flange cannot be obtained, wrap a very thin layer of insulating tape over the flange worm drive threads and carefully press the seal fully onto the flange shoulder, taking care not to damage the lip.

9 Whichever method is used, take great care not to damage the spiral formed on the sealing lip. On fitting the shaped seal note that it is installed with its open side *inwards*, towards the output shaft rear bearing (ie opposite to all other models). The manufacturer also recommends that the vent passage in the immediate vicinity of the seal is blocked with Three Bond 1207 B or similar sealant. When refitting the output flange, note that the seal will bed in more rapidly if it is installed dry (with no oil or grease present); again, take care not to damage the seal as the flange is inserted.

5.9 Gearbox output shaft oil seal is installed open side inwards – R80GS, R100GS

6 Recommended fuel: general – all models

Note: *The information contained in this Section and in the Specifications Section of this Chapter is correct at the time of writing. For updated information, or for more specific details, refer either to the rider's handbook supplied with the machine or to a local BMW dealer or the BMW importer.*

1 At one time choosing the fuel for a machine was a simple task, the main criterion being that of price. However, with the introduction for environmental and health reasons of unleaded fuel and the progressive lowering of permissible levels of lead in leaded fuels, the situation is more complicated. Modern engines are also much more sensitive to the octane rating of the fuel used as they become more and more finely tuned to meet the conflicting demands of the greater performance and economy demanded by legislation. This Section expands on the basic information given in the Specifications Section of this Chapter.

2 First note that all recommendations are the minimum required. Depending on the quality of fuel locally available, on the operating conditions, on its owner's riding style or on its engine's particular characteristics or condition, any motorcycle may perform poorly on the specified grade of fuel and may require a higher grade to achieve normal performance.

3 Secondly, note that BMW advise against the use of any additives such as upper cylinder lubricants, octane boosters etc. Owners of machines used in the US should note that pure gasoline only is recommended – fuels containing a percentage of alcohol must **not** be used since alcohol will cause corrosion in aluminium, brass, rubber and plastic components and can cause severe engine damage. It may also cause bad starting and performance problems such as misfires or erratic idling.

4 Unleaded fuels should be used only as recommended. It is generally believed that the continuous use of unleaded fuels can cause accelerated wear of conventional valve seats, particularly on the exhaust; BMW have therefore fitted toughened exhaust valve seats to all 800 cc models built from late 1984 onwards. The seats have two grooves 1 mm wide and 0.2 mm deep machined on their inside edges and all cylinder heads fitted with them have a spot of blue paint on the cooling fin immediately under the bottom cylinder head nut. UK models thus modified start with frame numbers 6 440 512 (R80/1985), 6 470 498 (R80RT/1985), and 6 283 306 (R80G/S). Equivalent information is not available for US models (although all modified machines should have the blue spot marking); it should be noted, however, that BMW have allowed the use of unleaded fuel in all US models since 1980. Owners of US 1980–84 models are strongly advised to seek the advice of a competent BMW dealer or the BMW importer for confirmation of their machines' suitability for unleaded fuel.

5 For all models, note that it is unleaded fuel which is recommended, rather than 'low-lead' or 'lead-free' fuels.

6 At any time, if problems such as pinking (knocking) are experienced which could be attributed to poor quality fuel, attempt to solve the problem by changing the fuel before looking for a fault in the machine. First of all check carefully that the octane rating of the fuel used complies with BMW's minimum recommendations (see Specifications) then try higher grades and different types of fuel (eg leaded instead of unleaded) as well as different brands. Sometimes a cure can be effected by changing to a different filling station. If the fault persists, seek the advice of a good BMW dealer. Above all do not resort to unwarranted modifications to the machine; it should not, for example, be necessary to retard the ignition timing on any model covered in this manual that is described as suitable for unleaded fuel.

7 For owners of earlier models the situation can be summed up as follows:

   a) Any twin-cylinder BMW designed to run on super/premium grade fuel (see Chapter 4 Specifications) must use only the fuel recommended; unleaded is **not** suitable
   b) Any twin-cylinder BMW designed to run on regular grade fuel (see Chapter 4 Specifications) **may** use unleaded regular if required, but every third tankful at least must be leaded fuel to protect the valve seats
   c) Any 1985 or later BMW twin with the blue spot marking should use unleaded rather than leaded fuel to prolong spark plug life, as well as for obvious environmental reasons

7 Evaporative Emission Control System: general – US R80, R80RT, R100RS and R100RT models

General

1 All 1985 on models sold in California and all 1986 on 49-state models (except the R65) are fitted with an EEC system to comply with legislation controlling the escape of unburned hydrocarbons into the atmosphere as a result of evaporation.

2 When the machine is parked, heat from the sun or the hot engine causes the fuel in the tank to expand, thus increasing the pressure in the tank and producing evaporation through the tank air vent and, if the fuel taps are left switched on, through the carburettor breather vents.

3 To prevent this a sealed filler cap is fitted which has two valves. One opens at a negative pressure (vacuum) of 0.1 bar/1.5 psi to admit air and replace the fuel consumed as the engine is running. The second opens if the pressure (when the machine is stopped) inside the tank exceeds 0.3 – 0.4 bar/4.4 – 5.8 psi, thus acting as a safety valve in the event of excessive fuel expansion.

4 When the machine is parked, the switching off of the ignition closes the air vent and fuel shut-off solenoids. This allows vapour to pass through the tank vent hose, through the air vent solenoid and into the crankcase via a pressure relief valve which opens when tank pressure exceeds 0.15 bar/2.2 psi and prevents any reverse flow (into the tank) of engine vapours generated while the engine is running. The fuel shut-off solenoid cuts off the fuel supply to the carburettors, thus preventing any excessive tank pressure from venting through the carburettors if the owner should inadvertently leave the machine parked with the fuel taps switched on. This, incidentally, should cure the carburettor flooding fault which affects all BMW twins from time to time.

5 When the ignition is switched on, the air vent and fuel shut-off solenoids are both opened, restoring fuel supply to the carburettors (once the taps are switched on) and routing fuel vapours from the tank through another passage in the air vent solenoid, then into the air filter housing bottom half. While the engine is running it consumes through its own breather system the fuel vapour accumulated in the crankcase while the machine was parked and any excessive vapour generated subsequently in the tank.

6 The final component of the assembly is the flap door set at the bottom of a small compartment under the fuel tank filler cap. The compartment deliberately prevents the tank from being filled to the brim so that an air space is always left in the tank to allow for the expansion of fuel. The flap door is fitted to prevent neat fuel from swilling into the compartment and passing through the venting system into the engine. Its secondary function is to prevent fuel spraying out if the filler cap is removed when the tank pressure is excessive. Note that some pressure will always escape when the filler cap is removed, so be careful to keep your face well away when unscrewing the cap in case any fuel should spray out. **Warning:** *The flap door is an essential part of the system and must not be removed, modified or damaged in any way. It is designed to be opened by the insertion of a filling station's pump nozzle and should remain closed at all other times.*

Maintenance

7 The system requires no maintenance other than a check that all hoses are clear, undamaged, and correctly routed, with securely fastened connections. All electrical connections must be clean and secure.

8 Whenever the tank is removed and refitted do not forget to disconnect the vent hose as well as the fuel feed pipes and water drainage hose.

9 The system components are secured by clamps under the starter motor cover (see Fig. 4.13). Remove the retaining screws to release each solenoid as required. Ensure that all hose and electrical connections are correctly secured on refitting. If the pressure relief valve is removed, an arrow on its body indicates the direction of flow, and should point downwards.

Fault diagnosis

8 If the engine starts, but then stops after a short while or shows other signs of fuel starvation, first check that there is sufficient fuel in the tank and that both taps are switched on (main or reserve supply). If the fault persists, try running the engine with the filler cap unscrewed. If the fault disappears then it is in the breather system, but if it persists it

is in the fuel system.

9 If the fault is in the fuel system pull off the fuel feed pipe to each carburettor in turn and check whether fuel flows out when the ignition is switched off. If not, switch the ignition on; if fuel still does not flow the fuel shut-off solenoid is defective and must be renewed, although it is worth checking first whether fuel is flowing to the solenoid to ensure that the fault is not due to blocked fuel taps or feed pipes.

10 If fuel does flow out when the ignition is switched off and continues to flow when the ignition is switched on, the solenoid is defective and must be renewed. If, however, the flow stops when the ignition is switched on then the solenoid merely is incorrectly wired and the fault can be cured by reversing its connections.

11 If the fault lies in the breather system pull the vent hose off its union on the tank underside and blow gently through it with the ignition switched on. If resistance is felt switch off the ignition and blow again – if no resistance is felt the solenoid is incorrectly wired and the fault can be cured by reversing its connections.

12 If resistance is felt whether the ignition is on or off disconnect the air vent solenoid-to-air filter hose at the solenoid union and blow through the vent hose again. If no resistance is encountered check the air filter vent hose for blockages or kinking. If resistance is encountered the solenoid is defective and must be renewed.

13 If a fault develops which produces a severe pressure build-up when the machine is parked check the breather system as described in paragraph 11 above. If resistance is felt regardless of the ignition switch position disconnect the air vent solenoid-to-crankcase vent hose and pressure relief valve for bloackages; check also that the pressure relief valve is fitted the correct way up. If resistance is encountered the solenoid is defective and must be renewed.

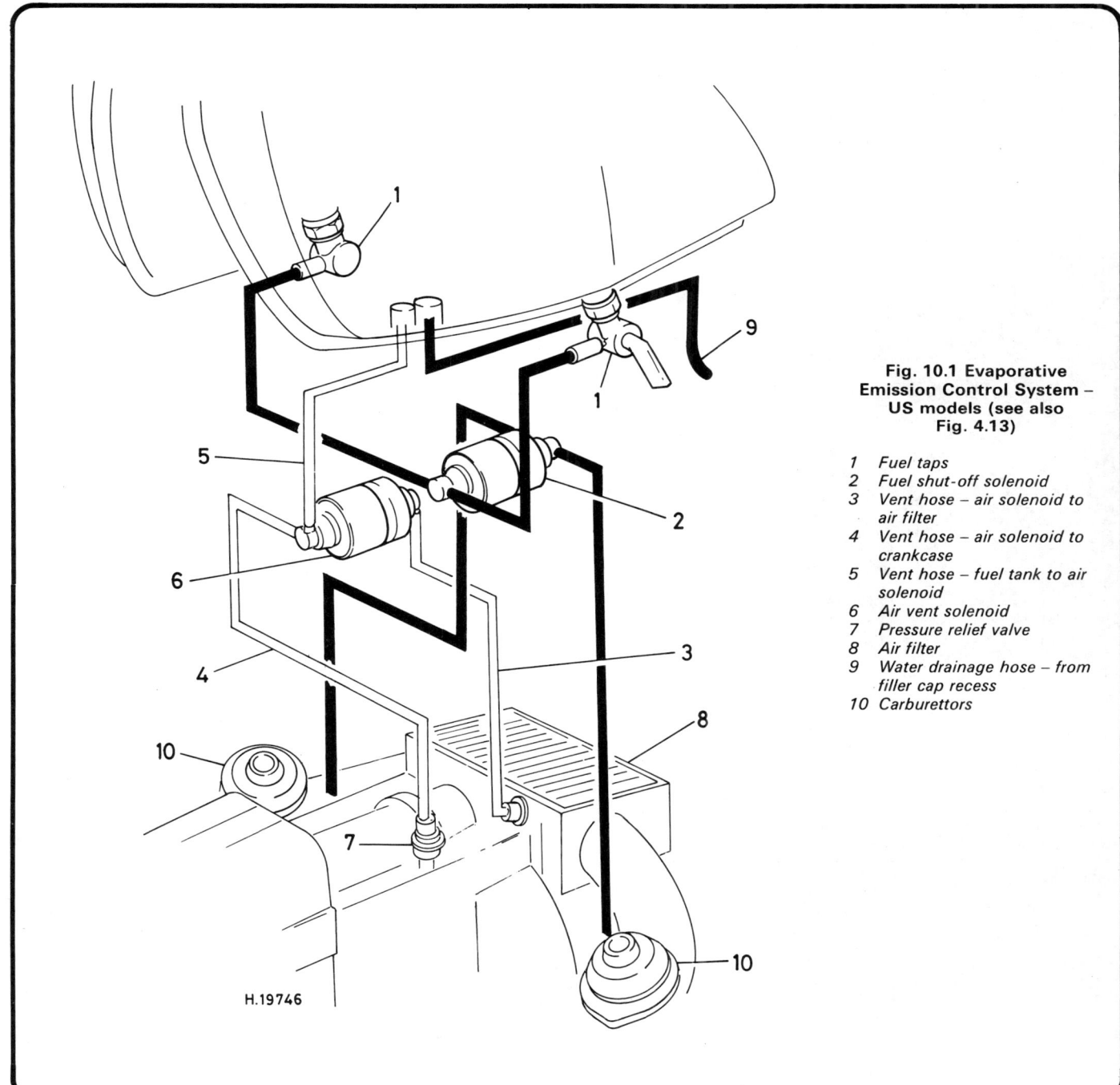

Fig. 10.1 Evaporative Emission Control System – US models (see also Fig. 4.13)

1 Fuel taps
2 Fuel shut-off solenoid
3 Vent hose – air solenoid to air filter
4 Vent hose – air solenoid to crankcase
5 Vent hose – fuel tank to air solenoid
6 Air vent solenoid
7 Pressure relief valve
8 Air filter
9 Water drainage hose – from filler cap recess
10 Carburettors

8 Exhaust system: general

All later models
1 Note that some modifications appear to have been made to the exhaust pipe/cylinder head seals. In some cases, particularly on later 800 cc models the (outer) compression ring may have been deleted and a modified type of sealing/clamp ring and finned nut may have been used instead. Removal, refitting and servicing procedures remain unchanged.

R65, R100RT, R100RS
2 Note that all these models use the R80/R80RT 1985 on type of exhaust system, using two separate exhaust pipes, a primary silencing expansion chamber and two separate silencers. Removal and refitting are as described for the R80/R80RT 1985 on models in Chapter 4.

R80GS, R100GS
3 To remove and refit the exhaust system on these models, follow the instructions given in Chapter 4 for the R80G/S model. Note however, that the silencer cover is retained by a single screw on the later models, and that the rear silencer is secured to the frame by a nut and bolt arrangement at the front and top, and by a (rubber-mounted) nut at the rear end.

9 Front forks: damper rod assembly overhaul – all R45/65 models and all other models from 1981 on

1 The front forks fitted to all later models in this manual use damper rod assemblies which are secured by the damper piston, which is screwed onto the rod upper end and secured by the application of Loctite 273 or 638 thread-locking compound.
2 While the overhaul procedure remains as described in Chapter 6, Sections 3 to 5, the following additional information relating to the damper rod assembly should be noted:
3 Prior to dismantling the damper assembly first measure carefully the length of the rod from the top of the piston to the bottom of the rod's lower end and record it. Remove the piston ring and wash the assembly carefully in hot soapy water to clean off any remaining oil or dirt and to remove any traces of flammable solvents. Heat the piston using a gentle flame until the Loctite starts to burn (approximately 250°C/482°F), whereupon the piston can be gripped with a pair of pliers or similar and unscrewed.
4 The damper components can then be removed, after making a careful note of exactly which way round each is fitted.
5 On reassembly ensure that all damper components are fitted the correct way round, then thoroughly degrease the threads of the piston and rod. Ensuring that the piston is fitted the correct way up (where appropriate), apply a single drop of thread-locking compound to the rod threads and screw the piston on to the rod until the rod's overall length is exactly as noted prior to dismantling (usually the top of the rod will be flush with the top of the piston). On all R65/85, R80 and R80RT/85, R100RS and R100RT models with K100-type forks, the rod's length is 258 ± 0.5 mm (10.16 ± 0.02 in). When the piston is correctly positioned put the assembly to one side until the Loctite has cured; this will take 24 hours at room temperature, but can be speeded up by warming the assemby with a hot air blower (eg a fan heater).
6 Do not forget to refit the piston ring before reassembling the fork.

10 Front forks: modifications – R65, R80, R80RT, R100RS and R100RT models

Fork top plug
1 All models from late 1985 (model year) on were fitted with a modified fork top plug pressed into the (unthreaded) stanchion and secured by a wire circlip against fork spring pressure. The plug is sealed by an O-ring; the filler plug arrangement remains the same. The plug passes up through the fork top yoke and is secured by a nut.
2 From the point of view of regular oil changes, the servicing procedure remains as described in the Routine maintenance section of this manual, the only difference being the revised torque wrench setting specified for the oil filler plug (see Specifications).
3 During fork leg removal and refitting, prise off the black plastic cap and unscrew the top nut, noting the presence of the washer underneath it. Slacken the bottom yoke pinch bolts and withdraw the fork leg complete with the top plug and spring, as described in Chapter 6.2. Refitting is the reverse of the above, noting the torque wrench setting specified for the top nut (see Specifications).

8.3a Rear silencer mountings – R80GS, R100GS models – front bolt ...

8.3b ... front upper bolt ...

8.3c ... rear upper nut (rubber mounted) ...

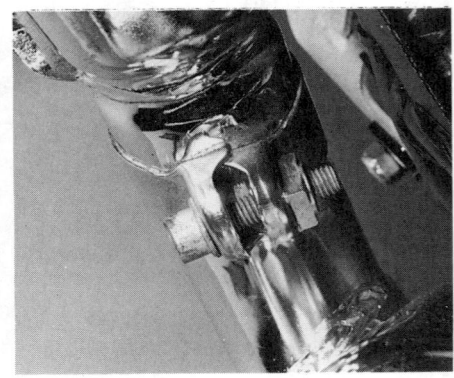

8.3d ... and pipe clamp

4 If the fork legs are to be dismantled they must first be removed from the machine; the top plug cannot be withdrawn upwards through the top yoke. Drain the oil as described in Chapter 6 then clamp the fork lower leg by the caliper mounting or wheel spindle lugs in a vice equipped with soft jaws to avoid marking the soft alloy, then use a suitable rod to press in the top plug until the retaining circlip is exposed. Push the circlip down into the leg on one side only so that it can be gripped with a pair of pliers and withdrawn. Allow the spring pressure to push the top plug out of the stanchion; in some cases the sealing O-ring may be such a tight fit that the top plug must be extracted using a pair of pliers to grip a bolt screwed into the filler plug thread.

5 On reassembly, always renew the sealing O-ring and note that it may be easier to add the fork oil before the plug is refitted, rather than risk wasting oil in trying to pour it through the rather small filler hole. Push the plug into the stanchion, fit the retaining circlip to its groove and allow the spring pressure to push the plug back up against the circlip. Refill the fork leg with the correct amount of the specified oil and refit the filler plug and sealing washer.

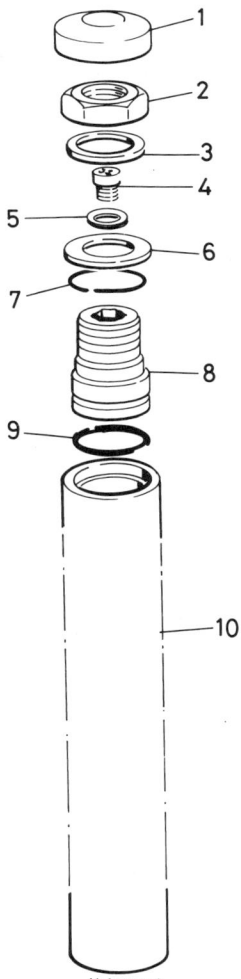

Fig. 10.2 Fork leg top plug modification – late 1985 models on

1	Top cap	7	Circlip
2	Top nut	8	Top plug
3	Washer	9	O-ring
4	Filler plug	10	Stanchion
5	Sealing washer		
6	Hardened steel shim (where fitted)		

Top yoke mounting

6 It has been discovered that the top yoke can be worn slightly by contact with the sharp-edged stanchions to the point where the joint can become loose, with a recess being eroded in the underside of the top yoke.

7 If this is found, hardened steel shims are available which when placed between the stanchion upper end and the underside of the top yoke, provide a bearing surface.

8 To fit the shims remove the top caps and top plugs (early type) or top nut (later type). Place the machine on its centre stand and slacken the bottom yoke pinch bolts until the stanchions can be dropped far enough to insert the shims (one per leg), whereupon the stanchions should be raised to their correct height and all disturbed nuts and bolts retightened to their specified torque settings. On R65 and R80 models the situation may be complicated by having to remove the shim from between the headlamp bracket bottom rubber mounting and the turn signal lamp mounting bracket, in order to make room for the new component; this may necessitate removal of the front wheel and mudguard before the stanchions can be lowered far enough to remove the shim.

9 On later 1988 models this modification should not be necessary due to modified machining of the stanchion upper end to provide a larger bearing surface.

Fork brace bolts

10 Later models may be fitted with fork brace bolts of the Torx type, which will require a special key to unscrew or fasten. Unfortunately, no details are available of the key size.

Dust excluder and oil seal

11 To reduce the amount of dirt which gets through to the oil seal, causing premature fork wear and resulting oil leaks, during 1988 the manufacturer introduced a modified oil seal with an extra dust seal lip which can be fitted to earlier models when necessary. The extra height of the oil seal requires the fitting of a spacer ring above the seal to prevent the dust excluder from fouling the seal lip and damaging it. (Note that later production machines will not require this spacer as the fork seal recess is machined deeper.) On models with black-painted forks the subsequent raising of the dust excluder exposes a strip of bare metal; this must be painted over.

12 In addition to this the manufacturer stresses the importance of only fitting dust excluders whose sealing lips are absolutely square to the stanchion (some are noticeably chamfered) and packing the excluder grooves with grease; they recommend Gleitmo 805 or Shell Retinax A.

---

11 Front forks: damping components alignment – R65, R80, R80RT, R100RS and R100RT models

1 Due to their long travel and relatively complex construction, these forks can be noisy in operation or, especially after they have been disturbed, they can become stiff in operation. While the standard procedure described in Chapter 6 is sufficient in most cases to prevent this, on occasion a stiff or noisy fork can be cured only by the more elaborate procedure described below. Note that the procedure starts with the premise that the stanchions are in place on the machine, with the damper rods fitted, and that the lower legs are attached loosely by the damper rod Allen screws. The fork oil must be drained and the fork top plugs, fork springs, mudguard, front wheel and fork brace must be removed. Note that on all 1985 on models with the modified top plugs (see Section 10), the top yoke, handlebars and instruments must be removed.

2 Push each lower leg sharply upwards until it is heard to make contact, then rotate it two or three times around the stanchion to centre the damper rods before tightening the damper rod Allen screw to the specified torque setting; use one of the methods described in Chapter 6.3 to prevent the damper rod from rotating. Check that the lower leg still slides smoothly and easily and rotates without stiffness; if necessary slacken the Allen screw and repeat the procedure until results are satisfactory.

3 Refit the fork brace, tightening its bolts only lightly at this stage, then temporarily refit the fork top plugs (and top yoke, later models) to centre the stanchions in the fork yokes. Refit the wheel spindle and clamp it on one side only. Push both lower legs upwards simultaneously until contact is heard again then tighten the fork brace

mounting bolts evenly and in a diagonal sequence to the specified torque setting; also tighten the second pair of spindle clamp bolts to the specified torque setting.

4 Pump the lower leg assembly up and down several times to check for any signs of stiffness or distortion, then check that the wheel spindle can be easily removed and refitted. If any stiffness or difficulty is found, check the fork components for distortion.

5 Refit the oil drain plugs, the front mudguard, the front wheel and the brake components then fill each leg with the specified quantity and type of fork oil and refit the fork springs and on later models refit the top yoke.

6 Raise the front wheel from the ground and support the machine with a wooden box or similar under the crankcase so that the forks are fully extended. Refit the fork top plugs (early models) and the oil filler plugs, then lower the machine to the ground and check the fork action.

7 Note that some stiffness will be inevitable in a freshly-rebuilt fork and a running-in period of 600 miles (1000 km) will probably prove necessary before the fork operates with absolute smoothness.

12 Front forks: general – R80GS and R100GS models

General

1 Apart from their greater travel and different appearance, the Marzocchi forks fitted to these models feature bushes which can be renewed separately to compensate for wear. They also have different damping components in the left- and right-hand legs. When dismantling, therefore, it is *essential* that each fork leg is overhauled separately and that all components are stored in separate, clearly marked containers to avoid any risk of confusion.

Fork oil change

2 Apart from the different oil quantities and grades, and the torque wrench settings, given in the Specifications Section of this Chapter, this operation is the same as described for the later models in the Routine maintenance section of this manual.

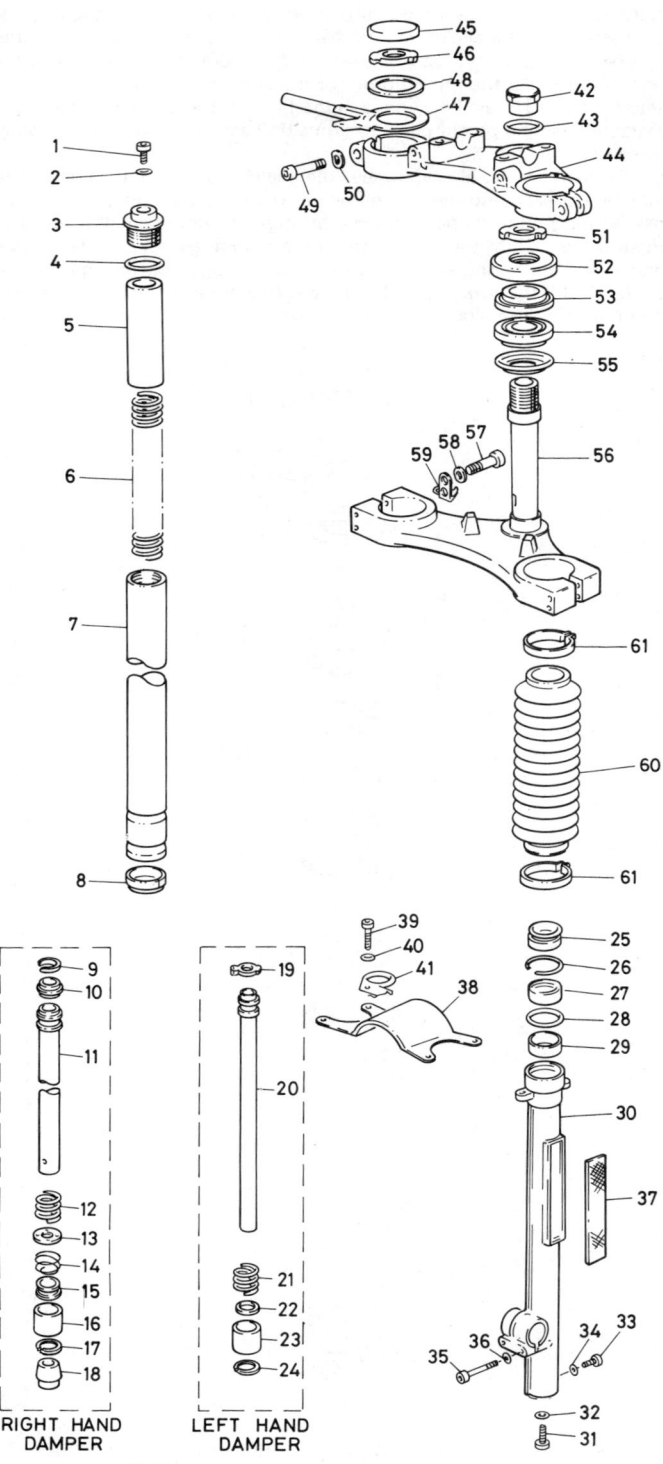

Fig. 10.3 Marzocchi front forks – R80GS and R100GS models

1 Oil filler plug
2 Gasket
3 Top plug
4 O-ring
5 Spacer
6 Spring
7 Stanchion
8 Bottom bush
9 Piston ring
10 Piston
11 Damper rod
12 Rebound spring
13 Spring retainer
14 Valve spring
15 Valve
16 Valve housing
17 Circlip
18 Damper rod seat
19 Piston ring
20 Damper rod
21 Rebound spring
22 Washer
23 Valve housing
24 Circlip
25 Dust excluder
26 Circlip
27 Oil seal
28 Backing washer
29 Top bush
30 Lower leg
31 Allen screw
32 Sealing washer
33 Oil drain plug
34 Sealing washer
35 Bolt – 2 off
36 Washer – 2 off
37 Reflector
38 Fork brace
39 Bolt – 4 off
40 Washer – 4 off
41 Brake hose guide
42 Bolt
43 Washer
44 Top yoke
45 Top cap
46 Slotted nut
47 Turn signal lamp bracket
48 Shim
49 Bolt – 2 off
50 Washer – 2 off
51 Adjuster nut
52 Dust cover
53 Tapered roller bearing
54 Tapered roller bearing
55 Dust seal
56 Bottom yoke/steering stem
57 Bolt – 4 off
58 Washer – 4 off
59 Brake hose guide
60 Gaiter
61 Gaiter clamps

Fork legs – removal and refitting

3 Remove the front wheel (Chapter 8.2). Unscrew the four bolts and remove the fork brace and release the brake hose guide, then remove the brake caliper mounting bolts and tie the brake caliper to the frame downtubes out of harm's way. Wedge a spacer of clean wood or similar between the pads to prevent their movement.
4 Prise the black plastic top cap off each fork leg and use a C-spanner to unscrew the top slotted nut, noting the shim underneath it. Remove the nut, shim and turn signal lamp assembly from the top of each leg.
5 Remove the oil drain and filler plugs and drain the fork oil.
6 While the legs are still clamped in the fork yokes, use an Allen key to slacken the fork top plug; it is fitted with a 17 mm internal hexagon to permit removal and refitting. Slacken both gaiter clamps on each leg.
7 Slacken the top and bottom yoke pinch bolts fully and withdraw the fork legs as described in Chapter 6.2.
8 On refitting, use fine abrasive paper to polish away any burrs, raised edges or deposits of corrosion from the fork stanchions and their location in the yokes. Smear a light coat of grease over the stanchion upper end and slide the legs into place.
9 Lightly tighten the pinch bolts so that the legs are just held in the yokes, then check that the tops of the stanchions are flush with the top of the top yoke. Slide the wheel spindle through the spindle lugs to ensure that the fork legs are correctly aligned, then tighten first the top yoke pinch bolts to their specified torque setting, followed by the bottom yoke pinch bolts which must also be tightened to their specified setting. Refit the turn signal lamp assembly, shim and slotted nut. Tighten the slotted nut securely, to its specified torque setting if the necessary equipment is available. If not yet done, refill the fork legs with the specified amount and type of oil, then refit the filler plug and black plastic cap to the top of each leg.
10 Refit the fork brace and brake hose guide, followed by the front wheel and the brake caliper.
11 When the front wheel has been refitted, push the machine off its stand, apply the front brake and pump the forks up and down to align the legs and their mountings. Working from the top downwards tighten all fasteners to their specified torque setting. Slide the fork gaiters into place and fasten their clamps.
12 Check that all controls are correctly adjusted, that all components are securely fastened and that the suspension works smoothly before using the machine.

Left-hand fork leg – dismantling and reassembly

13 Remove the fork leg from the machine as described above. Slacken the damper rod Allen screw in the base of the fork lower leg. This task is sometimes complicated by the fact that the damper rod assembly rotates with the screw so that nothing is achieved; to prevent this happening, tap smartly on the head of the Allen screw with a suitable hammer and a soft metal drift to jar the threads free, then push the fork lower leg up the stanchion as far as possible to compress the fork spring and to lock the damper assembly using spring pressure. If this fails, use a more positive means of locking the damper assembly.
14 Using a vice whose jaws have been padded with soft alloy or wooden covers, clamp the fork lower leg securely in the horizontal position, ensuring that the vice is clamped only on the wheel spindle lug to prevent damage to the lower leg. Unscrew the top plug (see below) and remove the spacer and spring. Obtain a length of wooden dowel that will fit inside the stanchion and is long enough to rest on the head of the damper assembly while projecting beyond the stanchion upper end, then grind a coarse taper on one end of the dowel so that it fits securely into the head of the damper assembly. Using a pair of Mole grips or a similar tool to provide the necessary leverage, apply pressure to the damper assembly to prevent it from rotating and unscrew the Allen screw.
15 To remove the fork spring and spacer, first unscrew the fork top plug. If it was not slackened while still clamped in the fork yokes, obtain two blocks of wood and cut V-shaped notches in them so that the stanchion can be clamped securely upright in a vice at its upper end without risk of distorting it; failing this, refit the fork leg to the machine and tighten the top and bottom yoke pinch bolts. With the stanchion held securely, unscrew the top plug taking care as it is under some pressure from the fork spring and may be ejected forcibly, as the last threads are reached; maintain firm pressure on the Allen key to counter this. Withdraw the spacer, followed by the spring. Note which way up the spring is fitted as a guide to correct reassembly.
16 Remove the damper rod Allen screw, noting its Dowty-type sealing washer. Pull the fork lower leg off the stanchion and remove the gaiter.

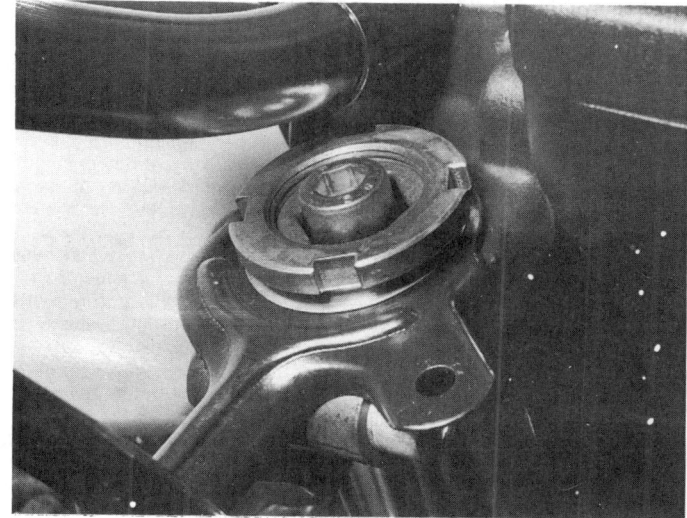

12.4 Unscrew slotted nut to release shim and turn signal bracket

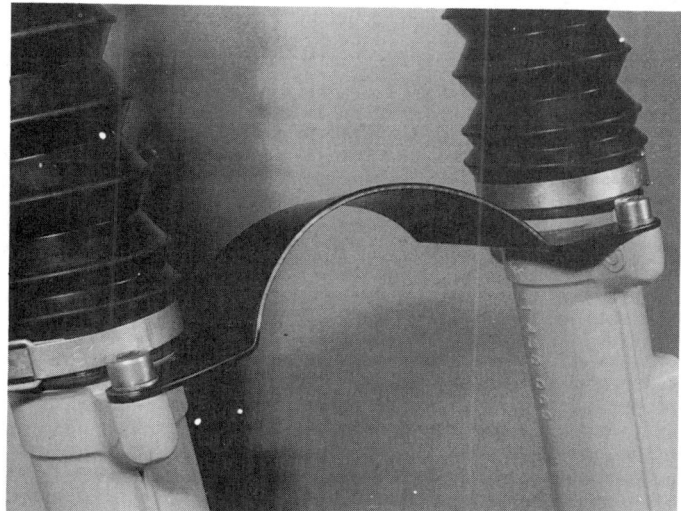

12.10 Refit the fork brace and fasten the gaiter clamps

12.16 Damper rod Allen screw is fitted with Dowty-type sealing washer

17 Remove the circlip from the bottom of the stanchion and pull out the damper rod with the valve housing (noting which way up this is fitted), the washer, and the rebound spring. Note that the rebound spring was found to be a very tight fit inside the stanchion. Note the white plastic piston ring fitted to the head of the damper rod. If the bottom bush requires renewal prise it apart just enough to slide it off the stanchion lower end.

18 If the fork top bush or oil seal are to be renewed, carefully prise out the dust excluder and the wire circlip beneath it. Using a large screwdriver or similar lever with rounded edges, carefully lever the oil seal out of the lower leg; take care not to scratch or damage the seal housing. If the seal proves particularly tight, pour boiling water over the lower leg upper end to loosen its grip on the seal by expansion – *take care to prevent any risk of personal injury while doing this*. With the seal removed, withdraw the metal backing washer underneath it. The top bush may be slack enough to drop out, especially if the lower leg is heated using boiling water, but if not an internally-expanding puller of the required dimensions must be obtained. The manufacturer specifies service tool No. 00.8.560. Do not attempt to lever or prise the bush out, its bearing surface may be severely damaged.

19 Examine all components, cleaning them thoroughly and looking for any signs of wear or damage (see Chapter 6.4). If any defective or worn components are found, they must be renewed. If the bush bearing surfaces are visibly worn, scratched or damaged, the bushes must be renewed as a set.

20 Ensure that all components are absolutely clean on reassembly and smear clean fork oil over each component as it is refitted.

21 Reassembly is the reverse of the dismantling procedure, noting the following points.

22 To refit the top bush oil it liberally and deburr its housing, then push it in as far as possible by hand, finally tapping it fully into its housing. If necessary temporarily refit the stanchion to the lower leg to support the bush as it is tapped home. Refit the metal backing washer, smear the new oil seal with grease (Shell Retinax A) and drive it into the lower leg using a socket spanner or similar as a drift which bears only on the seal's hard outer edge. When the circlip groove is exposed do not force the seal any further. Refit the circlip and press the dust excluder in by hand.

23 Liberally oil the bottom bush and press it over the stanchion lower end with its chamfered end facing downwards; check that it fits correctly into its groove.

24 Fit the piston ring to the damper rod and fit the rod into the stanchion (this is easiest if the rod is dropped in from the upper end). Fit the rebound spring into the stanchion lower end and push it up above the shoulder machined inside the stanchion. The metal washer butts against the shoulder and is followed by the valve housing, which is fitted with its internal taper facing downwards. Refit the circlip to secure the assembly.

25 Fit the fork spring with its tapered end downwards, followed by the spacer and fork top plug; fit a new sealing O-ring to the plug. Check that the damper rod protrudes fully from the stanchion lower end. Smear the stanchion with fork oil.

26 Carefully insert the stanchion into the lower leg, taking care not to damage the bushes or the seal lips. Refit the damper rod Allen screw and fork oil drain plug, using new sealing washers if required and tightening both to the torque settings specified. Refit the fork gaiter and fasten its clamps loosely.

27 It may be easier to remove the fork top plug again and to fill the fork leg with the correct amount of the specified fork oil, rather than risk wasting oil by trying to pour it through the small filler hole.

28 Clamp the stanchion, either in the wooden blocks in the vice or in the fork yokes, and tighten the fork top plug to the specified torque setting. If the oil has been added, refit and tighten the filler plug.

Right-hand fork leg – dismantling and reassembly

29 The right-hand leg is identical to the left apart from the damper assembly. It can therefore be dismantled following the instructions given above from paragraph 13 to paragraph 16. Then proceed as follows:

30 Remove the circlip from the bottom of the stanchion and pull out the damper rod assembly with the valve housing (noting which way round it is fitted), which incorporates the valve, spring and spring retainer, and the rebound spring. Note the white plastic piston ring fitted to the damper piston. Invert the lower leg to tip out the damper rod seat. Remove the bottom bush, if necessary, as described in paragraph 17.

12.17a Remove circlip from bottom of stanchion ...

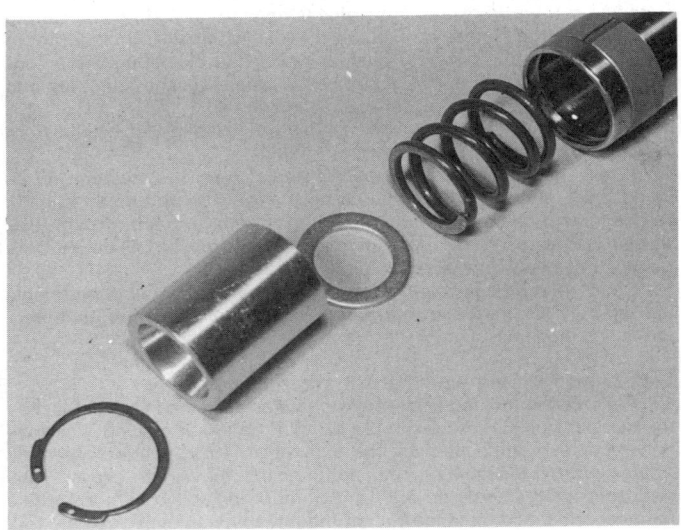

12.17b ... to release damper components – left-hand leg shown – note slotted bottom bush

12.18 Prise out circlip to permit removal of oil seal and/or bush

12.24 Do not forget to refit damper rod piston ring

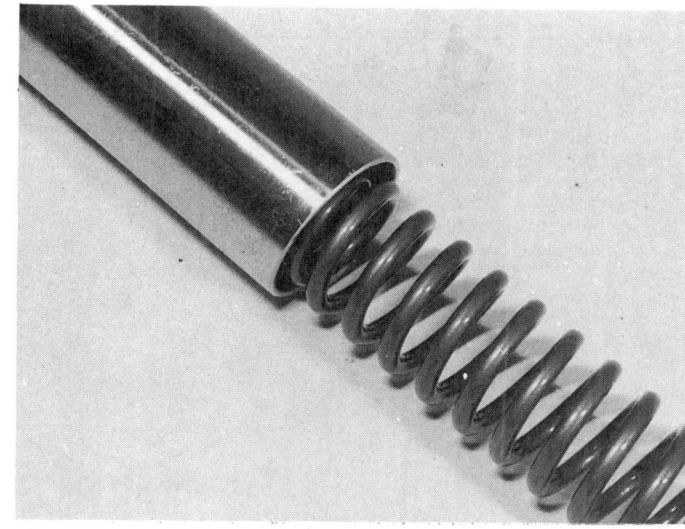

12.25a Fork spring is fitted with its tapered end downwards ...

12.25b ... and is followed by plastic spacer ...

12.25c ... and fork top plug – renew O-ring as a matter of course

12.26 Take care not to damage seal lips or bushes when refitting stanchion

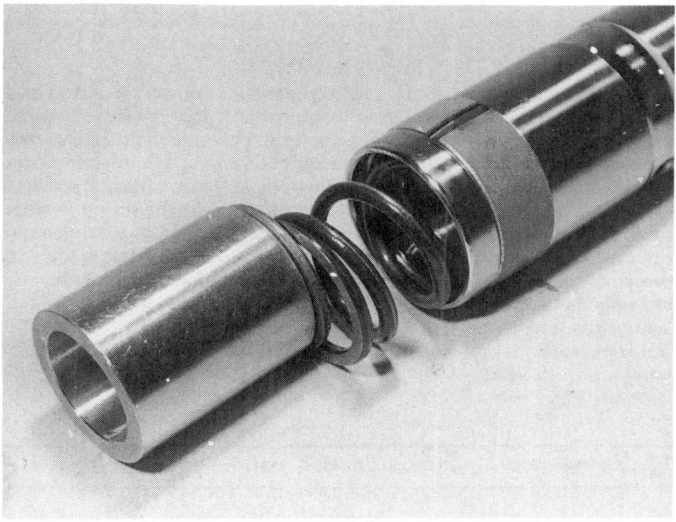

12.30 Removing circlip from bottom of stanchion releases right-hand leg damper components

12.32a Note different piston ring and piston in right-hand leg

12.32b Fit spring to valve and insert into valve housing ...

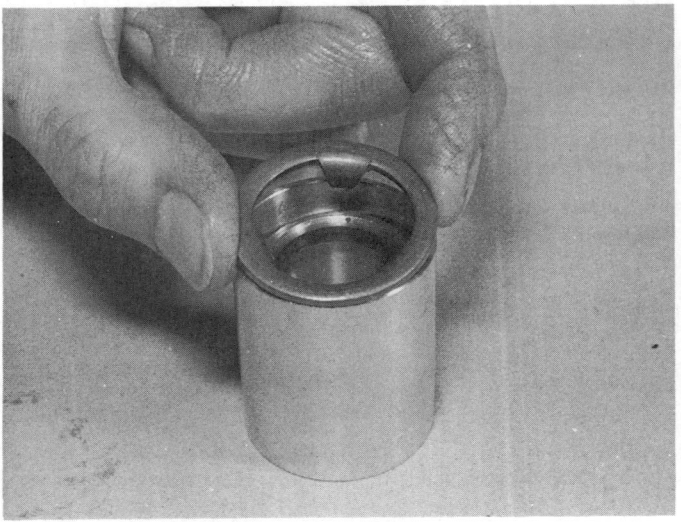

12.32c ... then fit spring retainer as shown

12.32d Do not forget to refit damper rod seat – right-hand leg only

32 To reassemble the damper rod fit the piston ring to the piston and fit the rod into the stanchion from the upper end. Use the fork spring to press the rod down until it protrudes from the stanchion lower end, then refit the rebound spring. Fit the light coil spring's narrow end over the valve then fit the two into the valve housing so that the coil spring's wider end is fully compressed inside the housing. Fit the spring retainer over the end of the housing with its three inner tangs projecting downwards, then refit the assembly over the end of the damper rod and press it up inside the stanchion. Secure the damper assembly by refitting the circlip, then use a dab of grease to stick the damper rod seat to the end of the rod.

33 The remainder of the rebuilding procedure is as described in paragraphs 25 to 28.

13 Fairing mounting: modification – all RT models

1 If the fairing storage compartments rub against the fuel tank remove the luggage locker lids, slacken the bolts securing the fairing to its rear upper mounting bracket and push the fairing as far outwards as the slotted mounting will allow, before tightening the bolts securely again. On later models the slotted mounting will be replaced by a carefully-spaced hole.

2 If this proves insufficient, remove the fuel tank and drill a 7 mm (0.28 in) hole in the fairing locker at the point of contact (usually in the top corner of each locker). A rubber grommet (the manufacturer recommends those used in the dual seat base) can then be inserted to protect the tank.

14 Dualseat mounting: repair – R80GS and R100GS models

1 The dualseat front mounting on these models consists of a prong which is attached to the seat base on early models by ultrasonic welding. The prong is intended to project into the rear of the frame top tube, in conjunction with the smaller prong which engages the fuel tank catch.

2 However if the seat is incorrectly fitted, with the prong resting on top of the frame tube, the prong may break under the weight of the rider. In this event it is possible to purchase a repair kit rather than renewing the seat. The manufacturer has introduced a repair kit

Chapter 10 The 1986 to 1988 models

consisting of a separate prong which is attached by two rivets. This requires the drilling of two 6.5 mm (0.26 in) holes in the seat base, following instructions supplied with the kit.
3 On all later models the prong will be a separate item bolted to the seat base.

15 Instrument mountings: general – R100RS and R100RT models

Cases of instrument vibration and of damage such as tachometer (rev-counter) needles dropping off have been cured by the fitting of softer black-coloured rubber mounting grommets in the fork top yoke mounting bracket. Note that the standard light-coloured grommets are quite satisfactory on all other models. An authorised BMW dealer should be able to obtain the correct replacement parts, if required.

16 Final drive and rear suspension: general – all models except the R80GS and R100GS

1 Note that the R65, R100RS and R100RT models covered in this Chapter are fitted with the R80, R80RT 1985-type of Monolever rear suspension. For all information, therefore, refer to the relevant instructions in Chapter 7.
2 Although the R80G/S model remained unchanged until it was discontinued, a modified rear suspension unit bottom mounting eye was introduced during 1988 for some 1986 US and 1986 – 87 UK models, as a result of cracks appearing in the eye in some cases. The strengthened eye has 4 mm/0.16 in of material (formerly 2.5 mm/0.10 in) surrounding the steel/rubber mounting bush. An authorised BMW dealer will have full details of the modification which was carried out as part of a safety recall campaign.

17 Rear bevel drive housing: removal – R80GS and R100GS models

1 Remove the rear wheel from the machine. See Chapter 8.3.
2 If the housing is to be dismantled drain its oil, as described in Routine maintenance.
3 Prise off the black plastic cap and slacken the housing pivot bearing stub (left-hand side) and pivot shaft locknut (right-hand side). **Note:** On the machine featured in the photographs both these fasteners were found to be extremely tight, particularly the pivot stub which is secured with Loctite 273. It was necessary for one or two people to steady the machine while another used an Allen key and a 3 – 4 ft long extension bar. Unless a very large vice is available and great care is taken to prevent damage by padding the vice jaws, it is unlikely that these fasteners can be slackened on the bench. Note also that high quality Allen keys are required for this degree of pressure.
5 Unscrew the brake adjuster nut and pull the cable clear of the cam lever trunnion and the housing abutment. Refit all components on the cable end to prevent their loss and secure the cable clear of the rear suspension.
6 Remove the right-hand side panel and slacken the suspension unit top mounting bolt and nut. Obtain a piece of wood long enough to support the housing at its normal working height, then remove the suspension unit bottom mounting nut, pull the unit off its mounting stud and tie it to the frame, out of the way. *Do not allow the rear suspension to drop sharply or components such as the swinging arm gaiter or casting may be damaged.*
7 Slacken the housing torque arm front mounting nut and unscrew the rear mounting nut and bolt. Lower the torque arm away from the housing.
8 Slacken the housing/swinging arm gaiter clamps and pull the gaiter clear of either component.

17.5 Unscrew adjusting nut and disconnect rear brake cable

17.6a Before removing suspension unit bottom mounting nut ...

17.6b ... support swinging arm as shown to prevent damage

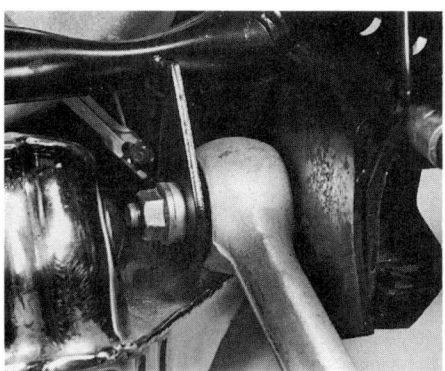

17.7a Slacken torque arm front mounting nut ...

17.7b ... and remove rear mounting bolt

17.8 Release gaiter clamps and peel back gaiter

9 Ensuring that the housing and swinging arm *both* remain fully supported unscrew the pivot stub and pivot shaft, put both to one side and withdraw the housing from the swinging arm and driveshaft.

10 Withdraw the two pivot bearing inner races immediately and mark or store them so that they cannot be confused and are refitted in their original locations.

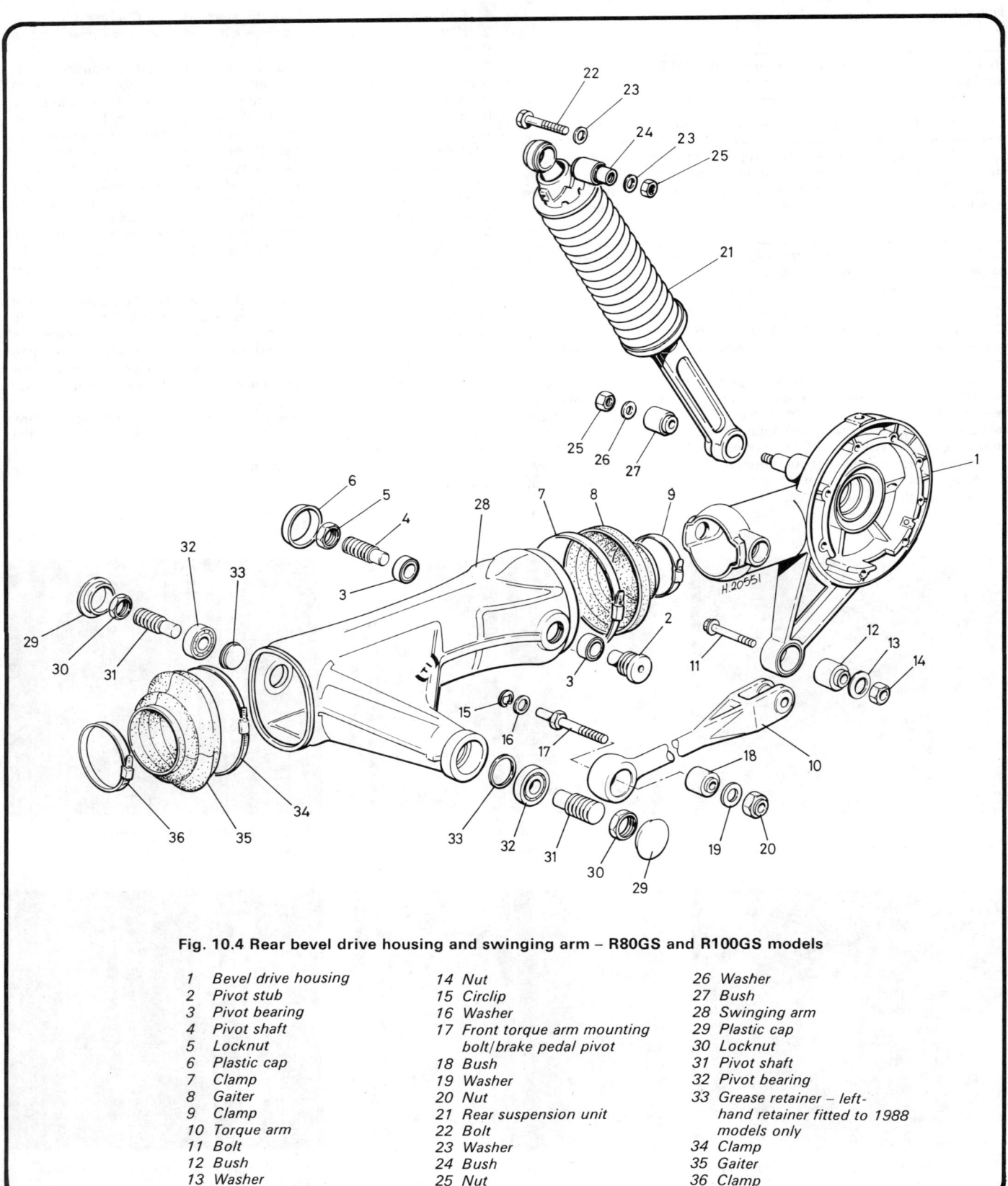

Fig. 10.4 Rear bevel drive housing and swinging arm – R80GS and R100GS models

1 Bevel drive housing
2 Pivot stub
3 Pivot bearing
4 Pivot shaft
5 Locknut
6 Plastic cap
7 Clamp
8 Gaiter
9 Clamp
10 Torque arm
11 Bolt
12 Bush
13 Washer
14 Nut
15 Circlip
16 Washer
17 Front torque arm mounting bolt/brake pedal pivot
18 Bush
19 Washer
20 Nut
21 Rear suspension unit
22 Bolt
23 Washer
24 Bush
25 Nut
26 Washer
27 Bush
28 Swinging arm
29 Plastic cap
30 Locknut
31 Pivot shaft
32 Pivot bearing
33 Grease retainer – left-hand retainer fitted to 1988 models only
34 Clamp
35 Gaiter
36 Clamp

18 Rear bevel drive housing: refitting – R80GS and R100GS models

1 All components should be clean and dry, particularly mounting bolts and nuts and components such as the pivot shaft, locknut and pivot stub. In the latter case the threads should be carefully cleaned to remove all traces of old thread locking compound and the whole stub should be degreased; do not forget to clean the threads in the swinging arm casting as well, and do a 'dry run' to check that both threads are in good condition.

2 The driveshaft splines and pivot bearings should be coated with lubricant; those recommended by the manufacturer are given in the Specifications Section of this Chapter. If none are available locally, a good BMW dealer should be able to recommend a suitable alternative. Coat the driveshaft and input bevel drive pinion splines and both needle roller pivot bearings with lubricant and apply a thin smear of grease to the suspension unit and torque arm mounting bolts to prevent corrosion. Apply a thin coat of Never Seez or Copaslip to the pivot shaft and pivot stub bearing journals and to the pivot bearing inner races. Fit the inner races to the pivot bearings, using the lubricant to stick them in place.

3 When all is ready support the swinging arm at approximately normal working height, select top gear and refit the housing to the driveshaft, rotating the rear wheel drive flange to engage the splines.

4 As soon as the driveshaft is connected refit the torque arm and insert its bolt from right to left, ie nut against the rear wheel. Support the housing on a block of wood and refit the pivot shaft and stub, then refit the rear suspension unit. Tighten the suspension unit and torque arm mountings firmly but do not apply full torque at this stage.

5 Check that the housing is correctly installed and properly aligned on its pivot bearings. If necessary disconnect the torque arm and suspension unit again so that the housing's movement can be checked. If all is well unscrew the pivot stub until the full width of thread can be seen, apply one or two drops of Loctite 273 or equivalent thread-locking compound and tighten the pivot stub to the specified torque wrench setting.

6 Using normal firm hand pressure on a standard length Allen key, securely tighten the pivot stub to preload the bearings (check the housing moves smoothly, if possible) then slacken off and tighten again to the specified torque wrench setting. Hold the shaft steady while tightening the locknut securely with a ring spanner, then check-tighten it (ensuring that the shaft does not move) using a torque wrench set to the specified setting. Check that the housing pivots smoothly and easily throughout its full movement with no trace of free play. Refit the black plastic cap.

7 Refit the gaiter over the swinging arm and housing lips, then fasten its clamps securely. Reconnect the brake cable. Refit the rear wheel, select neutral and push the machine off its centre stand.

8 Bounce the rear suspension vigorously to settle all components and to ensure that everything is in good order, then stand the machine upright on its wheels with the rider seated normally.

9 With all suspension components arranged as nearly as possible in their normal working positions, tighten to the specified torque settings the suspension unit top and bottom mountings and the torque arm front and rear mountings. This procedure prolongs the life of the rubber bushes at these points by minimising the distortion they suffer when in use.

10 Place the machine on its centre stand again and either refill the rear bevel drive housing with oil or check its level. See Routine maintenance. Check and adjust the rear brake and stoplamp switch setting. Check that all suspension, drive and brake components are correctly fastened and working properly before taking the machine out on the road.

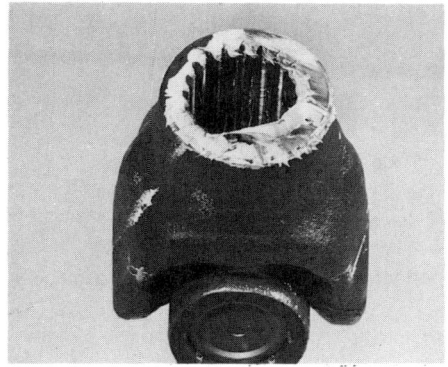

18.2a Apply a good coat of specified lubricant to driveshaft splines ...

18.2b ... and to housing pivot bearings

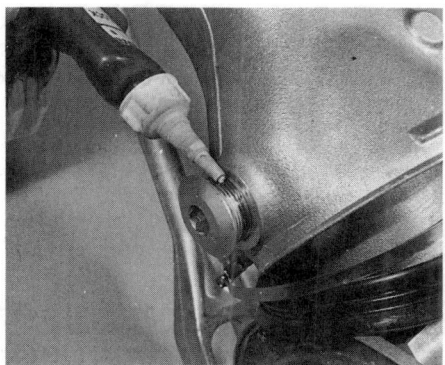

18.5a Apply one or two drops of thread-locking compound ...

18.5b ... and tighten housing pivot stub to specified torque setting

18.6a Preload bearings as described in text ...

18.6b ... then tighten locknut to specified torque setting – check housing movement

19 Swinging arm and driveshaft: removal and refitting – R80GS and R100GS models

1 Once the rear bevel drive housing has been removed (see Section 17) the procedure required to remove and refit the swinging arm and driveshaft is substantially the same as that described in Chapter 7, Sections 5, 6 and 8.
2 The major difference is that the large Paralever-type swinging arm casting can be withdrawn over the driveshaft and can be manoeuvred into place with the driveshaft still bolted to the gearbox output flange. Since the remarks made about the driveshaft bolts in Chapter 7.8 apply equally to these later models, servicing operations which do not actually require driveshaft removal should be simpler on Paralever models.
3 Note that the driveshaft cannot be pulled back through the swinging arm and therefore, the swinging arm must be removed to permit removal of the driveshaft.
4 The swinging arm pivot bearings are sealed. They should be checked for wear whenever the swinging arm is removed and if possible, repacked with fresh grease.
5 The rear brake pedal pivot forms part of the torque arm front mounting, necessitating the brake pedal to be removed before the mounting bolt is withdrawn. Remove the circlip and washer and pull the brake pedal off its pivot. The torque arm nut can then be unscrewed and the bolt can be withdrawn. Carefully clean and grease it on refitting. Note that a torque wrench cannot be applied easily with the exhaust in place.
6 The bonded rubber bushes at each end of the torque arm should be checked for signs of wear or damage, such as cracking or perishing. If faulty they can be pressed out using a drawbolt arrangement and renewed. A drawbolt tool will also be required to press the bushes into their housings.

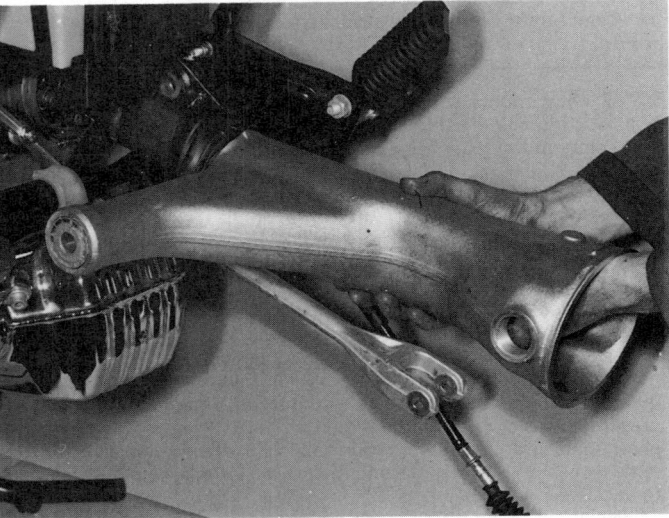

19.2 Swinging arm can be removed and refitted with driveshaft in place – R80GS, R100GS

20 Driveshaft: general – R80GS and R100GS models

Both universal joints can be checked as described in Chapter 7.7. To check the damper clamp the front end in a vice and twist the rear end backwards and forwards in the normal direction of rotation, using a lever passed through the rear joint. If any signs of wear or free play are discovered the shaft must be renewed; individual component parts are not available.

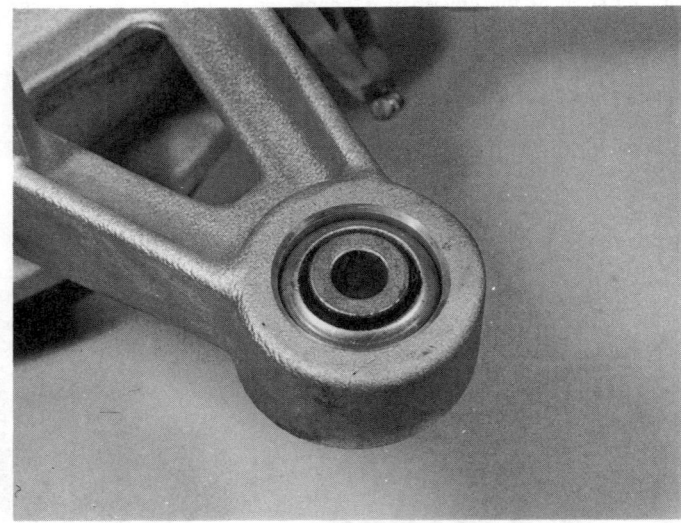

19.6 Check torque arm bonded rubber bushes for wear or damage

21 Wheel track offset: all models

1 On all machines covered in this manual, the centre lines of the front and rear wheels should be aligned exactly. However, to allow for production tolerances a maximum difference (or offset) of 4 mm (0.16 in) is permissible. This is usually adjustable by means of the swinging arm pivot bearings.
2 While a difference of up to 12 mm (0.47 in) offset is physically possible with the swinging arm set to the right, the pivot bearings should always be set so that the offset is reduced to a minimum. If adjustment of the pivot bearings cannot bring the wheels into line, the machine should be taken to an authorised BMW dealer or competent repairer who has the necessary jigs to check frame alignment.
3 On machines with wire-spoked wheels note that the rim is usually centred on the hub but in certain cases (particularly the R80G/S and ST models) a degree of offset is designed in. If the wheels are ever taken for repair, always ensure that the relative positions of the rim and hub are checked before the wheel is dismantled, so that it can be correctly rebuilt.
4 Owners should note that if the wheel track offset is outside the specified tolerance, there could be some risk of the driveshaft fouling the inside of the swinging arm. Whenever the swinging arm is disturbed, always check that there is sufficient clearance at all suspension positions between the universal joint and the swinging arm.

20.1 Paralever driveshaft has two universal joints and an integral damper

22 Rear suspension unit: general – R80GS and R100GS models

The unit fitted to these models has four spring preload settings. When removing and refitting the unit note that its top mounting eye is offset to the outside edge of the bracket (photo).

23 Wheels, brakes and tyres: general

1 The R65, R100RS and R100RT models are fitted with the same wheel, brake and tyre components described in Chapter 8 for the 1985 on R80/R80RT models. For these later models, therefore, follow the appropriate instructions for the servicing procedure required.
2 The R80GS and R100GS models also use similar wheel, brake and tyre components to the 1985 on R80/R80RT models. With the obvious exception of the wire-spoked wheels, therefore, follow the appropriate instructions for the servicing procedure required. Note the revised torque setting for the brake disc mounting nuts, 27-31 Nm (20-23 lbf ft).
3 On all models, care must be taken when ordering replacement parts for hydraulic brake systems, since several minor modifications have been made, principally to the master cylinder cover and rubber diaphragm to improve venting and to minimise the possibility of moisture contaminating the brake fluid.
4 Whenever the rear brake is dismantled, check the return springs with great care and renew them if there is the slightest doubt about their condition or if they show signs of stretching, fatigue, or wear. Later models will have a rubber damper fitted around the rearmost (camshaft side) return spring to prevent any risk of the spring vibrating to the point of breaking, a problem which also produces severe brake squeal. If a machine is found without a rubber damper, one should be fitted on reassembly. Note that the manufacturer also recommends that both return springs must be renewed whenever an unmodified machine is found.
5 On reassembly, fit the rubber damper to the rearmost return spring so that the damper flat rear face touches the brake shoes and cam, and its chamfered side face is towards the wheel.

24 Rear wheel: removal and refitting

The bolts used to fasten the rear wheel are marked with their length (in millimetres) stamped into the bolt head. For example, R80 and R80RT models use 50 mm long bolts which are marked '50'. *To ensure that the wheel is correctly fastened, ensure that the number on all four bolt heads is the same, and that it matches the number stamped into the wheel hub.*

25 Wheel rim: repair – R80GS and R100GS models

1 Owners should note that the unusual design of the spokes and rims on these models will mean that repair work, whether it involves the renewal of the rim and/or spokes or just truing-up, is a task for the expert. Always take the machine to a good authorised BMW dealer for the repair to be carried out.
2 If replacement parts are required, they can only be obtained from a BMW dealer, due to the unique design. Furthermore, major repair work must start with the careful checking and measurement of the rim's position relative to the hub, so that the correct offset can be built in on reassembly (see Section 21). This requires a great deal of skill and equipment. Given the potential for poor handling and machine instability that could result from a poorly-built wheel, it is essential that owners do not attempt repairs themselves.

26 Tubeless tyre valves: renewal – later models

1 The 1985 R80 and R80RT models were first fitted with threaded-type tyre valves which use an 8 mm hole in the cast alloy wheel rim. From June 1985 on, a rubber-bodied car-type valve was used, which fits into a 15 mm hole in the wheel rim; note that the wheels and valves are not interchangeable. All R65, R100RS and R100RT models should be fitted with the car-type valves.
2 To renew a valve first remove the wheel from the machine (Chapter 8, Section 2 or 3, as appropriate) and then remove the tyre (Chapter 8, Section 14). Cut off the valve's inner retaining shoulder and pull the remains out of the rim. To fit a new valve, lubricate it thoroughly and push it through the rim from the outside towards the centre (having first removed its cap). It must then be drawn into place by screwing the correct tool on to its threaded end to provide purchase (the tool should be available at any tyre-fitting establishment). If great care is taken to avoid crushing the valve end it is possible to screw a suitably-sized nut on to the valve threads and to grip this with a large pair of pliers. Check that the rubber locating shoulders lock securely into place on each side of the rim. Refit the tyre and wheel.
3 Note that the R80GS and R100GS models retain the early 8 mm threaded-type valve assembly.

27 Battery: removal and refitting

R65, R80, R80RT, R100RS, R100RT
1 Depending on the make and capacity of battery fitted, it may prove necessary to remove the seat front mounting as well as the retaining strap or rubber bands (as appropriate) before the battery can be manoeuvred out of its carrier. Take great care not to damage the battery or to allow the electrolyte to spill.

R80GS, R100GS
2 To remove the battery proceed as described for the R80G/S model in Chapter 9.4, but note that only one screw secures the silencer cover on these later models and that there is no need to remove the suspension unit top mounting. Instead, the battery can be eased out of its carrier once both retaining straps have been withdrawn.

22.1 Note offset of rear suspension unit top mounting eye – R80GS, R100GS

23.5 Note correct positioning of brake return spring rubber damper

26.3 R80GS, R100GS wheel rims are fitted with early type of tubeless tyre valve – ensure locknut is securely fastened

28 Diode board (rectifier): testing – all models

1 Owners should note that if the tests given in Chapter 9.6 reveal the diode board to be faulty, it should be replaced only by the latest improved version which can be identified by its finish; it is either painted black or has a black stripe across the grey finish.
2 Note that an occasional cause of failure of the older type was the melting of soldered joints at their contacts, principally on machines with a fairing.
3 Although it is of academic interest unless the facilities are available to renew individual diodes, it is possible to test each diode of the unit using either a multimeter set to the resistance scale or a battery and bulb test circuit. Diodes act as one-way valves, allowing current to flow in one direction only.
4 If a meter or test lamp is connected across a diode's terminals, first in one direction and then (by reversing the test connections) in the opposite, continuity (or little resistance) should be found in one direction only. If continuity is found in both directions, or in none, then that particular diode is at fault.

29 Fuses: general – R80GS and R100GS models

1 The fuse holder on these models is mounted on the battery left-hand side, behind the silencer cover. Remove its single retaining screw and carefully withdraw the cover.
2 Unclip the cover from the fuse holder. The fuses are of the spade type common on many modern cars; always ensure that sufficient spares of the correct rating are kept on the machine.
3 Always refit the fuse holder cover correctly to prevent the entry of dirt and water sprayed up from the rear wheel.

30 Valeo starter motor: servicing – R80GS and R100GS models

General

1 The R80GS and R100GS are fitted with a Valeo French-built pre-engaged starter motor. This starter may eventually be fitted to other new models in the range and may also be supplied as a replacement part for older models.
2 In design and function it is identical to the Bosch unit described in Chapter 9. Given below are the only significant differences in servicing procedures.

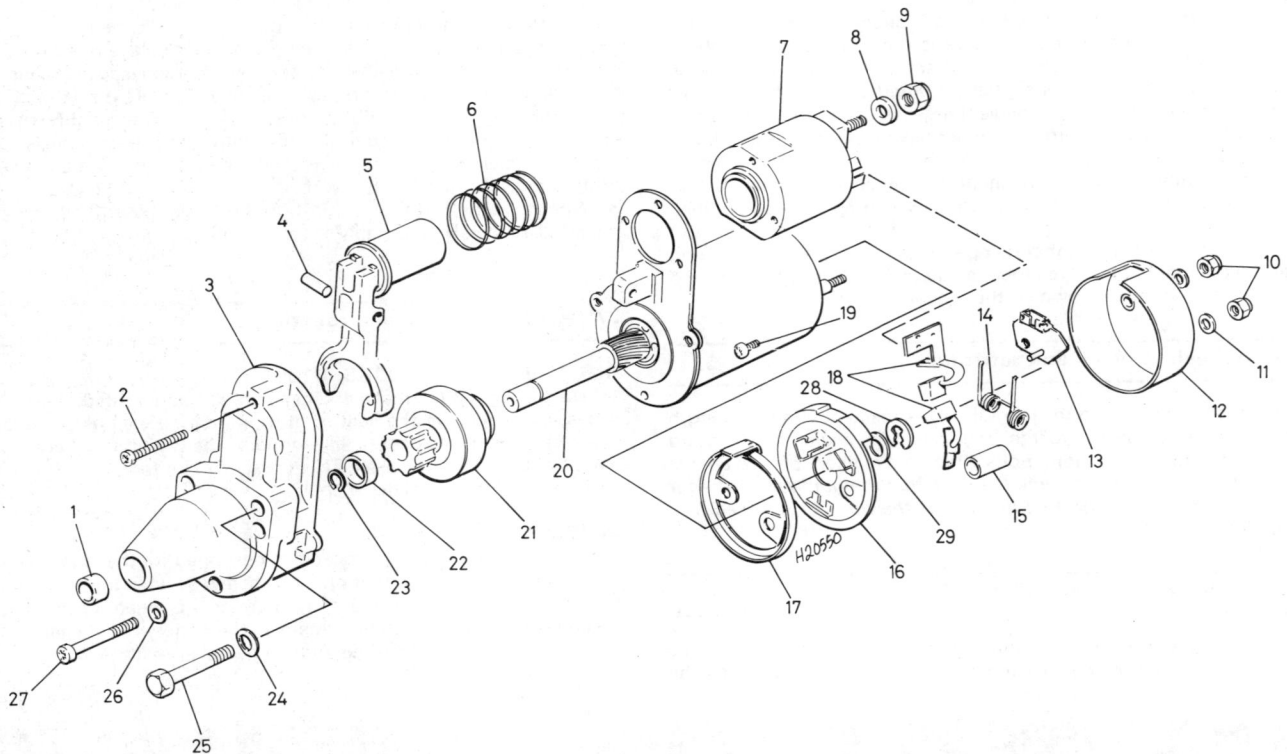

Fig. 10.5 Valeo starter motor

1   Bush
2   Screw
3   Drive housing
4   Pivot pin
5   Pinion engaging lever assembly
6   Coil spring
7   Starter solenoid
8   Lock washer
9   Nut
10 Nut – 2 off
11 Washer – 2 off
12 Commutator cover
13 Rubber plug
14 Brush spring
15 Spacer
16 Brush holder
17 Seal
18 Brush set
19 Screw – 2 off
20 Starter motor body and armature assembly
21 Starter pinion/clutch assembly
22 Bush
23 Circlip
24 Wave washer – 2 off
25 Mounting bolt – 2 off
26 Washer – 3 off
27 Screw – 3 off
28 Circlip
29 Shim – as required

Chapter 10 The 1986 to 1988 models

29.2 Fuses are of spade type – always carry spare of correct rating

29.3 Ensure cover is properly sealed to exclude moisture and dirt

Removal and refitting
3 Remove the seat and fuel tank, followed by the air filter top cover and element. Unscrew the two retaining Allen screws (one on each side) and withdraw the starter cover; this may be a tight fit, but should yield to gentle pressure.
4 Disconnect the battery earth (negative) lead at its connection to the gearbox cover, then unscrew the large nut and spring washer and withdraw the heavy-gauge black starter lead and the smaller red wire. Disconnect the black wire from the solenoid spade terminal.
5 Unscrew the two mounting bolts from the motor rear end, then withdraw the motor.
6 Refitting is a reversal of the above.

Overhaul
7 The starter motor must be removed from the machine before any part of it can be dismantled.
8 Remove the two nuts and washers and withdraw the commutator cover, noting the rubber plug and the way one of the brush lead terminals is retained on the stud by the cover.
9 Prise back the brush retaining spring, noting the presence of the small white insulating pieces. Withdraw the brushes and measure their length. As with the Bosch unit the brushes should be renewed if they have worn to half their original length or more, but the original length is not specified. As a guide, the nearly-new brushes on the machine featured in the accompanying photographs were found to be 14 mm (0.55 in) long which would indicate a minimum length of 7 mm (0.28 in). Check that the brushes are free to slide in their holders and use a clean, lint-free rag to remove any particles of dust or dirt.
10 Remove the retaining clip from the armature end, noting the presence and number of any shims behind it. Carefully withdraw the brush holder and seal.
11 Working from the drive end, remove the retaining screws and withdraw the drive housing. Check the armature bush for wear and renew it if necessary.
12 Unscrew its retaining screws and withdraw the solenoid, separating it from the pinion engaging lever assembly. Drift out the pivot pin to release the lever from the housing.
13 Prise off the retaining circlip and slide off the starter pinion assembly The bush at its centre can be renewed if worn, but if the pinion clutch is worn or defective, the unit must be renewed complete.
14 There is little point in removing the armature from the motor body as the two cannot be renewed individually, only as part of the assembly. If the armature or field coils are ever found to be defective it may be possible for an auto-electrical specialist to attempt a repair, rather than resorting to renewal of the unit.
15 Check and clean the commutator as described for the Bosch unit in Chapter 9.

30.5 Valeo starter motor is retained by two bolts (arrowed) at rear end

30.8 Remove commutator cover to reach brushes

30.9a Prise back brush retaining spring to release brushes – note brush leads and insulating pieces

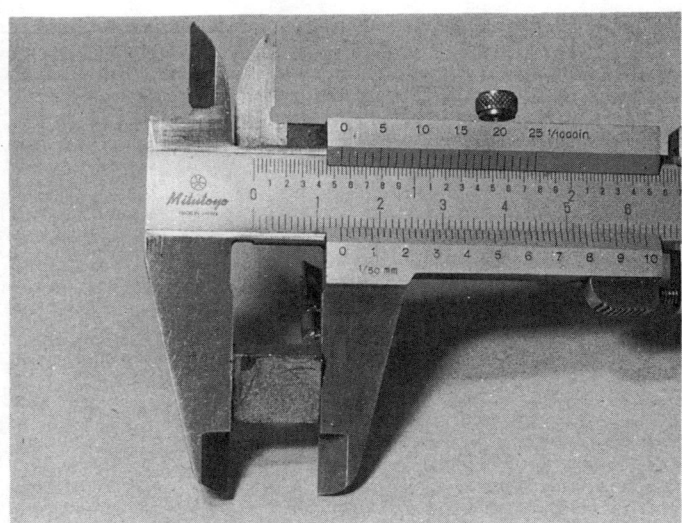

30.9b Measuring brush length

31 Stop lamp and clutch interlock switches: general

1 The plunger-type switches fitted to the handlebar master cylinder or clutch lever assembly on all later models and to the rear brake pedal assembly on some models have been replaced by a modified type which is more resistant to the entry of dirt or water and the resulting arcing across the contacts.

2 The modified switch must be installed by hand only (maximum torque of 5 Nm/3.5 lbf ft) and must be secured using a drop of Loctite 242 or similar thread-locking compound.

3 Before installing the modified type of switch to the handlebar levers, however, check that the lever recess is large enough so that the plunger makes contact squarely and not on one edge, which could cause it to bend and break the switch. If necessary open out the recess until the plunger operation is correct.

4 For rear brake switches the pedal stop screw can in some cases contact the switch body and damage it, hindering the free movement of the plunger. A cap is available from BMW dealers which will prevent this, but its fitment will mean that the switch setting will have to be adjusted by appoximately 3.5 mm (0.14 in).

5 Don't forget that the regular application of a water dispersant lubricant such as WD40 or CRC56 will preserve a switch of this type and greatly prolong its life.

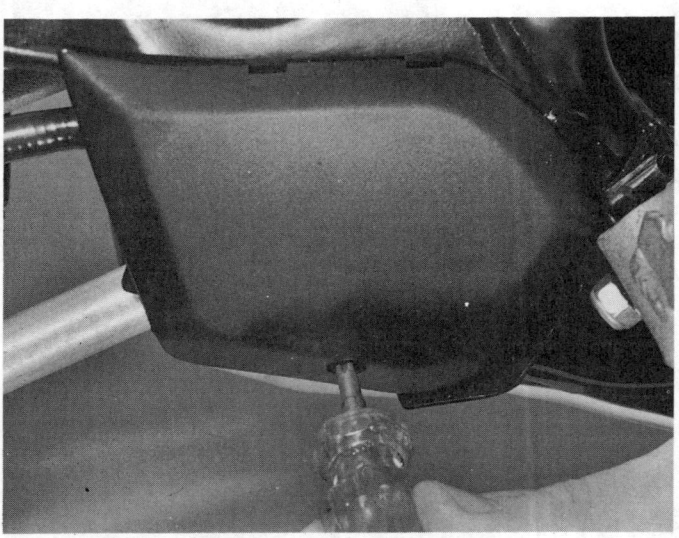

31.5a Stop lamp rear switch – R80GS, R100GS – remove single screw to release cover ...

31.5b ... regular maintenance will prolong switch life

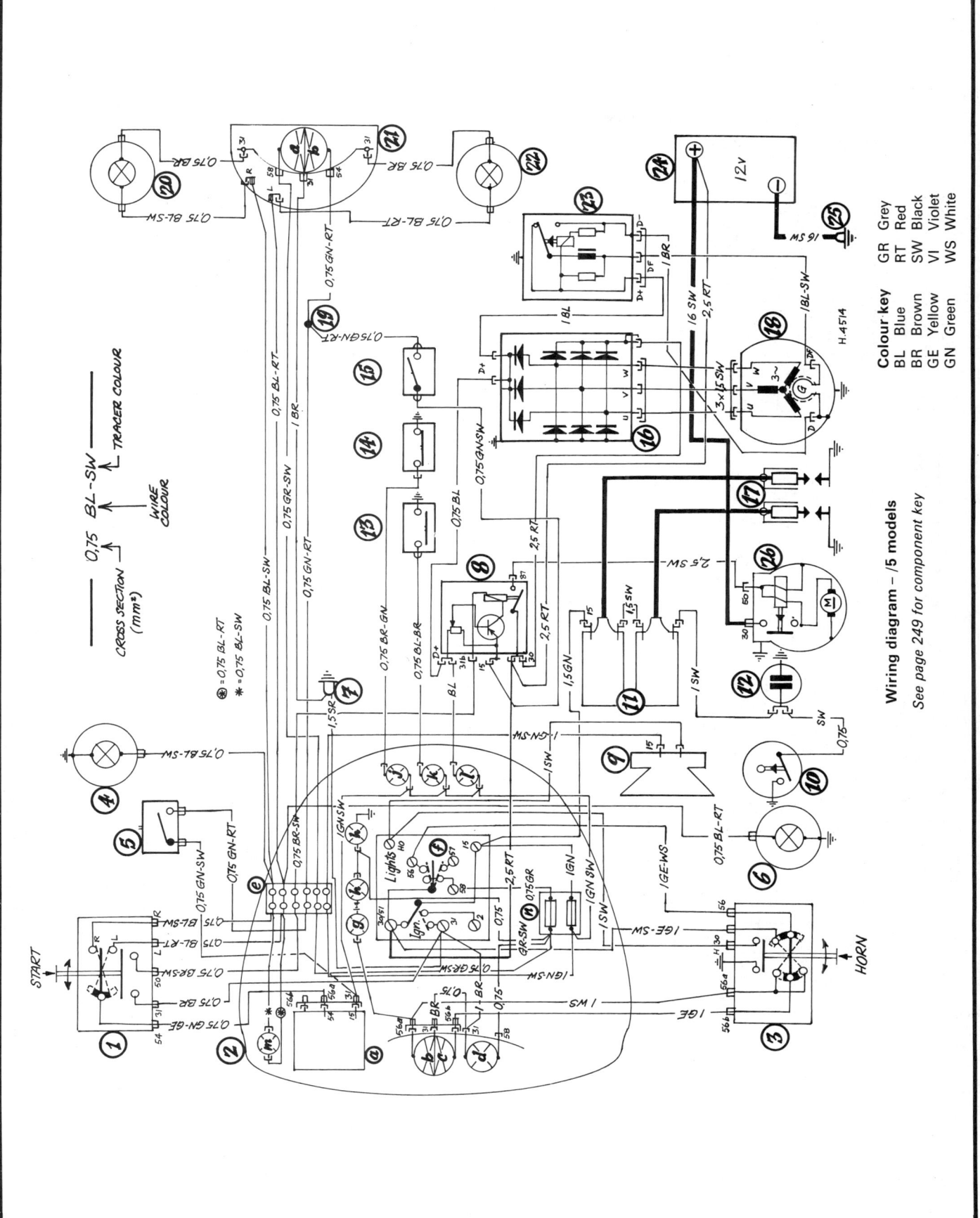

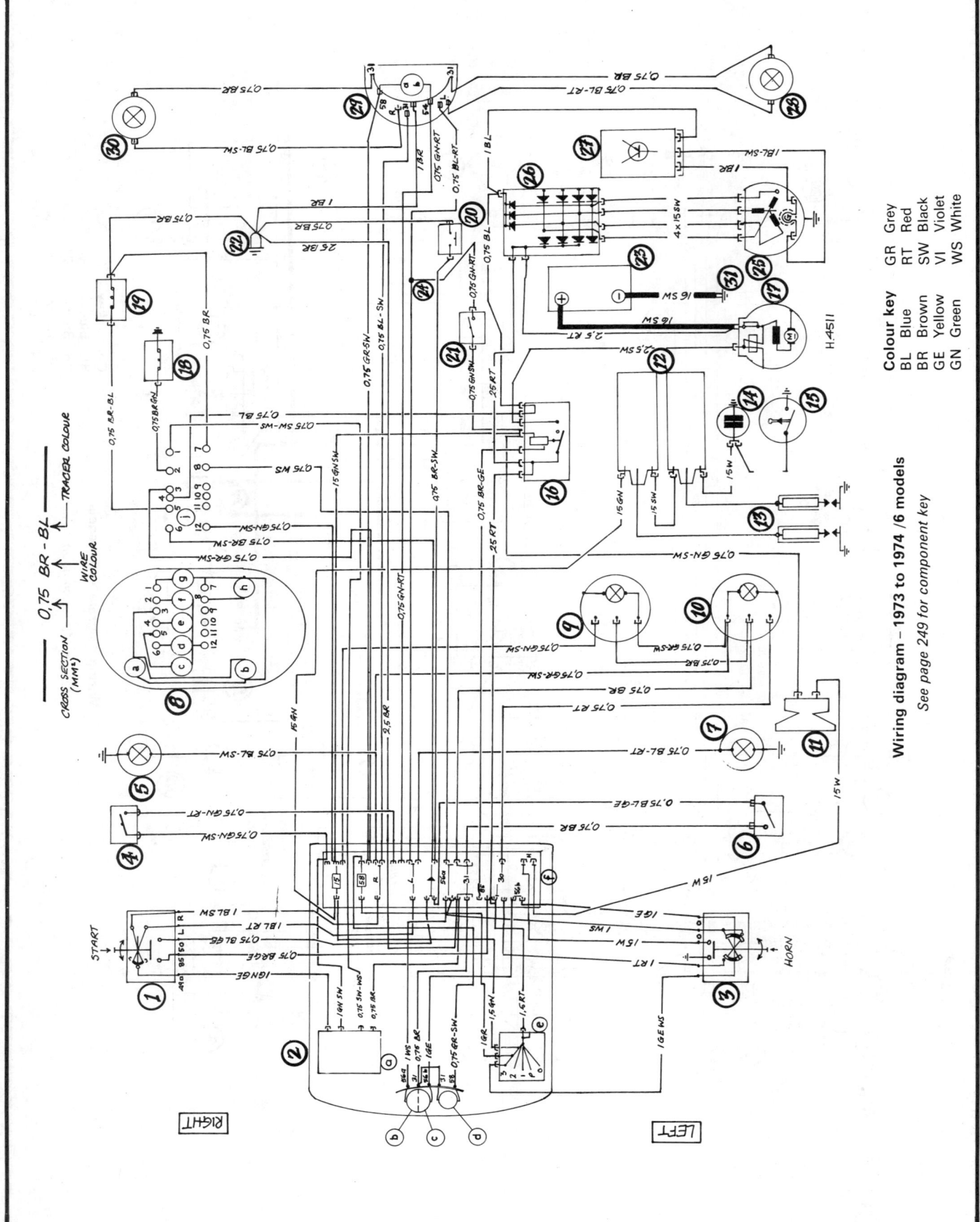

Component key – /5 models

1. Indicator switch and starter button
2. Headlamp:
   a. Flasher unit
   b. Main beam
   c. Dip beam
   d. Pilot light
   e. Connector
   f. Ignition and lighting switch
   g. Main beam warning lamp (blue)
   h. Instrument lighting
   i. Oil pressure warning lamp (orange)
   k. Neutral warning lamp (green)
   l. Charge warning lamp (red)
   m. Indicator warning lamp (green)
   n. Fuses (2)
3. Dipswitch, headlamp flasher and horn
4. Front right-hand indicator
5. Front brake stop light switch
6. Front left-hand indicator
7. Frame earth near ignition coil
8. Starter relay
9. Horn
10. Contact breaker
11. Ignition coils
12. Capacitor
13. Neutral warning lamp switch
14. Oil pressure switch
15. Rear brake stop light switch
16. Diode plate
17. Spark plugs
18. Alternator
19. Connector
20. Rear right-hand indicator
21. Rear/stop light:
    a. Rear lamp
    b. Stop lamp
22. Rear left-hand indicator
23. Voltage regulator
24. Battery
25. Battery earth on gearbox
26. Starter and solenoid

Component key – 1973 to 1974 /6 models

1. Indicator switch and starter button
2. Headlamp:
   a. Flasher unit
   b. Main beam
   c. Dipped beam
   d. Pilot light
   e. Ignition and lighting switch
   f. Connector
3. Dipswitch, headlight flasher and horn push
4. Front brake stop light switch
5. Front right-hand indicator
6. Starter cut-out switch
7. Front left-hand indicator
8. Instrument housing:
   a. Speedometer illumination
   b. Rev-counter illumination
   c. Brake fluid level warning lamp (red)
   d. Neutral warning lamp (green)
   e. Charge warning lamp (red)
   f. Oil pressure warning lamp (orange)
   g. Indicator warning lamp (orange)
   h. Main beam warning lamp (blue)
   j. Connector
9. Voltmeter – R90S only
10. Clock – R90S only
11. Horn
12. Ignition coils
13. Spark plugs
14. Capacitor
15. Contact breaker
16. Starter relay
17. Starter and solenoid
18. Oil pressure switch
19. Brake fluid level switch
20. Neutral indicator switch
21. Rear stoplight switch
22. Earth point at ignition coil
23. Battery
24. Connector
25. Alternator
26. Diode plate
27. Voltage regulator
28. Rear left-hand indicator
29. Rear/stop light:
    a. Rear lamp
    b. Stop lamp
30. Rear right-hand indicator
31. Battery earth at gearbox

Component key – 1975 to 1976 /6 models

1. Turn indicator switch, starter button and emergency cutout
2. Headlight:
   a. Flasher relay
   b. High beam
   c. Low beam
   d. Parking light
   e. Light relay
   f. Ignition/Lighting switch
   g. Contact board with fuses
3. Dip switch, headlight flasher and horn button
5. Front right-hand indicator
6. Starter, cut-out switch
7. Front left-hand indicator
8. Left horn
9. Front stoplight switch
10. Combined instrument:
    a. Speedometer dial lighting
    b. Revolution counter dial lighting
    c. Brake fluid level telltale (red)
    d. Neutral telltale (green)
    e. Battery charge telltale (red)
    f. Oil pressure telltale (orange)
    g. Turn indicator repeater (orange)
    h. Headlight high beam telltale (blue)
11. Starter relay
12. Coils
13. Condenser
14. Ignition contact breaker
15. Spark plugs and caps
16. Oil pressure switch
17. Earth (ground)
18. Rear stoplight switch
19. 2-pin connector
20. Neutral switch
21. Brake fluid level sensing switch
22. 4-pin connector
23. 1-pin connector
24. Diode carrier
25. Battery
26. Starter motor
27. Alternator
28. Voltage regulator
29. Rear right-hand indicator
30. Rear light:
    a. Rear and licence plate light
    b. Brake light
31. Rear left-hand indicator
32. Voltmeter (R90S)
33. Clock (R90S)

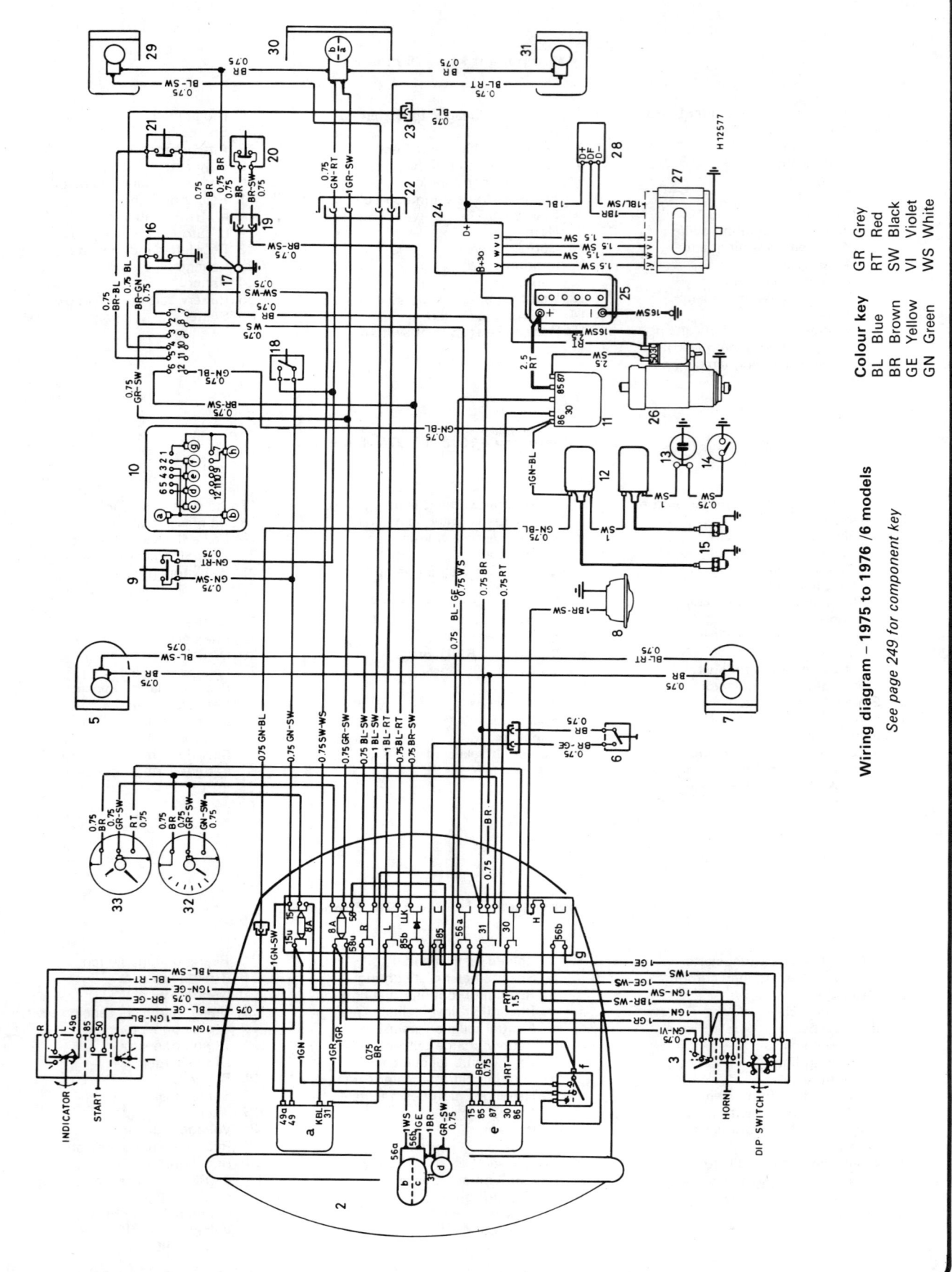

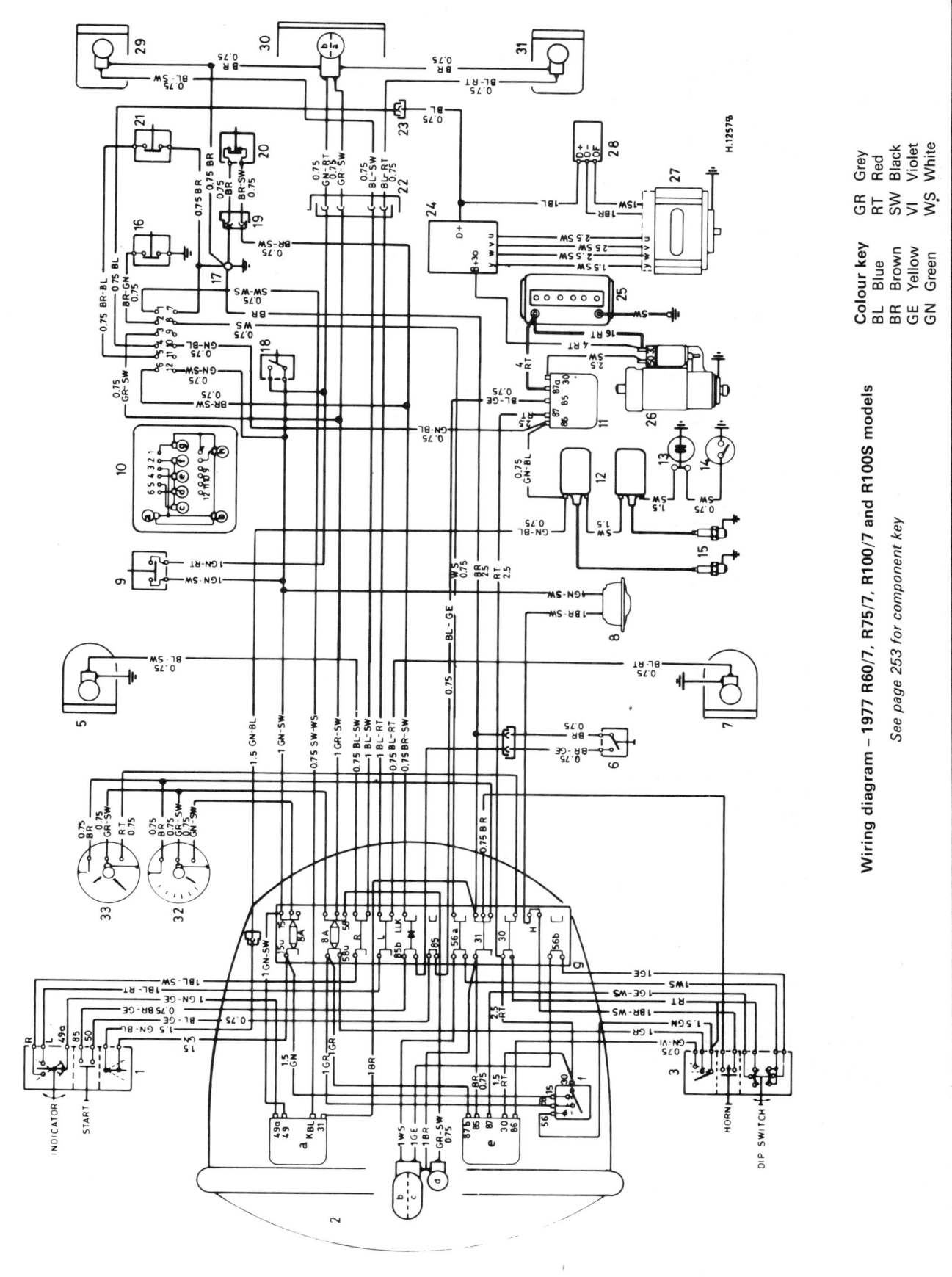

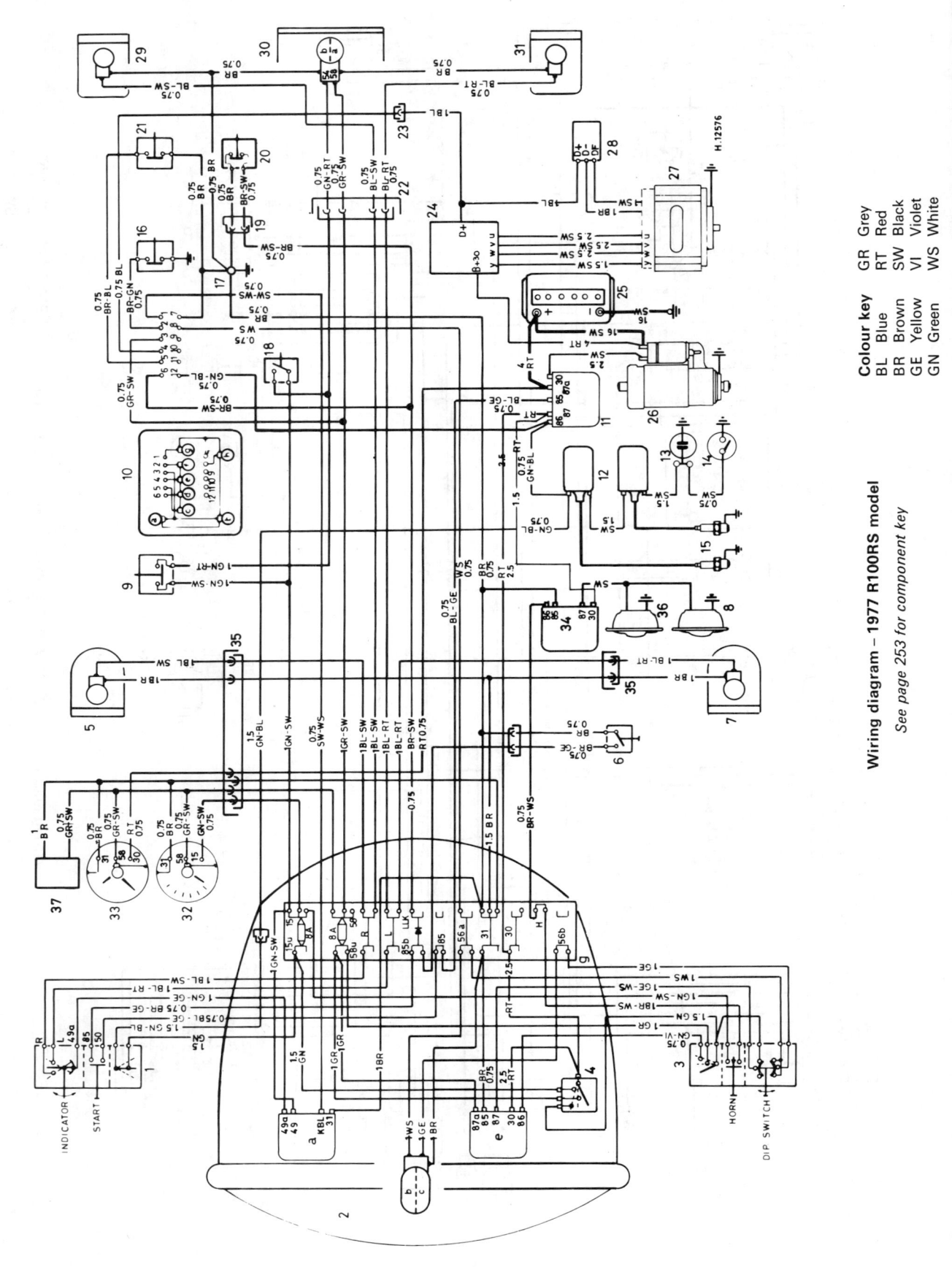

Component key – 1977 R60/7, R75/7, R100/7, R100S and R100RS models

1 Turn indicator switch, starter button and emergency cutout
2 Headlight:
   a Flasher relay
   b High beam
   c Low beam
   d Parking light
   e Light relay
   f Ignition/Lighting switch (except R100RS)
   g Contact board with fuses
3 Dip switch, headlight flasher and horn button
4 Ignition and light switch (RS100RS only)
5 Front right-hand indicator
6 Starter, cut-out switch
7 Front left-hand indicator
8 Left horn
9 Front stoplight switch
10 Combined instrument:
   a Speedometer dial lighting
   b Revolution counter dial lighting
   c Brake fluid level telltale (red)
   d Neutral telltale (green)
   e Battery charge telltale (red)
   f Oil pressure telltale (orange)
   g Turn indicator repeater (orange)
   h Headlight high beam telltale (blue)
11 Starter relay
12 Coils
13 Condenser
14 Ignition contact breaker
15 Spark plugs and caps
16 Oil pressure switch
17 Earth (ground)
18 Rear stoplight switch
19 2-pin connector
20 Neutral switch
21 Brake fluid level sensing switch
22 4-pin connector
23 1-pin connector
24 Diode carrier
25 Battery
26 Starter motor
27 Alternator
28 Voltage regulator
29 Rear right-hand indicator
30 Rear light:
   a Rear and licence plate light
   b Brake light
31 Rear left-hand indicator
32 Voltmeter (R100S and R100RS)
33 Clock (R100S and R100RS)
34 Horn relay (R100RS only)
35 6-pin plug connector (R100RS only)
36 Right horn (R100RS only)
37 Front parking/marker light (R100RS only)

Component key – 1978 R60/7 and R100/7, 1978 to 1980 R80/7 and R100S, 1979 to 1980 R100T

1 Starter button and emergency cutout (with indicator switch, '78 models)
2 Headlight:
   a Flasher relay
   b High beam
   c Low beam
   d Parking light
   e Light relay
   f Ignition/light switch
   g Contact board with fuses
3 Dip switch, headlight flasher and horn switch (with indicator switch, '79 models)
4 Front RH indicator
5 2-pin connector
6 Clutch switch
7 Voltmeter
8 Clock
9 Front LH indicator
10 Horn
11 Single-pin connector
12 Front stoplight switch
13 Combined instrument:
   a Speedometer light
   b Revolution counter light
   c Brake fluid telltale
   d Neutral indicator
   e Battery charge indicator
   f Oil pressure light
   g Indicator repeater
   h High beam indicator
14 Starter relay
15 Buzzer relay
16 Single-pin connector
17 Ignition coils
18 Spark plugs with caps
19 Contact breaker assembly
20 Starter motor
21 Socket
22 Flying fuse
23 Battery
24 Alternator
25 Regulator
26 Diode board (rectifier)
27 Single-pin connector
28 Diode
29 Rear stoplight switch
30 2-pin connector
31 Single-pin connector
32 Brake fluid switch
33 Oil pressure switch
34 2-pin connector
35 Neutral switch
36 6-pin connector
37 2-pin connector
38 Buzzer
39 Rear LH indicator
40 Rear light:
   a Rear and licence plate light
   b Brake light
41 Rear RH indicator

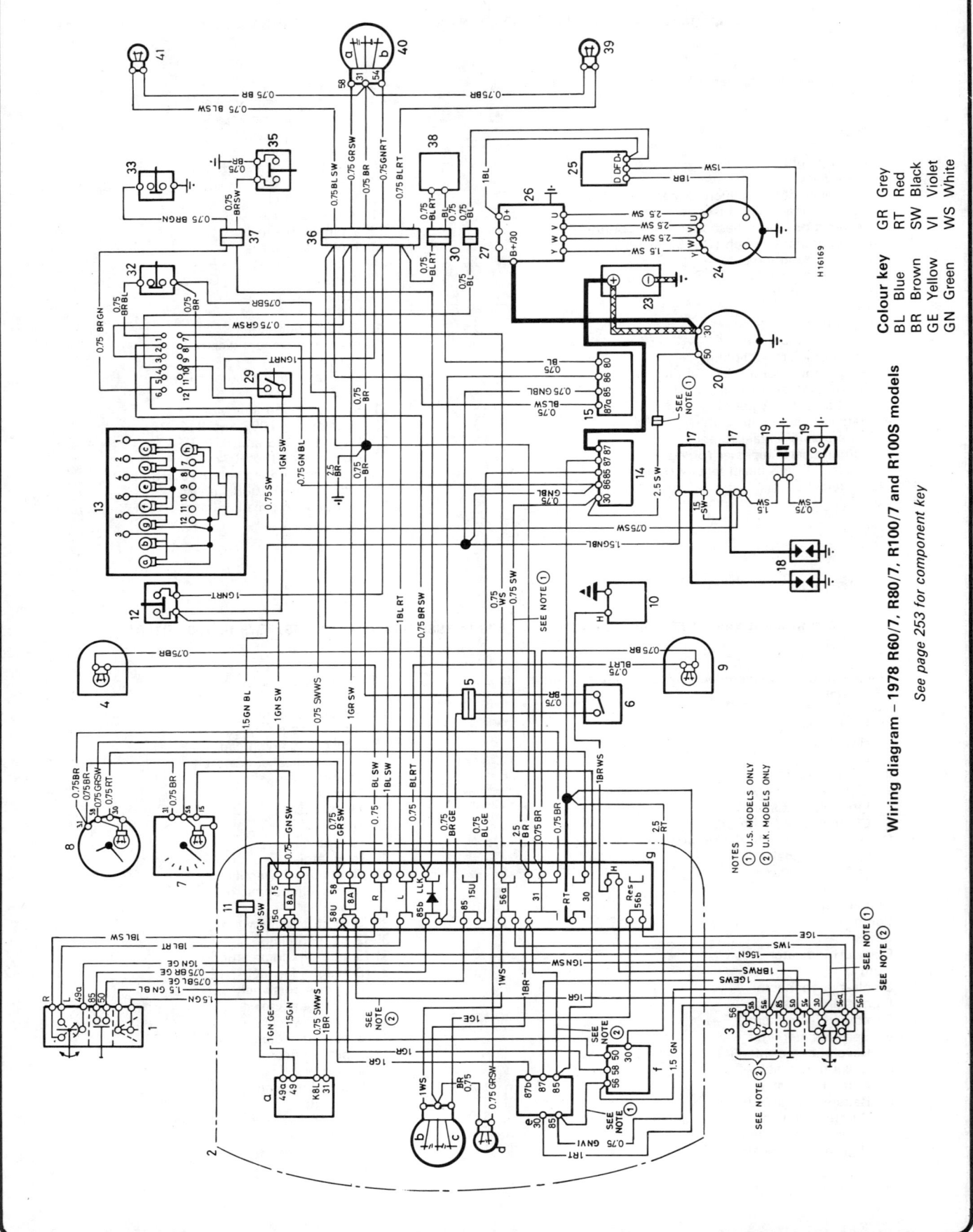

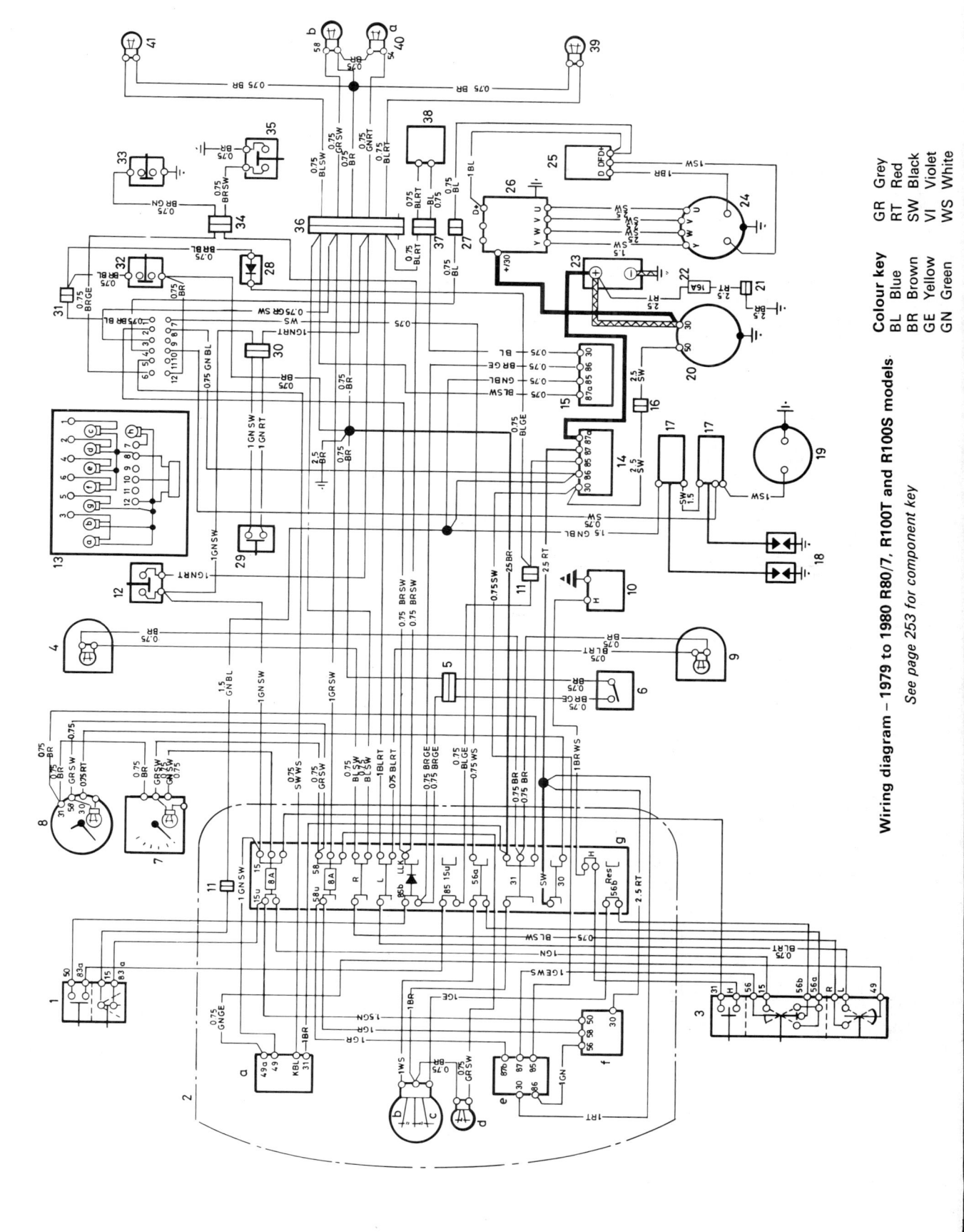

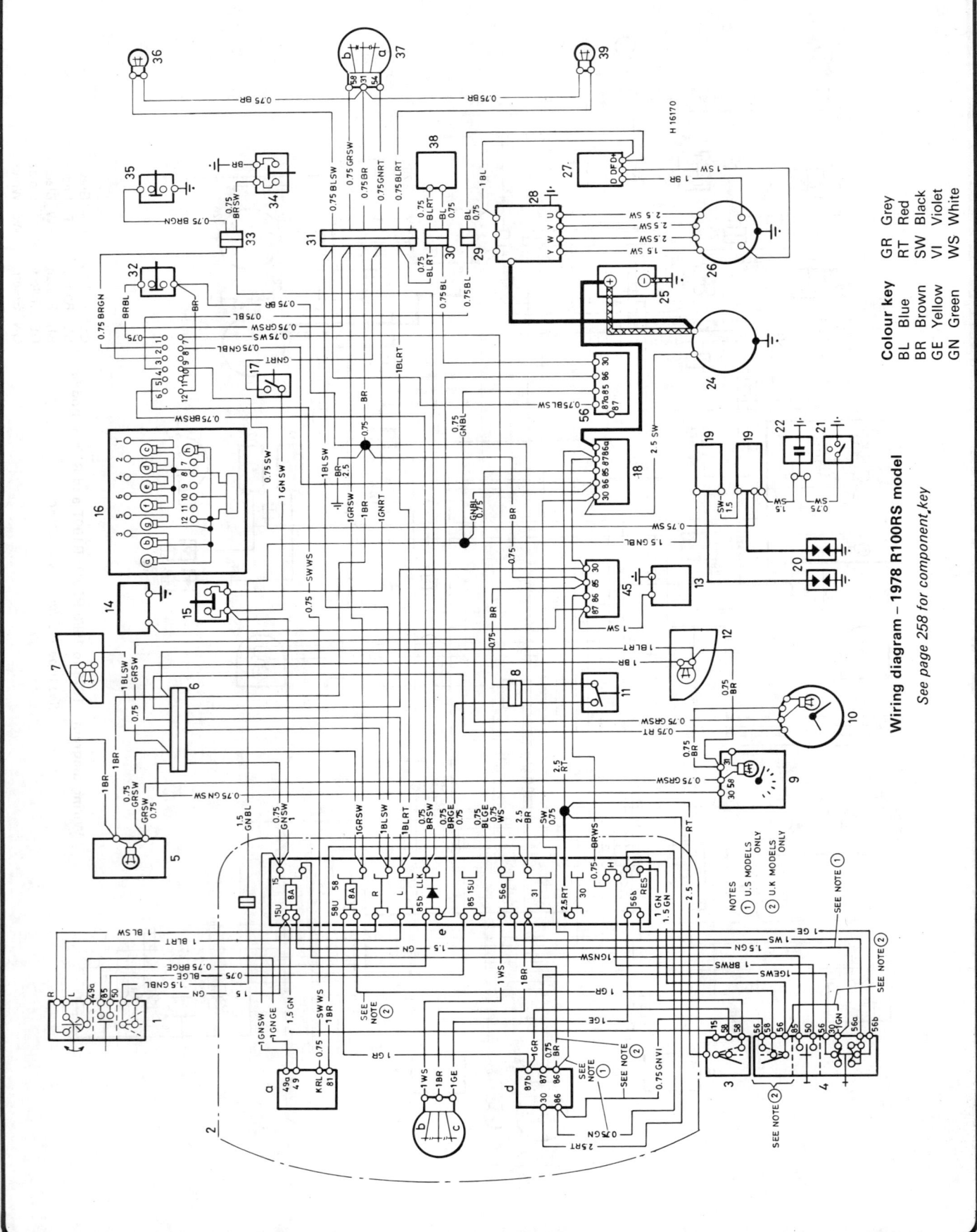

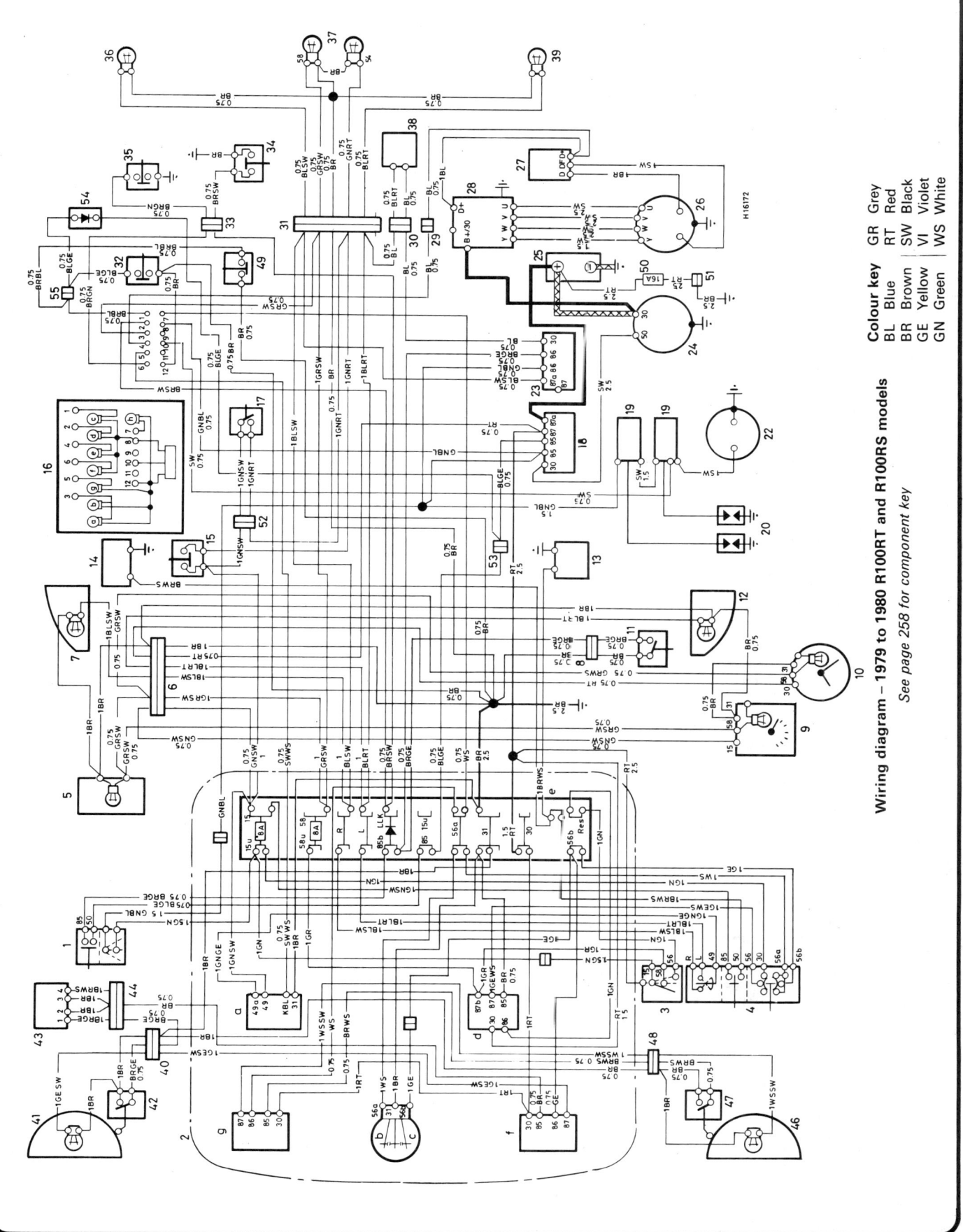

Wiring diagram – 1979 to 1980 R100RT and R100RS models
See page 258 for component key

Component key – 1978 to 1980 R100RS and 1979 to 1980 R100RT

1. Starter button and emergency cutout (with indicator switch, '78 model)
2. Headlight:
   a. Flasher relay
   b. High beam
   c. Low beam
   d. Light relay
   e. Contact board with fuses
   f. Fog light relay (1979 models)
   g. Auxiliary driving light relay (1979 models)
3. Ignition/light switch
4. Dip, headlight flasher and horn switch (with indicator switch, '79 models)
5. Running light
6. 6-pin connector
7. Front RH indicator
8. 2-pin connector
9. Voltmeter
10. Clock
11. Clutch switch
12. Front LH indicator
13. Left horn
14. Right horn
15. Front stoplight switch
16. Combined instrument:
    a. Speedometer light
    b. Revolution counter light
    c. Brake fluid telltale
    d. Neutral indicator
    e. Battery charge indicator
    f. Oil pressure light
    g. Indicator repeater
    h. High beam telltale
17. Rear stoplight switch
18. Starter relay
19. Ignition coils
20. Spark plugs and caps
21. Capacitor (1978 model)
22. Contact breaker assembly
23. Buzzer relay
24. Starter motor
25. Battery
26. Alternator
27. Regulator
28. Diode board (rectifier)
29. Single-pin connector
30. 2-pin connector
31. 6-pin connector
32. Brake fluid switch
33. 2-pin connector
34. Neutral switch
35. Oil pressure switch
36. Rear RH indicator
37. Rear light:
    a. Rear and licence plate light
    b. Brake light
38. Buzzer
39. Rear LH indicator
40. 3-pin connector
41. Fog light
42. Limit switch
43. Fog light switch
44. 3-pin connector
45. Horn relay (1978 models)
46. Auxiliary driving light
47. Limit switch
48. 3-pin connector
49. Rear brake fluid switch
50. Flying fuse
51. Socket
52. 2-pin connector
53. Single-pin connector
54. Diode
55. Single-pin connector
56. Relay

Component key – 1983 to 1984 R80RT and 1981 on R100, R100CS, R100RT, R100RS models

1. Starter button and emergency cutout
2. Headlight:
   a. Flasher relay
   b. High beam
   c. Low beam
   d. Parking light
   e. Light relay
   f. Ignition/light switch (R100, R100CS)
   g. Contact board with fuses
3. Ignition/light switch (R100RS, RT)
4. Dip switch, headlight flasher and horn button
5. Running light (R100RS, RT)
6. 6-pin connector (R100RS, RT)
7. Front RH indicator
8. Voltmeter
9. Clock
10. Clutch switch
11. Front LH indicator
12. Left horn
13. Right horn (R100RS, RT)
14. Front stoplight switch
15. Combined instrument:
    a. Speedometer light
    b. Revolution counter light
    c. High beam tell tale
    d. Neutral indicator
    e. Battery charge indicator
    f. Oil pressure light
    g. Indicator repeater
16. Rear stoplight switch
17. Starter relay
18. Ignition coils
19. Spark plugs and caps
20. Ignition trigger
21. Starter motor
22. Battery
23. Alternator
24. Regulator
25. Diode board (rectifier)
26. 6-pin connector
27. Oil pressure switch
28. Neutral switch
29. Rear RH indicator
30. Rear light:
    a. Rear and licence plate light
    b. Brake light
31. Rear LH indicator
32. TCI unit

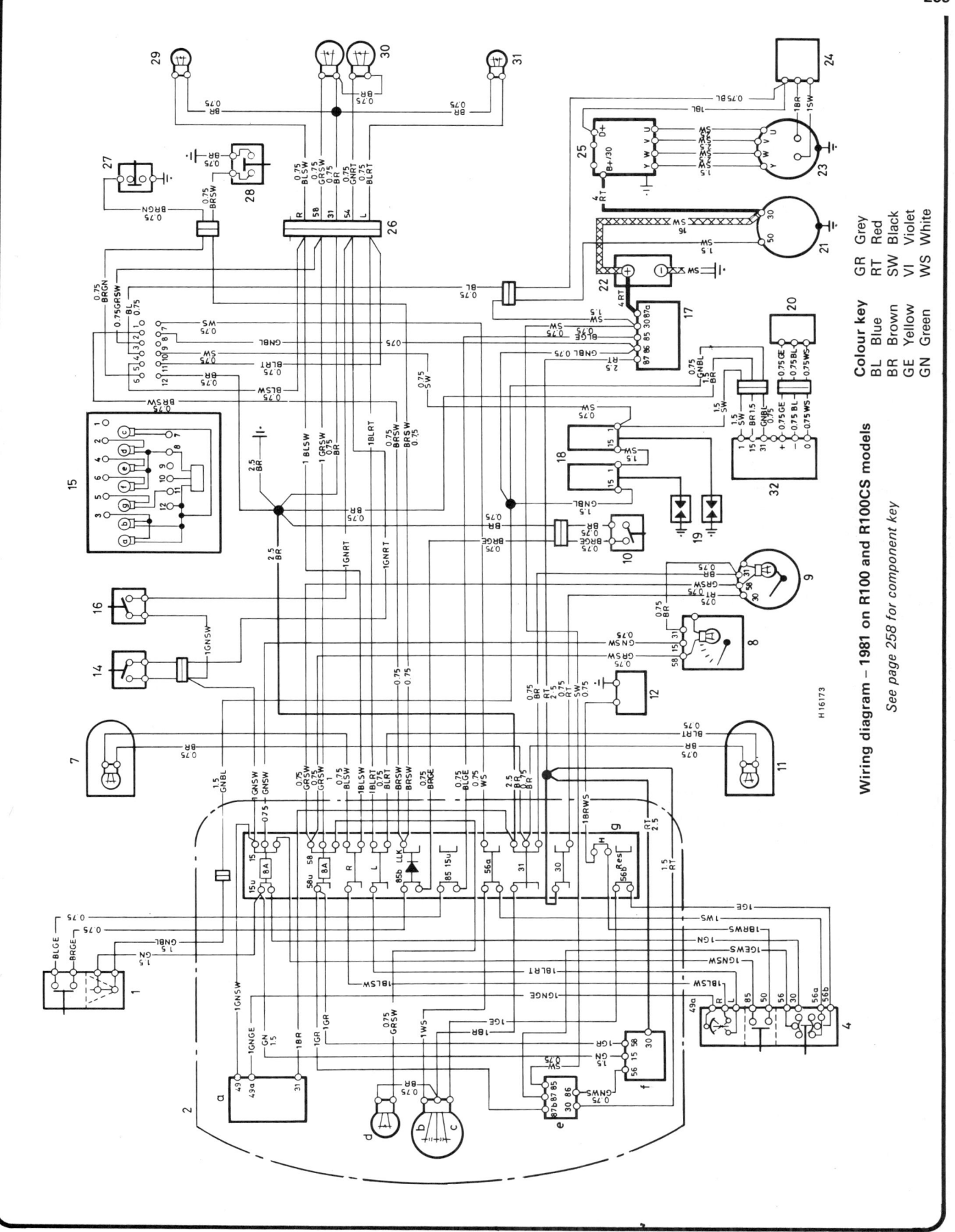

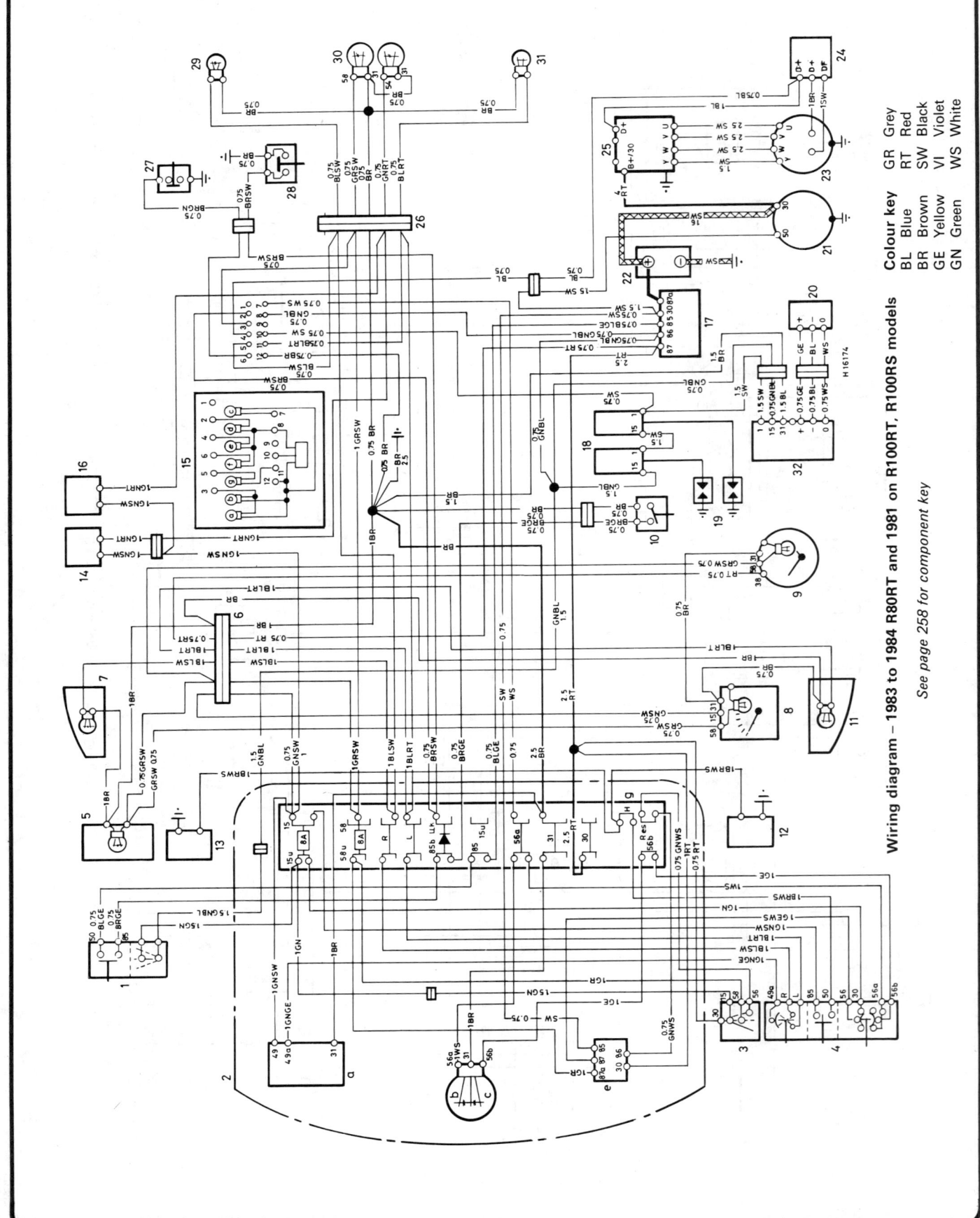

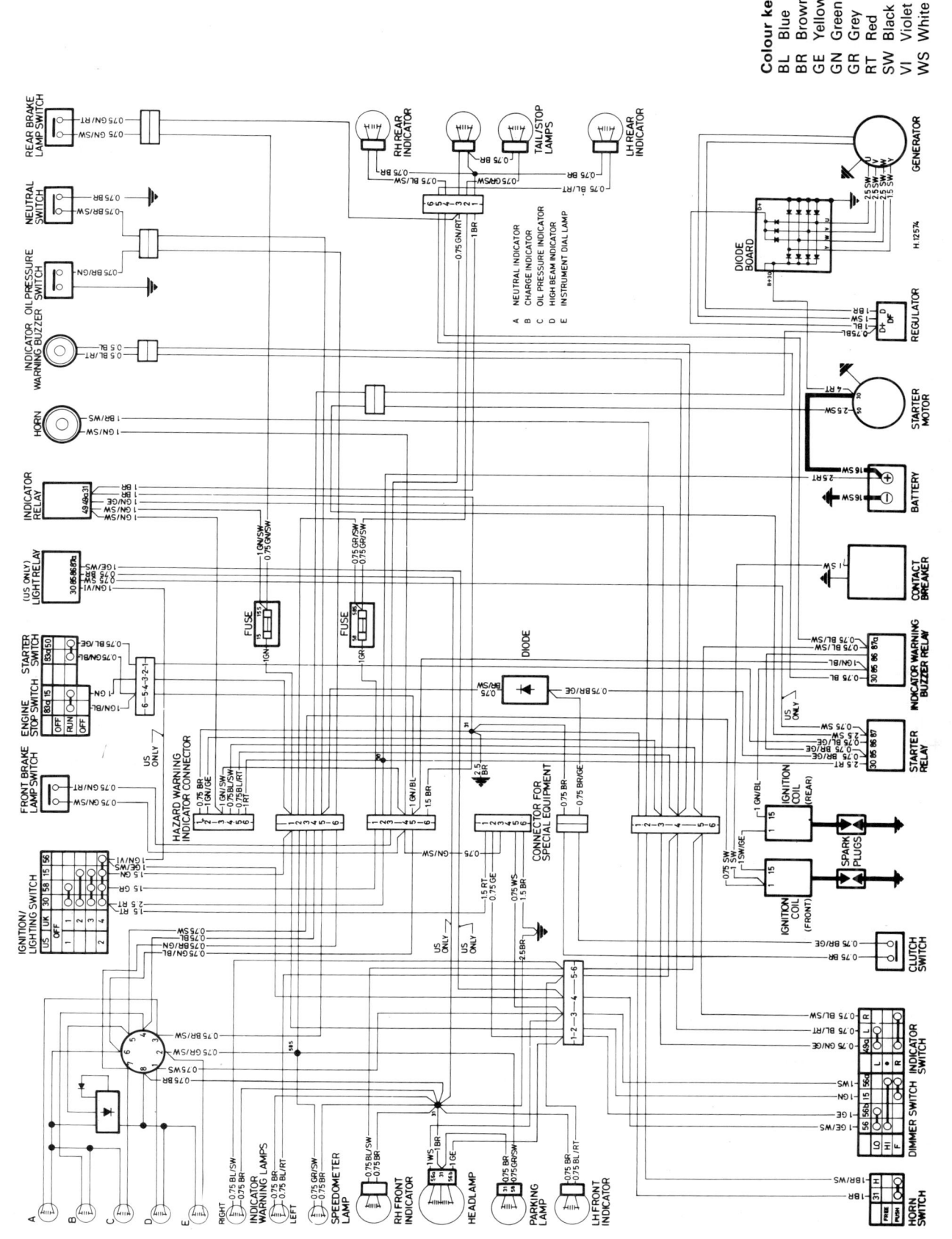

Wiring diagram – 1979 to 1980 R45 and R65 models

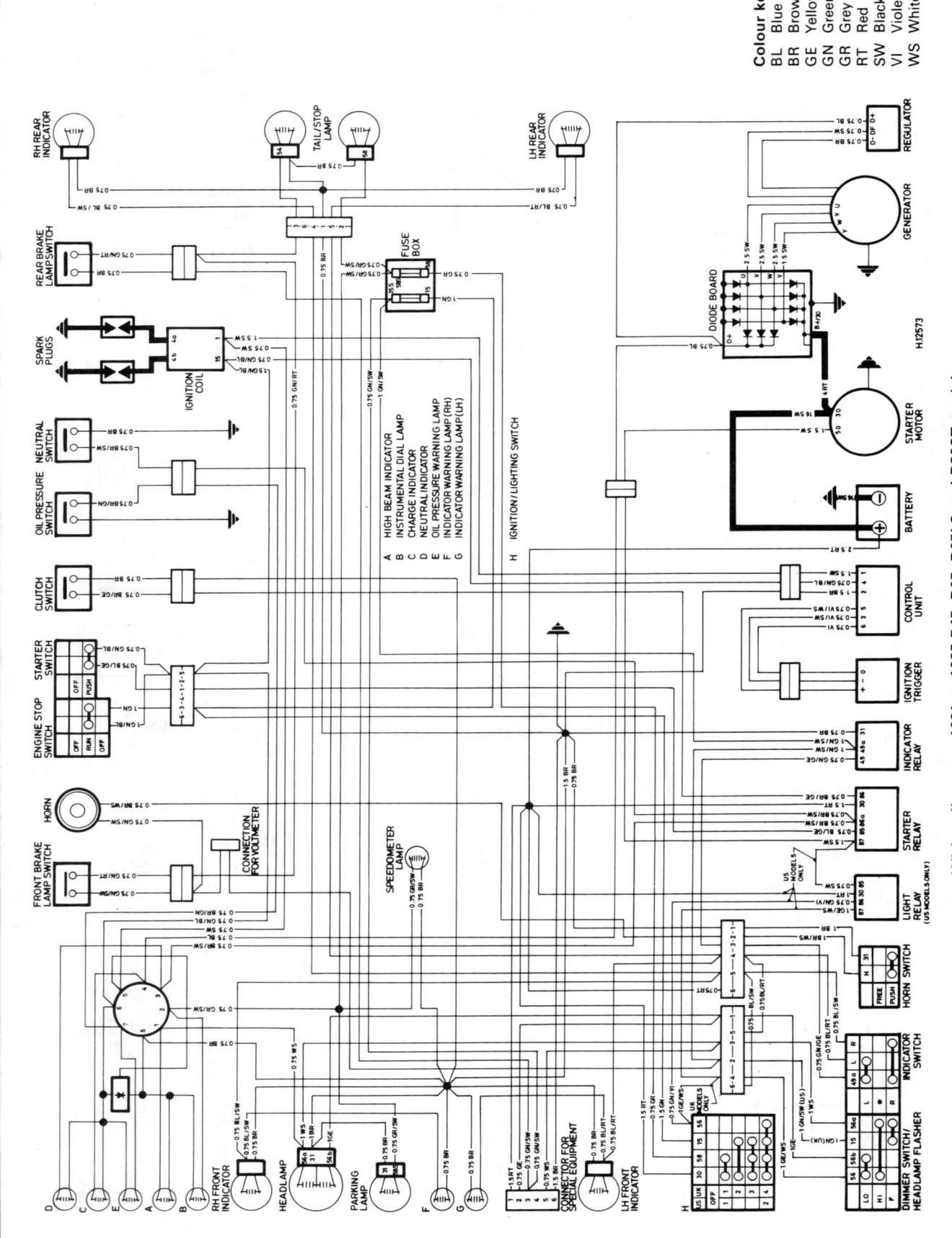

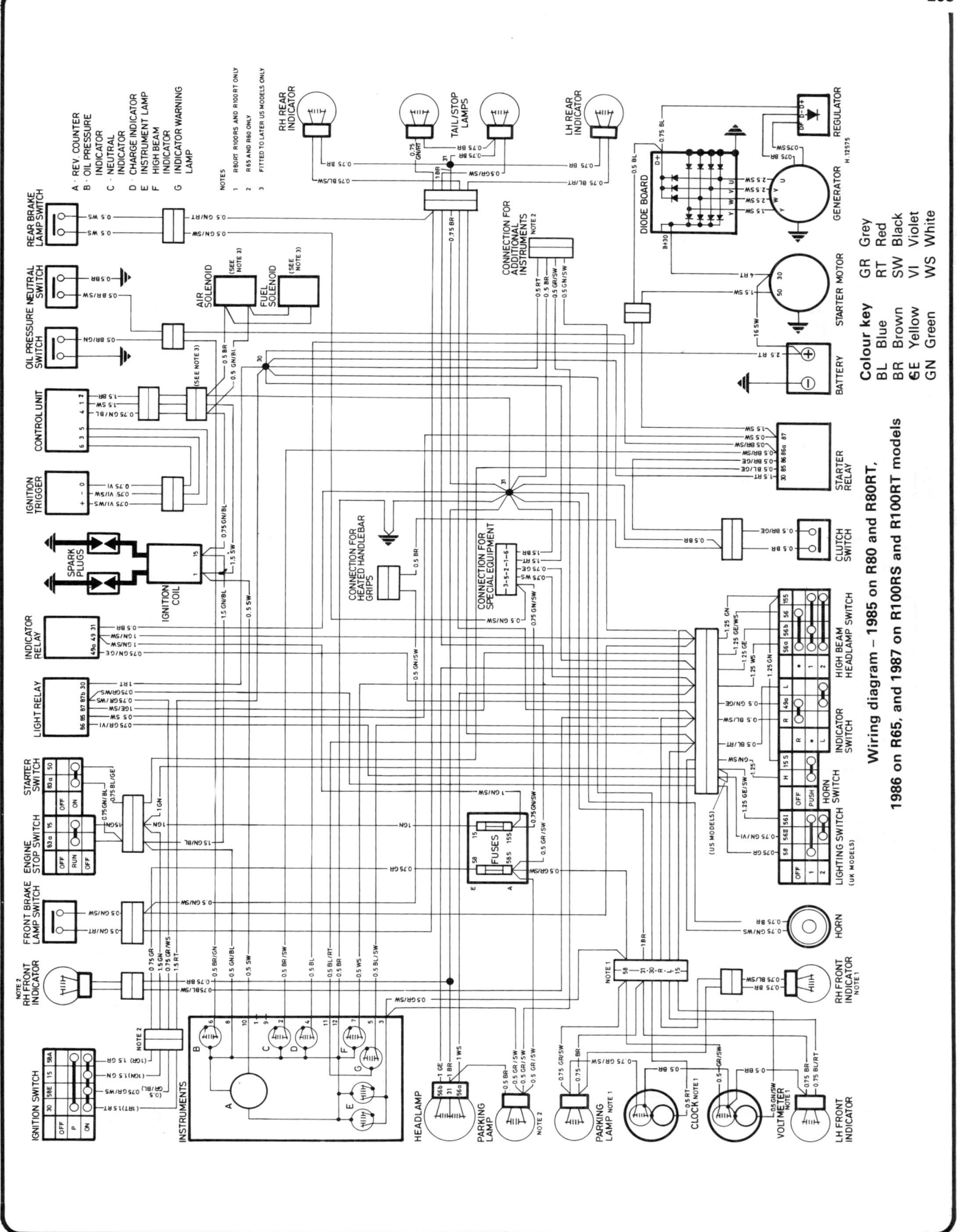

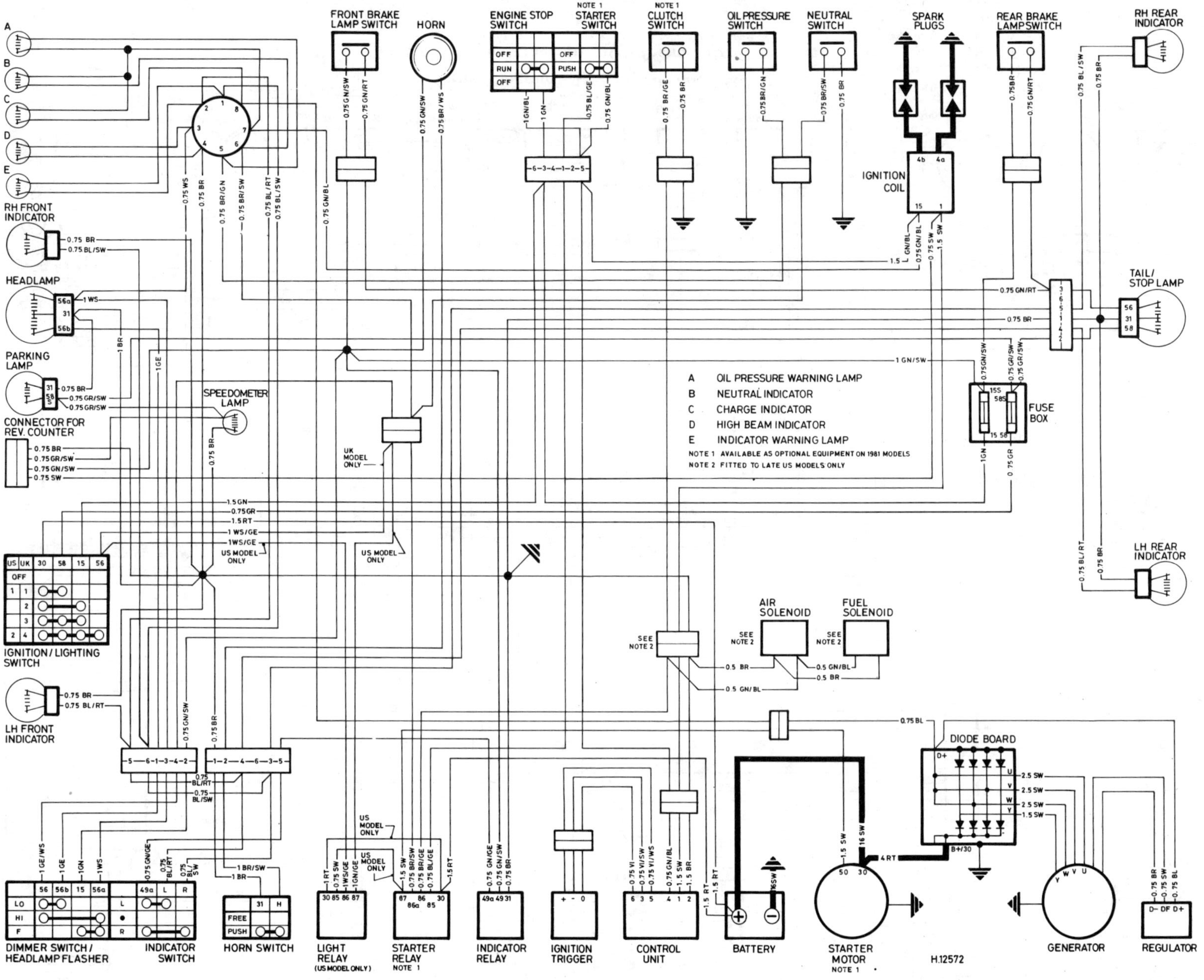

Wiring diagram – R80G/S model

Colour key
BL Blue
BR Brown
GE Yellow
GN Green
GR Grey
RT Red
SW Black
VI Violet
WS White

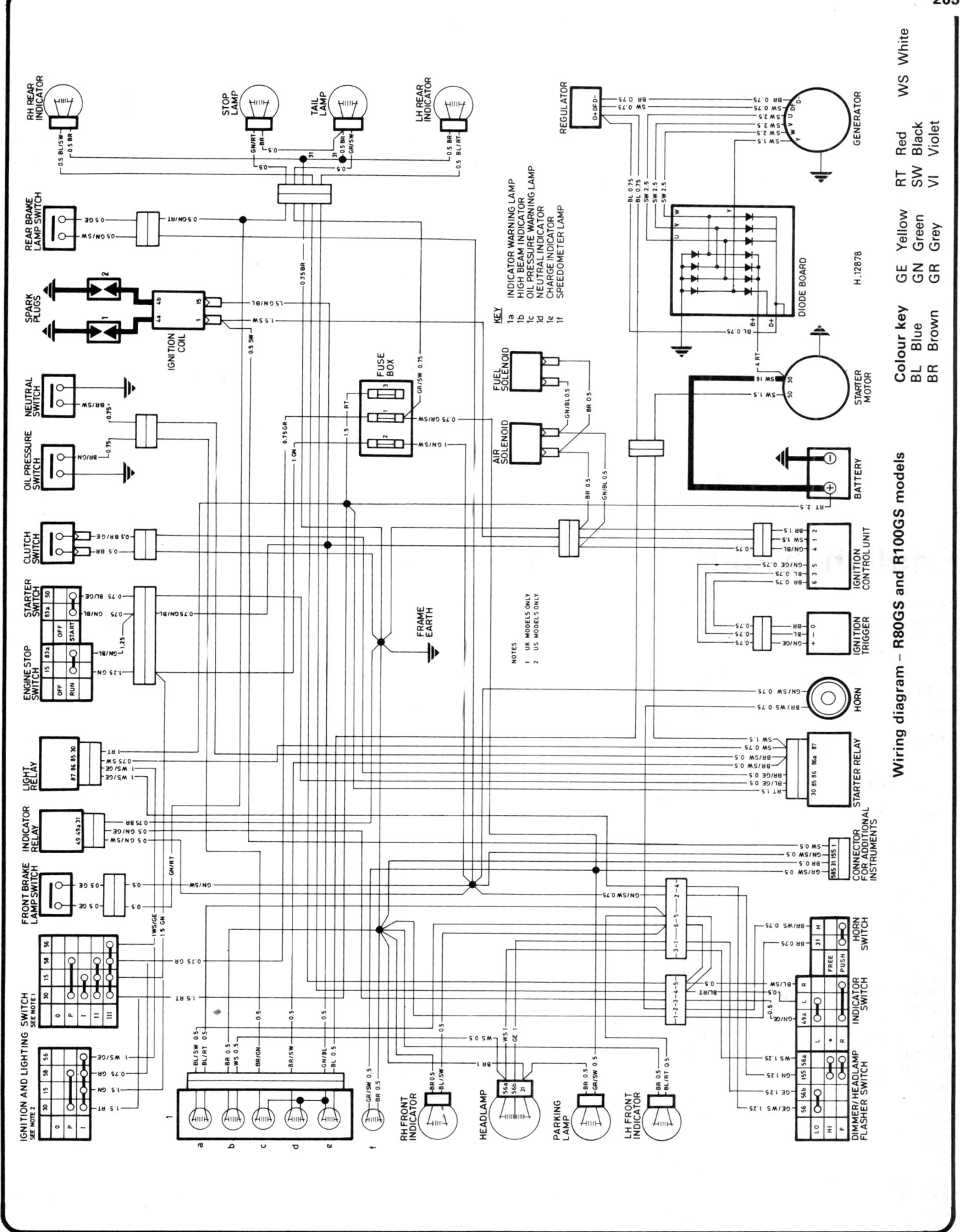

English/American terminology

Because this book has been written in England, British English component names, phrases and spellings have been used throughout. American English usage is quite often different and whereas normally no confusion should occur, a list of equivalent terminology is given below.

English	American	English	American
Air filter	Air cleaner	Number plate	License plate
Alignment (headlamp)	Aim	Output or layshaft	Countershaft
Allen screw/key	Socket screw/wrench	Panniers	Side cases
Anticlockwise	Counterclockwise	Paraffin	Kerosene
Bottom/top gear	Low/high gear	Petrol	Gasoline
Bottom/top yoke	Bottom/top triple clamp	Petrol/fuel tank	Gas tank
Bush	Bushing	Pinking	Pinging
Carburettor	Carburetor	Rear suspension unit	Rear shock absorber
Catch	Latch	Rocker cover	Valve cover
Circlip	Snap ring	Selector	Shifter
Clutch drum	Clutch housing	Self-locking pliers	Vise-grips
Dip switch	Dimmer switch	Side or parking lamp	Parking or auxiliary light
Disulphide	Disulfide	Side or prop stand	Kick stand
Dynamo	DC generator	Silencer	Muffler
Earth	Ground	Spanner	Wrench
End float	End play	Split pin	Cotter pin
Engineer's blue	Machinist's dye	Stanchion	Tube
Exhaust pipe	Header	Sulphuric	Sulfuric
Fault diagnosis	Trouble shooting	Sump	Oil pan
Float chamber	Float bowl	Swinging arm	Swingarm
Footrest	Footpeg	Tab washer	Lock washer
Fuel/petrol tap	Petcock	Top box	Trunk
Gaiter	Boot	Torch	Flashlight
Gearbox	Transmission	Two/four stroke	Two/four cycle
Gearchange	Shift	Tyre	Tire
Gudgeon pin	Wrist/piston pin	Valve collar	Valve retainer
Indicator	Turn signal	Valve collets	Valve cotters
Inlet	Intake	Vice	Vise
Input shaft or mainshaft	Mainshaft	Wheel spindle	Axle
Kickstart	Kickstarter	White spirit	Stoddard solvent
Lower leg	Slider	Windscreen	Windshield
Mudguard	Fender		

Conversion factors

Length (distance)
Inches (in)	X	25.4	= Millimetres (mm)	X 0.0394	= Inches (in)
Feet (ft)	X	0.305	= Metres (m)	X 3.281	= Feet (ft)
Miles	X	1.609	= Kilometres (km)	X 0.621	= Miles

Volume (capacity)
Cubic inches (cu in; in³)	X	16.387	= Cubic centimetres (cc; cm³)	X 0.061	= Cubic inches (cu in; in³)
Imperial pints (Imp pt)	X	0.568	= Litres (l)	X 1.76	= Imperial pints (Imp pt)
Imperial quarts (Imp qt)	X	1.137	= Litres (l)	X 0.88	= Imperial quarts (Imp qt)
Imperial quarts (Imp qt)	X	1.201	= US quarts (US qt)	X 0.833	= Imperial quarts (Imp qt)
US quarts (US qt)	X	0.946	= Litres (l)	X 1.057	= US quarts (US qt)
Imperial gallons (Imp gal)	X	4.546	= Litres (l)	X 0.22	= Imperial gallons (Imp gal)
Imperial gallons (Imp gal)	X	1.201	= US gallons (US gal)	X 0.833	= Imperial gallons (Imp gal)
US gallons (US gal)	X	3.785	= Litres (l)	X 0.264	= US gallons (US gal)

Mass (weight)
Ounces (oz)	X	28.35	= Grams (g)	X 0.035	= Ounces (oz)
Pounds (lb)	X	0.454	= Kilograms (kg)	X 2.205	= Pounds (lb)

Force
Ounces-force (ozf; oz)	X	0.278	= Newtons (N)	X 3.6	= Ounces-force (ozf; oz)
Pounds-force (lbf; lb)	X	4.448	= Newtons (N)	X 0.225	= Pounds-force (lbf; lb)
Newtons (N)	X	0.1	= Kilograms-force (kgf; kg)	X 9.81	= Newtons (N)

Pressure
Pounds-force per square inch (psi; lbf/in²; lb/in²)	X	0.070	= Kilograms-force per square centimetre (kgf/cm²; kg/cm²)	X 14.223	= Pounds-force per square inch (psi; lbf/in²; lb/in²)
Pounds-force per square inch (psi; lbf/in²; lb/in²)	X	0.068	= Atmospheres (atm)	X 14.696	= Pounds-force per square inch (psi; lbf/in²; lb/in²)
Pounds-force per square inch (psi; lbf/in²; lb/in²)	X	0.069	= Bars	X 14.5	= Pounds-force per square inch (psi; lbf/in²; lb/in²)
Pounds-force per square inch (psi; lbf/in²; lb/in²)	X	6.895	= Kilopascals (kPa)	X 0.145	= Pounds-force per square inch (psi; lbf/in²; lb/in²)
Kilopascals (kPa)	X	0.01	= Kilograms-force per square centimetre (kgf/cm²; kg/cm²)	X 98.1	= Kilopascals (kPa)
Millibar (mbar)	X	100	= Pascals (Pa)	X 0.01	= Millibar (mbar)
Millibar (mbar)	X	0.0145	= Pounds-force per square inch (psi; lbf/in²; lb/in²)	X 68.947	= Millibar (mbar)
Millibar (mbar)	X	0.75	= Millimetres of mercury (mmHg)	X 1.333	= Millibar (mbar)
Millibar (mbar)	X	0.401	= Inches of water (inH$_2$O)	X 2.491	= Millibar (mbar)
Millimetres of mercury (mmHg)	X	0.535	= Inches of water (inH$_2$O)	X 1.868	= Millimetres of mercury (mmHg)
Inches of water (inH$_2$O)	X	0.036	= Pounds-force per square inch (psi; lbf/in²; lb/in²)	X 27.68	= Inches of water (inH$_2$O)

Torque (moment of force)
Pounds-force inches (lbf in; lb in)	X	1.152	= Kilograms-force centimetre (kgf cm; kg cm)	X 0.868	= Pounds-force inches (lbf in; lb in)
Pounds-force inches (lbf in; lb in)	X	0.113	= Newton metres (Nm)	X 8.85	= Pounds-force inches (lbf in; lb in)
Pounds-force inches (lbf in; lb in)	X	0.083	= Pounds-force feet (lbf ft; lb ft)	X 12	= Pounds-force inches (lbf in; lb in)
Pounds-force feet (lbf ft; lb ft)	X	0.138	= Kilograms-force metres (kgf m; kg m)	X 7.233	= Pounds-force feet (lbf ft; lb ft)
Pounds-force feet (lbf ft; lb ft)	X	1.356	= Newton metres (Nm)	X 0.738	= Pounds-force feet (lbf ft; lb ft)
Newton metres (Nm)	X	0.102	= Kilograms-force metres (kgf m; kg m)	X 9.804	= Newton metres (Nm)

Power
Horsepower (hp)	X	745.7	= Watts (W)	X 0.0013	= Horsepower (hp)

Velocity (speed)
Miles per hour (miles/hr; mph)	X	1.609	= Kilometres per hour (km/hr; kph)	X 0.621	= Miles per hour (miles/hr; mph)

*Fuel consumption**
Miles per gallon, Imperial (mpg)	X	0.354	= Kilometres per litre (km/l)	X 2.825	= Miles per gallon, Imperial (mpg)
Miles per gallon, US (mpg)	X	0.425	= Kilometres per litre (km/l)	X 2.352	= Miles per gallon, US (mpg)

Temperature

Degrees Fahrenheit = (°C x 1.8) + 32 Degrees Celsius (Degrees Centigrade; °C) = (°F - 32) x 0.56

*It is common practice to convert from miles per gallon (mpg) to litres/100 kilometres (l/100km), where mpg (Imperial) x l/100 km = 282 and mpg (US) x l/100 km = 235

Index

A

About this manual 5
Accessories 14
Acknowledgements 2
Adjustments:-
   carburettors 134, 138
   clutch 39, 53
   horn 218
   spark plugs 42
   valve clearances 40
   wheel track offset 242
Air filter:-
   cleaning 37
   element renewal 53
   modification 229
Alternator:-
   overhaul 214
   removal 213

B

Battery:-
   check 36, 53
   examination and maintenance 211
   removal and refitting 210, 243
Bearings:-
   big-end 81
   gearbox 111, 229
   main 81
   steering head 57, 165
   swinging arm 52, 54, 174, 228
   wheel 57, 193
Big-end bearings:-
   examination and renovation 81
   specifications 63
Bleeding the hydraulic brake system 203
Brakes:-
   bleeding 203
   caliper 198
   check 30, 46
   description 184
   drum:
      front 195
      rear 197, 243
   hydraulic system 198, 203
   modifications 243
   overhaul 54
   specifications 182
   torque wrench settings 184
Bulbs:-
   renewal 218
   specifications 209, 227

C

Cables:-
   rev-counter 170
   speedometer 170
Caliper – brake:-
   removal, examination and refitting 198
   specifications 183
Cam followers:-
   examination and renovation 79
   specifications 63
Camshaft:-
   examination and renovation 79
   refitting 82
   removal 72
   specifications 62
Carburettors:-
   adjustment 138
   adjustment and exhaust emissions – general note 134
   checking the settings 134
   checks – general 45, 54
   overhaul:
      Bing constant-depression type 134
      Bing slide type 131
      Dell'orto 132
   removal and refitting 130
   specifications 119, 225
Charging system 212
Checks:-
   battery 36, 53
   brakes 30, 46
   carburettors 45, 54, 134
   contact breaker gap and ignition timing
   (all models up to 1980) 42, 54
   controls 30
   cylinder head nuts tightness 40, 53
   driveshaft oil level 36, 228
   electrical system 210, 212
   engine oil level 29, 228
   fuel level 30
   gearbox oil level 36
   legal 30
   nuts and bolts tightness – general 30, 52, 58
   rear bevel drive oil level 36, 229
   spark plugs 42, 229
   steering head bearings 57
   swinging arm pivot bearings 54, 228
   tyres 29
   valve clearances 40, 53
   wheels 56
Cleaning:-
   air filter 37
   cylinder and sump cooling fins 34, 53
   fuel tap filter 53

oil pump pick-up filter gauze 145
the machine 28
Clutch:-
   adjustment 39, 53
   description 90
   dismantling 91
   examination and renovation 94
   operating mechanism removal, examination and reassembly 96
   reassembly 94
   removal 91
   specifications 90, 224
   torque wrench settings 90
Compression – engine:-
   specifications 60, 224
   testing 67
Condenser:-
   capacity 147
   removal and refitting 148
Connecting rods:-
   examination and renovation 81
   refitting 84
   removal 72
Contact breaker:-
   cam felt and ATU pivots greasing 53
   gap check 42, 54
   removal and refitting 148
Controls:
   check 30
   general 167
   lubrication 34
Conversion factors 267
Crankcase breather 145
Crankshaft:-
   examination and renovation 81
   refitting 82
   removal 75
   seal modification 229
Cylinder and sump cooling fins 34, 53
Cylinder barrels:-
   examination and renovation 79
   refitting 86
   removal 67
Cylinder heads:-
   examination and renovation 77
   nuts tightness check 40, 53
   refitting 87
   removal 67

D

Description – general:-
   clutch 90
   electrical system 210
   engine 66
   final drive and rear suspension 173
   frame and forks 154
   fuel system and lubrication 122
   gearbox 100
   ignition system 148
   wheels, brakes and tyres 184
Dimensions – model 8, 223
Diode board 215, 244
Driveshaft:-
   examination 176, 242
   oil change 52
   oil level check 36, 228
   refitting 176, 179, 242
   removal 174, 176, 242
Drum – brake:-
   adjustment 51
   examination and renovation:
      front 195
      rear 197, 243
Dualseat mountings – R80GS and R100GS 238

E

Electrical system:-
   alternator 213, 214
   battery 36, 53, 210, 211, 243
   bulbs 218
   charging system 212
   description 210
   diode board 215, 244
   fuses 215, 244
   general information and preliminary checks 210
   horn 218
   relays 218
   specifications 208, 227
   starter motor 216, 244
   switches 218, 246
   torque wrench settings 209
   voltage regulator 215
   wiring 210
   wiring diagrams 247-265
Electronic ignition system 150
Engine:-
   big-end bearings 81
   cam followers 79
   camshaft 72, 75, 79, 82
   compression test 67
   connecting rods 72, 81, 84
   crankshaft 81, 82, 229
   cylinder barrels 67, 79, 86
   cylinder heads 67, 77, 87
   description 66
   dismantling:
      general 67
      preliminaries 75
   examination and renovation 76
   front engine and starter covers 67
   lubrication system 121, 122
   main bearings 81
   oil and filter changing 30, 52, 228
   oil level check 29
   oil pump 75, 82
   oil seals 80, 229
   operations with unit in frame 66
   piston rings 80
   pistons 71, 80, 84
   pushrods 79
   reassembly 82
   refitting in the frame 89
   removing from the frame 75
   rocker assemblies 77, 87
   specifications 59, 224
   starting and running a rebuilt engine 89
   taking a rebuilt engine on the road 89
   timing chain 72, 79, 82
   timing chain cover 72, 80
   timing chain sprockets and tensioner 79
   torque wrench settings 66
   valves, springs and guides 76
Engine lubrication system:-
   description 122
   oil pressure relief valve 146
   oil pressure warning light 146
   oil pump 143, 145
   specifications 121, 225
   torque wrench settings 122
Evaporative Emission Control System 230
Exhaust system 141, 232

F

Fairing 168, 238
Fault diagnosis:-
   brakes 24
   clutch 21
   electrical system 25

engine:
- abnormal noise 21
- acceleration poor 20
- fails to start 18
- knocking or pinking 20
- overheating 20
- poor running at idle and low speed 19
- poor running or lack of power at high speed 20
- stalls after starting 19
- exhaust smokes excessively 22
- frame and suspension – abnormal noise 24
- gear selection 21
- handling or roadholding poor 23
- oil pressure indicator lamp goes on 22
- starter motor 18
- transmission – abnormal noise 22

Filters:-
- air 37, 53, 229
- engine oil 30, 52, 228
- fuel tap 53
- oil pump pick-up 145

Final drive:-
- description 173, 239
- driveshaft 36, 52, 174, 176, 179, 228, 242
- Paralever models 228, 239-242
- rear bevel drive 173, 174
- specifications 171, 226
- torque wrench settings 172, 226

Footrests 167

Frame and forks:-
- description 154
- dualseat mountings – R80GS and R100GS 238
- fairing 168, 238
- footrests, stands and controls 167, 229
- frame 167
- front forks 55, 154-165, 232-238
- instruments 170, 239
- specifications 152, 225
- speedometer and rev-counter cables 110
- steering damper 167
- steering head bearings 165
- torque wrench settings 153, 225

Front brake 195, 200, 243

Front engine and starter covers 67

Front forks:-
- alignment 165, 233
- dismantling 156, 232, 235
- examination and renovation 163
- modifications 232, 233
- oil change 55, 234
- reassembly 163, 232, 235
- refitting 165, 235
- removal 154, 235

Front wheel:-
- bearings 57, 193
- removal and refitting 184

Fuel system:-
- carburettors 130-139
- description 122
- evaporative emission control system 230
- fuel grades 118, 224, 230
- fuel tank 126
- fuel tap filter 53
- fuel taps 130
- pure air system 140
- specifications 118, 224
- torque wrench settings 122

Fuel tank:-
- capacity 118, 224
- removal and refitting 126

Fuel taps:-
- filter cleaning 53
- removal, examination and refitting 130

Fuses 215, 244

G

Gearbox:-
- bearings, seals, gear and selector forks 111, 229
- examination and renovation 111
- description 100
- five-speed:
  - dismantling and reassembling the gear assemblies 111
  - modifications 229
  - reassembly 116
  - removing the gear shafts and selector forks 107
- four-speed:
  - adjusting the selector forks and reassembling 116
  - dismantling and reassembling the gear assemblies 108
  - removing the gear shafts and selector forks 107
- oil change 52
- oil level check 36
- modifications 229
- refitting in the frame 116
- removing and replacing the end cover bearings and seals 107
- removing from the frame 101, 229
- removing the end cover 104
- specifications 99
- torque wrench settings 100

Gearchange mechanism:-
- dismantling; examination and reassembly (five-speed) 114
- removal, examination and reassembly (four-speed) 113

H

Headlamp and parking lamp 218
Horn 218
Hydraulic brake system:-
- bleeding 203
- overhaul 198

I

Ignition system:-
- condenser 148
- contact breaker 42, 53, 54
- control unit 149
- electronic system 150
- HT coil(s) 149
- ignition trigger 148
- pre-ignition – all R60 models 151
- spark plugs 41, 42, 53, 229
- specifications 147, 225
- timing 44, 54
- torque wrench settings 148
- trigger 148

Instrument and warning lamps 218
Instruments 170, 239

K

Kickstart:-
- removal, examination and reassembly:
  - five-speed 114
  - four-speed 114

L

Lubrication:-
- contact breaker cam felt and ATU pivots greasing (all models up to 1980) 53
- controls and stand pivots 34, 53
- driveshaft:
  - oil changing 52
  - oil level check 36, 228

Index

engine:
  description 122
  oil and filter changing 30, 52, 228
  oil level check 29
  specifications 121, 225
front fork oil change 55
gearbox:
  oil change 52
  oil level check 36
rear bevel drive:
  oil change 52, 229
  oil level check 36
swinging arm pivot bearings greasing 52, 228

M

Main bearings 81
Maintenance – routine 28-58, 228
Master cylinder:-
  removal, examination and refitting:
    front brake 200
    modifications 243
    rear disc brake 202

N

Neutral warning lamp switches 114
Nivomat suspension units 180

O

Oil pressure relief valve 146
Oil pressure warning light 146
Oil pump:-
  examination and renovation 143
  pick-up filter gauze cleaning 145
  refitting 82
  removal 75
Oil seals – engine 80, 229

P

Paralever rear suspension 239-242
Piston rings:-
  examination and renovation 80
  specifications 65
Pistons:-
  examination and renovation 80
  refitting 84
  removal 71
  specifications 64
Pre-ignition fault – all R60 models 151
Pure air system 140
Pushrods:-
  examination and renovation 79
  specifications 63

R

Rear bevel drive:-
  examination and renovation 173
  housing:
    refitting 174, 241
    removal 173, 239
  oil change 52, 229
  oil level check 36
Rear brake:-
  disc 202
  drum 197, 243

Rear suspension units:-
  check 30, 180, 229
  description 173
  modifications 239
  Nivomat units 180
  settings 30, 243
  specifications 172, 226
  torque wrench settings 172, 226
  units adjustment, removal and examination 180, 239, 241
Rear wheel:-
  removal and refitting 191, 243
  specifications 182, 226
Relays 218
Rev-counter and cable 170, 239
Rocker assemblies:-
  examination and renovation 77
  refitting 87
  specifications 62
Routine maintenance 28-58, 228

S

Safety precautions 10
Service intervals 28, 228
Spanner size comparison 13
Spare parts 9
Spark plugs:-
  check 42
  operating conditions – colour chart 41
  renewal 53, 229
  specifications 148, 225
Specifications:-
  clutch 90, 224
  electrical system 208, 227
  engine 59, 224
  final drive and rear suspension 171, 226
  frame and forks 152, 225
  fuel system and lubrication 118, 224
  gearbox 99
  ignition system 147, 225
  wheels, brakes and tyres 182, 226
Speedometer and cable 170, 239
Stands:-
  general 167, 229
  pivots lubrication 34
Starter motor:-
  overhaul 216, 245
  removal 216, 245
  specifications 209
Steering damper 167
Steering head bearings:-
  check 57
  removal, examination and refitting 165
Swinging arm:-
  examination and renewal of bearings and seals 174, 242
  pivot bearings:
    check 54, 242
    greasing 52, 228
Swinging arm and driveshaft:-
  refitting 179, 242
  removal 174, 242
Switches:-
  general 218, 246
  neutral warning lamp 114

T

Tachometer and cable 170, 239
Timing chain:-
  examination and renovation 79
  refitting 82
  removal 72

Timing chain cover:-
   refitting 84
   removal 72
Timing chain sprockets and tensioner 79
Timing – ignition:-
   check 44, 54
   specifications 147
Tools 11
Torque wrench settings 13, 66, 90, 122, 153, 172, 184, 209, 225, 226
Turn signal and stop/tail lamp 218
Tyres:-
   check 29
   pressures 183, 227
   specifications 183, 226
   tubed:
      fitting instructions – colour 207
      removal, repair and refitting 204
      valve cores and caps 205
   tubeless:
      puncture repair and tyre renewal 206
      removal and refitting 205
      valves description and removal 206, 243

V

Valve clearances:-
   adjustment 40, 53
   specifications 60

Valves, springs and guides:-
   examination and renovation 76
   specifications 61, 62, 224
Valves – tyre 205, 206, 243
Voltage regulator:-
   removal 215
   specifications 209

W

Weights – model 8, 223
Wheel bearings:-
   check 57
   removal, examination and refitting 193
Wheels:-
   balancing 206
   bearings 57, 193
   check 56, 243
   description 184
   front 184
   rear 191, 243
   specifications 182, 226
   track offset 242
   torque wrench settings 184
Wiring diagrams 247-265
Wiring layout 210
Working facilities 11